A Reader's Guide
to the Short Stories of

SHERWOOD ANDERSON

A
Reference
Publication
in
Literature

Everett Emerson
Editor

A Reader's Guide
to the Short Stories of
SHERWOOD ANDERSON

Judy Jo Small

G. K. Hall & Co.
An Imprint of Macmillan Publishing Company
New York

Maxwell Macmillan Canada
Toronto

Maxwell Macmillan International
New York   Oxford   Singapore   Sydney

G. K. Hall & Co.

Maxwell Macmillan Canada, Inc.

An Imprint of Macmillan Publishing Company

1200 Eglinton Avenue East

866 Third Avenue

Suite 200

New York, NY 10022

Don Mills, Ontario M3C 3N1

Macmillan Publishing Company is part of the Maxwell Communication Group
of Companies.

Library of Congress Catalog Card Number: 93-7883

Printed in the United States of America

97-98

printing number
1 2 3 4 5 6 7 8 9 10

Library of Congress Cataloging-in-Publication Data

Small Judy Jo.
    A reader's guide to the short stories of Sherwood Anderson / Judy
    Jo Small.
446   p.   cm.
    Includes bibliographical references and index.
    ISBN 0-8161-8968-4
    1. Anderson, Sherwood, 1876-1941—Criticism and interpretation.
    2. Short story.
    PS3501.N4Z845 1994
    813'.52—dc20   93-7883
                                                       CIP

The paper used in this publication meets the minimum requirements of American
National Standard for Information Sciences—Permanence of Paper for Printed Library
Materials. ANSI Z39.48-1984. ™

Contents

The Author

Judy Jo Small is an assistant professor of English at North Carolina State University in Raleigh. Her first book, *Positive as Sound: Emily Dickinson's Rhyme,* was published by the University of Georgia Press. In addition, she is the author of several published articles on American literature.

Dr. Small has degrees from Duke University, the University of Pennsylvania, and the University of North Carolina at Chapel Hill, where she was awarded the C. Hugh Holman Fellowship in American Literature. She previously taught at Wake Forest University and at Meredith College.

Foreword

Judy Jo Small's *A Reader's Guide to the Short Stories of Sherwood Anderson* is itself something of a compositional feat. She has provided us with an extraordinary amount of information about Anderson's stories—materials relating to their historical and biographical background, synopses of the important critical readings, the facts surrounding their composition, publication, and reception—and done so in a way that is eminently readable. Her work will be a godsend to teachers preparing classes and scholars engaged in research on Anderson. Students and general readers will find their enjoyment of the stories (i.e., the best of Anderson) deepened as they turn the pages of this compendium. Anderson himself would have heartily approved.

—Kim Townsend

Preface

This volume provides a compendium of historical and critical information about the short stories of Sherwood Anderson, whose works—especially the stories of *Winesburg, Ohio*—inspired a generation of modern American writers. Though Anderson's novels and tales earned an international reputation that continues to this day, most of his novels are now seldom read. Even during his lifetime, it seems to have been understood that whatever enduring name Anderson would have would depend on his short fiction. This book discusses, individually, sixty-one of Anderson's short stories. It offers a concise compilation of biographical, critical, and bibliographical material for many kinds of readers. General readers will find here, readily accessible, discussions that enable deeper understanding of Anderson and his work. Students may consult the volume either to learn more about a particular story or to gain an overview of a broad spectrum of Anderson's most important writings. Teachers will discover that the book provides a usable, compact gathering of pertinent facts and interpretive insights about individual stories. Scholars will find it helpful as a review and reference tool that facilitates further criticism and research.

Each chapter of this guide is devoted to one of the stories that Anderson collected into four volumes of short fiction—*Winesburg, Ohio, The Triumph of the Egg, Horses and Men,* and *Death in the Woods.* Anderson wrote a number of other stories that he never collected for publication in book form; those stories are not treated separately here, except "The Rabbit-pen," which is included for reasons stated in the chapter devoted to it. Whenever Anderson omitted a story that had received magazine publication from a subsequently published collection, he seems to have indicated his judgment that the story was inferior in quality; critics, concurring with his judgment, have given scant attention to stories outside the four volumes. Anderson was contemplating a fifth collection of his stories some time before his death, but there is no record of the contents he planned for it. So far, no one has undertaken serious textual study of the uncollected late stories, some of which were published posthumously by other editors, and these stories too have been little discussed. Indeed, scholars have not agreed upon anything that could be called a canon, or even a list, of Anderson's short fiction. His voluminous magazine publications include miscellaneous essays, documentary sketches, and autobiographical reminiscences as well as pure fiction—

and the lines of demarcation between those various categories is by no means always clear. Establishing a canon of authoritative Anderson texts is a significant task that remains to be accomplished. Nevertheless, the present book covers the bulk of his important short fiction and discusses it in relation to the entire body of his work.

Each chapter here treats one short story. The stories from each of Anderson's four collections are grouped together and arranged in the same order in which they appear in those volumes. For convenient reference, each chapter follows the overall format of this series, which derives in large part from Lea Newman's exemplary *A Reader's Guide to the Short Stories of Herman Melville*.

The first section reports on circumstances surrounding the composition of a story—when and where it was written and what is known about the process of its evolution and revision prior to publication. Because the stories in *Winesburg, Ohio* make up a loose narrative unity and because most of them were composed during a period of several months as part of that unity (even though they were not published together until some years later), a general statement about circumstances related to the composition of the whole cycle introduces the twenty-two separate chapters concerning these stories.

The second section of each chapter sets forth sources and influences that may have contributed to a specific story. Sometimes these sources are works of literary or visual art that may have inspired some element in Anderson's story. Frequently, though, the sources are biographical, and I have included here significant connections between Anderson's fiction and his purportedly autobiographical works. Readers should be cautious. Anderson did not always tell the straight truth in his memoirs: he delighted in the inevitable distortions wrought by imagination and memory, and he presented himself as a flagrant "storyteller."

The third part of each chapter records information pertaining to the story's publication. Most of Anderson's stories appeared first in magazines, and data about initial publication is accompanied here by facts about Anderson's relations with his several publishers, including such things as rejections, payments, and contracts. No attempt is made to list all reprintings of each story, but major reprintings are indicated, as are revisions of the originally published text in successive publications. In addition to the publications listed, readers may wish to know that all of Anderson's stories have been reprinted in Kichinosuke Ohashi's twenty-one volume edition of *The Complete Works of Sherwood Anderson* (Kyoto, Japan: Rinsen Book Company, 1982).

The fourth subdivision of each chapter discusses relationships between the story and Anderson's other works. Here again *Winesburg, Ohio* has required special handling. The complex interrelationships among the stories within the Winesburg cycle have been a primary topic of critical commentary, and for these stories my discussion first identifies connections between a given story and others in the cycle, then turns to relationships between the story and work outside the cycle. To some extent, the collected stories in *The Triumph of the Egg* are united by a common theme as well, which is suggested by the title and the introductory and valedictory prose poems that frame the volume ("The Dumb Man" and "The Man with the Trumpet"); this rarely noticed theme is treated in the separate chapters concerning the individual stories.

The fifth section presents critical and interpretive commentary. My aim has been to survey in a succinct, organized fashion all the substantial critical analysis that has been published in English between the time of the story's first publication and 1991. In addition, I have included some pertinent material from Robert Allen Papinchak's *Sherwood Anderson: A Study of the Short Fiction* (Twayne 1992), which appeared as I was completing this project. I do not mention all the reviews of Anderson's short story collections or, though doubtless some of them are of real value, the many passing references that hundreds of other writers have made. With the exception of William L. Phillips's "Sherwood Anderson's *Winesburg, Ohio,*" often cited by scholars and critics, I do not include dissertations. For *Winesburg, Ohio* and the handful of other much-discussed stories, I have sought primarily to review in accurate synopsis what others have said, accompanied by a modicum of connective and evaluative commentary. (That two new books have been published on the Winesburg stories since I began attests to their persistent fame.) For stories that have been neglected by critics—and there are a surprising number of these—I have briefly offered my own critical remarks. While I do not argue that many of the lesser-known stories are among Anderson's finest, some of them deserve and reward closer study than they have received. The discussions here contribute some fresh, new material to Anderson scholarship. My study of "The Fight," notably, brings to light a previously unrecognized aspect of the controversy between Anderson and Hemingway.

The final section of each chapter is a list of works cited. It establishes a fairly comprehensive bibliography for each of the collected stories. Readers will note that for standard reference, where it is not otherwise indicated, I use the latest authorized texts, that is, the versions of the stories that appear in the four Anderson story collections rather than earlier, magazine versions. For *Winesburg, Ohio* I use the text emended by Malcolm Cowley and published by Viking Press in 1960, which has become the standard text.

My study owes its existence to the devoted labor and sensitive understanding of a host of earlier literary scholars. It has been my pleasure to learn from their work. It remains true, however, as H. L. Mencken said years ago, that Anderson has offered considerable difficulty for academic critics because his method is unorthodox and irreducible to formula: "His uncertain, speculative, inquiring manner only too often leaves the impression that he doesn't know what he is about—that his story is too much for him. Now and then, perhaps, it actually is. But not often. Nine times out of ten his groping is no more than concealment of a highly deft and competent artistry. He turns his characters around slowly, inspecting them leisurely and from all sides. He pauses to wonder about them. . . . In the end, instead of labeling them, he asks questions about them"[1] The existing work on Anderson's short fiction consequently leaves a great deal of room for further study. Textual work needs to be done, as I have said. Fuller criticism, moreover, is in order. With the exception of "I Want to Know Why," "Death in the Woods," and a few others, the stories outside *Winesburg, Ohio*, have not been adequately scrutinized and interpreted. Even the stories within the *Winesburg* collection, often glossed over by interpreters with eyes focused on the whole cycle, would profit from more attention to their value as separate entities. Newer critical approaches, if applied to Anderson's stories, could also produce fresh, worthwhile insights. Needed above all is better explanation of Anderson's contribution to modern fictional technique. Though the influence of his narrative style upon the younger writers of his generation is almost universally acknowledged, only the barest account has yet been given of the secrets of his prose.

A number of acknowledgments are in order, for I have not produced this book without the assistance of others. I offer my thanks to Diana Haskell of the Newberry Library for help with the Sherwood Anderson Papers and for permission to quote from them. I am indebted to seasoned Anderson scholars Charles Modlin, Walter Rideout, William V. Miller, and Welford Taylor for their advice and information. Charlie Modlin has been especially generous, reading sections of manuscript and sharing with me the benefits of his research. Walter Rideout has liberally supplied accurate dates and other details from his biographical work in progress, *Sherwood Anderson: A Writer in America,* forthcoming form Oxford University Press. I also appreciate the kind help of Kit Knowles, Mike Reynolds, and Mike Grimwood, my colleagues at North Carolina State University. Diligent bibliographical work, proofreading, and indexing carried out cheerfully by graduate students Caroline Maun, Lisa Covington, Steve Brandon, and Chad Lewis have been invaluable. My whole family has been wonderfully understanding and encouraging, but I owe special thanks to my dear daughter, Jane, who has labored over index cards, solved my computer problems, and smoothed out much tangled prose. Above all I am grateful to the general editor of this series, Everett Emerson, for his patient support, solid editorial criticism, and steadfast friendship.

[1]H. L. Mencken, *The Impossible H. L. Mencken: A Selection of His Best Newspaper Stories.* Ed. Marion Elizabeth Rodgers (New York: Doubleday, 1991), p. 529.

Abbreviations

WO   *Winesburg, Ohio*

TE   *The Triumph of the Egg*

HM   *Horses and Men*

DW   *Death in the Woods*

The Rabbit-pen

Circumstances of Composition

This story, the first one Anderson published, may have been written before he moved to Chicago in 1913. In his *Memoirs* Anderson recounts its genesis in a conversation with "Trilena" White, an old friend, a teacher whom he had met when he was a student at Wittenberg College. On a visit to his house, he explains, she had expressed her admiration for William Dean Howells, editor of "The Easy Chair" for *Harper's,* whereupon Anderson sharply criticized Howells: "'They are all of them, Howells, Twain, Hawthorne, too much afraid,' I had declared. 'In all their writing there is too much of life left out'" (White, *Memoirs* 334). She in turn challenged him to "write a story that *Harper's* [would] print," and he did. Since "it was not the kind of story [he] was already feeling [his] way toward," he says (perhaps oversimplifying), he was neither very proud of it nor "much excited by its publication" (White, *Memoirs,* 334–35). (Trillena White is the correct spelling, and actually Anderson never went to college, but he did meet her when he was a student at Wittenberg Academy.) A slightly different version of this story appears in the earlier edition of the *Memoirs.* Here the conversation with Miss White took place not at Anderson's own house but in the garden behind a house where both he and she were visitors, and in the garden there was a pen of rabbits where a buck rabbit killed the newborn babies; in this version he admits that he felt pride in having his work published in "such a respected magazine" (Rosenfeld, *Memoirs* 212–13).

Elsewhere Anderson stated that he wrote and submitted the story while he lived in Elyria, Ohio, and that he received word of its acceptance while he was hospitalized in Cleveland after his nervous collapse in December 1912; scholars have been reluctant to accept that statement because the story was not published until the middle of 1914 (Sutton 195–96). Phillips thinks Anderson may have written it not in Elyria but in an isolated cabin in the Ozark Mountains in Missouri, where Anderson and his wife, Cornelia (with their three small children), spent the winter of 1913–14, miserable and bitter as they faced the failure of their marriage (30). No matter which account is correct, whether the story was composed immediately before his breakdown or in the following year, certainly it came out of a turbulent period in Anderson's life, when he was fleeing from a middle-class life as president of the Anderson Manufacturing Company and preparing to desert his wife and children, all for a nebulous hope that he might somehow find his way as a writer.

Sources and Influences

As the account above indicates, the chief influence on this story was the standard genre of fiction recognized by genteel commercial magazines such as *Harper's*. The "stock characters" and "trick ending" are some of the conventional "'poison plot' elements that Anderson came to detest" (White, "Critical Analysis" 36).

The frustrations of Anderson's personal life, too, are reflected in the Harkness children's noise and clutter, which disturb the writer Fordyce, and in the refined but distressing distance that exists between Joe Harkness and his wife.

Publication History

"The Rabbit-pen" appeared in *Harper's Magazine* in July of 1914 (129:207–10). It was the only thing Anderson ever published there. He reported that he was paid seventy-five dollars for it (Rosenfeld, *Memoirs* 213).

Recently the story has been republished in an appendix to the critical edition of *Marching Men* and in *Sherwood Anderson: Early Writings* (White 127–35).

Relation to Other Works

Possibly the most important thing about Anderson's first story is its difference from his later stories. It stands as "in almost every conceivable way the antithesis of the concept of writing in 'The New Note,'" which Anderson wrote for the initial issue of Margaret Anderson's antiestablishment "little magazine" *The Little Review* (D. Anderson 33). Its "language is stilted, cliché-ridden, and consciously grammatical" (Phillips 99). Its plot is based on an obvious, artificial contrast between the wild life of the caged rabbits and the tame life of human characters who are penned in by their own timidity. Its polite, upper-class world seems alien from that of the grotesques of *Winesburg, Ohio*.

Yet the suppressed emotions surging beneath the surface politeness of these genteel characters *do* bear a resemblance to those within the citizens in Winesburg; sexuality especially is a source of quiet torment in both. Moreover, the envious longing with which an effete upper class views a less inhibited, more vital servant class in this story markedly resembles the similar longing in the novel *Dark Laughter* (1925). And the theme of the impotent male and the strong, decisive female appears again and again in Anderson's writings, in stories such as "His Chest of Drawers" as well as in *Perhaps Women* (1931) and in the novels *Beyond Desire* (1932) and *Kit Brandon* (1936). Miller discusses Gretchen as one of a number of "manager" women in Anderson's work (73–74). Aligning sex with death, this story is particularly like "Vibrant Life," as Sutton points out; though it is "a highly-watered down version" of the theme, it reveals "concern with the impulses of life" (350). In this regard, the story is a fitting prelude to Anderson's later works.

Critical Studies

Applause for the new form of short story Anderson pioneered elsewhere has been accompanied, perhaps inevitably, by disdain for this beginning publication in an "establishment" periodical. Schevill's indictment of "The Rabbit-pen" reflects the critical consensus: "Although Anderson claimed that this was one of his first efforts to describe some of the realism of life, there is very little 'realism' in this story. The hazy symbolism of a buck rabbit who runs wild in his pen is not at all fused into the narration. . . . " (80). The concluding "twist," Schevill adds, is almost laughable.

A psychobiographical interpretation, offered by Townsend, sees the significance of the tale in its revelation of the author's divided self; he was torn between his roles as "suburban host" and as "wandering writer," and also between half affectionate "frustration with Cornelia . . . and what must have been his attraction to Trillena [White] (85). The killer rabbit, according to this view, was "caged in Anderson" himself.

In the story's treatment of the contrast between the sentimental impotence of Fordyce and the Harknesses on the one hand and the earthy vitality of rabbits and servants on the other, it is also possible to read a sly parable (right in the pages of *Harper's!*) of the contrast between the effete art that Howells and his kindred writers ordained and the fearless living art that Anderson himself hoped to inaugurate.

Works Cited

Anderson, David. "*The Little Review* and Sherwood Anderson." *Midwestern Miscellany* 8 (1980):28–38.

Anderson, Sherwood. "His Chest of Drawers." *Household Magazine* 39 (August 1939):4–5. Rpt. in *The Sherwood Anderson Reader*. Ed. Paul Rosenfeld. Boston: Houghton Mifflin, 1947, 831–35. Rpt. in *Sherwood*

Anderson: Short Stories. Ed. Maxwell Geismar. New York: Hill and Wang, 1962, 277–81. Rpt. in *Sherwood Anderson's Memoirs: A Critical Edition*. Ed. Ray Lewis White. Chapel Hill: University of North Carolina Press, 1969, 218–22.

———. "Vibrant Life." *Little Review* 3 (March 1916):10–11.

Miller, William V. 1974. "Earth-Mothers, Succubi, and Other Ectoplasmic Spirits: The Women in Sherwood Anderson's Short Stories." In *Midamerica* I. Ed. David D. Anderson. East Lansing, MI: Midwestern Press, 64–81. Rpt. in *Critical Essays on Sherwood Anderson*. Ed. David D. Anderson. Boston: G. K. Hall, 1981, 196–209.

Phillips, William L. "Sherwood Anderson's *Winesburg, Ohio:* Its Origins, Composition, Technique, and Reception." Ph.D. diss., University of Chicago, 1950.

Rosenfeld, Paul, ed. 1942. *Sherwood Anderson's Memoirs*. New York: Harcourt, Brace.

Schevill, James. 1951. *Sherwood Anderson: His Life and Work*. Denver: University of Denver Press.

Sutton, William A. 1972. *The Road to Winesburg: A Mosaic of the Imaginative Life of Sherwood Anderson*. Metuchen, NJ: Scarecrow Press.

Townsend, Kim. 1987. *Sherwood Anderson*. Boston: Houghton Mifflin.

White, Ray Lewis. "A Critical Analysis." *Readers & Writers* 1, no. 6 (April 1968):32–36.

———, ed. 1969. *Sherwood Anderson's Memoirs: A Critical Text*. Chapel Hill: University of North Carolina Press.

———, ed. 1972. *Marching Men: A Critical Text*. Cleveland and London: Press of Case Western Reserve University.

———, ed. 1989. *Sherwood Anderson: Early Writings*. Kent, OH, and London: Kent State University Press.

Winesburg, Ohio

Winesburg, Ohio

Circumstances of Composition

"When I wrote the stories in the book called *Winesburg, Ohio*," Sherwood Anderson would recall in his *Memoirs*, "I was living in a cheap room in a Chicago rooming house" (346). The roominghouse, now no longer standing, was located at 735 Cass Street, since renamed Wabash Avenue (Duffey 136). The other tenants, younger than he, were bohemian artists, writers, musicians, and actors (White, *Memoirs* 350). During the day, Anderson earned his living writing advertising copy at the Long-Critchfield Company, and at night he wrote fiction (Daugherty 33, 37). His bed, like that of the old man in "The Book of the Grotesque," was situated by a window and had been built up "so that he could look out over the Loop" from his third-floor room (Phillips 14). Gazing at the people passing below, Anderson imagined the secrets of their lives and dreamed ambitiously that he "could tell all of the stories of all the people of America" (White, *Memoirs* 351–52).

It was the fall of 1915 when he began to produce the Winesburg stories, and Anderson was thirty-nine. He had come a long way from the small Ohio towns where he had grown up, and he had brought with him a rich fund of memories. His family had once lived uncomfortably near poverty, and he had nearly always worked at one job or another in an effort to get ahead. After his mother's death, he had left his hometown, gone to work in the city, done a brief tour of duty in the Spanish–American War, spent a year completing his high school education, and begun a career as an advertising writer. He had married and become fairly successful in business. In 1912, however, he had suffered a nervous collapse. One day, in Elyria, Ohio, he had quite suddenly walked out of the paint manufacturing plant of which he was president and wandered in an amnesiac fugue state for several days before at last he was brought to a hospital to recover (Townsend 76–82. There are many accounts of this famous episode. Sutton, in *Exit to Elsinore,* gives details). Tensions in his marriage, financial difficulties in his business, and emotional turmoil over his compelling inner need to write all had led to this breakdown, and Anderson thereafter embarked on a new course in life.

In 1913 he moved to Chicago. There he lived for several months among the writers, artists, and intellectuals of the 57th Street group centered around Floyd Dell, editor of the *Friday Literary Review,* and his wife, Margery Currey. Anderson was introduced into the Dell-Currey circle by his brother Karl Anderson, a painter and one of the planners of the famous Armory

Show, which had come to Chicago in the spring of 1913, shocking and fascinating the public with works by Cezanne, Van Gogh, Matisse, Brancusi, and other Post–Impressionists, Fauves, Cubists, and antiacademic American artists. The Chicago group included painter B. J. O. Nordfelt and sculptor Mary Randolph (Duffey 134–35). Anderson also became acquainted with Ben Hecht, Arthur Ficke, Burton Rascoe, Carl Sandburg, and other leading figures of the widespread cultural and artistic movement known as the Chicago Renaissance (White, *Memoirs* 336–37). Waging a protest against the prevailing doctrine that defined success in terms of materialism and respectability, they proclaimed "the necessity of liberation from the business culture, to the point at times of preaching outright anarchy" (Duffey 133). They revolted against middle-class conventionality, complacency, and inhibition—which they dubbed "Puritanism." They called for a new and fearless vitality of conduct and expression. Enthusiastically they applauded such new heroes as Henrik Ibsen, George Bernard Shaw, and Sigmund Freud.

Though this period was in one sense the dawning of Anderson's artistic career, he had been writing for years. He wrote advertisements for a living, and he had written a number of essays and sketches for the trade journal *Agricultural Advertising* (White, *Early Writings*). Moreover, he had begun writing fiction about 1909 or 1910, in the attic of his Elyria, Ohio, home; he brought with him to Chicago the manuscripts of four unpublished novels. One of them had as a central figure "a Talbot Whittingham who had lived in a town called Winesburg, Ohio" (Phillips 14). In July 1914 Anderson published his first short story, "The Rabbit-pen," in the highly respected and respectable *Harper's Magazine*. He must have been pleased. But he had his sights set on something much higher.

In the fall of 1914, he moved—alone—to the Cass Street roominghouse. Though he still worked as an advertising writer to cover his expenses, his primary energies were devoted to his art. At times during these years he was miserable with his job and bemoaned his lot: having to "go into a room with other men and drone for hours over the question of the advisability of advertising a new kind of hose supporters," he said, made him feel how delightful it would be to "take a revolver from [his] pocket and begin shooting the men in the room" (Sutton, *Letters* 8). But his spirits were lifted by the thrill of bold new ideas and by the recognition of friends who lauded him as a native Midwestern genius.

Anderson had never been to college, but he had always been a great reader (Karl Anderson 26). He was particularly fond of the picaresque works of George Borrow, whose *Lavengro* and *The Romany Rye* presented common folk who were twisted by the strains of life (Schevill 71). Ivan Turgenev's *Annals of a Sportsman* (translated sometimes as *Sportsman's Sketches*) was another favorite; passionately he admired its "love of human life, tenderness, [and] lack of the eternal preaching and smart-aleckness so characteristic of much Western writing" (Jones-Rideout, *Letters* 118). The form of Turgenev's book, a gathering of related sketches rounded by an epilogue, may also have contributed to the short story cycle Anderson would write (Ingram 14, 23; Howe 93). Anderson's discovery of Gertrude Stein's *Three Lives* and *Tender Buttons* awakened him to the possibilities of using simple words and phrases poetically, as artistic tools; he would always acknowledge that he owed her "a lot" (Campbell and Modlin 10; Kramer 297; Townsend 100). When Edgar Lee Masters's *Spoon River Anthology* appeared in book form (April 1915), Anderson "stayed up all night reading" it (Phillips 16–17). Probably Masters's collection of poetic portraits of "thwarted village lives" further stimulated Anderson toward writing his own account of the inner life of a small town in America (Howe 95; Wrenn 181).

At last—evidently around November of 1915—he produced a piece of writing that he knew was "solid, . . . like a rock." That was the story "Hands," and he experienced its composition as a miracle (White, *Memoirs* 352–53). The other Winesburg tales followed rapidly, he said, "the words and ideas flowing freely" in a "joyous" phase of confidence (White, *Memoirs* 348). By November 1916, he had completed fifteen of the Winesburg stories, and two others were still in progress (Jones-Rideout, *Letters* 4).

It is impossible to be certain of the precise order of composition of the Winesburg stories. After careful study of the sole extant manuscript of the Winesburg tales and after comparison of that manuscript with the published versions of the stories, William L. Phillips attempted to establish such an order, in his article "How Sherwood Anderson Wrote *Winesburg, Ohio*." Phillips's scholarship has long been a landmark in Anderson criticism, and most other scholars have accepted his conclusions without question. For example, in the introduction to the 1960 Viking edition of *Winesburg, Ohio*, which is now the standard edition, Malcolm Cowley depends on Phillips's work when he states that the stories were composed "in roughly the same order in which they appear in the book" (13). Phillips based his conclusions largely on a manuscript of eighteen *Winesburg* tales handwritten by Anderson on the backs of pages of an earlier effort at a novel concerning a Talbot Whittingham; seven other stories appear "on the cheap, now yellowed print paper used in blocking out advertisements" (Phillips, "How" 10). For the most part, the Whittingham narrative makes it possible to determine the sequence of the stories on the other side of the paper, and Phillips argues that the order of the stories in the existing manuscript represents "the order of composition of the tales" (13). Phillips discounts Anderson's own statement that the *Winesburg* manuscript is not a first draft containing revisions, but a later manuscript "prepared for the making of a fair copy by a stenographer" (10, 13). Furthermore, he concludes that "the *Winesburg* stories were written during a relatively short period of time, one leading to another, and that this period of time was late 1915 and early 1916" (13). Many of

Phillips's assertions seem plausible, and much of what he says is undeniably correct. But the evidence needs to be reexamined, for some of his conclusions are mistaken and others violate common sense.

Letters that have since come to light indicate that Anderson wrote a number of the *Winesburg* stories later than "early 1916." The composition of "The Untold Lie" can be traced to November 1916, "Tandy" plainly was not made into a story until after November 1916, and "Godliness" did not become a story until 1918. (For details, see the discussions of individual stories, below.) "Tandy" appears as the fourth story in Phillips's "chain of composition," yet facts place it much later; therefore, Phillips's major conclusion is cast into doubt. (Phillips's idea that Anderson reworked the manuscripts of "Hands" and "The Untold Lie" for the periodical publication of those stories and then returned to the manuscript version for the book is also suspicious.) "Death" had been written by December 1916 (Jones-Rideout, *Letters* 5). It seems probable that "Sophistication" and "Departure" were written still later, "to round out" the volume, as Phillips surmises (28–29).

In the summer of 1916 Anderson married a second time. He had liked and respected his first wife, Cornelia Lane Anderson, and he felt guilty about abandoning her and their three children. Nevertheless, they had been unable to establish between them the understanding intimacy he felt he needed, and he had found the obligations and noisy confusion of a household full of small children intolerable. His second wife, Tennessee Mitchell, was a free spirit. She seemed a living example of the "new woman" exalted by the liberationists with whom he associated. She was the former mistress of Edgar Lee Masters, and she had a career of her own. Determined to be modern and not to encumber each other, the newlyweds maintained separate residences. In a way, the contrast between his first wife and his second mirrored Anderson's dramatic switch from bourgeois conventionality to bohemian aestheticism. His emotional conflicts about women and sexuality were far from settled, however, and his uncertainties continued to animate his fiction.

In October 1916, with the help of Floyd Dell, Anderson would publish the first of his novels, *Windy McPherson's Son*. By that time, four of his Winesburg stories had been published, in the little magazines *Masses* and the *Little Review*. In November, Waldo Frank hailed Anderson's new novel as proof of "Emerging Greatness." Thereafter, Anderson's stories appeared in the new magazine *Seven Arts,* which Frank edited with James Oppenheim and Van Wyck Brooks. Although the magazine foundered before long and Anderson again had to turn to the *Little Review* and other periodicals, his relationship with this group of New York intellectuals was profoundly enriching. The uncultivated businessman-turned-writer who had who grown up in Clyde, Ohio, was launched as an eminent artist of modern American fiction.

It was to be a dizzying, adventurous journey, full of painful bumps and sloughs of despondency. But Anderson would never forget that the *Winesburg* stories were abiding evidence of his pioneering style and his devotion to his craft as well as enduring testament to human efforts to achieve significant forms of expression. "The influence of the work cannot be overstated: as a consequence of its publication, the American short story was never to look the same again" (Kimbel 62).

Works Cited

Anderson, Karl James. "My Brother, Sherwood Anderson." *Saturday Review of Literature* 31 (September 4, 1948):6–7, 26–27.

Campbell, Hilbert H., and Charles E. Modlin. 1976. *Sherwood Anderson: Centennial Studies*. Troy, NY: Whitston.

Cowley, Malcolm. 1960. "Introduction." *Winesburg, Ohio*. By Sherwood Anderson. New York: Viking, 1–15. Rpt. in Sherwood Anderson, Winesburg, Ohio: *Text and Criticism*. Ed. John H. Ferres. New York: Viking, 1966, 357–68. Rpt. in *Sherwood Anderson: A Collection of Critical Essays*. Ed. Walter B. Rideout. Englewood Cliffs, NJ: Prentice-Hall, 1974, 49–58.

Daugherty, George H. "Anderson, Advertising Man." *Newberry Library Bulletin* 2, no. 2 (December 1948):29–38.

Duffey, Bernard. 1954. *The Chicago Renaissance in American Letters: A Critical History*. East Lansing: Michigan State College Press.

Frank, Waldo. "Emerging Greatness." *Seven Arts* 1 (November 1916):73–78. Rpt. in *The Achievement of Sherwood Anderson: Essays in Criticism*. Ed. Ray Lewis White. Chapel Hill: University of North Carolina Press, 1966, 9–24. Rpt. in *Sherwood Anderson: A Collection of Critical Essays*. Ed. Walter B. Rideout. Englewood Cliffs, NJ: Prentice-Hall, 1974, 13–17.

Howe, Irving. 1951. *Sherwood Anderson*. New York: William Sloane Associates.

Ingram, Forrest L. 1971. *Representative Short Story Cycles of the Twentieth Century: Studies in a Literary Genre*. The Hague: Mouton.

Jones, Howard Mumford, and Walter B. Rideout, eds. 1953. *Letters of Sherwood Anderson*. Boston: Little, Brown.

Kimbel, Ellen. 1984. "The American Short Story: 1900–1920." In *The American Short Story, 1900–1945: A Critical History*. Ed. Philip Stevick. Boston: Twayne, 33–69.

Kramer, Dale. 1966. *Chicago Renaissance: The Literary Life in the Midwest, 1900–1930*. New York: Appleton-Century.

Phillips, William L. "How Sherwood Anderson Wrote *Winesburg, Ohio.*" *American Literature* 23 (1951):7–30. Rpt. in *Sherwood Anderson:* Winesburg, Ohio: *Text and Criticism.* Ed. John H. Ferres. New York: Viking, 1966. 263–86. Rpt. in *The Achievement of Sherwood Anderson: Essays in Criticism.* Ed. Ray Lewis White. Chapel Hill: University of North Carolina Press, 1966, 62–84. Rpt. in *The Merrill Studies in* Winesburg, Ohio. Comp. Ray Lewis White. Columbus, OH: Charles E. Merrill, 1971, 2–24. Rpt. in *Sherwood Anderson: A Collection of Critical Essays.* Ed. Walter B. Rideout. Englewood Cliffs, NJ: Prentice-Hall, 1974, 18–38.

Schevill, James. 1951. *Sherwood Anderson: His Life and Work.* Denver: University of Denver Press.

Sutton, William A. 1967. *Exit to Elsinore.* Muncie, IN: Ball State University Press.

———, ed. 1985. *Letters to Bab: Sherwood Anderson to Marietta D. Finley, 1916–33.* Foreword by Walter B. Rideout. Urbana and Chicago: University of Illinois Press.

Townsend, Kim. 1987. *Sherwood Anderson.* Boston: Houghton Mifflin.

White, Ray Lewis, ed. 1969. *Sherwood Anderson's Memoirs: A Critical Edition.* Chapel Hill: University of North Carolina Press.

———, ed. 1990. *Sherwood Anderson: Early Writings.* Kent, OH: Kent State University Press.

Wrenn, John H., and Margaret M. Wrenn. 1976. "'Tennessee Mitchell': The Forgotten Muse of Sherwood Anderson and Edgar Lee Masters." In *Sherwood Anderson: Centennial Studies.* Eds. Hilbert H. Campbell and Charles E. Modlin. Troy, NY: Whitston, 175–84.

The Book of the Grotesque

Circumstances of Composition

Phillips's dating of the composition of "The Book of the Grotesque"—"at least as early as November, 1915" ("How" 9)—is reasonable, given the publication date the following February. Phillips understandably concludes that this was "the first of the *Winesburg* tales to be written" ("How" 9). Because the "earliest extant table of contents" shows this title as an addition to an original list of nineteen stories, White suggests that "The Book of the Grotesque" was composed somewhat later ("Table"). Nevertheless, it seems likely that this story and "Hands" were written at "about the same time," as Kramer states (293); they appeared in print only a month apart.

In this story Anderson reworked some of the ideas included in the unpublished novel about Talbot Whittingham that he had been composing in 1914 and 1915. Like the old writer here, Talbot envisions all the people he has known longing for him to tell their stories (Rideout, "Talbot" 53). In that attempted novel, too, Anderson wrote that life has "twisted" people into "grotesques," and Talbot finally realizes that "Everything is grotesque and the beautiful is beyond the grotesque"; moreover, he understands that it is the artist's task to reveal that beauty (Rideout 54).

Sources and Influences

Sherwood Anderson's own experience was a chief source for this sketch. The procession of figures before the old writer's eyes is one piece of autobiography: Anderson often wrote of how the faces and figures of people would march through his brain (see, for example, "An Apology for Crudity," *A New Testament* 69, and Modlin, *Love Letters* 131). Anderson's living alone in an upstairs room with a raised bed placed beside the window is another obvious parallel to the situation in the story (Taylor 20). Moreover, like the old writer, Anderson had not yet published the books he had written, and at thirty-nine he felt himself to be rather old. The oblique self-portrait exhibits a wry mixture of pride and anxiety.

A passage in *A Story Teller's Story* also suggests that the old writer's not publishing his book may derive from Anderson's ambivalent feelings about publishing. In this somewhat fictionalized autobiography, the author says that when he first began to write he imagined himself as "a kind of heroic figure, a silent man creeping into little rooms, writing marvelous tales, poems, novels—that would never be published" until some day after he had died in obscurity, when his writings would be romantically discovered "in a garret" and his genius declared (72). A Twain-like humor plays over the passage, and he adds: "It might have been a good card had I found within myself the courage to play it, but I didn't." The old writer in "The Book of the Grotesque" is in part like the romantic figure imagined here, while the narrative voice of the unheroic fellow who has descended from the garret and published the book is a bit of a Sancho Panza (or a Huck Finn), resigned to the condition of the everyday and the grotesque.

The old carpenter in the tale originated in a Civil War veteran from Clyde, Ohio, whom Anderson recalls in his *Memoirs*. With "tears running down his gaunt old cheeks," the real-life carpenter, named Jim Lane, watched the local militia (including young Sherwood Anderson) leaving for the Spanish–American War (White 166–67). Lane "had been in Andersonville prison" and "had seen his brother die of hunger there" (166). The Confederate prison camp at Andersonville, Georgia, was notoriously horrible; thousands of Union prisoners died miserably there, unclothed, exposed to the elements, and scarcely fed.

Various sources have been proposed for the word "grotesque." David D. Anderson suggests as a specific source "an experimental play, *Grotesque,* by Cloyd Head and Maurice Brown, which was produced at the Chicago Little Theatre in 1915" and which was reviewed in the same issue of *The Little Review*—December, 1915—that published Anderson's story "Sister" ("Idea" 12–13). In 1951, Schevill argued that Anderson had "installed a new word in the American language," stripping it of the satirical note attached to Poe's use of the grotesque (*Sherwood* 101–102). In 1977, however, he traced the grotesque mode in American letters back from Anderson to Hawthorne, Melville, and Poe and forward to West, Faulkner, Heller, Pynchon, and Hawkes, as well as connecting it more broadly to "European Epic and Absurdist styles," especially that of Bertolt Brecht ("Notes" 230, 232). So the word is hardly traceable to a single source. The first issue of *Little Review* had included a set of poems by Arthur Davison Ficke called "Ten Grotesques," but as Townsend states simply, "The word *grotesque* was in the air" (110).

The influence of Anderson's reading of the King James Bible on this story has been noted by Welford Taylor, who remarks here an echo of Old Testament language ("in the beginning . . . ," *WO* 23), by means of which the voice of the narrator achieves the tone of "an ancient sage" (38).

The old writer's idea about "truths," the central philosophical proposition in *Winesburg, Ohio,* has prompted much discussion of possible sources. Ciancio calls attention to the philosophical likeness between the central thought in the book written by the old man and the doctrine in Plato's *Meno* that knowledge is recollection of an eternal self beyond "the finite mind"; since truths "came into being with man's consciousness," yearnings for the "Universal Truth . . . , which is undifferentiated and suprarational," cannot be satisfied, Ciancio explains (1001). This interpretation is brought into question by Anderson's text, which denies that universal truth ever existed: "in the beginning when the world was young there were a great many thoughts but no such thing as a truth" (*WO* 23). The thrust of this passage, evidently, is profoundly anti-Platonic.

Two commentators have remarked that the old writer's theory that adherence to a truth can lead to "falsehood" (*WO* 24) may be traceable to Ralph Waldo Emerson. Phillips pointed out in 1976 the "striking echo" in Anderson of a passage from Emerson's essay "Intellect," which states that when someone attends to only "a single aspect of truth . . . for a long time, the truth becomes distorted and not itself but falsehood" ("Emerson" 5). Less than a year later, Park showed the connection between Anderson's story and the same Emersonian passage and others in Emerson's journals and in *Natural History of the Intellect*.

A provocative statement made by Anderson's friend George Daugherty suggests that Nietzsche's perspectivist notion of truth contributed to the old writer's theory. Daugherty remembered that Anderson was interested in Nietzsche during the period when he wrote *Winesburg, Ohio* and that he sometimes quoted a Nietzschean idea: "This is true—but the opposite is also true" (37). "This fitted in admirably with Anderson's well-known theory of the relation of truth and romance," Daugherty remarks. Though critics have long recognized the influence of Nietzsche's thought on Anderson's first two novels, they have overlooked the specific connection between the old writer's thought about truths in this tale and Nietzsche's insistence that there is no such thing as absolute truth, only the multitude of seeming truths that human beings manufacture (for example, in the essay "On Truth and Falsity in Their Ultramoral Sense" 180). In this philosophical view, old convictions appear to carry the weight of truth only because human beings have forgotten the fictionality, the rhetoricity, of their own constructions. Accordingly, taking (constructed) truths seriously—and living by them—is the origin of the condition of the grotesque, as Anderson defines it.

Two critics argue the influence of Mark Twain, a writer whom Anderson much admired and to whom he acknowledged a debt. Schevill sees in the old writer "a symbolic Mark Twain–like figure with his white mustache, cigars, and Joan of Arc fantasies" ("Notes" 232). Alsen points out the correspondence between the old writer's idea about the danger of embracing a truth and the very similar idea developed in Twain's "What Is Man?" (privately published in 1906). Alsen argues that both Twain and Anderson use the old man figure as a "self-portrait" and that in each instance that portrait is colored by an "ironic self-awareness" that in pursuing truth themselves they risk slipping into the delusion of having found it even though they know "there is no absolute truth" (12–14).

Admitting that it is difficult to determine whether Anderson had read Chekhov before writing the stories of *Winesburg* (and he denied that he had), Stewart points out important similarities between the works of the two writers, including skepticism about absolute truth and "sympathy for pathetic individual graspings for a meaningful order" by means of "necessarily false and incomplete" beliefs (35).

Publication History

This story, the first of the stories later collected in *Winesburg, Ohio* to appear in print, was originally published in February 1916 in *Masses* 8:17. The date given in Paul Rosenfeld's *Sherwood Anderson Reader*—1918—is incorrect (v). It was the third of Anderson's short stories to be published, for "The Rabbit-pen" had come out in 1914, followed by "Sister" in 1915.

"The Book of the Grotesque" was the first of three of Anderson's stories published in the radical weekly *Masses,* edited by Max Eastman. The magazine promoted the liberation of women, candid talk about sexuality and methods of contraception, and the socialist cause. It billed itself as "frank, arrogant, impertinent" and declared its opposition to "Rigidity and Dogma wherever it is found." That editorial stance accorded well with the denial of absolute truth set forth in Anderson's sketch. Anderson submitted the story to Floyd Dell, the associate editor of *Masses,* who was already reviewing the manuscript of *Windy McPherson's Son* (Phillips, "How" 24). Since *Masses* did not offer money for contributions, Anderson received no payment for the story.

In 1919, it became the opening story of *Winesburg, Ohio.* In the first edition, its placement indicates its nature as a prologue to the volume; the title *Winesburg, Ohio* follows it, as a headline for the story "Hands." Other editions have treated it in various ways. The edition prepared by Malcolm Cowley for Viking Press (1960) and the Penguin reprint place it before the map of Winesburg; the Viking Critical Edition (1966), in contrast, situates it merely as the first story of the volume (Mann 62n).

One error has remained constant since the first edition of the book. In the discussion of "truths" there are four pairs of opposite truths listed—"the truth of virginity and the truth of passion, the truth of wealth and of poverty, of thrift and of profligacy, of carelessness and abandon" (*WO* 23). The *Masses* version of the story reads correctly not "*carelessness* and abandon," which in context does not make good sense, but "*carefulness* and abandon" (emphasis added). In the Newberry Library manuscript of *Winesburg,* Anderson (though with his characteristically poor spelling) wrote "carefullness" (Phillips, "Editions" 154).

Relation to Other Works

Anderson originally intended that the title of this story, "The Book of the Grotesque," should be the title of the whole book. B. W. Huebsch, the first publisher of *Winesburg, Ohio,* assured William Phillips that he himself had suggested to Anderson that the title of the collection should be changed to *Winesburg, Ohio* (Phillips, "How" 30n); nearly all critics have accepted this as a statement of fact. In 1980, however, Curry expressed doubt about the accuracy of Huebsch's memory; she cites two letters Anderson wrote to John Lane Publishing Company, which considered and rejected the book, as clear proof that in 1918, before Huebsch looked at it, Anderson had begun referring to the volume as *Winesburg* and already intended to use that as a title (239). Though Baker thinks the title change was fortunate because the definition of the grotesque the sketch contains is so slenderly related to *Winesburg* as a whole (574), Bresnahan argues that the original title, "The Book of the Grotesque," is more appropriate to the focus of the larger work than the title finally selected (45).

Most critics have agreed that this short tale functions as a prologue to the rest of the collection and serves to unify the group. There have been a few exceptions: Kramer, like Baker, thinks the first tale "has little bearing on what follows" (239; similarly, White, *Exploration* 24). But the majority of critics think otherwise. The book is "knit together, however loosely, by the idea of the first tale," says Phillips ("How" 7). The tale serves "as a statement of purpose," writes David D. Anderson ("Moments" 158). It provides "the introduction" to a unified work, agrees Bluefarb (43–44). And Fertig says that, along with "Departure," this tale serves as a "frame" for the collection (70).

Indeed it does. Anderson endeavors in *Winesburg, Ohio* to create a little world and people it with lifelike characters. So he begins his book with a fable about artistic creation, alluding to the Judeo-Christian myth of creation. Acutely aware of his position as a member of the modernist movement in the arts, Anderson presents a metafictional meditation concerned with the process by which art is created—in particular, the process by which a narrative writer creates characters. The meditation sets up an analogy between God's role as primal originator (the Word) and the writer's role as belated originator (in words), but with a profoundly ironic reversal. For Anderson emphasizes his modernist ontology and its aesthetic results. The artist, impelled by a spontaneous instinct for expression, seems to imitate what has been understood as the divine act; but since no truth exists except for the manifold truths that the human mind has produced (the creation story being merely a story), there is no solid ontological ground, no foundation of absolute truth upon which the artist, or anyone else, can build. The artistic function subsumes the divine function—but with inescapable imperfection. The writer dreams; the dreams leave impressions; the writer seeks to describe the impressions. Inevitably, he risks being trapped in his own epistemological circles. As Anderson would write in *Tar* (1926), "I am a story teller starting to tell a story and cannot be expected to tell the truth. Truth is impossible to me" (ix).

It has become customary to call various characters in the collected stories "grotesques." Thurston draws specific parallels to the types of grotesques referred to in the opening tale, offering Joe Welling (of "A Man of Ideas") as an example of those that are "amusing," Doctor Reefy (of "Paper Pills") as an example of those that are "almost beautiful," and Elizabeth Willard as a likely candidate for the "one, a woman all drawn out of shape" who elicits a whimper from the old writer (120).

Several critics remark that this story introduces a key theme in *Winesburg, Ohio,* the theme of the artist. In one of its aspects the story cycle resembles the genre of the *Künstlerroman*. Burbank interprets the old writer as an "artist of life." Although he is mistaken in calling him "a writer who does not write," he properly remarks in him the combination appropriate for an artist of accepting isolation and sympathizing with others (67). More pessimistic in emphasis, Stouck argues that the story "defines the relationship of the artist to his characters," which is that the artist "cannot really express anything for his characters . . . and must be left to whimper like a small dog" at them like the old writer here ("Dance" 541; in the same vein, see his "Failure" 151 and "Postmodern" 312).

The relationship between the old writer in this tale, the potential writer George Willard in the other tales, and the narrator of the whole collection (and, finally, Anderson himself) is a complex subject, and that subject will be discussed below, under the heading "Critical Studies." Here it will suffice to mention Bluefarb's comment that the old man "is, in a sense, the George Willard who never left home" and "a kind of anticipatory persona of George," the chief character of the collection, who at the end seems destined to write a book "very much like" the book the old man did not publish and like the one that Sherwood Anderson at last did publish (44).

The idea in this introductory tale that there are many truths is borne out by several tales that show the painful effects of partial truths, including fragmentary views of sex, as Murphy explains. Those few, the "spiritual elite," who come to grasp the paradox of both "the truth of virginity and the truth of passion" (*WO* 23) he argues, are Doctor Reefy (of "Paper Pills"), Curtis

Hartman (of "The Strength of God,") Kate Swift (of "The Teacher"), Tom Foster (of "Drink"), and—eventually—George Willard (241–42).

The idea of manifold truths Tanner finds relevant to the form of the whole story cycle, which is composed not, by his definition, of stories, but merely of "incidents" that reveal isolated "truths"; disparagingly, Tanner finds no unifying vision in the book, "no complex moral attitude toward life, no adjudicating subtleties, no finely drawn discriminations . . . (213). The disparagement is needless. The fragmented form of the various tales is distinctly modern, and their incomplete truths reflect a complex vision of a town (and a nation) and of perennial human problems.

Several commentators have found more specific connections between the opening story and those that follow. Especially, the connection between the "truths" of the opening story and the thoughts that Doctor Reefy puts on scraps of paper has been frequently noted (for example, San Juan 143; Berland 138). Stouck points out the similarity between the old man's avoidance of "absolute judgment" and Ray Pearson's insight in "The Untold Lie" that "Whatever I told him would have been a lie" (*WO* 209).

The passage that compares the old writer to a pregnant woman has also stirred much interpretive comment. Fludernik connects "the womb-tomb metaphor" here with an intricate web of symbolic imagery that runs throughout the story cycle (124). Bidney presents a compelling argument that the passage (which states that within the writer stirs "a youth" who is instead "a woman" dressed "like a knight") should be understood as an introduction to "the androgyny myth" that provides "the organizing principle of Anderson's complex book" (261). According to Fertig, the maiden in armor is of key importance to the theme of romantic inspiration and transformation that runs throughout the book (66); he asserts that she stands as "a representative of the ideal dream world to which the artist aspires," like the young woman Enoch Robinson imagines in his painting (in "Loneliness") and like Elizabeth Willard once she is transformed into someone young and lovely (in "Death") (69). A parallel between this young woman dressed in mail and the vision of a "golden age" in "Hands" (*Winesburg* 30) is suggested by Berland (136). Bredahl observes that "The Teacher" reinforces the ideas in the opening story of "[t]he young thing within" and personal and artistic growth (432). McAleer, similarly, sees the young woman as linked with the "woman with a sword" in "Loneliness" (*WO* 173) and with the other questing "knightly women" Elizabeth Willard, Louise Bentley, and Kate Swift (in "Mother," "Godliness," and "The Teacher," respectively (173). Lorch notes the significant contrast between Enoch Robinson (of "Loneliness") and the old writer, "who peoples his room" like Enoch but who, in accepting the carpenter, "shows that unlike Enoch he has not rejected the world" (60).

Broader links between ideas set forth in "The Book of the Grotesque" and Anderson's work generally have been widely recognized. As Weber aptly puts it, the statement in this sketch about the multiplicity of truth "epitomizes the philosophy of uncertainty that dominated Anderson's thought and art" (23). Moreover, grotesque distortions of life are prominent in most of Anderson's works, most memorably in the literal grotesques that hatch from hen's eggs in one of of his greatest stories, "The Egg." The symbolic value of those misshapen chicks lends that story a mournful, ironic undertone that is discernible in almost all of Anderson's writing. The central figures of the early novels *Windy McPherson's Son* and *Marching Men* are both "grotesques, who not only embrace a specific truth but also seem to float in and out of reality" (Williams 130). The episode in *Poor White* involving Joe Wainsworth, the harnessmaker who goes berserk when his craft is made obsolete by industrialism, "suggests the grotesquerie of *Winesburg*" (Howe 127). It is easy to locate dozens of other characters in Anderson's fiction who also can be categorized as grotesque.

The pregnancy metaphor in "The Book of the Grotesque" links it with *A Story Teller's Story* (260), in which a tale kicks inside the storyteller at night, driving away sleep and impelling him to write (Curry "Writer's," 282n). Anderson repeats the metaphor in the opening section of his *A New Testament* (1927). As early as 1914, in his essay "The New Note," Anderson was emphasizing the importance of youthful vision, which he states "is as old as the world": whenever writers "speak out of the body and soul of youth," he said, they participate in "a perpetual sweet new birth of the world" (23).

Anderson's own understanding of the idea of the grotesque may be made clearer by his use of words directly from the text of the story in a letter of May 1917, wherein he laments that "all the big radicals" had become rigidified by the war: "They had got hold of a truth you see and had become not thinkers but scientists. They are so very sure that two and two make four. In embracing their truth they have become grotesque" (Sutton, 446). That philosophy made Anderson unwilling to adopt a rigid political stance. Characteristically, when he bought and wrote editorials for two newspapers in Marion, Virginia, in 1927, one supported the Republican Party and the other supported the Democratic Party (Gregory, *Talks* 16). Always, Anderson maintained the conviction that one may pursue truth eternally yet never grasp it.

Critical Studies

A review written upon the publication of *Winesburg* in 1919 comments that the introductory episode of the writer and the carpenter is "a kind of allegory" (W. S. B. 31). That reviewer does not interpret further, but the reference may point to the introduction in this sketch of themes important to the whole book—the suffering of human beings, the ridiculous forms in which that suffering is sometimes expressed, and the importance to the writer of understanding the human stories that lie beneath the surfaces of social and professional roles people play and beneath their sometimes absurd behavior. As Stouck wrote in 1969, this brief episode initiates *Winesburg's* "theme of failure and the figure of the sympathetic listener" ("Failure" 147).

The old writer who is the central character in the story is the subject of critical disagreement. Stouck contends that "we are meant to view the old writer as ineffectual" ("Failure" 147). Stouck sees the procession of figures before the old man's eyes as "a dance of the dead" and the "youth in the coat of mail" as "the writer's imagination and also his death consciousness" ("Dance" 532). Most other critics, however, view the old writer in a far more positive light. Thurston finds the writer's "dream that was not a dream" (*WO* 22) to be a genuine visionary power (120). The writer's imaginative capacity extends by implication, Thurston proposes, both to the narrator and to "Anderson's conception of himself as a 'story-teller.'" The narrator's question "Why quarrel with an old man concerning his thoughts?" may be merely the half-humorous self-deprecation of an author who fears that he may have overreached himself by claiming special powers of insight.

The connections among the old writer in the prologue, the aspiring young writer in the following tales (George Willard), the narrator, and Sherwood Anderson himself are highly problematic. The links and the gaps among those four figures are almost certainly deliberate. Like a number of other interpreters, Alsen assumes that the old writer is Anderson's self-portrait (13). Numerous specific correlations between the old man's situation and Anderson's at the time of writing make that interpretation tenable. (See "Circumstances of Composition.") Loosely speaking, as the old writer is a portrait of the artist as an old man, so George Willard is a portrait of the artist as a young man.

The narrator's relationship with the old writer is explained by Papinchak in terms of the motif of fruition that runs through the collection; the old man is "like a pregnant woman" (*WO* 22) but is unable to produce until the narrator serves "as midwife"(2). The close relationship of the old writer with the narrator is also argued by Lawry, who says they are "distinct" but "nearly one," the writer providing for the narrator "a model for the art of Winesburg" and the carpenter representing "its subject and audience" ("Arts" 57–58). Lawry is further concerned with the relations between the old writer and George Willard, who, by leaving behind his village at the end of the book, in a sense rejects his past; the old writer, in contrast, dreams of a procession of figures from his past. George, instead of containing some "young thing inside" (*WO* 24), says Lawry, "is only young." The narrator, who publishes such a work as the old writer wrote but did not publish, mediates between

George and the old writer in his story, reaching out to an audience in the present with a story recovered from the past. Thus Lawry not only suggests how Anderson resolved the American dilemma of moving into the future without forgetting the past but also seeks himself to reconcile the dispute about whether *Winesburg, Ohio* constitutes a revolt from the village or a nostalgic glimpse of the past. Lawry recognizes the complexities of these linked storyteller figures as "faces of Janus" (58).

The most sophisticated treatment of these relationships can be found in Forrest Ingram's study of *Winesburg, Ohio.* Ingram posits that the "fictively realized narrator, . . . as a *persona* who yet is the implied author, . . . fuses the fictional world of the characters in the book with the real world of Anderson the author" (155). (Fuses, but also separates, it might more accurately be said.) The narrator's "first creation" is the character of the old writer.

> From this point on, levels of reality and myth intermingle; the real is brother to the imaginary. The old carpenter who "became the nearest thing to what is understandable and lovable of all the grotesques in the writer's book" may be a mere creation of the old writer as the old writer is of the narrator and the narrator is of Anderson. The people whose intimate lives are strung out across the pages of *Winesburg*—are they figures of the old writer's fancy, or of the narrator's fancy, or of Anderson's? Are they, perhaps, George Willard's people? George himself, of course, is only a fictional character. He, too, however, intends to be a writer . . . [and] George's future mimics the old writer's past. . . . It is possible, then, that the old writer stands at the head of the work as a later George Willard, a prototype of the George Willard to come. It is possible, too, that the narrator, by summoning to fictional life the figures of the old writer and of George Willard, fictionalized his own initiation into, and projected culmination of his creative career. (156)

This interrelationship, argues Ingram, is the key to the structural "looseness" that Anderson manages in his cycle, where lives flow past one another, "touching and not quite touching, connected and yet not really connected" (157).

Stouck develops a similar idea to explain the kinship of this story with the postmodern novel. The narrator, having seen the book that the old writer has written according to a "vision he once had," has "presumably set its contents down for the reader"; hence the sketch does not present the ensuing stories to the reader as realistic but calls attention to the fact that they stand "at several removes from 'reality'" ("Postmodern" 315). It seems odd, if not unwarranted, to affix the label "postmodernist" to a work that became a modernist icon to a whole generation. But undoubtedly "The Book of the Grotesque" worries over and celebrates the fictive status of the text it serves to introduce.

Formalist approaches to the story classify it variously. Berland argues that the mode of *Winesburg, Ohio* is not tragic but pathetic because it sees human beings as fated by the very nature of things and deprived of "real moral choice" (136). The form of this story according to James Mellard is epiphanic (1304). Grouping it with four other *Winesburg* stories that are structured around a movement toward a revelation, Mellard states that this story leads to the epiphany that "people who are 'grotesques' are not necessarily horrible, some being 'amusing,' 'beautiful,' and even . . . 'lovable." Another critic who has commented on Anderson's formal maneuvers in this tale shows specifically how the pathos here "escapes sentimentalism by a careful juxtaposition of objective statement to pathetic insight" (Berland 135).

Much of the critical attention to this tale has centered on its statement about truths, which culminates in the assertion that "It was the truths that made the people grotesques" (*WO* 24). The meaning of this passage has been much debated. Massa's interpretation may be dismissed as insufficient—that beneath the apparent determinism of the passage is the simple message "that what we need are *common* truths, *shared* values" (95). Some critics accept the statement as an indication that at the core of each of the stories there is or should be a grotesque espousal of some particular "truth"; others, for various reasons, disagree. Typical of critics who take the first approach is Walcutt, who defines the grotesque as a "person who has become obsessed by a mannerism, an idea, or an interest to the point where he ceases to be Man in the ideal sense" (227). Schevill, similarly, states that the grotesque characters have tried to make truth a personal possession and thus have cut themselves off from society (102–102; similarly, Bort 443–44).

A number of interpreters, however, argue that the theory of truths is inadequate. Asselineau finds the style of the "passage on the different kinds of 'truths'" to be "confused, probably because the ideas the author is trying to express have not been completely formulated" (352); possibly he would have withdrawn this objection had he known of the textual error in the passage (see "Publication History," above). Howe's objection, however, is more precise and more far-reaching: "The one conspicuous disharmony in the book is that the introductory 'Book of the Grotesque' suggests that the grotesques are victims of their wilful fanaticism, while in the stories themselves grotesqueness is the result of an essentially valid resistance to forces external to its victims" (107). Cowley also objects: the problem of the twisted characters in *Winesburg,* he says, is not "their each having seized upon a single truth," but "their inability to express themselves" (14; similarly, Voss 185). Baker similarly concludes that here "Anderson's philosophizing appears at its most inchoate" and that the theory applies to only two of the stories in the collection, "Godliness" and "The Philosopher" (574–75; similarly, Kimbel 63, 64). Fussell contends that, while the general idea—the advantage of "flexibility" as opposed to "rigidity"—is clear, the "modern 'humours' theory" Anderson has concocted is flawed by an "eccentric use of the word *truth*) and by the idea that not publishing has prevented the old writer from becoming a grotesque. Yet he allows that the broad distinctions made in the opening story "are entirely continuous with" important distinctions made thereafter between George Willard, who in freeing himself from the "entanglements" of life paradoxically enables artistic expression of "the common passion," and the other characters, whose excessive involvement with life distorts and prevents "complete self-realization" (111).

Attempting to reconcile Schevill's view that people turn themselves into grotesques with Howe's view that except in the misleading statement in the prologue the grotesques are victims of external forces, Ciancio argues that the truths are "pure and unsullied ideals" that, when pursued, bring characters into conflict with social repression, which in turn brings awareness of "existential guilt," the impossibility of achieving "Universal Truth," and finally "a refusal to grow" (1000, 998, 1001). The blame, then, lies partly outside them and partly in them. Similarly, Berland says that the origin of grotesqueness "is not an improper manipulation of truths so much as the truths themselves" because ideals by their very nature become false when translated into practice (136). That view manages to explain the statement that the old writer did not become a grotesque "for the same reason that he never published the book" (*WO* 24). Yet, as Berland adds, grotesqueness seems inevitable, and "the young thing inside" the old writer, which Anderson credits with saving him from grotesqueness, is also a presence in the striving searchers in the rest of the book, who are meant to be understood as grotesque. The irony, Berland speculates, may be intentional since, of course, the published book lies in the reader's hands.

The problem of this passage, though, extends to a larger interpretive issue related to the whole book. Critics have followed Howe in drawing a contrast between the grotesques, who are distinguished by their "sentient striving," and the banal but apparently normal characters in the tales, whom Howe calls "simply clods" (100; likewise, Ciancio 996). Similarly, critics have relied heavily on the contrast between the potential artist George Willard and the grotesque characters he meets. There is a strong suggestion, though, that all of the characters, if looked at closely enough, would reveal shapes of the grotesque, as Berland insists: "each of them has a dream," and each of them dreads becoming a clod (136). A letter Anderson wrote in the late 1930s indicates clearly that, by then at least, he thought his characters were "like all people I have known . . . no more normal or abnormal" (Curry, "Writer's," 231n). To be lonely, to be queer—in greater or lesser degree, that is the human condition. The distinctions that critics draw, when measured against the text they are interpreting, seem to succumb to the grotesque fate that is the subject of their discussion. They formulate interpretive truths that are useful, but the text itself finally eludes those truths.

The point that surfaces in *Winesburg,* again and again, is that there are many and opposing truths—in the world, and in the world of the text in hand. Something is amiss—from the beginning—within those who strive, within those who do not strive, within society and all its institutions, within ourselves and all our efforts. That is grotesque. But the perpetual drama of individual human beings struggling toward fulfillment, while it may be "horrible" or "amusing" or "almost beautiful," provides a basis for mutual understanding and love. Likewise, something is amiss when critics try to affix blame for the sufferings of the characters of *Winesburg, Ohio* (or for the sufferings of any of its individual characters) to any one cause, such as provincialism or puritanical repression or industrialism or capitalism or egotism or patriarchal oppression. Those truths may be found within the text, to be sure. But the roots of trouble, "The Book of the Grotesque" indicates, lie far deeper. A single truth, or a "dozen," will not explain the whole. In keeping with the philosophy it expounds, this tale avoids setting forth any unambiguous "truth." The book it introduces is a cycle of stories, after all, not a treatise; and the stories are presented as the outgrowth of an old writer's dreams. Consequently, this prologue would have us understand, the book demands understanding of a different order altogether.

Works Cited

Alsen, Eberhard. "The Futile Pursuit of Truth in Twain's 'What Is Man' and Anderson's 'Book of the Grotesque.'" *Mark Twain Journal* 17, iii (Winter 1974–75):12–14.

Anderson, David D. "Sherwood Anderson's Idea of the Grotesque." *Ohio-ana* 6 (Spring 1963):12–13.

———. 1967. *Sherwood Anderson: An Introduction and Interpretation.* New York: Holt, Rinehart.

———. 1981. "Sherwood Anderson's Moments of Insight." In *Critical Essays on Sherwood Anderson.* Boston: G. K. Hall, 155–71. Originally printed in *Critical Studies in American Literature: A Collection of Critical Essays.* By David D. Anderson. Karachi: University of Karachi, 1964, 99–141. Rpt. in Part in *Sherwood Anderson:* Winesburg Ohio: *Text and Criticism.* Ed. John H. Ferres. New York: Viking, 1966, 421–31. Revised version incorporated into the next work cited, 37–54.

Anderson, Sherwood. "The New Note." *Little Review* 1 (March 1914):23.

———. "Sister." *Little Review* 2 (December 1915):3–4.

———. "An Apology for Crudity." *Dial* 63 (November 8, 1917):437–38.

———1924. *A Story Teller's Story.* New York: B. W. Huebsch. Rpt. *A Story Teller's Story: A Critical Text.* Ed. Ray Lewis White. Cleveland:

Press of Case Western Reserve University, 1969. Rpt. New York: Viking, 1969.

———. 1926. *Tar: A Midwest Childhood*. New York: Boni and Liveright. Rpt. *Tar: A Midwest Childhood: A Critical Text*. Ed. Ray Lewis White. Cleveland: Press of Case Western Reserve University, 1969.

———. 1927. *A New Testament*. New York: Boni & Liveright.

———. 1960. "The Book of the Grotesque," *Winesburg, Ohio*. New York: Viking, 21–24.

Asselineau, Roger. "Language and Style in Sherwood Anderson's *Winesburg, Ohio*." *In Sherwood Anderson:* Winesburg, Ohio: *Text and Criticism*. Ed. John H. Ferres. New York: Viking, 1966, 345–56. From "Langue et Style de Sherwood Anderson Dans *Winesburg, Ohio*." Trans. John H. Ferres *Configuration Critique de Sherwood Anderson. La Revue des Lettres Modernes* 78–80 (1963):121–35.

Baker, Carlos. "Sherwood Anderson's Winesburg: A Reprise." *Virginia Quarterly Review* 48 (1972):568–79.

Berland, Alwyn. "Sherwood Anderson and the Pathetic Grotesque." *Western Review* 15 (1951):135–38.

Bidney, Martin. "Anderson and the Androgyne: 'Something More Than Man or Woman.'" *Studies in Short Fiction* 25 (1988):261–73.

Bluefarb, Sam. 1972. "George Willard: Death and Resurrection." In *The Escape Motif in the American Novel: Mark Twain to Richard Wright*. Columbus: Ohio State University Press, 42–58.

Bort, Barry D. "*Winesburg, Ohio:* The Escape from Isolation. *Midwest Quarterly* 11 (Summer 1970):443–56.

Bresnahan, Roger J. "The Village Grown Up: Sherwood Anderson and Lewis Bromfield." *Midamerica* 12 (1985):45–52.

Burbank, Rex. 1964. *Sherwood Anderson*. New York: Twayne.

Ciancio, Ralph. "'The Sweetness of the Twisted Apples': Unity of Vision in Winesburg, Ohio." *PMLA* 87 (1972):994–1006.

Cowley, Malcolm. 1960. "Introduction." *Winesburg, Ohio*. New York: Viking, 1–15.

Curry, Martha Mulroy. 1975. *The "Writer's Book" by Sherwood Anderson: A Critical Edition*. Metuchen, NJ: Scarecrow Press.

Curry, Sister Martha. "Sherwood Anderson and James Joyce." *American Literature* 52 (1980):236–49.

Daugherty, George H. "Anderson, Advertising Man." *Newberry Library Bulletin,* Second Series, no. 2 (December 1948):29–38.

Duffey, Bernard. 1954. *The Chicago Renaissance in American Letters: A Critical History*. East Lansing: Michigan State College Press.

Fertig, Martin J. "'A Great Deal of Wonder in Me': Inspiration and Transformation in *Winesburg, Ohio.*" *Markham Review* 6 (Summer 1977:65–70).

Fludernik, Monika. "'The Divine Accident of Life': Metaphoric Structure and Meaning in *Winesburg, Ohio.*" *Style* 22 (1988):116–35.

Gregory, Horace. 1949. "Editor's Note." *The Portable Sherwood Anderson.* New York: Viking, 40–42.

———. 1968. "On Sherwood Anderson." In *Talks with Authors*. Ed. Charles F. Madden. Carbondale: Southern Illinois University Press, 12–22.

Howe, Irving. 1951. *Sherwood Anderson*. New York: William Sloane.

Ingram, Forrest. 1971. *Representative Short Story Cycles of the Twentieth Century: Studies in a Literary Genre*. The Hague: Mouton.

Jones, Howard Mumford, and Walter B. Rideout, eds. 1963. *Letters of Sherwood Anderson*. Boston: Little, Brown.

Kimbel, Ellen. 1984. "The American Short Story: 1900–1920." In *The American Short Story, 1900–1945: A Critical History*. Ed. Philip Stevick. Boston: Twayne, 33–69.

Kramer, Dale. 1966. *Chicago Renaissance: The Literary Life in the Midwest, 1900–1920*. New York: Appleton-Century.

Lawry, Jon S. "The Arts of Winesburg and Bidwell, Ohio." *Twentieth Century Literature* 23 (February 1977):53–66.

Lorch, Thomas M. "The Choreographic Structure of *Winesburg, Ohio.*" *College Language Association Journal* 12 (1968):56–65.

McAleer, John J. "Christ Symbolism in *Winesburg, Ohio.*" *Discourse* 4 (1961):168–81.

Mann, Susan Garland. 1989. "Sherwood Anderson's *Winesburg, Ohio.*" *The Short Story Cycle: A Genre Companion and Reference Guide*. New York: Greenwood Press, 49–69.

Massa, Ann. 1982. "Sherwood Anderson." *American Literature in Context IV: 1900–1930*. London: Methuen, 88–101.

Mellard, James M. "Narrative Forms in Winesburg, Ohio." *PMLA* 83 (1968):1304–1312.

Modlin, Charles E., ed. 1989. *Sherwood Anderson's Love Letters to Eleanor Copenhaver Anderson*. Athens: University of Georgia Press.

Murphy, George D. "The Theme of Sublimation in Anderson's *Winesburg, Ohio.*" *Modern Fiction Studies* 13 (1967):237–46.

Nietzsche, Friedrich. 1964. "On Truth and Falsity in the Ultramoral Sense."

Early Greek Philosophy and Other Essays. Trans. Maximilian A. Mugge. Vol. 2, *The Complete Works of Friedrich Nietzsche*. Ed. Oscar Levy. New York: Russell & Russell.

Papinchak, Robert Allen. "'Something in the Elders': The Recurrent Imagery in Winesburg, Ohio." *Winesburg Eagle* 9, no. 1 (November 1983):1–7.

Park, Martha M. "How Far from Emerson's Man of One Idea to Anderson's Grotesques?" *CLA Journal* 20 (1977):374–79.

Phillips, William L. 1976. "The Editions of *Winesburg, Ohio*." In *Sherwood Anderson: Centennial Studies*. Ed. Hilbert H. Campbell and Charles E. Modlin. Troy, NY: Whitston, 151–55.

———. "Emerson in Anderson." *American Notes and Queries* 15 (1976):4–5.

———. "How Sherwood Anderson Wrote *Winesburg, Ohio*." *American Literature* 23 (1951):7–30. Rpt. in *Sherwood Anderson:* Winesburg, Ohio: *Text and Criticism*. Ed. John H. Ferres. New York: Viking, 1966, 263–86. Rpt. in *The Achievement of Sherwood Anderson: Essays in Criticism*. Ed. Ray Lewis White. Chapel Hill: University of North Carolina Press, 1966, 62–84. Rpt. in *The Merrill Studies in* Winesburg, Ohio. Comp. Ray Lewis White. Columbus, OH: Charles E. Merrill, 1971, 2–24. Rpt. in *Sherwood Anderson: A Collection of Critical Essays*. Ed. Walter B. Rideout. Englewood Cliffs, NJ: Prentice-Hall, 1974, 18–38.

Rideout, Walter. "Talbot Whittingham and Anderson: A Passage to *Winesburg, Ohio*." Rpt. in *Sherwood Anderson:* Winesburg, Ohio: *Text and Criticism*. Ed. John H. Ferres. New York: Viking, 1966, 287–300. Rpt. in *Critical Essays on Sherwood Anderson*. Ed. David D. Anderson. Boston: G. K. Hall, 1981, 146–54.

Rogers, Douglas. "Development of the Artist in *Winesburg, Ohio*." *Studies in the Twentieth Century*, no. 10 (Fall 1972):91–99.

Rosenfeld, Paul, ed. 1947. *The Sherwood Anderson Reader*. Boston: Houghton Mifflin.

San Juan, Epifanio, Jr. "Vision and Reality: A Reconsideration of Sherwood Anderson's *Winesburg, Ohio*." *American Literature* 35 (1963):137–55. Rpt. in part in *Sherwood Anderson:* Winesburg, Ohio: *Text and Criticism*. Ed. John H. Ferres. New York: Viking, 1966, 468–81.

Schevill, James. "Notes on the Grotesque: Anderson, Brecht, and Williams." *Twentieth Century Literature* 23 (May 1977):229–38.

———. 1951. *Sherwood Anderson: His Life and Work*. Denver: University of Denver Press.

Stewart, Maaja A. "Scepticism and Belief in Chekhov and Anderson." *Studies in Short Fiction* 9 (1972):29–40.

Stouck, David. "*Winesburg, Ohio* and the Failure of Art." *Twentieth Century Literature* 15 (1969):145–51.

—— "*Winesburg, Ohio* as a Dance of Death." *American Literature* 48 (1977):525–42. Rpt. in *Critical Essays on Sherwood Anderson*. Ed. David D. Anderson. Boston: G. K. Hall, 1981, 181–95.

——. "Sherwood Anderson and the Postmodern Novel." *Contemporary Literature* 26 (1985):302–316.

Sutton, William A. 1972. *The Road to Winesburg: A Mosaic of the Imaginative Life of Sherwood Anderson*. Metuchen, NJ: Scarecrow Press.

Tanner, Tony. 1965. "Sherwood Anderson's Little Things." *The Reign of Wonder: Naïvety and Reality in American Literature*. Cambridge: Cambridge University Press.

Taylor, Welford Dunaway. 1977. *Sherwood Anderson*. New York: Frederick Ungar.

Thurston, Jarvis. "Anderson and 'Winesburg': Mysticism and Craft." *Accent* 16 (1956):107–128.

Townsend, Kim. 1987. *Sherwood Anderson*. Boston: Hougton Mifflin.

Voss, Arthur. 1973. *The American Short Story: a Critical Survey*. Norman: University of Oklahoma Press.

Walcutt, Charles Child. 1956. *American Literary Naturalism, A Divided Stream*. Minneapolis: University of Minnesota Press.

Weber, Brom. 1964. *Sherwood Anderson*. Minneapolis: University of Minnesota Press.

White, Ray Lewis, ed. 1969. *Sherwood Anderson's Memoirs: A Critical Edition*. Chapel Hill: University of North Carolina Press.

——. "*Winesburg, Ohio:* The Table of Contents." *Notes on Modern American Literature* 8 (1984): Item 8.

——. 1990. *Winesburg, Ohio: An Exploration*. Boston: Twayne.

Williams, Kenny J. 1988. *A Storyteller and A City: Sherwood Anderson's Chicago*. De Kalb: Northern Illinois University Press.

W. S. B. 1971. "Ohio Small Town Life: Commonplace People and Their Everyday Existence." In *The Merrill Studies in* Winesburg, Ohio. Comp. Ray Lewis White. Columbus, OH: Charles E. Merrill, 30–32. Rpt. from the *Boston Transcript,* 11 June 1919, p. 6.

Hands

Circumstances of Composition

The story "Hands" was of tremendous personal importance to Sherwood Anderson. He considered it his "first authentic tale" (White, *Memoirs* 237). Although he had published two stories and written several unpublished books before he wrote this story, it was the writing of "Hands" that convinced him he might be able to be a writer he could respect, for it was "solid," with "structure, beauty, strength"; moreover, "it did not come out of reality . . . but out of that strange, more real life into which [he had] so long been trying to penetrate" (White, *Memoirs* 238). He vividly describes the circumstances of the story's composition in several accounts, which vary slightly in detail (White, *Memoirs* 237–38, 352–53, and 417; Jones-Rideout, *Letters* 314–15, 317, 387). Common to all of them, however, is the sense of exaltation he felt when he had completed the story, feeling certain of its fine quality. It was, he said, "the greatest moment of my life" (White, *Memoirs* 353).

Another element repeated in Anderson's various accounts of the composition of "Hands" is his insistence that he wrote it in a burst of inspiration, at one sitting, and never changed a word of it afterward. Phillips refutes that claim on the evidence of revisions that appear in the manuscript, which is written on the back of pages of the unpublished novel about Talbot Whittingham. Although the revisions do not include addition or deletion of paragraphs or sentences, and although "the order of narration" has not been altered, the author certainly did some polishing, for there are "almost two hundred instances in which earlier words and phrases are deleted, changed, or added to, to provide the readings of the final published version of the story" ("How" 9, 20). Phillips judges that "about nine-tenths of the changes" followed the completion of the first draft ("How" 21). Specific revisions, which Phillips details, included "changing a more formal, Latinate expression to a colloquial, Anglo-Saxon one" and muting the homoerotic elements (for example, "he still hungered for the boy" became "he still hungered for the presence of the boy" [WO 33]) ("How" 22–23).

Sources and Influences

Anderson describes his changing feelings about homosexuals in several passages in his *Memoirs*. When he came to Chicago for the first time and was working "in a North Side warehouse" (1896–97), his encounters with homosexuals were disturbing to him and left him feeling "a strange unhealth"; later (around 1913), when he was living on 57th Street and "all the young intellectuals" he was associating with were talking about Freud and "analyzing each other and everyone they met," Anderson's inquiry on the subject led his friends to conclude he himself had secret homosexual desires (White, *Memoirs* 339–40). Though Anderson scoffs at their amateur psychologizing, and though in time his puzzled uneasiness yielded to sympathy for the "plight" of homosexuals, still all this had left its mark: he looks back on that time of Freudian consciousness as "a time when it was well for a man to be somewhat guarded in the remarks he made, what he did with his hands" (339–40). Anderson's declaration that he had not read Freud when he wrote "Hands" is probably true, but that he "had scarcely heard of him" (White, *Memoirs* 473) cannot be believed.

Two other episodes in Anderson's life may have influenced this story. He recalls encountering, on the stairs of his Cass Street roominghouse, a young woman dressed in a man's suit, weeping because her love for another woman was unreturned; he goes on to say—though without specific reference to "Hands"—that when he read the Winesburg tales to his fellow boarders, they were quick to recognize in his fictional characters the "inner truth" of some member of their group (White, *Memoirs* 347–48). A slightly different version of this episode appears in *No Swank* (108–109). Anderson also recalls that when he and an advertising colleague were sardonically calling each other "Mable" and "Eva"—an allusion to their "common whoredom" within the commercial establishment—the suspicious stares of men in bars gave him a sense of what a homosexual pariah feels; that, he says, entered into the story (White, *Memoirs* 414–17).

The originality of this short story is indicated by the scarcity of critical comment concerning other sources. Cargill states that the influence of Gertrude Stein's *Three Lives* is visible in the story's "studied, conscious simplicity of style" and in its "intelligent sympathy . . . fenced off a little by attempted objectivity" (325). Wagner adds that Stein's stylistic impact can be detected in the "incremental adjectives" and "figurative language" Anderson used in the description of Wing's hands (82). Elledge offers "many specific parallels" between the story of Wing Biddlebaum and the story of Paolo and Francesca in the *Inferno:* that the characters are the first to interact with writers who will someday tell their tales (George Willard and Dante), that they suffer torment for their love (though with the difference that Wing's love is not "carnal"), that "Winesburg is a modernized version of Dante's hell," and that Wing's picking up crumbs as if he were going through a rosary seems a "futile" act of "penance" (11–15). These parallels could be coincidental; the extent of Anderson's knowledge of Dante is not clear, and Elledge does not mention it, though the oculist in *Marching Men* had quoted from Dante, as Phillips notes ("Origins" 146).

The radical nature of the subject matter is perhaps indicated by the fact that of the 220 stories analyzed by Wright in his *The American Short Story in the Twenties,* only three others deal with homosexuality—Anderson's "The Man Who Became a Woman," Hemingway's "Simple Enquiry," and Faulkner's "Divorce in Naples" (56n).

Publication History

"Hands" first appeared in *Masses* (8:5, 7) in March 1916. It was the second of the *Winesburg* tales to be published, following "The Book of the Grotesque" by one month. The managing editor of this radical little magazine, Floyd Dell, was an enthusiastic advocate of Freudian psychology and a central figure in the 57th Street group of Chicago intellectuals and artists whom Anderson met in 1913 (see "Sources and Influences"). Dell left his position as editor of the literary review of the Chicago *Evening Post* and went to New York, where his editorial work, first with *Masses* and then with the *Liberator,* became increasingly dedicated to socialist causes (see "The Strength of God," Publication History).

The first five paragraphs of the story in *Masses* differ considerably from the version finally published in *Winesburg, Ohio* (and also from the existing manuscript). The magazine version begins with a quotation: "On, you Wing Biddlebaum, comb your hair, it's falling into your eyes." The "slightly more abrupt opening" of that version was the author's own work, not that of the editors, Phillips concludes ("How" 9n).

Edward O'Brien listed "Hands" as one of the fifty best short stories of 1916 in the February 1917 issue of *Bookman.*

"Hands" was published again in 1919 in *Winesburg, Ohio.* In addition to the revision and rearrangement of the material in the opening paragraphs, two other significant changes appear in the *Winesburg* version of the text. In the magazine, George Willard is a reporter for the *Winesburg Democrat,* whereas in the book he works for the *Winesburg Eagle.* Additionally, the magazine version states that Wing Biddlebaum is "one of those men in whom sex is diffused," while the later version substitutes the euphemism "the force that creates life" for the word "sex." Anderson's fondness for the story is indicated by his including it in his Marion, Virginia, newspaper the *Smyth County News* in 1929. Paul Rosenfeld included it in the *Sherwood Anderson Reader* after Anderson's death (21–26).

Relation to Other Works

"Hands" develops the theme of isolation suggested in "The Book of the Grotesque" and introduces a further aspect of that theme by depicting one of the many communication problems that thrust the people of Winesburg into grotesque loneliness. The emotional withdrawal of Wing Biddlebaum typifies the characters of *Winesburg* (Wright 49). His "inability to communicate feeling" links him with the central characters of the next two stories, who are unable "to communicate thought" and "love" (D. Anderson 41; similarly, Frank 30, and Howe 101).

The story also introduces a major symbolic motif that runs throughout the story cycle—hands. They are especially significant in "Paper Pills," "An Awakening," "Queer," "The Untold Lie," and "Sophistication." Hand gestures provide an index of characters' emotions and relations with each other. Picht traces the motif through several tales, showing that hand contact allows the characters "to communicate their deepest feelings" (51). Bresnahan lists the numerous references to hands in the book, arguing that the ineffectuality of the older characters, including Wing, is doubly pathetic because they "should have been the town's leading citizens—its old hands" (22). Anderson's sensitivity to the expressive capacity of hands is evident outside *Winesburg, Ohio* as well—indeed, in most of his writings. In *Tar: A Midwest Childhood,* the title character recalls his mother's workworn hands and speculates that it was her hands that led him to "think so much about other people's hands" (276).

The energy "trapped inside" the old teacher now turned berry picker is allied with the pattern common to many of the stories of vitality and youthful vision stirring within characters who manifest symptoms of physical or spiritual decrepitude; even the opening paragraph of the story offers "a world of youth . . . buried syntactically within a statement of decay and frustration" (Bredahl 427–28).

The story also marks the first appearance of George Willard, the central figure of the book. Wing is the first of several in Winesburg who offer him advice; like Kate Swift and Wash Williams, he urges George to behave unconventionally (Wright 124). Eventually George will learn to dream, as Wing advises. But George's immediate response marks an early phase of his development: he wonders what lies behind Wing's strange hands but decides he does not "want to know what it is" (*WO* 31). This excessively timid reaction differs dramatically from his growing determination to understand other people in subsequent stories, notably "Loneliness" and "Drink." Wing's hands, both expert at "berry-picking (hence money-making)" and poetically expressive of his need to communicate his dream, are significantly related to George Willard's ambivalence (in "Mother" and other tales) with regard to the conflicting goals represented by his father and mother—respectively, "practical affairs and dreams" (Rideout 26).

The "religious symbolism" introduced in the final scene of the story links "Hands" with "Godliness" and "The Strength of God" as well as with religious, mystical language throughout the collection (Thurston 113–14). Moreover, Wing's suffering marks him as a Christ symbol, the first of a "succession of figures" that includes every person in Winesburg, thus fulfilling the declaration of Doctor Parcival that "everyone in the world is Christ and they are all crucified" (McAleer, "Christ" 178, quoting *WO* 57). Many of these figures, like Wing, are depicted kneeling in prayer. McAleer also notes a parallel between Wing and Hugh McVey, protagonist of *Poor White;* each is "[u]njustly accused by the people he tries to help" and "reviled, scourged, rejected" ("Christ" 178).

But Wing Biddlebaum is reviled because a community judges him guilty of homosexual acts (or, at least, homosexual tendencies). "Hands" is the story in which Anderson most fully treats the topic of homosexual desire. It is related to "The Man Who Became a Woman," in which an adolescent boy discovers the strangely feminine and masculine aspects of himself. Even more closely, Wing Biddlebaum's experience resembles that of Judge Arthur Turner in *A Story Teller's Story,* which was published in 1924 (White 120–38). Like Wing, Judge Turner is fat and old, a dreamer with delicate hands who recalls having been beaten by rougher associates and who re-presses an urge to embrace the boy he confides in, a youth who, like George, dimly intuits but does not understand the significance of what he hears. Turner has suffered ridicule and disgrace after writing a note filled with idealized love to a male college friend; for that, he was labeled a "pervert" (137). Moreover, just as Wing earns the admiration of the town for his speed in berrypicking, Turner has turned to "money making as the only sure method to win respect from the men of the modern world." Unlike Wing, he counsels his youthful confidant to do likewise; Wing retains his faith in dreaming.

A line in Anderson's *A Writer's Book* also relates to the sexual theme of "Hands." Anderson there envisions the photographer who took his mother's picture as "a small-town fairy, an unconscious one. . . ." (37). Wing Biddlebaum likewise, despite the fact that he is ostracized for sexual misconduct involving his pupils, is quite unconscious of harboring any sexual impulses. Anderson's sympathetic attitude toward Wing Biddlebaum can be contrasted with his satiric treatment of highly conscious homosexuals and lesbians in the later short story "That Sophistication."

Critical Studies

Most criticism of "Hands" has treated it in the context of some larger perspective on the whole of *Winesburg, Ohio*. Love finds in it the pattern he identifies as central to the story cycle, the conflict of urban torment and natural pastoral stillness. In the opening paragraph, Love notes the opposition between "the felicitous landscape" and the "uninhibited relationships" of the berrypickers on the one hand and Wing's grotesque isolation on the other (46); the contrast is emphasized by two metaphors applied to Wing Biddlebaum's hands, one mechanical—"piston rods of his machinery of expression"—and one natural—"the beating of the wings of an imprisoned bird" (Love 47). Furthermore, Wing's idealized dream of Socrates communicating with his students ironically relates to the harsh facts of his past, when, "like Socrates, he had been attacked as a corrupter of youth" (47). The allusion to Socrates is further elaborated by White's article "Socrates in Winesburg."

Abcarian points out in this story the pattern he considers central to the whole cycle, that "of blighted hope" whereby a character is "at a single blow . . . turned into a grotesque" (96–97).

Bort remarks that the story represents an extreme of isolation that significantly contrasts with the remembered moments of communication in the story that follows it, "Paper Pills" (444–46). As he argues, Wing Biddlebaum "is last seen furtively using his wonderful hands only to nourish himself" (446); nevertheless, the negative thrust of this commentary overlooks the important fact that Wing has continued to reach out to George, urging him to live a richer life.

Ciancio also sees "Hands" as "paradigmatic" of the *Winesburg* tales, but his interpretive emphasis is on the repeated pattern in which characters are brought to "conscious awareness of their flesh and hence of their existential guilt" (997, 998). Wing, who has been "unconsciously homosexual" (997) up to the moment he caresses George, discovers in "his sexual ecstasy" the truth about himself; this confrontation with "the radical paradox of being mortal" is typical, argues Ciancio, as is withdrawal into a paralysis of "subconscious longing and conscious dread" (998). Ciancio overstates the case when he claims that "Like Socrates, Wing is both a teacher and a pederast" (997). Moreover, his interpretation of Wing's gesture of thrusting his hands into his pockets as "onanism" is open to question (998). And surely critics have not agreed that Wing attains the conscious awareness of his homosexual desires that Ciancio asserts. The narrative states plainly, "Although he *did not understand* what had happened [to prompt the mob action in the Pennsylvania town] he felt that the hands must be to blame" (*WO* 33, italics mine).

Fertig, who is interested in the pattern of inspiration and artistic imagination in the collection, shows that in this story the motif of dreams introduced in the prologue takes a peculiar twist. Wing teaches his students to dream and urges George to dream, but dreams become problematic when the dream of a half-witted student leads to Wing's humiliation and exile from the community. The story indicates, concludes Fertig, that "the inspiration of a single character can lead to momentary confusion"; dreams may contain insight but also may be perilous (67).

Sociological critics have stressed the force of industrialism evident in the tale. Frank comments that "the tragic ambivalence of hands" has to do with the displacement of the proper function of hands—"loving"—by the turning of hands to "things" in the machine age (30); this argument would be stronger if the characters were given occupations more technological than berrypicking. More plausibly, Glicksberg emphasizes the "pressure of social conformity" in an "increasingly mechanized" era as the force that has reduced Wing to cowering anxiety (50–51). Stewart identifies the roots of Wing's suffering in "American Materialism and Puritanism" and points out that the story shifts its focus between "the town's perspective" and that of the private self, illuminating both the distinct differences of the two and the encroachment of the social upon the personal (32–33). Calverton, who focuses on Anderson's "proletarian class-consciousness" (91), is impressed with the story's psychological penetration and with the tragic dignity it endows upon such a plain man (100–101). Calverton touches on the key to Anderson's compassion as he explains that the "scientific attitude" that behavior is determined by environmental forces had led to "a broad change in judgment" by artists and the disappearance of moralizing (102; similarly, Wright 98).

Social attitudes regarding unconventional behavior are a prime cause of the tragedy in "Hands," and some critics have focused on that aspect of the story. Certainly Wing is "fatally misunderstood" (Howe 100) and "a victim of mob psychology" (Orvis 191). The "mob action" carried out in the Pennsylvania town can be seen as evidence of a "weakness . . . in the community structure"; significantly, representation of social violence in stories of the 1920s far exceeds that in stories of the previous twenty years (Wright 40). Kimbel's assertion that the townspeople are motivated by resentment at Wing's "awakening the imaginative and poetic in their sons" (65) is surely mistaken. However stupid and cruel their action is, at its base there is fear of real child molestation, not of anything so abstract as poetry. Still, a crucial and often overlooked point of the story is that it is they who are carried away by a half-wit's dream and by their own worst imaginings. As Yingling points out, "Hands" is "more overtly concerned with homosexual panic" than it is with homosexuality as such (115).

Psychological commentary on the story has been frequent, but it remains far from adequate. Acknowledging Wing's acquiescence to social dictates as a factor in his own victimization, Hoffman has noted the compulsive nature of Wing's hand movements, which manifest his repressed emotional needs (242). That view has become more or less standard. Beyond that, however, critical confusion abounds. About the central character's sexual identity there is little agreement. Some interpreters quite simply call Wing Biddlebaum a "homosexual" (Geismar 234), while others refer to him as "[p]robably . . . no homosexual" (DeJovine 26) or "non-sexual" (Mellard 1306) or even "thoroughly good and wholesome" (Taylor 28). More nearly accurate are Baker's reference to "half-suppressed homosexuality" and Bucco's emphasis on what Anderson calls the "diffused, not centralized nature of Wing's sexuality (Baker 571; Bucco 6; *WO* 32). Bucco says, "A Freudian critic might call Biddlebaum's love of the ideal a sublimation of his sexual instinct," but the Platonic reference in the tale suggests a different perspective by recalling a time when homosexual activity was socially acceptable yet when philosophers understood that "sexual love was subaltern, after all, to love of the ideal" (6). Anderson's portrait of Wing Biddlebaum differs significantly from Freud's portrait of Leonardo da Vinci, as Friend explains: for Freud the higher, creative life springs from the central fact of "sex perversion" whereas in Anderson's tale "*eros* is diffused" and there is "no dualism of the sensual and the spiritual" (57). To explain Wing Biddlebaum's dedication to teaching exclusively in terms of his latent sexual orientation is unnecessarily reductive. It is worth remembering that sexuality in general and sexual orientation in particular are still far from being well understood. Discussions of *latent* homosexual tendencies especially are inevitably extremely speculative. Above all, adult sexual desire directed toward children is surrounded by strong taboos; it is curious that this aspect of Anderson's story is almost never discussed. Commentators who eagerly see the story as a denunciation of conventional morality, sexual repression, and homophobia scarcely admit that the story also raises this other issue: if there is a sexual component in a teacher's feeling for a student (or vice versa, as the child's dream indicates), should that not be repressed? Like George Willard, most readers have not wanted to confront that question.

The idea of "sublimation" has been a convenient if not entirely satisfactory way of getting around it. Much as the Freudian critic Bucco hypothesizes, Murphy argues that "Wing's sexual urges had been most exquisitely sublimated" until "recognition of the essential truth" of the accusations against him paralyzes his psyche (239). A similar view is elaborated a few years later by Ciancio (997–98, discussed above), who, however, sees Wing as nearly typical of the characters of Winesburg, while Murphy places Wing's aversion to his own sexual desires at the opposite extreme from the ideal Platonic love of other characters in the collection (especially in "Death" and "Sophistication").

Possibly, the story is a protest against labeling (Townsend 106), just such labeling as many of the critical commentators indulge in. But "Hands" is more open-ended than most interpreters have realized. As Murphy remarks, "very little about Anderson is straightforward and uncomplicated" (237). And "Hands" raises far more questions than it answers. It presents a character, a story. It is not reducible to any one truth.

Anderson's formal innovations in short story technique have been important to his reputation and influence. He deliberately departed from conventional plot stories and took just pride in having freed the short story from rigid formulas and having given it a looser structure (Schevill 97; White, *Memoirs* 349–50). Not surprisingly, then, critics have paid close attention to the narrative structure and style of "Hands," a story of which he was particularly proud. Morgan argues that the image that likens the protagonist's hands to "piston rods" is an artistic flaw. Barker decries the "clumsy mechanics" of the tale, particularly Anderson's beginning in a "dramatic" mode, then abruptly introducing the voice of the storyteller referring to the story he is telling: "The story of Wing Biddelbaum is a story of hands" (437, quoting *WO*). But most commentators admire the artful arrangement of a story that only *seems* "discursive and loosely organized" (Voss 71). The omniscient authorial approach, though it is a "highly 'unrealistic' method of narrating," is also "evocative and effective," argues Mahoney (246). In particular, the "risky" passage where the narrator calls for a poet is "appropriate . . . to a narrator whose wisdom is more of the heart than the head" (Thurston 121) and to the Platonic emphasis of the story (Bucco 8). Also artful are the contrasted details of the setting—decayed veranda and neat kitchen, land seeded for clover but filled with mustard weeds—and a further pattern of ironic contrasts among the schoolteacher's gentle hands, the saloonkeeper's threatening fist, and the hands carrying a rope for lynching, between hatred in Pennsylvania and pride in Winesburg for the same man's hands, and between Eucharistic imagery and a lonely man "more like a bird" than a priest (Bucco 8, 6).

The narrative violations of chronology have been a particular subject of discussion for formalist critics. Classifying the story as a tale of "caustic pathos" with an "exposed situation," Wright shows that, in accord with the formal demands of that type of plotless tale, certain "crucial information" is withheld until it is most effective, thus arousing suspense and achieving something like the effect of a tragic reversal and discovery (389, 236, 262, 320). The story does not proceed by a conventional flashback but by "a kind of box-within-a-box structure": showing Wing first from the perspective of the townspeople, then from that of George Willard, and last from that of Wing himself, Anderson manages to convey to readers the complex understanding "that we are all Wing Biddlebaum and that we are also the men who cast him out . . . " (Joselyn 71). The "circularity of structure," which begins in the present, moves to the recent past and then a further past, and finally returns to the present, also supports the theme of entrapment (Bucco 5).

Possibly, says Townsend, there is even a relation between Wing's "diffused" sexuality and the narrative structure, which is "not focused, not building to a climax, not phallic as it were"; the narrative moves in gracefully wrought digressions; what seems only a "lovable weakness" (*WO* 31) is in fact the mark of "an accomplished storyteller" (106–107).

Gerlach shows Anderson here working out "a more flexible approach to closure" (94). The framing device Anderson employs, depicting the old teacher walking up and down on the decayed veranda both in the opening sentence and again at the end, is indicative of the "irresolution" of the narrative, in which nothing progresses and the protagonist does not achieve understanding of himself; yet the narrative offers an appropriate "feeling of termination" by referring to nightfall and offering an image of Wing kneeling in a posture that has "overtones . . . of eternity" (95–96). Rather implausibly, though, Gerlach refuses to grant that Anderson realized the value of the device he used, thinking he "might genuinely have meant those invocations to a storyteller," not realizing "that the device was precisely what allowed him to conceal the extent of his innovation" (99). The persistent tendency to see Anderson's technique as clumsy even when it is demonstrated to be skillful marks a critical blindness that seems to have carried over from earlier portraits of Anderson as a "groping" homespun storyteller and from a general confusion of the narrators of the tales with the author himself. Certainly Anderson's repeated praise of this story as "authentic" and "solid" is some evidence that he understood its worth (White, *Memoirs* 238).

Mellard finds in the story structure a movement toward an epiphany that reveals the meaning of the central symbol. In the final scene, Wing's picking up the crumbs allows the reader to see "the nature of Wing's gift, the tragic irony of his situation, and the meaning of his hands in their divine expression of love and faith" (1304–1305; similarly, Kimbel 66). Mellard, then, finds the key moment of recognition in the story to be the reader's, whereas Murphy (239) and Ciancio (998) find it to be Wing's. This is a crucial point of interpretive disagreement, and it draws attention to important matters that the story leaves to a reader's inference. One critic proposes that "Hands" is "an almost perfect example of an explicit or context-free story"; numerous linguistic features within the text support his contention that the story "places minimal reliance on the ability of the [reader] to supply items of content necessary either to flesh out the body of the [story] or to place it in the correct interpretive context" (Fischer 17, 30). But Wright, persuasively, argues otherwise. The authorial statement defining Wing as "one of those rare, little-understood men" whose gentleness makes them "not unlike the finer sort of women in their love of men" (*WO* 31) is not so complete as it seems, Wright asserts, for it omits such other important matters as "his exceptional naïveté, his fear of society, and his disastrous inability to understand the strain of homosexuality in himself" (333–34). The range of critical response to Wing Biddlebaum is in part owing to the tendency in Anderson (like that in other writers of the nineteen-twenties) to leave readers to draw inferences that most earlier writers had made explicit. In effect, the reader must be "the poet" who understands the story of "Hands."

An essay by Asselineau gives the fullest discussion of stylistic features in this story such as the poetic prose and the diction, a mixture of modern technical terms and archaisms with ordinary mainstream vocabulary (354, 349). A minor divergence of taste appears when Wagner praises a simile (82) that Asselineau finds "extraneous" (353), the comparison of Wing's motion when he begins to talk to that of "a fish returned to the brook by the fisherman" (*WO* 28). Gold's somewhat overblown comment that the term "maidens" in the opening paragraph shows that "For Anderson women have a strange holy power" (555) overlooks the point nearer at hand: the bookish flavor of the phrase "youths and maidens" participates in creating the subtle tensions of the opening paragraph, in which fields and laughing berry-pickers and quaintness of language lend a pastoral mood that is then effectively shattered by harsh realism as a "girlish voice" cruelly taunts an old, bald man: "Oh, you Wing Biddlebaum, comb your hair . . . " (*WO* 27).

One inference no one seems to have made is that the symbolic field of mustard weed in the opening scene is not purely negative in its import. Though critics rightly see here a parallel to the grotesque twisting of Wing Biddlebaum, there is also a hint of promise. For not only is a field of yellow-flowering mustard a thing of beauty; it is also productive of mustard seed, which Jesus likened to the kingdom of heaven because though it "is the least of all seeds, when it is grown, it is the greatest among herbs, and becometh a tree, so that the birds of the air come and lodge in the branches thereof" (Matt. 13:31–32). This biblical passage resonates suggestively with a name allied with both birds ("Wing") and trees ("baum"). Jesus also speaks of faith like "a grain of mustard seed," which can move mountains (Matt. 17:20). Wing demonstrates that his living faith remains uncrushed by persecution when in a moment of inspiration he tells George to dream (thus planting a seed in the boy's fallow mind), and the spiritual promise implicit in the first scene is reiterated in the last scene where Wing kneels, eating crumbs. Though this seems abstruse, far more subtle than Anderson is generally assumed to be, further evidence that he intended just such an inference to be drawn appears in the episode in *A Story Teller's Story* that tells the story of Judge Turner, a character similar to Wing Biddlebaum (see "Relation to Other works" above). When, as a boy, Turner finds a poisonous mushroom, Amanita Phalloides, his father tells him, "A bit of it no larger than a mustard seed would destroy your life" (White 130). The significance of this line extends, in Turner's story, to the symbolic poison of homophobic ridicule that does indeed warp Turner and to the symbolic poison he dispenses to the youth he tells to devote himself to money-making. Wing's teaching may be, by implication, more positive, for the seed he plants in George Willard's mind at length grows into the dreams by which he sees beneath the surfaces of many lives.

Works Cited

Abcarian, Richard. "Innocence and Experience in *Winesburg, Ohio.*" *University Review Kansas City* 35 (1968):95–105.

Anderson, David. 1967. *Sherwood Anderson: An Introduction and Interpretation*. New York: Holt, Rinehart.

Anderson, Sherwood. "Hands." *Masses* 8 (March 1916): 5–7.

———. 1926. *Tar: A Midwest Childhood*. New York: Boni & Liveright.

———. 1934. *No Swank*. Philadelphia: Centaur Press.

———. 1960. *Winesburg, Ohio*. New York: Viking.

Asselineau, Roger. 1966. "Language and Style in Sherwood Anderson's *Winesburg, Ohio*." In *Sherwood Anderson:* Winesburg, Ohio: *Text and Criticism*. Ed. John H. Ferres. New York: Viking, 345–56. Rpt. from "Langue et Style de Sherwood Anderson dans *Winesburg, Ohio*." Trans. John H. Ferres. *La Revue des Lettres Modernes* 78–80 (1963):121–35.

Baker, Carlos. "Sherwood Anderson's Winesburg: A Reprise." *The Virginia Quarterly Review* 48 (1972):568–79.

Barker, Russell H. "The Storyteller Role." *College English* 3 (1942):433–42.

Bort, Barry D. "*Winesburg, Ohio:* The Escape from Isolation." *Midwest Quarterly* 11 (1970):443–56.

Bredahl, A. Carl. "'The Young Thing Within': Divided Narrative and Sherwood Anderson's *Winesburg, Ohio*." *Midwest Quarterly: A Journal of Contemporary Thought* 27 (1986):422–37.

Bresnahan, Roger J. "The 'Old Hands' of Winesburg." *Midwestern Miscellany* 11 (1983):19–27.

Bucco, Martin. "A Reading of Sherwood Anderson's 'Hands.'" *Colorado State Review* 1 (1966):5–8.

Calverton, V. J. "Sherwood Anderson: A Study in Sociological Criticism." *Modern Quarterly* 2 (1924):82–118. Rpt. in *The Newer Spirit: A Sociological Criticism of Literature*. Introduction by Ernest Boyd. New York: Boni & Liveright, 1925, 52–118.

Cargill, Oscar. 1941. *Intellectual America: Ideas on the March*. New York: Macmillan.

Ciancio, Ralph. "The Sweetness of the Twisted Apples: Unity of Vision in *Winesburg, Ohio*." *PMLA* 87 (1972):994–1006.

Curry, Martha Mulroy, ed. 1975. *The "Writer's Book" by Sherwood Anderson: Text and Criticism*. Metuchen, NJ: Scarecrow Press.

De Jovine, F. Anthony. 1971. *The Young Hero in American Fiction: A Motif for Teaching Literature*. New York: Appleton-Century-Crofts.

Elledge, Jim. "Dante's Lovers in Sherwood Anderson's 'Hands.'" *Studies in Short Fiction* 21 (1984):11–15.

Fertig, Martin J. "'A Great Deal of Wonder in Me': Inspiration and Transformation in *Winesburg, Ohio*," *Markham Review* 6 (1977):65–70.

Fischer, Andreas. 1988. "Context-Free and Context-Sensitive Literature: Sherwood Anderson's *Winesburg, Ohio* and James Joyce's *Dubliners." Reading Contexts*. Ed. Neil Forsyth. Swiss Papers in English Language and Literature 4.

Frank, Waldo. "Winesburg, Ohio after Twenty Years." *Story* 19, 91 (September–October 1941):29–33. Rpt. in *Sherwood Anderson:* Winesburg, Ohio: *Text and Criticism*. Ed. John H. Ferres. New York: Viking, 1966, 369–76. Rpt. in *Achievement of Sherwood Anderson: Essays in Criticism*. Ed. Ray Lewis White. Chapel Hill: University of North Carolina Press, 1966, 116–121. Rpt. in *Homage to Sherwood Anderson, 1876–1941*. Ed. Paul P. Appel. Mamaroneck, NY: Appel, 1970, 41–47.

Friend, Julius, W. "The Philosophy of Sherwood Anderson." In *Homage to Sherwood Anderson, 1876–1941*. Ed. Paul P. Appel. Mamaroneck, NY: Appel, 1970, 55–62.

Geismar, Maxwell. "Sherwood Anderson: Last of the Townsmen." In *The Last of the Provincials: The American Novel, 1915–1925*. Boston: Houghton Mifflin, 1947, 223–84. Rpt. in part in *Sherwood Anderson:* Winesburg, Ohio: *Text and Criticism*. Ed. John H. Ferres. New York: Viking, 1966, 377–82.

Gerlach, John. 1985. *Toward the End: Closure and Structure in the American Short Story*. University: University of Alabama Press, 94–100.

Glicksberg, Charles J. 1971. *The Sexual Revolution in Modern American Literature*. The Hague: Martinus Nijhoff.

Gold, Herbert. "The Purity and Cunning of Sherwood Anderson." *Hudson Review* 10 (1957–58):548–57. Rpt. in *The Age of Happy Problems*. New York: Dial Press, 1962, 57–67. Rpt. in part in *Sherwood Anderson:* Winesburg, Ohio: *Text and Criticism*. Ed. John H. Ferres. New York: Viking, 1966, 396–404. Rpt. in *Critical Essays on Sherwood Anderson*. Ed. David D. Anderson. Boston: G. K. Hall, 1981, 138–45.

Hoffman, Frederick J. 1957. *Freudianism and the Literary Mind*. Rev. ed. Baton Rouge: Louisiana State University Press. Rpt. in *Sherwood Anderson:* Winesburg, Ohio: *Text and Criticism*. Ed. John H. Ferres. New York: Viking, 1966, 309–20. Rpt. in *The Achievement of Sherwood Anderson: Essays in Criticism*. Ed. Ray Lewis White. Chapel Hill: University of North Carolina Press, 1966, 174–92.

Howe, Irving. 1951. *Sherwood Anderson*. New York: William Sloane.

Jones, Howard Mumford, and Walter B. Rideout, eds. 1953. *Letters of Sherwood Anderson*. Boston: Little, Brown.

Joselyn, Sister Mary. 1966. "Sherwood Anderson and the Lyric Story." In *The Twenties: Poetry and Prose*. Richard E. Langford and William E. Taylor

(Eds.). DeLand, FL: Everett Edwards Press, 70–73. Rpt. in *Sherwood Anderson:* Winesburg, Ohio: *Text and Criticism*. Ed. John H. Ferres. New York: Viking, 1966, 444–54.

Kimbel, Ellen. 1984. "The American Short Story: 1900–1920." In *The American Short Story, 1900–1945: A Critical History*. Ed. Philip Stevick. Boston: Twayne, 33–69.

Love, Glen A. *"Winesburg, Ohio* and the Rhetoric of Silence." *American Literature* 40 (1968):38–57.

Mahoney, John J. "An Analysis of *Winesburg, Ohio." Journal of Aesthetics and Art Criticism* 15 (1956):245–52.

McAleer, John J. "Christ Symbolism in *Winesburg, Ohio." Discourse* 4 (1961):168–81. Rpt. in *The Merrill Studies in* Winesburg, Ohio. Comp. Ray Lewis White. Columbus, OH: Charles E. Merrill, 1971, 60–74.

Mellard, James M. "Narrative Forms in *Winesburg, Ohio." PMLA* 83 (1968):1304–1312.

Modlin, Charles E., ed. 1984. *Sherwood Anderson: Selected Letters*. Knoxville: University of Tennessee Press.

Morgan, Gwendolyn. "Anderson's 'Hands.'" *Explicator* 48 (Fall 1989):46–47.

Murphy, George D. "The Theme of Sublimation in Anderson's *Winesburg, Ohio." Modern Fiction Studies* 13 (1967):237–46.

Orvis, Mary Burchard. 1948. *The Art of Writing Fiction*. New York: Prentice-Hall.

Phillips, William L. "How Sherwood Anderson Wrote *Winesburg, Ohio." American Literature* 23 (1951):7–30. Rpt. in *Sherwood Anderson:* Winesburg, Ohio: *Text and Criticism*. Ed. John H. Ferres. New York: Viking, 1966, 263–86. Rpt. in *The Achievement of Sherwood Anderson: Essays in Criticism*. Ed. Ray Lewis White. Chapel Hill: University of North Carolina Press, 1966, 62–84. Rpt. in *The Merrill Studies in* Winesburg, Ohio. Comp. Ray Lewis White. Columbus, OH: Charles E. Merrill, 1971, 2–24. Rpt. in *Sherwood Anderson: A Collection of Critical Essays*. Ed. Walter B. Rideout. Englewood Cliffs, NJ: Prentice-Hall, 1974, 18–38.

————. "Sherwood Anderson's *Winesburg, Ohio:* Its Origins, Composition, Technique, and Reception." Ph.D. diss. University of Chicago, 1950.

Picht, Douglas R. 1971. "Anderson's Use of Tactile Imagery in *Winesburg, Ohio."* In *The Merrill Studies in* Winesburg, Ohio. Comp. Ray Lewis White. Columbus, OH: Charles E. Merrill, 48–51. Originally printed in *Research Studies* 35 (1967):176–78.

Rideout, Walter B. "The Simplicity of *Winesburg, Ohio." Shenandoah* 13

(1962): 20–31. Rpt. in *Sherwood Anderson:* Winesburg, Ohio: *Text and Criticism.* Ed. John H. Ferres. New York: Viking, 1966, 287–300. Rpt. in *Critical Essays on Sherwood Anderson.* Ed. David D. Anderson. Boston: G. K. Hall, 1981, 146–54.

Rosenfeld, Paul, ed. 1947. *The Sherwood Anderson Reader.* Boston: Houghton Mifflin.

Schevill, James. 1951. *Sherwood Anderson: His Life and Work.* Denver: University of Denver Press.

Stewart, Maaja A. "Scepticism and Belief in Chekhov and Anderson." *Studies in Short Fiction* 9 (1972):29–40.

Taylor, Welford Dunaway. 1977. *Sherwood Anderson.* New York: Frederick Ungar.

Thurston, Jarvis. "Anderson and 'Winesburg': Mysticism and Craft." *Accent* 16 (1956):107–28. Rpt. in part in *Sherwood Anderson:* Winesburg, Ohio: *Text and Criticism.* Ed. John H. Ferres. New York: Viking, 1966, 331–44.

Townsend, Kim. 1987. *Sherwood Anderson.* Boston: Houghton Mifflin.

Voss, Arthur. 1973. *The American Short Story: A Critical Survey.* Norman: University of Oklahoma Press.

Wagner, Linda W. 1976. "Sherwood, Stein, the Sentence, and Grape Sugar and Oranges." In *Sherwood Anderson: Dimensions of His Literary Art: A Collection of Critical Essays.* Ed. David D. Anderson. East Lansing: Michigan State University Press, 75–89.

Wright, Austin McGiffert. 1961. *The American Short Story in the Twenties.* Chicago: University of Chicago Press.

White, Ray Lewis. "Socrates in Winesburg." *Notes on Modern American Literature* 10 (1986):Item 2.

———, ed. 1969. *Sherwood Anderson's Memoirs: A Critical Edition.* Chapel Hill: University of North Carolina Press.

———, ed. 1968. *A Story Teller's Story: A Critical Text.* Cleveland: Press of Case Western Reserve University.

Yingling, Thomas. 1990. "*Winesburg, Ohio* and the End of Collective Experience." In *New Essays on* Winesburg, Ohio. Ed. John W. Crowley. Cambridge: Cambridge University Press.

Paper Pills

Circumstances of Composition

Originally Anderson seems to have used the title "Pills" for this tale, a title subsequently revised to "Paper Pills," then to "The Philosopher" (at its first publication), and finally again to "Paper Pills" (White, "Story Titles" 6–7). The character Doctor Reefy evidently is in part a reworking of the father of Talbot Whittingham in the unpublished novel Anderson brought with him to Chicago from Elyria; each figure is "a smalltown doctor with radical ideas" (Phillips, "How" 15).

Sources and Influences

In Elyria, Ohio, where Anderson had resided between 1907 and 1912 and where he had been president of a paint manufacturing company, one of his friends was a newspaper editor named Reefy (Phillips, "Origins" 50; Duffey 208). In fact, "there were two Dr. Reefy's in Elyria while Anderson was living there between 1908 and 1913," both of them graduates of the Eclectic Medical Institute in Cincinnati and both of them probably known to Anderson; since the eclectic physicians "refused to be limited to the 'regular' body of medical truths" and used Indian and herbal remedies as well as conventional medicines, they were looked upon as rather "odd," and Phillips argues a relationship between them and the doctor of "Paper Pills" (Eclectic" 3–4).

In *Tar*, there is an old doctor with memorable hands ("like old grape vines") known to the autobiographical figure Tar in his childhood and remembered by him for his "gentleness" (71). "Afterward Tar used the doctor in several of his printed tales," Anderson writes, commenting that the man was defeated by life: "Something had gone wrong with [him] as something had gone wrong with Tar's mother" (71–72). Later, Anderson relates, the old doctor married a young wife, who "only lived for a year"; his few friends included "an old tree nurseryman named John Spaniard" (170, 330). Researchers have found that there was in fact a nurseryman in Anderson's hometown of Clyde, Ohio, named French (Phillips, "How" 18).

Several passages in Anderson's *Memoirs* mention other autobiographical experiences that may have influenced some details of the story. It is well to be circumspect, however: even in this most autobiographical of his works,

Anderson does some fictionalizing. He recalls that when he was "very young," an old woman to whom he had delivered newspapers willed to him a weed-filled lot with "gnarled old apple trees" of which his brothers were scornful but which nourished his dreams till he discovered that the unpaid taxes on the lot exceeded its value (57–62); the episode forms a nice parable about a fall from innocence. He further recalls a time when he was wooing a wealthy young woman by writing flowery romantic letters full of praise of "purity" and "virginity" in love; his protestations are belied when he impulsively grabs her in a passionate embrace (381–85). If those facts are accurate, the young suitor who "talked continually of virginity" (*WO* 37) is perhaps a self-caricature. Likewise, the bite the other suitor inflicts on the young woman's shoulder may have originated in an incident Anderson recalls with self-loathing from his days as a businessman, when he impulsively bit a whore on the shoulder: "It was a vicious bite," he says (265). So the *other* young suitor may be a self-caricature, too. Together they may reflect his own divided attitude toward sex—and his awareness of it.

Stouck suggests that one of Oliver Herford's illustrations in the first edition of Edgar Lee Masters's *Spoon River Anthology,* showing "Death approaching an older man who has just taken a young wife," may have influenced this tale ("Dance" 531).

Massa notes Stein's influence in the device of repetition of key words in the tale (100). Phillips asserts that the overall style of the tale—flat statements and casual, digressive manner—derive from the tradition of oral storytelling ("Origins" 82).

Publication History

"Paper Pills" was first published in *The Little Review* (3:7–9) in the June–July issue of 1916 under the title "The Philosopher." When Anderson wrote the story now titled "The Philosopher" for *Winesburg, Ohio,* he changed the title of this story to "Paper Pills" (apparently reverting to an earlier title). Otherwise, the revisions Anderson made for the book version of the tale are fairly minor (correcting "knarled" to "gnarled," for example), with one exception: "going to have a child" and "pregnant" are both changed to the phrase "in the family way" (*LR* 8 and *WO* 37, 38). Phillips points out that the extant manuscript is like the text of *Winesburg* in this detail ("Origins" 151); either Anderson's final revision was a reversion to an earlier choice of phrase, as Phillips surmises, or the manuscript is a later one than Phillips believes it to be. The story was again published in the *Winesburg, Ohio* in 1919.

This is the first of three Winesburg tales to be published in *The Little Review,* but Anderson's association with the magazine had begun with his contribution of his article "The New Note" to the inaugural issue (March

1914). Before "Paper Pills" appeared, the magazine had published other articles and several of his tales and sketches, including "Sister," "Vibrant Life," and "The Struggle" (later "War" in *TE*). The magazine did not pay its contributors and took pride in being a forum for avant-garde work. Its editor, Margaret Anderson, wrote later, "Practically everything the *Little Review* published during the first years was material that would have been accepted by no other magazine in the world at the moment" (44). She boasts that Anderson and others, later on, when they were in demand, would offer work as a gift to her magazine in preference to sending it to paying magazines (44), but she was mistaken; as Howe puts it, "to the *Little Review* circle, [Anderson seemed] a delightfully innocent primitive—a misapprehension for which the magazine was properly punished by becoming the receptacle for his worst writing" (67). Increasingly, as he tried to support himself independently by his pen, pay became important to him. But in 1916 publication itself was gratifying.

Relation to Other Works

The most-quoted passage in "Paper Pills" is the paragraph about "the sweetness of the twisted apples" (*WO* 36); it is closely akin to the reference to the beauty of grotesques in the introductory "The Book of the Grotesque" (*WO* 23). Critics generally seem to agree that the passage is the "central symbolic statement of the book" (Bridgman 156), for it combines a naturalistic sense of the ravages of life with compassionate tenderness, especially for ordinary folk in nonurban backwaters. Further, the theory of "truths" in "The Book of the Grotesque" is allied to the discussion in this story about Doctor Reefy's making truths out of his thoughts and then letting them fade away. By his habit of filling his pockets with bits of writing that are later thrown away, Reefy is linked with the old writer in the introductory story, who, because he does not publish his work or embrace one truth exclusively, is saved from becoming grotesque.

The pregnancy motif introduced in "The Book of the Grotesque," where the old writer is likened to "a pregnant woman" (*WO* 22), is related to Reefy's practice of forming thoughts that grow "gigantic in his mind" (37) and also to the pregnancy of the young woman in this tale, who becomes Reefy's wife. Since this pregnancy ends without bringing forth new life, thematic emphasis falls on blighted fruit or unripened hope, as in "Mother," where Elizabeth Willard laments that the thing growing within her son "is the thing I let be killed in myself" (*WO* 43).

The close description of Doctor Reefy's hands in evocative similes links this story to "Hands." As Wing Biddlebaum stuffs his hands into his pockets, so Doctor Reefy stuffs his written thoughts into his pockets; the parallel imagery makes the point explicated by Howe, that these grotesque characters "rot because they are unused, their energies deprived of outlet" (101).

The story is also tied to "Mother" through another story, almost at the end of the whole cycle—"Death"—that brings the central characters of the two earlier stories together. The main portion of that tale is set at a time earlier than "Paper Pills" and shows Doctor Reefy, in middle age, meeting Elizabeth Willard in understanding friendship and sharing with her a brief, dramatic embrace. There is also an encounter between Doctor Reefy and George Willard, who does not appear in "Paper Pills."

Two Winesburg stories center on doctors, Doctor Reefy and Doctor Parcival (of "The Philosopher"). Both "are philosophers and writers," says Miller, and both "should be sued for malpractice" ("Portraits" 6). Cowan, however, contrasts the two, arguing that "[u]nlike Dr. Parcival's suffering, Dr. Reefy's suffering is ultimately redemptive" (100). Surely Anderson associated them closely in his own mind, as the earlier title of this story indicates. Like Doctor Parcival, Doctor Reefy exemplifies a key theme of the whole book, "the loneliness of human life, the baffled search of every personality for meanings and purposes deeper than anything that may be said or done, answers that will cut under the superficial axioms by which we are judged" (M. A. 87–88).

The importance of this story to Anderson is indicated by his later references to it. In 1928, he offered a summary of the story to *The Bookman* for an article about the "credos" of American authors ("Statements" 204). He says plainly that his "philosophy of life" is contained in Doctor Reefy's way of writing out his thoughts, sometimes being "o'ermastered . . . for the time" by an idea, and tossing the bits of paper from his pocket at a friend, laughing. Evidently Anderson intends here a serious statement about not taking oneself too seriously, about balancing passionate convictions with philosophical skepticism. He also suggests a lot about his own writing practices. As Curry points out, two passages in *Writer's Book* are related to "Paper Pills." In one, Anderson recommends that "every young writer" should read the story about Doctor Reefy because "clinging to ideas" is poisonous, and it is better to keep "a continual flow," to "write and throw away" (83, 84). In the other, Anderson likens writing a short story to "pick[ing] an apple in an orchard"; both are "grasped whole" (85). Doctor Reefy's laughter is perhaps illuminated by a passage in *A Story Teller's Story* in which Anderson speaks of his own effort to be an artist: "I am tremendously serious about it all, but at the same time I laugh constantly at myself for my own seriousness" (White 222).

The metaphorical parallel between the production of children and the production of art was of continuing interest to Anderson. In two novels Anderson wrote before this story, *Windy McPherson's Son* (1916) and *Marching Men* (1917), children are of immense importance in marriage and in a sense are the justification for sex; against that background, the loss of the child in this story is even more pathetic.

Critical Studies

"Paper Pills" is one of Anderson's many stories of the buried life. Although Doctor Reefy is old and physically unattractive, he has within him "the seeds of something very fine" (*WO* 35). The story reveals his hidden sensitivity, generous soul, and creative mind (Way 112). But there is also a terrible sense of waste about this man, a doctor who no longer practices his profession and who sits shut up by himself in an office into which fresh air never enters.

The story is virtually plotless, and critics have been interested in its techniques. An early reviewer admired it as a welcome change from "the snappy short story form, with its planned proportions of flippant philosophy, epigrammatic conversation, and sex danger," for it is simply "a bit from the lives of" its characters, "told effortlessly, almost carelessly . . . " (MA 88, 87). Several commentators have focused on Anderson's use of the telling detail to convey meaning; Schevill compares the technique to that of Expressionist painting (100), Burbank notes that the "disconnected images which are thematically and symbolically related and coalescent" are like Impressionist painting (62), and Thomas finds a stylistic likeness to Alfred Stieglitz's photographic technique in the paper pills, which, associated with both twisted apples and the doctor's knuckles, "become symbols of Dr. Reefy's inability to communicate" (72). San Juan thinks the repeated figure of round balls in hands, paper pills, and apples lends "unity" to the story (143), but Stouck finds something "postmodern" in these stylized images ("Postmodern" 312). And Pawlowski comments that with the knuckles, the balls of paper, and the apples, Anderson brings in "the implicit tree of knowledge" and manages to "achieve a spatial concept" (295), though it is not quite clear what that means.

Critics have by no means reached a consensus, however, on the general question of whether Anderson's technique is that of a talented bumbler or an accomplished stylist. This story in particular has aroused the accusation that Anderson's sloppiness appears in the "jaded white horse" that becomes a "jaded grey horse" two pages later in the first edition and in the awkward juxtaposition of "knuckles and nibbling" in the passage about the sweetness of gnarled apples (*WO* 36); the same critic admires the fine way that passage plays "rural nostalgia" against urban sterility (Bridgman 164, 156–57). Cowley emended the text so that in the 1960 edition the horse is white both times it is mentioned. As for "knuckles" and "nibbling," however, it is reasonable to suppose that the conjunction is quite deliberate; images of teeth, biting, and fruit are central in the story. The young woman's lover, impelled by lust and greed, has literally taken a cruel bite of her, but as she grows to understand the doctor, she metaphorically tastes the sweetness of a gentle man twisted by life, of which the gnarled old hands are an emblem. He himself is like the apples rejected by the pickers, which only the knowing few may savor. Anderson draws a further parallel: as Reefy goes about "filling his pockets with the scraps of paper," so one may gather the misshapen apples, "filling his pockets with them" (*WO* 36). The story itself thus is identified with the character and the apple as a "paper pill"—not forbidden fruit but overlooked fruit, more beautiful than the perfectly round but tasteless commodity usually consumed in the literary marketplace.

Another stylistic comment is offered by Baker, who wryly notes that though *Winesburg* was for its time very candid about sex, the "terminology" is quaintly "euphemistical," as when the woman in this tale "is put 'in the family way'" (571, quoting *WO* 37). Baker overlooks the fine irony of the phrase, which underlines the pathetic absence of family for the lonely man who married her. Since Anderson's first published version is blatantly modern in referring to the woman as "pregnant," the revision suggests Anderson's intent to draw attention to the specific promise conveyed by the word "family" and to the loss Reefy endures.

The structural arrangement of the story, which does not follow a chronological sequence, has also received some analysis. Mellard classifies this as one of five symbolic stories with an "epiphanic" structure, arguing that the events narrated at the end—Reefy's marriage, his wife's death, and the couple's shared moments when he read her his thoughts—offer the reader an epiphanic insight into the meaning of his life (1305). Wright classifies it as a tale of "romantic pathos" with an "exposed situation" where, as in "Hands," the narrator withholds vital information until it will make the most effective impact, providing an artificial version of a tragic reversal; Wright points out that it is "almost entirely narrated," largely dispensing with dialogue and dramatic scenes (388, 262, 292–93). Further, he shows that the story exhibits characteristics that were to become typical of stories of the twenties—the protagonist's withdrawal from society, the treatment of illicit sexual relationships, and the demand that a reader draw significant inferences (in this story, about the depth of the doctor's grief over his wife's death) (49n, 57, 408). The structure of the smaller story embedded in the larger, the tale of the heiress with her two suitors, has elicited one appreciative comment, from a critic who admires in it the "psychological comedy" of expectations that are built up and then surprised in "a doubly ironic reversal in which one expectation is fulfilled but in an unexpected and ridiculous manner" (Hilfer 151).

Doctor Reefy's wife has received less attention than she deserves. Chase, who criticized *Winesburg, Ohio* as excessively preoccupied with sex, calls her "an hysterical pregnant girl" (35). Two feminist critics, however, have seen in her story the significant "abuse of women" that permeates the book (Rigsbee 236) and the "powerlessness" and passivity (evidenced especially when she silently accepts the pain of the dental patient) that characterize the women of Winesburg (Atlas 256–57). Neither of those critics, though, adequately addresses Doctor Reefy's intuitive understanding of and tenderness toward the victimized woman, which make the story more complex in its treatment of gender relationships than they allow. The young woman's motives in seeking out Doctor Reefy have scarcely been mentioned; although White states that she goes to Reefy "for childbearing advice" (*Exploration* 60), it is more likely that she goes seeking release from an unwanted pregnancy.

The real, and unresolved, critical issue concerning "Paper Pills," however, is the evaluation of Doctor Reefy's character. Is he or is he not a "grotesque"? Waldo Frank, Sherwood Anderson's friend, argued in 1941 that he is: the thing that "goes wrong" in this story "is *thought,*" says Frank, which the doctor turns into "ineffectual scraps of wisdom . . . cluttering his pocket" (30). Howe, in 1951, agreed, adding that Reefy is one of those with "instincts curdled in isolation" (101). Similarly, Thurston, in 1956, found the paper pills to be a clear indication of "the compulsive symptomatic act" that marks "the blockage of the spiritual quest" (113).

More recent critics, in contrast, have admired Doctor Reefy, and sometimes have elevated him to almost heroic status. David D. Anderson, for example, while nodding to Frank's view, explains Reefy's motivations as far more conscious and wise; the doctor, he argues, pockets these scraps of thought because "he knows they would be misinterpreted" and "voluntarily" withdraws from social contact to avoid "inevitable misunderstanding" (43). The discrepancy between the real communication Reefy had shared with his wife and the supposed impossibility of communicating with anyone else remains unclear in that interpretation. Similarly, Bort, although he acknowledges that the cobweb-filled office is "emblematic of the man," implies that Reefy is somehow redeemed by "a moment of wordless understanding and the remembrance of that communion" (445, 454).

The foundation on which praise of Reefy is usually based is his apparent fulfillment of the wisdom implicit in the theory of truths set forth in the introductory tale, "The Book of the Grotesque." "He does not try to live by his thoughts," and his skepticism saves him "from the distortion of . . . mediate truths" (Berland 138; similarly, Taylor 26). Lorch goes further: Reefy has "succeeded" in passing the test of life, remaining "flexible and open" like the old writer in the initial tale (61; similarly, Phillips, "Eclectic" 3, and White, *Exploration* 59–60). Ciancio goes further still: not only does Reefy "resist the temptation" to believe in his truths (1004), he restores the soul of a young girl in a disillusioned "spiritual condition" with his "medicinal paper pills" so that she "dies happily" (1002) and so that he becomes "the only man in Winesburg" who "truly communicates" (1004). It is not clear exactly how Ciancio deduces that Reefy's marriage is "chaste" and "disembodied." Moreover, his conclusion that Reefy's vision "is complete, finished, whole" and attains "total communication, speech divested of words, those gross impediments which fragment and confound the vision of the ordinary artist" (1004) sidesteps the fact that the doctor fills scraps of paper with *words* and then, laughing, pelts his friend with those *fragments (WO* 36). This is hardly the ideal communication Ciancio describes. But even Ciancio does not go so far as Massa, who makes Reefy a moral exemplar of "the marvelously active life of the inquiring mind" and unselfish love, "the healer," "the perfect man," and the agent of readers' redemption: "to eat of the apples which are like the story of his life, to touch his hands, to acquire his wisdom is to rise from the fallen, corrupted state of America and to ascend to innocence, happiness and goodness" (93–99). His redemption had been accomplished by the dark girl he loved, who had saved him from the temptation of truths and made him "whole" (Massa 99–100).

Noting a reference to the fall of mankind in the twisted apple symbol (Pawlowski 295; Ciancio 999; Massa 94), critics also disagree about whether the implication extends to Reefy as fallen Adam or as redeemer. Cowan, like Massa, views him as identified with "Christ" (99–100). The idea of many critics that the "paper pills" symbolize Reefy's "healing power" (Curry 288n) is disputed by Carl Bredahl, who remarks that they "do not restore health" to his wife (425). Though he acknowledges "the seeds of something very fine" (*WO* 35) in Reefy, Bredahl claims the story "is finally a story of sterility" (425). The woman's "large fertile farm" mentioned in the opening paragraph is also symbolic, but ironically there is no issue from this union. What has become of "the young thing inside" (*WO* 24)? Of all the critics, only Fludernik suggests that the doctor induced the illness in which she lost the baby (123–24). The tooth-pulling scene leads Bredahl to the conclusion that, symbolically at least, "we are left finally with an abortion as Reefy extracts and discards a dead tooth" (425); Fludernik reads the symbolism of the episode as indicative of a subsequent literal abortion. Murphy gives that scene a different interpretation, arguing that the young woman's nightmare reveals her subconscious grasp of "a connection between sexual ardor and violence" and that the pulling of the tooth "symbolically castrat[es] the ravenous sexual monster of her dreams" (239–40). The specific imagery of the scene—the patient's groans, the screams, the blood running down the white dress—suggests that Bredahl's and Fludernik's interpretations may be the most plausible. A miscarriage follows weeks during which the woman is with the doctor nearly every day, but the subject is handled obliquely and left ambiguous.

Further evidence that the girl comes to the doctor seeking an abortion is the dramatization of *Winesburg, Ohio,* first performed in 1934 and printed in *Plays: Winesburg and Others.* The play does not mention Reefy's ever having a wife, but Belle Carpenter (a character from the story "An Awakening") comes to Doctor Reefy to request "an operation" to relieve her of an out-of-wedlock pregnancy. In the play, he urges her to respond to "the stirrings of the new life" and denies her request (30); she goes on to have the baby. While the later work does not *prove* anything about the characters in tales composed nearly two decades before, it does indicate the likelihood that abortion is an issue in the story.

One neglected matter is the doctor's inheritance of his wife's property. In a book where the corrupting influence of wealth is prominent, his acquisition of money seems significant. His clothes and his manner of living prove that he is no materialist, but his giving up his practice of going from house to house in order to sit alone in a "musty office . . . above the Paris Dry Goods Company's store" (*WO* 35), if actuated by sorrow over the loss of his wife, is *enabled* by her money. Together, grief and property have contributed to his professional and spiritual drying up.

Possibly a full interpretation of the story requires that it be considered along with "Death" near the end of the volume. It is true that Doctor Reefy is "defeated . . . by death" (Burbank 73), but the events of the story "Death" show traits in Reefy's character that also contribute to his defeat. Worth considering, too, is Wright's comment that this story is unusual among stories of the twenties in showing "true resignation," a trait common in earlier stories (113). The question is whether resignation is wisdom proper to a true "philosopher" (as in the earlier title)—and if so, whether wisdom need be so deadly.

Works Cited

Anderson, David. 1967. *Sherwood Anderson: An Introduction and Interpretation.* New York: Holt, Rinehart.

Anderson, Margaret. 1969. *My Thirty Years' War: The Autobiography, Beginnings and Battles to 1930.* New York: Horizon Press.

A[nderson], M[axwell]. "A Country Town." *New Republic* 19 (June 25, 1919): 257, 260. Rpt. in *Sherwood Anderson: Winesburg, Ohio: Text and Criticism.* Ed. John H. Ferres. New York: Viking, 1966, 253–54. Rpt. in *The Achievement of Sherwood Anderson: Essays in Criticism.* Ed. Ray Lewis White. Chapel Hill: University of North Carolina Press, 1966, 86–88. Rpt. in *The Merrill Studies in Winesburg, Ohio.* Comp. Ray Lewis White. Columbus, OH: Charles E. Merrill, 1971, 35–37.

Anderson, Sherwood. "Sister." *Little Review* 2 (December 1915):3–4. Rpt. in *Sherwood Anderson: Early Writings*. Ed. Ray Lewis White. Kent, OH, and London: Kent State University Press, 1989, 138–40.

———. *Windy McPherson's Son*. 1916. New York: John Lane. Rev. ed. New York: B. W. Huebsch 1922; Chicago and London: University of Chicago Press, 1965. Introduction by Wright Morris.

———. "The Philosopher." *The Little Review* 3 (June–July 1916):7–9.

———. 1917. *Marching Men*. New York: John Lane. Rpt. in *Marching Men: A Critical Text*. Ed. Ray Lewis White. Cleveland and London: Press of Case Western Reserve University, 1972.

———. 1919. *Winesburg, Ohio*. New York: B. W. Huebsch. Rpt. New York: Viking, 1960.

———. "Vibrant Life." *Little Review* 3 (March 1916):10–11. Rpt. in *Sherwood Anderson: Early Writings*. Ed. Ray Lewis White. Kent, OH, and London: Kent State University Press, 1989, 155–57.

———. 1926. *Tar: A Midwest Childhood*. New York: Boni & Liveright. Rpt. *Tar: A Midwest Childhood: A Critical Text*. Ed. Ray Lewis White. Cleveland: Press of Case Western Reserve University, 1969.

———. "Statements of Belief II." *Bookman* 68 (1928):204–207.

———. 1937. *Plays: Winesburg and Others*. New York: Scribners.

Atlas, Marilyn Judith. 1981. "Sherwood Anderson and the Women of Winesburg." In *Critical Essays on Sherwood Anderson*. Ed. David D. Anderson. Boston: G. K. Hall, 250–66.

Baker, Carlos. "Sherwood Anderson's Winesburg: A Reprise." *The Virginia Quarterly Review* 48 (1972):568–79.

Berland, Alwyn. "Sherwood Anderson and the Pathetic Grotesque." *Western Review* 15 (1915):135–38.

Bort, Barry D. "*Winesburg, Ohio:* The Escape from Isolation." *Midwest Quarterly* 11 (1970):443–56.

Bredahl, A. Carl. "'The Young Thing Within': Divided Narrative and Sherwood Anderson's *Winesburg, Ohio*." *Midwest Quarterly: A Journal of Contemporary Thought* 27 (1986):422–37.

Bridgman, Richard. 1966. *The Colloquial Style in America*. New York: Oxford University Press.

Burbank, Rex. 1964. *Sherwood Anderson*. New York: Twayne. Rpt. in part in *The Achievement of Sherwood Anderson: Essays in Criticism*. Ed. Ray Lewis White. Chapel Hill: University of North Carolina Press, 1966, 32–

43. Rpt. in part in *Sherwood Anderson: A Collection of Critical Essays*. Ed. Walter B. Rideout. Englewood Cliffs, NJ: Prentice-Hall, 1974, 70–83.

Chase, Cleveland B. 1927. *Sherwood Anderson*. New York: Robert M. McBride. Rpt. Folcroft, PA.: Folcroft Press, 1969.

Ciancio, Ralph. "The Sweetness of the Twisted Apples: Unity of Vision in *Winesburg, Ohio.*" *PMLA* 87 (1972):994–1006.

Cowan, James C. "The *Pharmakos* Figure in Modern American Stones of Physicians and Patients." *Literature and Medicine* 6 (1987):94–109.

Cowley, Malcom. 1960. "Introduction." In *Winesburg, Ohio*. By Sherwood Anderson. New York: Viking, 1–15. Rpt. in *Sherwood Anderson:* Winesburg, Ohio: *Text and Criticism*. Ed. John H. Ferres. New York: Viking, 1966, 357–68. Rpt. in *Sherwood Anderson: A Collection of Critical Essays*. Ed. Walter B. Rideout. Englewood Cliffs, NJ: Prentice-Hall, 1974, 49–58.

Curry, Martha Mulroy. 1975. *The "Writer's Book" by Sherwood Anderson: A Critical Edition*. Metuchen, NJ: Scarecrow Press.

Duffey, Bernard. 1954. *The Chicago Renaissance in American Letters: A Critical History*. East Lansing: Michigan State College Press.

Fludernik, Monika. "'The Divine Accident of Life': Metaphoric Structure and Meaning in *Winesburg, Ohio*," *Style* 22 (1988):116–35.

Frank, Waldo. "Winesburg, Ohio after Twenty Years." *Story* 19, 91 (September–October 1941):29–33. Rpt. in *Sherwood Anderson:* Winesburg, Ohio: *Text and Criticism*. Ed. John H. Ferres. New York: Viking, 1966, 369–76. Rpt. in *Achievement of Sherwood Anderson: Essays in Criticism*. Ed. Ray Lewis White. Chapel Hill: University of North Carolina Press, 1966, 116–21. Rpt. in *Homage to Sherwood Anderson, 1876–1941*. Ed. Paul P. Appel. Mamaroneck, NY: Appel, 1970, 41–47.

Howe, Irving. 1951. *Sherwood Anderson*. New York: William Sloane.

Hilfer, Anthony Channel. 1969. *The Revolt from the Village, 1915–1930*. Chapel Hill: University of North Carolina Press.

Massa, Ann. "Sherwood Anderson." In *American Literature in Context IV: 1900–1930*. London: Methuen, 1982, 88–101.

Mellard, James M. "Narrative Forms in *Winesburg, Ohio*." *PMLA* 83 (1968):1304–12.

Miller, William V. 1976. "Portraits of the Artist: Anderson's Fictional Storytellers." In *Sherwood Anderson: Dimensions of His Literary Art: A Collection of Critical Essays*. Ed. David D. Anderson. East Lansing: Michigan State University Press, 1–23.

Murphy, George D. "The Theme of Sublimation in Anderson's *Winesburg, Ohio." Modern Fiction Studies* 13 (1967):237–46.

Pawlowski, Robert S. "The Process of Observation: *Winesburg, Ohio* and *The Golden Apples." University Review Kansas City* 37 (1971):292–98.

Phillips, William L. "The Eclectic Dr. Reefy." *American Notes and Queries* 15 (1976):2–4.

———. "How Sherwood Anderson Wrote *Winesburg, Ohio." American Literature* 23 (1951):7–30. Rpt. in *Sherwood Anderson: Winesburg, Ohio: Text and Criticism.* Ed. John H. Ferres. New York: Viking, 1966, 263–86. Rpt. in *The Achievement of Sherwood Anderson: Essays in Criticism.* Ed. Ray Lewis White. Chapel Hill: University of North Carolina Press, 1966, 62–84. Rpt. in *The Merrill Studies in* Winesburg, Ohio. Comp. Ray Lewis White. Columbus, OH: Charles E. Merrill, 1971, 2–24. Rpt. in *Sherwood Anderson: A Collection of Critical Essays.* Ed. Walter B. Rideout. Englewood Cliffs, NJ: Prentice-Hall, 1974, 18–38.

———. "Sherwood Anderson's *Winesburg, Ohio:* Its Origins, Composition, Technique, and Reception." Ph.D. diss. University of Chicago, 1950.

Rigsbee, Sally Adair. "The Feminine in *Winesburg, Ohio." Studies in American Fiction* 9 (1981):233–44.

San Juan, Epifanio, Jr. "Vision and Reality: A Reconsideration of Sherwood Anderson's *Winesburg, Ohio." American Literature* 35 (1963):137–55. Rpt. in part in *Sherwood Anderson:* Winesburg, Ohio: *Text and Criticism.* Ed. John H. Ferres. New York: Viking, 1966, 468–81.

Schevill, James. 1951. *Sherwood Anderson: His Life and Work.* Denver: University of Denver Press.

Stouck, David. "Winesburg, Ohio as a Dance of Death." *American Literature* 48 (1977):525–42. Rpt. in *Critical Essays on Sherwood Anderson.* Ed. David D. Anderson. Boston: G. K. Hall, 1981, 181–95.

———. "Sherwood Anderson and the Postmodern Novel." *Contemporary Literature* 26 (1985):302–16.

Taylor, Welford Dunaway. 1977. *Sherwood Anderson.* New York: Frederick Ungar.

Thomas, F. Richard. 1983. "Sherwood Anderson (1876–1941)." *Literary Admirers of Alfred Stieglitz.* Carbondale: Southern Illinois University Press, 65–78.

Thurston, Jarvis. "Anderson and 'Winesburg': Mysticism and Craft." *Accent* 16 (1956):107–28. Rpt. in part in *Sherwood Anderson:* Winesburg, Ohio: *Text and Criticism.* Ed. John H. Ferres. New York: Viking, 1966, 331–44.

Way, Brian. 1971. "Sherwood Anderson." In *The American Novel and the*

Nineteen Twenties. Malcolm Bradbury and David Palmer (Eds.). Stratford-upon-Avon Studies 13. London: Edward Arnold, 107–26.

White, Ray Lewis, ed. 1968. *A Story Teller's Story: A Critical Text.* Cleveland: Press of Case Western Reserve University.

———, ed. 1969. *Sherwood Anderson's Memoirs: A Critical Edition.* Chapel Hill: University of North Carolina Press.

———. "*Winesburg, Ohio:* The Story Titles." *Winesburg Eagle* 10, no. 1 (November 1984):6–7.

———. 1990. *Winesburg, Ohio: An Exploration.* Boston: Twayne.

Wright, Austin McGiffert. 1961. *The American Short Story in the Twenties.* Chicago: University of Chicago Press.

Mother

Circumstances of Composition

Originally Anderson seems to have entitled this story "George Willard's Mother," later shortening that to the present title (White, "Story Titles" 6–7).

Sources and Influences

"Mother" is deeply rooted in autobiography. In his *Memoirs,* Anderson reports, "I tried to write of my own boyhood but couldn't do it so I invented a figure called George Willard and about his figure I built a series of stories and sketches called *Winesburg, Ohio*" (White 22). Anderson's mother, Emma Smith Anderson, was clearly the model for Elizabeth Willard, and his father, Irwin McLain Anderson, was the model for Tom Willard. The characters in the story, however, are idealized images. Numerous inconsistencies in the stories Anderson told over the years about his parents demonstrate the workings of his imagination, as he frankly admitted: "Facts elude me. . . . When, for example, I wrote of my own father and mother I depicted people my brothers and sisters could not recognize" (White, *Memoirs* 21; similarly, *Dark Laughter* 90; Curry, *Writer's Book* 39).

The mother Anderson remembered in his *Memoirs,* like Elizabeth Willard, worked hard all her life, doing drudge work her son considered demeaning, and in her last years she was ill—silent, "tall," and "gaunt" (67), with "bony hands" (White, *Memoirs* 115). She was uncomplaining of her lot and able to convey to her children her love and belief in their special talents "without the words being actually said" (White, *Memoirs* 68). All these traits entered into the fictional mother.

The father Anderson remembered in the *Memoirs* was, in essentials, like Tom Willard—a man who "hadn't made good," yet a big talker (White, *Memoirs* 274). He had a certain boyish charm and was, like Tom Willard, a Civil War veteran proud of his past (44, 156, 80–81). He, too, was neglectful of his wife. Anderson wrote that, whereas it is often said that "fathers want their sons to be what they cannot themselves be," in his case he wished that his father were a better man.

The facts of Anderson's boyhood are available in William Sutton's unpublished dissertation and in his *The Road to Winesburg*. In an appendix to the critical edition of *Tar* (219–30), Sutton reports on early diaries of Anderson's parents. These diaries reveal a woman more fun-loving and a man more dutiful and pious than any of the son's accounts indicates. There is no evidence, however, that Emma Anderson had sexual relationships prior to her marriage. That aspect of Elizabeth Willard's life is probably the author's invention. In addition, the portrayal of the Willards' marriage must have been colored by the miseries of Anderson's own broken first marriage.

A profound tension in Anderson's nature is represented in the story by the conflicting aspirations of the two parents for their adolescent son George—the father's ambition that he should become a material success and the mother's desire that he should develop a capacity for artistic expression. The protagonist of Anderson's unpublished novel "Talbot Whittingham" has a double-sided personality, part "imaginative . . . and sensitive," part "self-centered, arrogant, and manipulative," just like the author during his years of growing up (Rideout, "Talbot" 43). Throughout his life, Anderson sought to avoid being like his father—by success in business and by a different kind of success in art. At the same time, he sought somehow to redeem his mother's silent suffering. Paul Rosenfeld traces the story to "an influence stilly goading [the author] all his days to live his life and not settle down into cheap ambition, to grow and to learn; it is perhaps to this influence that the man owes his art" (39).

Publication History

"Mother" was first published in March 1917, in the New York "little magazine" *Seven Arts* (1:452–61). It was the seventh of the Winesburg stories to be printed, and the third of four to be printed in *Seven Arts* (following "Queer" and "The Untold Lie"). Anderson wrote to Waldo Frank, associate editor of the magazine, on December 14, 1916, thanking him for accepting the story and for sending a check in payment (Jones-Rideout, *Letters* 5). Of the three magazines that published the stories subsequently collected in *Winesburg, Ohio, Seven Arts* was the only one that paid its contributors; Anderson later recalled that for all the *Winesburg* stories he received a total of only $85 (Rosenfeld, *Memoirs* 288).

He also said that this story, about a mother who had several premarital love affairs, so offended the advertising manager of *Seven Arts* that he resigned: "'I wouldn't have minded your printing the story,' he said. 'It's giving it that title'" (White, *Memoirs* 409). There may be some correlation between the advertising manager's response and the fact that, for the magazine publication, the title was enclosed in quotation marks. Or possibly, as White suggests, the marks indicate Anderson's own ironic intent ("Story Titles" 7). The quotation marks were dropped, though, when "Mother" was published again in *Winesburg, Ohio* (1919).

The magazine version differs in several minor details from that in the collected story cycle.

Relation to Other Works

The central character of this story appears again in "Death," near the end of *Winesburg, Ohio*. The later story explains Elizabeth Willard's reasons for her unwise marriage and develops the idea in the earlier story of her longing for release from isolation, and for self-expression, communication, and love. It relates events around the time of her death at forty-five, which occurs not long after the main action of "Mother," where she is forty-five and her son is eighteen. But "Death" also extends back several years into the past, treating Elizabeth Willard's conversations with Doctor Reefy during a period in her life when "her son George was a boy of twelve or fourteen" (*WO* 221) and dramatizing a moment of interrupted lovemaking between her and the doctor when she was "forty-one" (*WO* 225). Thus "Death" ties together the central figures of "Paper Pills" and "Mother," two adjacent stories early in the story cycle. Since when Elizabeth Willard is introduced, "she is forty-five and broken," in one sense "[h]er death hovers over the length of the novel and her wish for George Willard's creativity increases our own investment in it" (Atlas 257).

"Mother" carries forward an important theme from "The Book of the Grotesque" and "Hands"—the value of dreams. The "young thing" within the old writer in the introductory sketch, Bredahl observes, is implicit in Elizabeth Willard's desire to bring forth the "something unexpressed in herself" and in the "secret something" she sees "striving to grow" in her son (428–29). Elizabeth's aspirations for George correlate closely with the advice Wing Biddlebaum gives him in the previous tale. Furthermore, whereas

"Hands" and "Paper Pills" show the loneliness of a bachelor and a widower, this story shows the equally pathetic loneliness that can exist within marriage.

In her abject drudgery, Elizabeth Willard is like Katherine Bentley of the first part of "Godliness." In her frustrated longing, she is also much like Louise Bentley of the third part of "Godliness" and Alice Hindman of "Adventure"; in the final analysis, of course, they all in a sense merely epitomize the human condition in *Winesburg, Ohio* and even in Anderson's works as a whole.

This is the first tale in which George Willard has an active role. With the desire expressed by both mother and son to leave Winesburg, the story introduces the motif of departure that runs through subsequent tales and culminates in the final one; it is also the first to mention George's aim of becoming a writer (Ingram 156; see also Baker 579).

Not surprisingly, Elizabeth Willard resembles many other mother figures in Anderson's fictionalized autobiographies and in his rather autobiographical fiction. In *Windy McPherson's Son* (1916) Sam McPherson's mother silently suffers through a barren life with an improvident, blustering husband. The mother in *A Story Teller's Story* (1924) is wise and quietly tender, but "outworn and done for at thirty" (21); her fingers are "long" and gentle (11). Tar Moorehead's mother, the strong one in the family, rules "by silence" (*Tar* 236); Tar is fascinated by her "long work-roughened fingers" and thinks later that "the memory of his mother's hands" is responsible for his "think[ing] so much about other people's hands" (276). A subsequent development of the same maternal figure appears in the patient, silent, nurturing old woman in "Death in the Woods" (Curry 184n). Anderson himself confessed, "I have seen something of my mother in every woman I have loved and in every woman of whom I have written . . . " (Curry 41).

Tom Willard, similarly, is related to many of Anderson's fictional fathers. The father in *Windy McPherson's Son* is "an obscure housepainter" who shores up his injured pride by bragging of his military background (11). His son, who longs to leave home, hates him and tries to kill him. Interestingly, the attempted murder of the father is transferred in "Mother" from the son to the mother. Moreover, whereas McPherson's son reacts to his father's failure with a determination to become rich, George reacts to his father's failure with a vague artistic impulse—"to go away and look at people and think" (*WO* 48). In *A Story Teller's Story* the father, humiliated by failure, persists in his pretensions to grandeur, but there at last the son admits with bemused humility that he and his father "are of the same breed" (21). This evidence suggests that Anderson may have "gradually resolved" his resentment of his father, finally recognizing how much he himself was like his father, even in a certain "slickness" (Geismar 260).

The conflict between Tom and Elizabeth Willard over their son's direction in life is reflected in another form in Hugh McVey of *Poor White* (1920), "a man in whom two natures, that of a vagabond dreamer and of a constructive exploiter, fought for dominance" (Hansen 112). Essentially, that inner struggle is central in Bruce Dudley of *Dark Laughter* (1925) as well. The struggle between the married couple in the short story "Brother Death" also resembles the Willards' conflict; there, too, it is the wife who is more sensitive to things of the spirit and the husband who is caught up in the pursuit of material success.

The author's intent for the character of Elizabeth Willard is summed up vividly in a 1932 letter to Arthur Barton, who was then planning a dramatic production of the *Winesburg* tales. "She is the kind of girl and woman not so beautiful on the outside but having in her a lot of inner fire," Anderson wrote; when her spirit is stirred "she becomes again a living thing" but when "the excitement is past swings again into this rather tired defeated woman" (Modlin 155).

Barton's project never reached completion. In 1934, though, a dramatization of *Winesburg, Ohio,* based largely on "Mother," was produced by the Hedgerow Theatre, under the direction of Jasper Deeter; the play has been printed in *Plays: Winesburg and Others.* Anderson wrote to a friend that the drama centered on the mother's efforts "to turn the son away from the father's influence—embodying all the cheapness of American individualism" (Campbell and Modlin 46). In the play, Elizabeth Willard dies, scissors in hand, just after she vengefully announces to her husband that George is not his son. This revision may have been motivated by a desire to add dramatic interest, but it also suggests that Anderson had not yet entirely overcome his old hostility toward his father.

Critical Studies

"Mother" is "[o]ne of the simplest and most poignant" of the Winesburg stories (Way 109). As such, it has aroused a great deal of comment and little controversy. The two most frequent topics of critical discussion are the mother's inability to communicate and the parents' conflict over George.

"The form of the mother, frustrated, lonely, at last desperate, pervades the variations that make the rest of the book," as Waldo Frank long ago observed (30). The mother's longing for significant life and for self-expression causes her to try to break out of the dull round of conventional behavior—donning bloomers, taking lovers, dreaming of a career on stage, and finally transferring her defeated hopes to her son. The suggestion of some critics that her only mistake was in succumbing to convention by marrying (Glicksberg 51; Rigsbee 238) is not borne out by the facts of the story. Yingling's claim that Elizabeth's misery derives from sexual repression and the frustration imposed by morality is likewise unfounded (100–101). Obviously her marriage to Tom Willard is a failure. But before her marriage, when her need for communication found an outlet in promiscuous sexuality, the satisfaction turned out to be "specious" and "ephemeral" (Murphy 240). Love affairs with traveling men who slept in her hotel brought happiness only "for a time" and ended in "sobbing repentance" (*WO* 46); her lovers did not share her emotions. Significantly, she now spends her days changing the soiled linens of just such men. Her youthful dreams of becoming an actress and traveling around the world become doubly ironic in light of reports by traveling actors that their lives are "as dull and uninteresting" as lives in Winesburg (46). At last, "when she determines to murder her husband in the grand tragic manner of a Lady Macbeth or Tosca," the pity of it all is underscored by the sudden collapse of her strength and by her paltry weapon—a pair of sewing scissors (Way 109–110).

Worst of all, she is unable to communicate her thoughts and feelings to her son (Howe 101; similarly, Voss 189). Though "inwardly she violently defies anything that threatens her son, outwardly she is perfunctory, almost apologetic in his presence" (D. Anderson 44). Pathetically, even though she feels a surge of delight when George tells her he has no desire to go into business, "the expression of joy had become impossible to her" (*WO* 48). Her prayer, that George "be allowed to express something for us" (*WO* 40), is indirectly "the representative prayer of all the grotesques: (Fussell 109; similarly, Rogers 92–93). Since George is a potential writer, this prayer "appears to describe the motivation behind" *Winesburg, Ohio* itself: noting, as others have, that Anderson dedicated the book to the memory of his mother, Stouck finds in the cycle a failed desire "to expiate . . . filial guilt" and to express thwarted lives (146, 151). That opinion is not representative of critical opinion generally, for most interpreters agree that the stories succeed in giving voice to the silent, struggling souls of a typical American town, thus expressing the inner life hidden beneath the surface of Elizabeth Willard and of a great many other commonplace people. Notably, the mother's crippling silence is coupled here with an opposite but equally crippling verbosity in Tom Willard, who cannot articulate his pain except by sputtering, "Damn such a life, damn it!" (*WO* 39), and whose blithering lectures fail of their intended effect, alienating his son instead (see Love 44; Fagin 133; Ward 36–38).

The other primary focus of critics has been the rivalry between George's parents over the direction his life is to take, a rivalry Bluefarb finds "patently Oedipal" and "overwhelmingly reminiscent of" the rivalry of Paul Morel's parents in Lawrence's *Sons and Lovers* (49). The father's desire that his son become conventionally successful is countered by the mother's desire that he develop his imaginative and creative capacities (Burbank 69–70). Their hopes for George spring from their need to have him satisfy vicariously their own frustrated dreams and thus may be a bit "vampiric" or "parasitical" (Bluefarb 51). George reflects the parental conflict in his shifting passages through the public life of the town on the one hand and through its buried lives on the other—"the 'daylight world' of the minor characters," whom he includes in his reports for the newspaper, and "the 'night world' of the major ones, the grotesques," whom he increasingly comes to understand (Rideout, "Simplicity" 27). Tom is a "philistine," one might say, whereas Elizabeth is a grotesque (Miller, "Portraits" 5–6). Anderson clearly implies that the mother's desire that George *not* "become smart and successful" (*WO* 41) is the deeper wisdom, that George's growth depends on his disregard of conventional success and his cultivation of his artistic capacities (Fagin 84; Fertig 68–69). It may be, as Bunge argues, that the women of Winesburg more often than the men are deeply in touch with *true* values. But the cautionary statement concerning truth in "The Book of the Grotesque" should be remembered; it is also true that deep sensitivity and disregard of convention can lead to misery, as many of the tales (including this one) attest.

One minor difference of critical opinion pertains to the evaluation of the mother's character. McAleer calls attention to the Christ symbolism of the tale, which appears when in prayer Elizabeth "offers herself as a vicarious sacrifice" for her son (178–79). A feminist analyst looks askance at that passage in the text, noting the way in which Elizabeth voluntarily directs violence against herself; female victimization is further highlighted by the mother's identification with the sufferings of the alley cat (Atlas 257). The text, however, emphasizes not only Elizabeth's weakness but also the vital power of the dream within her, which she transmits to her son.

The technique of this story has stirred some comment. Mellard and Wright employ different systems of classification, but their analysis of the story's structure is essentially the same. Mellard classifies it as one of six "emblematic" tales in *Winesburg,* each of which portrays in its central character a "universal" *type* indicated by the title. In these stories, essentially "static" presentation of character heightens the sense of the typical, even the archetypical; the movement of each story rises to a pitch of "lyrical excitement," as Howe puts it (in describing what he calls "parabolic" structure), and then is frustrated, so that there is "no significant change" (Mellard 1309–1311). Wright classifies the story as a tale of "caustic pathos" with an "episode of suffering" (389); its structure is typical in that Elizabeth's long sufferings erupt in an episode of "uncharacteristic behavior" (planning murder) and then return to a state much like the former (231–32). Wright also describes the narrative technique in the passage about Elizabeth's dressing in men's garments and riding a bicycle, relating its manner to that of other writers in the twenties (303–306). Ingram analyzes the references to her hands, which at different times express "despair," "aggressiveness," and yearning for "communion" (188). Nims argues that the setting, the shabby hotel, is used as a symbol of the family's entrapment in an Oedipal night-mare. Finally, San Juan refutes Trilling's charges that Anderson's works lack "the stuff of actuality" by showing how vivid realistic details and images—faded wallpaper, soiled beds, smallpox scars, a "grey cat crouched behind barrels filled with torn paper and broken bottles above which flew a black swarm of flies"—serve to engrave Elizabeth Willard on the mind (*WO* 41). The metamorphosis of that cat into Elizabeth's mental image of herself as a fierce tigress coming to defend her injured cub spotlights her brief "imaginative transcendence" of sordid defeat (San Juan 149). The woman's complex character is encapsulated in those two contrasting feline images.

Works Cited

Anderson, David. 1967. *Sherwood Anderson: An Introduction and Interpretation.* New York: Holt, Rinehart.

Anderson, Sherwood. 1916. *Windy McPherson's Son.* New York: John Lane. Rev. ed. B. W. Huebsch 1922; Chicago & London: University of Chicago Press, 1965. Introduction by Wright Morris. Grosset and Dunlap, 1925.

———. 1924. *A Story Teller's Story.* New York: B. W. Huebsch. Rpt. in *A Story Teller's Story: A Critical Text.* Ed. Ray Lewis White. Cleveland: Press of Case Western Reserve University, 1968. Rpt. New York: Viking, 1969.

———. 1925. *Dark Laughter.* New York: Boni & Liveright. Grosset and Dunlap, 1925.

———. 1926. *Tar: A Midwest Childhood.* New York: Boni & Liveright. Rpt. in *Tar: A Midwest Childhood: A Critical Text.* Ed. Ray Lewis White. Cleveland: Press of Case Western Reserve University, 1969.

———. 1937. *Plays: Winesburg and Others.* New York: Scribners.

Atlas, Marilyn Judith. 1981. "Sherwood Anderson and the Women of Winesburg." In *Critical Essays on Sherwood Anderson.* Ed. David D. Anderson. Boston: G. K. Hall, 250–66.

Baker, Carlos. "Sherwood Anderson's Winesburg: A Reprise." *The Virginia Quarterly Review* 48 (1972):568–79.

Bluefarb, Sam. 1972. "George Willard: Death and Resurrection." *The Escape Motif in the American Novel: Mark Twain to Richard Wright.* Columbus: Ohio State University Press, 42–58.

Bredahl, A. Carl. "'The Young Thing Within': Divided Narrative and Sherwood Anderson's *Winesburg, Ohio.*" *Midwest Quarterly: A Journal of Contemporary Thought* 27 (1986):422–37.

Bunge, Nancy. "Women as Social Critics in *Sister Carrie, Winesburg, Ohio, and Main Street." Midamerica* 3 (1976):46–55.

Burbank, Rex. 1964. *Sherwood Anderson.* New York: Twayne. Rpt. in part in *The Achievement of Sherwood Anderson: Essays in Criticism.* Ed. Ray Lewis White. Chapel Hill: University of North Carolina Press, 1966, 32–43. Rpt. in part in *Sherwood Anderson: A Collection of Critical Essays.* Ed. Walter B. Rideout. Englewood Cliffs, NJ: Prentice-Hall, 1974, 70–83.

Campbell, Hilbert H., and Charles E. Modlin, eds. 1976. *Sherwood Anderson: Centennial Studies.* Troy, NY: Whitston.

Curry, Martha Mulroy. 1975. *The "Writer's Book" by Sherwood Anderson: A Critical Edition.* Metuchen, NJ: Scarecrow Press.

Fagin, N. Bryllion. 1973. *The Phenomenon of Sherwood Anderson: A Study in American Life and Letters.* New York: Russell & Russell. Originally printed Baltimore: Rossi-Bryn, 1927.

Fertig, Martin J. "'A Great Deal of Wonder in Me': Inspiration and Transformation in *Winesburg, Ohio." Markham Review* 6 (1977):65–70.

Geismar, Maxwell. 1947. "Sherwood Anderson: Last of the Townsmen." In *The Last of the Provincials: The American Novel, 1915–1925.* Boston: Houghton Mifflin, 223–84. Rpt. in part in *Sherwood Anderson:* Winesburg, Ohio: *Text and Criticism.* Ed. John H. Ferres. New York: Viking, 1966, 377–82.

Glicksberg, Charles J. 1971. *The Sexual Revolution in Modern American Literature.* The Hague: Martinus Nijhoff.

Hansen, Harry. 1923. *Midwest Portraits: A Book of Memories and Friendships.* New York: Harcourt, Brace.

Howe, Irving. 1951. *Sherwood Anderson.* New York: William Sloane.

Jones, Howard Mumford, and Walter B. Rideout, eds. 1953. *Letters of Sherwood Anderson.* Boston: Little, Brown.

Ingram, Forrest L. 1971. *Representative Short Story Cycles of the Twentieth Century: Studies in a Literary Genre.* The Hague: Mouton.

Love, Glen A. "*Winesburg, Ohio* and the Rhetoric of Silence." *American Literature* 40(1968):38–57.

McAleer, John L. "Christ Symbolism in *Winesburg, Ohio." Discourse* 4 (1961):168–81. Rpt. in *The Merrill Studies in* Winesburg, Ohio. Comp. Ray Lewis White. Columbus, OH: Charles E. Merrill, 1971, 60–74.

Mellard, James M. "Narrative Forms in *Winesburg, Ohio." PMLA* 83 (1968):1304–1312.

Miller, William V. 1976. "Portraits of the Artist: Anderson's Fictional Storytellers." In *Sherwood Anderson: Dimensions of His Literary Art: A Collection of Critical Essays*. Ed. David D. Anderson. East Lansing: Michigan State University Press, 1–23.

Modlin, Charles E., ed. 1984. *Sherwood Anderson: Selected Letters*. Knoxville: University of Tennessee Press.

Murphy, George D. "The Theme of Sublimation in Anderson's *Winesburg, Ohio*." *Modern Fiction Studies* 13 (1967):237–46.

Nims, Margaret. "Sherwood Anderson's Use of Setting and Sexual Symbolism in 'The Mother.'" *Journal of Evolutionary Psychology* 8 (1987):219–22.

Phillips, William L. "How Sherwood Anderson Wrote *Winesburg, Ohio*." *American Literature* 23 (1951):7–30. Rpt. in *Sherwood Anderson: Winesburg, Ohio: Text and Criticism*. Ed. John H. Ferres. New York: Viking, 1966, 263–86. Rpt. in *The Achievement of Sherwood Anderson: Essays in Criticism*. Ed. Ray Lewis White. Chapel Hill: University of North Carolina Press, 1966, 62–84. Rpt. in *The Merrill Studies in* Winesburg, Ohio. Comp. Ray Lewis White. Columbus, OH: Charles E. Merrill, 1971, 2–24. Rpt. in *Sherwood Anderson: A Collection of Critical Essays*. Ed. Walter B. Rideout. Englewood Cliffs, NJ: Prentice-Hall, 1974, 18–38.

Rideout, Walter B. "The Simplicity of *Winesburg, Ohio*." *Shenandoah* 13 (1962):20–31. Rpt. in *Sherwood Anderson:* Winesburg, Ohio: *Text and Criticism*. Ed. John H. Ferres. New York: Viking, 1966, 287–300. Rpt. in *Critical Essays on Sherwood Anderson*. Ed. David D. Anderson. Boston: G. K. Hall, 1981, 146–54.

———. 1976. "Talbot Whittingham and Anderson: A Passage to *Winesburg, Ohio*." In *Sherwood Anderson: Dimensions of His Literary Art*. Ed. David D. Anderson. East Lansing: Michigan State University Press, 41–60.

Rigsbee, Sally Adair. "The Feminine in *Winesburg, Ohio*." *Studies in American Fiction* 9 (1981):233–44.

Rosenfeld, Paul. "Sherwood Anderson." *Dial* 72 (1922):29–42. Rpt. in *The Port of New York*. New York: Harcourt, Brace, 1924, 175–98. Rpt. in *Critical Essays on Sherwood Anderson*. Ed. David D. Anderson. Boston: G. K. Hall, 1981, 74–85.

———, ed. 1952. *Sherwood Anderson's Memoirs*. New York: Harcourt, Brace.

San Juan, Epifanio, Jr. "Vision and Reality: A Reconsideration of Sherwood Anderson's *Winesburg, Ohio*." *American Literature* 35 (1963):137–55.

Rpt. in part in *Sherwood Anderson:* Winesburg, Ohio: *Text and Criticism.* Ed. John H. Ferres. New York: Viking, 1966, 468–81.

Stouck, David. *"Winesburg, Ohio* and the Failure of Art." *Twentieth Century Literature* 15 (1969):145–51.

Sutton, William A. 1972. *The Road to Winesburg: A Mosaic of the Imaginative Life of Sherwood Anderson.* Metuchen, NJ: Scarecrow Press.

Townsend, Kim. 1987. *Sherwood Anderson.* Boston: Houghton Mifflin.

Trilling, Lionel. 1950. "Sherwood Anderson." *The Liberal Imagination: Essays on Literature and Society.* New York: Viking, 22–33. Originally in *Kenyon Review* 3 (1941):293–302. Rpt. in *Sherwood Anderson: Winesburg, Ohio: Text and Criticism.* Ed. John H. Ferres. New York: Viking, 1966, 455–67. Rpt. in *The Achievement of Sherwood Anderson: Essays in Criticism.* Ed. Ray Lewis White. Chapel Hill: University of North Carolina Press, 1966, 212–24. Rpt. in *Sherwood Anderson: A Collection of Critical Essays.* Ed. Walter B. Rideout. Englewood Cliffs, NJ: Prentice-Hall, 1974, 130–38.

Voss, Arthur. 1973. *The American Short Story: A Critical Survey.* Norman: University of Oklahoma Press.

Ward, J. A. 1985. *"Winesburg, Ohio:* Habitual Silence and the Roaring of Voices." *American Silences: The Realism of James Agee, Walker Evans, and Edward Hopper.* Baton Rouge: Louisiana State University Press, 35–50.

Way, Brian. 1971. "Sherwood Anderson." In *The American Novel and the Nineteen Twenties.* Eds. Malcolm Bradbury and David Palmer. Stratford-upon-Avon Studies 13. London: Edward Arnold, 107–126.

White, Ray Lewis. *"Winesburg, Ohio:* The Story Titles." *Winesburg Eagle* 10 (1984):6–7.

———, ed. 1969. *Sherwood Anderson's Memoirs: A Critical Edition.* Chapel Hill: University of North Carolina Press.

Wright, Austin McGiffert. 1961. *The American Short Story in the Twenties.* Chicago: University of Chicago Press.

The Philosopher

Circumstances of Composition

This, the fifth story in *Winesburg, Ohio,* was not the fifth in order of composition, but instead seems to have been among the last stories Anderson wrote for the volume. In the extant manuscript it is not included in the sequence of tales on the back of manuscript pages for an unpublished novel concerning Talbot Whittingham. Rather, it is one of seven stories written on cheap paper used for writing advertisements, and may have been composed in the office of the Long-Critchfield Agency where Anderson was employed, or at a hotel when he was traveling to visit advertising clients (Phillips 12). It almost surely was written after June of 1916, when the story now entitled "Paper Pills" was published in the *Little Review* with the title "The Philosopher," since it is improbable Anderson would have used the name of a story waiting for publication as the title for a second story; moreover, on the basis of the number of internal details of setting (which became more abundant in the later stories), Phillips conjectures that the story was one of the last to be written (28).

Sources and Influences

The name Parcival is derived from the medieval legend of the knights in search of the Holy Grail. The idea of Doctor Parcival may have come to Anderson by way of Henry Adams's *Mont-Saint-Michel and Chartres,* which includes an account of Chrétien de Troyes's legend of Sir Perceval and his vision of the sacred cup that Christ passed to his disciples at the Last Supper; this is the likely source of the Christ symbolism in the story, according to McAleer (170).

Oddly enough, Friedrich Nietzsche's philosophy, particularly the idea of the *übermensch* in *Thus Spoke Zarathustra,* is reflected in Doctor Parcival's philosophy of contempt (White 39). It is through "hatred and contempt," Parcival tells George, that one can become "a superior being" (*WO* 55). Ironically, Parsifal is the hero of Richard Wagner's sacred drama of that title, which Nietzsche despised for its Christian view of morality. In this story, Doctor Parcival's final assertion "that everyone in the world is Christ and they are all crucified" (*WO* 57) clashes with his Nietzschean doctrine of contempt, for Anderson believed that "the main importance of Jesus Christ lay in the fact that he preached the doctrine of pity" (Schevill 330). The doctor's name and his conflicting doctrines indicate a crucial division in his personality.

The unpublished novel on which Anderson was working in 1914 and 1915, about a character named Talbot Whittingham, contains elements that seem to relate to Doctor Parcival's contradictory philosophical doctrines. As Rideout explains, Talbot "becomes involved" in a debate between two of his colleagues about the merits of Christ's teachings as opposed to those of Nietzsche; Talbot kills one man without remorse and is influenced to plan a second murder (stalking his prey through the streets of Chicago to a point "in full view from" the room on Cass Street where Anderson lived when he wrote the tale), but he finally rejects the Nietzschean position and affirms the compassion of Jesus (44–49, 59n). Less overtly, the conflicting claims of the superman philosophy and the impulse to pity appear in Doctor Parcival.

An allusion to the Sermon on the Mount appears in Doctor Parcival's boast, "Why should I concern myself with what I eat" (*WO* 51): Jesus had taught, "Take no thought for your life, what ye shall eat. . . . Behold the fowls of the air . . . ; your heavenly Father feedeth them" (Matt. 7:26–25). Parcival has learned the text but missed the message of humility and the promise.

Zlotnick argues that the story was influenced by a tale from James Joyce's *Dubliners,* "The Sisters." In both stories, a physically repulsive man talks compulsively to a "sensitive and uninitiated" boy, advising and mystifying him; in both, the man serves as "surrogate father" to a boy whose own father is inadequate; in both, the man is significantly "warped" by his religion; and in both, the boy experiences "an epiphany" (406). Zlotnick's assertion that Anderson retells Joyce's tale is cast into doubt, however, by Curry's carefully supported argument that Anderson had not read *Dubliners,* or indeed, any of Joyce's writing before 1920 (236–40).

The mob violence Doctor Parcival fears (violence that actually occurs in "Hands") may have been an idea Anderson derived from his reading of Mark Twain (Gregory, *Talks* 18).

But Doctor Parcival's reference to the murder of a "Doctor Cronin" (*WO* 52) is based on a real event. As Williams reports, this famous Chicago case involved the murder of Dr. Patrick Henry Cronin, a leader in the Irish secret society Clan-na-Gael (283n). One of the seven men indicted "escaped from the city and was not brought to trial," and Parcival implies that he himself may be that man (Williams 185–86, 284n).

Certain autobiographical events also suggested some of the story details. As Parcival remembers his mother taking in other people's washing to maintain her children, so Anderson (with more obvious pain) repeatedly recalled his mother washing other folks' dirty clothes (White, *Memoirs* 28, 38, 43–45, 62, 67, 114–15, 156, 205). It is interesting that he did not put that detail in the story "Mother," although Elizabeth Willard suffers a similarly demeaning drudgery. Furthermore, the paint-splattered clothes of his brother, which so offend Parcival's aesthetic sense, are like a detail included in "Death," where Elizabeth Willard recalls the distaste she felt for her husband when he always had paint on his hands. Both images almost certainly originated in Anderson's memories of his boyhood, when he and his brothers helped their father, who was a house painter.

The saloon where Will Henderson goes to drink was probably remembered from Clyde, Ohio. When Anderson was growing up there, the town of 2,500 had seventeen saloons (Hurd 31).

Publication History

This story was not published in a periodical. It appeared in *Winesburg, Ohio* in 1919.

Relation to Other Works

Doctor Parcival is the first of the grotesques actually to tell his story to George Willard. In "Hands," George prefers not to know Wing Biddlebaum's story, which is presented directly by an omniscient narrator. In this story, George sits passively and listens as Parcival rambles on about his life and philosophy. In some of the following stories, however, George takes a more active role in encouraging the grotesques to tell their tales, and a pattern of developing interest becomes still more apparent.

By placing this later-composed story just after "Mother," then, Anderson allows a reader to see some immediate results of George's plan to "look at people and think," as he has confided it to Elizabeth Willard (*WO* 48). This story also continues the theme of suffering from "Mother," even presenting a portrait of Doctor Parcival's overworked mother that is linked with that of George's mother; further, it makes explicit "the submerged Christian symbolism of the volume," which culminates in Elizabeth Willard's dying at 3 PM on a Friday in March, in the story "Death" (Ingram 197n).

The death of Parcival's brother is related to the deaths of other brothers in the *Winesburg* stories. Jesse Bentley (of "Godliness"), who like Parcival has been trained for the Presbyterian ministry, has lost four brothers in the Civil War. The old carpenter in "The Book of the Grotesque" weeps over his dead brother. Since Parcival's brother is run over by a train, he is allied with Old Windpeter Winters in "The Untold Lie." In both instances, the crushing force of industrialism is implicit symbolically.

There is also a link between the climactic "adventure" of this story and Alice Hindman's "adventure" in the story with that title. As Alice Hindman's desperate plea falls on deaf ears, so Parcival's refusal to attend to a dead child goes unheard. In each instance, the character is shattered as a result.

Even the structurelessness of Parcival's tales may be related to Anderson's narrative manner; like the stories of *Winesburg, Ohio,* Parcival's narratives "began nowhere and ended nowhere" (Tanner 209). Tanner is harsh in calling Anderson's endings "pointless cessations"; the formal quality he is noticing, also noted by Anderson's first readers, was quite deliberate. (See the discussion of "Loneliness," and in particular, its publication history.) Pickering explains that just as Parcival's talks push George's mind "to see beyond dead objects into an imaginative world," the unconventional structure of *Winesburg* "force[s] the reader's imagination to fill in the narrative gaps" (35).

Doctor Parcival is a figure in some respects like Mike McCarthy in *Windy McPherson's Son* (1916), a man who, when jailed for assaulting another man with a pocket knife, delivers a half-insane tirade. Declaring himself to be "Michael, Son of God," he first hurls abuse at the respectable folk of the town, then prays that God will send them "a new Christ" to shout, "Be ashamed! Be ashamed of your cowardly . . . lives, so miserably lived . . . ," and at last bursts into sobs of repentance (44–45). The boy who listens to McCarthy gleans an essential truth from these ravings—"the idea of brotherhood" (45)—as, presumably, George Willard extracts some "essence of truth" from the ramblings of Doctor Parcival (*WO* 51). Both McCarthy and Parcival instinctively try "to justify [themselves] before God" (*Windy* 46).

More important, perhaps, is the resemblance between Doctor Parcival and Beaut McGregor of *Marching Men* (1917). Parcival tells George, "I want to fill you with hatred and contempt so that you will be a superior being" (*WO* 55). As with Beaut McGregor, Parcival's own abject sufferings and his vision of the disorder and squalor of other lives lead him to feel fanatical contempt for the mass of mankind and admiration for strength and power. A "proletarian class-consciousness" lies behind both works, and though "the Nietzschean war-cry," as Calverton puts it (91, 93), drops out of *Winesburg* for the most part, Parcival's emulation of his brother and his own efforts to elevate himself to heroic status are an echo of the earlier work. At the end of *Marching Men,* Beaut had relinquished his aim to master men. In this tale, too, as Parcival quakes with fear that he will be lynched for failing to attend to an accident victim, there is a shift away from his pose as a superman to a recognition of human mutuality. Self-pity overshadows the germ of generous pity for others, and yet the germ is there.

Doctor Parcival appears again in the play *Winesburg, Ohio,* produced in 1934 by the Hedgerow Theatre just outside Philadelphia. His character is somewhat altered there: sardonically, he preaches the saving power of drunkenness and practices what he preaches, guzzling whiskey from first scene to last. A letter from Anderson to the producer, Jasper Deeter, expresses misgivings about the Parcival of the play and provides some insight into the author's conception of the character. Anderson wrote that Parcival is "mystic and poet," a man who "is wiser than all the others about him" and is thereby isolated from them; longing for "human brotherhood" is "so intense in him that he identifies himself with a Chicago murderer" and with the crucified Christ; Anderson urged that the actor portraying Parcival should bring more poetic sensitivity into his character (Jones-Rideout, *Letters* 305–06). The Parcival of the play no longer tries to teach George contempt for others, but teaches him—in George's words—"about God and people and you being every one and every one being you" (51). Thus the Parcival of the play is closer than the Parcival of the tale to the protagonist of the story "Brothers," who identifies with, among others, a pathetic murderer. The Parcival of the tale shares that capacity, but there is more of the will to power in his character, more of a desire to stand beyond good and evil in his admiration for his cruel brother, in his suggestion that he is a murderer, and in his effort to display his contempt by refusing to come to the accident victim. The different handling of the theme in these several works suggests that Anderson, in his wrestlings with his own need to assert himself and his own need to understand others sympathetically, increasingly moved away from contempt and toward pity.

Critical Studies

There is general agreement among critics that in some sense Doctor Parcival's climactic statement is central in *Winesburg, Ohio:* "Dr. Parcival had spoken for Anderson when he told the lad 'Everyone in the world is Christ'" (Rosenfeld 10). But interpretive analyses of this story are on the whole sketchy, and consensus about the meaning of the story is limited to the most obvious points.

Many critical references to the story are isolated comments enmeshed in general discussions of the book as a whole. Burbank calls Doctor Parcival "a recluse tortured by guilt" and mentions his entreaties that George write a book incorporating the philosophical insight that crucifixion is the universal fate (70). White finds Parcival a victim of an "inferiority complex," "misanthropic," masochistic, and eager for "martyrdom" (*Exploration* 64–65). Love remarks that Parcival is one of the town's garrulous talkers, one who recoils from his own effusiveness with "self-disgust" (44). Baker sees Parcival as one of those characters who fulfill the idea in "The Book of the Grotesque" that embracing truths makes people grotesque; in this instance, Parcival preaches his truth and "is nailed to the cross of inaction" (574–75). Stouck notes that Parcival is one of Winesburg's "failed artists" (535). And Atlas sees a pattern of female victimization here, both in Parcival's mother and in the little girl thrown from the buggy (258), a perception that should be qualified by the obvious male victimization also present in the story.

More penetrating, but still brief, comments illuminate other aspects of the story. David Anderson explains that Parcival tells George the past events "that taught him to hate," but at the last the old man "lets his mask slip" and reveals his compassion (45). Yet even then, Parcival's fear and pity for himself are far stronger than any genuine feeling for others. Stewart explains that the doctor's "adventure," like Elizabeth Willard's (in "Mother"), involves a "melodramatic self-dramatization" in which the repressed inner self is asserted; whereas on the one hand Parcival "identifies with all the people he has read about and gives them to George as possible bits of his own experience," on the other hand, he slavishly admires his cruel and selfish brother; when these opposite parts of himself are brought into a conflict with the potential for bringing about a better understanding of himself, Parcival's habitual philosophy thwarts that chance (36). These insights deserve fuller treatment. The same can be said of the succinct commentary of Abcarian, who notes that the flashback to Parcival's youth reveals the trauma that left his innocence irreparably wounded: the brutality of his drunken brother is the source of his obsession, "a kind of paranoiac distortion of the crucifixion" (98).

A more extended but eccentric interpretation is offered in San Juan's article on *Winesburg, Ohio,* which begins from the assumption that the crucial distinction in the work is that between "fixed schematic ways of doing, feeling, and thinking" and more flexible modes of self-expression (138–39). San Juan asserts that Doctor Parcival is the embodiment of Anderson's most prized qualities—"energy and amplitude of imagination" and an "inherently ironical temper" (139). The doctor's not always reliable statements about his past are evidence of "the triumph of possibility and free initiative" (139). His fearful prophecy that he will be lynched is an imaginative transcendence over "the realm of facts," and his "slightly cynical prayer" over his dead father is evidence of "critical awareness" and an ironical "comic spirit" (140, 152). Parcival's fantastic visionary powers contrast with the conformist mentality of the average citizen, represented by such men as Will Henderson and Tom Willard. But San Juan confuses Tom Willard, the hotel keeper, with Tom Willy, the saloon keeper (147). And his interpretation, though intriguing, does not reckon with the distasteful and pathetic aspects of Parcival's character, such as his symptoms of paranoia. Still, the positive emphasis of San Juan's interpretation serves to counterbalance critical emphasis on Parcival's repulsive traits. And it may be an important reminder that the prologue of *Winesburg* states that single "truths" lead to falsehood. The intrinsic contradictions in Parcival's philosophy possibly are meant to be seen as truer than any one truth alone.

The closest approximation to a full analysis of the story is McAleer's

"Christ Symbolism in *Winesburg, Ohio.*" This article recognizes a truth in Parcival's final pronouncement, a truth relevant to the whole book, but argues that obsession with this truth has paralyzed the doctor's will and led him to despair (169). As Sir Perceval in Chrétien de Troyes's version of the legend glimpsed the Holy Grail but did not ask its meaning, so Anderson's Doctor Parcival fails to see the full meaning of his "truth," which it becomes the task of George Willard, modern knight-errant, to find (170). The key, thinks McAleer, lies in the story of Parcival's brother, which reveals the cause of man's suffering in the railroad car, symbol of destructive power of a materialistic industrial age; this symbolism is made comprehensible by the story "Godliness" (171–74; see "Godliness," under "Relation to Other Works"). A further glimpse of the clash "between the agrarian and industrial ways of life" appears in the accident where a little girl in a buggy is killed after a train frightens her horses (175). Even Tom Willy, the saloon keeper, bears in the birthmarks on his hands the stigmata of Christ, McAleer indicates (178)—a point that should reduce the tendency of critics to divide the people of Winesburg into "grotesques" and "clods" (see San Juan, above; Howe 100; Ciancio 996). McAleer states in a later essay that this tale marks the first appearance of Christ symbolism in modern American literature ("Biblical" 317).

Ciancio's comments about Parcival are consonant with McAleer's; he emphasizes the doctor's "fanaticism" and the "self-aggrandizing visions that estrange [him] from the brotherhood of man" and points out the final irony that Parcival "is denied his martyrdom" (995). Moreover, Ciancio states, all "the grotesques are self-crucified" (999).

Cowan proposes an interesting interpretation related to Jacques Derrida's explanation of the play of multiple meanings associated with the Greek word *pharmakon,* which can mean "'remedy,' 'recipe,' 'poison,' or 'drug,'" and which is associated with the word *pharmakos,* or "scapegoat" (94–95). Doctor Parcival's behavior situates him in complex relation to all these terms.

Two formalist analysts of the structure of the tale use differing terminology but are otherwise in general agreement. Mellard classifies it as an "emblematic" tale, a type in which description and action are arranged so as to explain a character, a universal type who is thus essentially static; the story reaches its highest pitch, Mellard explains, when Parcival announces that he will surely be lynched but the expected climax does not arrive and there is "no significant change in [his] condition" (1309–1311). Wright classifies the tale as one of caustic pathos, with an episode of suffering (389); the structure reflects long-repressed feelings that erupt in Parcival's irrational panic that he will be hanged (231–32). Wright notes the doctor's "extreme egotism" and his need that others acknowledge his identity as a suffering martyr, but he also stresses that Anderson leaves important inferences to be made by the reader, chiefly, "What feeling causes the hero's final remarks?" (136, 126, 407–408).

Other inferences must be made by a reader as well. Was Parcival indeed involved in the murder of Doctor Cronin? Where *does* he get his money? How did he feel about the death of his father? Does this son of an insane father show signs of incipient madness? Why does he want George's admiration? Which parts of his ramblings are "a pack of lies" and which are "the very essence of truth" (*WO* 51)?

Much remains to be explored about this puzzling tale and its wise and ridiculous central character. But enough has already been said about its multiple ironies to refute Herbert Gold's assertion that Anderson identifies completely, and morbidly, with Doctor Parcival (552). The inconsistencies in the old man's philosophy and character—which make him at once better and worse than the "average" citizens of Winesburg—are intimately related not only to the tensions within his young fellow-quester George Willard but also to the ambivalences in the author, which are conveyed to readers as they survey the grotesques, and in them the human condition, with fluctuating contempt, bemusement, pity, and fear.

Works Cited

Abcarian, Richard. "Innocence and Experience in *Winesburg, Ohio. University Review Kansas City* 35 (1968):95–105.

Anderson, David. 1967. *Sherwood Anderson: An Introduction and Interpretation*. New York: Holt, Rinehart.

Anderson, Sherwood. 1919. "The Philosopher.": In *Winesburg, Ohio*. New York: B. W. Huebsch. Rpt. New York: Viking, 1960.

———. 1937. *Plays: Winesburg and Others*. New York: Scribner's.

Atlas, Marilyn Judith. "Sherwood Anderson and the Women of Winesburg." In *Critical Essays on Sherwood Anderson*. Ed. David D. Anderson. Boston: G. K. Hall, 1981, 250–66.

Baker, Carlos. "Sherwood Anderson's Winesburg: A Reprise." *The Virginia Quarterly Review* 48 (1972):568–79.

Burbank, Rex. 1964. *Sherwood Anderson*. New York: Twayne. Rpt. in part in *The Achievement of Sherwood Anderson: Essays in Criticism*. Ed. Ray Lewis White. Chapel Hill: University of North Carolina Press, 1966, 32–43. Rpt. in part in *Sherwood Anderson: A Collection of Critical Essays*. Ed. Walter B. Rideout. Englewood Cliffs, NJ: Prentice-Hall, 1974, 70–83.

Calverton, V. J. "Sherwood Anderson: A Study in Sociological Criticism." *Modern Quarterly* 2 (1924):82–118. Rpt. in *The Newer Spirit: A Sociolog-*

ical Criticism of Literature. Introduction by Ernest Boyd. New York: Boni & Liveright, 1925, 52–118.

Ciancio, Ralph. "The Sweetness of the Twisted Apples: Unity of Vision in *Winesburg, Ohio*." *PMLA* 87 (1972):994–1006.

Cowan, James C. "The *Pharmakos* Figure in Modern American Stories of Physicians and Patients." *Literature and Medicine* 6 (1987), 94–109.

Curry, Martha Mulroy. "Sherwood Anderson and James Joyce." *American Literature* 52 (1980–81):236–49.

Gold, Herbert. "The Purity and Cunning of Sherwood Anderson." *Hudson Review* 10 (1957–58):548–57. Rpt. in *The Age of Happy Problems*. New York: Dial, 1962, 56–67. Rpt. in part in *Sherwood Anderson: Winesburg, Ohio: Text and Criticism*. Ed. John H. Ferres. New York: Viking, 1966, 396–404. Rpt. in *Critical Essays on Sherwood Anderson*. Ed. David D. Anderson. Boston: G. K. Hall, 1981, 138–45.

Gregory, Horace. 1968. "On Sherwood Anderson." In *Talks with Authors*. Ed. Charles F. Madden. Carbondale: Southern Illinois University Press, 12–22.

Howe, Irving. 1951. *Sherwood Anderson*. New York: William Sloane.

Hurd, Thaddeus B. "Fun in Winesburg." *Midwestern Miscellany* 11 (1983):28–39.

Ingram, Forrest L. 1971. *Representative Short Story Cycles of the Twentieth Century: Studies in a Literary Genre*. The Hague: Mouton.

Jones, Howard Mumford, and Walter B. Rideout, eds. 1953. *Letters of Sherwood Anderson*. Boston: Little, Brown.

Love, Glen A. "*Winesburg, Ohio* and the Rhetoric of Silence." *American Literature* 40 (1968):38–57.

McAleer, John J. "Biblical Symbols in American Literature: A Utilitarian Design. *English Studies* 46 (1965):310–22.

———. "Christ Symbolism in *Winesburg, Ohio*." *Discourse* 4 (1961):168–81. Rpt. in *The Merrill Studies in* Winesburg, Ohio. Comp. Ray Lewis White. Columbus, OH: Charles E. Merrill, 1971, 60–74.

Mellard, James M. "Narrative Forms in *Winesburg, Ohio*." *PMLA* 83 (1968):1304–12.

Phillips, William J. "How Sherwood Anderson Wrote *Winesburg, Ohio*." *American Literature* 23 (1951):7–30. Rpt. in *Sherwood Anderson:* Winesburg, Ohio: *Text and Criticism*. Ed. John H. Ferres. New York: Viking, 1966, 263–86. Rpt. in *The Achievement of Sherwood Anderson: Essays in Criticism*. Ed. Ray Lewis White. Chapel Hill: University of North Carolina

Press, 1966, 62–84. Rpt. in *The Merrill Studies in* Winesburg, Ohio. Comp. Ray Lewis White. Columbus, OH: Charles E. Merrill, 1971, 2–24. Rpt. in *Sherwood Anderson: A Collection of Critical Essays*. Ed. Walter B. Rideout. Englewood Cliffs, NJ: Prentice-Hall, 1974, 18–38.

Pickering, Samuel. "*Winesburg, Ohio:* A Portrait of the Artist as a Young Man." *Southern Quarterly* 16 (1977):27–38.

Rideout, Walter B. "Talbot Whittingham and Anderson: A Passage to *Winesburg, Ohio.*" In *Sherwood Anderson: Dimensions of His Literary Art*. Ed. David D. Anderson. East Lansing: Michigan State University Press, 1976, 41–60.

Rosenfeld, Paul. "The Man of Good Will." *Story* 19 (September–October 1941), pp. 5–10. Rpt. in *Homage to Sherwood Anderson, 1876–1941*. Ed. Paul P. Appel. Mamaroneck, NY: Paul P. Appel, 1970, 3–10.

San Juan, Epifanio, Jr. "Vision and Reality: A Reconsideration of Sherwood Anderson's *Winesburg, Ohio.*" *American Literature* 35 (1963):137–55. Rpt. in part in *Sherwood Anderson:* Winesburg, Ohio: *Text and Criticism*. Ed. John H. Ferres. New York: Viking, 1966, 468–81.

Schevill, James. 1951. *Sherwood Anderson: His Life and Work*. Denver: University of Denver Press.

Stewart, Maaja A. "Scepticism and Belief in Chekhov and Anderson." *Studies in Short Fiction* 9 (1972):29–40.

Stouck, David. "*Winesburg, Ohio* as a Dance of Death." *American Literature* 48 (1977):525–42. Rpt. in *Critical Essays on Sherwood Anderson*. Ed. David D. Anderson. Boston: G. K. Hall, 1981, 181–95.

Tanner, Tony. 1965. "Sherwood Anderson's Little Things." *The Reign of Wonder: Naïvety and Reality in American Literature*. Cambridge: Cambridge University Press, 205–227.

White, Ray Lewis, ed. 1969. *Sherwood Anderson's Memoirs: A Critical Edition*. Chapel Hill: University of North Carolina Press.

———. 1990. *Winesburg, Ohio: An Exploration*. Boston: Twayne.

Williams, Kenny J. 1988. *A Storyteller and a City: Sherwood Anderson's Chicago*. De Kalb: Northern Illinois University Press.

Wright, Austin McGiffert. 1961. *The American Short Story in the Twenties*. Chicago: University of Chicago Press.

Zlotnick, Joan. "Dubliners in *Winesburg, Ohio:* A Note on Joyce's 'The Sisters' and Anderson's 'The Philosopher.'" *Studies in Short Fiction* 12 (1975):405–407.

Nobody Knows

Circumstances of Composition

In the extant manuscript of the *Winesburg* tales, "Nobody Knows" appears eighth in a sequence of the tales, following immediately after the third part of "Godliness" and immediately followed by "Respectability"; the two tales most closely related to it in subject matter ("An Awakening" and "Sophistication") do not appear in the same sequence but in separate stacks of manuscript (Phillips, "How" 11). Consequently it is difficult to be certain of the order of composition of these tales, though Phillips plausibly suggests that these and other stories which mention George Willard's romantic relationships led Anderson's imagination from one episode to another (18–19).

This is the only *Winesburg* tale of which there exists a second manuscript. The alternate draft, which Anderson in 1938 called a "re-draft," consists of eight pages handwritten in pencil, whereas the other draft is nine pages long and is in blue ink (White, "Unique" 3). In addition to a few variant commas and paragraph breaks, there are minor differences of wording ("it's all right," for example, as opposed to the "it'll be all right" of the other manuscript and the final text).

A novel concerning Talbot Whittingham on which Anderson had been working before he began composing the stories about the people of Winesburg included a sexual initiation scene (of Talbot with Lillian Gale) that "prefigures" the one in this story (Rideout, "Talbot" 53); it is likely that Anderson drew from that earlier work for this story, as he did with other stories in the cycle.

When Anderson arranged the stories for the collection *Winesburg, Ohio* (1919), this story became the sixth in the sequence.

Sources and Influences

Autobiographical sources for this story are indicated by Anderson's *Memoirs* (White 85–100) and by the reminiscences gathered in *Tar* (153–69). The *Memoirs* records three adolescent sex adventures. The first involved "a little village pushover," the daughter of a man who makes his living by traveling about with a stuffed whale, which people may look at for ten cents apiece; Anderson recalls his nervousness when he responded to her invitations, his telling himself that his mother "could not know," the way he felt when the girl "put her little hand in mine," and the terrible humiliation he suffered when they were discovered undressing in the moonlight and were subjected to public ridicule (White 85–89). The second adventure concerned the arousal of his lust when, delivering newspapers at night, he saw through a window a nude girl warming herself before the stove as she changed into her nightclothes (White 89–90). The third adventure was a brief affair, when he was "perhaps fourteen," with a bold girl who invited him to her grandparents' house and made him feel at last that he "had become a man"; this "paradise" ended when his fear of pregnancy caused him to break it off (White 90–100). The second of these memories was transformed into the story "Girl by the Stove." The first and third were reshaped into an episode in *Tar* (see "Relation to Other Works").

Townsend discusses Anderson's sexual awakenings in his biography (19–27).

Publication History

This story was first published in *Winesburg, Ohio* in 1919.

Relation to Other Works

The autobiographical novel *Tar* contains a close parallel to this story. The two early sexual encounters recorded in the *Memoirs* (see "Sources and Influences") were reshaped into an integrated narrative in *Tar* (1926), where it becomes a classic nice-girl/bad-girl conflict for the adolescent boy. The newsboy's adoration for a rich girl visiting her grandparents gets "all mixed up with" his desire to go up to a hayloft with a poor girl; the story concludes with the mother's entry into the barn and the ashamed boy's conviction that he can never talk to the rich girl again (153–69). Details of the episode in *Tar* that correlate closely with "Nobody Knows" are the boy's trembling nervousness, the poor girl's dirty face and dirty dress, and her need "to be reassured," exhibited when, after inviting him to the loft, she says, "If you saw me on Main Street I bet you wouldn't speak to me. You're too stuck up" (166). White points to other episodes, showing Tar's sexual curiosity, that he suggests are connected to "Nobody Knows" (*Tar* 143n), but the relationships are far less direct.

Within *Winesburg, Ohio*, this is the first story in which George Willard appears as protagonist. Like his mother (in "Mother"), he has a casual affair that fails to bring him lasting satisfaction (Wright 71). The story is most importantly related, though, to "An Awakening" and "Sophistication." All three stories deal with George Willard's developing understanding of sex and of women, and "they are arranged in an ascending order of progression," as Rideout notes ("Simplicity" 28). Rideout goes on to say that Anderson's "subtle sense of design" is indicated by the placement of the tales—one early in the volume, one two-thirds of the way through, and one nearly at the end. "Nobody Knows" presents George's first sexual experience, and the other two stories show his growing maturity as he learns about some of the complexities beneath the superficial acts of love; Rideout's analysis of the relationships of these three tales is illuminating (28–31). Lorch elaborates on Rideout's interpretation (57). Their perceptions are covered under the "Critical Studies" section for each individual story.

Phillips asserts that this tale is connected to the introductory sketch by its illustration of the point that "the 'truth' of abandon to mere sex" can make people grotesque.

Less direct relations exist between "Nobody Knows" and other stories in *Winesburg, Ohio*. Louise Trunnion is like Elizabeth Willard (of "Mother") in her unfulfilled longing, and each of them suffers both from the insensitivity of men and from her own confusion about what she wants (Atlas 258). The same might be said of Louise Bentley (of "Godliness"), Alice Hindman (of "Adventure"), and Kate Swift (of "The Teacher"). Louise's father, old Jake Trunnion, is "half deaf" (*WO* 60), a symbolic handicap that links him to the "somewhat deaf" old fellow Alice Hindman meets (*WO* 120) and that underlines the barriers to communication that afflict all these people.

Anderson's candor about sex led him to be praised by the rebels of the twenties and reviled by the conservative establishment. But he was always repelled by loveless sex, and that attitude is marked not only in this story but also in "Respectability" and, outside *Winesburg, Ohio,* in "I Want to Know Why" and "Unused" (Chapman 39). Loveless sex within marriage is sometimes even more distasteful than sex with a loose girl of the town, and in his novels *Many Marriages* (1922) and *Dark Laughter* (1925) Anderson approves of the choice of passionate love over a stultifying conventional relationship.

But the more important point regarding this story is the way the characters use sex as a means to some goal of more urgent importance than mere physical desire: Louise is using sex in hopes of getting attention, respect, and love, while George is using sex to get a sense of masculine pride and power. An interesting variation on this theme appears in the late novel *Kit Brandon* (1936), where the heroine uses her sexual assets shrewdly and deliberately to manipulate men and to acquire money, status, and power. The pathetic strivings of poor girl Louise Trunnion are transformed in Kit to a kind of magnificence, as—expertly—she leaves her poverty permanently behind. Still, the loneliness of Kit's success is dramatized by an episode much like that in "Nobody Knows": Kit entices a half-eager, half-frightened stranger to the outskirts of town, where on a grassy bank they engage in another "blind, dumb effort of perplexed hungry humans to draw close" (266).

Critical Studies

Two early critics of Anderson touch briefly on this story's significance. Chase remarks that George is "not sure whether he is seducing or being seduced" by Louise Trunnion (35). Fagin calls the tale a "mere statement" of a sex adventure, "truthful but pointless," and sees in it testimony not only to the adolescent's view that his encounter is "a stupendous achievement" but also to the adolescent vision of its author, who speaks for a nation still adolescent in its attitudes towards sexuality; American literature has been so "devoid . . . of the simplest statements of sex life" that the story is as much an initiation for the country as it is for the nervous young hero (115).

Although the story has not received much critical attention, recent critics who have discussed it have, for the most part, been better attuned to its ironies. Baker rightly considers the tale "a triumph of controlled understatement" but misses a key point when he describes Louise as "complacently certain of her adolescent charms," "healthy," and "nubile" (571, 573). This splendid, wryly tender portrait of a village slut shows a starved soul doing its tawdry, valiant best to fulfill itself in a world where the poor and the female are routinely exploited. More accurate is Burbank's assessment of Louise as "pathetic" and of George as immature (68, 70). Rideout emphasizes George's self-centeredness throughout the tale, from initial nervous timidity, through a spurt of talkativeness and subsequent aggressiveness, to final guilty listening for a voice that does not speak ("Simplicity" 28–29). George at this stage of his development is "coarse" and "egotistical," and his consciousness is limited to the physical dimension of love (Murphy 244). He treats Louise simply as an object to satisfy his needs (Rigsbee 239). And the failure of sexual union to satisfy his deeper needs is betrayed by his anxiety at the close, where he tries to buck up his flagging spirits by assuring himself that no one will find out about his adventure (Bort 448–49). He "wins only a pathetic victory," and it is Anderson's strength as a writer that he can subtly indicate the churlishness and "question the manhood" of the initiation accomplished (Townsend 116–17, 24).

The form and technique of the story have received some comment. Mellard classifies it as one of five stories "of incident" in *Winesburg,* a type characterized by narrative simplicity and scant symbolism; Mellard notes that the story leads up to George's discovery "that the 'nobody knows' rational-

ization has two sides —"first to coax the girl and at last to still his own
doubts" (1306–1307). That nice twist Ingram calls a "reversal of insight," and
he shows it to be a technique in several *Winesburg* tales (197). Ingram also
remarks that the symbolism of hands in the story cycle takes a rather "ludicrous" turn here as George's ardor idealizes Louise's greasy, rough hands
(188–89). Wright classifies the tale as an "episode of choice" of the type he
calls "caustic comedy" because the main character, as a result of "emotional
cowardice," refuses to acknowledge an obvious problem (388, 214). Wright
mentions aspects of the story that are characteristic of stories of the twenties—the youthful protagonist, the treatment of illicit sex, the transitory satisfaction sex brings, and the interference by the "force of conventionality"
(31, 57, 89, 128). But the most valuable part of his discussion is his analysis
of Anderson's use of dramatic inference in the concluding paragraphs of the
tale, where the narrative indirectly conveys that George is not at all confident that Louise has not "gotten anything on" him; the doubts that mar
George's "triumph" are indicated by movement and by "dogged" mutterings,
which a reader must appreciate as evidence of George's real feelings (348–
49). The reader, then, becomes the one who sees beneath the surface of
lives, as George has not yet learned to do.

Works Cited

Anderson, Sherwood. 1926. *Tar: A Midwest Childhood.* New York: Boni &
    Liveright. Rpt. *Tar: A Midwest Childhood: A Critical Text.* Ed. Ray Lewis
    White. Cleveland: Press of Case Western Reserve University, 1969.

———. 1936. *Kit Brandon: A Portrait.* New York and London: Scribners.

———. "Girl by the Stove." *Decision* 1 (January 1941):19–22. Rpt. in *The Sher-
    wood Anderson Reader.* Ed. Paul Rosenfeld. Boston: Houghton Mifflin,
    1947, 704–707.

Atlas, Marilyn Judith. 1981. "Sherwood Anderson and the Women of Wines-
    burg." In *Critical Essays on Sherwood Anderson.* Ed. David D. Ander-
    son. Boston: G. K. Hall, 250–66.

Baker, Carlos. "Sherwood Anderson's Winesburg: A Reprise." *The Virginia
    Quarterly Review* 48 (1972):568–79.

Bort, Barry D. "*Winesburg, Ohio:* The Escape from Isolation." *Midwest
    Quarterly* 11 (1970):443–56.

Burbank, Rex. 1964. *Sherwood Anderson.* New York: Twayne. Rpt. in part
    in *The Achievement of Sherwood Anderson: Essays in Criticism.* Ed. Ray
    Lewis White. Chapel Hill: University of North Carolina Press, 1966, 32–

43. Rpt. in part in *Sherwood Anderson: A Collection of Critical Essays.* Ed. Walter B. Rideout. Englewood Cliffs, NJ: Prentice-Hall, 1974, 70–83.

Chapman, Arnold. "Sherwood Anderson and Eduardo Mallea." *PMLA* 69 (1954):34–45.

Chase, Cleveland B. 1927. *Sherwood Anderson.* New York: Robert M. McBride. Rpt. Folcroft, PA: Folcroft Press, 1969.

Fagin, N. Bryllion. 1973. *The Phenomenon of Sherwood Anderson: A Study in American Life and Letters.* New York: Russell & Russell. Originally printed Baltimore: Rossi-Bryn, 1927.

Ingram, Forrest L. 1971. *Representative Short Story Cycles of the Twentieth Century: Studies in a Literary Genre.* The Hague: Mouton.

Lorch, Thomas M. "The Choreographic Structure of *Winesburg, Ohio.*'" *College Language Association Journal* 12 (1968–69):56–65.

Mellard, James M. "Narrative Forms in *Winesburg, Ohio.*" *PMLA* 83 (1968):1304–1312.

Murphy, George D. "The Theme of Sublimation in Anderson's *Winesburg, Ohio.*" *Modern Fiction Studies* 13 (1967):237–46.

Phillips, William L. "How Sherwood Anderson Wrote *Winesburg, Ohio.*" *American Literature* 23 (1951):7–30. Rpt. in *Sherwood Anderson: Winesburg, Ohio: Text and Criticism.* Ed. John H. Ferres. New York: Viking, 1966, 263–86. Rpt. in *The Achievement of Sherwood Anderson: Essays in Criticism.* Ed. Ray Lewis White. Chapel Hill: University of North CarolinaP ress, 1966, 62–84. Rpt. in *The Merrill Studies in* Winesburg, Ohio. Comp. Ray Lewis White. Columbus, OH: Charles E. Merrill, 1971, 2–24. Rpt. in *Sherwood Anderson: A Collection of Critical Essays* Ed. Walter B. Rideout. Englewood Cliffs, NJ: Prentice-Hall, 1974, 18–38.

Rideout, Walter B. "The Simplicity of *Winesburg, Ohio.*" *Shenandoah* 13 (1962):20–31. Rpt. in *Sherwood Anderson:* Winesburg, Ohio: *Text and Criticism.* Ed. John H. Ferres. Viking, 1966, 287–300. Rpt. in *Critical Essays on Sherwood Anderson.* Ed. David D. Anderson. Boston: Hall, 1981, 146–54.

———. 1976. "Talbot Whittingham and Anderson: A Passage to *Winesburg, Ohio.*" In *Sherwood Anderson: Dimensions of His Literary Art.* Ed. David D. Anderson. East Lansing: Michigan State University Press, 41–60.

Rigsbee, Sally Adair. "The Feminine in *Winesburg, Ohio.*" *Studies in American Fiction* 9 (1981):233–44.

Townsend, Kim. 1987. *Sherwood Anderson.* Boston: Houghton Mifflin.

White, Ray Lewis. "*Winesburg, Ohio:* The Unique Alternate Draft of 'Nobody Knows.'" *Winesburg Eagle* 8, no. 1 (November 1982):3–5.

———, ed. 1969. *Sherwood Anderson's Memoirs: A Critical Edition.* Chapel Hill: University of North Carolina Press.

Wright, Austin McGiffert. 1961. *The American Short Story in the Twenties.* Chicago: University of Chicago Press.

Godliness

Circumstances of Composition

"Godliness" was composed later than many of the other tales in *Winesburg, Ohio.* As Thurston has pointed out, the story came out of an abandoned attempt at a novel (126). From June through August of 1917, Anderson vacationed at Lake Chateaugay in upstate New York, near the Canadian border, close to a camp run by Alys Bentley; he had stayed at the camp the previous summer, too, and had married his second wife, Tennessee Mitchell, in the village of Chateaugay (Townsend 127–28). In the relaxed summer of 1917, he enjoyed the company of Tennessee and also of his first wife and children, who stayed nearby; he had long talks with author and editor Waldo Frank and psychoanalyst Trigant Burrow; he danced in Bentley's eurhythmic classes; and he worked on a novel to be titled *Immaturity.* In a letter of August 27, 1917, Anderson wrote to Frank:

> As I have loafed and danced and waited in the sun up here this summer, a peculiar thing has taken place in me. My mind has run back and back to the time when men tended sheep and lived a noma[d]ic life on hillsides and by little talking streams. I have become less & less the thinker and more the thing of earth and the winds. When I awake at night and the wind is howling, my first thought is that the gods are at play in the hills here. My new book, starting with life on a big farm in Ohio, will have something of that flavor in its earlier chapters. There is a delightful old man, Joseph Bentley by name, who is full of old Bible thoughts and impulses. (Jones-Rideout, *Letters* 15)

He had begun the novel earlier that year. In a letter of January 12, 1917, he mentioned his "new book" in which Winesburg passes through a "hurried transition from an agricultural to an industrial community"; John Hardy was to be in it "a banker and industrial leader," and his son Tom Hardy would leave, "striving, hoping, hungering" (Sutton, *Letters* 44). The theme of the book, he said, was to be "the terrible immaturity and crudeness of all our lives." (44).

Anderson reworked material from that attempted novel into the four-part story "Godliness." Back in Chicago in September, he wrote Frank that he had finished five chapters but was finding his job distracting (Jones-Rideout, *Letters* 17). In November, he wrote that his novel had begun to "ramble . . . and chatter about the most absurd and unexpected things," and by December it had "gone insane" because its author was "a really delicious, garrulous, heavy lame fellow with shaggy eyebrows" (Jones-Rideout *Letters* 25, 27). Sometime after that, when his frisky mood turned to sobriety, he must have seen the possibility of turning his story into a sort of historical background for the *Winesburg* tales. Transforming Joseph Bentley into Jesse Bentley, he fitted the material into its present shape. When Waldo Frank saw the completed *Winesburg, Ohio* in 1919, he expressed surprise that Anderson had included "four parts of the 'boy Jesus'" in it (Phillips, "Origins" 167n); that remark gives special resonance to the name "Joseph" and may suggest something about the novel Anderson had begun in 1917.

In the existing manuscript of *Winesburg*, Part Three of the tale stands seventh in the sequence of eleven tales on the backs of the "Talbot Whittingham" manuscript (between "Mother" and "Nobody Knows"), and Part Four is eleventh (following "The Thinker"). Parts One and Two are on pages removed from the fragment of the "Talbot Whittingham" manuscript on which "Mother" appears (Phillips, "How" 11). That does not necessarily indicate anything about the order of composition, though it may. Kramer states that "Anderson mixed a portion of *Immortality* [Kramer's misreading of *Immaturity;* he refers to Parts One and Two, presumably] with two earlier short tales" (305). Ingram, too, argues, on the basis of Phillips's work with the manuscript, that Parts Three and Four "were composed as an integral part of the first eleven stories" and speculates that Parts One and Two were written afterward (146 and 146n). The manuscript evidence does suggest at least that Anderson did not always intend to place all four parts together as a unit.

White concludes, from his study of the tables of contents for *Winesburg, Ohio,* that the four parts of "Godliness" once stood together as ninth in the sequence of tales (after "The Thinker") and were subsequently moved up to their present position, sixth ("Table").

Sources and Influences

Two historical figures have been identified as the man on whom Jesse Bentley was modeled. Jesse Benton, who (with his family) was the first person to settle in Clyde, Ohio, may have been a source for Anderson's character, as Duffey suggests (208). The Bentley farm has been traced to an actual location three miles south of Clyde, Anderson's boyhood home (Hurd 173). But Sykes makes a convincing case that Jesse Bentley was based on Joseph F. Glidden of De Kalb, Illinois: parallels between Glidden and the fictional character include the amount of land each originally owned (600 acres), their subsequent acquisition of much more land, their laying vast quantities of tile to drain the fields, their early education for the ministry, and their invention of a machine for making wire fence (80–81). Sykes surmises that the author might have met Glidden on one of his advertising trips to Illinois; Anderson's employer, the Critchfield Company, was the advertising agent for several of the "farm tools and conveniences" Glidden had invented (82). Supporting that possibility is a 1916 letter in which Anderson refers to a friend who is both a manufacturer of wire fence and a man of incipient artistic sensitivity (Sutton, *Letters* 13). The letter quoted above (in "Circumstances of Composition") makes clear that Anderson originally called his character Joseph Bentley, using Glidden's first name and his dancing instructor's last name. The alteration of "Joseph" to "Jesse" may have been influenced by the original settler in Clyde and by the biblical father of David.

Clearly the Old Testament was a major source for this tale. David Bentley is in several important ways like the biblical David, and something of the poetic aspect of the biblical David is suggested in Part Two of the tale, where the boy delights in the pastoral life of the farm. Jesse Bentley is a figure that ironically incorporates David's father, old Jesse the Bethlehemite; Saul, first king of Israel; and Goliath, the Philistine. Like the biblical Jesse, Anderson's character is a wealthy owner of land and flocks and a patriarch; he aspires to emulate Jesse by fathering a race of "sons who shall be rulers" (*WO* 70). More important, he is like Saul, who ruled Israel during a period of transition (from a tribal to a national society), who organized mostly successful battles against the neighboring Philistines, who suffered from fits of madness and wild zeal, who tenderly loved young David, and who was cursed for disobeying God's law (1 Samuel 11–16). But Saul also persecuted David, who then fled from him (1 Samuel 18–21), as David flees from his grandfather at the end of "Godliness." In Anderson's character the dark side of Saul merges into the figure of the enemy Goliath, whom David slew with a stone (1 Samuel 17). This complex blending of scriptural antecedents is powerfully evocative.

Furthermore, as Laughlin explains, the story contains an ironic and tragic allusion to the story of Abraham's sacrifice of Isaac (57–58). Moreover, "a biblical vocabulary" enters the story, as Asselineau remarks, but one cannot imagine why he thinks Anderson is trying "to break free from it" (349); it belongs.

Another influence on the story was Mark Twain. Anderson himself wrote to a friend in the fall of 1917 about a spirit he found in works by Twain: "Is it not likely that when the country was new and men were often alone in the fields and forests, they got a sense of bigness outside themselves that has now in some way been lost? . . . I am old enough to remember tales that strengthen my belief in a deep, semi-religious influence that was formerly at work among our people. The flavor of it hangs over the best work of Mark Twain" (Jones-Rideout, *Letters* 23). Contrasting that spirit with the "shrill-ness" of modern America, Anderson mentions his "fancy" that the pioneers "had a savagery superior to our own" (Jones-Rideout, *Letters* 22, 23); this idea was surely connected with the novel he had been working on, and it shows up in the first part of "Godliness" in the contrast between the "crude and animal-like poetic fervor" of the settlers and "the shrill cries of millions of new voices" that crowd into minds of the industrial age (*WO* 65, 70).

Publication History

This story made its first appearance in *Winesburg, Ohio* (1919).

Relation to Other Works

A chief critical question concerning "Godliness" has been its relation, or lack of relation, to the rest of *Winesburg, Ohio*. George Willard does not appear in the story. Most of the events in the story take place not in Winesburg, but on a farm outside the town, and the chronology of the tale stands outside the time frame of the rest of the tales. Howe said in 1951 that the story does not "fit into" the pattern of the book (106). Thurston, who had noticed the story's source in an abortive novel, declared in 1956 that it "rests uneasily among the other stories," especially because its "heavy-handed preaching about industrialism," "overt spiritual seeking," and "almost burlesque use of biblical symbols" are too "mystical" to be consonant with *Winesburg, Ohio*; these mystical elements, he stated, are in the vein of *Marching Men* and *Many Marriages* (126). Burbank in 1964 agreed, arguing that it also "violates the symbolic structure of the book" and "lapses into direct statement and contrived allegory" (76).

But a great many critics have insisted that the four-part story does indeed fit integrally into the structure of the book. It reiterates and expands the theme of isolation (D. Anderson 46–46). It is linked with the other tales by the motif of departure, the motif of adventure, the motif of dreams, and the symbols of fire and rooms (Ingram 168, 173–76, 180, 182). In addition to offering numerous symbolic relationships with the other tales, it gives the historical and sociological background essential to an understanding of the town (Laughlin 98–99). It reaches behind the "sexual and imaginative frustrations of the townspeople" into the religious and moral distortions at their root (Schevill 103). In fact, in Jesse Bentley, it presents the character who more than any other in the book "personifies" the oppressive morality and materialism that constitute the destructive conventional values of the community (Lorch 65). He has become warped because, as "The Book of the Grotesque" says, from his thoughts he has fashioned a "truth" which he then embraces—that God will bless those who serve Him by working hard and acquiring material prosperity (Laughlin 97).

Moreover, Louise Bentley's longing for love and her husband's misunderstanding of her longing are more or less paradigmatic of all the *Winesburg* stories (Geismar 235), especially those involving Elizabeth and Tom Willard (McDonald 238). As with other characters, Louise's desire for understanding takes "a sexual form that is both expression and betrayal" (Hilfer 153); Louise Trunnion (of "Nobody Knows"), Alice Hindman (of "Adventure"), and Kate Swift (of "The Teacher") are particularly like her in this respect.

The story is, furthermore, linked with "The Strength of God" by the idea that religion can be a destructive force (Bowden 120–21). Both Jesse Bentley and the Reverend Curtis Hartman show "a certain weirdly adolescent desire" for God's approval (O'Neill 68). The "triangular relationship" of Jesse, Louise, and David resembles that of Hartman, Kate Swift, and George Willard (Dewey 257). Moreover, the story is linked with both "The Strength of God" and "Tandy" by its emphasis on love gestures between parents and children (Maresca 282). The emotional starvation inflicted on the daughter by a religion-absorbed father in "Tandy" bears a particularly close relation to the sources of Louise Bentley's grotesque behavior.

In several specific ways "Godliness" is related to "The Philosopher." Both Jesse Bentley and Doctor Parcival are fanatics, "motivated by self-aggrandizing visions that estrange them from the brotherhood of man" (Ciancio 995). Both were ministerial students in their youth (Abcarian 101). Each of them has a twitch in his left eye, a handicap that suggests a strange, partly sinister combination of visionary insight and blindness. Finally, according to McAleer's rather elaborate argument, the story of Jesse Bentley holds the key to the crucifixion of humankind (to which Doctor Parcival refers) because it reveals the new sin of the industrial age—materialism—from which they must escape in order to find the "Grail" (171–73).

There is also a broad parallel between David Hardy and the character central to the whole cycle, George Willard, who, like David, breaks away from a community that alternately nurtures and threatens him and toward which he in turn feels a mixture of yearning affection and bewildered terror. As O'Neill points out, "David too had been sought out by at least one of the town's obsessed, his own grandfather"; and his recoil, like George's, "expresses for us some of the fear experienced by the artist, ultimately by Anderson himself, as the dark and violent underside of Winesburg, which is to say, of American life, is revealed" (81).

In other important ways, "Godliness" is similar to works by Anderson besides those collected in *Winesburg*. In the spring of 1917, Anderson had composed a series of free verse poems in which he promises, "I will renew in my people the worship of gods." The themes of *Mid-American Chants* (1918) reappear in the story of Jesse Bentley; the world of the old "sweet . . . Biblical . . . makers of wagons and harness and plows" is transformed into a world of toiling millions "choked" by words and industrial smoke, and the sense of mystery and reverence is nearly crushed by factories and trade (11, 16). The mode of the *Chants* is prophetic, that of the tale tragic.

Most of all, however, "Godliness" approaches in theme and tone the novel *Poor White* (1920), which also treats an Ohio town in transition from agriculture to industry. The central figure of *Poor White* is Hugh McVey, a dreamy Midwestern boy who is prodded by a New England aunt to be industrious and get ahead in the world; Hugh is like Jesse Bentley in determinedly redirecting his natural bent into sustained, and successful, efforts to achieve worldly success. Both Hugh and Jesse become inventors of products for farmers. Both remain loners and social misfits, characterized by a weird combination of acuteness to large, abstract ideas and insensitivity to the simplest, most obvious needs of people near them. Both have a certain warped grandeur, for while in one sense they are totally self-absorbed, in another they are visionary innocents whose aims are so large that the selfishness inherent in them is almost coincidental. It is not money and fame they want, but to participate in the highest good they can imagine. The tragic results of their efforts are attributable to larger forces in Western civilization as much as, or more than, to personal wrongheadedness. Critics have often remarked the influence of *Huckleberry Finn* on the early chapters of *Poor White,* and Anderson mentioned the sense in Twain of "a deep, semi–religious influence" (Jones-Rideout, *Letters* 23), which he was trying to catch, too, in his 1917 manuscript. "Godliness," more than any other Anderson story, approximates *Poor White,* for both depict the cultural shift by which a pastoral world with all its peaceful beauty and brutal ignorance developed into an industrialized world where property dominates men's minds and bruises their souls. More than any other story, too, this story approaches the historical reach of *Poor White,* tracing the roots of America's problems to the unholy alliance of religion and profit present from the first arrival of the Europeans and offering a prophetic warning for a nation that in 1917 was still, like Jesse, "too greedy for glory" (*WO* 102).

Louise Bentley's anguished struggle to use her talents and to find loving relationships is allied with the similar struggle of Clara Butterworth, the woman who becomes a major focus in the middle and later portions of *Poor White*. Though Clara lacks Louise's angry bitterness, they both have been neglected by their fathers, and as a consequence emotional neediness limits their potential for independent womanhood. Moreover, the affectionate gestures they each make to men other than their fathers are misunderstood as invitations to mere sexual contact. Louise is thus an early instance of Anderson's repeated attempts to deal with women's longings amid the changing social conditions that would increasingly offer to women the chimerical promise of liberating themselves from subservience to men and from slavish domestic drudgery (which killed Louise's mother). The way out for women was supposed to be education, and Louise with her books is a precursor of other Anderson heroines who approach in various ways independent selfhood—Clara, Aline Gray (in *Dark Laughter*, 1925), and Kit Brandon (in the novel of that name, 1936). The frustration of their attempts owes something to the author's sense that there is an "age-old woman's desire to be possessed" (*WO* 94), as well as to the historical facts of women's struggle both to be themselves and to fulfill themselves in love.

The heroine most resembling Louise Bentley, though, is Ethel Long in *Beyond Desire* (1932). Like Louise, Ethel grows bitter because her father is so much more devoted to his sons than to her. When her brothers die, he is more interested in begetting another son than in developing a genuine relationship with his living daughter. Her efforts to satisfy her emotional longings are, like Louise's, desperate and confused. Incisively, Louise articulates her awareness of the "poison" of the old patriarchal devaluation of females when, violating her deep love for her son, she relinquishes the boy to her father: Jesse's farm, she says, "is a place for a man child, although it never was a place for me" (*WO* 78). Whereas Louise sees the problem as specific to one man, however, Ethel grasps its broadly cultural nature: "Ethel felt it was rather absurd, the determination of the male about sons . . . a vanity that went on and on in men . . . wanting to reproduce themselves . . . thinking that so terribly important. . . . It was all a part of the immaturity of men a woman got so tired of (*Beyond Desire* 142). The masculine vanity of wanting sons in order to magnify a family's status reappears in the obsession of Tom Halsey in *Kit Brandon* (216 and passim).

The climactic moment of encounter in "Godliness," it may be added, is one of the most vivid enactments of an archetypal scene that appears repeatedly in Anderson's fiction. When David hurls the stone at Jesse, proclaiming to himself, "I have killed the man of God and now I will myself be a man and go into the world" (*WO* 102), it relates not only to the episode mentioned in the opening section of the four-part tale, where Enoch Bentley nearly kills his father, but also to patricidal sequences in *Windy McPherson's Son* (1916), in "A Chicago Hamlet" (1923), and in *Kit Brandon* (1936).

Critical Studies

This story is unique among the stories of *Winesburg, Ohio* in comprising four related tales. As a miniature cycle of stories culminating in the flight of a youth from his community, it approximates the pattern of the larger cycle in which it is contained. It is unique also in that it reaches back into times previous to the short span of years in which the actions of the other stories occur; "Godliness" alone encompasses the history of four generations. Partly because of these differences, the story has received a considerable measure of critical blame. Some recent critics, however, have recognized its merit.

Howe dismissed it simply as "a failure" (106), and many other critics have followed suit. Thurston specifies its flaws: "[t]he heavy-handed preaching about industrialism there, the overt spiritual seeking, and the almost burlesque use of Biblical symbols and allusions" (126; similarly, Love 48, Ingram 160, Burbank 76). (See also "Relation to Other Works," above.) Abcarian argues that the story fails because it "veers toward the novelistic," diluting the power of Jesse Bentley's story by the addition of the essentially irrelevant story of his daughter Louise and by the awkward shifting of the point of view "from Jesse to Louise to David" (101). Baker expands these charges: "In seeking to combine the classical doctrine of hubris with the Old Testament stories of Abraham and Isaac and David and Goliath, Anderson not only strains the reader's capacity for belief but also comes close to the edge of unintentional parody by invoking these heroic Biblical figures to serve as models for his bucolic midwesterners" (574). Even one of the story's staunchest defenders, Rosemary M. Laughlin, considers that the final "David-Goliath encounter" is a flaw; though the story has established the probability of that climax by describing the youth's hunting squirrels with his sling, she says, the imposition of the second myth "distracts and detracts from" the myth of Abraham and Isaac, which she considers central (103 n. 5).

Mellard's analysis of narrative forms in *Winesburg, Ohio,* however, comments appreciatively on the multiple ironies of the story and indirectly counters the complaint that it too explicitly "tells" its thesis. He classifies "Godliness" as belonging to the "thematic" group of tales, each of which "subordinates character, event, and symbol to the exposition of the 'truth,'" or central idea, indicated in the story title (1307). By calling attention to "the nearly allegorical nature" of all the thematic stories (1309), Mellard points to a difference of approach that need not be viewed as a weakness. The more traditional narrative approach of "Godliness," as O'Neill explains, integrates the stories of *Winesburg* and enables a deeper understanding of the psychological, emotional, and moral forces at work in them by placing them in a broader context of social and cultural history (70).

The fullest treatment of the story from a sociohistorical perspective is

Laughlin's "Godliness and the American Dream in Winesburg, Ohio." It delineates the parallels between this story and the history of American Protes-
tants as recounted by authors from John Smith and William Bradford
through Franklin and Edwards and "nineteenth century historians like Pres-
cott and Parkman" (100). The "two influences at work in Jesse Bentley" (*WO*
80), Laughlin states, are precisely those two conflicting influences wedded
so incompatibly in American history: Jesse "sees himself in history as a tool
of God's Providence, a chosen servant," and he believes that "material prosperity [is] the sign of divine favor." The parallel with the Biblical story of
Abraham and Isaac, Laughlin observes, associates Jesse's tragedy—easily
and naturally—with that of the nation (102). Whereas Jesse, like Abraham,
desires only "to sire a new nation and a great race," David misinterprets his
intention to sacrifice the lamb as a personal threat; having been initiated in
the bloody scene at the end of Part Two "into the contorted world of his
grandfather," he flees that world at the end of Part Four (101–102). The loss
of innocence inflicted upon them both is an outgrowth of the industrialism
and materialism that swept away the whole nation's "rustic innocence and
virtue" (102).

O'Neill extends these insights, correcting as he does so Laughlin's over-
emphasis on the innocence of the preindustrial world. The fundamental
sociological reality in Anderson's story is the ignorant, "brute work" of farmers engaged in a "pressing economic struggle" with a primitive land (70–71,
73)—a fact that goes far in explaining Jesse's materialism. "The harshness of
life in the middle west just after the Civil War revived and kept alive an
unlovely creed, a Calvinism long since judged too unyielding and graceless
for the new commercial sections of Boston, but grimly satisfying for those
who found the earth as uncompromising as the Hebrews' God" (72).
Anderson's particular achievement, as O'Neill explains, is dramatizing "the
emotional dynamic" by which poetic impulses submerged in the lives of
these crude farmers rose in the minds of men like Jesse to "visionary exaltation" as "the Old Testament became a living metaphor" for their lives (73–
74). In exemplifying the "fusion of the ordinary and the deranged," Jesse—
"resourceful American business-man farmer" and fanatic—epitomizes the
pattern of the grotesque in *Winesburg, Ohio* (75).

Neither of these critics treats the section of the story dealing with Louise
Bentley as an important part of its historical content. O'Neill correctly notes
that Louise's academic success indicates that horizons were expanding in
the 1880s for young women with brains, luck, and wealthy fathers (76). But
since the overall story is so clearly related to the American historical process,
it is valid to emphasize, as Lorch does, the representative nature of Jesse's
carelessness with his wife and daughter and of John Hardy's misunderstanding of his wife (64). The great tradition, whether envisioned by those who
imagined a city on a hill or by those who planned a noble nation of liberty

and justice for all, has always tended to leave women out of the picture. It seems hardly fair, then, to blame *Anderson* for "dooming [Louise] to an unhappy life," as Atlas does (259); the tale shows that deeply ingrained habits in the American character have denied women their birthright, and it demonstrates the author's considerable sympathy for the struggling soul within the cold, angry, unstable woman known to the citizens of Winesburg. Atlas is right in suggesting that Anderson's authorial comment about the "age-old woman's desire to be possessed" (*WO* 94) indicates a bias in his view of the sexes (258–59), but in the main Louise is a victim. Her "complete defeat . . . is expressed in her rejection of her child" (Rigsbee 234). The sins of her father are here visited upon the next two generations.

Dewey proposes that Louise represents "a difficult middle stage between the failing religion of her father and the emerging artistic sense of her son" (255). According to this interpretation, the story traces the process of three generations, each of which tries to satisfy its spiritual hunger in a different way. Jesse seeks in vain for communion with "an absent God" (253), Louise seeks futilely for communion in sex, and David (named after the psalmist) is an "embryonic artist" who prefigures George Willard, who presumably will find communion through art (256).

Two critics call attention to "the debasement of the (printed) word" in the modern era (Colquitt 81). Yingling attributes Winesburg's "loss of an authentic cultural wisdom" and modern "alienation" to the rise of "print culture" (109, 123). Colquitt observes that Jesse Bentley's "perversion of 'the Word'" has a much earlier origin, in the original fall of mankind (81).

Abcarian properly emphasizes the tragic dimension of Jesse's story and the tragic recognition revealed in his last words "that 'greed' and 'glory' are not complementary but inimical" (100). Similarly, McAleer sees in the tale the essential cause of "the suffering of man in Winesburg and the world"— the process by which materialism crowded out lifegiving love (172–73). He points out the crucial irony that, when David hurls a stone at Jesse with his sling, "the man who sees his neighbors as Philistines is himself identified as a Philistine, whose presence taints the promised land," and he also calls attention to "David's kinship . . . with Christ"—by virtue of the genealogy that traces Jesus back to "the seed of David" and of "the head wound" David receives in Part Two (173).

Still, critics have not yet adequately interpreted the complex overlay of myth in the story, which is Anderson's boldest experiment in this vein. Laughlin astutely observes that different myths are associated with different viewpoints: from David's point of view, the scene in which Jesse intends to anoint his grandson with the blood of the lamb assumes "the form of the Abraham–Isaac myth" (102) while in Jesse's mind it is simply another part of his attempted reenactment of the success of the biblical Jesse and Saul through the boy-hero David. David's rejection of the role of Isaac, however, and his adoption of the role of the giant-slayer constitute a shift of crucial significance not merely for Jesse but for the whole sequence of stories in *Winesburg*. Since Isaac is a figure typologically linked with Jesus, David's defiant refusal to accept the role of sacrificial sufferer places him in rebellion not only against all the fathers who would transfer their sins to subsequent generations but also against the philosophy enunciated by Doctor Parcival, that "everyone in the world is Christ and they are all crucified" (*WO* 57). Ironically, in his final gesture, by which he hopes to find freedom, David inflicts a wound and becomes a man, a man in whom pride and poetry and murderous violence and suffering and dreams of a better life make up an amalgam of primal emotion much like that which animated his ancestral lineage. Though the story charts profound cultural changes, it also traces the persistence of the past in the present.

Works Cited

Abcarian, Richard. "Innocence and Experience in *Winesburg, Ohio*." *University Review–Kansas City* 35 (1968):95–105.

Anderson, David. 1967. *Sherwood Anderson: An Introduction and Interpretation*. New York: Holt, Rinehart.

Anderson, Sherwood. 1916. *Windy McPherson's Son*. New York: John Lane. Rev. ed. New York: B. W. Huebsch, 1922. Chicago and London: University of Chicago Press, 1965. Introduction by Wright Morris.

———. 1918. *Mid-American Chants*. New York: John Lane. Rpt. New York: B. W. Huebsch, 1923.

———. 1919. *Winesburg, Ohio*. New York: B. W. Huebsch. Rpt. New York: Viking, 1960.

———. 1920. *Poor White*. New York: B. W. Huebsch. Rpt. New York: Viking, 1966. Introduction by Walter B. Rideout.

———. 1925. *Dark Laughter*. New York: Boni & Liveright. Grosset and Dunlap, 1925.

———. 1932. *Beyond Desire*. New York: Liveright. Rpt. New York: Liveright, 1961. Introduction by Walter B. Rideout.

———. 1936. *Kit Brandon: A Portrait*. New York and London: Scribners.

Asselineau, Roger. 1966. "Language and Style in Sherwood Anderson's *Winesburg, Ohio*." In *Sherwood Anderson:* Winesburg, Ohio: *Text and Criticism*. Ed. and trans. John H. Ferres. New York: Viking, 345–56. Rpt. from "Langue et Style de Sherwood Anderson dans *Winesburg, Ohio*."

Configuration Critique de Sherwood Anderson. La Revue des Lettres Modernes 78–80 (1963):121–35.

Atlas, Marilyn Judith. 1981. "Sherwood Anderson and the Women of Winesburg." In *Critical Essays on Sherwood Anderson*. Ed. David D. Anderson. Boston: G. K. Hall, 250–66.

Baker, Carlos. "Sherwood Anderson's Winesburg: A Reprise." *The Virginia Quarterly Review* 48 (1972):568–79.

Bowden, Edwin T. 1961. *The Dungeon of the Heart: Human Isolation and the American Novel*. New York: Macmillan, 114–24.

Burbank, Rex. 1964. *Sherwood Anderson*. New York: Twayne. Rpt. in part in *The Achievement of Sherwood Anderson: Essays in Criticism*. Ed. Ray Lewis White. Chapel Hill: University of North Carolina Press, 1966, 32–43. Rpt. in part in *Sherwood Anderson: A Collection of Critical Essays*. Ed. Walter B. Rideout. Englewood Cliffs, NJ: Prentice-Hall, 1974, 70–83.

Ciancio, Ralph. "The Sweetness of the Twisted Apples: Unity of Vision in *Winesburg, Ohio*." *PMLA* 87 (1972):994–1006.

Colquitt, Clare. 1990. "Motherlove in Two Narratives of Community: *Winesburg, Ohio* and *The Country of the Pointed Firs*." *New Essays on Winesburg, Ohio*. Ed. John W. Crowley. Cambridge and New York: Cambridge University Press, 73–97.

Crowley, John W., ed. 1990. *Winesburg, Ohio*. New York and Cambridge: Cambridge University Press, 99–128.

Dewey, Joseph. "No God in the Sky and No God in Myself: Godliness' and Anderson's *Winesburg*." *Modern Fiction Studies* 35 (1989):251–59.

Duffey, Bernard. 1954. *The Chicago Renaissance in American Letters: A Critical History*. East Lansing: Michigan State College Press.

Geismar, Maxwell. 1947. "Sherwood Anderson: Last of the Townsmen." In *The Last of the Provincials: The American Novel, 1915–1925*. Boston: Houghton Mifflin, 223–84. Rpt. in part in *Sherwood Anderson:* Winesburg, Ohio: *Text and Criticism*. Ed. John H. Ferres. New York: Viking, 1966, 377–82.

Hilfer, Anthony Channel. 1969. *The Revolt from the Village, 1915–1930*. Chapel Hill: University of North Carolina Press.

Howe, Irving. 1951. *Sherwood Anderson*. New York: William Sloane.

Hurd, Thaddeus B. 1992. "Excerpts from *Winesburg* and Clyde, Fictional/Real Places." Appendix in *Sherwood Anderson: A Study of the Short Fiction*. By Robert Allen Papinchak. New York, Twayne.

Ingram, Forrest L. 1971. *Representative Short Story Cycles of the Twentieth Century: Studies in a Literary Genre*. The Hague: Mouton.

Jones, Howard Mumford, and Walter B. Rideout, eds. 1953. *Letters of Sherwood Anderson*. Boston: Little, Brown.

Kramer, Dale. 1966. *Chicago Renaissance: The Literary Life in the Midwest, 1900–1930*. New York: Appleton-Century.

Laughlin, Rosemary M. "'Godliness' and the American Dream in *Winesburg, Ohio*." *Twentieth Century Literature* 13 (1967):97–103. Rpt. in *The Merrill Studies in* Winesburg, Ohio. Comp. Ray Lewis White. Columbus, OH: Charles E. Merrill, 1971, 52–60.

Lorch, Thomas M. "The Choreographic Structure of *Winesburg, Ohio*." *College Language Association Journal* 12 (1968–69):56–65.

Love, Glen A. "*Winesburg, Ohio* and the Rhetoric of Silence." *American Literature* 40 (1968):38–57.

Maresca, Carol J. "Gestures as Meaning in Sherwood Anderson's *Winesburg, Ohio*." *College Language Association Journal* 9 (1966):279–83.

McAleer, John J. "Christ Symbolism in *Winesburg, Ohio*." *Discourse* 4 (1961):168–81. Rpt. in *The Merrill Studies in* Winesburg, Ohio. Comp. Ray Lewis White. Columbus, OH: Charles E. Merrill, 1971, 60–74.

McDonald, Walter R. "*Winesburg, Ohio:* Tales of Isolation." *University Review Kansas City* 35 (1969):237–40.

Mellard, James M. "Narrative Forms in *Winesburg, Ohio*." *PMLA* 83 (1968):1304–1312.

O'Neill, John. "Anderson Writ Large: 'Godliness' in *Winesburg, Ohio*." *Twentieth Century Literature* 23 (1977):67–83.

Phillips, William L. "Sherwood Anderson's *Winesburg, Ohio:* Its Origins, Composition, Technique, and Reception." Ph.D. diss., University of Chicago, 1950.

———. "How Sherwood Anderson Wrote *Winesburg, Ohio*." *American Literature* 23 (1951):7–30. Rpt. in *Sherwood Anderson: Winesburg, Ohio: Text and Criticism*. Ed. John H. Ferres. New York: Viking, 1966, 263–86. Rpt. in *The Achievement of Sherwood Anderson: Essays in Criticism*. Ed. Ray Lewis White. Chapel Hill: University of North Carolina Press, 1966, 62–84. Rpt. in *The Merrill Studies in* Winesburg, Ohio. Comp. Ray Lewis White. Columbus, OH: Charles E. Merrill, 1971, 2–24. Rpt. in *Sherwood Anderson: A Collection of Critical Essays*. Ed. Walter B. Rideout. Englewood Cliffs, NJ: Prentice-Hall, 1974, 18–38.

Rigsbee, Sally Adair. "The Feminine in *Winesburg, Ohio*." *Studies in American Fiction* 9 (1981):233–44.

Schevill, James. 1951. *Sherwood Anderson: His Life and Work*. Denver: University of Denver Press.

Sutton, William A., ed. 1985. *Letters to Bab: Sherwood Anderson to Marietta D. Finley, 1916–33*. Foreword by Walter B. Rideout. Urbana and Chicago: University of Illinois Press.

Sykes, Robert H. "The Identity of Anderson's Fanatical Farmer." *Studies in Short Fiction* 18 (1981):79–82.

Thurston, Jarvis. "Anderson and 'Winesburg': Mysticism and Craft." *Accent* 16 (1956):107–128. Rpt. in part in *Sherwood Anderson:* Winesburg, Ohio: *Text and Criticism*. Ed. John H. Ferres. New York: Viking, 1966, 331–44.

Townsend, Kim. 1987. *Sherwood Anderson*. Boston: Houghton Mifflin.

White, Ray Lewis. "*Winesburg, Ohio:* The Table of Contents." *Notes On Modern American Literature* 8 (1984):Item 8.

Yingling, Thomas. 1990. "*Winesburg, Ohio* and the End of Collective Experience." *New Essays on* Winesburg, Ohio. Ed. John W. Crowley. Cambridge and New York: Cambridge University Press, 99–128.

A Man of Ideas

Sources and Influences

In his *Memoirs,* Anderson states that he may have gotten "the figure of Joe" Welling, the central character in "A Man of Ideas," from a friend he had known in Elyria, Ohio—a printer who talked excitedly "in little rushes," sometimes "for hours" (281).

Schevill's observation that Welling is "a parody on the good-natured American promoter" (103) serves as a reminder that the author himself played the role of adman with gusto for years, though by the time he wrote the stories that were to ensure his fame he had come to look askance at that role and the platitudes he had once enthusiastically promulgated.

The baseball club in the story derives from the author's earlier memories. Clyde, Ohio, the town on which the fictional Winesburg was modeled, had a new baseball club in 1882, two years before the Anderson family, with the seven-year-old Sherwood, moved there (Hurd 35). When he grew older, "he played right field for the Clyde Stars, and then he became their manager" (Townsend 16).

Publication History

Under the title "The Man of Ideas," this story made its first appearance in *Little Review* (5:22–28) in June of 1918. It was the ninth of the Winesburg stories to be published in a periodical, and the second in *Little Review*. This magazine did not give payments to contributors.

It was reprinted in *Winesburg, Ohio* (1919) as "A Man of Ideas," the title that appears in the extant manuscript.

Anderson liked the story well enough to reprint it in the *Smyth County News* (January 19, 1927, 6–7), one of two Virginia newspapers he bought in 1927 and edited until 1932.

Relation to Other Works

"The Man of Ideas" is one of several stories in *Winesburg, Ohio* that Mellard classifies as an "emblematic" narrative, that is, one focused on a character type who undergoes no change in the course of the story (1310). Of the six stories in that category, this one is most like the series of character sketches, called "Business Types," that Anderson wrote for *Agricultural Advertising* in 1904, particularly "The Man of Affairs" (White, *Early* 70–75).

Silent, inarticulate characters are prominent in *Winesburg, Ohio,* but the main character of this tale is an interesting exception (Love 44). Although Joe Welling is like Wing Biddlebaum (in "Hands") and Kate Swift (in "The Teacher") in that he vacillates between periods of silence and outbursts of emotion-charged talk, the other grotesque characters typically suffer under their inability to express themselves; Joe's "boyish loquacity" saves him from threatened disaster (Ward 42, 38). Correlating with this difference in character is a stylistic difference in the narration: whereas in *Winesburg, Ohio,* as a whole "the voice of the author predominates over the characters' voices in a proportion of about five parts to one," in this story nearly one-fourth of the text is direct speech attributed to the main character (Mahoney 246).

Moreover, Joe is an exception to the pattern common in the Winesburg tales of entrapment by codes of conventional morality. He conducts his love life with a mind utterly free from such concern. Consequently, he evokes the most overt and sinister attempt to enforce the moral code that occurs in the whole collection. Happily, he also averts that attempt—without even becoming aware that anything is amiss. That is the key element in the story's comedy.

Comedy is not Anderson's usual mode, and his attempts in that vein are marked by varying degrees of success. Among the *Winesburg* tales, "Queer" comes closest to "A Man of Ideas" in accentuating the absurdity of its protagonist more than his pain, but the very notion of the grotesque depends on an ironic discrepancy that holds comic potential. The earnest minister peeping out the church window at a naked woman (in "The Strength of God"), the strutting adolescent smoking a cigar after his first sexual experience (in "Nobody Knows"), the desperate race of a henpecked farmhand to prevent a young rowdy from doing his duty by a girl he has gotten pregnant (in "The Untold Lie")—all spring from the sensibility that would produce the tragicomic masterpiece "The Egg." The sensibility is one Anderson shared, and knew he shared, with Mark Twain.

Ingram, in his analysis of interrelationships among stories in the *Winesburg* cycle, offers an interesting discussion of the way in which this story develops the symbol of fire that runs through the series. Joe Welling himself has a fiery vitality, and his disquisition on decay as fire reveals a secret about the town, Ingram says: the "human beings we meet in the stories show signs" of the capacity for warm, passionate humanity, but at the same time most of them "are burning out" (180). The warm glow amid the decay is something like "the sweetness of the twisted apples" (*WO* 36).

Joe's empty, compulsive talk makes him a descendent of Windy Mc-Pherson, an obscure housepainter who hides his humiliation with loud joviality (*Windy McPherson's Son,* 1916). A fictional portrait of Anderson's father, Windy is much like George Willard's father as well. In that context, this story can be seen to mark a phase of George's development, for Tom Willard's exhortations to his son to stop dreaming and "wake up" (*WO* 44) are of a kind with Joe's insistent claims that he would be a livelier newspaper reporter than George: "Here and there I would run finding out things you'll never see" (*WO* 106). Subsequently, in "The Thinker," George seems to be trying to live up to that standard, for he is described as "[l]ike an excited dog," running "here and there, noting on his pad of paper . . . little facts" (*WO* 134). The shallow philosophy of the man of ideas, then, is a seduction George will eventually have to overcome in order to become an artist with depth of insight. Still, of Anderson's many portrayals of his father's type, Joe Welling is surely one of the most genial.

Critical Studies

This tale has stirred little controversy or extended discussion. There is agreement that, bizarre as he is, Joe Welling is "a happy man" (Bowden 114) and that "his apparent deformity" enables his triumph (Hilfer 152; similarly, Burbank 75, Ciancio 995). He is a grotesque character who is "amusing" (*WO* 23). Though everyone who knows him shrinks from Joe's intermittent fits of inane loquacity, Joe wins over the town, gains a sweetheart, and with his ebullient chatter overmasters her violent relatives when they come to enact vengeance on him. The story turns on the rising tension as the town (like the reader) waits for what seems an inevitable "tragedy" (*WO* 109), and then on the surprising release of tension when Joe's stream of ideas saves the day.

Several critics have appreciated the story's ironies. Raymund finds it a "delightful irony" that the community accepts Joe, whose "every moronic utterance refutes popular opinion" (139). San Juan stresses Joe's uncanny creativity, which parodies his "routine existence" as a Standard Oil agent (152). Thomas suggests that the reference to the ten-dollar fine against Tom King for his wanton killing of a harmless dog is "a highly charged emotional indictment" of the whole society (69). That indictment extends to the town's passive waiting for the Kings to beat up or kill Joe Welling without doing anything to prevent it.

Lorch comments that although Joe does not achieve genuine communication and although his "apocalyptic visions of flood, fire, and famine indicate that he is a deeply unbalanced person," he "represents the potential power and influence of the artist in society" (60). Atlas, on the other hand, infers from the story that Joe and Sarah King *have* achieved "a meaningful relationship" (259). It is noteworthy that Joe's "apocalyptic" imaginings always have a positive thrust. Even when he contemplates the destruction of "all the fruits of the earth," he is buoyantly confident that people will develop new foods: "they couldn't down us. I should say not," he exudes (*WO* 110). His charm, his indomitable good nature, and his optimism typify the adman and the politician more than the artist. If the artist's sober truths were as alluring as Joe's trivial "news," Winesburg—and the world—would be wiser.

Works Cited

Anderson, Sherwood. 1916. *Windy McPherson's Son*. New York: John Lane. Rev. ed. New York: B. W. Huebsch, 1922. Chicago and London: University of Chicago Press, 1965. Introduction by Wright Morris.

———. 1919. *Winesburg, Ohio*. New York: B. W. Huebsch. Rpt. New York: Viking, 1960.

Atlas, Marilyn Judith. 1981. "Sherwood Anderson and the Women of Winesburg." In *Critical Essays on Sherwood Anderson*. Ed. David D. Anderson. Boston: G. K. Hall, 250–66.

Bowden, Edwin T. 1961. *The Dungeon of the Heart: Human Isolation and the American Novel*. New York: Macmillan, 114–24.

Burbank, Rex. 1964. *Sherwood Anderson*. New York: Twayne. Rpt. in part in *The Achievement of Sherwood Anderson: Essays in Criticism*. Ed. Ray Lewis White. Chapel Hill: University of North Carolina Press, 1966, 32–

43. Rpt. in part in *Sherwood Anderson: A Collection of Critical Essays.* Ed. Walter B. Rideout. Englewood Cliffs, NJ: Prentice-Hall, 1974, 70–83.

Ciancio, Ralph. "The Sweetness of the Twisted Apples: Unity of Vision in *Winesburg, Ohio.*" *PMLA* 87 (1972):994–1006.

Hilfer, Anthony Channel. 1969. *The Revolt from the Village, 1915–1930.* Chapel Hill: University of North Carolina Press.

Hurd, Thaddeus, B. "Fun in Winesburg." *Midwestern Miscellany* 11 (1983):28–39.

Ingram, Forrest L. 1971. *Representative Short Story Cycles of the Twentieth Century: Studies in a Literary Genre.* The Hague: Mouton.

Jones, Howard Mumford, and Walter B. Rideout, eds. 1953. *Letters of Sherwood Anderson.* Boston: Little, Brown.

Lorch, Thomas M. "The Choreographic Structure of *Winesburg, Ohio.*'" *College Language Association Journal* 12 (1968–69):56–65.

Love, Glen A. "*Winesburg, Ohio* and the Rhetoric of Silence." *American Literature* 40 (1968):38–57.

Mahoney, John J. "An Analysis of *Winesburg, Ohio.*" *Journal of Aesthetics and Art Criticism* 15 (1956):245–52.

Mellard, James M. "Narrative Forms in *Winesburg, Ohio.*" *PMLA* 83 (1968):1304–1312.

Phillips, William L. "How Sherwood Anderson Wrote *Winesburg, Ohio.*" *American Literature* 23 (1951):7–30. Rpt. in *Sherwood Anderson:* Winesburg, Ohio: *Text and Criticism.* Ed. John H. Ferres. New York: Viking, 1966, 263–86. Rpt. in *The Achievement of Sherwood Anderson: Essays in Criticism.* Ed. Ray Lewis White. Chapel Hill: University of North Carolina Press, 1966, 62–84. Rpt. in *The Merrill Studies in* Winesburg, Ohio. Comp. Ray Lewis White. Columbus, OH: Charles E. Merrill, 1971, 2–24. Rpt. in *Sherwood Anderson: A Collection of Critical Essays.* Ed. Walter B. Rideout. Englewood Cliffs, NJ: Prentice-Hall, 1974, 18–38.

Raymund, Bernard. "The Grammar of Not-Reason: Sherwood Anderson." *Arizona Quarterly* 12 (1956):48–60, 137–48.

San Juan, Epifanio, Jr. "Vision and Reality: A Reconsideration of Sherwood Anderson's *Winesburg, Ohio.*" *American Literature* 35 (1963):137–55. Rpt. in part in *Sherwood Anderson:* Winesburg, Ohio: *Text and Criticism.* Ed. John H. Ferres. New York: Viking, 1966, 468–81.

Schevill, James. 1951. *Sherwood Anderson: His Life and Work.* Denver: University of Denver Press.

Thomas, F. Richard. 1983. "Sherwood Anderson (1876–1941)." *Literary Ad-*

mirers of Alfred Stieglitz. Carbondale: Southern Illinois University Press, 65–78.

Townsend, Kim. 1987. *Sherwood Anderson*. Boston: Houghton Mifflin.

White, Ray Lewis, ed. 1989. *Sherwood Anderson: Early Writings*. Kent, OH, and London: Kent State University Press.

———, ed. 1969. *Sherwood Anderson's Memoirs: A Critical Edition*. Chapel Hill: University of North Carolina Press.

Ward, J. A. 1985. "*Winesburg, Ohio:* Habitual Silence and the Roaring of Voices." *American Silences: The Realism of James Agee, Walker Evans, and Edward Hopper*. Baton Rouge: Louisiana State University Press, 35–50.

Adventure

Circumstances of Composition

White's study of several tables of contents indicates that "Adventure" does not appear on the earliest extant list of *Winesburg* tales but was added subsequently ("Table"). Its title in the existing manuscript was "Her Adventure" ("Story Titles" 6–7).

Sources and Influences

Anderson had met many lonely young women by the time he came to write this story, and there is probably no one model for Alice Hindman. In his *Memoirs,* however, he tells a story of an evening during his youth when he became aware of his sister's desperate loneliness and longing for romance (White, *Memoirs* 106–109). If the story is true, it must have contributed to the tale of Alice Hindman.

Later in his *Memoirs,* he recounts a period, during his days as a businessman, when he began to engage in some obsessive behaviors—such as scrubbing his room and stripping himself naked; he correlates his behavior with the idea of Carlyle's *Sartor Resartus* and with self-deception—"the naked fact of myself . . . [that] I couldn't face" (White, *Memoirs* 250). The passage suggests that Alice Hindman's nakedness, too, should be understood as in part an attempt to reckon with the truth of herself.

Peden sees this story as a classic of the genre of the "sick" short story, which has roots in Poe, Hawthorne, and Bierce (112).

Publication History

"Adventure" first appeared in *Winesburg, Ohio* (1919).

Relation to Other Works

Critics have devoted more comment to relationships between this story and other tales in *Winesburg, Ohio* than to analysis of the story itself, probably because the story is "an epitome of Anderson's theory and demonstration of pathetic grotesquerie and sexual frustration" (White "Table"). Alice's sense of loneliness and dislocation is common to virtually all the inhabitants of Winesburg. They all might say, with her, "What is the matter with me?" As Geismar observes, the closing line of the story, where Alice "began trying to force herself to face bravely the fact that many people must live and die alone, even in Winesburg" (*WO* 120), is virtually "the central meaning of the volume" (236; similarly, Bowden 114).

George Willard, the primary character linking the various stories of *Winesburg, Ohio,* does not appear in "Adventure." He is merely mentioned in the first sentence as having been a child when Alice was twenty-seven. Lorch notices that Anderson strengthens "the book's over-arching structure" here, though, by associating Alice's lover, Ned Currie, with George; Ned has preceded George as reporter for the *Winesburg Eagle* and as one who leaves town to go to the city, and with him "the story introduces . . . [the idea] of the first love the young man outgrows and leaves behind" (63).

A more important motif linking this tale to the others in the cycle is that of "adventure" itself, as Ingram points out (172–74). Elizabeth Willard has "an adventure" when she plans to protect her son by killing her husband ("Mother," *WO* 42). Doctor Parcival has "an adventure" when he refuses medical assistance to a little girl ("The Philosopher," *WO* 55). George Willard has "an adventure" in his first furtive sexual encounter ("Nobody Knows," *WO* 58). Louise Bentley has "an adventure" when she sees a couple making love ("Godliness," *WO* 92), and her son, David Hardy, has "an adventure" that drives him away from his family and his town ("Godliness," *WO* 97). Similarly, in "The Thinker," "The Teacher," "Drink," "Death," and "Departure," characters reach out beyond the dull routines of their lives in adventure (*WO* 131, 162, 211, 224, 246). Alice's "adventure" in the rain (*WO* 119), Ingram explains, "best exemplifies the generalities of the motif . . . : the attempt to establish contact with another . . . ; and, since the act emerges from a soul starved for loving and being loved, the setting up of such an attempt (unconsciously) as a substitute for true communion" (173).

Mellard shows an interesting connection between "Adventure" and "The Untold Lie," for the two tales offer "ironically complementary recognitions": that a life spent alone will be hard, and that a loveless married life, which will also be hard, "might not be the worst thing that can happen to one" (1307).

Several critics have focused on the close links between Elizabeth Willard ("Mother" and "Death"), Louise Bentley ("Godliness"), Kate Swift ("The Teacher"), and Alice Hindman. Of these female characters, two are married, two unmarried, but all—symbolically, at least—"call to deaf men" (Bunge 49–50). Rigsbee declares that these women are deprived of both physical and spiritual fulfillment by a patriarchal society that devalues their finer qualities and that will not respond to women's needs for "equal and reciprocal" relationships; she applauds Anderson for his "loving sensitivity" to women and their moral superiority (234–35, 242). Atlas, in contrast, while she acknowledges Anderson's sympathy for women, urges that his limited understanding is revealed in the fact that these women succumb to the "traditional trap" of seeking "love first" rather than "finding a healthy outlet for [their] needs" (253, 259–60). Atlas's standard, however, is alien to the notion of the grotesque that is central in *Winesburg, Ohio*. Certainly Anderson never saw it as his artistic aim to provide positive role models for readers. If there was some imbalance in Anderson's comprehension of women, the portrait of Alice Hindman—sympathetic and believable to the last detail—is hardly the example to demonstrate it.

Alice Hindman also resembles a number of other Anderson heroines—especially the woman from Iowa in "Seeds," Elsie Leander in "The New Englander," and Rosalind Wescott in "Out of Nowhere into Nothing." Repressed sexuality as well as longing for love and understanding torments them all, but Rosalind and Alice are less pathological than the other two, more intelligent and more "modern" in their willingness to flout convention. Yet, both of them are deeply bruised when their timid entreaties for support meet with rejection. Clara Butterworth in *Poor White* is a woman of the same type, but stronger (and novelistically developed). She achieves maturity and independence out of necessity when it becomes plain that her husband is hopelessly dependent and needs her guidance. The novel, of course, hardly sees that as any solution to women's problems.

The motif of nakedness links "Adventure" to "Respectability" and "The Strength of God." Alice bares her body spontaneously to the rain and to whatever other lonely person should walk by. In contrast, the nakedness in "Respectability" is a calculated and cynical gesture, and the nakedness in "The Strength of God," meant to be private, is observed only surreptitiously, by a Peeping Tom. All these fictional episodes are related, however, to the most notorious of Anderson's books, *Many Marriages* (1923), in which the male protagonist stands naked throughout most of the book delivering a monologue to his wife and daughter about the necessity of shedding the constricting bonds of civilized life that make one ashamed of natural impulses. That novel was parodied by Hemingway in a scene in *The Torrents of Spring,* where Yogi Jonson strips off his garments and walks beside an Indian squaw (Flanagan 514). Nevertheless, Anderson went on to write the short story "Death in the Woods," in which nakedness is part of a haunting apotheosis.

Critical Studies

Although numerous critics have commented briefly on this story, few have offered extended analyses. Generally, the pattern that a critic sees as dominant in the whole story cycle is the meaning he or she assigns to "Adventure." Glicksberg, who views Anderson as a prophet of Freud and the emancipation of sexual instinct, states that Alice Hindman is one of the many victims of sexual frustration and social conformity in Winesburg (50–52). Similarly, Way, who stresses that the story illustrates the Puritan inhibitions in American society that obstruct the expression of sexual desire, finds the old man, who cannot grasp what Alice is trying to say, to be a symbol of the whole society's lack of understanding of sexuality (110). Murphy, on the other hand, who views Anderson as "more Platonic than Lawrencian or Freudian" in his attitude toward sex, explains that Alice is one of a number of characters who are injured by sex and that she suffers not from sexual frustration but from confusing sexual contact with genuine communication (237, 240). Consistent with that view is O'Neill's interpretation that Alice, with her "Griselda-like . . . fidelity," typifies the tendency of Anderson's women to "believe with disastrous purity of intent in the symbolical, the instrumental power of sex" (69). Somewhat less plausibly, Pickering sees Alice as one of the artist-figures of Winesburg, an "artistic dreamer" whose fatal mistake is to try "to find her dream in the objective world" (34). Abcarian is convincing, however, in connecting Alice's blighted hopes to the larger theme of innocence and experience in *Winesburg, Ohio;* from this perspective, her gesture of running out naked into the rain is an attempt "to recapture the lost innocence of youth" (98–99). Other critics have added that in the rain scene there are "overtones of fertility ritual and myth" (Mellard 1306; similarly, Papinchak 4).

Taylor discusses the psychological dimension of the story, in which Anderson transforms the basic plot of "a sentimental melodrama" about "a country maiden whose lover is seduced by the evils of the city" into a study of a mind made grotesque by the notion of "romantic love" and its distorting fantasies (24). His conclusion that Alice learns "something useful" when she begins to resign herself to solitude (25), however, is too pat to do justice to the richly evocative ending of the story.

Wright is more accurate in stating that Alice's "fundamental problem has not been solved" at the conclusion of the story, merely repressed (232). The disjunction of conscious and unconscious elements in her personality remains at the end, because she is still "shocked by her own acts" (265). Wright also offers insight into the progressive movement of the story from emphasis on the distortion of Alice's character to an eruption of feeling that stirs pity by revealing the intensity of her suffering; he classifies the story as one of "caustic pathos" (230–31).

Another formalist critic similarly focuses on the "dislocation of the narrative line" in the story: a "poetic" and contrapuntal interaction joins the report of Alice's "outward existence [which] appears to run steadily downhill into dull meaninglessness" and the account of her "inward life [which] climbs with increasing intensity toward a climax of desperation and hysteria" (Joselyn 72).

Anderson's narrative technique is also the topic of the longest analysis the story has received. Stegner explains that "until the adventure itself" an omniscient narrator summarily reports and comments on eleven years of the central character's life, presenting her experiences in terms that make them seem to be typical aspects of a "sociological and psychological" study (142–43). Then the method suddenly shifts to dramatic treatment that involves the reader in the character's feelings and brings about "emotional understanding" (144). Finally—in the last sentence—the perspective widens again to extend the meaning of this one incident to embrace the whole town and, by implication, all the world.

Two other brief comments on Anderson's narrative technique deserve mention. Thomas compares the objective presentation of carefully selected details in the rain scene to Alfred Stieglitz's photographic method (69). Stouck points out a likeness to postmodern fiction in the narrator's reference (in paragraph two) to Alice Hindman's stepfather; since the character is never mentioned again, the reference emphasizes the discontinuous, incomplete nature of the work (316). This kind of criticism, though less than definitive, is useful. Anderson's conception of artistic form helped to revolutionize modern fiction. He developed a looser, less rigid form that would correspond more closely to reality as it is experienced. And "Adventure" is a splendid example of his looser form and the content—the view of life—that called it into being. Despite life's pain and grotesque incoherences, he always held—and wrote it for his epitaph—that it is "life" that is "the great adventure."

Works Cited

Abcarian, Richard. "Innocence and Experience in *Winesburg, Ohio*." *University Review Kansas City* 3 (1968):95–105.

Anderson, Sherwood. 1919. *Winesburg, Ohio*. New York: B. W. Huebsch. Rpt. New York: Viking, 1960.

———. 1923. *Many Marriages*. *New York:* B. W. Huebsch.

Atlas, Marilyn Judith. 1981. "Sherwood Anderson and the Women of Winesburg." In *Critical Essays on Sherwood Anderson*. Ed. David D. Anderson. Boston: G. K. Hall, 250–66.

Bowden, Edwin T. 1961. *The Dungeon of the Heart: Human Isolation and the American Novel*. New York: Macmillan, 114–24.

Bunge, Nancy. "Women as Social Critics in *Sister Carrie, Winesburg, Ohio,* and *Main Street*." *Midamerica* 3 (1976):46–55.

Flanagan, John J. "Hemingway's Debt to Sherwood Anderson." *Journal of English and Germanic Philology* 54 (1955):507–520. Rpt. in *Studies by Members of the English Department, University of Illinois, in Memory of John Jay Perry*. Urbana: University of Illinois Press, 1955, 47–60. Rpt. in part in *Sherwood Anderson:* Winesburg, Ohio: *Text and Criticism*. Ed. John H. Ferres. New York: Viking, 1966, 482–86.

Geismar, Maxwell, 1947. "Sherwood Anderson: Last of the Townsmen." In *The Last of the Provincials: The American Novel, 1915–1925*. Boston: Houghton Mifflin, 223–84. Rpt. in part in *Sherwood Anderson:* Winesburg, Ohio: *Text and Criticism*. Ed. John H. Ferres. New York: Viking, 1966, 377–82.

Glicksberg, Charles J. 1971. *The Sexual Revolution in Modern American Literature*. The Hague: Martinus Nijhoff.

Ingram, Forrest L. 1971. *Representative Short Story Cycles of the Twentieth Century: Studies in a Literary Genre*. The Hague: Mouton.

Joselyn, Sister Mary. 1966. *"Sherwood Anderson and the Lyric Story."* In *The Twenties: Poetry and Prose*. Richard E. Langford and William E. Taylor (Eds.). DeLand, FL: Everett Edwards Press, 70–73. Rpt. in *Sherwood Anderson:* Winesburg, Ohio: *Text and Criticism*. Ed. John H. Ferres. New York: Viking. 1966, 444–54.

Lorch, Thomas M. "The Choreographic Structure of Winesburg, Ohio.'" *College Language Association Journal* 12 (1968–69):56–65.

Mellard, James M. "Narrative Forms in *Winesburg, Ohio*." *PMLA* 83 (1968):1304–1312.

Murphy, George D. "The Theme of Sublimation in Anderson's *Winesburg, Ohio*." *Modern Fiction Studies* 13 (1967):237–46.

O'Neill, John. "Anderson Writ Large: 'Godliness' in *Winesburg, Ohio*." *Twentieth Century Literature* 23 (1977):67–83.

Papinchak, Robert Allen. "Something in the Elders: The Recurrent Imagery in *Winesburg, Ohio.*" *Winesburg Eagle* 9 (1983):1–7.

Peden, William. 1964. *The American Short Story: Front Line in the National Defense of Literature.* Boston: Houghton Mifflin.

Phillips, William L. "How Sherwood Anderson Wrote *Winesburg, Ohio.*" *American Literature* 23 (1951):7–30. Rpt. in *Sherwood Anderson:* Winesburg, Ohio: *Text and Criticism.* Ed. John H. Ferres. New York: Viking, 1966, 263–86. Rpt. in *The Achievement of Sherwood Anderson: Essays in Criticism.* Ed. Ray Lewis White. Chapel Hill: University of North Carolina Press, 1966, 62–84. Rpt. in *The Merrill Studies in* Winesburg, Ohio. Comp. Ray Lewis White. Columbus, OH: Charles E. Merrill, 1971, 2–24. Rpt. in *Sherwood Anderson: A Collection of Critical Essays.* Ed. Walter B. Rideout. Englewood Cliffs, NJ: Prentice-Hall, 1974, 18–38.

Pickering, Samuel. "*Winesburg, Ohio:* A Portrait of the Artist as a Young Man." *Southern Quarterly* 16 (1977):27–38.

Rigsbee, Sally Adair. "The Feminine in *Winesburg, Ohio.*" *Studies in American Fiction* 9 (1981):233–44.

Stegner, Wallace Earle, Richard Scowcroft, and Boris Ilyin, eds. 1950. *The Writer's Art: A Collection of Short Stories.* Boston: Heath.

Stouck, David. "Sherwood Anderson and the Postmodern Novel." *Contemporary Literature* 26 (1985):302–316.

Taylor, Welford Dunaway. 1977. *Sherwood Anderson.* New York: Frederick Ungar.

Thomas, F. Richard. "Sherwood Anderson (1876–1941)." The *Literary Admirers of Alfred Stieglitz.* Carbondale: Southern Illinois University Press, 1983, 65–78.

Way, Brian. 1971. "Sherwood Anderson." In *The American Novel and the Nineteen Twenties.* Eds. Malcolm Bradbury and David Palmer. Stratford-upon-Avon Studies 13. London: Edward Arnold, 107–126.

White, Ray Lewis. "*Winesburg, Ohio:* The Story Titles." *Winesburg Eagle* 10, 1 (November 1984):6–7.

———. "*Winesburg, Ohio:* The Table of Contents." *Notes On Modern American Literature* 8 (1984):Item 8.

———, ed. 1969. *Sherwood Anderson's Memoirs: A Critical Edition.* Chapel Hill: Univeristy of North Carolina Press.

Wright, Austin McGiffert. *The American Short Story in the Twenties.* Chicago: University of Chicago Press, 1961.

Respectability

Circumstances of Composition

The extant manuscript of this story is ninth in the sequence of manuscript stories (Phillips 11). An earlier title seems to have been "Wash Williams" (White, "Titles" 6).

Sources and Influences

No one has suggested a model for the protagonist of "Respectability." In Anderson's *Memoirs,* however, there is an episode, purportedly remembered from Anderson's days as an up-and-coming businessman in Elyria, Ohio, that bears interesting parallels with this story and that may reveal something about its psychological origins. Describing himself at that period of his life, Anderson emphasizes his working-class background and his loathing for the respectably middle-class life he was leading, for his "so respectable neighborhood," for the sordid women with whom he and his respectable friends entertained themselves, and for his educated middle-class wife—whom he did not really know very well but whom he fiercely resented because she seemed allied with everything that was stifling him (White, *Memoirs* 254–65). He paints a scene of himself then standing at his window, feeling trapped and "stale," and watching with longing admiration his Italian neighbor with his wife and children—undesirables in the eyes of the respectable community—as they work lovingly together in the backyard planting a new spring garden (White, *Memoirs* 266).

A similar revulsion against a perversion he felt in American life appears in a letter of November 1916 to Marietta Finley: "Chicago is horrible. The living impulses that drive the men I meet day by day are materialistic. They want to preserve the respectability of their homes and keep alive the institution of prostitution. . . . At times there comes over me a terrible conviction that I am living in a city of the dead" (Sutton 15). Presumably he refers here to his business associates and acquaintances. The bohemian, artistic circles he became aligned with in Chicago were animated by a spirit of revolt against bourgeois hypocrisy and inhibition, which they dubbed "Puritanism." In these circles Freud's theories were eagerly discussed.

109

Publication History

"Respectability" first appeared in *Winesburg, Ohio* (1919).

Relation to Other Works

This tale is linked with others in the *Winesburg* sequence in several ways. Its protagonist, like the central characters of "Hands," "Paper Pills," and other stories, is a person outwardly grotesque but inwardly sensitive and rather fine (Way 112). His well-cared-for hands betray a delicacy of sentiment beneath his filthy, corpulent aspect, and his passionate hatred transforms his voice into "something almost beautiful" (*WO* 125). Like the chief characters of "Hands" and "Loneliness," he is unable "to accept the gross fact of sex" (Murphy 238). Like the grotesques in "Drink," "The Thinker," "The Strength of God," and "Loneliness," he displays an "intense need of the feminine" combined with "an inability to establish relationships with real women" (Rigsbee 236).

George Willard, the character who serves to link most of the stories in the cycle, plays a small role here. Wash Williams is one of several characters who give George advice; others include Wing Biddlebaum ("Hands"), George's parents ("Mother"), Doctor Parcival ("The Philosopher"), and Kate Swift ("The Teacher"). In this story, George demonstrates a growing ability to listen with empathy and to understand what is beneath the surface of another person's life. Moreover, George's walking out with Belle Carpenter, which prompts Wash to warn him about women, lays the groundwork for the plot of "An Awakening." Wash's warning, the later story shows, did little good.

Ingram points out that the story is also related to the rest of the cycle by its use of the dream motif, with Wash trying to destroy George's dreams (176), and by its use of the symbol of touch, which here reflects the shifts in Wash's feelings for his wife (189). Moreover, the symbolic pattern of "the seed fallen on barren ground," central in *Winesburg, Ohio,* is repeated by the husband and wife in their garden (Hilfer 153).

Anderson uses similar images of fertility outside *Winesburg, Ohio* as well. In *Dark Laughter* (1925) Bruce Dudley works as a gardener for Aline Grey, digging in the earth and planting seed, before they both "drop back into nature" and he impregnates her (250). In *Kit Brandon* (1936) appears a scene even more curiously resembling the garden scene of "Respectability." The young mountain girl, Kit, drops seed corn into the holes her father makes in the earth (30). Shortly thereafter, tenderly, the father begins to bathe his daughter in a mountain stream, whereupon she flees in terror from his incestuous overtures (34). The connection of natural vitality and sexual impulse—along with the ambivalent recoil—is common to both episodes.

Wash Williams's occupation as telegraph operator connects him with other characters in Anderson's fiction. Hugh McVey, in *Poor White* (1920), is another desperately lonely character who works as a telegraph operator. In *Tar* (1926) there is another telegraph operator named Wash Williams, who keeps secret the contents of a telegram received by a lonely woman in the town (324). But otherwise that short passage sheds little light on "Respectability."

Critical Studies

The relationship between Wash Williams's physical appearance and his moral character has received interpretative remark. Millichamp, who notes the irony of Wash's name, finds a correlation between his repulsive looks and his "psychological aberrations" (341). Fertig, however, stresses the "strange transformation" of this filthy, ugly man into "something almost beautiful" in George Willard's eyes as he hears Wash telling his story (68). San Juan points out the additional irony that Wash's "poetic nature" is deeply sensitive to the moral ugliness in his mother-in-law's stylish house (151). Likewise, Calverton appreciates the "trace of sublimity" that invests "this proletarian" (101).

Several commentators have regarded Wash as a mere victim of society or of cynical women (Burbank 72; Abcarian 97; Bunge 53). More detailed and more penetrating studies, though, are attentive as well to his responsibility for his own undoing. Mellard, for example, explains that this story dramatizes the theme that Wash becomes a "simian" grotesque alienated from humankind because he has seized upon one inadequate "truth" (1307, 1309). Bredahl notes the irony that, as a telegraph operator, Wash is "expert . . . at impersonal communication" but inept at establishing genuine contact with his wife; mistakenly viewing her "as a symbol" rather than as a real human being, Wash grovels at her feet instead of establishing a healthy sexual relationship with her (426; similarly, Jacobsen 62). Ciancio astutely remarks that the title carries a double irony since it "not only refers to [the] ex-wife's promiscuity and her mother's voyeurism . . . [but also] refers to the ironic respect paid to Wash by men who envy the seeming courage and uninhibitedness with which he hurls down curses upon women; his misogyny and show of masculine strength are sheer bravado, the mask of a gentlehearted man who recoils from sex . . . " (999). Ciancio further discusses the Edenic imagery of the garden scene, in which the bride tries unsuccessfully to tempt her husband to consummate the marriage while he clings to the "truth" of virginity (1000).

The finest interpretation of this story, however, is scattered among the pages of Wright's *The American Short Story in the Twenties*. Classifying the tale as one of caustic pathos with an episode of exposure, Wright accounts for the formal structure of the tale, its effects on the reader, the psychological and moral character of its protagonist, and the connection between the story Wash tells and the larger story that contains it. The caustic emphasis of the whole story, which makes clear Wash's "perverse egotism" and impossible idealization of love, yields ultimately to pity as George, and the reader, come to understand the reasons for his suffering (229–30, 235–36). The intensity of Wash's rage against women is revealed to be a disproportionate response to his mother-in-law's behavior, which reflects "at worst, stupidity and bad taste rather than malice" (97). Yet even in the excess of his perfectionism can be seen a "passion and integrity" of feeling that is admirable (269). Anderson's narrative technique here is in the main dramatic, and the peculiar blend of the contemptible, the lofty, and the ridiculous in Wash's character is left to be inferred (335, 355).

Works Cited

Abcarian, Richard. "Innocence and Experience in *Winesburg, Ohio.*" *University Review Kansas City* 35 (1968):95–105.

Anderson, Sherwood. 1919. *Winesburg, Ohio.* New York: B. W. Huebsch. Rpt. New York: Viking, 1960.

———. 1920. *Poor White.* New York: B. W. Huebsch. Rpt. New York: Viking, 1966

———. 1925. *Dark Laughter.* New York: Boni & Liveright; Grosset and Dunlap, 1925.

———. 1926. *Tar: A Midwest Childhood.* New York: Boni & Liveright. Rpt. in *Tar: A Midwest Childhood: A Critical Text.* Ed. Ray Lewis White. Cleveland: Press of Case Western Reserve University, 1969.

———. 1936. *Kit Brandon: A Portrait.* New York and London: Scribners.

Bredahl, A. Carl. "'The Young Thing Within': Divided Narrative and Sherwood Anderson's *Winesburg, Ohio.*" *Midwest Quarterly: A Journal of Contemporary Thought* 27 (1986):422–37.

Bunge, Nancy. "Women as Social Critics in *Sister Carrie, Winesburg, Ohio,* and *MainStreet.*" *Midamerica* 3 (1976):46–55.

Burbank, Rex. 1964. *Sherwood Anderson.* New York: Twayne. Rpt. in part in *The Achievement of Sherwood Anderson: Essays in Criticism.* Ed. Ray Lewis White. Chapel Hill: University of North Carolina Press, 1966, 32–43. Rpt. in part in *Sherwood Anderson: A Collection of Critical Essays.* Ed. Walter B. Rideout. Englewood Cliffs, NJ: Prentice-Hall, 1974, 70–83.

Calverton, V. J. "Sherwood Anderson: A Study in Sociological Criticism." *Modern Quarterly* 2 (1924):82–118. Rpt. in *The Newer Spirit: A Sociological Criticism of Literature*. Introduction by Ernest Boyd. New York: Boni & Liveright, 1925, 52–118.

Ciancio, Ralph. "The Sweetness of the Twisted Apples: Unity of Vision in *Winesburg, Ohio.*" *PMLA* 87 (1972):994–1006.

Fertig, Martin J. " 'A Great Deal of Wonder in Me': Inspiration and Transformation in *Winesburg, Ohio.*" *Markham Review* 6 (1977):65–70.

Hilfer, Anthony Channel. 1969. *The Revolt from the Village, 1915–1930*. Chapel Hill: University of North Carolina Press.

Ingram, Forrest L. 1971. *Representative Short Story Cycles of the Twentieth Century: Studies in a Literary Genre*. The Hague: Mouton.

Jacobsen, Marcia. 1990. "*Winesburg, Ohio* and the Autobiographical Moment." In *New Essays on* Winesburg, Ohio. Ed. John W. Crowley. Cambridge and New York: Cambridge University Press, 53–72.

Mellard, James M. "Narrative Forms in *Winesburg, Ohio.*" *PMLA* 83 (1968):1304–12.

Millichamp, Joseph R. "Distorted Matter and Disjunctive Forms: The Grotesque as Modernist Genre." *Arizona Quarterly* 33 (1977):339–47.

Murphy, George D. "The Theme of Sublimation in Anderson's *Winesburg, Ohio.*" *Modern Fiction Studies* 13 (1967):237–46.

Phillips, William L. "How Sherwood Anderson Wrote *Winesburg, Ohio.*" *American Literature* 23 (1951):7–30. Rpt. in *Sherwood Anderson:* Winesburg, Ohio: *Text and Criticism*. Ed. John H. Ferres. New York: Viking, 1966, 263–86. Rpt. in *The Achievement of Sherwood Anderson: Essays in Criticism*. Ed. Ray Lewis White. Chapel Hill: University of North Carolina Press, 1966, 62–84. Rpt. in *The Merrill Studies in* Winesburg, Ohio. Comp. Ray Lewis White. Columbus, OH: Charles E. Merrill, 1971, 2–24. Rpt. in *Sherwood Anderson: A Collection of Critical Essays*. Ed. Walter B. Rideout. Englewood Cliffs, NJ: Prentice-Hall, 1974, 18–38.

Rigsbee, Sally Adair. "The Feminine in *Winesburg, Ohio.*" *Studies in American Fiction* 9 (1981):233–44.

San Juan, Epifanio, Jr. "Vision and Reality: A Reconsideration of Sherwood Anderson's *Winesburg, Ohio.*" *American Literature* 35 (1963):137–55. Rpt. in part in *Sherwood Anderson:* Winesburg, Ohio: *Text and Criticism*. Ed. John H. Ferres. New York: Viking, 1966, 468–81.

Sutton, William A. *Letters to Bab: Sherwood Anderson to Marietta D. Finley, 1916–33*. Foreword by Walter B. Rideout. Urbana and Chicago: University of Illinois Press.

Way, Brian. 1971. "Sherwood Anderson." In *The American Novel and the Nineteen Twenties*. Eds. Malcolm Bradbury and David Palmer. Stratford-upon-Avon Studies 13. London: Edward Arnold, 107–126.

White, Ray Lewis. "Winesburg, Ohio: The Table of Contents." *Notes on Modern American Literature* 8 (1984):Item 8.

———. "Winesburg, Ohio: The Story Titles." *Winesburg Eagle* 10, no. 1 (November 1984):6–7.

———, ed. 1969. *Sherwood Anderson's Memoirs: A Critical Edition*. Chapel Hill: University of North Carolina Press.

Wright, Austin McGiffert. 1961. *The American Short Story in the Twenties*. Chicago: University of Chicago Press.

The Thinker

Sources and Influences

Anderson's memories of his boyhood in Clyde, Ohio, contributed to the setting of this and the other *Winesburg* stories. Electric lights were installed in Clyde in 1893, three years before Anderson left it; the author nostalgically recalls his town in its preindustrial days in the romantic scene where Seth and Helen walk along the street as the lamplighter lights the lamps (Rideout 24). It seems likely that Anderson's shame concerning his father and his ambivalent feelings about his mother contributed in some way to the family situation of Seth Richmond, the adolescent who is central in this story. The young Anderson's resemblance to George Willard is clearly manifest; though he never held a job as a newspaper reporter, his enterprising spirit and eager industry selling newspapers, running errands, mowing lawns, harvesting crops, and grooming horses earned him the respect of citizens of Clyde and the nickname "Jobby." Helen White seems to be based on a wealthy and attractive girl in Clyde whom Anderson recalls in his *Memoirs* (White, *Memoirs* 165–67). No prototype for Seth, however, has been suggested.

Publication History

"The Thinker" appeared first in the September 1917 issue of *Seven Arts* (2:584–97). The editors of this influential New York "little magazine," James Oppenheim, Waldo Frank, and Van Wyck Brooks, Eastern intellectuals eager to encourage the growth of an American literature independent of genteel and British models, had embraced the new Chicago author as a native genius, and Anderson was immensely gratified by their attentions. After they had accepted "Queer" for publication in their second issue, he offered to send the remaining tales in the *Winesburg* series for their consideration (Jones-Rideout 4). They subsequently published three others, of which "The Thinker" was the last. Anderson received payments for these stories, and by March 1917, he was complaining to Waldo Frank: "I'm damned, Frank, if I am going to let you pull and haul among my stories, taking the cream at $40 per. It isn't fair, and you know it. I will send you the stories one at a time, and you accept or reject" (Jones-Rideout, *Letters* 9–10). The implication here that Anderson received $40 for each of his *Seven Arts* stories does not seem to tally with his later statement that for all the *Winesburg* tales he was paid only $85 (Rosenfeld, *Memoirs* 288), though the periodicals that brought out the other *Winesburg* tales did in fact pay nothing. To Anderson's regret, the magazine's subsidy was withdrawn in response to the pacifist position of the editors concerning World War I; the October 1917 issue was the last (Jones-Rideout, *Letters* 17n).

Relation to Other Works

Various details of this story serve to integrate it with the rest of the *Winesburg* cycle. In the opening paragraph, the reference to the boy living alone in a house with his mother is reminiscent of the opening of "A Man of Ideas," and the description of the chattering, joking berrypickers watched by an isolated figure recalls the opening of "Hands." Subsequent references to Tom Willard's blustering political talk and to Abner Groff's glowering rage against an alley cat, which appeared previously in "Mother," reiterate the themes of pretentious shallowness and impotent frustration found in the earlier story. Particularly noticeable is the realistic portrait of Seth's mother, which, like the portrait of Elizabeth Willard, shows remarkable understanding of maternal ambivalences and hesitancies in dealing with a son who is almost a man.

Seth Richmond, the central character, is like other grotesques in having seized hold of a truth—in his case, "the conviction that silence is a virtue" (Phillips, "Origins" 182). His inability to articulate his feelings defeats him, as it does Louise Bentley (in "Godliness"), Elmer Cowley (in "Queer"), and Ray Pearson (in "The Untold Lie") (Burbank 72). As a result, he longs to escape to the anonymity of the city, like characters in "Queer," "The Strength of God," and "Departure" (Baker 576). The imagery of hands and touch, which plays a significant role in revealing the "ebb and flow" of feelings in the relationship between Seth and Helen, is an important motif in the whole cycle (Ingram 189–90). And Seth, the silent "thinker," bears an ironic likeness to Joe Welling, the verbose "man of ideas" who seems to be his opposite: neither has any real or deep insight (Ingram 195).

The story also shows a phase of George's development; it thus plays a part in the unifying action of the cycle that has led critics to note its affinity with the genre of the bildungsroman. For the first time, the reader is told of George's desire to be a writer. But George's immaturity is evident in his notion of writing, which "centers on externals, . . . fame and fun," and in his decision to fall in love so that he can write a love story (Rideout 27). George is running about rather foolishly "[l]ike an excited dog" to gather news items (*WO* 134), and the tale suggests that "exactly insofar as George remains a newspaper reporter, he is committed to the surface of life, not its depths" (Rideout 22; similarly, Burbank 70). George at this point seems more naïve than Seth, but George's progress is pointed up in the later story "Sophistication," where his walk with Helen White significantly contrasts with the walk she and Seth take here (Lorch 59).

Several later works show Anderson's continuing interest in the character types in "The Thinker." Ed, in the story "Milk Bottles," and John, in the unpublished "Brother Earl," are like George Willard at this stage in their falsely "romantic view of writing" (Miller 19–20). Hugh McVey, the leading figure in *Poor White* (1920), resembles Seth. Hugh is a silent youth given to dreamy fantasies and inept at communicating with other people; as a consequence, the citizens of his town imagine him to be a profound man who is "always thinking great thoughts" (70). Ironically, as in "The Thinker," the community's approbation cooperates with the character's personal inadequacies to intensify his alienation. Hugh, however, seems more merely naïve and less hostile than Seth, and he develops at last into a fuller (though still immature) understanding of life.

The play *Winesburg, Ohio,* produced in 1934 in a Philadelphia suburb by the Hedgerow Theatre, presents a rather different Seth Richmond from the one in the original story. In letters written in 1932 to Arthur Barton, the man with whom he originally collaborated on the play (though it was Jasper Deeter who finally produced it), Anderson articulates his conception of the character of Seth, a conception entirely consistent with that which emerges in the drama. Seth, he says, is "a boy who sees life absolutely in terms of himself"; "[h]e wants to succeed in life, make money, be a big man, and he would like to have Helen decorate his own successful life" (Modlin, *Letters* 154). Seth is to be a foil for George Willard; he is "mean spirited" like George's father and with the same sort of "cheap dream"; he is "shrewd," while George is "the imaginative lovable one" (Modlin, *Letters* 155, 157). By making the contrast between the two youths analogous to that of George's father and mother, Anderson manages to tighten the unity of the play, but the contrast is rather different from that in the story, where both young men are fairly self-centered and where Seth is anything but shrewd. George, at this stage of his development, stands out in the story as the one who is motivated by the drive for success and personal eminence, while Seth is dreamily ineffectual.

Critical Studies

Critical comment about "The Thinker" has been scant. There has been nothing approaching disagreement, but neither has there been a full and adequate interpretation.

Only one commentator approaches the story with a view to its criticism of society. Identifying it as a tale "in the naturalistic tradition," Walcutt argues that, while Seth's need for self-expression and intimacy is normal, the absence of a "tradition of manners" in the small towns of America makes it impossible for him to establish a relationship with Helen (228–29).

Most commentators, however, have tended to stress Seth's personal shortcomings. Bowden points out the irony of Seth's lack of perception: while he "believes himself alone and unloved in the world," there is in fact love all around him (114). San Juan remarks his weak will, his indecisiveness, his "endless efforts at rationalization" (150–51). Ward attributes Seth's silence to "extreme shallowness" rather than to depth of feeling (as the community mistakenly supposes) and notices that Seth's "simple obtuseness" is a parody of George's "more profound bewilderment" in the face of a troubled family situation and an urge to escape from the little world of Winesburg (40, 45n). Wright effectively summarizes these views when he states that Seth "defeats himself because of his misconception of himself": he misunderstands both his own emotions and the readiness of others (especially Helen White) to love and appreciate him (163).

Consistent with those interpretations, and amplifying them, is Ciancio's analysis, which detects archetypal and Freudian dimensions of the story. The garden where the young couple walks carries Edenic echoes, and Helen is "a modern-day, atavistic Eve" who awakens Seth's sexuality, but Seth—haunted by his mother's "sharp reproofs"—is unable to free himself from maternal attachment into manhood (1000). Ciancio's assertion that the mother's harsh reprimands have inhibited the boy's development is evidently mistaken, since she has been unable to reprove her son and has on the contrary voiced approval of his escapade; yet he must be right in discovering a trace of mockery in Helen's parting remark: "You go and talk with your mother" (*WO* 142).

Several studies have focused attention on the form and techniques of the story. Though Joselyn's study is hardly what it purports to be, an analysis of the story's structure, and though it misconstrues some story details, it does explain the importance of "the arrangement of actions," in which various "talkers" surround the silent protagonist, and of the symbolic final scene, where—imagining a field of blossoms and bees—Seth finds himself "unable either to go forward into a meaningful existence or to . . . return to innocence" (73). More useful, however, is Mellard's classification of "The Thinker" as an "emblematic tale": as in other tales of this type, the aim is to sketch a "universal" or "archetypal" figure, who does not change in the course of the story (1309–10). As a result, the movement of the story is toward an ironic moment when, by behaving typically, the character fails to elude the forces that entrap him (1311). Similarly, Wright explains in some detail that what happens in the story constitutes an "episode" rather than a "plot" because it contains no change (160–64). Wright classifies the tale as one of what he calls "horror modified" because in it, what seems at first to be merely pathetic gradually emerges as a much more "serious perversity" (245–49). Further, he offers a perceptive analysis of the dialogue between Seth and Helen (295–96), and discusses Anderson's narrative shifts from generalized summary statements to particular speeches and acts (302–307). Ingram points out the ironic effects that accrue as Seth's disdainful remark that his mother thinks of him as a mere "boy" is followed first by the narrator's description of his "boyish earnestness," then by Helen's thought that he is a "purposeful man," and finally by Seth's vague comment that he does not know or "care much" what he will do after leaving Winesburg (159).

Feminist critics have briefly noted that Mrs. Richmond is a victim of male dominance (Bunge 53), that establishing a proper relation with the feminine—Helen—is the key that Seth needs to establish his freedom (Rigsbee 236), and that Helen shows no desire for independent selfhood (Atlas 262). Ingram notes that communication between Mrs. Richmond and her son has been interrupted (183). But very little has been said about the first four-and-a-quarter pages of the story, which deal with the Richmond house, the father's death, the public shame attached to it, and the mother's anguished inability to communicate with her son. Moreover, there has been not even a serious attempt at an explication of the relationship between those early pages and the action in the later, more-discussed, parts of the story. Several issues need to be considered with regard to their effects on the boy's character: the financial decline of the family; the mother's sentimental insistence that her highest hope for her son is that he turn out "as good a man as your father" (*WO* 129) though the father was obviously irresponsible, adulterous, and violent; the son's "adventure" running away with friends to a fair; and his subversion of his mother's effort to provide discipline. Is he under his mother's thumb? Or is she under his? Or both? These early experiences surely hold crucial clues to the psychological roots of Seth's entrapment in thought that does not eventuate in action. Critics need to probe the significance of these experiences so that Seth's character and the structure of the tale may be seen in their integrity. Properly handled, such criticism would elucidate the theme, prominent throughout *Winesburg,* of parents' influence on children's lives.

Works Cited

Anderson, Sherwood. 1919. *Winesburg, Ohio.* New York: B. W. Huebsch. Rpt. New York: Viking, 1960.

———. 1920. *Poor White.* New York: B. W. Huebsch. 1920. Rpt. New York: Viking, 1966.

———. 1937. *Plays: Winesburg and Others.* New York: Scribners.

Atlas, Marilyn Judith. 1981. "Sherwood Anderson and the Women of Winesburg." In *Critical Essays on Sherwood Anderson.* Ed. David D. Anderson. Boston: G. K. Hall, 250–66.

Baker, Carlos. "Sherwood Anderson's Winesburg: A Reprise." *The Virginia Quarterly Review* 48 (1972):568–79.

Bowden, Edwin T. 1961. *The Dungeon of the Heart: Human Isolation and the American Novel.* New York; Macmillan, 114–24.

Bunge, Nancy. "Women as Social Critics in *Sister Carrie, Winesburg, Ohio,* and *Main Street." Midamerica* 3 (1976):46–55.

Burbank, Rex. 1964. *Sherwood Anderson.* New York: Twayne. Rpt. in part in *The Achievement of Sherwood Anderson: Essays in Criticism.* Ed. Ray Lewis White. Chapel Hill: Univ. of North Carolina Press, 1966, 32–43. Rpt. in part in *Sherwood Anderson: A Collection of Critical Essays.* Ed. Walter B. Rideout. Englewood Cliffs, NJ: Prentice-Hall, 1974, 70–83.

Ciancio, Ralph. "The Sweetness of the Twisted Apples: Unity of Vision in *Winesburg, Ohio." PMLA* 87 (1972):994–1006.

Ingram, Forrest L. 1971. *Representative Short Story Cycles of the Twentieth Century: Studies in a Literary Genre.* The Hague: Mouton.

Jones, Howard Mumford, and Walter B. Rideout, eds. 1953. *Letters of Sherwood Anderson.* Boston: Little, Brown.

Joselyn, Sister Mary. 1966. "Sherwood Anderson and the Lyric Story." In *The Twenties: Poetry and Prose.* Richard E. Langford and William E. Taylor (Eds.). DeLand, FL: Everett Edwards Press, 70–73. Rpt. in *Sherwood Anderson:* Winesburg, Ohio: *Text and Criticism.* Ed. John H. Ferres. New York: Viking, 1966, 444–54.

Lorch, Thomas M. "The Choreographic Structure of *Winesburg, Ohio.*'" *College Language Association Journal* 12 (1968–69):56–65.

Mellard, James M. "Narrative Forms in *Winesburg, Ohio.*" *PMLA* 83 (1968):1304–1312.

Miller, William V. 1976. "Portraits of the Artist: Anderson's Fictional Storytellers." In *Sherwood Anderson: Dimensions of His Literary Art: A Collection of Critical Essays.* East Lansing: Michigan State University Press, 1–23.

Modlin, Charles E., ed. 1984. *Sherwood Anderson:Selected Letters.* Knoxville: University of Tennessee Press.

Phillips, William L. "How Sherwood Anderson Wrote *Winesburg, Ohio.*" *American Literature* 23 (1951):7–30. Rpt. in *Sherwood Anderson:* Winesburg, Ohio: *Text and Criticism.* Ed. John H. Ferres. New York: Viking, 1966, 263–86. Rpt. in *The Achievement of Sherwood Anderson: Essays in Criticism.* Ed. Ray Lewis White. Chapel Hill: University of North Carolina Press, 1966, 62–84. Rpt. in *The Merrill Studies in* Winesburg, Ohio. Comp. Ray Lewis White. Columbus, OH: Charles E. Merrill, 1971, 2–24. Rpt. in *Sherwood Anderson: A Collection of Critical Essays.* Ed. Walter B. Rideout. Englewood Cliffs, NJ: Prentice-Hall, 1974, 18–38.

——. "Sherwood Anderson's *Winesburg, Ohio:* Its Origins, Composition, Technique, and Reception." Ph.D. Diss., University of Chicago, 1950.

Rideout, Walter B. "The Simplicity of *Winesburg, Ohio.*" *Shenandoah* 13 (1962):20–31. Rpt. in *Sherwood Anderson:* Winesburg, Ohio: *Text and Criticism.* Ed. John H. Ferres. New York: Viking, 1966, 287–300. Rpt. in *Critical Essays on Sherwood Anderson.* Ed. David D. Anderson. Boston: G. K. Hall, 1981, 146–54.

Rigsbee, Sally Adair. "The Feminine in *Winesburg, Ohio.*" *Studies in American Fiction* 9 (1981):233–44.

Rosenfeld, Paul, ed. 1942. *Sherwood Anderson's Memoirs.* New York: Harcourt, Brace.

San Juan, Epifanio, Jr. "Vision and Reality: A Reconsideration of Sherwood Anderson's *Winesburg, Ohio.*" *American Literature* 35 (1963):137–55. Rpt. in part in *Sherwood Anderson:* Winesburg, Ohio: *Text and Criticism.* Ed. John H. Ferres. New York: Viking, 1966, 468–81.

Walcutt, Charles Child, "Sherwood Anderson: Impressionism and the Buried Life." *Sewanee Review* 60 (1952):28–47. Rpt. in *American Literary Naturalism, a Divided Stream.* Minneapolis: University of Minnesota Press, 1956, 222–39. Rpt. in part in *Sherwood Anderson:* Winesburg, Ohio: *Text and Criticism.* Ed. John H. Ferres. New York: Viking, 1966, 432–43.

Ward, J. A. 1985. "Winesburg, Ohio: Habitual Silence and the Roaring of Voices." *American Silences: The Realism of James Agee, Walker Evans, and Edward Hopper*. Baton Rouge: Louisiana State University Press, 35–50.

White, Ray Lewis, ed. 1969. *Sherwood Anderson's Memoirs: A Critical Edition*. Chapel Hill: University of North Carolina Press.

Wright, Austin McGiffert. 1961. *The American Short Story in the Twenties*. Chicago: University of Chicago Press.

Tandy

Circumstances of Composition

It is generally assumed that "Tandy" was the fourth of the *Winesburg* tales to be written, following only "The Book of the Grotesque," "Hands," and "Paper Pills." This opinion is based on the scholarship of William L. Phillips, whose dissertation and subsequent article "How Sherwood Anderson Wrote *Winesburg, Ohio*" have long been landmarks in Anderson criticism. Phillips, after close study of the sole extant manuscript of the *Winesburg* tales, concluded that the "chain of manuscripts," in which "Tandy" appears fourth, indicated the order of composition of the tales (11–13). Letters since published, however, seem to indicate otherwise. Phillips reports that Anderson "had told his friends in the rooming house that he was writing a trilogy about a woman named Tandy Hard," whereupon "Max Wald, the musician [and fellow roomer] has said the name reminded him of nothing but hard candy" (15). There is no reason to doubt that statement, but letters Anderson wrote to Marietta D. Finley suggest that he was writing about Tandy, not in "late 1915 and early 1916," as Phillips believed (13), but in late 1916 and early 1917. On November 23, 1916, Anderson wrote to Miss Finley, whom Anderson called "Bab," that he was engaged in "a big piece of work" which he was writing "blindly, pouring myself and my character Tandy into it," and which he expected at length to make into "a book" (Sutton, *Letters* 9). The fact that "Tandy" remained unpublished while, by November of 1916, four *Winesburg* tales had been printed and a fifth accepted for publication may also argue for a later date of composition than Phillips suggests. Moreover, on the earliest extant table of contents of *Winesburg, Ohio*, "Tandy" does not appear; it is added to the end of a revised list of stories, then removed in a subsequent revision, and finally restored to the position it occupies in the published collection (White, "Table"). Finally, in a letter of December 1916 to Finley, Anderson wrote:

> I am trying with all my might to be and remain a lover. All this writing is addressed to my beloved.
>
> I am writing these snatches of things to women, to all women, to one woman. I am telling her of my life, of a man actively engaged in the grim wrestle of modern industrial life. (Sutton, *Letters* 30)

Though the evidence is circumstantial, the passage may indicate that the writer was then at work on either the novel or the story about Tandy.

It may be, as Rideout conjectures, that the "drunken young man" in "Tandy" was "borrowed" from a novel Anderson began in Elyria, Ohio, before 1912 and never published, "Talbot Whittingham" (53).

Sources and Influences

In his *Memoirs* Anderson states that he modeled Tandy not on a child but on a blonde woman he had known some time after his first marriage had gone sour (White, *Memoirs* 305–308). It was a "temporary passionate love" on his part and the woman was a virgin with conflicting feelings, but at length she agreed "to sin with" him (White, *Memoirs* 305). For her and her "sweet graciousness," he says, he wrote the "little prose poem, the woman strong to be loved" that he called "Tandy" (White, *Memoirs* 306). Then he remembers his expounding to her his theories about the nature of "the artist's relations with women" (something that he admits was totally inappropriate under the circumstances), and he connects that memory by association to another affair in which it was brought home to him that he did not love individual women so much as he used them in order "to be set free of self" (White, *Memoirs* 307–308). However different the situation in the *Winesburg* story, Anderson's reminiscence suggests the biographical origin of the questing drunkard's romantic, abstract love. It also accounts for the awareness implicit in the narrative that such a love, metaphysical as well as physical in nature, places a heavy burden on the woman who becomes its momentary symbolic embodiment.

A literary source for the story has been proposed by Luedtke (531–40). He believes that Tandy's agnostic father, Tom Hard, is "a half jocular, half critical sketch of Thomas Hardy" (532). The desperate, longing stranger, he suggests, is connected with Hardy's character Jude Fawley, who had a weakness for women and liquor, idealized Sue Bridehead in finally hopeless longing, and—in Hardy's words—"wanted something to love" (533–34).

No one has proposed any origin of the strange name "Tandy." In view of the Nietzschean current that runs through the *Winesburg* collection, however, Tandy's last name may have some connection with Zarathustra's exhortation to "Be hard!" (259). Moreover, the stranger's speech resembles Zarathustra's seven-times repeated refrain "Never yet have I found the woman by whom I should like to have children, unless it be this woman whom I love: for I love thee, O Eternity!" (272–75).

Publication History

On April 5, 1917, Anderson submitted this tale to Waldo Frank, editor of the New York monthly little magazine *The Seven Arts*. In his letter to Frank, Anderson referred to the story as a "little piece of rather colorful writing called 'Tandy Hard'" (Sutton, *Road* 432). Evidently the editors rejected it, for "Tandy" made its first published appearance in *Winesburg, Ohio* (1919).

A curious episode involving "Tandy" occurred in 1926, when Dreiser was accused of plagiarizing the tale. He published a short free-verse poem, entitled "Beautiful," in *Vanity Fair,* and most of its lines were obviously taken directly from Anderson's story. When New York newspaperman Franklin P. Adams printed Dreiser's poem side by side with passages from "Tandy" in the *World,* "a literary squall blew up" (Swanberg 313). Anderson's response was characteristically magnanimous; in a public statement he praised Dreiser, whom he had always admired, and referred to the whole thing as an "accident" (Swanberg 314). In a letter to his friend Marietta Finley, he expressed regret about Dreiser's embarrassment, guessing that he must have composed the poem from the story and then "put it aside and forgot the circumstances under which he wrote it" (Sutton, *Letters* 376; also see White, *Memoirs* 459). Dreiser, however, did not publicly admit any mistake and subsequently included the poem in his book *Moods: Philosophic and Emotional, Cadenced and Declaimed* (Swanberg 314, 429).

Relation to Other Works

Readers have understood that "Tandy" expresses a feeling that is central in Anderson's works. The stranger articulates not only "the underlying if always obscurely felt emotion of the town" of Winesburg but also "the crux of [Anderson's] message" (Geismar 236). The stranger's quest is essentially the same quest that all the characters pursue in their various confused ways. It is, ultimately, "not-finding-the-thing-to-love" that turns them all into grotesques (Thurston 113).

The kinship between this tale, where Tom Hard "never saw God manifesting himself in the little child" (*WO* 143) and the story that follows it, where the minister does see (or thinks he sees) God "manifested . . . in the body of a woman" (*WO* 155), has been pointed out by Ingram (196). If Luedtke is correct in his contention that Tom Hard's name alludes to Thomas Hardy (see "Sources and Influences"), then Louise Hardy (of "Godliness") is involved in that allusion; Louise's father—a religious zealot—is as cold toward her as Tom Hard—the zealous atheist—is toward Tandy, with the result that the two daughters are equally victims. But each father's neglect is countered by other examples of men's reverence for women. Tom Foster (in "Drink"), like the stranger here, tries alcohol as a means to experience love and attains a vision of Helen White clothed in "mythic garments" (Ingram 197). Similarly, Wash Williams's worshipful adoration of his wife resembles the drunken stranger's when he falls to his knees and kisses the little girl's hands "ecstatically" (*WO* 145; Fludernik 127). Further, that scene forms an interesting parallel to the minister's window in "The Strength of God," which shows Christ blessing a child, who gazes raptly at his face (Ciancio 1006n).

But an important qualification of the stranger's "truth" is suggested by the relationship of "Tandy" to the two paired tales that follow it. Although "The Strength of God" does, as Ingram notes, show another man who beholds in a mortal woman an incarnation of the divine, the tale after it looks beneath the physical surface of the same woman to reveal a suffering human soul longing in its own way for something to love. A story such as "Adventure," furthermore, makes it obvious that "strength and fidelity in a woman . . . will not assure [her] enduring happiness" (Ingram 196). The stranger's statement that "the quality of being strong to be loved . . . is something men need from women and that they do not get" (*WO* 145), like his insistence (only partly true) that he understands the little girl, recalls earlier tales such as "Godliness," where a woman (Louise Hardy), longing for love and deeply misunderstood by everyone around her, finds that the thing she needs most from men is what she does not get. While the stranger seems to have spoken a truth, then, it is revealed to be only a one-sided truth because it is embedded in false distinctions concerning gender. In fact, by elevating Tandy to the status of God/Virgin/Superman, he fails to understand her as also a human sufferer, a "Christ . . . crucified" (see "The Philosopher").

George Willard's role in "Tandy" is minimal. He merely sits on the sidewalk as the stranger delivers his monologue. The significance to George of what he observes is left for the reader to infer. There is a connection, though, between the action in this tale and his own behavior in the later tale "Sophistication," where he, in a boastful mood, rather imperiously makes demands of Helen White that echo the stranger's plea that the little girl grow up to realize his ideal: "I want you to try to be different from other women. . . . I want you to be a beautiful woman. You see what I want" (*WO* 236–37). His approach indicates his immaturity. Later, as Rogers observes, George and Helen "share a moment of pure understanding, of love, . . . [and] transcendence of their physical being" (95), but when Rogers equates that love with the stranger's "insight" in the earlier tale, he overlooks a crucial difference: the *mutuality* of their respect, understanding, and love, which is utterly lacking in the romanticized vision of love the self-pitying stranger carelessly imposes on a child he barely knows.

The mutuality of feeling achieved in "Sophistication" may in fact point to a crucial detail most critics have overlooked in "Tandy"—namely, the insistence that the girl "Be something more than man or woman" (*WO* 145). As Bidney argues, the vision of the "mysterious stranger" includes a faith in the androgynous ideal, a hope that the child will grow to "transcend male and female" (263). This ideal, as Bidney states, is set forth in the introductory "The Book of the Grotesque" in the image of the old writer who is pregnant with a youth who is also a woman dressed as a knight; the ideal is at last achieved momentarily in the penultimate story, "Sophistication" (261, 263). Bidney's insight is an important one, but it overlooks in the stranger's speech repetitions that contradict the androgynous ideal: "There is a woman coming. . . . You may be the woman. . . . Out of her defeats has been born a new quality in woman. . . . It is something men need from women . . ." (*WO* 145). If the stranger's confusion does attain a dim intuition of a richer and more life-giving truth, it is well to remember that the intuition is very dim indeed and that his confusions are hurtful.

Longing for some perfect love is a theme that runs throughout Anderson's works. In *Mid-American Chants* (1918), it characterizes the prophetic voice of the Whitmanian poet calling readers to renewed vitality: "I am a lover. I love life. In the end love shall save me. . . . Look upon me, my beloved, my lover who does not come" (13). These lines, composed in 1916 and first printed in 1917 with an essay in *Seven Arts,* "From Chicago," were included also in *Sherwood Anderson's Notebook* (1926). Translating such longing into actual male–female relationships is problematic, however, as Anderson's fiction shows. In *Many Marriages* (1923), the same longing stirs in the hopeful declaration of a sex-starved washing machine manufacturer about to embark on an adulterous love affair with his secretary: "O, my Natalie, you are a woman strong to be loved" (70). The religious intensity of his idealization begins to fade, though, as they leave town together; she is silent and weeping, while he reflects that he barely knows her, wonders if he is merely "using her" to escape a boring life, and finally begins to order her about (252–64). In *Dark Laughter,* Bruce Dudley thinks, "The lover must love. It is his nature" (96). But the same novel contains another curious parallel to the story "Tandy." In an Indiana hotel, the owner's daughter had once been "a pretty little thing with yellow curls" whom "traveling men petted and fussed with," taking her on their laps and giving her pennies and candy (89); in later years, ironically, growing "stout" and "gray," she is still unmarried, maybe because "she had seen too much of men" (92).

Critical Studies

For the most part, this story, the shortest in *Winesburg, Ohio,* has been judged harshly by critics. An early reviewer, writing for the *Chicago Evening Post,* while finding the tale to be "a significant poem," acknowledged that the plot was "fugitive and unimportant" (Jones 34). Chase deemed it "a romantic trifle" (37), and Howe declared that it was the only *Winesburg* story "so bad that its omission would help the book" (106). More recent critics frequently have concurred. Hilfer has found that the author's "attempts at abstract formula . . . lead to bathos" (151). White thinks the story seems "incomplete" and is "the most unsatisfying" of all the *Winesburg* stories ("Table"); its meaning, he holds, is "obscure" (*Exploration* 41–42).

Critical treatments of the story generally are abbreviated in the extreme; only a few commentators have analyzed it in any detail. Luedtke's article, though ostensibly about "Tandy," is mainly a discussion of broad connections between Anderson's works and Thomas Hardy's. It finds "Tandy" significant primarily as a "simple manifesto" answering Hardy's despair with faith that men and women can restore "a natural relation with one another and the world in which they live" (540). Other critics, too, have attended almost exclusively to the words spoken by the stranger—interpreting them either as a "vision of wholeness" that is communicated to the child (D. Anderson 46) or as an "invocation of the woman of the future" who will transcend sexual roles (Rigsbee 242; similarly, Bidney 263). Stouck, simplistically, finds "the point of the sketch" to be a call for "courage for sexual expression in women" (40). Ciancio also states that the stranger, who manages to communicate his feelings, thus differentiates himself from most of the grotesque characters in the *Winesburg* cycle (1001); like the other grotesques, though, the stranger is self-persecuted, pursuing a transcendental ideal "to his inevitable destruction" (997). Bredahl locates something positive in the tale: almost at the midpoint of the book the "young thing within" mentioned in the very first story is beginning to be expressed—or "brought forth" in the symbolic child (429). But Bredahl also sees signs of a "debilitating attitude" in the reverence given to a "female," who is also referred to as "the manifestation of God" (429).

Formalist analyses, likewise, accept the drunkard's speech as the climax of the tale. The story moves from an account of his previous life to the moment when he speaks, releasing "the ache and tension in his soul," according to Mahoney (247). In a somewhat more sophisticated analysis, Mellard labels "Tandy" one of five "symbolic stories" in the cycle, with the child serving as the central symbol and the speech itself providing the epiphany, the stranger's "moment of insight and understanding" (1304–1305). With a slightly different emphasis—on the child's "admiration" for the man—Wright considers the tale to be one of Anderson's stories of "caustic pathos" because it progresses from presentation of what is ugly about the stranger to the child's "sympathetic judgment" (389, 236–37).

In all the commentaries, the child's own suffering has been almost entirely ignored. The final line of the story leaves her "sobbing as though her young strength were not enough to bear the vision the words of the drunkard had brought to her" (*WO* 146). Taylor glibly remarks that she will probably "grow into a happy, normal adult" because she has received a "pleasant and uplifting" hope (32). Contesting that interpretation, Arcana argues that the stranger imposes a "burden" and a "curse" on the neglected little girl, which will turn her into a grotesque; recognizing her emotional hunger, he "exploits" it by placing her on a pedestal and pouring forth all his desires on her, expecting her image to sustain him (68–69). Arcana's insight offers an important corrective to most critics' tendency to overlook the role of the little girl, who wants to relinquish her old identity but finds the new one assigned to her almost crushing. Somewhat implausibly, Arcana asserts that the meaning she derives from the tale was not part of the author's "conscious intent" because he saw in women just what the drunkard does: "the primitive magic mother" (68–69). The tale itself, which begins and ends with a clear depiction of a very human little girl who needs from men a strength and love she does not get, argues otherwise.

While critics seem unanimously to endorse the notion that "the story is presented without irony" (Atlas 264), there is evidence that their conclusion should be revised. It has long been easy to dismiss Anderson as "the perpetual adolescent in love with love" (Gold 556). And no doubt he was sympathetic to the "truth" the drunkard speaks. But that sympathy should not blind readers to the obvious fact that it is a *partial* truth. The man who speaks it is not only a romantic visionary but also a selfish *grotesque*. His histrionic idealization is finally as cruel—and unloving—as the father's callous neglect. Anderson would hardly have written the tale this way if his own romanticizing tendency were not counterbalanced by a measure of cynical judgment. Bidney's interpretation may come nearest to appreciating both the truth and the falsehood in the stranger's speech, but his is not a fully articulated analysis. (See "Relation to Other Works.")

Works Cited

Anderson, David. 1967. *Sherwood Anderson: An Introduction and Interpretation*. New York: Holt, Rinehart.

Anderson, Sherwood. 1918. *Mid-American Chants*. New York: John Lane. Rpt. New York: B. W. Huebsch, 1923.

——. 1919. *Winesburg, Ohio.* New York: B. W. Huebsch. Rpt. New York: Viking, 1960.

——. 1923. *Many Marriages.* New York: B. W. Huebsch. Rpt. Metuchen, NJ: Scarecrow, 1978.

——. 1925. *Dark Laughter.* New York: Boni & Liveright; Grosset and Dunlap, 1925.

——. 1970. *Sherwood Anderson's Notebook.* Mamaroneck, NY: Appel. Originally printed New York: Boni Liveright, 1926.

Arcana, Judith. "'Tandy': At the Core of Winesburg." *Studies in Short Fiction* 24 (1987):66–70.

Atlas, Marilyn Judith. 1981. "Sherwood Anderson and the Women of Winesburg." In *Critical Essays on Sherwood Anderson.* Ed. David D. Anderson. Boston: G. K. Hall, 250–66.

Bidney, Martin. "Anderson and the Androgyne: 'Something More than Man or Woman.'" *Studies in Short Fiction* 25 (1988):261–73.

Bredahl, A. Carl. "'The Young Thing Within': Divided Narrative and Sherwood Anderson's *Winesburg, Ohio.*" *Midwest Quarterly: A Journal of Contemporary Thought* 27 (1986):422–37.

Chase, Cleveland B. 1927. *Sherwood Anderson.* New York: Robert M. McBride. Rpt. Folcroft, PA: Folcroft Press, 1969.

Ciancio, Ralph. "The Sweetness of the Twisted Apples: Unity of Vision in *Winesburg, Ohio.*" *PMLA* 87 (1972):994–1006.

Fludernik, Monika. "'The Divine Accident of Life': Metaphoric Structure and Meaning in *Winesburg, Ohio.*" *Style* 22 (1988):116–35.

Geismar, Maxwell. 1947. "Sherwood Anderson: Last of the Townsmen." In *The Last of the Provincials: The American Novel, 1915–1925.* Boston: Houghton Mifflin, 223–84. Rpt. in part in *Sherwood Anderson:* Winesburg, Ohio: *Text and Criticism.* Ed. John H. Ferres. New York: Viking, 1966, 377–82.

Gold, Herbert. "The Purity and Cunning of Sherwood Anderson." *Hudson Review* 10 (1957–58):548–57. Rpt. in *The Age of Happy Problems.* New York: Dial Press, 1962, 56–67. Rpt. in part in *Sherwood Anderson:* Winesburg, Ohio: *Text and Criticism.* Ed. John H. Ferres. New York: Viking, 1966, 396–404. Rpt. in *Critical Essays on Sherwood Anderson.* Ed. David D. Anderson. Boston; G. K. Hall, 1981, 138–45.

Hilfer, Anthony Channel. 1969. *The Revolt from the Village, 1915–1930.* Chapel Hill: University of North Carolina Press.

Howe, Irving. 1951. *Sherwood Anderson.* New York: William Sloane.

Ingram, Forrest L. 1971. *Representative Short Story Cycles of the Twentieth Century: Studies in a Literary Genre.* The Hague: Mouton.

Jones, Llewellyn. 1971. "The Unroofing of Winesburg: Tales of Life That Seem Overheard Rather Than Written." In *The Merrill Studies in* Winesburg, Ohio. Comp. Ray Lewis White. Columbus, OH: Charles E. Merrill, 32–34. Originally printed in *Chicago Evening Post,* 20 June 1919, p. 9.

Luedtke, Luther S. "Sherwood Anderson, Thomas Hardy, and 'Tandy.'" *Modern Fiction Studies* 20 (1974–75):531–40.

Mahoney, John J. "An Analysis of *Winesburg, Ohio.*" *Journal of Aesthetics and Art Criticism* 15 (1956):245–52.

Mellard, James M. "Narrative Forms in *Winesburg, Ohio.*" *PMLA* 83 (1968):1304–1312.

Nietzsche, Friedrich. 1964. *Thus Spake Zarathustra: A Book for All and None.* Trans. Thomas Common. Vol. 11 of *The Complete Works of Friedrich Nietzsche.* Ed. Oscar Levy. New York: Russell & Russell.

Phillips, William L. "How Sherwood Anderson Wrote *Winesburg, Ohio.*" *American Literature* 23 (1951):7–30. Rpt. in *Sherwood Anderson:* Winesburg, Ohio: *Text and Criticism.* Ed. John H. Ferres. New York: Viking, 1966, 263–86. Rpt. in *The Achievement of Sherwood Anderson: Essays in Criticism.* Ed. Ray Lewis White. Chapel Hill: University of North Carolina Press, 1966, 62–84. Rpt. in *The Merrill Studies in Winesburg, Ohio.* Comp. Ray Lewis White. Columbus, OH: Charles E. Merrill, 1971, 2–24. Rpt. in *Sherwood Anderson: A Collection of Critical Essays.* Ed. Walter B. Rideout. Englewood Cliffs, NJ: Prentice-Hall, 1974, 18–38.

———. "Sherwood Anderson's *Winesburg, Ohio:* Its Origins, Composition, Technique, and Reception." Ph.D. diss., University of Chicago, 1949.

Rideout, Walter B. 1976. "Talbot Whittingham and Anderson: A Passage to *Winesburg, Ohio.*" In *Sherwood Anderson: Dimensions of His Literary Art.* Ed. David D. Anderson. East Lansing: Michigan State University Press, 41–60.

Rigsbee, Sally Adair. "The Feminine in *Winesburg, Ohio.*" *Studies in American Fiction* 9 (1981):233–44.

Rogers, Douglas G. "Development of the Artist in Winesburg, Ohio." *Studies in the Twentieth Century* 10 (1972):91–99.

Stouck, David. 1990. "Anderson's Expressionist Art." In *New Essays on Winesburg, Ohio.* Ed. John W. Crowley. Cambridge and New York: Cambridge University Press, 21–51.

Sutton, William A., ed. 1985. *Letters to Bab: Sherwood Anderson to Marietta*

D. Finley, 1916–33. Foreword by Walter B. Rideout. Urbana and Chicago: University of Illinois Press.

——. 1972. *The Road to Winesburg: A Mosaic of the Imaginative Life of Sherwood Anderson*. Metuchen, NJ: Scarecrow Press.

Swanberg, W. A. 1965. *Dreiser*. New York: Scribners.

Taylor, Welford Dunaway. 1977. *Sherwood Anderson*. New York: Frederick Ungar.

Thurston, Jarvis. "Anderson and 'Winesburg': Mysticism and Craft." *Accent* 16 (1956):107–28. Rpt. in part in *Sherwood Anderson: Winesburg, Ohio: Text and Criticism*. Ed. John H. Ferres. New York: Viking, 1966, 331–44.

White, Ray Lewis. "*Winesburg Ohio:* The Table of Contents." *Notes On Modern American Literature* 8 (1984):Item 8.

——. 1990. *Winesburg Ohio: An Exploration*. Boston: Twayne.

——, ed. 1969. *Sherwood Anderson's Memoirs: A Critical Edition*. Chapel Hill: University of North Carolina Press.

Wright, Austin McGiffert. 1961. *The American Short Story in the Twenties*. Chicago: University of Chicago Press.

The Strength of God

Sources and Influences

Commentators have noticed affinities between this story and certain classics of the American tradition. Curtis Hartman is a "lineal descendant of Hawthorne's Arthur Dimmesdale," according to Glicksberg (54). Bredahl states that Hartman's struggle between carnal desire and obedience to God reflects the theme of the sermon preached by Father Mapple in Herman Melville's *Moby Dick* (431). Doubtless other literary precursors might also be suggested.

No one has identified any specific real-life person as model for Curtis Hartman. But his Presbyterian Church is said to be the same Presbyterian Church that Anderson remembered from his hometown, Clyde, Ohio (Hurd 170). One commentator has reported, "You can even today verify the Reverend Curtis Hartman's angle of vision, from his study window in the belfry, across and down into Kate Swift's bedroom" (Ferres 238). Clearly, though, the ethos of the time also was an influence, with new attitudes toward sexuality, questioning of old assumptions about God and man's duty, and the growth of an ethic of self-expression.

Publication History

"The Strength of God" was first published in August 1916 in the radical New York little magazine titled *Masses* (8:12–13). It was the third of Anderson's stories to appear there—it was also the last. An editor of the magazine, Floyd Dell, was sometimes referred to by Anderson as his "literary father" (Jones-Rideout, *Letters* 405). Dell had been an influential Chicago editor in 1913 when Anderson, then an unknown writer, met him. Anderson was always grateful to Dell for showing enthusiasm for his early works, for introducing him to new ideas and people, and for making extensive efforts to get his writing published. In 1933, Anderson was still praising the editors of *Masses* (Max Eastman and John Reed as well as Floyd Dell) for the "feeling of bold[ness] and joy and life" they had brought into their magazine (Jones-Rideout, *Letters* 275). But as Dell, and the magazine, became more focused on proletarian issues and socialist crusading, Anderson's work became unacceptable (Tanselle 533). Anderson, for his part, was unwilling to fit himself into Dell's mold.

The story was collected into *Winesburg, Ohio* in 1919.

Relation to Other Works

The relationships between this tale and the rest of the *Winesburg* cycle are manifold. Although the Reverend Curtis Hartman, the central character, is a more prominent and respected figure in the community than most of the grotesques, his story is, like the others, a story of the buried life. Here as elsewhere, "there are two modes of perception operating"—one focused on the minister's respectable public life, and the other on his inner struggle for fulfillment (Stouck 148). His yearning for life and love, which conflicts with the demands of his social role and the limits placed on him by polite convention, is essentially the same kind of yearning that all the grotesques feel. He dreads becoming a meaningless "clod" (*WO* 69), and in his case the desire for significance takes the form of longing that "the spirit of God [would be] made manifest in him" (*WO* 148). There are specific parallels between his story and that of Jesse Bentley, a religious man of another generation who also yearns for a divine sign (Ingram 194). Hartman's desires, like those of so many of the other main characters, are ambiguously sexual *and* spiritual. The near impossibility of separating these two strands of desire is one of Anderson's primary insights.

Hartman senses, as does Ray Pearson (in "The Untold Lie"), that "marriage has cheated [him] out of life" (Abcarian 98). However, Hartman finds an ecstatic ideal vision apparently embodied in a specific woman; just as the drunken stranger in "Tandy" sees "God manifesting himself in the little child," Tom Hard's daughter (*WO* 143), the minister sees God manifest in Kate Swift's naked body as she kneels in prayer (*WO* 155). Some essential germ of truth in this vision is underscored by the narrator's comment in the following story, "The Teacher," that Kate Swift looks "lovely" as she walks on a winter night, like "a tiny goddess on a pedestal in a garden" (*WO* 160). The woman's naked body here reiterates a motif introduced in Alice Hindman's tale, "Adventure," and appearing again in Wash Williams's tale, "Respectability." In the first of these stories, the reader understands the nakedness sympathetically, from the woman's point of view; in the next, the reader is shocked and repulsed, from the man's point of view; in the two stories concerning the minister and the teacher, the reader is able to understand the gesture from both points of view—the minister's guilt-ridden lust transformed to compassionate religious veneration and the teacher's torment of fleshly desire, entrapment, vulnerability, shame, and spiritual need.

"The two most closely interwoven narratives" in the *Winesburg* cycle, as David Anderson observes, are "The Strength of God" and "The Teacher" (46). Both the Reverend Curtis Hartman and Kate Swift "interpret their personal loneliness and need for love as sin" (D. Anderson 46). Symbols of fire and wind, important throughout *Winesburg, Ohio,* are especially prominent in these two tales (Ingram 180–81; Fludernik 128–30). Hartman yearns for "the flame of the spirit" to burn in him and for inspiration to "come like a great wind into his voice" (*WO* 148), and at the story's end his triumph is marked by "eyes glowing" and "voice ringing with fervor" (*WO* 155).

Other motifs also connect this story with the rest of the collection. The minister's thought of escaping to some city links him with characters in "The Thinker," "Queer," and "Departure" (Baker 576). The window through which first he peeps and that finally he smashes in order to achieve his "liberation" contrasts with the cobweb-covered windows in "Paper Pills," which keep Doctor Reefy almost completely isolated. The hand with which the minister breaks the window, freeing himself "from the passivity which has made him grotesque in his own eyes" (Bresnahan 26), is linked with all the other expressive hands in the book. His bleeding fist shows that his liberation was costly; it also serves as a reminder of Parcival's pronouncement in "The Philosopher" that "everyone in the world is Christ and they are all crucified" (*WO* 57).

George Willard's role in the story is minimal. He merely listens, uncomprehending, as the minister bursts into the newspaper office and proclaims his vision and his victory.

Yet one can discern here a fascinating parallel with Anderson's later story "Death in the Woods." Both stories revolve around a naked female body; a male watcher in "The Strength of God" is replaced by a group of men in the later story; and in both a boy who does not fully comprehend the episode is connected with the artist/narrator who understands the inner feelings of each participant.

Furthermore, Glicksberg relates the story to Anderson's novel *Many Marriages* (1923), which he calls a "version of the tragedy of sex-starved America" (54). Indeed, there is a close parallel between the marriages of Hartman and John Webster, the protagonist of *Many Marriages:* both men feel welling resentment against passionless wives who have settled into acceptance of a kind of "death-in-life" (53, 55). But Glicksberg is too quick to identify Webster's naive celebration of "the Dionysian life of instinct" simply as Anderson's own (55). When these characters reach out for fulfillment in their various and somewhat ridiculous ways, it is generally clear that "sexual need . . . is often supplemented or overshadowed by a personal need of another sort" (Wright 85). This theme is most obvious in "Seeds," which stands as Anderson's plainest critique of the oversimplifications of Freudian psychology, but it is more subtly present in nearly all of his work. His characters desire a more vital life. For those who are deprived of sexual gratification by circumstance or puritanical fear, sex is a dramatic need. Sex alone, though, is never sufficient. Beaut McGregor in *Marching Men* (1917) gets his sexual needs met in eminently practical fashion, but he still yearns toward another woman and toward being a leader who can stir men to orderly lives. Similarly, the Reverend Curtis Hartman longs not only for woman's flesh but also for a spiritual flame that will enable him to touch the souls of his congregation. Just as Elizabeth Willard ("Mother"), Louise Bentley ("Godliness"), and Wash Williams ("Respectability") want more than sex, so it cannot be believed that a Dionysian experience with either his wife or the schoolteacher could successfully calm the upthrusting lust for life and significance in the minister's heart.

Another theme that enters this story links it to a major concern of Anderson throughout his writing career. As McAleer points out, Hartman's marriage to the daughter of a wealthy manufacturer of underwear marks him as "a typical victim of the age of materialism"; thinking himself secure, Hartman discovers "money [is] no substitute for love" (175). McAleer's emphasis explains Hartman's vision of the naked woman as a triumph over materialism and connects the tale with others in *Winesburg,* especially "The Philosopher" and "Godliness," and with several of Anderson's novels, where the pressures of industrial-commercial society are more nearly central.

Critical Studies

No single article has been devoted primarily to "The Strength of God," though Anderson's interpreters frequently refer to the story. A reviewer in 1919, evidently objecting to the notion of a preacher-turned-Peeping Tom, called it "the one unconvincing and manufactured story in the book" (Rascoe 29). More recent critics, however, have appreciated the story for its frankness in dealing with repressed desires (Bowden 116) and its violation of "Victorian and puritanical taboos" (Geismar 235). Its brilliant delineation of the minister's fluctuating psychological responses to temptation of the flesh has been analyzed and admired (White 90). Another critic who applauds Anderson as the prophet of sexual liberation finds it "[o]ne of the most powerful stories in the collection" because of its compassionate understanding of a man whose "raging, pent-up desires . . . override the protests of his moral self" (Glicksberg 53). Most scholars now agree with that view.

Variant interpretations of the story's conclusion, though, tend to divide commentators into two groups—those who see chiefly irony or pathology and those who believe that the Reverend Curtis Hartman achieves a genuine spiritual triumph. First, the ironic interpretations. From a psychoanalytical viewpoint, states a Freudian critic, the minister's final revelation is an example of "symbolic substitutes for actual sensual gratification" (Hoffman 242). This kind of insight has led some readers to conclude that Hartman's epiphany is a "delusion" (Fertig 67), or "a renewal of a perverted faith by fright and a neurotic conviction of sin" (D. Anderson 47), or even "the destruction of the imagination by Calvinist dogma" (Pickering 32). Similarly, Bidney states that Hartman's final act is "nothing but self-defeat, a relapse into passive celibacy-within-marriage" (267). Kenner, accepting this line of interpretation, argues that the story shows how "facile" Anderson's sophistication is: there is something fundamentally false about it because it is meant to appeal to people "more knowing" than the character himself, people who will "recognize sexual energy" in what Hartman naively calls "the strength of God" (149). But these readings are probably too simple.

To other critics, who acknowledge a positive counterforce to the irony, the story seems less facile. "Despite the 'naturalism,' despite the skepticism," argues Gregory, there is an "an atmosphere of vision" and an undertone of "symbolic, almost transcendental, meaning" (11). Stone agrees: not only does the destruction of the minister's temptation have "a redemptive effect," but the story conveys the intuition Anderson shared with Whitman—that flesh itself is holy (116). Temptation transforms the minister's dull sermons into moving, forceful communications fired by personal knowledge of weakness, which expands to become compassionate fellow-feeling. As he moves from seeing the woman as an emblem of carnal desire to understanding her "as a symbol of suffering humanity, kneeling naked and weeping before God," Hartman learns "humility," "compassion," and "spiritual perception" (Browning 146–47). Ultimately, McAleer states, the minister attains "a veritable Grail vision," which "reignites" his faith (175). Murphy argues that, in spite of "the comic elements" in his portrait, the Reverend Curtis Hartman becomes one of Winesburg's "spiritual elite"; by sublimating their physical desire, these elect few avoid "the trap of a merely sensual mode of communication" and achieve "a plane of consciousness where communication operates in terms of an imaginative, mystical sympathy" (241–43). Hartman's final triumphant cry, Ingram adds, reveals "as deep an insight into incarnational spirituality as one may gather from poems of Donne or Herbert" (163–64).

The design on Hartman's stained-glass window has been a specific topic of interpretive discussion. The child who gazes "with rapt eyes into the face of Christ" (*WO* 150) is symbolically linked with the minister, and the pictured Christ is to the child as the teacher is to the minister (Howe 108). The chip the minister breaks out, in the boy's heel, suggests "his own Achilles heel" (Ingram 163). The comforting gesture of the pictured Christ—laying his hand on the child's head—is reiterated in Hartman's sermon when he says "the hand of God, placed beneath [his] head" (*WO* 151) has lifted him (Maresca 281–82). But his release from guilty lust is not achieved until he is able to see in the teacher "the nakedness of humanity" as representative of "weakness and suffering rather than sex and temptation" (Wright 143–44). The symbol works both ways; that is, Hartman's victory comes when he assumes the role both of child and of comforter and when he can see in Kate both a suffering child in need of redemption and a manifestation of God with power to redeem him.

A feminist interpretation insists, correctly, that Hartman's religion is "warped" because he sees Kate Swift as a symbol rather than "as a human being" (Rigsbee 236). But a structuralist interpretation, which asserts that Hartman can overcome his self-division when he ceases "to see her as a person" and imagines her as a symbol (Bredahl 432), seems equally correct. The irony persistent in the victory, the sardonic element in the compassion—these constitute the clash that places this story properly in the book that Anderson indirectly identified as a book of the grotesque.

Formalist critics, consequently, have classified this as a story of caustic pathos (Wright 230–32) or as a "thematic" story, where in almost allegorical fashion the protagonist finds a "truth" that is extremely ironic (Mellard 1307–1308).

The narrative technique of the tale has received some deserved attention. Wright analyzes the admixture of narration and dramatic scene, of generalized summary and particularized detail, and of explicit statement and inferences left to the reader (292–93, 304, 333–34, 408). Gold admires the prose style, which seems simple in its "curious archaic directness" but is in fact highly sophisticated (554). Grimaud applies George Lakoff's method of analysis of names to Anderson's use of the minister's proper name, class name ("the man"), or periphrasis at various points in the story. The most significant points in Grimaud's study show Anderson's skillful handling of language. The class names "man" and "woman" are employed when the characters' erotic nature is being highlighted. At the story's turning point appears a superb antithesis: "the woman of sin began to pray" (488).

Yingling observes that Curtis Hartman's "voyeuristic relation" to Kate Swift is also the reader's "relation to the people of the text" (104). The inaccessibility of the object of desire and the incommunicability of psychic experience, which are dramatized in the story, seem to Yingling to be a result of "the collapse of collective experience" in Western culture and a determining characteristic of the condition of the grotesque (103–105). Yingling perceives that "the figure of George Willard as artist" promises to deliver an intelligible synthesis of "universal reality" (121–22). Yingling states that George will not fulfill that promise but will be alienated, "wholly taken up by the modern world of interiority" (125). The text of *Winesburg, Ohio,* of course, leaves George's future vague, open to readers' varied speculations. But the artist who produced "The Strength of God" communicates richly through that text, providing desired access to the heart of man.

Works Cited

Abcarian, Richard. "Innocence and Experience in *Winesburg, Ohio*." *University Review Kansas City* 35 (1968):95–105.

Anderson, David. 1967. *Sherwood Anderson: An Introduction and Interpretation*. New York: Holt, Rinehart.

Anderson, Sherwood. 1917. *Marching Men*. New York: John Lane. Rpt. in *Marching Men: A Critical Text*. Ed. Ray Lewis White. Cleveland and London: Press of Case Western Reserve University, 1972.

——. 1919. *Winesburg, Ohio*. New York: B. W. Huebsch. Rpt. New York: Viking, 1960.

——. 1923. *Many Marriages*. New York: B. W. Huebsch. Rpt. Metuchen, NJ: Scarecrow, 1978.

Baker, Carlos. "Sherwood Anderson's Winesburg: A Reprise." *The Virginia Quarterly Review* 48 (1972):568–79.

Bidney, Martin. "Anderson and the Androgyne: 'Something More than Man or Woman.'" *Studies in Short Fiction* 25 (1988):261–73.

Bowden, Edwin T. 1961. *The Dungeon of the Heart: Human Isolation and the American Novel*. New York: Macmillan, 114–24.

Bredahl, A. Carl. "'The Young Thing Within': Divided Narrative and Sherwood Anderson's *Winesburg, Ohio*." *Midwest Quarterly: A Journal of Contemporary Thought* 27 (1986):422–37.

Bresnahan, Roger J. "The 'Old Hands' of Winesburg." *Midwestern Miscellany* 11 (1983):19–27.

Browning, Chris. "Kate Swift: Sherwood Anderson's Creative Eros." *Tennessee Studies in Literature* 13 (1968):141–48.

Ferres, John H. "The Nostalgia of *Winesburg, Ohio*. " *Newberry Library Bulletin* 6, no. 8 (July 1971):235–42.

Fertig, Martin J. "'A Great Deal of Wonder in Me': Inspiration and Transformation in *Winesburg, Ohio*." *Markham Review* 6 (1977):65–70.

Fludernik, Monika. "'The Divine Accident of Life': Metaphoric Structure and Meaning in *Winesburg, Ohio*." *Style* 22 (1988):116–35.

Geismar, Maxwell. 1947. "Sherwood Anderson: Last of the Townsmen." In *The Last of the Provincials: The American Novel, 1915–1925*. Boston: Houghton Mifflin, 223–84. Rpt. in part in *Sherwood Anderson:* Winesburg, Ohio: *Text and Criticism*. Ed. John H. Ferres. New York: Viking, 1966, 377–82.

Glicksberg, Charles J. 1971. *The Sexual Revolution in Modern American Literature*. The Hague: Martinus Nijhoff.

Gold, Herbert. "The Purity and Cunning of Sherwood Anderson." *Hudson Review* 10 (1957–58):548–57. Rpt. in *The Age of Happy Problems*. New York: Dial Press, 1962, 56–67. Rpt. in part in *Sherwood Anderson:* Winesburg, Ohio: *Text and Criticism*. Ed. John H. Ferres. New York: Viking, 1966, 396–404. Rpt. in *Critical Essays on Sherwood Anderson*. Ed. David D. Anderson. Boston: G. K. Hall, 1981, 138–45.

Gregory, Horace. 1949. "Editor's Introduction." *The Portable Sherwood Anderson*. Ed. Horace Gregory. New York: Viking, 1–31. Rev. ed. New York: Viking Penguin, 1972.

Grimaud, Michel. "Spinning Names: Reference in Narratives." *Poetics* 17 (1988):483–96.

Hoffman, Frederick J. 1957. *Freudianism and the Literary Mind*. Rev. ed. Baton Rouge: Louisiana State University Press. Rpt. in *Sherwood Anderson:* Winesburg, Ohio: *Text and Criticism*. Ed. John H. Ferres. New York: Viking, 1966, 309–20. Rpt. in *The Achievement of Sherwood Anderson: Essays in Criticism*. Ed. Ray Lewis White. Chapel Hill: University of North Carolina Press, 1966, 174–92.

Hurd, Thaddeus B. 1992. "Excerpts from '*Winesburg* and Clyde, Fictional/Real Places.'" In *Sherwood Anderson: A Study of the Short Fiction.* Ed. Robert Allen Papinchak. New York: Twayne, 163–81.

Ingram, Forrest L. 1971. *Representative Short Story Cycles of the Twentieth Century: Studies in a Literary Genre.* The Hague: Mouton.

Jones, Howard Mumford and Walter B. Rideout, eds. 1953. *Letters of Sherwood Anderson.* Boston: Little, Brown.

Kenner, Hugh. 1975. *A Homemade World: The American Modernist Writers.* New York: Knopf.

Maresca, Carol J. "Gestures as Meaning in Sherwood Anderson's *Winesburg, Ohio.*" *College Language Association Journal* 9 (1966):279–83.

McAleer, John J. "Christ Symbolism in *Winesburg, Ohio.*" *Discourse* 4 (1961):168–81. Rpt. in *The Merrill Studies in* Winesburg, Ohio. Comp. Ray Lewis White. Columbus, OH: Charles E. Merrill, 1971, 60–74.

Mellard, James M. "Narrative Forms in *Winesburg, Ohio.*" *PMLA* 83 (1968):1304–1312.

Murphy, George D. "The Theme of Sublimation in Anderson's *Winesburg, Ohio.*" *Modern Fiction Studies* 13 (1967):237–46.

Phillips, William L. "How Sherwood Anderson Wrote *Winesburg, Ohio.* "*American Literature* 23 (1951):7–30. Rpt. in *Sherwood Anderson:* Winesburg, Ohio: *Text and Criticism.* Ed. John H. Ferres. New York: Viking, 1966, 263–86. Rpt. in *The Achievement of Sherwood Anderson: Essays in Criticism.* Ed. Ray Lewis White. Chapel Hill: University of North Carolina Press, 1966, 62–84. Rpt. in *The Merrill Studies in* Winesburg, Ohio. Comp. Ray Lewis White. Columbus, OH: Charles E. Merrill, 1971, 2–24. Rpt. in *Sherwood Anderson: A Collection of Critical Essays.* Ed. Walter B. Rideout. Englewood Cliffs, NJ: Prentice-Hall, 1974, 18–38.

Pickering, Samuel. "*Winesburg, Ohio:* A Portrait of the Artist as a Young Man." *Southern Quarterly* 16 (1977):27–38.

Rascoe, Burton. 1937. *The Joys of Reading: Life's Greatest Pleasure.* Garden City, NY: Doubleday.

Rigsbee, Sally Adair. "The Feminine in *Winesburg, Ohio.*" *Studies in American Fiction* 9 (1981):233–44.

Stone, Edward. 1969. *A Certain Morbidness: A View of American Literature.* Preface by Harry T. Moore. Carbondale: Southern Illinois University Press.

Stouck, David. "Winesburg, Ohio and the Failure of Art." *Twentieth Century Literature* 15 (1969):145–51.

Tanselle, G. Thomas. "Realist or Dreamer: Letters of Sherwood Anderson and Floyd Dell." *Modern Language Review* 58 (1963):532–37.

White, Ray Lewis. 1990. Winesburg, Ohio: *An Exploration*. Boston: Twayne.

Wright, Austin McGiffert. 1961. *The American Short Story in the Twenties*. Chicago: University of Chicago Press.

Yingling, Thomas. 1990. "*Winesburg, Ohio* and the End of Collective Experience." In *New Essays on* Winesburg, Ohio. Ed. John W. Crowley. Cambridge and New York: Cambridge University Press, 99–128.

The Teacher

Circumstances of Composition

The earliest prepublication title of this story was "The School Teacher" (White 6).

Sources and Influences

It seems probable that one of Anderson's own teachers was the model for Kate Swift. In his *Memoirs,* he mentions that one of his teachers in Clyde, Ohio, encouraged him, trying tenderly and with "some difficulty" to tell him that he "must read a lot" and get the benefit of his education (White, *Memoirs* 102). A more likely model, however, is Trillena White, a teacher (not his own) who became Anderson's friend when he was a student at Wittenberg Academy. She was ten years older than he. Tall, athletic, and well read, she was the principal of Central High School in Springfield in 1900 (Baker 51). The two frequently walked together and discussed authors and books (Schevill 29). Later Anderson said that "she was the first person to really introduce me to literature, for which she had a very fine feeling" (Sutton 94). She seems to be the teacher who appears in the piece called "To George Borrow."

It has also been suggested that Anderson's mother influenced this portrait, since she stimulated him to "see beneath the surface of lives"; this phrase from the dedication to *Winesburg, Ohio* closely resembles Kate Swift's advice to young George Willard (Browning 142).

Benvenuto Cellini, the topic of some of Kate Swift's stories, was the hero of a play that Anderson and Ben Hecht tried to write; in his autobiography, Hecht describes Anderson acting out the role of Cellini (227).

Publication History

This story was first published in the collection *Winesburg, Ohio* (1919).

Waldo Frank, editor of *Seven Arts,* which had published four *Winesburg* tales, wrote to the author after the book came out asking why "The Teacher" and "The Strength of God" had not been submitted to him; "I'd have snatched them," he said (Sutton 432). The reason, apparently, is that "The Strength of God" had already appeared in *Masses* and Anderson did not think "The Teacher" could stand alone.

Relation to Other Works

"The Teacher" is integrally related to other stories in *Winesburg, Ohio,* particularly to "The Strength of God," to which it is virtually a companion piece. The culminating episodes of both tales are set on the same snowy January night, and in this story the reader discovers the train of events that, ironically, have produced the climax of Curtis Hartman's story, immediately preceding. George Willard plays a minor role in both stories; he is a "catalyst" who "unwittingly stimulates Kate Swift's self-revelatory insight, which in turn has an effect on Curtis Hartman's flash of discovery," and George Willard witnesses, without comprehension, the outward effects of their inner turmoil (Ingram 166). These two stories, as vividly as any in the collection, show "the gropings and cross-purposes" and "the failure of communication" that augment the misery of the grotesques (Walcutt 230).

This is one of several stories in which older characters give advice to young George Willard; other characters who offer themselves as teachers are Wing Biddlebaum ("Hands"), Doctor Parcival ("The Philosopher"), Joe Welling ("A Man of Ideas"), and Wash Williams ("Respectability"). (See Fussell 109 on this topic.) Of all these, though, Kate Swift's advice—"to know what people are thinking about, not what they say" (*WO* 163)—comes closest to expressing Anderson's own intention in the *Winesburg* stories (Rideout 28; similarly, Voss 191, and Ward 38). Ironically, however, to some extent her "words fail to convey even *this* truth," for George Willard admits having "missed something" she was trying to say (Love 54).

The story marks a stage in George Willard's development, a key chapter in his bildungsroman. In the early stories he is unable "to see beneath the surface," but as time goes on, gradually, he approaches artistic maturity (Rogers 94–95). In "The Teacher," even as he realizes that he has "missed something," George "begins to understand something of the complexity of human motives and behavior" (Burbank 70). Subsequently, in "The Awakening," he displays his insensitivity to thoughts and feelings and a foolish reliance on words, but thereafter, in "Sophistication," he shows that he has finally grasped the message Kate Swift was attempting to teach (Lorch 58).

Kate Swift's own capacity to generate energy "in the minds of" her students connects her with the theme of "the young thing inside" first mentioned in the introductory sketch, "The Book of the Grotesque" (Bredahl 432). Like Elizabeth Willard ("Mother"), she yearns "for love and beauty" with passionate idealism, but they both "have repressed their feelings" for so long that their attempts to express themselves are muddled (Bunge 49; similarly, Bidney 264–65). Kate Swift also provides a prime instance of the motif of transformation in *Winesburg* when she is described as walking at night in the snow: although her neighbors see her as ill-complexioned and rather homely, her figure has a straight-backed dignity and her features are like those "of a tiny goddess on a pedestal in a garden" (*WO* 160). Such transformations, explains Fertig (who ably analyzes the pattern in *Winesburg, Ohio* but overlooks this instance of it), artistically reveal the "essential nature" of a character (70).

Kate Swift is a type of woman prevalent in Anderson's writing, intense and imaginative but incomplete. Specifically, according to Miller, she fits the pattern of giving women like Lillian in "Not Sixteen," Kate in "Daughters," Alice in "Like a Queen," and the woman in "A Man's Story" (76).

A particularly close parallel exists between Kate Swift and Mary Underwood of *Windy McPherson's Son*. Mary Underwood, too, is a teacher in a small town, a loner whose vigorous, independent mind causes her to be misunderstood by the townspeople. She, too, lives with an aunt and takes walks to relieve her tension. And Mary takes an interest in young Sam McPherson, whose promise she recognizes. Mary's passion for Sam is purely maternal, however, not confusedly combined with physical desire. The element of ambiguity inherent in Kate Swift's reaching out to George enters the novel only in the response of Sam and the townspeople, who are unable to comprehend the purity of her intent; he absurdly proposes marriage, and they gossip as if she were carrying on an illicit affair. The complexity of motive absent in Mary Underwood but active in Kate Swift may reflect either Anderson's growth of understanding or his increased daring.

Critical Studies

Discussions of this story for the most part are sketchy. Gold describes it disparagingly as a "simple" tale of pathos inviting readers to indulge in dreamy, nostalgic fantasies over their "own past" sorrows (550–51). Phillips sums it up, in the terms of "The Book of the Grotesque," as a cautionary tale concerning "the 'truth' of virginity . . . too closely held" (Origins" 183). More accurately, but still rather summarily, Berland labels it merely another instance of the theme that characters are grotesque because their beautiful dreams are incommunicable and "unrealizable" (137–38).

The chief concern of most critics has been Kate Swift's psychology, but again there has been a tendency to oversimplify in one direction or another. Consequently, sharp disagreement has arisen over the evaluation of her character. Howe states that she is "distraught," estranged, looking to George for some miraculous "salvation" (103–104). Burbank views her as "socially defeated," a victim of the "callousness or indifference" of others (72). These assessments are insufficiently complex. Browning argues, against such interpretations, that the teacher is "far from defeated," that she is in fact Anderson's "ideal woman"—possessing "intelligence, education, energy and passion for life, independence of spirit" and effectively symbolizing the "creative Eros" for both the Reverend Curtis Hartman and George Willard (144, 141). Since George "is not yet mature enough to understand more than the sexual promise of her actions," Browning declares, Kate sensibly withdraws, saving him by refusing the merely physical "compromise" and thus propelling him to seek for the more spiritual "something" that he has missed (145). But Rigsbee corrects Browning's excessive idealization of the teacher by calling attention to the real confusion the character experiences as a result of "the intense pressure of her own sexual needs" (244n). Indeed, the story states plainly that, for a while, Kate Swift's "eagerness to open the door of life to the boy . . . had possession of her" (*WO* 164).

Murphy's analysis takes account of the difficulties Kate Swift faces: both this story and "The Strength of God," he explains, illustrate "Anderson's vision of the subtle connections which exist between *eros* and *agape*" (243). When "sexual excitement" obscures Kate's attempt to communicate "the import of life" to George, she experiences a "moment of despair" (243). Nevertheless, her sublimation of her desire elevates her "to a plane of consciousness where communication operates in terms of imaginative, mystical sympathy" (242), and George's elevation to that higher consciousness appears afterward, in "Death" and "Sophistication" (243–46). In contrary interpretations, Atlas views Kate Swift merely as "frustrated, unwilling to be sexual," "stern and cold toward her students," and repressed by a sheltering mother (actually, an aunt) (261), and Bidney argues that she is "a failed artist/androgyne" with "sadomasochistic" behavior, "in love with" George but prevented from fulfillment by an imprisoning "idealism" (265). Whereas Murphy's interpretation may be overly positive, Atlas and Bidney tend to suggest, implausibly, that an uninhibited sexual relationship with George Willard would somehow resolve the teacher's problems. In fact, it is hard to see how recoil from sexual involvement with an adolescent pupil can reasonably be held against her.

The stories Kate tells her students have aroused similarly differing judgments. According to Lorch, she is "an effective teller of stories about artists" such as Lamb and Cellini (58). But Bidney finds the stories revealingly perverse expressions of her internal conflict between "female" mildness and "male" aggression (265).

One may conclude that the moral principles by which Kate should be judged (and on which she should base her behavior) are not easily reducible to formula. Neither "virginity" nor "passion" is the true answer to the teacher's predicament, and the whole approach of the storyteller aims to elicit from the reader a complex understanding that is more than either of these intellectual antipodes.

Critics who have centered attention on the form of the story and its techniques have written some of the most illuminating criticism. Mellard classifies the story as one of the "emblematic" type—that is, as one of six stories in *Winesburg, Ohio* whose primary purpose is to draw a portrait of a universal or archetypal figure (1310). Consequently, says Mellard, the characterization is relatively static, and past events are used to explain the teacher's "conflicting attitude toward the maturing George"—her attraction (maternal and sexual) to him as pupil, man, and artist, and the "confusion of desire and duty" she experiences (1310–11). Wright classifies the story as one of caustic pathos with an episode of exposure in which the central character erupts into an uncharacteristic expression of long-pent-up feeling (231). He points out that Anderson's treatment of the action is primarily narrative; though the narrative voice is occasionally explicit in making evaluations, more important conclusions such as "the nature of Kate Swift's repression" are left to be gathered by the reader "through inference from the story as a whole" (399, 293n, 333–34, 408). Ingram shows how symbolic details of the story guide readers toward appropriate inferences—specifically, the way gestures reflect the ebb and flow of characters' feelings and the way the elaborate patterned references to fire and snow throughout the narrative indicate the undercurrent of passion in both main characters and their isolation (190, 180–81).

Tanner remarks that the narrative approach in this story, where one "can see into every home," differs from the detached stance more common in the *Winesburg* tales (211–12). Though he judges this lack of perspective to be a weakness, it is possible to see the more comprehensive point of view here in relation to the multiplicity of viewpoints that have accumulated by this point in the collection. The incomplete viewpoints of the Reverend Curtis Hartman, Kate Swift, and George Willard are immediately relevant, but the viewpoints of all the other characters in Winesburg, too, are present in a sense as the narrator here reaches toward some more encompassing vision. As Thurston notices, the ending of "The Teacher" is unnecessary to the story as an independent entity but vital to the cycle as a whole (127). The reader is enabled to see more broadly than any of the characters, almost with the benign wisdom of an adult tucking troubled children into bed, as the narrative voice closes: "and in all Winesburg he was the last soul on that winter night to go to sleep" (*WO* 166). This is a very *told* story, artful and evocative as George's final line beckons the reader as well as himself toward a deeper, intuitive understanding: "I have missed something. I have missed something Kate Swift was trying to tell me."

Works Cited

Anderson, Sherwood. 1919. *Winesburg, Ohio*. New York: B. W. Huebsch. Rpt. New York: Viking, 1960.

————. 1970. "To George Borrow." In *No Swank*. Mamaroneck, NY: Appel, 35–46.

Atlas, Marilyn Judith. 1981. "Sherwood Anderson and the Women of Winesburg." In *Critical Essays on Sherwood Anderson*. Ed. David D. Anderson. Boston: G. K. Hall, 250–66.

Baker, William. "Sherwood Anderson in Springfield." *American Literary Realism* 15 (1982):47–61.

Berland, Alwyn. "Sherwood Anderson and the Pathetic Grotesque." *Western Review* 15 (1951):135–38.

Bidney, Martin. "Anderson and the Androgyne: 'Something More than Man or Woman.'" *Studies in Short Fiction* 25 (1988):261–73.

Bredahl, A. Carl. "'The Young Thing Within': Divided Narrative and Sherwood Anderson's *Winesburg, Ohio*." *Midwest Quarterly: A Journal of Contemporary Thought* 27 (1986):422–37.

Browning, Chris. "Kate Swift: Sherwood Anderson's Creative Eros." *Tennessee Studies in Literature* 13 (1968):141–48. Rpt. in *The Merrill Studies in Winesburg, Ohio*. Comp. Ray Lewis White. Columbus, OH: Charles E. Merrill, 1971, 74–82.

Bunge, Nancy. "Women as Social Critics in *Sister Carrie, Winesburg, Ohio,* and *Main Street*." *Midamerica* 3 (1976):46–55.

Burbank, Rex. 1964. *Sherwood Anderson*. New York: Twayne. Rpt. in part in *The Achievement of Sherwood Anderson: Essays in Criticism*. Ed. Ray Lewis White. Chapel Hill: University of North Carolina Press, 1966, 32–43. Rpt. in part in *Sherwood Anderson: A Collection of Critical Essays*. Ed. Walter B. Rideout. Englewood Cliffs, NJ: Prentice-Hall, 1974, 70–83.

Fertig, Martin J. "'A Great Deal of Wonder in Me': Inspiration and Transformation in *Winesburg, Ohio*." *Markham Review* 6 (1977):65–70.

Fussell, Edwin. "*Winesburg, Ohio:* Art and Isolation." *Modern Fiction Studies*

6 (1960):106–14. Rpt. in *Sherwood Anderson: Winesburg, Ohio: Text and Criticism.* Ed. John H. Ferres. New York: Viking, 1966, 383–95. Rpt. in *Achievement of Sherwood Anderson: Essays in Criticism.* Ed. Ray Lewis White. Chapel Hill: University of North Carolina Press, 1966, 104–113. Rpt. in *Sherwood Anderson: A Collection of Critical Essays.* Ed. Walter B. Rideout. Englewood Cliffs, NJ: Prentice-Hall, 1974, 39–48.

Gold, Herbert. "The Purity and Cunning of Sherwood Anderson." *Hudson Review* 10 (1957–58):548–57. Rpt. in *The Age of Happy Problems.* New York: Dial Press, 1962, 56–67. Rpt. in part in *Sherwood Anderson: Winesburg, Ohio: Text and Criticism.* Ed. John H. Ferres. New York: Viking, 1966, 396–404. Rpt. in *Critical Essays on Sherwood Anderson.* Ed. David D. Anderson. Boston: G. K. Hall, 1981, 138–45.

Hecht, Ben. 1954. *A Child of the Century.* New York: Simon and Schuster.

Howe, Irving. 1951. *Sherwood Anderson.* New York: William Sloane.

Ingram, Forrest L. 1971. *Representative Short Story Cycles of the Twentieth Century: Studies in a Literary Genre.* The Hague: Mouton.

Jones, Howard Mumford, and Walter B. Rideout, eds. 1953. *Letters of Sherwood Anderson.* Boston: Little, Brown.

Lorch, Thomas M. "The Choreographic Structure of *Winesburg, Ohio.*'" *College Language Association Journal* 12 (1968–69):56–65.

Love, Glen A. "*Winesburg, Ohio* and the Rhetoric of Silence." *American Literature* 40 (1968):38–57.

Mellard, James M. "Narrative Forms in *Winesburg, Ohio.*" *PMLA* 83 (1968):1304–1312.

Miller, William V. 1974. "Earth-Mothers, Succubi, and Other Ectoplasmic Spirits: The Women in Sherwood Anderson's Short Stories." In *Midamerica I.* Ed. David D. Anderson. East Lansing, MI: Midwestern Press, 64–81. Rpt. in *Critical Essays on Sherwood Anderson.* Ed. David D. Anderson. Boston: G. K. Hall, 1981, 196–209.

Murphy, George D. "The Theme of Sublimation in Anderson's *Winesburg, Ohio.*" *Modern Fiction Studies* 13 (1967):237–46.

Phillips, William L. "How Sherwood Anderson Wrote *Winesburg, Ohio.*" *American Literature* 23 (1951):7–30. Rpt. in *Sherwood Anderson: Winesburg, Ohio: Text and Criticism.* Ed. John H. Ferres. New York: Viking, 1966, 263–86. Rpt. in *The Achievement of Sherwood Anderson: Essays in Criticism.* Ed. Ray Lewis White. Chapel Hill: University of North Carolina Press, 1966, 62–84. Rpt. in *The Merrill Studies in* Winesburg, Ohio. Comp. Ray Lewis White. Columbus, OH: Charles E. Merrill, 1971, 2–24. Rpt. in *Sherwood Anderson: A Collection of Critical Essays.* Ed. Walter B. Rideout. Englewood Cliffs, NJ: Prentice-Hall, 1974, 18–38.

———. "Sherwood Anderson's *Winesburg, Ohio:* Its Origins, Composition, Technique, and Reception." Ph.D. diss., University of Chicago, 1950.

Rideout, Walter B. "The Simplicity of *Winesburg, Ohio.*" *Shenandoah* 13 (1962):20–31. Rpt. in *Sherwood Anderson:* Winesburg, Ohio: *Text and Criticism.* Ed. John H. Ferres. New York: Viking, 1966, 287–300. Rpt. in *Critical Essays on Sherwood Anderson.* Ed. David D. Anderson. Boston: G. K. Hall, 1981, 146–54.

Rigsbee, Sally Adair. "The Feminine in *Winesburg, Ohio.*" *Studies in American Fiction* 9 (1981):233–44.

Rogers, Douglas G. "Development of the Artist in *Winesburg, Ohio.*" *Studies in the Twentieth Century* 10 (1972):91–99.

Schevill, James. 1951. *Sherwood Anderson: His Life and Work.* Denver: University of Denver Press.

Sutton, William A. 1972. *The Road to Winesburg: A Mosaic of the Imaginative Life of Sherwood Anderson.* Metuchen, NJ: Scarecrow Press.

Tanner, Tony. 1965. "Sherwood Anderson's Little Things." *The Reign of Wonder: Naïvety and Reality in American Literature.* Cambridge: Cambridge University Press, 205–27.

Thurston, Jarvis. "Anderson and 'Winesburg': Mysticism and Craft." *Accent* 16 (1956):107–28. Rpt. in part in *Sherwood Anderson:* Winesburg, Ohio: *Text and Criticism.* Ed. John Ferres. New York: Viking, 1966, 331–44.

Voss, Arthur. 1973. *The American Short Story: A Critical Survey.* Norman: University of Oklahoma Press.

Walcutt, Charles Child. "Sherwood Anderson: Impressionism and the Buried Life." *American Literary Naturalism, a Divided Stream.* Minneapolis: University of Minnesota Press, 1956, 222–39. Originally in *Sewanee Review* 60 (1952):28–47. Rpt. in part in *Sherwood Anderson:* Winesburg, Ohio: *Text and Criticism.* Ed. John H. Ferres. New York: Viking, 1966, 432–43.

Ward, J. A. 1985. "*Winesburg, Ohio:* Habitual Silence and the Roaring of Voices." *American Silences: The Realism of James Agee, Walker Evans, and Edward Hopper.* Baton Rouge: Louisiana State University Press, 35–50.

White, Ray Lewis. "*Winesburg, Ohio:* The Story Titles." *Winesburg Eagle* 10, no. 1 (November 1984):6–7.

———, ed. 1969. *Sherwood Anderson's Memoirs: A Critical Edition.* Chapel Hill: University of North Carolina Press.

Wright, Austin McGiffert. 1961. *The American Short Story in the Twenties.* Chicago: University of Chicago Press.

Loneliness

Circumstances of Composition

In the extant manuscript of *Winesburg, Ohio,* "Loneliness" is one of five tales on the backs of fragments of old writings; Phillips believes it probably was placed between "The Teacher" and "An Awakening" ("How" 12). The original title of the story seems to have been "Alone," and it appears as "The Lonely Man" on a draft of the table of contents of *Winesburg* (White, "Titles" 6–7). The position of the story in the collection shifted as, in planning the volume, the author considered various arrangements; earlier "Loneliness" was placed between "Godliness" and "Queer," then between "The Thinker" and "Queer," and then between "Adventure" and "Queer" (White, "Table"). That may explain why, as it now stands, "Loneliness" disrupts the chronology of the surrounding stories: it is set in October, while the stories both before and after it are set in January.

Sources and Influences

The chief sources of the story, evidently, are biographical. Many features of Enoch Robinson's life are drawn almost directly from Sherwood Anderson's personal experience. Like his character, Anderson had grown up in small towns of Ohio, and chiefly in Clyde, on which Winesburg is modeled. He had wanted, or thought he wanted, the life conventionally defined as successful in America—rising in the world of business, becoming a respectable citizen, enjoying polite prosperity and domestic comforts with a wife and children. He had married and worked in the commercial world of the American middle class and then become deeply dissatisfied. He had gone on long walks at night, seeking release. He had isolated himself in a room in his house, where he wrote, inventing "imaginary figures" and "trying to find a cure-all" (Anderson, "To George Borrow" 37). Then he had fled from all that life to go to Chicago and pursue his art. Mingling there with writers of what came to be called the Chicago Renaissance and with such artists as his brother Karl Anderson, post–Impressionist painter B. J. O. Nordfelt, and sculptor Mary Randolph, Anderson was exhilarated by the ideas and enthusiasms of his new bohemian companions (Duffey 134–35). Yet, amid the impassioned talk of the writers and intellectuals, Anderson seemed to be listening with "a certain amazement (resembling fear) and indicating clearly that nothing would induce him into such fancy realms. . . . He didn't talk ideas—he told stories" (Margaret Anderson 38). At the time he wrote this story, Anderson lived alone in a room, as Robinson does. A new woman, Tennessee Claflin Mitchell, entered Anderson's life in Chicago, but he did not let her move into his room. Even after their marriage, in the summer of 1916, they lived separately; he kept his room as his own. One critic surmises that Enoch Robinson's "fear of strong women" reflects Anderson's own fear of Tennessee Mitchell, the independent, creative woman "who may at times have felt too 'large' for his room" (Atlas 254–55).

Unlike his character, who gets married after he has been an artist for years, Anderson had abandoned bourgeois conventionality—and wife and children—*before* joining the world of artists. Moreover, Anderson's wife, Cornelia Lane Anderson, unlike Mrs. Robinson, did not have the benefit of her husband's gift of an $8,000 inheritance; she had to go to work to support three children and received little financial assistance from her ex-husband, who remarried quickly after their divorce. (She herself did not remarry.) But like Mrs. Robinson, Cornelia believed her husband was "not mentally sound," and that idea, her husband thought, had helped to ease the separation (Jones-Rideout, *Letters* 8).

Townsend believes that Anderson's younger brother, Earl, a timid and unsuccessful artist, "comes through" in the characterization of Enoch Robinson (69).

Publication History

"Loneliness" was first published in *Winesburg, Ohio* (1919); before that it was twice rejected by magazines. First, Anderson submitted it to *Masses,* of which Floyd Dell was associate editor. Though *Masses* had accepted "The Book of the Grotesque," "Hands," and "The Strength of God," the editorial board rejected this story. Then, on November 20, 1916, Anderson submitted the story to *Seven Arts,* writing to editor Waldo Frank, "Personally, I like the Enoch Robinson thing better than anything I have done" (Sutton, *Road* 347). *Seven Arts,* too, rejected it. Anderson expressed his disappointment, telling Frank that when Floyd Dell had complained that the story was "damn rot" and "[did] not get anywhere," Anderson had replied, "It gets there, but you are not at the station" (Jones-Rideout, *Letters* 5). Dell was later to dispute Anderson's understanding of his letter, explaining his comment as having meant only that the story was more in the vein of Chekhov than of de Maupassant (Sutton 610). Another likely factor in the rejection was that the *Masses* by this time was interested in more political material.

The story is the only *Winesburg* tale reprinted in *The Teller's Tales,* a collection edited by Frank Gado in 1983.

Relation to Other Works

This story is related to the rest of the *Winesburg* cycle in a number of significant ways. Placed immediately after "The Teacher," it extends and reinforces the idea that there is more to writing than words, more to painting than "line and values and composition." Just as George realizes there was "something Kate Swift was trying to tell" him, so Enoch knows there is "something else" in his painting, some hidden essence that his friends have not seen at all (*WO* 169, 166). The "something" hidden behind the elders is connected closely, too, with the dedication to the book, in which Anderson commemorates his mother for awaking his "hunger to see beneath the surface" of things (Papinchak, "Something" 6). The fact that the hidden thing is a woman suggests a connection with "Tandy" as well.

This story "fuses . . . recurring themes and images" of "corn," "darkness," "man," "woman," "fruition," and "thwarted potential" that permeate the cycle (Papinchak, *Sherwood* 25). Moreover, Enoch's ambivalence about speaking to George is typical of the conflict many of the grotesques feel about whether to speak or keep silent (Mahoney 250; similarly, Fagin 139–40). Enoch's flight from the city to the sanctuary of the town links him with Doctor Parcival in "The Philosopher," the stranger in "Tandy," and Tom Foster and his grandmother in "Drink" (Williams 186–87). His imaginary woman carrying a sword recalls the woman dressed like a knight who is inside the old writer in "The Book of the Grotesque." Enoch's attempt to show a woman how big and powerful he is anticipates George's strutting before Belle Carpenter in "An Awakening," and both characters experience a jolt that awakes them to reality (Lorch 59; similarly, Ingram 176–77). Enoch's loneliness, according to Winther, expresses "the idea which unites all the stories into a composite view of life. Exile is the price a man pays for imagination and insight into the meaning of life" (148).

The separation of lives in Winesburg is wryly underlined by a detail that links this story with "Adventure." In this story the lonely Enoch Robinson meets George Willard on a rainy fall night to tell his story about the woman who left him bereft; in that story Alice Hindman, a woman left behind by her lover, runs out in a fall rain longing "to find some other lonely human and embrace him" (*WO* 119). Had the stories been juxtaposed, as Anderson once intended (see "Circumstances of Composition" above), this relationship would have been more readily noticed.

The story also marks a stage in George Willard's development, the aspect of the cycle that partakes of the genre of the bildungsroman or the künstlerroman. As various citizens of Winesburg tell the news reporter their stories, he progresses from completely passive listening (in "Hands") to increasingly active questioning. Here, his curiosity is not only piqued by the old artist, who is said to be "a little off his head" (*WO* 174), but when Enoch breaks off his story and tells him to go away, George, undeterred, insists on finding out more: "Don't stop now. Tell me the rest of it" (*WO* 177). He is beginning to understand what Kate Swift meant when she admonished him to find out "what people are thinking about, not what they say" (*WO* 163).

In its narrative form the story closely resembles "Respectability" (Wright 235–36.

Examining Anderson's works outside *Winesburg, Ohio,* one can find numerous examples of characters whose artistic impulses clash with the social world of commerce, citizenship, families, lovers, and current notions about what constitutes art; but the work that most closely resembles "Loneliness" in content is, perhaps, the uncollected tale "The Story Writers." Both stories center on the conflict between ordinary life and the life of art, and in both, success is blocked by the artists themselves. Whereas the *Smart Set* story is decidedly in a comic-satiric vein, with characters who are patently foolish, "Loneliness" reaches for a more serious understanding of real threats any artist encounters: superficial talk about art, distracting desires for human contact, solipsistic retreat.

"Unused" also has some affinity with this story. Enoch's imaginary world is akin to the towering fantasies May Edgely constructs after she has been wounded by the actual world. Later, just as he is attracted to and then retreats from the threatening reality of a woman, she too reacts with ambivalence and understandable but abnormal fear to the sexual threat of a man. Her suicide is literal, Enoch's metaphorical.

In "Prelude to a Story" in his *Writer's Book,* when Anderson describes his own early efforts to become a writer, he remembers himself in his room, overhearing the sounds of women on the stairs and dreaming of an imaginary woman he had named Cecelia; and he explicitly compares himself then to Enoch Robinson (Curry 14). The "Prelude to a Story" concludes with two scenes that may illuminate "Loneliness." In one, Anderson, now a well-known writer who still struggles with some of the same old problems, hears in the rustle of a stream the sound of voices and footsteps of real, remembered people "mingled" with those of imaginary people. In the other, he burns a manuscript written to conform to the standards of a popular magazine and joyfully acknowledges himself to be "an eternal child" happily in thrall to "the people of [his] imaginary world" (Curry 58–60).

Finally, there is a suggestive parallel between the hurt, suffering woman lying "white and still" and beautiful in the elders of Robinson's painting and the long-abused old woman who is the powerful central figure of the artist's imagination in Anderson's great short story "Death in the Woods." Evidently

Anderson wrote a draft of "Death in the Woods" around the time that he wrote "Loneliness" and most of the other tales about Winesburg. (See "Death in the Woods," "Circumstances of Composition.") Though he tried again and again over the years to rework the idea of this woman, not until 1926 did the story achieve a form that he considered publishable. It is significant that Enoch cannot paint this figure, who is yet the key to his work; one of Anderson's triumphs is that he did at last succeed in painting her in his prose.

Critical Studies

This story is important as an indirect statement of Anderson's ideas about art. Critical interpreters vary, though, in their evaluation of Enoch Robinson's character and in their assessment of his significance. Some commentators have stressed, perhaps unduly, Enoch's similarity to Sherwood Anderson and/or to George Willard. Gold finds in Enoch's "romantic idealism" the "boyish" limitation that is central to Anderson's own artistic imperfection (552–53). Stouck, similarly, pointing out the biographical parallels between Enoch and the author and the resemblance between "the pathetic little artist" and George Willard (both of whom retreat from reality in the face of the death of their mothers), argues that the story reveals Anderson's "sense of despair" about the ability of art "to communicate" ("Failure" 149–50). Along the same lines, Way thinks the story itself is "poor" but "interesting" because it "reflects Anderson's difficulties" (112). Pickering goes so far as to contend that the story belies the "apparently happy ending" of the book; he argues that "Enoch is effectually George" and implies that both figures "poignantly" predict the fate of their romantic author, who wrote crude, unfinished tales and "lost his vital imagination in the twenties" (35–38).

Like these critics in treating Enoch as more or less identical with Anderson, but unlike them in expressing tolerant approval of both character and author, Gado focuses attention on what the story reveals about Anderson's "concept of language." He sees in the story Anderson's commitment to an art that acknowledges "the irreducibility of the word to experience" and that consequently uses words to "evoke" experience "beyond language's power of containment" (4–5). The distinction he draws between Hemingway's approach and Anderson's is a useful one.

Other studies, however, point out significant differences between Enoch's personality and both George's and Anderson's. Stouck, in a later interpretation than that mentioned above, surmises that Enoch belongs to the impressionist school and that his failure "to communicate anything to the audience of friends" contrasts significantly with "Anderson's expressionist art" ("Expressionist" 47). Fertig considers the story to be a *parody* of Anderson's experience: despite the similarities, Enoch is "unlike Anderson" in "his immaturity and his inarticulateness," and, finally, in his insanity (67–68). Similarly, Fussell explains Enoch as an "artist *manqué*" whose childishness provides a significant contrast with the maturity of George Willard at the end of the *Winesburg* cycle, particularly in "Sophistication" (112). Ingram concurs, judging Enoch "partially responsible for his own isolating egotism" and envisioning George as he departs from Winesburg as one who may transcend the limitations of all the grotesques, including Enoch (196, 198–99). These interpretations suggest a more balanced view of a character who, however much he may derive from the author's own self-knowledge, is also held up to the reader as an object of pity and contempt. This statement, which Anderson made in his "A Note on Realism," seems particularly relevant: " . . . the imagination must constantly feed upon reality or starve. Separate yourself too much from life and you may at moments be a lyrical poet, but you are not an artist. Something dries up, starves for the want of food" (Curry 71–78).

Specific psychological interpretations of Enoch usually avoid conflating him with the author. Murphy regards the character as "schizoid" and groups him with those grotesques who are unable "to accept the gross fact of sex," in contradistinction to others who cannot get beyond mere sensuality and to those who successfully achieve the proper relation of the sexual and the spiritual (238). In more detail, Ciancio explicates "the sexual drama of Enoch Robinson's crippled mentality:" having grown up with a mother who kept the shades drawn between their house and the world, Enoch betrays an impotence that is figured in his lameness, evidenced by his panic in an encounter with a prostitute, and perpetuated by a return to the womb in a lonely room where figments of his imagination "shadow forth his fears" while he practices an art that paints women "in the ethereal rather than in the flesh" (998–99).

A feminist analysis by Rigsbee emphasizes Enoch's "intense need of the feminine and his inability to establish relationships with real women," which results from his being "so open to the power of the feminine" that he fears being drowned (236). Rigsbee points to "the suffering woman" in Enoch's painting as a "source of creative inspiration" whose "invisibility" reflects a sad fact of contemporary society (243).

Formalist critics have called attention to the story's use of repetitions (San Juan 144), imagery of "harvested grain" and rain (Papinchak, "Something" 5–6), authorial intrusions in the manner of an oral storyteller (Phillips, "Origins" 189–91; Ingram 158, 160–61), and symbolic settings (Ingram 184). Thurston comments on its prose style, which blends colloquial language with "the 'literary'" and "the Biblical poetic" (122–23). Mellard classifies it as one of the *Winesburg* tales having a "thematic" narrative form; that is, the story uses its central character to convey the *idea* of loneliness (1307). More fully than other tales, says Mellard, stories of this type illustrate the statement in "The Book of the Grotesque" that seizing upon a "truth" causes one to become a grotesque; for Enoch, that means, ironically, driving away the woman he does and does not want and clinging to a loneliness he deplores (1307, 1309). Wright classifies the story as one of a kind he calls "caustic pathos" which includes, in Enoch's narrative-within-the-narrative, an episode of exposure (235–36). Wright casts further light on Enoch's peculiar behavior by explaining that a feature common to many stories of the twenties is the replacement of clearly defined moral principles (characteristic of stories of an earlier period) with a vaguely understood but fiercely held intuitive sense of integrity, which sometimes results in "extreme egotism" and often in intense ambivalence combined with unwillingness to compromise (199, 133–34, 136–39). Wright notes that although the story is primarily narrated and contains only one scene, it still achieves "a strongly dramatic impact" and leaves the evaluation of the character to be inferred (293, 325, 335).

Some commentators have found specific flaws in the story. Thurston thinks that George Willard's "appearance as listener" obtrudes unnecessarily on "the role of the 'wise' author-narrator" (127). Phillips ("Origins" 191) and Wright (236) disagree with that judgment. Bridgman asserts that Anderson displays his carelessness when he writes of "dry shrivelled potato vines" in the same setting where there is "a drizzly wet October rain" (164; quoting *WO* 174). In fact, Anderson's agricultural detail is perfectly accurate: potato vines wither naturally in autumn in Ohio, and rain cannot restore the vines any more than it restores vitality to Enoch. The image of the vines works particularly well, moreover, because the senescence of the potato plant is accompanied by what might be deemed a kind of underground fruition. As Papinchak points out, the rain makes George Willard "glad" and is associated with his ripening potential (*Sherwood* 26).

Works Cited

Anderson, Margaret. 1969. *My Thirty Years' War: The Autobiography, Beginnings and Battles to 1930.* New York: Horizon Press.

Anderson, Sherwood. "The Story Writers." *Smart Set* 48 (January 1916):243–48.

———. 1919. *Winesburg, Ohio.* New York: B. W. Huebsch. Rpt. New York: Viking, 1960.

———. 1970. "To George Borrow." In *No Swank.* Mamaroneck, NY: Appel, 35–46.

Atlas, Marilyn Judith. "Sherwood Anderson and the Women of Winesburg."

In *Critical Essays on Sherwood Anderson*. Ed. David D. Anderson. Boston: G. K. Hall, 1981, 250–66.

Bridgman, Richard. 1966. *The Colloquial Style in America*. New York: Oxford University Press.

Ciancio, Ralph. "The Sweetness of the Twisted Apples: Unity of Vision in *Winesburg, Ohio*." *PMLA* 87 (1972):994–1006.

Curry, Martha Mulroy. 1975. *The "Writer's Book" by Sherwood Anderson: A Critical Edition*. Metuchen, NJ: Scarecrow Press.

Duffey, Bernard. 1954. *The Chicago Renaissance in American Letters: A Critical History*. East Lansing: Michigan State College Press.

Fagin, N. Bryllion. 1973. *The Phenomenon of Sherwood Anderson: A Study in American Life and Letters*. New York: Russell & Russell. Originally printed Baltimore: Rossi-Bryn, 1927.

Fertig, Martin J. "'A Great Deal of Wonder in Me': Inspiration and Transformation in *Winesburg, Ohio*." *Markham Review* 6 (1977):65–70.

Fussell, Edwin. "*Winesburg, Ohio*: Art and Isolation." *Modern Fiction Studies* 6 (1960):106–14. Rpt. In *Sherwood Anderson:* Winesburg, Ohio: *Text and Criticism*. Ed. John H. Ferres. New York: Viking, 1966, 383–95. Rpt. in *Achievement of Sherwood Anderson: Essays in Criticism*. Ed. Ray Lewis White. Chapel Hill: University of North Carolina Press, 1966, 104–13. Rpt. In *Sherwood Anderson: A Collection of Critical Essays*. Ed. Walter B. Rideout. Englewood Cliffs, NJ: Prentice-Hall, 1974, 39–48.

Gado, Frank. 1983. "Introduction." *The Teller's Tales*. New York: Union College Press, 1–20.

———, ed. 1983. *The Teller's Tales*. Signature Series. Schenectady, NY: Union College Press.

Gold, Herbert. "The Purity and Cunning of Sherwood Anderson." *Hudson Review* 10 (1957–58):548–57. Rpt. in *The Age of Happy Problems*. New York: Dial Press, 1962, 56–67. Rpt. in part in *Sherwood Anderson:* Winesburg, Ohio: *Text and Criticism*. Ed. John H. Ferres. New York: Viking, 1966, 396–404. Rpt. in *Critical Essays on Sherwood Anderson*. Ed. David D. Anderson. Boston: G. K. Hall, 1981, 138–45.

Ingram, Forrest L. 1971. *Representative Short Story Cycles of the Twentieth Century: Studies in a Literary Genre*. The Hague: Mouton.

Jones, Howard Mumford, and Walter B. Rideout, eds. 1953. *Letters of Sherwood Anderson*. Boston: Little, Brown.

Lorch, Thomas M. "The Choreographic Structure of *Winesburg, Ohio*.'" *College Language Association Journal* 12 (1968–69):56–65.

Mahoney, John J. "An Analysis of *Winesburg, Ohio.*" *Journal of Aesthetics and Art Criticism* 15 (1956):245–52.

Mellard, James M. "Narrative Forms in *Winesburg, Ohio.*" *PMLA* 83 (1968):1304–1312.

Murphy, George D. "The Theme of Sublimation in Anderson's *Winesburg, Ohio.*" *Modern Fiction Studies* 13 (1967):237–46.

Papinchak, Robert Allen. 1992. *Sherwood Anderson: A Study of the Short Fiction*. New York: Twayne.

——. "Something in the Elders: The Recurrent Imagery in *Winesburg, Ohio.*" *Winesburg Eagle* 9 (1983):1–7.

Phillips, William L. "How Sherwood Anderson Wrote *Winesburg, Ohio.*" *American Literature* 23 (1951):7–30. Rpt. in *Sherwood Anderson:* Winesburg, Ohio: *Text and Criticism*. Ed. John H. Ferres. New York: Viking, 1966, 263–86. Rpt. in *The Achievement of Sherwood Anderson: Essays in Criticism.* Ed. Ray Lewis White. Chapel Hill: University of North Carolina Press, 1966, 62–84. Rpt. in *The Merrill Studies in* Winesburg, Ohio. Comp. Ray Lewis White. Columbus, OH: Charles E. Merrill, 1971, 2–24. Rpt. in *Sherwood Anderson: A Collection of Critical Essays*. Ed. Walter B. Rideout. Englewood Cliffs, NJ: Prentice-Hall, 1974, 18–38.

——. "Sherwood Anderson's *Winesburg, Ohio:* Its Origins, Composition, Technique, and Reception." Ph.D. diss., University of Chicago, 1950.

Pickering, Samuel. "*Winesburg, Ohio:* A Portrait of the Artist as a Young Man." *Southern Quarterly* 16 (1977):27–38.

Rigsbee, Sally Adair. "The Feminine in *Winesburg, Ohio.*" *Studies in American Fiction* 9 (1981):233–44.

San Juan, Epifanio, Jr. "Vision and Reality: A Reconsideration of Sherwood Anderson's *Winesburg, Ohio.*" *American Literature* 35 (1963):137–55. Rpt. in part in *Sherwood Anderson:* Winesburg, Ohio: *Text and Criticism.* Ed. John H. Ferres. New York: Viking, 1966, 468–81.

Stouck, David. 1990. "Anderson's Expressionist Art." In *New Essays on Winesburg, Ohio*. Ed. John W. Crowley. Cambridge: Cambridge University Press, 27–51.

——. "*Winesburg, Ohio* and the Failure of Art." *Twentieth Century Literature* 15 (1969):145–51.

Sutton, William A. 1967. *Exit to Elsinore*. Muncie, IN: Ball State University Press.

——. 1972. *The Road to Winesburg: A Mosaic of the Imaginative Life of Sherwood Anderson*. Metuchen, NJ: Scarecrow Press.

Thurston, Jarvis. "Anderson and 'Winesburg': Mysticism and Craft." *Accent* 16 (1956):107–128. Rpt. in part in *Sherwood Anderson:* Winesburg, Ohio: *Text and Criticism*. Ed. John H. Ferres. New York: Viking, 1966, 331–44.

Townsend, Kim. 1987. *Sherwood Anderson*. Boston: Houghton Mifflin.

Way, Brian. 1971. "Sherwood Anderson." In *The American Novel and the Nineteen Twenties*. Eds. Malcolm Bradbury and David Palmer. Stratford-upon-Avon Studies 13. London: Edward Arnold, 107–126.

White, Ray Lewis. "*Winesburg, Ohio:* The Story Titles." *Winesburg Eagle* 10, 1 (November 1984):6–7.

———. "*Winesburg, Ohio:* The Table of Contents." *Notes on Modern American Literature* 8 (1984):Item 8.

Williams, Kenny J. 1988. *A Storyteller and a City: Sherwood Anderson's Chicago*. De Kalb: Northern Illinois University Press.

Winther, S. K. "The Aura of Loneliness in Sherwood Anderson." *Modern Fiction Studies* 5 (1959–60):145–52.

Wright, Austin McGiffert. 1961. *The American Short Story in the Twenties*. Chicago: University of Chicago Press.

An Awakening

Circumstances of Composition

The original manuscript title of this story was "George Willard's Awakening" (White "Story Titles" 6).

As Anderson considered various arrangements of the tales for collection into the volume *Winesburg, Ohio,* he first planned to place this story as fifth from the end of the volume, before "Drink," "Death," "Sophistication," and "Departure"; but a revised table of contents places it next to last, *after* "Sophistication" and just before "Departure"—a change that would dramatically alter the meaning of the cycle (White "Table"). Subsequent revisions return "An Awakening" to an earlier position and thus restore the implications that George Willard's relations with women progress from youthful folly and a humiliating lesson in "An Awakening" to some genuine and rewarding understanding in "Sophistication."

Sources and Influences

No source has been suggested for the figure of Belle Carpenter, though some critics surmise that George Willard's feelings are derived from Anderson's personal experiences with women. Townsend, for example, comments that the author "never wholly freed himself" from his awe of women or from his uncertainty about whether "he was man enough" to subdue a woman (116). But one hardly needs to probe Anderson's psychology to uncover the feelings he attributes to George in the face of the "belle": every man knows them first-hand.

Zlotnick detects a resemblance between this story and James Joyce's "Araby"; without claiming an influence, she notes in both stories the ironic treatment of self-aggrandizing adolescent "flights of fancy" and the protagonists' discovery of "the crass nature of the things to which they have themselves attributed spiritual meaning" (34–35).

Publication History

"An Awakening" was first published in December of 1918 in Margaret Anderson's *Little Review* (5:13–21). It was the third of the *Winesburg* stories printed in that magazine, but Anderson had printed numerous other articles and stories there, beginning with the very first issue.

It was printed again in *Winesburg, Ohio* in 1919, and in Edward J. O'Brien's *The Best Short Stories of 1919* (24–33).

Relation to Other Works

This story plays an important role in the cycle, which partakes of the genre of the bildungsroman (Fussell 108). That is, it details a significant episode in George Willard's maturation, showing him reaching beyond the usual circumference of his life but still boyishly foolish (Fussell 113). It is the second of three stories that dramatize George's growth in relationships with women, standing between "Nobody Knows," with his first, nervous sexual conquest, and "Sophistication," with his achievement of mature, satisfying communication; in "An Awakening" he is no longer timid and afraid, as he was in "Nobody Knows," but he has no more sympathetic understanding of Belle Carpenter than he had of Louise Trunnion; he actually "hears" a voice that he had listened for at the end of the earlier story, but "his intense self-centeredness about his inspiration" renders it somewhat ridiculous; and his humiliating defeat here stands in contrast to his "triumph" in "Sophistication," where voices that "whisper a message concerning the limitations of life" enable him to achieve "self-awareness but not self-centeredness" and a "feeling of oneness" with Helen White and with the people of Winesburg (Rideout 29–30).

The imaginary community that George creates in "An Awakening" as he fantasizes about the day laborers' houses is connected both with the more realistic community he recalls in "Sophistication" and the figures that appear before the old writer in "The Book of the Grotesque," which presumably resemble the dream-figures George himself may one day create (Ingram 171). But, like "Loneliness," this story presents a rough shattering of a dream world; as Enoch Robinson's feelings of self-importance vanish when a woman comes into his room, so George's sense of masculine largeness crumbles when he is cast aside by a more powerful man, and the setting that had seemed to him so radiantly vital and rank at last appears "utterly squalid and commonplace" (Ingram 177, quoting *WO* 189).

The lesson in reality that Ed Handby physically delivers to George in this story reinforces the meaning of Kate Swift's advice in "The Teacher": enamored of his own words and trusting Belle's words, George has forgotten to be attentive to that deeper level of "what people are thinking" (De Jovine 60). The warning against dreams that Wash Williams offered George, in "Respectability," after seeing him kissing Belle Carpenter, also is revealed at last to be founded on real insight (Ingram 195).

This is one of several stories in "the last third of the collection" that initiate George into suffering. Ed Handby hurls him to the ground repeatedly in this tale, Elmer Cowley knocks him semiconscious in the next ("Queer"), Tom Foster's "effort to understand and experience suffering" moves him deeply in "Drink," and he loses his mother in "Death" (Rigsbee 240).

Several critics have commented on the importance of the bodily gestures in the story and their relations to the themes of the cycle. Maresca remarks that Ed Handby's use of his fists to vent his frustrations is linked with the fists of Belle Carpenter, of Elizabeth Willard (in "Mother"), and of Curtis Hartman (in "The Strength of God") (280; similarly, Reid, 141). Way adds that in both "An Awakening" and "Queer" violence results from "inarticulateness," as it does in such characters as Melville's Billy Budd and Faulkner's Joe Christmas (111).

In the play *Winesburg,* Belle Carpenter's character and circumstances are considerably altered; made pregnant in a liaison with Banker White, she consults a doctor to request an abortion but ends by having the child.

Rideout points out the relationship between George's desire for order, expressed in both cosmic and military terms, and Anderson's desire for "universal order" in *Marching Men* (1917) and *Mid-American Chants* (1918), though in this story the notion is made to seem boyish (29).

A central episode in the late novel *Beyond Desire* (1932) resembles this tale. In that book, Red Oliver's yearnings for sex and manhood set him up to be used by a woman less naïve than he; he, too, winds up rejected, confused, humiliated. The psychological entanglements in the novel are more complex and have more sinister, more permanent results than those in the story; Red Oliver literally throws his life away in a labor uprising and Ethel Long figuratively throws hers away in a loveless marriage, whereas George simply grows up. Belle Carpenter's ambivalent feelings of hostility and attraction to domineering men, however, and Ed Handby's harsh methods of communicating his emotions do not bode well for their union; this side of the story, like the novel, contains dark social implications as it shows abusive parents passing on their perversities to their children.

Critical Studies

There are no studies devoted to this story alone, and there is no serious disagreement about its interpretation.

The primary subject of critical attention to the story has been its treatment of George Willard's maturation, most of which is covered above under "Relation to Other Works." Much of that commentary is consistent with Bluefarb's summary statement that the main episode of the story "paradoxically brings George to the beginnings of manhood" by "convincing him that he is still a boy with a boy's limitations" (53). A feminist commentator similarly concludes that the defeat of George's "grandiose egocentricity" and of his plan to assert "sexual mastery over a potent and challenging woman" is just what he needs to deepen his sensitivity (Rigsbee 240).

A few critics, however, suggest that some qualification of the emphasis on George's immaturity is warranted. Fussell remarks that George's "inchoate impulses" toward order, profound words, and detachment from life are at least "more or less in the right direction" (113). Fertig points out the ambiguity in a key passage of the story, where George says "words without meaning. . . . because they were brave words, full of meaning" (*WO* 185); somehow, it seems, his fervor is both "a delusion" and "a valid inspiration" (68). Pickering's highly romanticized interpretation that George's detached fantasy is the ideal creative state and that his only error is in trying "to objectify his vague feelings" is probably too extreme (33–34).

The sexual element of the story has stimulated only brief comment. Murphy remarks that Art Wilson, who brags about whores in the pool room, is one of the "sensualists" of Winesburg (239). Colquitt states that the story "reveals that women are capable of using men sexually as well" (91). McDonald notes that while "spiritual communion" is Anderson's ideal, this story reveals "a grudging admiration for Ed Handby's aggressive break from his own isolation" and for the "elementary communion" he achieves with Belle Carpenter (240).

Unexplored by critics are the complexities of Belle Carpenter's psychology—her hatred of her father for "his brutal treatment of her mother" (*WO* 180), her desire to maintain control in her relationships, and especially her fear of and attraction to Ed Handby's rude male power. The grotesque realism of her portrait merits more attention. So does the surprising blend of the pathetic, the comic, and the horrific in the portrayal of a bartender whose wooing takes the form of threats to break bones. San Juan defends Anderson against Trilling's charge that "his fiction lacks 'the stuff of actuality'" by pointing to Belle Carpenter's "dark skin, gray eyes, and thick lips" (146–47); he might better have pointed to the power struggles in her love life.

A Marxist interpretation of the story argues that George's momentary feeling of sublimity is "based in an Oedipal structure" that is "wholly masculine" and that depends "on repression of the material signs of economic difference" in the laborers' cheap houses (Yingling 119–20). That George's "heightened interiority is no genuine awakening but a fictional moment framing a transitive desire" becomes in this interpretation an indication that the "construction of the artist's solitary access to universal reality is determined within an ideological script it is designed to conceal" (121–122).

Formalist critics have commented on the story in a variety of ways. Tanner takes a swipe at Anderson by asserting that George's adolescent outpourings of words typify Anderson's writing, its "fragmentary sensations and inchoate emotions" (214–15). But other critics acknowledge the art. An important corrective to Tanner's view is offered by Mellard, who points out that the tale is a narrative of an initiation experience and that it contains "parody elements of the romantic quest, with its hero's battle, defeat, and 'rebirth'" (1306). Far more than most commentators have acknowledged, "An Awakening" is simply funny. Wright classifies the tale as a caustic romance; that is, while readers sympathize with the protagonist's youth and "idealism," they also understand the events more clearly than he does and observe his "vanity" and "ignorance" (210–11). Wright admires the technique whereby the story presents complex thought with dramatic effect, using the device of a divided mind and "explicit summaries and direct and indirect quotations" while leaving the reader to infer the irony that George's new romantic egotism, which he considers "an 'awakening' of his spirit," is in fact only "a typically adolescent upwelling of sexual anticipation and vanity," while his "real awakening does not come until later when he discovers that he is indeed being used, that he is not too big to be thrust aside like a child by Ed Handby" (404–405, 349–50). Wright points out "the change in the words George mutters" when alone ("Death," "night, the sea, fear, loveliness") and later when he holds Belle in his arms ("lust and night and women") (405, quoting *WO* 185, 188). This splendid comic stroke is followed, hilariously, by a deadpan statement: "George did not understand what happened to him that night on the hillside" (*WO* 188).

Works Cited

Anderson, Sherwood. 1919. *Winesburg, Ohio*. New York: B. W. Huebsch. Rpt. New York: Viking, 1960.

Bluefarb, Sam. 1972. "George Willard: Death and Resurrection." In *The Escape Motif in the American Novel: Mark Twain to Richard Wright*. Columbus: Ohio State University Press, 42–58.

Colquitt, Clare. "Motherlove in Two Narratives of Community: *Winesburg, Ohio* and *The Country of the Pointed Firs*." In *New Essays on* Winesburg, Ohio. Ed. John W. Crowley. Cambridge and New York: Cambridge University Press, 1990, 73–97.

De Jovine, F. Anthony. 1971. *The Young Hero in American Fiction: A Motif for Teaching Literature*. New York: Appleton-Century Crofts.

Fertig, Martin J. "'A Great Deal of Wonder in Me': Inspiration and Transformation in *Winesburg, Ohio*." *Markham Review* 6 (1977):65–70.

Fussell, Edwin. "*Winesburg, Ohio:* Art and Isolation." *Modern Fiction Studies* 6 (1960):106–14. Rpt. in *Sherwood Anderson:* Winesburg, Ohio: *Text and Criticism*. Ed. John H. Ferres. New York: Viking, 1966, 383–95. Rpt. in *Achievement of Sherwood Anderson: Essays in Criticism*. Ed. Ray Lewis White. Chapel Hill: University of North Carolina Press, 1966, 104–113. Rpt. in *Sherwood Anderson: A Collection of Critical Essays*. Ed. Walter B. Rideout. Englewood Cliffs, NJ: Prentice-Hall, 1974, 39–48.

Ingram, Forrest L. 1971. *Representative Short Story Cycles of the Twentieth Century: Studies in a Literary Genre*. The Hague: Mouton.

Maresca, Carol J. "Gestures as Meaning in Sherwood Anderson's *Winesburg, Ohio*." *College Language Association Journal* 9 (1966):279–83.

Mellard, James M. "Narrative Forms in *Winesburg, Ohio*." *PMLA* 83 (1968):1304–1312.

McDonald, Walter R. "*Winesburg, Ohio:* Tales of Isolation." *University Review Kansas City* 35 (1969):237–40.

Murphy, George D. "The Theme of Sublimation in Anderson's *Winesburg, Ohio*." *Modern Fiction Studies* 13 (1967):237–46.

O'Brien, Edward J., ed. 1920. *The Best Short Stories of 1919*, 24–33.

Phillips, William L. "How Sherwood Anderson wrote *Winesburg, Ohio*." *American Literature* 23 (1951):7–30. Rpt. in *Sherwood Anderson:* Winesburg, Ohio: *Text and Criticism*. Ed. John H. Ferres. New York: Viking, 1966, 263–86. Rpt. in *The Achievement of Sherwood Anderson: Essays in Criticism*. Ed. Ray Lewis White. Chapel Hill: University of North Carolina

Press, 1966, 62–84. Rpt. in *The Merrill Studies in* Winesburg, Ohio. Comp. Ray Lewis White. Columbus, OH: Charles E. Merrill, 1971, 2–24. Rpt. in *Sherwood Anderson: A Collection of Critical Essays*. Ed. Walter B. Rideout. Englewood Cliffs, NJ: Prentice-Hall, 1974, 18–38.

Pickering, Samuel. "*Winesburg, Ohio:* A Portrait of the Artist as a Young Man." *Southern Quarterly* 16 (1977):27–38.

Reid, Randall. *The Fiction of Nathanael West: No Redeemer, No Promised Land*. Chicago: University of Chicago Press, 1967.

Rideout, Walter B. "The Simplicity of *Winesburg, Ohio.*" *Shenandoah* 13 (1962):20–31. Rpt. in *Sherwood Anderson:* Winesburg, Ohio: *Text and Criticism*. Ed. John H. Ferres. New York: Viking, 1966, 287–300. Rpt. in *Critical Essays on Sherwood Anderson*. Ed. David D. Anderson. Boston: G. K. Hall, 1981, 146–54.

Rigsbee, Sally Adair. "The Feminine in *Winesburg, Ohio.*" *Studies in American Fiction* 9 (1981):233–44.

Tanner, Tony. 1965. "Sherwood Anderson's Little Things." *The Reign of Wonder: Naïvety and Reality in American Literature*. Cambridge: Cambridge University Press, 205–27.

Townsend, Kim. 1987. *Sherwood Anderson*. Boston: Houghton Mifflin.

Way, Brian. "Sherwood Anderson." In *The American Novel and the Nineteen Twenties*. Malcolm Bradbury and David Palmer (Eds.) Stratford-upon-Avon Studies 13. London: Edward Arnold, 1971, 107–126.

White, Ray Lewis. "*Winesburg, Ohio:* The Story Titles." *Winesburg Eagle* 10, 1 (November 1984):6–7.

———. "*Winesburg, Ohio:* The Table of Contents." *Notes on Modern American Literature* 8 (1984):Item 8.

Wright, Austin McGiffert. 1961. *The American Short Story in the Twenties*. Chicago: University of Chicago Press.

Yingling, Thomas. 1990. "*Winesburg, Ohio* and the End of Collective Experience." In *New Essays on* Winesburg, Ohio. Ed. John W. Crowley. Cambridge and New York: Cambridge University Press, 99–128.

Zlotnick, Joan. "Of Dubliners and Ohioans: A Comparative Study of Two Works." *Ball State University Forum* 17 (1976):33–36.

"Queer"

Circumstances of Composition

"Queer" must have been among the earliest of the *Winesburg* stories to be written. In a letter dated January 4, 1916, Anderson wrote to H. L. Mencken expressing regret that *Smart Set* had rejected the story and that the magazine's readers were so "limited in their outlook" (Modlin, *Letters* 3). This letter indicates that "Queer" must have been composed no later than early December of 1915. "The Book of the Grotesque" and "Hands" were the first *Winesburg* tales to be published, in February and March of 1916, respectively. "Queer" must have been written at about the same time.

Sources and Influences

"If anything is evident about Anderson's biography it is the fact that he never 'belonged.' If there is anything that we have to be grateful for, it is the fact that he wanted to, even if he had to reshape himself and the world in order to achieve it," Norman Holmes Pearson wrote in a 1948 essay (53–54). His remarks contain a fundamental truth about Anderson and about the characters in *Winesburg, Ohio,* who long to be part of society yet dread being like the society they see.

Sutton suggests the possibility that the model for Elmer Cowley may have been Anderson's brother Earl, whose "tortured life" was spent yearning for affection, which he felt was denied him (*Road* 442). In his *Memoirs,* though, Anderson describes his own similar yearnings: "Oh how I wanted the admiration and affection of people. I hungered and thirsted for admiration and affection"; moreover, he says, this is the universal longing, "the oldest and strongest hunger in the world" (White, *Memoirs* 15). At some level, then, Elmer Cowley is Anderson's portrait of Everyman. As Hoffman remarks, "the introduction of psychoanalytic theory" in the early years of the century brought about "a renewed interest in neurotics," who tended to be "regarded as a mirror of the world" (112–13).

Certainly Anderson's embarrassment about his own father's lack of worldly success entered into Elmer's feelings about Ebenezer Cowley. Elmer's suffering about clothes—his father's ruined coat in contrast to George Willard's new coat—was something the impoverished young Sherwood Anderson had known firsthand (see, for example, White, *Memoirs* 520).

Publication History

"Queer" was first published in the December 1916 issue of *Seven Arts* (1:97–108). It had earlier been rejected by *Smart Set* (see "Circumstances of Composition"). It was next published in *Winesburg, Ohio* (1919).

There has been a minor confusion about the submission of this story and "The Untold Lie" to *Seven Arts* that I believe is the result of a misleading sentence in Waldo Frank's 1948 essay "Sherwood Anderson: A Personal Note." Frank reports that he "first heard of Sherwood, in late 1915" when Edna Kenton returned to New York from Chicago and told him that Anderson might be a worthy contributor to the new magazine they were preparing to launch; after he wrote to Anderson, says Frank, "I got a batch of cheap copy paper scrawled in a long gangling script, each word of which looked like a lean hound in full chase across the page. I read *The Untold Lie* and wrote back to Anderson how luminous and exciting I found it" (39–40). But this cannot have been the first story Anderson submitted to *Seven Arts,* as most scholars have assumed (for example, David Anderson, "SA & the Seven Arts" 21). In a letter dated November 14, 1916, Anderson tells Frank that he has written "a series of intensive studies of people of my home town, Clyde, Ohio" and that "[t]he story called 'Queer' you are using in December is one of them"; he goes on to suggest that he could send the rest of them to Frank for his consideration (Jones-Rideout, *Letters* 4). That letter opens brightly, "I sent you a little thing the other day that I believe you will like." Then, in another letter, dated November 20, 1916, Anderson thanks Frank "for the check and for liking the story of the farm hands," which, he confides, he wrote only "last week" (Curry, *Writer's* 117–18n). Those two letters indicate plainly that "Queer" was accepted for publication before Frank read "The Untold Lie," which is probably the "little thing" Anderson mentions in the letter of November 14. This chain of events makes sense of the fact that "Queer" was published in the second issue of *Seven Arts* and "The Untold Lie" in the third.

The check Anderson received for "Queer" was the first money he received for his *Winesburg* stories; the magazines where he had published others previously, *Masses* and *Little Review,* did not pay contributors. The check was probably for $40, since in a letter of March, 1917, Anderson is complaining to Frank about their "taking the cream [of his stories] at $40 per" (Jones-Rideout, *Letters* 9). It might have been for less, though, for Anderson (who did sometimes bend facts) reports in his *Memoirs* that he received a total of only $85 for all the Winesburg tales (Rosenfeld 288).

Relation to Other Works

Walter Allen calls "Queer" the "archetypal" *Winesburg* story (78). In that judgment, he is agreeing with Irving Howe, who stated that the story presents the "most abstract version" of the book's theme: "Elmer Cowley has no specific deformity: he is the grotesque as such" (107, 105). It is no wonder, then, that commentators have found in Elmer Cowley's story numerous parallels with the other tales in the cycle. Chief among the characteristics he shares with other characters is his loneliness, his painful desire for social relationships and for recognition on his own terms (Wright 58, 126). Like many others, he is a victim of "conditions over which he had no control" (Taylor 30). He "cannot communicate" effectively (Gochberg 44; similarly, Mahoney 251–52), and his "manual gestures," like those of Wing Biddlebaum (in "Hands") and Joe Welling (in "A Man of Ideas"), indicate the emotions surging inside him (Ingram 190–91). Seeking to be understood, he approaches George Willard, as do the central characters of "Hands," "The Philosopher," "Nobody Knows," "Respectability," "The Teacher," "Loneliness," and "Drink." Like Seth Richmond (of "The Thinker"), Elmer mistakenly thinks that George Willard "belongs" to the town and is a contented embodiment of its spirit (Ingram 166; similarly, Lorch 63 and Voss 187). "Ironically, Elmer himself . . . comes closer than any other character in the book to typifying Winesburg grotesquerie" (Ingram 197). Like so many of the others, Elmer longs to escape the town that seems to stifle him (Baker 576; Ingram 169). And as his story closes, he is heading to the city on a train, as George will be at the end of the book.

Elmer realizes, however, "what most of the other grotesques have failed to perceive: George Willard does not understand them" (D. Anderson, *Sherwood Anderson* 48). Mook's warning to the cows "that Elmer is crazy" echoes George's earlier conclusion that Winesburg had gone insane after the minister and the teacher incoherently pour out their thoughts to him (Ward 45). Of course, in this story, "George does not get an opportunity to understand" (Stouck 534). George's eager willingness to understand here in fact marks his growing sensitivity to other people. But Elmer delivers a beating and sends George sprawling, in an echo of the story just before it, "An Awakening"; in both stories, "inarticulateness produces physical violence" (Way 111).

Half-witted characters appear in two *Winesburg* stories, "Hands" and "Queer." A half-witted boy charges Adolph Myers with sexual perversity in the former story, and Mook calls Elmer Cowley crazy in the latter. In both instances, ironically, the judgment masks and denies an evident likeness between accused and accuser: the boy's allegations spring from his own perverse imaginings, and Mook's conclusion is likewise rendered absurd by his own mental incompetence.

The story is not situated in the volume in strict chronological sequence. Its action is set in November; the stories before and after it are both set in October (Ingram 167).

The structure of "Queer," according to Howe, typifies "the choreography of *Winesburg*," where again and again a series of deformed figures "dances, with angular indirection and muted pathos, toward a central figure who seems to them young, fresh, and radiant," briefly drawing near him and at last retreating "painfully" and returning to the original posture (105–106).

Several of Anderson's later works repeat elements of "Queer." Notably, "The Egg" again uses the situation of the unhappy, unsuccessful farmer come to town and turned unhappy, unsuccessful shopkeeper; in both stories, a son participates in the family misery as he observes a worried father who cannot fully understand how his own strangeness interferes with his trade. The son in "The Egg," however, having achieved over time a philosophical distance from the situation, narrates that tale, whereas Elmer Cowley is both frantically, immediately embroiled and narrated about; the difference of perspective renders the stories quite different in effect.

Tar (1926) contains a character named Elmer Cowley, older than Tar and "stout but dumb"; the little boy thinks it would be nice to have Elmer do his fighting for him, but his older brother refuses Elmer's overtures of friendship and treats him with contempt (136–37). In *Tar,* too, there is "a half witted fellow" who looks at a field where there is a litter of pigs and laughs; "Life may be a comedy half witted people understand," thinks Tar (114). The passage resembles that in "Queer" where Elmer Cowley's monologue to the half-witted Mook is tinged with wistful regret that his life lacks such thoughtless simplicity.

Critical Studies

Evaluation of "Queer" has varied widely. Way terms it "rather weak" (111), while Allen considers it "the simplest and perhaps the most poignant story in the book, if only because of the very smallness of Elmer's ambitions" (79). Those differing evaluations probably depend on the extent to which readers are able to sympathize with the story's protagonist. Ciancio calls Elmer Cowley "an outright psychotic" (995; similarly, Bowden 114), whereas Wright sees isolation from society as typical of characters in stories of the twenties and Elmer Cowley's "desperate yearning for acceptance" as only the "most extreme" form of that loneliness (48, 58). Oddly enough, these differences of opinion have not been debated. Probably, though, one should be suspicious of a critical position that accepts a half-witted character's verdict that the protagonist is crazy.

There are no extended analyses of "Queer." A Marxist interpretation argues that it evidences "the fetishization of the commodity" in an economic system that subjects and alienates laborers (Yingling 112). But most criticism of the story appears in discussions of the story's relationships to the rest of *Winesburg, Ohio.* (See "Relations" above.)

Possibly the most useful comments about the story as a separate entity are those of formalist critics Mellard and Wright. Mellard classifies "Queer" as one of six "emblematic" narratives in *Winesburg* because it portrays a character type that represents an "archetypal" figure indicated in its title (1309–10). As in other stories of this kind, "past events and actions are shown in order to *explain*" the character, and though Elmer is seen struggling to escape his sense of entrapment, the structure of the story is ironic and the characterization relatively static because everything he does "solidifies the growing impression of [his] queerness"; at last he "lapses into a phrase that joins him unquestionably with the half-witted Mook and 'queer' old Ebenezer Cowley" (1310–12). (For a more positive interpretation of the phrase "I'll be washed . . . " as indicative of an impulse to order, see San Juan 144.)

Wright classifies "Queer" as a story of caustic pathos with an episode of suffering because on the one hand, Elmer causes his own unhappiness by drawing such a "sharp distinction . . . between normality and queerness" and the reader recoils from his perverse behavior, yet on the other hand, his suffering exceeds what he deserves (389, 136, 232–34). There is even a measure of courage in his stubborn determination to overcome his frustration (133). And, one might add, he displays integrity when he returns the cash he has stolen; he might have convinced himself he had a right to it, since he is a partner in the firm Cowley & Son.

"[T]he narrator allows Elmer Cowley to bring judgment on himself by his deeds—he protests loudly that he will not be queer, but continues to act like a lunatic" (Ingram 159). The subtlety of the story's tone springs from the careful blending of that exposure with the revelation of Elmer's own slow thoughts and his irrational but all-too-human anxiety that he is the only one who is visited by "unhappiness, . . . vague hungers and secret unnameable desires" (*WO* 194).

Works Cited

Allen, Walter. 1964. *The Modern Novel in Britain and the United States.* New York: Dutton.

Anderson, David. 1967. *Sherwood Anderson: An Introduction and Interpretation.* New York: Holt, Rinehart.

———. "Sherwood Anderson and *The Seven Arts.*" *Newsletter of the Society for the Study of Midwestern Literature* 10 (1980):18–30.

Anderson, Sherwood. 1919. *Winesburg, Ohio*. New York: B. W. Huebsch. Rpt. New York: Viking, 1960.1

———. 926. *Tar: A Midwest Childhood*. New York: Boni & Liveright. Rpt. in *Tar: A Midwest Childhood: A Critical Text*. Ed. Ray Lewis White. Cleveland: Press of Case Western Reserve University, 1969.

Baker, Carlos. "Sherwood Anderson's Winesburg: A Reprise." *The Virginia Quarterly Review* 48 (1972):568–79.

Bowden, Edwin T. 1961. *The Dungeon of the Heart: Human Isolation and the American Novel*. New York: Macmillan, 114–24.

Ciancio, Ralph. "The Sweetness of the Twisted Apples: Unity of Vision in *Winesburg, Ohio*." *PMLA* 87 (1972):994–1006.

Curry, Martha Mulroy. 1975. *The "Writer's Book" by Sherwood Anderson: A Critical Edition*. Metuchen, NJ: Scarecrow Press.

Frank, Waldo. "Sherwood Anderson: A Personal Note." *Newberry Library Bulletin* 2, no. 2 (December 1948):39–43.

Gochberg, Donald. 1971. "Stagnation and Growth: The Emergence of George Willard." In *Merrill Studies in* Winesburg, Ohio. Ed. Ray Lewis White. Columbus: Charles E. Merrill, 42–48. Originally published in *Expression* 4 (University of Maryland) (Winter 1960):29–35.

Hoffman, Frederick J. 1957. *Freudianism and the Literary Mind*. Rev. ed. Baton Rouge: Louisiana State University Press. Rpt. in *Sherwood Anderson:* Winesburg, Ohio: *Text and Criticism*. Ed. John H. Ferres. New York: Viking, 1966, 309–20. Rpt. in *The Achievement of Sherwood Anderson: Essays in Criticism*. Ed. Ray Lewis White. Chapel Hill: University of North Carolina Press, 1966, 174–92.

Howe, Irving. 1951. *Sherwood Anderson*. New York: William Sloane.

Ingram, Forrest L. 1971. *Representative Short Story Cycles of the Twentieth Century: Studies in a Literary Genre*. The Hague: Mouton.

Jones, Howard Mumford, and Walter B. Rideout, eds. 1953. *Letters of Sherwood Anderson*. Boston: Little, Brown.

Lorch, Thomas M. "The Choreographic Structure of *Winesburg, Ohio*." *College Language Association Journal* 12 (1968–69):56–65.

Mahoney, John J. "An Analysis of *Winesburg, Ohio*." *Journal of Aesthetics and Art Criticism* 15 (1956):245–52.

Mellard, James M. "Narrative Forms in *Winesburg, Ohio*." *PMLA* 83 (1968):1304–1312.

Modlin, Charles E., ed. 1984. *Sherwood Anderson: Selected Letters*. Knoxville: University of Tennessee Press.

Pearson, Norman Holmes. "Anderson and the New Puritanism." *Newberry Library Bulletin.* Second Series 2, no. 2 (December 1948):52–63. Rpt. in *Critical Essays on Sherwood Anderson.* Ed. David D. Anderson. Boston: G. K. Hall, 1981, 102–110.

Phillips, William L. "How Sherwood Anderson Wrote *Winesburg, Ohio.*" *American Literature* 23 (1951):7–30. Rpt. in *Sherwood Anderson:* Winesburg, Ohio: *Text and Criticism.* Ed. John H. Ferres. New York: Viking, 1966, 263–86. Rpt. in *The Achievement of Sherwood Anderson: Essays in Criticism.* Ed. Ray Lewis White. Chapel Hill: University of North Carolina Press, 1966, 62–84. Rpt. in *The Merrill Studies in* Winesburg, Ohio. Comp. Ray Lewis White. Columbus, OH: Charles E. Merrill, 1971, 2–24. Rpt. in *Sherwood Anderson: A Collection of Critical Essays.* Ed. Walter B. Rideout. Englewood Cliffs, NJ: Prentice-Hall, 1974, 18–38.

Rosenfeld, Paul, ed. 1942. *Sherwood Anderson's Memoirs.* New York: Harcourt, Brace.

San Juan, Epifanio, Jr. "Vision and Reality: A Reconsideration of Sherwood Anderson's *Winesburg, Ohio.*" *American Literature* 35 (1963):137–55. Rpt. in part in *Sherwood Anderson:* Winesburg, Ohio: *Text and Criticism.* Ed. John H. Ferres. New York: Viking, 1966, 468–81.

Stouck, David. "*Winesburg, Ohio* as a Dance of Death." *American Literature* 48 (1977):525–42. Rpt. in *Critical Essays on Sherwood Anderson.* Ed. David D. Anderson. Boston: G. K. Hall, 1981, 181–95.

Sutton, William A. 1972. *The Road to Winesburg: A Mosaic of the Imaginative Life of Sherwood Anderson.* Metuchen, NJ: Scarecrow Press.

Taylor, Welford Dunaway. 1977. *Sherwood Anderson.* New York: Frederick Ungar.

Voss, Arthur. 1973. *The American Short Story: A Critical Survey.* Norman: University of Oklahoma Press.

Ward, J. A. 1985. "*Winesburg, Ohio:* Habitual Silence and the Roaring of Voices." *American Silences: The Realism of James Agee, Walker Evans, and Edward Hopper.* Baton Rouge: Louisiana State University Press, 35–50.

Way, Brian. 1971. "Sherwood Anderson." In *The American Novel and the Nineteen Twenties.* Malcolm Bradbury and David Palmer (Eds.). Stratford-upon-Avon Studies 13. London: Edward Arnold, 107–126.

White, Ray Lewis, ed. 1969. *Sherwood Anderson's Memoirs: A Critical Edition.* Chapel Hill: University of North Carolina Press.

Wright, Austin McGiffert. 1961. *The American Short Story in the Twenties.* Chicago: University of Chicago Press.

Yingling, Thomas. 1990. "*Winesburg, Ohio* and the End of Collective Experience." In *New Essays on* Winesburg, Ohio. Ed. John W. Crowley. Cambridge and New York: Cambridge University Press, 99–128.

The Untold Lie

Circumstances of Composition

Anderson wrote "The Untold Lie" in early November 1916. The story can be dated fairly precisely by a letter of November 20 in which he thanks Waldo Frank, editor of the magazine *Seven Arts,* "for liking the story of the farm hands"; "I wrote the story last week," Anderson says (Curry, *Writer's* 117–18n). At that time, the author had completed fifteen of the stories that were to make up *Winesburg, Ohio* and had published four of them; another one, "Queer," had been accepted for publication in the December issue of *Seven Arts* (Jones-Rideout, *Letters* 4). Although there is no reason to question Anderson's statement that he had written the story in the week before he mailed it off, one can see that he had been toying with the idea of the story before that. A letter of October 24, 1916, to Marietta D. Finley sketches out a preliminary scene:

> Here before me is a long stretch of fields and in the distance a town. . . . Across the fields tramps a man in boots that are heavy with mud. He has a beard and wears an overcoat that is torn at the pockets. He is going to town to buy meat and has $3. Suddenly an impulse comes to him. He begins to run. Tears come into his eyes and he runs harder and harder. He is fifty years old and has been married thirty years. He is a farm hand. He has made up his mind to desert his wife and family and run away. He runs so hard across the field because he wants to get into town and board the train before his courage fails. (Sutton, *Letters* 6)

The surviving manuscript of the story is written on print paper of the kind used for writing advertisements; Anderson may have written it either in his office or on a trip to visit clients, as Phillips suggests ("How" 12). Phillips's surmise that the story was written before or during the spring of 1916 (27) is mistaken, however, for the reasons given above. His conclusion that the manuscript represents an original version that was subsequently revised for the magazine and then returned to for the volume *Winesburg, Ohio* (27–28) is, for the same reasons, doubtful. (See also "Publication History.")

The autobiographical *Tar* (1926) contains a brief reference to the composition of "The Untold Lie" (xiii).

Sources and Influences

The germ of this story was provided by the simplest of experiences. Anderson wrote to his son John in 1936, "I remember once being on a train in a day coach and seeing a man run across a field. The gesture stayed with me and resulted years afterward in a story called 'The Untold Lie'" (Sutton, *Road* 441). That image apparently combined in his mind with his own confused desires to run from the life he was living, something that in fact he did do in 1912, when he walked out of his office and disappeared, in his much-discussed breakdown.

The biographical fact that most obviously influenced the story, however, is the ambivalence Anderson felt about marriage. He was guilt-ridden about leaving his wife, Cornelia, and their three children. Yet he had felt trapped by the demands of domestic life in a household with small children. His November 20 letter to Waldo Frank (mentioned in "Circumstances of Composition" above) suggests how much the discomfitures of Anderson's personal life contributed to "The Untold Lie": just after thanking the editor for liking his story, Anderson remarks sardonically, "As a delightful old reprobate in my home town used to say, 'My life is an open ditch'" (Curry, *Writer's* 118n). Anderson thus aligns himself with the character Windpeter Winters as well as with the antinomies represented by Ray Pearson and Hal Winters.

The influence of Edgar Lee Masters's *Spoon River Anthology* on *Winesburg, Ohio* has been generally acknowledged. In 1915, Max Wald lent his copy of Masters's work to Anderson, who stayed up all night reading it (Phillips, "How" 16–17). Those poems about the frequently unpleasant undercurrents of small-town life bear an obvious resemblance to Anderson's *Winesburg* tales, and the issue of *Seven Arts* that published "The Untold Lie" promised that it was part of "a prose complement to" Masters's volume of poems (Sutton, *Road* 431). The candor with which this story speaks about out-of-wedlock pregnancies and marital strains, whether directly influenced by Masters or not, is certainly in a similar vein.

Zlotnick notes, without claiming that Anderson had read *Dubliners,* a similarity between this story and Joyce's "A Little Cloud"; in both stories a crisis is precipitated by an encounter between two men, a husband "burdened with responsibility" and a freewheeling adventurer (35–36).

Possibly Anderson's reading of Nietzsche entered into his sense that truth is a chimera. Zarathustra says, at the close of part three, for example, "Do not all words lie" (284).

Publication History

"The Untold Lie" was published in the January 1917 issue of *Seven Arts* (I:215–21). A revised version of the story appeared in *Winesburg, Ohio* (1919). Anderson reprinted it in his own newspaper the *Smyth County News* in 1928 (December 27, p. 7). And in 1947 Paul Rosenfeld included it in *The Sherwood Anderson Reader* (30–35).

The *Seven Arts* was a new "little magazine" with the idealistic aim of revolutionizing American arts and letters. Based in New York, it was edited by intellectuals James Oppenheim, Waldo Frank, and Paul Rosenfeld (and soon Van Wyck Brooks and Randolph Bourne). A member of the editorial board, Edna Kenton, went to Chicago looking for contributors and reported what she heard about Anderson to Waldo Frank, who wrote to him; the response was immediate, and Frank recalls his excitement as he read "The Untold Lie," "scrawled in a long gangling script, each word of which looked like a lean hound in full chase across the page" (Frank 39–40). Since the story was "virtually free of punctuation," however, Frank returned the manuscript, saying that it was "luminous" but asking "would [Anderson] mind throwing in a few commas?" Then, Frank recalls, relishing the memory of Anderson's "exuberance," the story came back, sprinkled with commas "after each half dozen words or so, irrespective of sense . . . ," and accompanied by a note "in which the author hoped he had provided enough punctuation; if not, would I please suit myself?" (40). Actually, "The Untold Lie" was not the first story by Anderson that Frank had read; *Seven Arts* accepted "Queer" for publication before they received the manuscript of "The Untold Lie." (See "Queer," "Publication History.") The second issue of the new magazine published "Queer," the third published "The Untold Lie," and the first published "Emerging Greatness," Frank's review of Anderson's novel *Windy McPherson's Son* (1916). The discovery of Anderson's talent must have been fairly sudden and intense for Frank, who says that "he personified for me the fecund sap of what he loved to call Mid-America" (40). For Anderson, forty years old and just beginning to have his work published, this recognition by highly educated Eastern intellectuals was deeply gratifying. (For a history of Anderson's connection with the magazine, see David Anderson's "Sherwood Anderson and *The Seven Arts*.")

The magazine version of the tale, unlike the version printed in *Winesburg, Ohio,* is written as a first-person narrative. In his doctoral dissertation Thurston surmises that Anderson revised the original first-person magazine version of the tale into a later omniscient-author version that appears in the book; Phillips disputes that conclusion on the basis of the manuscript version in the Newberry Library, an omniscient-author version that he considers original ("How" 26–27). But on the basis of the letter of November 20, 1916, uncovered by Curry, which indicates a later date of composition than Phillips guessed—a date less than a week before Anderson submitted it to the editors of *Seven Arts*—Phillips's assumption that the Newberry manuscript is original should be questioned. (See "Circumstances of Composition" above.)

Relation to Other Works

As clearly as any story in the *Winesburg* cycle, "The Untold Lie" reiterates the idea, set forth in "The Book of the Grotesque," that there is no such thing as absolute truth. The story culminates in Ray Pearson's recognition that "Whatever I told him would have been a lie" (*WO* 209). Struggling with the contradiction between the truth of acceptance of family responsibility and the truth of preservation of personal freedom, the character achieves the profound philosophic awareness at the heart of the book. Though Stouck argues that this idea suggests "that art cannot express the 'truth' or meaning of a life outside the individual artist's personal experience" and thus "completely undermines the book's purpose" ("Failure" 148), in fact Anderson's purpose was to convey precisely understanding of "the terrible vagueness and uncertainty" of life (Modlin, *Letters* 161), which he did not see as a cause for despair.

Commentators have noted various connections between this tale and the rest of the cycle. As a story in which an older character seeks to offer advice to a younger character, it is linked with several tales in which townspeople give advice to George Willard (Lorch 63). The symbolism of hands, which runs throughout the volume, is particularly prominent in the scene where Hal Winters "put his two hands on the older man's shoulders" in a moment of communion (Ingram 191, quoting *WO* 205). Also, the father's imagination of his children's "hands clutching at him" is related to the pattern of gestures between parent and child in "Godliness" and "Tandy" and between Christ and mankind in "The Strength of God" (Maresca 282). Other stories also treat illicit sex ("Paper Pills," "Mother," "Nobody Knows," "Adventure," "Respectability," and "Death"), marital hostility (especially "Mother" and "Godliness"), and characters whose integrity makes them reluctant to say things they do not feel ("The Thinker") (Wright 57, 77, 131–32). A similar technique of reversal of insight appears in "Nobody Knows," "The Teacher," and "An Awakening" (Ingram 197). The symbol of the overcoat appears both in "The Untold Lie" and in "Queer," which immediately precedes it. The close parallel between the life of the farm hands in this story and that of the pre–Civil War Bentleys in "Godliness"—brutal work all week, Saturdays in town where drink releases a "crude . . . poetic fervor"—shows Anderson's sociological insight into the persistence of traditional custom among rural, agrarian people in the age of machines.

The digressive passage concerning old Windpeter Winters's death has particularly interested interpreters. McAleer holds the old man's "fantastic defiance" to be "the supreme expression" of protest against life in an industrial, materialistic age, and relates it specifically to the wild rides that Louise Bentley and Elizabeth Willard take, in "Godliness" and "Mother," respectively, and to the accidents in "The Philosopher," where Parcival's brother is killed by a railroad car and a child is killed when her horses are frightened by a train (174–75). Similarly, Abcarian views the passage as one of "heroic passion and inspired rage" directed against the fatal "ethos of modern industrialism" (101). Baker connects it instead to the search for release from "repression" that characterizes most of the chief figures in the *Winesburg* cycle (575–76). The gesture, according to Stouck, is a "form of the expressionist scream" ("Expressionist" 45).

The significance to Anderson of Windpeter Winters's suicide is indicated by the fact that when, twenty years later, he wrote a play about the characters in *Winesburg, Ohio,* he set the opening scene in the cemetery at the old reprobate's funeral. Perceptively, Stouck points out the surging activity of life at the funeral and comments that " 'the road of life and the road of death' . . . [constitute] the two main narrative threads in the play" ("Dance" 538–39, quoting the play, 30). This analysis is consistent with the idea of contrary truths in "The Untold Lie," where Windpeter's "gloriously" drunken act is admired by adolescent boys and condemned by responsible members of the community (*WO* 203): a crazily vital death and a slow death-in-life are contrary faces of truth (Way 111).

The technique of the thematically central digression may be related to Anderson's "fondness for the exemplum," which Williams points out in the "fable of the fighting chickens" in *Windy McPherson's Son* and the "fable of the mice in *Poor White*" (270).

Anderson's interest in the impoverished, no-account Winters family extended beyond this story. An early version of "Death in the Woods" centers on "Mother Winters" (who was to become Mrs. Grimes in the final version of the story) and provides a brief glimpse of her husband "Pa Winters" (Hal?), whose milldam has fallen to ruin and who has purchased a steam engine. Business is meager, though, and his lusty youth of "hauling logs" and "roistering" has yielded to "sullen silent" age (Fanning 62–65).

Though "The Untold Lie" may be Anderson's "best presentation of the marriage dilemma," numerous other stories in his canon probe situations where women defend home values by trapping men—notably, "His Chest of Drawers," "The Door of the Trap," and "Brothers" (Miller 204–205). "Two Lovers" expands the theme that timid domestic fidelity and sexual freedom can be equally unfulfilling; that story strengthens the idea that men need masculine friendship and understanding (Townsend 312).

Critical Studies

This story has been recognized as one of Anderson's finest. He himself, in 1923, judged it second only to "The Egg" in what he called "solidity" (Modlin, *Letters* 52). Cowley, too, considers it the best tale in *Winesburg* (6), and Rideout identifies it as "the tale of perfect balance" that the author always aimed for. Gold admires the lyricism of the tale, along with its sense of epiphany, which "breathes the sadness, the beauty, the necessary risks of grownup desire" (551). Walcutt praises the "heartbreaking insight" that lays bare the "buried life" of a farmhand (231). Ciancio appreciates the blend of sympathy and irony aroused by the narration in passages such as those where Ray thinks of his children as mere "accidents of life" with which he "had nothing to do" (996, quoting *WO* 208). Similarly, Reid notes the mingling of "rueful and baffled humor" with a serious awareness of latent violence and despair (146–47).

A sociological perspective also responds to the story's masterful equipoise: while the story shows how "a puritan society obstructs the expression . . . of sexual desire," it also examines "what is worthwhile in the provincial mid-West puritan tradition" (Way 110).

The symbols in the tale have elicited sensitive critical explication. Mellard suggests that the horses represent freedom and that trains, on the other hand, represent the contingencies of freedom (1306). McAleer and Abcarian, however, associate the train with industrialism and materialism and horses with pastoral agrarianism (see "Relation to Other Works"). Rideout notices that there are actually four references to horses in the story, two of which are associated with wild freedom and two of which are associated with submission to the rider's domination; thus the references strike a balance between "the contrary themes of convention and revolt" (248–49). Rideout also states that the overcoat is a "Carlylean symbol, . . . the ugly outward husk of routine life being cast off" (248). Papinchak points out the symbolism of fertility and fruition in the cornfields where Ray and Hal work (2–3).

Others have observed the inspiriting effect of the autumn beauty on Ray Pearson's mood, the way it rallies his dormant aesthetic instincts against everything sordid in his life; the communication that takes place in the cornfield is silent, superior to any words that Ray could devise to tell his "truth" to his friend (Love 48–49, 54; similarly, San Juan 147–48).

Formalist critics have admired the structure and techniques of the story. Thurston delineates in it the features of oral storytelling that he sees as characteristic of Anderson's narrative method: the initial blocking in of background, the apparent digression, the authorial intrusions, the shifts in time, all of which seem artless but are subtly managed so as to allow a close relationship with the reader and a crafty manipulation of effect (118–20).

Wright classifies the tale as a simple romance with an episode of discovery in which the protagonist discovers his own ambivalent feelings with relief (386, 137). Mellard counts it among the five "stories of incident" in *Winesburg*, pointing out the "almost mythic simplicity of narrative" which moves toward a central incident when the protagonist gains "a crucial understanding" (1306–07); not all critics have agreed with the distinction Wright makes between this kind of understanding and the "epiphanies" he finds in the stories he calls "symbolic." Thomas finds that the moment in the field, when motion and time stop, reflects a "photographic" aesthetic sense that Anderson shared with his friend Alfred Stieglitz (71). The many comments on the principal digression in the story are treated above, under "Relation to Other Works."

There is only one article devoted exclusively to "The Untold Lie." Luckily, it is a rich interpretation. Rideout's "The Tale of Perfect Balance" offers a fine characterization of the narrator, an analysis of the Windpeter Winters digression, comments on the intricate arrangement of material and the handling of detail, and a sensitive treatment of the story's themes, particularly the tension between convention and revolt, "one of those many paradoxes in which human beings live, in which they die" (250).

Works Cited

Abcarian, Richard. "Innocence and Experience in *Winesburg, Ohio.*" *University Review Kansas City* 35 (1968):95–105.

Anderson, David. "Sherwood Anderson and *The Seven Arts.*" *Newsletter of the Society for the Study of Midwestern Literature* 10 (1980):18–30.

Anderson, Sherwood. 1919. *Winesburg, Ohio.* New York: B. W. Huebsch. Rpt. New York: Viking, 1960.

——. 1926. *Tar: A Midwest Childhood.* New York: Boni & Liveright. Rpt. in *Tar: A Midwest Childhood: A Critical Text.* Ed. Ray Lewis White. Cleveland: Press of Case Western Reserve University, 1969.

Baker, Carlos. "Sherwood Anderson's Winesburg: A Reprise." *The Virginia Quarterly Review* 48 (1972):568–79.

Ciancio, Ralph. "The Sweetness of the Twisted Apples: Unity of Vision in *Winesburg, Ohio.*" *PMLA* 87 (1972):994–1006.

Cowley, Malcolm. 1960. "Introduction." In *Winesburg, Ohio.* By Sherwood Anderson. New York: Viking, 1–15. Rpt. in *Sherwood Anderson: Winesburg, Ohio: Text and Criticism.* Ed. John H. Ferres. New York: Viking, 1966, 357–68. Rpt. in *Sherwood Anderson: A Collection of Critical Es-*

says. Ed. Walter B. Rideout. Englewood Cliffs, NJ: Prentice-Hall, 1974, 49–58.

Curry, Martha Mulroy. 1975. *The "Writer's Book" by Sherwood Anderson: A Critical Edition*. Metuchen, NJ: Scarecrow Press.

Fanning, Michael, ed. 1976. *France and Sherwood Anderson: Paris Notebook, 1921*. Baton Rouge: Louisiana State University Press.

Frank, Waldo. "Sherwood Anderson: A Personal Note." *Newberry Library Bulletin* 2, no. 2 (December 1948):39–43.

Gold, Herbert. "The Purity and Cunning of Sherwood Anderson." *Hudson Review* 10 (1957–58):548–57. Rpt. in *The Age of Happy Problems*. New York: Dial, 1962, 56–67. Rpt. in part in *Sherwood Anderson:* Winesburg, Ohio: *Text and Criticism*. Ed. John H. Ferres. New York: Viking, 1966, 396–404. Rpt. in *Critical Essays on Sherwood Anderson*. Ed. David D. Anderson. Boston: G. K. Hall, 1981, 138–45.

Ingram, Forrest L. 1971. *Representative Short Story Cycles of the Twentieth Century: Studies in a Literary Genre*. The Hague: Mouton.

Jones, Howard Mumford, and Walter B. Rideout, eds. 1953. *Letters of Sherwood Anderson*. Boston: Little, Brown.

Lorch, Thomas M. "The Choreographic Structure of *Winesburg, Ohio*." *College Language Association Journal* 12 (1968–69):56–65.

Love, Glen A. "*Winesburg, Ohio* and the Rhetoric of Silence." *American Literature* 40 (1968):38–57.

Maresca, Carol J. "Gestures as Meaning in Sherwood Anderson's *Winesburg, Ohio*." *College Language Association Journal* 9 (1966):279–83.

McAleer, John J. "Christ Symbolism in *Winesburg, Ohio*." *Discourse* 4 (1961):168–81. Rpt. in *The Merrill Studies in* Winesburg, Ohio. Comp. Ray Lewis White. Columbus, OH: Charles E. Merrill, 1971, 60–74.

Mellard, James M. "Narrative Forms in *Winesburg, Ohio*." *PMLA* 83 (1968):1304–1312.

Miller, William V. 1974. "Earth-Mothers, Succubi, and Other Ectoplasmic Spirits: The Women in Sherwood Anderson's Short Stories." In *Midamerica* I. Ed. David D. Anderson. East Lansing, MI: Midwestern Press, 64–81. Rpt. in *Critical Essays on Sherwood Anderson*. Ed. David D. Anderson. Boston: G. K. Hall, 1981, 196–209.

Modlin, Charles E., ed. 1984. *Sherwood Anderson: Selected Letters*. Knoxville: University of Tennessee Press.

Nietzsche, Friedrich. 1964. *Thus Spake Zarathustra: A Book for All and*

None. Trans. Thomas Common. Vol. 11 of *The Complete Works of Friedrich Nietzsche.* Ed. Oscar Levy. New York: Russell & Russell.

Papinchak, Robert Allen. "Something in the Elders: The Recurrent Imagery in *Winesburg, Ohio.*" *Winesburg Eagle* 9 (1983):1–7.

Phillips, William L. "How Sherwood Anderson Wrote *Winesburg, Ohio.*" *American Literature* 23 (1951):7–30. Rpt. in *Sherwood Anderson: Winesburg, Ohio: Text and Criticism.* Ed. John H. Ferres. New York: Viking, 1966, 263–86. Rpt. in *The Achievement of Sherwood Anderson: Essays in Criticism.* Ed. Ray Lewis White. Chapel Hill: University of North Carolina Press, 1966, 62–84. Rpt. in *The Merrill Studies in* Winesburg, Ohio. Comp. Ray Lewis White. Columbus, OH: Charles E. Merrill, 1971, 2–24. Rpt. in *Sherwood Anderson: A Collection of Critical Essays.* Ed. Walter B. Rideout. Englewood Cliffs, NJ: Prentice-Hall, 1974, 18–38.

Reid, Randall. 1967. *The Fiction of Nathanael West: No Redeemer, No Promised Land.* Chicago: University of Chicago Press.

Rideout, Walter B. " 'The Tale of Perfect Balance': Sherwood Anderson's 'The Untold Lie.'" *Newberry Library Bulletin* 6 (1971):243–50.

Rosenfeld, Paul, ed. 1948. *The Sherwood Anderson Reader.* Boston: Houghton Mifflin.

San Juan, Epifanio, Jr. "Vision and Reality: A Reconsideration of Sherwood Anderson's *Winesburg, Ohio.*" *American Literature* 35 (1963):137–55. Rpt. in part in *Sherwood Anderson:* Winesburg, Ohio: *Text and Criticism.* Ed. John H. Ferres. New York: Viking, 1966, 468–81.

Stouck, David. "*Winesburg, Ohio* and the Failure of Art." *Twentieth Century Literature* 15 (1969):145–51.

———. "*Winesburg, Ohio* as a Dance of Death." *American Literature* 48 (1977):525–42. Rpt. in *Critical Essays on Sherwood Anderson.* Ed. David D. Anderson. Boston: G. K. Hall, 1981, 181–95.

———. 1990. "Anderson's Expressionist Art." In *New Essays on Winesburg, Ohio.* Ed. John W. Crowley. Cambridge and New York: Cambridge University Press, 27–51.

Sutton, William A. 1967. *Exit to Elsinore.* Muncie, IN: Ball State University Press.

———. 1972. *The Road to Winesburg: A Mosaic of the Imaginative Life of Sherwood Anderson.* Metuchen, NJ: Scarecrow Press.

———, ed. 1985. *Letters to Bab: Sherwood Anderson to Marietta D. Finley, 1916–33.* Foreword by Walter B. Rideout. Urbana and Chicago: University of Illinois Press.

Thomas, F. Richard, 1983. "Sherwood Anderson (1876–1941)." *Literary Ad-*

mirers of Alfred Stieglitz. Carbondale: Southern Illinois University Press, 65–78.

Thurston, Jarvis. "Anderson and 'Winesburg': Mysticism and Craft." *Accent* 16 (1956):107–28. Rpt. in part in *Sherwood Anderson:* Winesburg, Ohio: *Text and Criticism*. Ed. John H. Ferres. New York: Viking, 1966, 331–44.

Townsend, Kim. 1987. *Sherwood Anderson*. Boston: Houghton Mifflin.

Walcutt, Charles Child. "Sherwood Anderson: Impressionism and the Buried Life." *American Literary Naturalism, a Divided Stream*. Minneapolis: University of Minnesota Press, 1956, 222–39. Originally in *Sewanee Review* 60 (1952): 28–47. Rpt. in part in *Sherwood Anderson:* Winesburg, Ohio: *Text and Criticism*. Ed. John H. Ferres. New York: Viking, 1966, 432–43.

Way, Brian. 1971. "Sherwood Anderson." In *The American Novel and the Nineteen Twenties*. Malcolm Bradbury and David Palmer (Eds.). Stratford-upon-Avon Studies 13. London: Edward Arnold, 107–126.

Williams, Kenny J. 1988. *A Storyteller and a City: Sherwood Anderson's Chicago*. De Kalb: Northern Illinois University Press.

Wright, Austin McGiffert. 1961. *The American Short Story in the Twenties*. Chicago: University of Chicago Press.

Zlotnick, Joan. "Dubliners in Winesburg, Ohio: A Note on Joyce's 'The Sisters' and Anderson's 'The Philosopher.'" *Studies in Short Fiction* 12 (1975):405–407.

Drink

Circumstances of Composition

Anderson originally titled this tale "The Drunkard" but revised it, on the manuscript, to "Drink" (White, "Titles" 6).

Sources and Influences

Rideout states that this story was prompted by the "drunkenness first from liquor then from life" of a "fellow lodger" at the Cass Street house, named Jack (48).

Freud's influence was being felt among intellectuals in the early decades of the century, and the repression of subconscious lusts became an important theme for many new writers, including Anderson. The warping of Tom Foster's sexual adjustment by the "sordid exhibitions" he has seen in the city is one manifestation of the new openness about such subjects (Hatcher 167–68). Interestingly, in his youth Anderson himself had been repulsed by witnessing "a crude manifestation of human lust" (White, *Memoirs* 111).

Publication History

"Drink" was first published in *Winesburg, Ohio* (1919). Evidently it had been submitted previously to *Seven Arts* and rejected; in a letter to editor Waldo Frank, tentatively dated April 1917, Anderson wrote, "Wish you had liked my story of the drunken boy. I liked it fine. It was true as hell. . . . Please don't always apply your reason to these things. They are to my mind fragments that will be more keenly realized in the minds of the reader than you fellows think" (Jones-Rideout, *Letters* 11).

Relation to Other Works

Critical comment about this story has been primarily devoted to its relationship to other stories in *Winesburg*. Its protagonist, Tom Foster, is one of the numerous lonely, inarticulate souls in the book (Fagin 134). Like Wash Williams (in "Respectability"), he has been "turned into a grotesque" by a single devastating experience (Abcarian 97). Both he and Wash recoil from all women because they cannot "conceive of gradations of value" (Wright 135). The apple orchard in the tale is connected to the apples in "Paper Pills." Tom's story, like that of the other grotesques, is a version of the fall from the paradise of "organic Oneness with Nature" into the pain of "the discontinuity of the psyche" and impossible yearnings (Ciancio 999). "His ideas about suffering link him to Doctor Parcival, a similar artistic nature," in "The Philosopher" (Lorch 59). The motif of dreams appears in his drunken fancies, and the symbols of fire and wind in his imaginings about Helen White (Ingram 177, 181). Like the drunken stranger in "Tandy," Tom finds his "thing to love" while intoxicated (Ingram 197). He is grotesque because he has embraced "the 'truth' of release only in alcohol" (Phillips, "Origins" 183). Of all the grotesques, only Tom Foster and Joe Welling (in "A Man of Ideas") find happiness, according to Bowden (114).

Tom Foster is one of the misfits who confides in George Willard and whom "George does not understand" (Stouck 533–34). But George's increasing maturity is revealed by his ability "to discriminate between" his anger at the yarn Tom tells about making love to Helen White and his own tenderness for the boy (Burbank 71; similarly, D. Anderson 48). It is also important that George is not satisfied with his own failure to understand and insists upon finding out more about Tom's motivations: "What makes you say you have? What makes you keep saying such things?" (*WO* 219).

Tom Foster and Seth Richmond in "The Thinker" "closely resemble George." Because all three are "sensitive" and "artistic," they all are in love with Helen White, and all are in the process of maturation; "they act as foils for each other" and place George "in perspective" (Lorch 63).

Beyond the *Winesburg* cycle, an interesting kinship to Tom Foster can be found in "A Meeting South" in the figure of David (William Faulkner), who is also gentle, wounded, poetic, and a heavy drinker. Tom's pained perplexity about the ugliness of prostitution and "the greedy look" in the eyes of a woman who tempted him into her room bears a likeness to the confusion and hurt of the narrator in "I Want to Know Why." The reveries of the aroused youth in "Drink"—poetic, sensuous, imaging nature with a palpable undercurrent of fleshly desire—are developed in "An Ohio Pagan" into a patently erotic nature-worship. And a similar adventure in stealing is developed at some length in "A Criminal's Christmas," but with utterly different effect: the sense of the grotesque that accompanies the detached narration in "Drink" gives way to warmth and charm when the child-narrator of the later story describes his own experience.

Critical Studies

Beyond remarks placing the story in the network of relationships in the *Winesburg* cycle, attention to "Drink" has been slight. Williams points out correctly that, far from representing any "revolt from the village," the story shows the harshness of urban life for Tom and his grandmother (186).

Assessments of Tom Foster's character have been rather superficial. San Juan accurately details Tom's "poetic sensitivity" (140–41). Lorch remarks that Tom approaches experience with a "purely artistic" detachment, learning what he can from stealing and drunkenness (59). Rigsbee, arguing that "all the male grotesques . . . struggle to expand their personalities to include" emotions of "affection and passion," asserts that Tom discovers "more order in his life after he gets drunk and fantasizes a romantic relationship with Helen White" (236). Bowden states that Tom "finds happiness by discovering the world in his own imagination" (114). Murphy declares Tom one of the "spiritual elite" of *Winesburg* who have learned to "sublimate their desire" in order to attain the highest plane of "mystical sympathy" that includes both "the truth of virginity and the truth of passion" (241–42, quoting *WO* 23).

These highly positive evaluations oversimplify the tale. No one mentions

Tom Foster's shiftlessness, which caused him to lose his job. The family background that has shaped his psychology likewise has rarely been mentioned, though his failure to assert himself certainly is connected both to the violent death of his father and to the self-sacrificial love of his "strong, capable little old grandmother," who has mopped and scrubbed and amended his misdemeanors (*WO* 210, 211, 213). Bidney's analysis, however, probes into the psychology of a character he argues is insufficiently "male"; "Brought up in rough circumstances, [Tom] edits the roughness out of consciousness—or tries to. It returns in his fantasies, transformed into masochistic pleasure" (268). Tom's horror of sex (which the character identifies as "hurting someone") remains a problem; the lesson he learned from a childhood theft is hardly analogous to the lesson he thinks he has learned by dousing the flames of desire with alcohol. When his insurgent desires again assert themselves, what will he do? Wright touches on this crucial issue, which is left unresolved at the end of the story: "a gentle boy . . . tries to adjust himself to the repression of his natural impulses by going on a solitary drinking spree during which he has fantasies of love, his ostensible motive being to satisfy his curiosity once and for all. The reader infers the fear of life that makes him think he can be satisfied by this experiment" (233). Such an inference does not negate Tom's attractive, poetic side, but it helps do justice to the complexities of the tale, which have seldom been acknowledged.

The style and form of the tale have received comment. San Juan notes that the spring season is an objective correlative to the protagonist's emotions (147). Mahoney analyzes the discontinuities in conversation between George and Tom (248–49). Mellard classifies the story as a "symbolic" tale leading to an epiphany that "presents an *affirmative* value" for the reader; through Tom's "initiatory loss of innocence and gaining of knowledge" the reader comes to appreciate the value of visionary experience (1304–1306). More attentive to the ironies in the drunken vision, Wright classifies the tale as one of caustic pathos containing an episode of suffering (389).

Works Cited

Abcarian, Richard. "Innocence and Experience in *Winesburg, Ohio*." *University Review Kansas City* 35 (1968):95–105.

Anderson, David. 1967. *Sherwood Anderson: An Introduction and Interpretation*. New York: Holt, Rinehart.

Anderson, Sherwood. "A Criminal's Christmas." *Vanity Fair* 27 (December 1926):89, 130. Rpt. in *Hello Towns!* New York: Liveright, 1929, 79–85. Rpt. in *Certain Things Last: the Selected Short Stories of Sherwood An-*

derson. Ed. Charles E. Modlin. New York: Four Walls Eight Windows, 1992, 252–57.

——. 1919. *Winesburg, Ohio.* New York: B. W. Huebsch. Rpt. New York: Viking, 1960.

Bidney, Martin. "Anderson and the Androgyne: 'Something More than Man or Woman.'" *Studies in Short Fiction* 25 (1988):261–73.

Bowden, Edwin T. 1961. *The Dungeon of the Heart: Human Isolation and the American Novel.* New York: Macmillan, 114–24.

Burbank, Rex. 1964. *Sherwood Anderson.* New York: Twayne. Rpt. in part in *The Achievement of Sherwood Anderson: Essays in Criticism.* Ed. Ray Lewis White. Chapel Hill: University of North Carolina Press, 1966, 32–43. Rpt. in part in *Sherwood Anderson: A Collection of Critical Essays.* Ed. Walter B. Rideout. Englewood Cliffs, NJ: Prentice-Hall, 1974, 70–83.

Ciancio, Ralph. "The Sweetness of the Twisted Apples: Unity of Vision in *Winesburg, Ohio.*" *PMLA* 87 (1972):994–1006.

Duffey, Bernard. 1954. *The Chicago Renaissance in American Letters: A Critical History.* East Lansing: Michigan State College Press.

Fagin, N. Bryllion. 1973. *The Phenomenon of Sherwood Anderson: A Study in American Life and Letters.* New York: Russell & Russell. Originally printed Baltimore: Rossi-Bryn, 1927.

Hatcher, Harlan. 1935. Creating the Modern American Novel. New York: Farrar & Rinehart.

Ingram, Forrest L. 1971. *Representative Short Story Cycles of the Twentieth Century: Studies in a Literary Genre.* The Hague: Mouton.

Jones, Howard Mumford, and Walter B. Rideout, eds. 1953. *Letters of Sherwood Anderson.* Boston: Little, Brown.

Lorch, Thomas M. "The Choreographic Structure of *Winesburg, Ohio.*" *College Language Association Journal* 12 (1968–69):56–65.

Mahoney, John J. "An Analysis of *Winesburg, Ohio.*" *Journal of Aesthetics and Art Criticism* 15 (1956):245–52.

Mellard, James M. "Narrative Forms in *Winesburg, Ohio.*" *PMLA* 83 (1968):1304–1312.

Murphy, George D. "The Theme of Sublimation in Anderson's *Winesburg, Ohio.*" *Modern Fiction Studies* 13 (1967):237–46.

Phillips, William L. "How Sherwood Anderson Wrote *Winesburg, Ohio.*" *American Literature* 23 (1951):7–30. Rpt. in *Sherwood Anderson:* Winesburg, Ohio: *Text and Criticism.* Ed. John H. Ferres. New York: Viking, 1966, 263–86. Rpt. in *The Achievement of Sherwood Anderson: Essays in*

Criticism. Ed. Ray Lewis White. Chapel Hill: University of North Carolina Press, 1966, 62–84. Rpt. in *The Merrill Studies in* Winesburg, Ohio. Comp. Ray Lewis White. Columbus, OH: Charles E. Merrill, 1971, 2–24. Rpt. in *Sherwood Anderson: A Collection of Critical Essays.* Ed. Walter B. Rideout. Englewood Cliffs, NJ: Prentice-Hall, 1974, 18–38.

———. "Sherwood Anderson's *Winesburg, Ohio:* Its Origins, Composition, Technique, and Reception." Ph.D. diss., University of Chicago, 1950.

Rideout, Walter B. 1976. "Talbot Whittingham and Anderson: A Passage to *Winesburg, Ohio.*" In *Sherwood Anderson: Dimensions of His Literary Art.* Ed. David D. Anderson. East Lansing: Michigan State University Press, 41–60.

Rigsbee, Sally Adair. "The Feminine in *Winesburg, Ohio.*" *Studies in American Fiction* 9 (1981):233–44.

San Juan, Epifanio, Jr. "Vision and Reality: A Reconsideration of Sherwood Anderson's *Winesburg, Ohio.*" *American Literature* 35 (1963):137–55. Rpt. in part in *Sherwood Anderson:* Winesburg, Ohio: *Text and Criticism.* Ed. John H. Ferres. New York: Viking, 1966, 468–81.

Stouck, David. "*Winesburg, Ohio* as a Dance of Death." *American Literature* 48 (1977):525–42. Rpt. in *Critical Essays on Sherwood Anderson.* Ed. David D. Anderson. Boston: G. K. Hall, 1981, 181–95.

White, Ray Lewis. "*Winesburg, Ohio:* The Story Titles." *Winesburg Eagle* 10, no. 1 (November 1984):6–7.

———, ed. 1969. *Sherwood Anderson's Memoirs: A Critical Edition.* Chapel Hill: University of North Carolina Press.

Williams, Kenny J. 1988. *A Storyteller and a City: Sherwood Anderson's Chicago.* De Kalb: Northern Illinois University Press.

Wright, Austin McGiffert. 1961. *The American Short Story in the Twenties.* Chicago: University of Chicago Press.

Death

Sources and Influences

The village of Winesburg is modeled on Clyde, Ohio, where Anderson spent much of his childhood (from 1884 to 1896). Elizabeth Willard is plainly modeled after his mother, Emma Smith Anderson, who died in Clyde on May 10, 1895, when she was forty-two and Sherwood was eighteen. Her death was a crucial event in Anderson's life, and he returned to it again and again in his writings. Tom Willard is based on Irwin McLain Anderson, Sherwood's father. The character Doctor Reefy may be remembered from an actual physician in Clyde, but that is not definite. (For a detailed discussion of sources for Doctor Reefy, see "Paper Pills.")

It is generally agreed that Edgar Lee Masters's *Spoon River Anthology,* which Anderson read shortly before he wrote the *Winesburg* stories, contributed in some way to the shape of Anderson's book (Phillips 16–17). Stouck suggests that the "formal design" of Masters's cycle of poems, in which voices of the dead tell their stories, influenced Anderson's story cycle, where the characters "are people from the narrator's memory of his home town, and many of them . . . long dead" (530–31). Stouck proposes that one of Oliver Herford's illustrations for Masters's volume, showing "Death in bed as a lover," is connected with "Elizabeth Willard's erotic personification of death" (531).

In *Tar* (1926), Anderson suggests that his memory of his mother's death has been "reconstructed in his imagination" under the impetus of a story by Chekhov in which there is an "anxious country doctor" with a "woman dying [and]—wanting love before she died" (326); White proposes that the story alluded to is "A Dead Body" (204n).

Publication History

This story was first published in *Winesburg, Ohio* (1919). Before that, evidently, it had been submitted to and rejected by *Seven Arts.* In a letter of December 14, 1916, Anderson wrote the editor, Waldo Frank, and mentioned that he had "another fine story" concerning the death of the woman in the story they had just accepted for publication, "Mother" (Jones-Rideout, *Letters* 5). On January 15, 1917, he apparently submitted "Death," advising that it "should not, I believe, be published too closely on the back of the first story about her" (Sutton 432). But *Seven Arts* did not publish it at all.

Relation to Other Works

Anderson wrote several autobiographical or semiautobiographical accounts of his mother's death; these appear in his *Memoirs* (White 114–15), in *A Story-Teller's Story* (1924) (62–63), and in *Tar* (1926) (326–41). All the accounts are slightly different, and that in *Tar* seems to be the most highly fictionalized. The dying woman's husband is not present in any of these versions of the death; Tom Willard's brief role at the deathbed in *Winesburg,* however, lends a moment of grotesque poignance to the story and helps round out the whole collection by repeating an image from the first page of the opening sketch, "The Book of the Grotesque," where the old carpenter, mourning his brother's death, weeps ludicrously into his mustache. There is no doctor in attendance at the scenes either in *A Story-Teller's Story* or in the *Memoirs;* in *Tar,* though, the boy (who represents Anderson) "liked to think" that his mother and her friend the doctor had had a "last talk" that was "full of significance to them both" because, as the boy "later found out, it is in their close relationships people live" (326).

"Death" is closely linked to two stories that appear almost at the beginning of *Winesburg, Ohio,* "Paper Pills" and "Mother." The earlier stories treat Doctor Reefy and Elizabeth Willard separately. "Death" brings the two lonely characters together, dramatizing an impetuous moment of fervid love and life. It also marks a key episode in George Willard's development, the aspect of the *Winesburg* cycle that partakes of the genre of the bildungsroman. The moment of understanding love that the mother and the doctor share is a fitting prelude to the similar moment that George shares with Helen White in the following story, "Sophistication." George's mother's death cuts him free of his ties to home and prepares him to carry out the intention he confided to her in "Mother," to go away from Winesburg; thus the story sets the stage for the final story, "Departure." Schevill states that "Death" contains the "climax of the book" because it joins the theme of "George Willard's rise to consciousness" with that of "the village grotesques" (104). Ironically, just as Elizabeth turns from a moment of love with Doctor Reefy to her lover Death, so George also forgets his moment of love with Helen White as he leaves town (Wright 72). But in seizing "the adventure of life," he is like the young aspect of his mother rather than her defeated, dying self.

The chronology of this story in relation to others is somewhat confusing. The two phases of the story—the romantic encounter with Doctor Reefy and the encounter with death—take place several years apart, though the transition between the two sections has the effect of eliding the lapse of time between those events. The dating is clearly set forth in several places: the time when the sick Elizabeth Willard visits the doctor is "when her son George was a boy of twelve or fourteen," the doctor embraces her when she is "forty-one," and she dies "in the year when her son George became eighteen (*WO* 221, 227, 229). Yet, when in one paragraph the woman flees trembling from Reefy's arms and in the next she is found spending "the last few months of her life hungering for death," it is extremely difficult for readers to remember that four or five years intervene (228). Evidently because he designed a dramatic juxtaposition of the woman's longing for love with her longing for death, Anderson has here sacrificed some clarity. In "Mother," Elizabeth Willard is forty-five; thus the main scenes in that story are set *between* the first and the last scenes of "Death." That fact is somewhat difficult to recognize. The natural inclination to read narrations as chronological also interferes with comprehension of the plain fact that "Paper Pills" is set some years after the events of "Death"; in "Death," Reefy is middle-aged, brown-mustached, awkward, and not yet married, whereas in "Paper Pills," he is old, white-bearded, graceful, and his wife has died.

McDonald remarks that Elizabeth Willard's quest to find an escape from the prison of isolation is repeated by all the major characters of *Winesburg*. Wright adds the interesting point that Elizabeth's "pursuit of love" is typical of short stories in the twenties in that her need "exists independently of any specific person," whereas in earlier stories characters usually consider "love only in connection with a specific person" who evokes it (70).

Fertig argues that the mother's transformation in death into "a vision of the ineffable beauty" makes it possible for George to fulfill himself as an artist and aligns her with other other "representative[s] of the ideal dream world" in *Winesburg*, "the young woman who leads the procession of grotesques" in "The Book of the Grotesque" and "the hurt and suffering woman Enoch Robinson is unable to paint" in "Loneliness" (69).

Ingram points out that "Death" is linked to the rest of the cycle by the motifs of adventure, of dream, of hunger, and the symbols of wind and of hands (174, 177, 179, 180, 191; on hand gestures, see also Maresca 282). He notes that both this story and the one after it open with a view of Doctor Reefy's stairway (198). Moreover, he states, this story "continues the submerged Christian symbolism of the volume" (most overt in "The Philosopher," which contains the line "everyone in the world is Christ and they are all crucified" [*WO* 27]) because "Elizabeth Willard dies in March, on Friday, at 3:00 P.M." (197n).

Ward asserts that "Death" contains a central statement relating to the theme of language, talk, and silence that runs throughout the cycle: he sees in Reefy's statement about the inexpressibility of love ("You must not try to make love definite.") Anderson's indication that "the proper attitude toward words" is "distrust" (44). Recurrent "thwarted climaxes," Reid remarks, characterize "Death," "Hands," and "Adventure" (141–42); "An Awakening" belongs with this group, too.

Beyond *Winesburg, Ohio,* there are other works that significantly resemble this story. The mother's death is of radical importance for the protagonists of *Windy McPherson's Son* (1916) and *Marching Men* (1917) (Phillips 29; Stouck 527). Moreover, suggestions of life as "a procession of the living dead" occur in "Out of Nowhere into Nothing" and *Dark Laughter* (1925) (Stouck 529). The story "Seeds" presents a woman much like Elizabeth Willard in her tormented need for love and appreciation, and in that story, too, fulfillment of the need is inhibited by fear and the forces of conventionality (Wright 85, 128). The theme of marriage as a trap is also important in Anderson's uncollected story "The Contract" (O'Connor 40–41). Finally, the transfiguration of an old woman into something young and beautiful prefigures the metamorphosis of Mrs. Grimes in "Death in the Woods" (Colquitt 92). One critic launches a lengthy argument that the thrice-repeated exclamation "You lovely dear!" (which indicates the mother's "entrapment" and defeat, Doctor Reefy's affection, and George's "belated" but "compassionate recognition of his mother as a distinct and separate 'other'") signals that George may achieve the fulfillment that has eluded her (Wentworth 36–39). Anderson's symbolic maneuverings here seem somewhat contrived, however, whereas in "Death in the Woods" a similar mystery is made not only plausible but haunting.

Critical Studies

There are no extended treatments of this story as a separate entity. Critical comments are scattered in various sources that treat *Winesburg* as a whole. Apart from the story's connections with other works, the topics that interest critics are the characters and the structure.

The pathetic ending of Elizabeth Willard's life has been variously explained. Winther sees in her only "the beautiful and the tortured spirit which is the true measure of man" (151). Taylor, however, describes her as "more willful than prudent," and blames her, as she blames herself, for having made an unwise marriage (32). Thurston considers that her aim—an "unnameable spiritual union with God, man, or nature"—is too high, too mystical, to be realized (112–13). Rigsbee, though, lays the blame squarely on society, that is, on the "conventional sexual mores" and "traditional role expectations" that first push Elizabeth into marriage and later interrupt her communion with a man who recognizes her full humanity; Elizabeth's aim, says Rigsbee, is simply "a more humane life" with relationships that are both intimate and *reciprocal* (235–39, 244n. 5).

Doctor Reefy assumes central importance in Ciancio's interpretation. For Ciancio, Elizabeth Willard is a victim, partly of men with a "strictly genital sexual attitude" and partly of her own choice (not of a beloved man but of the "abstraction" marriage) and of her own despair over the flesh (996, 1002). Reefy, too, suffers such "excruciating guilt" over his relations with this woman that he jerks away "the hand of consolation he had extended to George" (1003). But by the time he marries, Reefy has changed: he has "gained ascendancy over" grotesqueness and over despair and is able to express to his bride "a good many things he had been unable to express to Elizabeth" (1003, quoting *WO* 221). Thus, he becomes (in "Paper Pills") "the perfect artist and . . . the embodiment of all George aspires to and the hope of all the grotesques, who look upon George as their potential savior" (1004). This is a large claim, and Ciancio is distorting the facts when he says that Elizabeth "has abandoned George" and does not even try to tell him about the money she has saved for him; yet he seems close to the point when he argues that, when George echoes the words of both his mother's early lover and of Doctor Reefy, "he has become one with them in spirit" and that the mother is "eternalized in [his] imagination and restored at once to her innocence" (1005; similarly, Fertig 69).

Burbank notices that George's maturation is dramatized in this story as his "adolescent resentment at the inconvenience caused by his mother's death . . . gives way to realization of the finality of death and to conscious-ness of the tragic beauty his mother represented" (71). Murphy comments on the sexual fantasies George experiences beside his mother's corpse and their "conversion . . . into a vision of his mother as a young and desirable girl"; this symbolism is "more than simply Oedipal," for it reveals "the subtle connection which Anderson discerned between *eros* and *agape*—between a specific, egocentric sexual desire and a generalized love and sympathy for humanity" (244–45).

Formalistic critics have held several opinions about the story. Wright classifies it as a story of caustic pathos with an episode of choice (388). Mellard classifies it as one of the "thematic" stories in the cycle because its heroine has become obsessed with death, her one "truth"; the irony typical of this kind of story appears as one realizes that her dream of release from self is life-denying rather than life-affirming (1307–1309). The ending of the story, Thurston comments, is "unnecessary" to the story as an independent unit but makes sense as preparation for the conclusion of the cycle (127). Way complains that the story simply contains a lot of "bad writing," and Whitmanian transcendental intensities with little meaning (121). No one else has expressed such an opinion, and Way himself offers no evidence to sup-port it, but the story has not received much high praise, either.

Works Cited

Anderson, Sherwood. 1919. *Winesburg, Ohio*. New York: B. W. Huebsch. Rpt. New York: Viking, 1960.

———. 1924. *A Story Teller's Story*. New York: B. W. Huebsch. Rpt. in *A Story Teller's Story: A Critical Text*. Ed. Ray Lewis White. Cleveland: Press of Case Western Reserve University, 1968. Rpt. New York: Viking, 1969.

———. 1926. *Tar: A Midwest Childhood*. New York: Boni & Liveright. Rpt. in *Tar: A Midwest Childhood: A Critical Text*. Ed. Ray Lewis White. Cleveland: Press of Case Western Reserve University, 1969.

Burbank, Rex. 1964. *Sherwood Anderson*. New York: Twayne. Rpt. in part in *The Achievement of Sherwood Anderson: Essays in Criticism*. Ed. Ray Lewis White. Chapel Hill: University of North Carolina Press, 1966, 32–43. Rpt. in part in *Sherwood Anderson: A Collection of Critical Essays*. Ed. Walter B. Rideout. Englewood Cliffs: Prentice-Hall, 1974, 70–83.

Ciancio, Ralph. "The Sweetness of the Twisted Apples: Unity of Vision in *Winesburg, Ohio*." *PMLA* 87 (1972):994–1006.

Colquitt, Clare. 1990. "Motherlove in Two Narratives of Community: *Winesburg, Ohio* and *The Country of the Pointed Firs*." In *New Essays on Winesburg, Ohio*. Ed. John W. Crowley. Cambridge and New York: Cambridge University Press, 73–97.

Fertig, Martin J. "'A Great Deal of Wonder in Me': Inspiration and Transformation in *Winesburg, Ohio*." *Markham Review* 6 (1977):65–70.

Ingram, Forrest L. 1971. *Representative Short Story Cycles of the Twentieth Century: Studies in a Literary Genre*. The Hague: Mouton.

Jones, Howard Mumford, and Walter B. Rideout, eds. 1953. *Letters of Sherwood Anderson*. Boston: Little, Brown.

Maresca, Carol J. "Gestures as Meaning in Sherwood Anderson's *Winesburg, Ohio*." *College Language Association Journal* 9 (1966):279–83.

McDonald, Walter R. "*Winesburg, Ohio:* Tales of Isolation." *University Review Kansas City* 35 (1969):237–40.

Mellard, James M. "Narrative Forms in *Winesburg, Ohio*." *PMLA* 83 (1968):1304–12.

Murphy, George D. "The Theme of Sublimation in Anderson's *Winesburg, Ohio*." *Modern Fiction Studies* 13 (1967):237–46.

O'Connor, Frank [as O'Donovan, Michael]. 1963. *The Lonely Voice: A Study of the Short Story*. Cleveland: World Publishing.

Phillips, William L. "How Sherwood Anderson Wrote *Winesburg, Ohio*." *American Literature* 23 (1951):7–30. Rpt. in *Sherwood Anderson:* Winesburg, Ohio: *Text and Criticism*. Ed. John H. Ferres. New York: Viking, 1966, 263–86. Rpt. in *The Achievement of Sherwood Anderson: Essays in Criticism*. Ed. Ray Lewis White. Chapel Hill: University of North Carolina Press, 1966, 62–84. Rpt. in *The Merrill Studies in* Winesburg, Ohio. Comp. Ray Lewis White. Columbus, OH: Charles E. Merrill, 1971, 2–24. Rpt. in *Sherwood Anderson: A Collection of Critical Essays*. Ed. Walter B. Rideout. Englewood Cliffs, NJ: Prentice-Hall, 1974, 18–38.

Reid, Randall. 1967. *The Fiction of Nathanael West: No Redeemer, No Promised Land*. Chicago: University of Chicago Press.

Rigsbee, Sally Adair. "The Feminine in *Winesburg, Ohio*." *Studies in American Fiction* 9 (1981):233–44.

Schevill, James. 1951. *Sherwood Anderson: His Life and Work*. Denver: University of Denver Press.

Stouck, David. "*Winesburg, Ohio* as a Dance of Death." *American Literature* 48 (1977):525–42. Rpt. in *Critical Essays on Sherwood Anderson*. Ed. David D. Anderson. Boston: G. K. Hall, 1981, 181–95.

Sutton, William A. 1972. *The Road to Winesburg: A Mosaic of the Imaginative Life of Sherwood Anderson*. Metuchen, NJ: Scarecrow Press.

Taylor, Welford Dunaway. 1977. *Sherwood Anderson*. New York: Frederick Ungar.

Thurston, Jarvis. "Anderson and 'Winesburg': Mysticism and Craft." *Accent* 16 (1956):107–28. Rpt. in part in *Sherwood Anderson:* Winesburg, Ohio: *Text and Criticism*. Ed. John H. Ferres. New York: Viking, 1966, 331–44.

Ward, J. A. 1985. "*Winesburg, Ohio:* Habitual Silence and the Roaring of Voices." *American Silences: The Realism of James Agee, Walker Evans, and Edward Hopper*. Baton Rouge: Louisiana State University Press, 35–50.

Way, Brian. 1971. "Sherwood Anderson." In *The American Novel and the Nineteen Twenties*. Malcolm Bradbury and David Palmer (Eds.). Stratford-upon-Avon Studies 13. London: Edward Arnold, 107–126.

Wentworth, Michael. "'You Dear! You Dear! You Lovely Dear!': Failure and Promise in Sherwood Anderson's 'Death.'" *Midamerica* 15 (1988): 27–38.

White, Ray Lewis, ed. 1969. *Sherwood Anderson's Memoirs: A Critical Edition*. Chapel Hill: University of North Carolina Press.

Winther, S. K. "The Aura of Loneliness in Sherwood Anderson." *Modern Fiction Studies* 5 (1959–60):146–52.

Wright, Austin McGiffert. 1961. *The American Short Story in the Twenties*. Chicago: University of Chicago Press.

Sophistication

Sources and Influences

The village of Winesburg is based on Clyde, Ohio, where Anderson grew up. Like Winesburg, Clyde had a fairgrounds and an annual fair (Hurd, "Fun" 36). Nearby was Waterworks Pond, as in "Sophistication" (Hurd, "Excerpts" 170). And Helen White may be based on a real person. In his *Memoirs* the author recalls that on the night before he left Clyde, he called on a girl from a family "far above us in the social scale" and proposed marriage to her; when he returned, she was engaged to someone else (White 165–66). One scholar reports that citizens of Winesburg told him Anderson courted "a local belle" named Jenny Baker, who refused his offer of marriage and instead married Anderson's friend Herman Hurd, son of the grocer whose store became Hern's Grocery in *Winesburg,* and that Herman Hurd had vaguely corroborated that story: "As I recollect, my wife and one of the Winters girls were in Winesburg, but I don't remember what characters they were" (Sullivan 218–19).

Publication History

"Sophistication" was first published in *Winesburg, Ohio* (1919). After he moved to southwest Virginia, Anderson reprinted it in his own newspaper, *The Smyth County News* (August 30, 1928, pp. 1, 3), at the time of the Smyth County Fair and subtitled it "A Fair Story of Youth" (Rideout, "Why" 131).

Relation to Other Works

"Sophistication" is much less important as an independent story than as part of the whole novelistic cycle. It is "the unifying story of *Winesburg*" (Hilfer 153), the point where the themes most clearly come together. It shows George Willard crossing the threshold into manhood. And it shows two individuals overcoming their loneliness and frustration in a moment of genuine communion.

George Willard's growth to maturity reaches a climax in this story, one of the few in the book with a "happy ending"; enabled by his mother's death (in "Death") to "take the backward view of life," George senses the "meaninglessness of life" and yet at the same time "loves life . . . intensely" (Fussell

112–14), quoting *WO* 240–41). His acceptance of ambivalent feelings significantly contrasts with efforts of most of the other characters in the cycle to "crush" their own ambivalence (Wright 137).

George's relationships with women, beginning with his callow, "entirely self-centered" behavior in "Nobody Knows" and moving through his foolishly proud confidence in "An Awakening," develop in this story into a "triumph" based on insight into "the limitations of life" and fulfilled in a reverent "feeling of oneness" not only with a woman but also with all people of Winesburg (Rideout, "Simplicity" 29–30). "[F]or the first time," comments Bunge, "he wants to talk to a woman, not use her" (245). But talk is less important than understanding, and their experience of shared feeling is "almost entirely wordless" (Walcutt 231), also in contrast to the word-muddled episode in "An Awakening." Throughout *Winesburg,* bursts of talk fall short of real understanding. Silence, too, is "almost always a handicap" preventing inarticulate characters from communicating, but in "Sophistication" silence "becomes the only and the essential mode in which love and understanding can be achieved" (Ward 50).

Moreover, the story is "the culmination" of the relationship between George Willard and Helen White (Phillips 29). In "The Thinker," George shows his immaturity by deciding to fall in love with Helen so that he can do a better job of writing romances. Seth Richmond, in the same story, is also attracted to Helen White, and George does not even realize it. In "Drink," Tom Foster tells about his attraction to Helen, and George reacts with jealous confusion. But in "Sophistication" George works his way toward a mature relationship with the young woman they all desire.

While the young couple experience a "success in the pursuit of love" that is rare in *Winesburg* (and in stories of the twenties generally), the brevity of that success is apparent in the story that follows ("Departure") when George forgets Helen "in the excitement" of leaving town (Wright 72).

The symbols of fire and wind and of gestures, which run through the whole cycle, appear here as well, most clearly underlining the theme as George and Helen hold hands (*WO* 181, 192; see also Bresnahan 25).

The story contrasts with the one immediately before it, "Death," for its "impulse to joy, to animal spirits, to youth, . . . exists as a counter-balance to the necessity of the body's slow destruction" (Schevill 104). But perhaps it is more accurate to say that the life-impulse in the story is an outgrowth of a sense of the inevitability of destruction as well as a counterbalance to it; mature joy incorporates into itself knowledge of fleeting time and decay.

Ingram argues that "Sophistication" complements the cycle's opening story, "The Book of the Grotesque": whereas "the old writer has escaped being a grotesque because of the 'young thing' in him," George escapes the same fate "because of the old thing in him, 'the thing that reflects and remembers'" (170, quoting *WO* 24, 240).

There are several significant connections between this story and works other than *Winesburg*. In his "Foreword" to *Tar* (1926) Anderson writes, "Manhood, sophistication, is something worth striving for but innocence is somewhat sweeter. It may be the greater wisdom to remain innocent but it cannot be done. I wish it could" (x). In *Windy McPherson's Son* (1916), the first girl the protagonist ever walks out with is Banker Walker's daughter, and exhilarated by their daring, they feel things "beyond words" and then kiss in the shadows (54–56); the scene is obviously similar to George's walk with Banker White's daughter. Miller connects the wordless respect for deeper feelings in "Sophistication" with the theme of Anderson's uncollected story "Two Lovers" (15). Morgan finds a "fatalism" reminiscent of Crane and Dreiser both in the passage where George comes to know that human beings "must live and die in uncertainty" and in the similar passage in *Beyond Desire* (1932), where Red Oliver understands that "Life was an experience full of queer accidents" (90, quoting *WO* 234, *BD* 291).

The dramatic version of *Winesburg* that was produced in 1934 includes the wooing of Helen White by both Seth Richmond and George Willard. Anderson conveyed his intentions for the character of Helen White to a man with whom he collaborated on the play: "I think we should take the girl Helen White as a figure very much like George's mother when she was a young girl. There is this difference. Helen White belongs to one of the most prosperous families in the town . . . [and] is protected by all the forces of conservative society but like George's mother she is ready to break through conventions whenever she thinks she has found what she wants in a man" (Modlin, *Letters* 156).

Critical Studies

No individual articles are devoted to this story alone; because the story is thoroughly enmeshed with the rest of the cycle, most criticism treats its relationship to other works in *Winesburg*. One of the best and fullest analyses appears in Ward's *American Silences,* one of the few treatments that pays attention to the crucial difference between the couple's meeting in the summer and their meeting in late fall (47–50).

There is almost universal agreement that the story represents the "apex" of George's growth (De Jovine 61). But critics display different emphases and minor disagreements.

The nature of the love George and Helen experience is of prime interest to a number of commentators. Thurston states, "The asexual love" in this story is "Anderson's closest definition of love" (114–15; similarly, Rogers 96). Bort calls it an "I–Thou" relationship that would be ruined by any effort to possess it permanently in marriage (455). Murphy sees it as not quite asexual but "more than simply sexual," sublimated and reverential, "reminiscent of the arcane code of Courtly Love" as though physical expression "would constitute a profanation" of the love; this experience places the couple in the Platonic company of those who know love as "the delicate equipoise between 'the truth of virginity and the truth of passion'" (245–46, quoting *WO* 23). Abcarian argues that George and Helen's recovery of spontaneous, pagan innocence "is a state of grace making their communion possible" (102). For Ciancio, too, the love constitutes "an Edenic moment" in which the couple is freed from "existential guilt" in "unselfconscious harmony of body and spirit" expressed as "innocent animalism" (1005). Rigsbee, however, argues that the key to the communion is "mutual treasuring of those tender, vital feelings that Anderson associates with the feminine," freedom from gender "role expectations," and equality of the male–female relationship (241). Similarly, Bidney emphasizes George's desire "'to love and be loved by' Helen," a desire that would "combine . . . active and passive, boldness and vulnerability" in a love that is ideal because it is androgynous (263, quoting *WO* 241).

Some critics demur slightly from such plaudits for the perfection of love in this story. Fagin states that George is really "far from being sophisticated, he is just approaching sophistication," and reflects an America itself just emerging from a painfully immature sexual attitude (115). Bluefarb, for different reasons, says that George's relationship with Helen is "still in its idyllically romantic stage" (53). Bredahl worries that George's "reverence for Helen" is too much like the "groveling" of Wash Williams in "Respectability" and that it may be "debilitating" (427, 429, quoting *WO* 21). Most negative of all is Jacobson, who argues that "the narrator's overblown language" reflects not any specific deficiency of George Willard so much as a regression of the narrator and of Anderson himself to "mushy" sentiment and identification with his still-adolescent "protagonist" (68).

Against all those who see Helen White as representing some ideal, Atlas argues that she is only "the shadow of a strong woman," a "reflection" of George, and incapable of "independent action"; Atlas blames the author for missing the opportunity to develop a woman who uses "her impulses and intelligence to form a balanced, self-directed life" (263). Pickering expresses a still more divergent view: he considers Helen White "the epitome of self-satisfied respectability" and "the last and most dangerous threat to George's growth into an artist" (33). Pickering's interpretation, though, is heavily colored by a romantic reading of George Moore, and it is disputed by Fertig's assertion that Helen "has rejected the conventional middle-class values of her community in favor of an idealistic conception of the true value in life" (69). Yingling states that "Helen White's iconic significance for the young men of the town" derives largely from her social class, "from the privilege of being a banker's daughter" (103). While some of these arguments seem tangential, Bowden argues convincingly that the understanding George and Helen discover is hardly "a solution" to human loneliness, since it "cannot be actively sought" and can be found only "in rare intuitive moments" (119). More pessimistically still, Stouck states that the story "is shaped around George's growing awareness of life as a procession or dance toward death," which manifests itself in the activities surrounding the fair (537–38).

Formalist treatments of the story exhibit further differences. Several commentators discover a central "epiphany" in the story (Burbank 71; McDonald 240), and Wright classifies it among the romances with "an episode of discovery" (386, 184). Mellard, however, categorizes it as one of the "thematic" tales in *Winesburg* rather than as one of the "symbolic" tales, which move toward a final epiphany; he sees the story as moving allegorically toward George and Helen's finding of their "truth." It is not clear why he does not call their discovery an "epiphany," though he grants that the story is more "positive," less ironic, than others he places in this category (1307–1308). Howe says that this is the one story in the volume in which the movement toward a climax is not frustrated by interruption (107). Among specific techniques that critics discuss are repeated phrases, references to the cycle of seasons, and "modulations of mood" (San Juan 142–43); the absence of speech in the climactic scene, which reflects both George's and Helen's disgust with talk (Love 53–54; similarly, Mahoney 250); and the suggestive "symbol-like devices" and the "jerky, spasmodic focusing and refocusing" of narration that dramatize the protagonist's "restlessness and puzzlement" (Joselyn 72). The narrator's editorial commentary receives Ingram's approval (161), though Crawford regrets his "tendency to preach" (70). The "suggestive, implicit" language of the narrative, which requires the reader's "participation in the form of personal interpretation," is discussed matter-of-factly by Taylor (41–42; similarly, Wright 355, 408). But Way decries such language as "bad writing" and wants to be told explicitly what the "feelings" of the characters are (121).

The story, with its "door" and "leaf," has been identified as a possible source of Thomas Wolfe's closing scene in *Look Homeward, Angel,* for George's meditation in the empty fairground anticipates "Eugene's midnight vision in the deserted square of Altamont" (Budd 308–309; similarly, McDonald 240). The story has also been compared with "Big Two-Hearted River," the climactic story of Hemingway's *In Our Time,* where another protagonist silently discovers "the conditions in which the world may tolerably and validly be apprehended" (Ward 76–77).

It is Hilfer, though, who provides the best summary comment about the autumnal insight in "Sophistication":

> A disciple of Kenneth Burke's might even interpret the story as a perfect transposition of the classic tragic mode into modern naturalistic pathos

with a naturalistic "recognition" and "discovery" (of time and death) and a naturalistic "transcendence" and "catharsis" through the realization of the individual's participation in the universal fate. (155)

Words Cited

Abcarian, Richard. "Innocence and Experience in *Winesburg, Ohio.*" *University Review Kansas City* 35 (1968):95–105.

Anderson, Sherwood. 1916. *Windy McPherson's Son.* New York: John Lane. Rev. ed. New York: B. W. Huebsch, 1922; Chicago and London: University of Chicago Press, 1965. Introduction by Wright Morris.

——. 1919. *Winesburg, Ohio.* New York: B. W. Huebsch. Rpt. New York: Viking, 1960.

——. 1926. *Tar: A Midwest Childhood.* New York: Boni & Liveright. Rpt. in *Tar: A Midwest Childhood: A Critical Text.* Ed. Ray Lewis White. Cleveland: Press of Case Western Reserve University, 1969.

Atlas, Marilyn Judith. 1981. "Sherwood Anderson and the Women of Winesburg." In *Critical Essays on Sherwood Anderson.* Ed. David D. Anderson. Boston: G. K. Hall, 250–66.

Bidney, Martin. "Anderson and the Androgyne: 'Something More than Man or Woman.'" *Studies in Short Fiction* 25 (1988):261–73.

Bluefarb, Sam. 1972. "George Willard: Death and Resurrection." *The Escape Motif in the American Novel: Mark Twain to Richard Wright.* Columbus: Ohio State University Press, 42–58.

Bort, Barry D. "*Winesburg, Ohio:* The Escape from Isolation." *Midwest Quarterly* 11 (1970):443–56.

Bowden, Edwin T. 1961. *The Dungeon of the Heart: Human Isolation and the American Novel.* New York: Macmillan, 114–24.

Bredahl, A. Carl. "'The Young Thing Within': Divided Narrative and Sherwood Anderson's *Winesburg, Ohio.*" *Midwest Quarterly: A Journal of Contemporary Thought* 27 (1986):422–37.

Bresnahan, Roger J. "The 'Old Hands' of Winesburg." *Midwestern Miscellany* 11 (1983):19–27.

Budd, Louis J. "The Grotesque of Anderson and Wolfe." *Modern Fiction Studies* 5 (1959–60):304–310.

Bunge, Nancy. 1981. "Women in Sherwood Anderson's Fiction." In *Critical Essays on Sherwood Anderson.* Ed. David D. Anderson. Boston: G. K. Hall, 242–49.

Burbank, Rex. 1964. *Sherwood Anderson.* New York: Twayne. Rpt. in part in *The Achievement of Sherwood Anderson: Essays in Criticism.* Ed. Ray Lewis White. Chapel Hill: University of North Carolina Press, 1966, 32–43. Rpt. in part in *Sherwood Anderson: A Collection of Critical Essays.* Ed. Walter B. Rideout. Englewood Cliffs, NJ: Prentice-Hall, 1974, 70–83.

Ciancio, Ralph. "The Sweetness of the Twisted Apples: Unity of Vision in *Winesburg, Ohio.*" *PMLA* 87 (1972):994–1006.

Crawford, Nelson Antrim. 1981. "Sherwood Anderson, the Wistfully Faithful." In *Critical Essays on Sherwood Anderson.* Ed. David D. Anderson. Boston: G. K. Hall, 65–73. Originally printed in *The Midland* 8 (November 1922):297–308.

De Jovine, F. Anthony. 1971. *The Young Hero in American Fiction: A Motif for Teaching Literature.* New York: Appleton-Century-Crofts.

Fagin, N. Bryllion. 1973. *The Phenomenon of Sherwood Anderson: A Study in American Life and Letters.* New York: Russell & Russell. Originally printed Baltimore: Rossi-Bryn, 1927.

Fertig, Martin J. "'A Great Deal of Wonder in Me': Inspiration and Transformation in *Winesburg, Ohio.*" *Markham Review* 6 (1977):65–70.

Fussell, Edwin. "*Winesburg, Ohio:* Art and Isolation." *Modern Fiction Studies* 6 (1960):106–14. Rpt. in *Sherwood Anderson:* Winesburg, Ohio: *Text and Criticism.* Ed. John H. Ferres. New York: Viking, 1966, 383–95. Rpt. in *Achievement of Sherwood Anderson: Essays in Criticism.* Ed. Ray Lewis White. Chapel Hill: University of North Carolina Press, 1966, 104–113. Rpt. in *Sherwood Anderson: A Collection of Critical Essays.* Ed. Walter B. Rideout. Englewood Cliffs, NJ: Prentice-Hall, 1974, 39–48.

Hilfer, Anthony Channel. 1969. *The Revolt from the Village, 1915–1930.* Chapel Hill: University of North Carolina Press.

Howe, Irving. 1951. *Sherwood Anderson.* New York: William Sloane.

Hurd, Thaddeus B. "Excerpts from '*Winesburg* and Clyde, Fictional/Real Places.'" In *Sherwood Anderson: A Study of the Short Fiction.* Robert Allen Papinchak. New York: Twayne, 1992.

———. "Fun in Winesburg." *Midwestern Miscellany* 11 (1983):28–39.

Ingram, Forrest L. 1971. *Representative Short Story Cycles of the Twentieth Century: Studies in a Literary Genre.* The Hague: Mouton.

Jacobson, Marcia. 1990. "*Winesburg, Ohio* and the Autobiographical Moment." *New Essays on* Winesburg, Ohio. Ed. John W. Crowley. Cambridge and New York: Cambridge University Press, 53–72.

Joselyn, Sister Mary. 1966. "Sherwood Anderson and the Lyric Story." In *The*

Twenties: Poetry and Prose. Richard E. Langford and William E. Taylor (Eds.). DeLand, FL: Everett Edwards Press, 70–73. Rpt. in *Sherwood Anderson:* Winesburg, Ohio: *Text and Criticism.* Ed. John H. Ferres. New York: Viking, 1966, 444–54.

Love, Glen A. "*Winesburg, Ohio* and the Rhetoric of Silence." *American Literature* 40 (1968):38–57.

Mahoney, John J. "An Analysis of *Winesburg, Ohio.*" *Journal of Aesthetics and Art Criticism* 15 (1956):245–52.

McDonald, Walter R. "*Winesburg, Ohio:* Tales of Isolation." *University Review Kansas City* 35 (1969);237–40.

Mellard, James M. "Narrative Forms in *Winesburg, Ohio.*" *PMLA* 83 (1968):1304–1312.

Miller, William V. 1976. "Portraits of the Artist: Anderson's Fictional Storytellers." In *Sherwood Anderson: Dimensions of His Literary Art: A Collection of Critical Essays.* Ed. David D. Anderson. East Lansing: Michigan State University Press, 1–23.

Modlin, Charles E., ed. 1984. *Sherwood Anderson: Selected Letters.* Knoxville: University of Tennessee Press.

Morgan, H. Wayne. 1963. "Sherwood Anderson: The Search for Unity." *Writers in Transition: Seven Americans.* New York: Hill and Wang, 82–104.

Murphy, George D. "The Theme of Sublimation in Anderson's *Winesburg, Ohio.*" *Modern Fiction Studies* 13 (1967):237–46.

Phillips, William L. "How Sherwood Anderson Wrote *Winesburg, Ohio.*" *American Literature* 23 (1951):7–30. Rpt. in *Sherwood Anderson:* Winesburg, Ohio: *Text and Criticism.* Ed. John H. Ferres. New York: Viking, 1966, 263–86. Rpt. in *The Achievement of Sherwood Anderson: Essays in Criticism.* Ed. Ray Lewis White. Chapel Hill: University of North Carolina Press, 1966, 62–84. Rpt. in *The Merrill Studies in* Winesburg, Ohio. Comp. Ray Lewis White. Columbus, OH: Charles E. Merrill, 1971, 2–24. Rpt. in *Sherwood Anderson: A Collection of Critical Essays.* Ed. Walter B. Rideout. Englewood Cliffs, NJ: Prentice-Hall, 1974, 18–38.

Pickering, Samuel. "*Winesburg, Ohio:* A Portrait of the Artist as a Young Man." *Southern Quarterly* 16 (1977):27–38.

Rideout, Walter B. "The Simplicity of *Winesburg, Ohio.*" *Shenandoah* 13 (1962):20–31. Rpt. in *Sherwood Anderson:* Winesburg, Ohio: *Text and Criticism.* Ed. John H. Ferres. New York: Viking, 1966, 287–300. Rpt. in *Critical Essays on Sherwood Anderson.* Ed. David D. Anderson. Boston: G. K. Hall, 1981, 146–64.

——. 1966. "Why Sherwood Anderson Employed Buck Fever." In *The*

Achievement of Sherwood Anderson: Essays in Criticism. Ed. Ray Lewis White. Chapel Hill: University of North Carolina Press, 128–37. Originally in *Georgia Review* 13 (1959):76–85.

Rigsbee, Sally Adair. "The Feminine in *Winesburg, Ohio.*" *Studies in American Fiction* 9 (1981):233–44.

Rogers, Douglas G. "Development of the Artist in *Winesburg, Ohio.*" *Studies in the Twentieth Century* 10 (1972):91–99.

San Juan, Epifanio, Jr. "Vision and Reality: A Reconsideration of Sherwood Anderson's *Winesburg, Ohio.*" *American Literature* 35 (1963):137–55. Rpt. in part in *Sherwood Anderson:* Winesburg, Ohio: *Text and Criticism.* Ed. John H. Ferres. New York: Viking, 1966, 468–81.

Schevill, James. 1951. *Sherwood Anderson: His Life and Work.* Denver: University of Denver Press.

Stouck, David. *"Winesburg, Ohio* as a Dance of Death." *American Literature* 48 (1977):525–42. Rpt. in *Critical Essays on Sherwood Anderson.* Ed. David D. Anderson. Boston: G. K. Hall, 1981, 181–95.

Sullivan, John. "Winesburg Revisited." *Antioch Review* 20 (1960):213–21.

Taylor, Welford Dunaway. 1977. *Sherwood Anderson.* New York: Frederick Ungar.

Thurston, Jarvis. "Anderson and 'Winesburg': Mysticism and Craft." *Accent* 16 (1956):107–28. Rpt. in part in *Sherwood Anderson:* Winesburg, Ohio: *Text and Criticism.* Ed. John H. Ferres. New York: Viking, 1966, 331–44.

Walcutt, Charles Child. "Sherwood Anderson: Impressionism and the Buried Life." *Sewanee Review* 60 (1952):28–47. Rpt. in *American Literary Naturalism, a Divided Stream.* Minneapolis: University of Minnesota Press, 1956, 222–39. Rpt. in part in *Sherwood Anderson:* Winesburg, Ohio: *Text and Criticism.* Ed. John H. Ferres. New York: Viking, 1966, 432–43.

Ward, J. A. 1985. *"Winesburg, Ohio:* Habitual Silence and the Roaring of Voices." *American Silences: The Realism of James Agee, Walker Evans, and Edward Hopper.* Baton Rouge: Louisiana State University Press, 35–50.

Way, Brian. 1971. "Sherwood Anderson." In *The American Novel and the Nineteen Twenties.* Malcolm Bradbury and David Palmer (Eds.). Stratford-upon-Avon Studies 13. London: Edward Arnold, 107–126.

White, Ray Lewis. 1969. *Sherwood Anderson's Memoirs: A Critical Edition.* Chapel Hill: University of North Carolina Press.

Wright, Austin McGiffert. 1961. *The American Short Story in the Twenties.* Chicago: University of Chicago Press.

Yingling, Thomas. 1990. "*Winesburg, Ohio* and the End of Collective Experience." In *New Essays on* Winesburg, Ohio. Ed. John W. Crowley. Cambridge and New York: Cambridge University Press, 99–128.

Departure

Circumstances of Composition

This, the closing story of *Winesburg, Ohio,* seems to have been written, along with "Death" and "Sophistication," after the rest of the stories were completed. Phillips says that may have been in 1916 ("How" 13, 28), but it probably was somewhat later. In November of 1916 Anderson wrote to Waldo Frank, editor of *Seven Arts,* that he had completed fifteen *Winesburg* stories and planned a total of seventeen (Jones-Rideout, *Letters* 4); that suggests that Phillips miscalculated the dates of some of the stories. It was perhaps as late as 1918 when Anderson wrote "Departure." He had moved to Chicago in 1913 as an unpublished writer; by this time he would have seen a number of his stories and at least one of his novels in print. Though he was still earning his living as an advertising copywriter, he must have felt hopeful that he was launched at last on his true career.

The manuscript indicates that Anderson first titled the story "George Leaves Winesburg" and then revised it (White 6).

Sources and Influences

Though this story fits the archetypal pattern of the youth leaving home to seek his fortune, it is a slice of autobiography as well. The landscape and some of the people of Winesburg were remembered from Anderson's hometown of Clyde, Ohio. When he departed Clyde in 1896, his mother, like George Willard's, had recently died. Like George, he had left home with a twin heritage—an impulse to "be sharp" and an impulse to dream, tendencies he attributes in this book to George's father and mother, respectively. Evidence of both traits is manifest in George, but as Rideout argues, the "commitment to the world of dreams" that Anderson considered crucial to the imaginative writer is finally uppermost in the story (28). Like his character, Anderson had carried within him memories that provided the "background on which to paint the dreams of his manhood" (*WO* 247). But he had not found happiness quickly by any means. His first job in Chicago, "rolling barrels of apples in a cold-storage warehouse," was poorly paid and exhausting (Howe 27). Even his subsequent rise to "success," as that term is ordinarily defined, had left him miserable. When he wrote this story, Anderson in fact had moved to Chicago for the third time. (A succinct summary of these three moves—1896, 1900, and 1913—is given in David Anderson's "Sherwood Anderson, Chicago, and the Midwestern Myth," 58–59.) The author must have imagined that young George Willard's journey would not be easy.

Publication History

This story made its first appearance in *Winesburg, Ohio* (1919).

Relation to Other Works

The thread that ties together the varied stories of *Winesburg, Ohio* is the growth of a boy in his community. As Anderson put it in 1931, " . . . I told the story of the boy in *Winesburg* by telling the stories of other people whose lives touched his life" (Jones-Rideout, *Letters* 246). This makes the short story cycle in part a bildungsroman, as Fussell was the first to discern. "Departure" simply represents the completion of one phase of George Willard's growth. According to Phillips's analysis of the dating in the various stories, George leaves home two years and seven months after he had told his mother (in "Mother") that he expected to leave in a year or two ("Origins" 168).

Following the moment of achieved insight and understanding in "Sophistication," this story is "anticlimactic"; but George takes away with him "something of each of the grotesques who sought him out" in the course of the other stories (D. Anderson, *Sherwood* 49). Both the opening story and this one, which provide a framing perspective for the whole, present characters retrospectively transformed to "their essential nature," in the mind of the old writer in the first and in George's mind in the last (Fertig 70). Ingram argues that the book moves "from conception in 'The Book of the Grotesque,' to maturity in 'Departure,' of a fictive community in the distortive memory of the book's single narrator; and of a return, in 'Departure,' to the initial (now modified) situation" (147). Love, however, suggests that "Hands" and "Departure" frame the action of the whole, with pastoral images indicative of the context of the natural world (55).

A major device serving to connect the various *Winesburg* stories is the motif of departure. In one sense, George Willard's escape from Winesburg is significant because he "typifies all of the buried yearnings of his fellow townsmen" (Bluefarb 45). Other characters who leave Winesburg include David Hardy (in "Godliness"), Ned Currie (in "Adventure"), and Elmer Cowley (in "Queer"); Seth Richmond (in "The Thinker") decides to leave but evidently never acts on that decision (Ingram 168–69; similarly, Williams 185). Still other characters have arrived in Winesburg after departures from other places. Wing Biddlebaum had left Pennsylvania after a scandal (in "Hands"), Wash Williams had left Columbus after a decisive break with his wife (in "Respectability"), and Tom Foster and his grandmother had left Cincinnati hoping to escape from harsh poverty (in "Drink"); but "none of them has succeeded in escaping from himself" (Bowden 122). Moreover, since Enoch Robinson (in "Loneliness") "has already departed for the city as George does at the end, and failed," it is clear that "George's success is by no means assured" (Lorch 63–64). The book's numerous references to urban life (in sixteen different stories) show that, though characters frequently imagine that the city offers better opportunities, leaving the village does not solve life's problems: "both the city and the town suffer from false illusions and faulty interpretations" (Williams 183–84; similarly, Bowden 122).

Anderson drew on his own departure from Clyde not only in *Winesburg* but also in *Windy McPherson's Son* (1916) and *Tar* (1926); in both those works, however, the protagonists head for the city with money-making rather than artistic dreams uppermost in their minds (D. Anderson, "Sherwood Anderson, Chicago" 63; "Anderson and Myth" 135; and "From Memory" 83).

Critical Studies

This story, as Schevill comments, serves as "an epilogue" to *Winesburg, Ohio* (104). It has not received, and probably does not call for, extensive critical analysis.

One interpreter discovers social import in the story's evocation of "the inevitable disappearance of village life" (Love 55). A feminist critic chides Anderson for not letting any of the women of Winesburg escape as George does; in particular, she objects to the author's having "sacrificed Helen [White]'s potential in order to simplify George's exit" (Atlas 250, 256). Gold finds biographical significance in the ending, which he sees as a sad parallel to Anderson's own wrongheaded idea that the artist must withdraw from "decent connections with others in society" (553). Another psychobiographical speculator surmises that the story's inconclusive ending results from the fact that Anderson had not yet resolved his conflicts with his father; he would need "to outdo his father as a storyteller," Jacobson argues, "before he could define himself" (70). A formalist critic classifies the tale as one of the type he calls "the story of incident," noting the archetypal significance of the title (Mellard 1306). The symbolic appropriateness of the spring morning setting for the young man's journey has been noted by several critics (Hilfer 155; Abcarian 104). Others have mentioned his likeness to the numerous other characters in American novels who make escapes (Bluefarb 57), or, more specifically, to those who leave Midwestern towns for Chicago (D. Anderson, "Anderson and Myth" 123).

The most significant topic of critical discussion concerns the tone of this final episode and what it implies about George's departure in relation to his past and future. Ingram keenly observes that George's morning walk down "Trunion (true + union) Pike [which] had once been the center of Winesburg" (*WO* 210) shows his desire to connect with the town he has known "during its bleak and its green seasons" (170). But what of his actual departure? Gochberg gives the text a very positive reading, asserting that, from a "milieu of stagnation," "a cemetery" of twisted lives, George Willard "emerges growing healthily" as "a mean between grotesque extremes" (48). Similarly, in his book on Sherwood Anderson, David Anderson emphasizes George's position as a sort of paragon of empathy and understanding (50, 53). More accurately, in a later essay, he remarks: "In its ambiguity the ending approaches a Twain-like purity" ("Anderson and Myth" 123). In an analysis drawing upon Walter Benjamin's idea that oral culture (characterized by storytelling) is linked with wisdom and an integrated society whereas print culture is characterized by alienation, Yingling argues that although George, "the very figure of the storyteller" in whom others confide, serves as a "focus of collective experiences," the elegiac ending foresees that he will be absorbed by "the modern world of interiority" (122–25). Abcarian elaborates best the delicate balance between "the dominant tone of quiet joy" and "a countertone of sadness and the possibility of failure," the way the ending "turns out attention back to . . . the grotesques, each of whom once faced the world with the same youthful hope and expectation that George now carries with him" (104–105). The train conductor, Tom Little, seems to Abcarian a slightly "ominous" figure, reminiscent of Tiresias with his "timeless wisdom" (104). In contrast, the conductor seems to Ciancio "a Doubting Thomas" and a small-minded "clod," while George is assured of a successful return to Winesburg "from the transcendental perspective of the artistic imagination" (1006). If the statement about truths in "The Book of the Grotesque" is to be taken seriously, both critics may be right.

Works Cited

Abcarian, Richard. "Innocence and Experience in *Winesburg, Ohio*." *University Review Kansas City* 35 (1968):95–105.

Anderson, David. 1967. *Sherwood Anderson: An Introduction and Interpretation*. New York: Holt, Rinehart.

———. 1976. "Anderson and Myth." *Sherwood Anderson: Dimensions of His Literary Art*. East Lansing: Michigan State University Press, 118–41.

———. "From Memory to Meaning: The Boys' Stories of William Dean Howells, Clarence Darrow, and Sherwood Anderson." *Midamerica* 10 (1983).69–84.

———. "Sherwood Anderson, Chicago, and the Midwestern Myth." *Midamerica* 11 (1984):56–68.

Anderson, Sherwood. 1919. *Winesburg, Ohio*. New York: B. W. Huebsch. Rpt. New York: Viking, 1960.

Atlas, Marilyn Judith. 1981. "Sherwood Anderson and the Women of Winesburg." In *Critical Essays on Sherwood Anderson*. Ed. David D. Anderson. Boston: G. K. Hall, 250–66.

Bluefarb, Sam. "George Willard: Death and Resurrection." 1972. *The Escape Motif in the American Novel: Mark Twain to Richard Wright*. Columbus: Ohio State University Press, 42–58.

Bowden, Edwin T. 1961. *The Dungeon of the Heart: Human Isolation and the American Novel*. New York: Macmillan, 114–24.

Ciancio, Ralph. "The Sweetness of the Twisted Apples: Unity of Vision in *Winesburg, Ohio*." *PMLA* 87 (1972):994–1006.

Fertig, Martin J. "'A Great Deal of Wonder in Me': Inspiration and Transformation in *Winesburg, Ohio*." *Markham Review* 6 (1977):65–70.

Gochberg, Donald. 1971. "Stagnation and Growth: The Emergence of George Willard." In *Merrill Studies in* Winesburg, Ohio. Comp. Ray Lewis White. Columbus, OH: Charles E. Merrill, 42–48. Originally published in *Expression* 4 (Winter 1960):29–35.

Gold, Herbert. "The Purity and Cunning of Sherwood Anderson." *Hudson Review* 10 (1957–58):548–57. Rpt. in *The Age of Happy Problems*. New York: Dial Press, 1962, 56–67. Rpt. in part in *Sherwood Anderson: Winesburg, Ohio: Text and Criticism*. Ed. John H. Ferres. New York: Viking, 1966, 396–404. Rpt. in *Critical Essays on Sherwood Anderson*. Ed. David D. Anderson. Boston: G. K. Hall, 1981, 138–45.

Hilfer, Anthony Channel. 1969. *The Revolt from the Village, 1915–1930*. Chapel Hill: University of North Carolina Press.

Howe, Irving. 1951. *Sherwood Anderson*. New York: William Sloane.

Ingram, Forrest L. 1971. *Representative Short Story Cycles of the Twentieth Century: Studies in a Literary Genre*. The Hague: Mouton.

Jacobson, Marcia. 1990. "*Winesburg, Ohio* and the Autobiographical Moment." In *New Essays on* Winesburg, Ohio. Ed. John W. Crowley. Cambridge and New York: Cambridge University Press, 53–72.

Jones, Howard Mumford, and Walter B. Rideout, eds. 1953. *Letters of Sherwood Anderson*. Boston: Little, Brown.

Lorch, Thomas M. "The Choreographic Structure of *Winesburg, Ohio*." *College Language Association Journal* 12 (1968–69):56–65.

Love, Glen A. "*Winesburg, Ohio* and the Rhetoric of Silence." *American Literature* 40 (1968):38–57.

Mellard, James M. "Narrative Forms in *Winesburg, Ohio*." *PMLA* 83 (1968):1304–1312.

Phillips, William L. "How Sherwood Anderson Wrote *Winesburg, Ohio*." *American Literature* 23 (1951):7–30. Rpt. in *Sherwood Anderson:* Winesburg, Ohio: *Text and Criticism*. Ed. John H. Ferres. New York: Viking, 1966, 263–86. Rpt. in *The Achievement of Sherwood Anderson: Essays in Criticism*. Ed. Ray Lewis White. Chapel Hill: University of North Carolina Press, 1966, 62–84. Rpt. in *The Merrill Studies in* Winesburg, Ohio. Comp. Ray Lewis White. Columbus, OH: Charles E. Merrill, 1971, 2–24. Rpt. in *Sherwood Anderson: A Collection of Critical Essays*. Ed. Walter B. Rideout. Englewood Cliffs, NJ: Prentice Hall, 1974, 18–38.

——. "Sherwood Anderson's *Winesburg, Ohio:* Its Origins, Composition, Technique, and Reception." Ph.D. diss., University of Chicago, 1950.

Rideout, Walter B. "The Simplicity of *Winesburg, Ohio*." *Shenandoah* 13 (1962):20–31. Rpt. in *Sherwood Anderson:* Winesburg, Ohio: *Text and Criticism*. Ed. John H. Ferres. New York: Viking, 1966, 287–300. Rpt. in *Critical Essays on Sherwood Anderson*. Ed. David D. Anderson. Boston: G. K. Hall, 1981, 146–54.

Schevill, James. 1951. *Sherwood Anderson: His Life and Work*. Denver: University of Denver Press.

White, Ray Lewis. "*Winesburg, Ohio:* The Story Titles." *Winesburg Eagle* 10, no. 1 (November 1984):6–7.

Williams, Kenny J. 1988. *A Storyteller and a City: Sherwood Anderson's Chicago*. De Kalb: Northern Illinois University Press.

Yingling, Thomas. 1990. "*Winesburg, Ohio* and the End of Collective Experience." In *New Essays on* Winesburg, Ohio. Ed. John W. Crowley. Cambridge and New York: Cambridge University Press, 99–128.

The Triumph of the Egg

I Want to Know Why

Circumstances of Composition

This famous story was written in Chicago in August of 1919. The author was living "on the ground floor of a three-story brick building on Division Street" (Williams vi). Walter Rideout has set forth in illuminating detail the ways in which Anderson's personal experience around that time contributed to the story. In May, just after *Winesburg, Ohio* was published, Anderson had "watched the thoroughbred Sir Barton run a muddy track to victory in the Kentucky Derby"; in the following weeks, he returned to Chicago and "labored resentfully at his copywriting" for the Long-Critchfield Agency while Sir Barton went on to become the first Triple Crown Winner (7–8). Increasingly, Anderson felt that his work in advertising was self-defiling, a prostitution of his artistic talent (13). A restful July vacation with his second wife in Ephraim, Wisconsin, made his return to Chicago painful by contrast; Chicago had been torn by race riots, and "out of revulsion at white violence" Anderson sheltered five black acquaintants in his small apartment (8). During the previous year he had been discussing Mark Twain and *Huckleberry Finn* with Van Wyck Brooks, who was at work on *The Ordeal of Mark Twain;* Twain's idiom and cultural situation were much on his mind (12). On August 10 he read in the sports columns that "the thoroughbred Sun Briar had won the Champlain Handicap at the races at Saratoga Springs, New York, and had set a new track record"; shortly thereafter, he began to write this story (9).

Sources and Influences

In his childhood Anderson had developed a passion for the trotting and pacing horses at the Clyde racetrack. He later remembered himself as a boy leaning over the track fence, trembling: "Tears came into my eyes and a lump into my throat. It was my first love. Oh the beautiful, the courageous and aristocratic creatures. I grew sick with envy of the drivers . . . " (White, *Memoirs* 52). Among the jobs he had in his youth was grooming the horses in the Clyde livery stable; that was "a comedown" from dreams of driving splendid racing horses but also "a time of adventure" with swaggering roughs (White, *Memoirs,* 110–11). One experience in particular may have entered into this story. Anderson recalled that when his intoxicated co-worker Ed brought a red-headed prostitute to his cot in the stable office, "I heard the beginnings of a crude manifestation of human lust that sickened me"; fleeing, he "kept thinking how Ed's boastful lying about various women of the town" had aroused his own lust, and was ashamed (White, *Memoirs* 111–112).

Anderson's somewhat different speculation about the source of the story appears in a typescript at the Newberry Library, written about twenty years after the story was composed; possibly, he thinks, in "a glow" from having "written something solid" he may have gone to a prostitute "on the same day" and felt doubly "mean" upon hearing her child beyond a curtain— "And so I imagine myself . . . thinking of the theme of the story 'I Want to Know Why.' I would simply have been questioning the two sides of myself, being, in myself, both the boy who was a horse lover and the trainer who went off to the whore" (Curry, 113–14n).

Rideout points out the influence of Sun Briar, the horse that won the Champlain Handicap, on the name of the fictional stallion Sunstreak, who wins the Mullford Handicap (9), but he is convinced that the Derby winner Sir Barton must have contributed as well (11). Rideout also states that the name of Sunstreak's owner, "Mr. Van Riddle," was probably derived from Sam Riddle, the real owner of a popular horse at Saratoga, that "Middle-stride" was drawn after a gelding named "Exterminator," which Anderson saw win at Churchill Downs in 1918, and that Banker Bohon's name is imported into the story from an actual banker in Harrodsburg, Kentucky, father of two of Anderson's clients (10–11). The original "impulse to write the story," Anderson would recall in 1932, came during days he spent at the Saratoga tracks "with Dave Bohon" (White, *Letters* 39).

Critics agree that Twain's *Huckleberry Finn* was a major influence on the tale. The fullest treatment of the subject is offered by Gross, who explains that Anderson's story shows its indebtedness to Twain's novel in three ways: the "ironic point of view" of boy narrators "who are morally finer than most of the white world which they are describing" but who mistakenly believe that if they were "better" or "more grown up" they would be able to appreciate the wisdom of the society around them; the "symbolic dichotomy" between the track and the town that is akin to that between raft and shore in the novel—with the black man as "a kind of moral center" against which the cruelty and chicanery the dominant whites are judged; and the initiation of the protagonists into "realms of moral horror" that destroy their "idyllic world" and leave them isolated and withdrawn (3–5).

The narrator's revulsion at the trainer's ignoble sexuality may have been influenced by Anderson's attitude toward his father's adultery (White, *Memoirs* 115).

Publication History

"I Want to Know Why" was first printed in November of 1919 in *Smart Set* (60:35–40). Years later Anderson recalled that he "had difficulty selling it" and that he had received "perhaps thirty dollars" for it (Curry, 112–13n). If Rideout's research is reliable and the story was indeed composed in August of 1919, it does not seem that Anderson can have had much difficulty securing the story's publication. His memory of the payment, too, may or may not be not quite accurate: Rogers cites a letter saying that Anderson sold the story to "some little magazine for $25" (117). As Gullason observes, it is interesting that H. L. Mencken's *Smart Set,* "which prided itself on being the magazine of cleverness," was the forum of this tale, which, in spite of its "irony and paradox," speaks on behalf of old-fashioned, dyed-in-the-wool values (77). *Smart Set* had published two earlier tales much inferior to this one, "The Story Writers" and "The White Streak," and had rejected the fine story "Queer." Anderson wrote contemptuously of Mencken to Van Wyck Brooks in 1918: "One cannot surrender to the cheaper inclination in writing, to win perhaps the secondary approval of an ass like Mencken as his reward" (Jones-Rideout, *Letters* 37). The popularity and quality of the newly published *Winesburg, Ohio* may have paved the way for this story. But the "smart" sayings that fill the space on the page after Anderson's story in *Smart Set* are incongruous; for example, "A man often has heart enough to love two women at a time, but he seldom has wit enough to get away with it" (40).

In 1921 the story was reprinted in *The Triumph of the Egg* (5–20). That collection went through three printings in 1921 and 1922 and a fourth in 1924 (Campbell 169).

In November of 1937 the story was reprinted in the popular magazine *Redbook* (70:38–41, 114), which paid $500 for it (Curry 113n; Jones-Rideout, *Letters* 381n). Anderson had to pay one-quarter of that amount to Viking Press, which owned the rights to the volumes originally published by B. W. Huebsch (Jones-Rideout, *Letters* 381–83).

The story has been much reprinted since and often anthologized. Rosenfeld included it in *The Sherwood Anderson Reader* in 1947 (86–94). Geismar published it in his collection of Anderson's short stories in 1962 (5–13), as did Gado in 1983 (35–46) and Modlin in 1992 (8–17).

Relation to Other Works

"I Want to Know Why" is most clearly related to Anderson's other stories with racetrack settings, "I'm a Fool" and "The Man Who Became a Woman," both collected in *Horses and Men* (1923). All three stories, in an "idyllic," preindustrial setting, treat the "frustration," "guilt and confusion" of adolescent boys growing into manhood (Pecile 147–48). "I Want to Know Why" is more complex than "I'm a Fool," which also employs a boy as narrator. "The Man Who Became a Woman," though, has greater symbolic density than either and a richer perspective lent by an adult narrator looking back on his earlier experience. Howe's analysis of the comparative merits of these three tales is persuasive (153–57, 160–64).

Within the collection *The Triumph of the Egg,* "I Want to Know Why" introduces the central question to which the volume responds. The book's title alludes to Percy Bysshe Shelley's poem *The Triumph of Life,* which he left unfinished at his death. Shelley's poem opens with dawn lifting "the mask of darkness . . . from the awakened Earth" but soon gives way to the poet's vision of a sad procession of multitudes of anxious people hurrying along confusedly:

> . . . none seemed to know
> Whither he went, or whence he came, or why. . . .

As the great and famous personages of history pass by, all of them conquered by life, the poet asks the same question the narrator of Anderson's story poses—"Why?" Nobody knows what answer to that question Shelley would have written had he lived to conclude his poem. Anderson's volume, however, repeatedly evokes the images of Shelley's "Ode to the West Wind," which gathers symbols of destruction and senescence to hint prophetically at an anticipated spring. It would appear that Anderson tried to arrange the stories in *The Triumph of the Egg* in an order that moves from the initial "I Want to Know Why" through manifold versions of banal human struggle with stultifying material conditions, spiritual deprivation, and moral cruelty that reiterate the temper of the existing portion of *The Triumph of Life*. Increasingly discernible within this modern wasteland, though, are repeated signs of a new world waiting to be born, and these signs draw upon the affirmative direction of the "Ode to the West Wind." The stories in Anderson's collection are framed by two prose poems. "The Dumb Man," at the beginning, in which Anderson yearns for words to tell "a wonderful story," functions as a modernist version of the invocation of the muse. At the end, where Anderson hope that the words he has scattered (in the intervening stories) may be like seeds, "The Man with the Trumpet" is a prophetic call to individual and cultural regeneration. The scenes Anderson paints are as dark as those in Shelley's *The Triumph of Life,* and the characters' positive gestures are surrounded with irony, though the volume contains a strong, if subdued, current of revolutionary zeal. It is open-ended. The hope expressed is tentative. Life's enigmas are by no means resolved. And the situations and characters in the stories are so homely that readers have hardly noticed that *The Triumph of the Egg* is Anderson's boldest experiment in the symbolic and prophetic mode.

The experience of maturing adolescents is a favorite subject of Anderson's. It is important especially in *Winesburg, Ohio* (1919) and in *Poor White* (1920). Tom Foster, in "Drink," like the narrator of "I Want to Know Why," suffers from an episode of sordid sex. And horse racing is an important subject matter in *A Story Teller's Story* as well (1924). The contrast between the moral corruption of the boasters who gather at the livery stables and Alonzo Berners's humility before fine horses and his pessimism about humanity (118–25, 178–81) is much like the similar disparity that animates "I Want to Know Why." Furthermore, *A Story Teller's Story* draws a cameo portrait of a little, crooked, no-account gambler that resembles that of Jerry Tillford in this story: by a "soft light [that] came into his eyes" at the sight of a superb horse, the gambler reveals an aesthetic sensitivity not unlike that of a photographer or painter, and the narrator comments that what he shared with this man as they watched the horse run was "a kind of consciousness that perhaps the horses haven't . . . consciousness of one another. That is what love is, perhaps" (313–14).

Tar (1926) draws on racetrack scenes with more nostalgia; the child's viewpoint of this semiautobiographical narrative, as in the story, captures the sensuous enjoyment of simple food cooked out of doors and the innocent bewilderment of a boy trying to sort out the mysterious, twisted rules of the adult world.

The portrayal of the Negro in "I Want to Know Why" bears comparison with that in other works in the Anderson canon. Particularly notable is the similarity between the view expressed here and that in *Dark Laughter* (1925), which also "reflects a popularly-held primitivistic stereotype of the Negro during the 1920s" (Love 247n). The narrative approach of this story allows for considerable dramatic irony, however, and it is not just to equate the boy narrator's perception with the (adult) author's. Greater complexity of presentation appears both in "The Man Who Became a Woman" and in "Out of Nowhere into Nothing." This is not to say that Anderson's understanding of blacks is adequate: by any absolute standard, it is not. But neither is it so lacking in sensitivity as is sometimes supposed.

Critical Studies

"I Want to Know Why" has been tremendously admired. An early critic remarked that the story (and also "Out of Nowhere into Nothing") made him "wonder if there is any greater poignancy utterly free from sentimental claptrap, anywhere in American literature" (Crawford 71). Hansen applauded, as so many others have since, the forceful "genuineness" of the adolescent narrator's voice (153). Chase found in the boy's "fumbling inarticulateness" a lyric eloquence like that in Keats's "Ode to a Nightingale" (42). Fagin called it "one of the finest" American short stories (87), and subsequent critics have for the most part concurred. Cargill judged it a superb psychological study of a primitive mind: "No other American" except Twain, he said, "has such complete rapport with youth" (328). Voss ranks it without peer among twentieth-century initiation stories, "with the possible exception of Hemingway's 'My Old Man,'" which was strongly influenced by Anderson's story (194). West considers it to be one of the author's best, kept from being "one of the great stories of the century" only by its emphasis on "the natural beauty of the instinctive life" to the detriment of attention to the "opposite side of the problem," which has to do with human morality (50–52).

A common objection to the story involves the ending. Chase called it "an anticlimax so banal as to make one wonder whether it wasn't by pure chance that Anderson caught the lyric note at all" (42). Howe criticizes what he considers a stylistic lapse in the narrative perspective: the story "achieves a triumph of tone" with "echoes of the authentic Twain," he writes, "[e]xcept for two minor intrusions by an adult voice and several badly superfluous sentences at its end" (157; similarly, Raymund 141–42).

A few critics, however, have simply disliked the story as a whole. Calverton found it "lazy in motion, weak in construction, and unparsimoniously conceived, . . . redeemed largely by a unique and effective climax" (104). Nearly fifty years later, Way thought Anderson's "inability to handle vernacular first-person narration in the manner of Mark Twain" showed up in the story as "the flat stereotyped effect of Ring Lardner's weaker tales" (120–21).

Close analysis of the story essentially begins with the interpretation given in Brooks and Warren's *Understanding Fiction* in 1943. Labeling it an initiation story, they assert that the narrator's "discovery is that good and evil can be so intimately allied—can exist in the same person" (344, 347). They note that in his sense that "Negroes are 'squarer' with kids than white men are" and in his favorable evaluation of Henry Rieback's father, the boy is already questioning conventional societal values (345). They also place great weight on the phrase "who knows what he does" (*TE* 19) and extrapolate from it a thematic emphasis on "man's capacity for choice," which differentiates humans from horses and which confers on them moral responsibility" "Man, because he is capable of choice—because he 'knows' what he does—because he is capable of being better than the brute, becomes, when he fails to exercise his capacity, something worse than the brute" (348–49). They also point to two brief passages they consider to be violations of the style appropriate to the narrator (349–50).

Sherbo presents a brief but convincing dissent from that interpretation by observing that the phrase "knows what he does" points back to an earlier passage in which the narrator says he loved the trainer because, as they looked together at the stallion, "he knew what I knew" (*TE* 15). Thus, argues Sherbo, the emphasis belongs on the "almost mystical understanding of Sunstreak" that the trainer shares with the boy who tells the story rather than on the man's awareness of his actions (which in the boy's idiom would surely be phrased "who knows what he's doing"); the phrase indicates the boy's "painful suspicion" that he, too, like the man he has identified with, "may also someday be guilty of actions as disgusting as those he has witnessed" (351).

Howe restores a moral emphasis to the story by refining Brooks and Warren's analysis, stating that the boy's "displaced sexual energy has an esthetic and moral dimension of which he is only dimly aware but which is a major spring of his behavior" (155). He also incorporates Sherbo's point: "The degradation of the brothel is real enough and the boy's revulsion is certainly justified, but . . . [he also] fears the prospect of all adult sexuality, which can never be as 'pure' as his relation to horses" (156). The boy thus enters into knowledge of the real world and its ambiguities, Howe concludes.

Lesser offers a Freudian interpretation. The impact of the story, he argues, depends on elements of Oedipal significance latent in the adolescent narrator's yearning "for an ideal relationship with a man who is like his father but better than his father" and in his eagerness "to deny the sexuality of [his] parents" (386, 390). The boy's own father is "extremely permissive," cannot buy his son nice presents, and does not share his passion for horses (386). The boy feels he has found his pre–Oedipal ideal when he and Jerry Tillford share love for a stallion that is an ideal mother (this seems rather improbable, but Lesser offers as evidence the boy's comparison of the stallion to "a girl you think about sometimes but never see"); the scene at the farmhouse, however, destroys that illusion, revealing Jerry's boasting and sexuality, reminding the boy "of the sexuality of [his] parents, and also representing "a sexual rejection and betrayal"—duplicating that is, "the 'primal scene'" (388–90).

Ringe argues that the story has been misread because critics have been inattentive to the point of view of the story and to the difference between the narrator's immature, selfish judgment and what "the mature reader" understands (24–25). Ringe observes correctly that the track "Negroes are squarer because they do not have the sense of responsibility to the runaway boys' parents that a white man would have," that the boy cannot see "how a Negro may think of his own lot," and that the expensive presents Henry Rieback's absentee father sends scarcely make him as "good" as the boy believes (25–26). Ringe reduces the narrator's complex sensitivity, though, to sheer physical sensation and states that the climactic scene involves a revelation to the boy of his own kind of childish selfishness (26–29).

Parish disputes the analyses of both Lesser and Ringe. Against the former, he asserts that the boy's father is not too permissive but merely exhibiting admirable, old-fashioned wisdom in guiding his son "unobtrusively" while allowing him to learn for himself; the son, who has learned from his father "self- reliance and other values sometimes dismissed as bourgeois," already accepts his father's values (50–53; similarly, Love 239–40, 242). The boy does not realize, though, how "one-sided" is the ecstatic "communion" he imagines between himself and Jerry at the paddock (53). Refuting Ringe's view that the boy moves from mere "selfish sensuous gratification" to mature judgment, Parish argues that the story shows "his moral development" to have been "well under way" even at the outset and that it "depicts the inevitable dulling of childhood's acute sensations as a loss," after the manner of Wordsworth's "Intimations of Immortality from Recollections of Early Childhood" (55–56). Lawry emphasizes the aesthetic aspect of the boy's love of horses (which he finds not sexual in any significant way) and its betrayal by the connection, which the boy naïvely fails to recognize, between the love of horses and the world of gambling— almost allegorically represented by the whorehouse behind the beautiful track ("Love" 46–52). He suggests that a positive alternative for life lies somewhere between the "untainted" but irresponsible model represented by Bildad and the "steady" but dull father (54).

Fetterley provides a feminist interpretation, arguing that the narrator resists "not just growing up" but "specifically growing up *male*" (14). His own father, she says, "refuses to relate to" him, and Jerry Tillford's failure to be "an acceptable adult male role model" leaves him "stranded in a limbo" between youth and manhood (14–15). Women appear only "negatively" in the story—the mother is clingy, whiny, and contemptible, the whore is ugly, and "the good girl is the one you never see"; "the positive elements of the female role are co-opted by men"—mostly by Negroes (19, 24; similarly, Anneliese Smith 29). Intuitively, the boy understands that whores, horses, and children are "objects of exploitation by men" (20).

Anderson's treatment of the Negro in this story has stimulated a certain amount of critical controversy. Naugle points out that the name "Bildad" is significant both for its suggestion that the black man is a beneficent father-figure (dad) and for its allusion to the biblical figure who consoled Job, who, like the narrator, pondered "the mystery of human pain and divine justice" (592–94). Others object to the characterization as demeaning to blacks. Anneliese Smith stresses the stereotypical elements in the tale that identify Negroes as "happy savage[s]," good because they are asexual, contented Uncle Toms (29–31). Matthews, similarly, alleges that, despite the surface admiration, the story actually "has effectively emasculated" blacks "by reducing their talents to relating cooking tips and exacting favors from whites" (409). Like Smith, Matthews makes no distinction between the narrator's viewpoint and Anderson's own. Love argues, however, that the distinction is immaterial since the author's conception of blacks is as unacceptable as the narrator's (247n). (See also "Relation to Other Works.")

Formalist critics have commented on several aspects of the story. Schevill calls it "a triumph of style on the easiest level" (164). Barker, similarly, mentions that it is "relatively free from the kind of structural flaws" that mar Anderson's attempts at types of narration more ambitious than the direct first person (440). Those who do not grasp the ironic dimension of the story are quick to conclude that Anderson is primitive and sentimental—Beachcroft, for example (240), or Trilling (24). Love argues that the tale affirms not the primitive but the pastoral (239–43). Other critics, too, praise the "masterly handling" of "the naïve point of view" and its attendant ironies (Burbank 97–100; similarly, Brossard 612). Wright's comments about the dramatic effect of the discrepancy between the narrator's indirectly expressed moral judgments and the author's and reader's understanding are helpful (99, 133, 285, 360–61, 407). Wright classifies the story as a "caustic romance" (211).

Rideout sees the narrative digressions as particularly effective, for they "both build up a world of rapture and reveal the Boy's reluctance to get to the event that destroyed it for him"; here is a fine instance of Anderson's creating form to convey meaning "rather than imposing on his fiction some currently favored formula" (9,14; similarly, Orvis 88). David Anderson adds a defense of the "lapses in style" that critics, following Brooks and Warren, frequently mention: these "occasional glimpses of the adult narrator," he argues, "are conscious, artistic lapses" designed "to minimize misinterpretation" (64).

Brooks and Warren's classification of "I Want to Know Why" as an initiation story has also been questioned and refined. Marcus remarks that the story depicts an "uncompleted initiation" because there is no ritual and no "clear-cut entrance into the adult world" (224, 228). Gado observes a counterpointing of the conventional initiation pattern against an inverted pattern, which moves in "joke-like" fashion to subvert the logic it also confirms: "The narrator urgently wants to 'know why,' yet, just as urgently, he tries to retreat from that knowledge. The reader immediately knows the 'why's' that cause the narrator's distress, yet, from a farther remove, the more profound questions raised about human behavior remain unanswered—and unanswerable" (7–9).

In such stories as this, Anderson helped create the modern mode of fiction—dramatic and nondidactic. The advantage in lending immediacy to the action is obvious. But, necessarily, inferences about meaning are left to readers, and that is not without its perils. Critical disputes about whether the boy's father exhibits concerned good sense or uncaring laxity, for example, depend largely on readers' attitudes about how parents ought to behave; likewise, feelings about bought sex also noticeably color interpretations of the story. A striking difference in inference appears in conclusions drawn by Jon Lawry and Perry Miller: while Lawry discovers in the story an appeal to the audience to be more sympathetic with others—since everyone, like the trainer, betrays what he loves ("Artist" 21)—Miller finds there an appeal for "a masculine fraternity as will strengthen the manhood of the nation" against a threatening "matriarchy" (19).

The influence of this story on Ernest Hemingway's "My Old Man" was remarked soon after his first book, *Three Stories and Ten Poems,* was published in the summer of 1923. Hemingway denied it: "I know it wasn't inspired by him," he wrote to Edmund Wilson in November of 1923, adding that Anderson's "work seems to have gone to hell"; Wilson's review, then, simply reported that both Anderson and Hemingway were influenced by Gertrude Stein (117, 119–120). Critics generally disregard Hemingway's denial (Fenton 121; O'Connor 117; Burhans 326; Leary 141; Paul Smith 11–12). In a passage in his *Memoirs* composed in 1938, Anderson comments on the episode as well as on other aspects of his relationship with Hemingway: Gertrude Stein later told him, he reports, "that Hemingway's difficulty was that I had written two stories, 'I'm a Fool' and 'I Want to Know Why,' and that he could not bear the thought of my having written them" (White 462–64). A good discussion of Anderson's relationships with Hemingway is Phillips's "Sherwood Anderson's Two Prize Pupils." (See also "The Fight," p. 376.)

Works Cited

Anderson, David. 1967. *Sherwood Anderson: An Introduction and Interpretation.* New York: Holt, Rinehart.

Anderson, Sherwood. "The Story Writers." *Smart Set* 48 (January 1916):243–48. Rpt. in *Sherwood Anderson: Early Writings.* Ed. Ray Lewis White. Kent, OH, and London: Kent State University Press, 1989, 141–50.

——. "The White Streak." *Smart Set* 55 (July 1918):27–30.

——. 1924. *A Story Teller's Story.* New York: B. W. Huebsch. Rpt. in *A Story Teller's Story: A Critical Text.* Ed. Ray Lewis White. Cleveland: Press of Case Western Reserve University, 1969.

Barker, Russell H. "The Storyteller Role." *College English* 3 (1942):433–42.

Beachcroft, T[homas] O[wen]. 1968. *The Modest Art: A Survey of the Short Story in English.* London: Oxford University Press.

Brooks, Cleanth, and Robert Penn Warren. 1943. *Understanding Fiction.*

New York: Appleton-Century-Crofts, 344–40. 2nd. ed. New York: Appleton-Century-Crofts, 1959, 325–30.

Brossard, Chandler. "Sherwood Anderson: A Sweet Singer, 'A Smooth Son of a Bitch.'" *American Mercury* 72 (1951):611–16. Rpt. in *Critical Essays on Sherwood Anderson*. Ed. David D. Anderson. Boston: G. K. Hall, 1981, 120–24.

Burbank, Rex. 1964. *Sherwood Anderson*. New York: Twayne. Rpt. in part in *The Achievement of Sherwood Anderson: Essays in Criticism*. Ed. Ray Lewis White. Chapel Hill: University of North Carolina Press, 1966, 32–43. Rpt. in part in *Sherwood Anderson: A Collection of Critical Essays*. Ed. Walter B. Rideout. Englewood Cliffs, NJ: Prentice-Hall, 1974, 70–83.

Burhans, Clinton S., Jr. "The Complex Unity of *In Our Time*." *Modern Fiction Studies* 14 (1968):313–28.

Calverton, V. J. "Sherwood Anderson: A Study in Sociological Criticism." *Modern Quarterly* 2 (1924):82–118. Rpt. in *The Newer Spirit: A Sociological Criticism of Literature*. Introduction by Ernest Boyd. New York: Boni & Liveright, 1925, 52–118.

Campbell, Hilbert H. "Sherwood Anderson and the Viking Press, 1925–1941." *Resources for American Literary Study* 10 (1980):167–72.

Cargill, Oscar. 1941. *Intellectual America: Ideas on the March*. New York: Macmillan.

Chase, Cleveland B. 1927. *Sherwood Anderson*. New York: Robert M. McBride. Rpt. Folcroft, PA: Folcroft Press, 1969.

Crawford, Nelson Antrim. 1981. "Sherwood Anderson, the Wistfully Faithful." in *Critical Essays on Sherwood Anderson*. Ed. David D. Anderson. Boston: G. K. Hall, 65–73. Originally printed in *The Midland* 8 (November 1922:297–308).

Curry, Martha Mulroy. 1975. *The "Writer's Book" by Sherwood Anderson: A Critical Edition*. Metuchen, NJ: Scarecrow Press.

Fagin, N. Bryllion. 1973. *The Phenomenon of Sherwood Anderson: A Study in American Life and Letters*. New York: Russell & Russell. Originally printed Baltimore: Rossi-Bryn, 1927.

Fenton, Charles A. 1954. *The Apprenticeship of Ernest Hemingway: The Early Years*. New York: Farrar, Straus & Young.

Fetterley, Judith. 1978. "Growing Up Male in America" 'I Want to Know Why.'" In *The Resisting Reader*. Bloomington and London: Indiana University Press, 12–22.

Gado, Frank. 1983. *The Teller's Tales*. Signature Series. Schenectady, NY: Union College Press.

Geismar, Maxwell, ed. 1962. *Sherwood Anderson: Short Stories*. New York: Hill and Wang.

Gross, Seymour L. "Sherwood Anderson's Debt to *Huckleberry Finn*." *Mark Twain Journal* 11 (1960):3–5, 24.

Gullason, Thomas A. 1984. "The 'Lesser' Renaissance: The American Short Story in the 1920s." In *The American Short Story, 1900–1945: A Critical History*. Ed. Philip Stevick. Boston: Twayne, 71–101.

Hansen, Harry. 1923. *Midwest Portraits: A Book of Memories and Friendships*. New York: Harcourt, Brace.

Howe, Irving. 1951. *Sherwood Anderson*. New York: William Sloane.

Jones, Howard Mumford, and Walter B. Rideout, eds. 1953. *Letters of Sherwood Anderson*. Boston: Little, Brown.

Lawry, Jon S. "Love and Betrayal in Sherwood Anderson's 'I Want to Know Why.'" *Shenandoah* 13 (1962):46–54.

———. "The Artist in America: The Case of Sherwood Anderson." *Ball State University Forum* 7 (1966):15–26.

Leary, Lewis. 1969. "Sherwood Anderson" *The Man Who Became a Boy Again*." in *Literatur und Sprache der Vereinigten Staaten: Aufsätze zu Ehren von Hans Galinsky*. Hans Helmcke, Klaus Lubbers, Renate Schmidt-von Bardeleben (Eds.). Heidelberg: Carl Winter, 135–43.

Lesser, Simon O. "The Image of the Father" A Reading of 'My Kinsman, Major Molineux' and 'I Want to Know Why.'" *Partisan Review* 22 (1955):372–90. Rpt. as "Conscious and Unconscious Perception" in *Fiction and the Unconscious*. Boston: Beacon Press, 1957, 224–34.

Love, Glen A. 1976. "Horses or Men: Primitive and Pastoral Elements in Sherwood Anderson." In *Sherwood Anderson: Centennial Studies*. Hilbert H. Campbell and Charles E. Modlin (Eds.). Troy, NY: Whitston, 235–248.

Marcus, Mordecai. "What is an Initiation Story?" *Journal of Aesthetics and Art Criticism* 19 (1960–61):221–28.

Matthews, Jack. "Winesburg Today." *Columbus* (Ohio) *Dispatch Magazine* (November 29, 1959):40–43.

Miller, Perry. "A Curious Sense of Dirt." *New Republic* 128 (June 22, 1953):19–20.

Modlin, Charles E., ed. 1992. *Certain Things Last: The Selected Stories of Sherwood Anderson*. New York: Four Walls Eight Windows.

Naugle, Helen H. "The Name 'Bildad.'" *Modern Fiction Studies* 22 (1976–77):591–94.

O'Connor, William Van. 1962. *The Grotesque: An American Genre and Other Essays*. Carbondale: Southern Illinois University Press.

Orvis, Mary Burchard. 1948. *The Art of Writing Fiction*. New York: Prentice-Hall.

Parish, John E. "The Silent Father in Anderson's 'I Want to Know Why.'" *Rice University Studies* 51, no. 1 (1965):49–57.

Pecile, Jordan. 1977. "On Sherwood Anderson and 'I'm a Fool.'" In *The American Short Story*. Ed. Calvin Skaggs. New York: Dell, 145–49.

Phillips, William L. "Sherwood Anderson's Two Prize Pupils." *University of Chicago Magazine* 47 (1955):9–12. Rpt. in *The Achievement of Sherwood Anderson: Essays in Criticism*. Ed. Ray Lewis White. Chapel Hill: University of North Carolina Press, 1966, 202–10.

Raymund, Bernard. "The Grammar of Not-Reason: Sherwood Anderson." *Arizona Quarterly* 12 (1956):48–60, 137–48.

Rideout, Walter B. " 'I Want to Know Why' as Biography and Fiction." *Midwestern Miscellany* 12 (1984):7–14.

Ringe, Donald A. "Point of View and Theme in 'I Want to Know Why.'" *Critique* 3 (1959):24–29.

Rogers, W. G. 1965. *Wise Men Fish Here: The Story of Frances Steloff and the Gotham Book Mart*. New York: Harcourt, Brace, 114, 116–17, 209.

Rosenfeld, Paul ed. 1947. *The Sherwood Anderson Reader*. Boston: Houghton Mifflin.

Schevill, James. 1951. *Sherwood Anderson: His Life and Work*. Denver: University of Denver Press.

Sherbo, Arthur. "Sherwood Anderson's I Want to Know Why and Messrs. Brooks and Warren." *College English* 15 (1954):350–51.

Smith, Anneliese H. "Part of the Problem: Student Response to Sherwood Anderson's 'I Want to Know Why?'" *Negro American Literature Forum* 7 (1973):28–31.

Smith, Paul. 1989. *A Reader's Guide to the Short Stories of Ernest Hemingway*. Boston: G. K. Hall.

Trilling, Lionel. "Sherwood Anderson." *The Liberal Imagination: Essays on Literature and Society*. New York: Viking, 1950, 22–33. Originally in *Kenyon Review* 3 (1941):293–302. Rpt. in *Sherwood Anderson: Winesburg, Ohio: Text and Criticism*. Ed. John H. Ferres. New York: Viking, 1966, 455–67. rpt. in *The Achievement of Sherwood Anderson: Essays in*

Criticism. Ed. Ray Lewis White. Chapel Hill: University of North Carolina Press, 1966, 212–24. Rpt. in *Sherwood Anderson: A Collection of Critical Essays.* Ed. Walter B. Rideout. Englewood Cliffs, NJ: Prentice-Hall, 1974.

Voss, Arthur. 1973. *The American Short Story: A Critical Survey.* Norman: University of Oklahoma Press.

Way, Brian. 1971. "Sherwood Anderson." In *The American Novel and the Nineteen Twenties.* Eds. Malcolm Bradbury and David Palmer (Eds.). Stratford-upon-Avon Studies 13. London: Edward Arnold, 107–26.

West, Ray B., Jr. 1952. *The Short Story in America: 1900–1950.* Chicago: Regnery. Rpt. New York: Books for Libraries (Division of Arno Press), 1979.

White, Ray Lewis, ed. 1991. *Sherwood Anderson's Secret Love Letters.* Baton Rouge and London: Louisiana State University Press.

——, ed. 1969. *Sherwood Anderson's Memoirs: A Critical Edition.* Chapel Hill: University of North Carolina Press.

Williams, Kenny J. 1988. *A Storyteller and a City: Sherwood Anderson's Chicago.* De Kalb: Northern Illinois University Press.

Wilson, Edmund. 1952. "Emergence of Ernest Hemingway." *The Shores of Light: A Literary Chronicle of the Twenties and Thirties.* New York: Farrar, Straus, & Young, 115–24.

Wright, Austin McGiffert. 1961. *The American Short Story in the Twenties.* Chicago: University of Chicago Press.

Seeds

Circumstances of Composition

Anderson wrote "Seeds" in the fall and winter of 1917. He was living on the north side of Chicago at 735 North Cass Street, a boardinghouse he shared with other aspiring artists whom he called "The Little Children of the Arts." Since 1913, he had been associating with other leading figures of the Chicago Renaissance, participating in their bohemian revolt against the genteel tradition and against all the repressive forces they labeled as Puritanism. Anderson had spent that summer in upstate New York at Lake Chateaugay, where he had discussed Freudian theory with a friend, a psychoanalyst at Johns Hopkins University; he used their debate as the first episode in the story (see "Sources and Influences").

Around the same time, he was at work on a novel about life on an Ohio farm, parts of which he refashioned into the four-part story "Godliness." His stories were beginning to be regularly published, and many of the *Winesburg* tales had appeared in magazines. New York as well as Chicago editors were recognizing his worth; *Seven Arts* editor Waldo Frank had come to visit him at Lake Chateaugay. Though Anderson was frustrated with his advertising job, his confidence in himself as an artist was growing.

Anderson revised this story thoroughly, adding significant material to the ending and removing the original opening. Sutton has published a detailed account of the revisions that went into the four known versions of this tale, illustrating the point that "Anderson was not customarily a spontaneous writer" though he sometimes romanticized himself in those terms (1). The earliest extant manuscript begins by referring to a young man in Chicago who tells a story that sets the narrator's thoughts in motion; then immediately the narrative goes "back to the origion [*sic*] of the thought" by telling of the discussion with the psychoanalyst (Sutton, *Revision* 11).

Sources and Influences

In the summers of 1916 and 1917 Anderson vacationed in the Adirondacks, at Lake Chateaugay. During both summers he and his new wife, Tennessee Mitchell, enjoyed the company of Trigant Burrow and his wife. Burrow was one of the first to introduce Freudian psychoanalysis in America; he had studied with Jung in Zurich but had sided with Freud after the rift between

him and Jung. In 1911 he was one of the founders of the American Psychoanalytic Association. At the time of this story he was practicing in the Johns
Hopkins clinic. It was during the second of Anderson's summers at the lake
that the tense conversation referred to in the story took place (1917, that is;
Burrow misdates it 1916, and several scholars have repeated the mistake).

Burrow later recalled that, on a "delightful midsummer day," Anderson
had canoed over to his camp (Lifwynn Camp) early in the morning and
together they had hiked to Rocky Brook: "We sat there beside the brook and
talked the livelong day, and our talk was entirely along psychoanalytic lines"
(*Search* 558–59). It was "the social implications of the neurosis" that particularly interested Anderson, Burrow was to report. But as a result of this and
other contacts with Burrow, Anderson wrote letters to friends expressing his
irritation and disappointment with Burrow's apparent attempts to "clutch" at
him, to "reform" him (Sutton, *Letters* 85; Jones-Rideout, *Letters* 15).

However, the two men continued a friendly correspondence. At the end
of 1918, Anderson wrote Burrow that he had "found to be true" many of the
things Burrow had told him (Modlin, *Letters* 11). In 1921 he apologized for
having been unfair in his "sarcastic" judgment of Burrow: "My difficulty lay
in the fact that I continually thought of you as one who believed they had
found truth. . . . I have thought of the science to which you have given so
much of your life as one that could very well do wonders in making life and
its difficulties more understandable but that one person could in any way
cure the evils in life for another seemed to me impossible" (Burrow, *Search*
53–54). Burrow responded magnanimously, admitting that he, like other
Freudians, had been too "autocratic," employing a "*theory* of life" to keep
"aloof from the *actuality* of life" (56). By the time Anderson wrote his *Memoirs,* he described Burrow's attempts "to search out [his] very soul" and his
own resentful "resistance" as "a half comic situation" (White, *Memoirs* 284).
Burrow discussed the episode in a 1925 speech, subsequently printed in the
Psychoanalytic Review. Howe's commentary on this relationship is interesting; he says, "years later [Burrow] was to feel that Anderson's doubts about
individual therapy had constituted a brilliant intuition" (180). After the
author's death, Burrow wrote of Anderson, "socially he was one of the
healthiest men I have even known" (*Search* 442).

Townsend suggests that "Seeds" owes something to Anderson's encounter one night in 1913 with a slightly crippled woman in Jackson Park, which
Anderson wrote about in his *Memoirs* and in *Sherwood Anderson's Notebook*
(Townsend 140, 89; Rosenfeld, *Memoirs* 238–39; *Notebook* 32–35). More significantly, Townsend speculates, the woman in the story is modeled after
"the Tennessee that threw herself on his mercy after her affair with Edgar
Lee Masters" (140). Tennessee was, like the woman in the story, a music
teacher who had come to Chicago from a small town. Townsend also notes
the allusion to Shelley in the repeated cries for "fructifying winds" (140).

Burbank states that Anderson's reading of *The Education of Henry Adams* contributed to the idea that there is a need for a cultural rebirth, to cure the universal "disease" (108).

> Adams saw the popular influence of the Virgin Mary in the twelfth century as being basically sexual, and in her power he saw the fructifying effects of sex upon art. The art of the Middle Ages found in the Louvre and the hundreds of cathedrals built in the name of Mary were cultural testaments to the centrality of sex in human creativity. . . . Adams provided Anderson with a symbol for his belief . . . that Puritanism and industrialism were historically connected. (108–109)

Burbank's insight is valuable for calling attention to the symbolic role of the central figure in "Seeds," for she personifies the American Venus stifled by cultural forces that thwart her development. Modern science fails to meet her needs.

Publication History

"Seeds" was first published in *Little Review* in July of 1918 (5:24–31), the same month that the uncollected story "White Streak" was published in *Smart Set*. It was the second of the stories later collected in *The Triumph of the Egg* to appear in print, "War" having come out in 1916, also in Margaret Anderson's *Little Review*, which had been printing Anderson's stories and essays regularly since its first issue in March 1914. The magazine had moved from Chicago to New York City early in 1917.

The story was reprinted in *The Triumph of the Egg* in 1921 (21–32). The *English Review* reprinted it in January of the following year (34:13–20).

The *Little Review* version of the story begins, "There was a doctor from Johns Hopkins talked to me one day last summer concerning universal life and its universal insanity." The sentence was deleted in the version printed in *The Triumph of the Egg*, presumably because the reference to Burrow seemed too personal.

Relation to Other Works

Shelley's "Ode to the West Wind" evidently provides the controlling metaphor of the story "Seeds," and indeed the central metaphor of the whole volume *The Triumph of the Egg*. Shelley's poem begins with an autumn wind driving dead leaves like "Pestilence-driven multitudes" and carrying seeds "to their dark wintry bed" where they will lie until spring awakens them; the poem ends with a prayer that the poet's "dead thoughts" may be inspired so that they may serve "Like withered leaves to quicken a new birth" and that his "words" may be scattered "among mankind" like "The trumpet of a prophecy!" Analogously, Anderson's book begins with the prose poem "The Dumb Man," which is filled with images of Death, yearning Life, and a poet who lacks words to tell his story. It ends with "The Man with the Trumpet," a prophetic prose poem celebrating the words the poet has "scattered . . . like seeds" and "like building stones," which people might use "to build temples to their lives" (1–4, 268–69). The two prose poems serve as a frame for the intervening stories. Imagery of death and hints of rebirth run throughout the volume, leading sequentially to the climactic final scene of "Out of Nowhere into Nothing," where Rosalind Wescott runs through the darkness tingling with life, understanding herself to be "a creator of light" (*TE* 267). As a group, the stories in *The Triumph of the Egg* constitute Anderson's vision of a universal wasteland and his attempt to find words to quicken its dormant life. Comparison with a passage from his *A New Testament* (1927) is suggestive: "I am but one man but in my loins is the seed that shall be planted in fields and in town. The lords of life shall come into the land" (105).

The reference to the girl in the roominghouse as a "grotesque" links the story to the grotesques of *Winesburg, Ohio* (1919). Voss, in fact, holds that "Seeds" is "less interesting as a story than it is as a commentary on the themes of *Winesburg, Ohio*" (193). The statement that the girl needs primarily not a lover but "to be loved, to be long and quietly and patiently loved" (*TE* 31) associates her situation closely with that of Louise Bentley, in "Godliness," a story written about the same time. A number of Anderson's other characters, of course, especially women, fit that description as well. Alice Hindman's naked foray in confused pursuit of sex and love (in "Adventure") resembles that of the Iowa woman here. Curiously, LeRoy's statement that "[t]he life force within her" had become "decentralized" (*TE* 29) aligns her with Wing Biddlebaum, protagonist of "Hands," of whom the narrator says, "[h]e was one of those men in whom the force that creates life is diffused, not centralized" (*WO* 32). Moreover, the psychoanalyst who has "gone beneath the surface of the lives of men and women" is by that phrase associated with the effort of *Winesburg, Ohio* and its dedicatory phrase, though "Seeds" clearly implies that his methods are misguided.

The story relates to Anderson's handling of sexuality in other works. As Burbank suggests, the women in "The New Englander" and in "Out of Nowhere into Nothing" are also shut off from fulfillment "of their inner, imaginative lives"; overcoming Puritan inhibitions about sexual expression "could be the initial step toward breaking the barrier of loneliness" (89). In *Poor White* (1920), too, breaking free of sexual timidity is an important theme. *Many Marriages* (1923) is completely dominated "by the proposition that by lifting the lid of moral repression from the inner life one may release the manifold impulses of the subconscious and enjoy a multitude of beautiful relationships and many marriages'"; it insists, however, that genuine love unites flesh and spirit (Burbank 110–11).

Even after he completed *The Triumph of the Egg,* Anderson continued to play with the motifs of this story. In his *Paris Notebook,* a 1921 entry reads, "A little twisted girl came to me at night wanting my seed to carry away in her basket. I refused and now hells door clanks open for me too"; putting aside that "yesterday's night," he goes on to liken himself to a "living leaf" (Fanning 62). Bruce Dudley, in *Dark Laughter* (1925), thinks, "I am a seed, floating on a wind. Why have I not planted myself?" (60). He goes on to impregnate Aline Grey, who has longed to give in to her own dark, libidinous stirrings.

Protests against sexual repression was rapidly becoming commonplace among liberal artists and intellectuals. In the twenties, repression was "the peg upon which discontented Americans hung all of their resentment with the moral world around them" (Hoffman, *Freudianism* 30). The real originality of "Seeds" lies in its critique of the easy solutions so readily accepted by many of the modernists. In this vein, but more pointedly, Anderson would ridicule aspects of the new sexual and psychological glibness in "The Triumph of a Modern."

Critical Studies

Most critical discussion of this story has centered on its origin and its revelation of Anderson's attitude toward Freudian psychology. There has been little close analysis.

Hoffman, noting Burrow's belief that "Anderson was, like Freud, a genius" with intuitive psychological insight, interprets the story to mean that science cannot remedy the "universal illness," though the artist can describe it (*Freudianism* 236; similarly, D. Anderson 63). Cargill notes that the story shows Anderson "accepted the Freudian diagnosis" but rejected "the Freudian cure"; disparagingly, Cargill says that Anderson was "a far greater pessimist" than Freud because, unlike Freud, he poses as a "stupid ruminator on problems to which he knows there is no solution" (680).

Burbank observes a key parallel within the story: the psychologist offers a cure—rational analysis, which the narrator repudiates—and the narrator offers a cure—sex, which LeRoy refuses. Plainly, both proposed solutions are simplistic: "The point of this story is that the inner life is a myriad of often conflicting impulses," curable only by long, steady love (107–108). For that reason, Burbank judges "Seeds" to be far more successful than the thesis-ridden novels *Many Marriages* and *Dark Laughter.*

Wright classifies the story's form as caustic pathos with an episode of exposure (389). The woman's background helps explain why she has come to the city confusedly seeking love and adventure and why she cannot carry out the love affairs she invites: "old thoughts and beliefs—seeds planted [in her unconscious mind] by dead men, inhibit the fulfillment of her desires" (120, 128). The "essential thing" controlling the response to the story, Wright says, is the "sympathetic judgment" of the male characters, who acknowledge that her problem is universal (120–21, 236–37).

The most sophisticated, albeit brief, discussion of the story appears in Townsend's biography. He observes that "the narrator is too smart for his own good," as the analyst and the painter inform him "when he tries to chasten them"; hence, the positions of all three men are reduced to absurdity as they critique each other so that "nothing" is left but "the writing, in control as it levels each man in its turn" (140). Townsend thus properly emphasizes the fundamental skepticism that questions specific remedies. He overlooks, though, one other thing that is left: the twisted woman yearning for the creative fulfillment of life. Symbolically, that is a matter of some importance.

Works Cited

Anderson, David. 1967. *Sherwood Anderson: An Introduction and Interpretation*. New York: Holt, Rinehart.

Anderson, Sherwood. "The White Streak." *Smart Set* (July 1918):27–30.

———. 1919. *Winesburg, Ohio*. New York: B. W. Huebsch. Rpt. New York: Viking, 1960.

———. 1921. *The Triumph of the Egg*. New York: B. W. Huebsch. Rpt. New York: Four Walls Eight Windows, 1988. Introduction by Herbert Gold.

———. 1927. *A New Testament*. New York: Boni & Liveright.

Burbank, Rex. 1964. *Sherwood Anderson*. New York: Twayne. Rpt. in part in *The Achievement of Sherwood Anderson: Essays in Criticism*. Ed. Ray Lewis White. Chapel Hill: University of North Carolina Press, 1966, 32–43. Rpt. in part in *Sherwood Anderson: Collection of Critical Essays*. Ed. Walter B. Rideout. Englewood Cliffs, NJ: Prentice-Hall, 1974, 70–83.

Burrow, Trigant. 1958. *A Search for Man's Sanity: The Selected Letters of Trigant Burrow, with Biographical Notes*. Foreword by Sir Herbert Read. Ed. Lifwyn Foundation. New York: Oxford University Press.

———. "Psychoanalytic Improvisations and the Personal Equation." *Psychoanalytic Review* 13 (1926):173–86.

Cargill, Oscar. 1941. *Intellectual America: Ideas on the March*. New York: Macmillan.

Fanning, Michael, ed. 1976. *France and Sherwood Anderson: Paris Notebook, 1921*. Baton Rouge: Louisiana State University Press.

Hoffman, Frederick J. "The Voices of Sherwood Anderson." *Shenandoah* 13 (1962):5–19. Rpt. in *The Achievement of Sherwood Anderson: Essays in Criticism*. Ed. Ray Lewis White. Chapel Hill: University of North Carolina Press, 1966, 232–44.

———. 1957. *Freudianism and the Literary Mind*. Rev. ed. Baton Rouge: Louisiana State University Press. Rpt. in *Sherwood Anderson:* Winesburg, Ohio: *Text and Criticism*. Ed. John H. Ferres. New York: Viking, 1966, 309–20. Rpt. in *The Achievement of Sherwood Anderson: Essays in Criticism*. Ed. Ray Lewis White. Chapel Hill: University of North Carolina Press, 1966, 174–92.

Jones, Howard Mumford, and Walter B. Rideout, eds. 1953. *Letters of Sherwood Anderson*. Boston: Little, Brown.

Modlin, Charles E., ed. 1984. *Sherwood Anderson: Selected Letters*. Knoxville: University of Tennessee Press.

Rosenfeld, Paul, ed. 1942. *Sherwood Anderson's Memoirs*. New York: Harcourt, Brace.

Sutton, William A. 1976. *The Revision of 'Seeds.'* Ball State Monograph no. 25. Muncie, IN: Ball State University Press.

———. ed. 1985. *Letters to Bab: Sherwood Anderson to Marietta D. Finley, 1916–33*. Foreword by Walter B. Rideout. Urbana and Chicago: University of Illinois Press.

Townsend, Kim. 1987. *Sherwood Anderson*. Boston: Houghton Mifflin.

Voss, Arthur. 1973. *The American Short Story: A Critical Survey*. Norman: University of Oklahoma Press.

White, Ray Lewis, ed. 1969. *Sherwood Anderson's Memoirs: A Critical Edition*. Chapel Hill: University of North Carolina Press.

Wright, Austin McGiffert. 1961. *The American Short Story in the Twenties*. Chicago: University of Chicago Press.

The Other Woman

Circumstances of Composition

The date of this story's composition has not been established. Anderson's aims in writing it are suggested in a 1923 letter to his publisher Ben Huebsch. Editors, he said, were mistaken in their high admiration for this story: "These people go wrong because they have their eyes too much on conventional technique. 'The Other Woman' is so decidedly French in technique and spirit. It's a clever story—no less. I wrote it partly with my tongue in my cheek—bad little boy stuff. In a sense just wanted to show the mutts I know their damn technique" (Modlin, *Letters* 52).

Sources and Influences

Fagin mentions the obvious influence of Freud on "The Other Woman" and its disclosure that beneath the protagonist's conscious love for the "nice, clean woman" lies his unconscious "desire for another woman, a slatternly, common, vulgar woman" (122). Fagin's enthusiastic response to the story's probing into a taboo subject reveals a good deal about sexual attitudes in the twenties, both the force of repression and the thirst for more openness and freedom. The rejection of the genteel tradition was one of the things in Anderson's writing that seemed most valuable to the writers and critics of his time.

The painful experience of Anderson's first marriage, to Cornelia Lane, also must have contributed to the story. In a letter to his fourth wife, Eleanor Copenhaver, Anderson confided, "[Cornelia thought] that any expression of love through the body was nasty. She couldn't help it & I was ignorant but she did spoil that side of life for me—so that finally I couldn't bear to touch her" (Modlin, *Love Letters* 251).

Publication History

The *Little Review* first published this story in the May–June issue of 1920 (7:37–44). In 1921 it was reprinted in Anderson's *The Triumph of the Egg* (33–45). That year Edward O'Brien also selected it for inclusion in his *The Best Short Stories of 1920* (3–11), a volume he dedicated to Sherwood Anderson. Anderson later, correctly, remarked that "The Egg," written the same

year, was "an incomparably finer thing" (Modlin *Letters* 52). Geismar included it in his edition of Anderson's short stories (13–20) in 1962, as did
Modlin in 1992 (18–26).

Relation to Other Works

"The Other Woman" contains an allusion to "I Want to Know Why." The
passage "I was like a perplexed bare-footed boy standing in the dusty road
before a farm house" (*TE* 39) evidently is a deliberate attempt to associate
the predicament of the socially and artistically eminent married man here
with that of the adolescent swipe there. References to seeds and unlit lamps
also link this tale with other stories (with those titles) in the same volume,
connecting it to the overall theme of longing for rebirth and renewal.

Sexual inhibitions between married couples appear frequently in Anderson's works. Sometimes the woman is the reluctant one, but often the man's
timidity is as intense, or even more so, than hers. In *Winesburg, Ohio* (1919),
puritanical inhibitions within marriage play an important role in both "Respectability" and "The Strength of God." In *Poor White* (1920) a new husband is so terrified that he flees out the window on his wedding night and
has to be coaxed by his bride, a week later, to consummate their marriage.
The harshest expression of sexual loathing in any of Anderson's fiction, and
the most fully articulated, is that of Ma Wescott in "Out of Nowhere into
Nothing."

The uncollected story "A Moonlight Walk" (1937) contains an extramarital
adventure similar to that in "The Other Woman," but the handling there is
mellower; instead of cleverly revealing an inner conflict the protagonist cannot decipher but the reader can, the later story treats a long-married couple
who have shared real intimacy, physical and emotional, and conveys a sense
of genuine mystery about the husband's irrational desire for another woman.
For that reason, Anderson undoubtedly would have valued "A Moonlight
Walk" more than he did this story. (See "Circumstances of Composition.")

Critical Studies

Discussion of "The Other Woman" has been minimal. Hoffman states that in
the story "man finds the key to happiness by spending the night before his
wedding with a strange woman" (245). That the man has found happiness,
however, is far from clear; rather, he seems to have found, through repeated
fantasizing about a single sexual encounter, a way to endure a celibate marriage. Burbank is more nearly accurate in saying that the protagonist's one-
night stand "has released his inner, instinctive life—hitherto inhibited by
conventional moral pieties" (96). But the qualifier "hitherto" falsifies the con-

tinuing inhibition that keeps the still-reverential husband from arousing his wife, and himself, into full intimacy. The language of the closing scene indicates that, metaphorically, neither of them is yet awake.

Geismar and Cargill detect some of the irony. Geismar calls the tale one of Anderson's "wonderfully ironic parables of human weakness and conflict," yet he still sees the wife simply as "a noble creature indeed, full of sentiment" (xix). In fact, her nobility is thoroughly compounded with fear, and her sentiment is the insubstantial kind. Cargill correctly observes that the husband "insists almost too vehemently that he loves his wife" (680). But Cargill also mistakenly judges it a mark of the author's "stupidity" that the story contradicts the thematic basis of "Seeds" that Freudian techniques could not cure neuroses; he contends that the relief the husband finds in talking about his problem proves "there is something, after all, in the Freudian method of katharsis" (681). Something, yes; but the man's problem is by no means cured. Wright accurately classifies the story as "caustic pathos" (389, 233). Critics have rarely seen just how caustic.

Burbank admires the "groping" narrator and "the felicitous combination of wonder, sadness, and perplexity" his narrative achieves (95). No one has commented that there are actually *two* narrators, the troubled husband who tells the story of his marriage, and the more sophisticated narrator to whom he tells it. The latter, the narrator of the story as a whole, gives a kind of knowing wink to the reader in the opening lines as the husband twice makes the "superfluous remark" that he loves his wife; "I turned to look at him," says the narrator, indicating that such strange insistence betrays more than the husband realizes (*TE* 33). He then proceeds to summarize skillfully much of the man's narrative, establishing a tone before turning to direct quotation of the rest of it, and relying then on the reader to catch the ironies. In the telling, the husband's response to what he senses as his listener's "shrewdness" distinctly modifies his own self-scrutiny (*TE* 33).

Works Cited

Anderson, Sherwood. "A Moonlight Walk." *Redbook* 70 (December 1937):43–45, 100–104. Rpt. as "A Walk in the Moonlight" in *The Sherwood Anderson Reader*. Ed. Paul Rosenfeld. Boston: Houghton Mifflin, 1974, 817–30. Rpt. in *Sherwood Anderson: Short Stories*. Ed. Maxwell Geismar, New York: Hill and Wang, 1962, 263–76.

Burbank, Rex. 1964. *Sherwood Anderson*. New York: Twayne. Rpt. in part in *The Achievement of Sherwood Anderson: Essays in Criticism*. Ed. Ray Lewis White. Chapel Hill: University of North Carolina Press, 1966, 32–43. Rpt. in part in *Sherwood Anderson: Collection of Critical Essays*. Ed. Walter B. Rideout. Englewood Cliffs, NJ: Prentice-Hall, 1974, 70–83.

Cargill, Oscar. 1941. *Intellectual America: Ideas on the March*. New York: Macmillan.

Fagin, N. Bryllion. 1973. *The Phenomenon of Sherwood Anderson: A Study in American Life and Letters*. New York: Russell & Russell. Originally printed Baltimore: Rossi-Bryn, 1927.

Geismar, Maxwell, ed. 1962. *Sherwood Anderson: Short Stories*. New York: Hill and Wang.

Hoffman, Frederick J. 1957. *Freudianism and the Literary Mind*. Rev. ed. Baton Rouge: Louisiana State University Press. Rpt. in *Sherwood Anderson: Winesburg, Ohio: Text and Criticism*. Ed. John H. Ferres. New York: Viking, 1966, 309–20. Rpt. in *The Achievement of Sherwood Anderson: Essays in Criticism*. Ed. Ray Lewis White. Chapel Hill: University of North Carolina Press, 1966, 174–92.

Modlin, Charles E., ed. 1992. *Certain Things Last: The Selected Short Stories of Sherwood Anderson,* New York: Four Walls Eight Windows.

——, ed. 1989. *Sherwood Anderson's Love Letters to Eleanor Copenhaver Anderson*. Athens: University of Georgia Press.

——, ed. 1984. *Sherwood Anderson: Selected Letters*. Knoxville: University of Tennessee Press.

O'Brien, Edward J., ed. 1921. *The Best Short Stories of 1920*. Boston: Small, Maynard.

Wright, Austin McGiffert. 1961. *The American Short Story in the Twenties*. Chicago: University of Chicago Press.

The Egg

Circumstances of Composition

Anderson wrote this story, which some consider to be his masterpiece, in August or September of 1918. Schevill states that it was written in New York City, where Anderson spent the summer months on leave from his Chicago advertising job (118). During that summer, the author lived alone in a room on West 22nd Street, composing every morning and earning some money in the afternoons for nominal work as "location finder" for the movie company of his friends John Emerson and Anita Loos (Townsend 149). He was deep into the writing of *Poor White,* a novel that would appear in 1920. Schevill guesses plausibly that "The Egg" may have originated as a part of that novel, since both are set in Bidwell, Ohio, and since the story's chief character has once worked as a farm hand for Thomas Butterworth, a character in the novel (165).

Because of curious similarities of detail, West hypothesizes that the story may be the one that in his *Memoirs* Anderson mentions having begun in a train station in Harrodsburg, Kentucky, and completed on the train to Louisville (White, *Memoirs* 678–79); this conjecture places the story during roughly the same period as Shevill does.

In the years following its publication, Anderson repeatedly expressed his belief that "The Egg" was the finest thing he had written (Jones-Rideout, *Letters* 54, 110; Modlin, *Letters* 41, 52).

Sources and Influences

Despite the fact that there is no evidence Anderson had read any of James Joyce's work by 1918, West argues that stories in *Dubliners* influenced "The Egg," especially its narrative method (676 and n).

Joseph points out that Washington Irving presented "[t]he classic account of the Columbus egg story," which is the "first of all American success stories" in his *The Life and Voyages of Columbus* (132–33). That lineage establishes one important context of "The Egg" and its critique of that tradition.

The deepest impetus for the story lay in Anderson's childhood memories of discontent within his family because of his father's failure to "rise in the world." Irwin Anderson, as all the author's autobiographical accounts of him attest, was something of a showman, like the father in the tale. His "grandiose ideas" and his "ill-starred" desire for success perpetually disappointed himself and his family (Taylor 51). Though he "had a robust hardiness the character in the story does not have," his "ineptness" and "the world's unwillingness to take him seriously" caused them much pain (Howe 170). A keen sense of the family's economic hardship and social humiliation animated both Sherwood Anderson's drive for success in the business world and his recoil from that drive in a troubled effort to define success in different terms through his art. As he matured in his art, however, he came to see how much he resembled his father, how much of the showman he carried within his own nature, and how much his rejection of business success (or, it could be said, his failure in business) was rooted in the same preference for the life of imagination. In his *Paris Notebook,* written three years later, he was still ruminating about that peculiarly American notion "that it is our individual duty to rise in the world," a notion that has caused Americans who do *not* rise to feel "deep resentment" and has contributed to the "weariness" of the whole nation (Fanning 33).

Anderson's similarity to the father in the tale extends to their mutual fondness for grotesques. At the time he wrote "The Egg," Anderson had been presenting to the public the various grotesques of *Winesburg, Ohio.* Somewhat like the restaurant keeper with his bottled embryos, he had hoped people would see what strange and wonderful forms of life his grotesque characters represented, and he was appalled when so many readers responded by finding them sickening (White, *Memoirs* 389, 467).

Miller suggests that Anderson's image of his mother influenced the portrait of the mother in this tale: "Her competence serves as a foil for [her husband's] poignant frustration in the story's climax" (204).

Publication History

This story was first published in March of 1920 in the *Dial* (68:295–304). It was there titled "The Triumph of the Egg." The *Dial* had published Anderson's "Apology for Crudity" in November 1917, but this was the first of his stories to appear there. It was also his first publication there since the magazine's 1918 transit from Chicago to New York and the institution of new editorial policies that were to make it the most distinguished journal of letters in America. Anderson had originally submitted the story to the *Little Review,* which had brought out so many of his tales; it was scheduled for publication there early in 1919 (Modlin, *Letters* 11). Subsequently, however, considering the magazine "too dreadfully inartistic and bad," he withdrew the story and submitted it to the *Dial* (Jones-Rideout, *Letters* 44). Though he did publish a few more things in *Little Review,* his new relationship with the *Dial* was connected with his growing literary eminence.

Anderson altered the story's original title in July of 1921 when he decided to use it as the title for the volume of collected stories that Huebsch brought out in October (West 680 and n). Until that time, he had been calling the book "Unlighted Lamps." As "The Egg," then, this story appeared as the fourth tale in the collection (46–63). It was subsequently reprinted in Rosenfeld's *Sherwood Anderson Reader* (76–85), in Gregory's *The Portable Sherwood Anderson* (448–62), in Geismar's *Sherwood Anderson: Short Stories* (20–30), in Gado's *The Teller's Tales* (134–47), and in Modlin's *Certain Things Last* (27–38).

Relation to Other Works

In 1922 Raymond O'Neil adapted the story for stage presentation (Modlin, *Letters* 39). In February of 1925, the Provincetown Players produced the play as a curtain-raiser for Eugene O'Neill's *Different,* and Anderson called the production "very very nice" (Sutton, *Letters* 209). Anderson discussed the dramatic version of the story in a letter to the Dramatic Publishing Company, which served as a foreword to the printed text (Jones-Rideout, *Letters* 263–64 and n).

Horace Gregory's praise of "The Egg" still seems to hold true: "all the other stories and verses in the volume grow pale beside it" ("Editor's" 24). Yet its richness can be better appreciated in relation to the several motifs that link it with the rest of *The Triumph of the Egg.* The symbol of the egg, used in the book's title, is fundamentally significant in relation to the central theme of the connection between death and life. Personified types of death and life are introduced in the poetic introduction to the volume, "The Dumb Man." Images of stones, seeds, and birth run throughout the book, culminating in the exhortation to life in the final poetic piece, "The Man with the Trumpet." The egg is an ideal symbol: though apparently dead, rocklike, and inanimate, it contains secreted inside a kernel of life with the capacity to burst its prison walls and fulfill itself in open air. The egg is not a unidirectional symbol, however: as one phase of life's unending cycle, it is emblematic of the unsolved mystery of things. Every child knows it as the riddle of the chicken and the egg, and the protagonist of "Out of Nowhere into Nothing" ponders it in a song:

> Life the conquerer over death,
> Death the conquerer over life. (*TE* 262)

The seed (in "Seeds") is an analogous symbol.

The diseases that plague the helpless chickens carry out the idea of a "universal" disease set forth in "Seeds" and reiterated in "Senility." The farmyard problems are ultimately existential, and the bottled remedies that sound comic in this context hint obliquely at a deeper, spiritual redemption. "Wilmer's White Wonder Cholera Cure," advertised in the poultry papers, may or may not be efficacious in saving chickens from untimely death. Nevertheless, the final story in the volume, "Out of Nowhere into Nothing," shows Rosalind Westcott "pressed against the walls of her prison" and reaching outside herself toward the "white wonder of life," guessing that it may cure her distress and may have "something to do with God" (*TE* 237). The deep pessimism and the equally deep affirmation embedded at the heart of the book inhere in these carefully ordered, interwoven images.

Further ties also connect "The Egg" to the rest of the book. The narrator's final statement that "I wondered why" eggs and hens and the whole process of life go on as they do links him to the narrator of the first story in the book, "I Want to Know Why," and with Doctor Cochran of "Unlighted Lamps," who wonders as he dies, "Why are babies always being born?" (*TE* 91). The description of the narrator's family departing from the chicken farm like "refugees fleeing from a battlefield" (*TE* 49) connects them with the beleaguered Polish refugees in "War." The father's defeated ambitions likewise tie in with "The Man in the Brown Coat," where the historian refers to his father's failure to "rise in the world." And the narrator's imaginative filling in of the details of his father's experience is a leap of the same kind of creative sympathy that enables the old man and the narrator of "Brothers" to understand and identify with a murderer. Finally, the familial tenderness in the closing scene is a counterbalance to the strained, distant relations of husband, wife, and child that exist in so many of the other stories.

As for relationships beyond *The Triumph of the Egg*, the grotesque chickens in the father's collection obviously reiterate the idea of the grotesque that is central to *Winesburg, Ohio* (1919). Two stories in that earlier collection show particular similarities to this tale. Like the father here, Ebenezer Cowley in "Queer" is an unhappy farmer come to town and turned unhappy merchant, and he too is hopelessly unlikely ever to fit in with normal society; Cowley's son is driven to desperation, however, whereas the son in this story has turned philosophic. "Godliness" depicts the same social transition from a half-brutal, half-idyllic rural culture to a burgeoning town culture intoxicated with the idea of getting ahead.

"The Egg" is most closely linked, however, with *Poor White* (1920), which also treats America's "progress" from an old agricultural life to a new industrial civilization. Again, Anderson dramatizes the psychological trauma that results from social change. The setting is the same, near Bidwell, Ohio. The narrator's father, like Hugh McVey in the novel, follows the American dream of a better life and moves to Pickleville, outside the town of Bidwell, and there comes to realize his isolation from the community. The tale focuses on one family that runs a little all-night restaurant, but the novel's larger scope covers the broader economic situation—meteoric rise to wealth of a few and devastation of the lower classes. Yet the father in "The Egg," like Hugh, has a sensitive soul and a dream that is more than economic. Both men are unfulfilled emotionally; material success is not the only thing at stake (Gregory, *Talks* 17). Furthermore, Sarah Shepard, who instills ambition into Hugh, resembles the mother in the short story: both women have read the popular literature touting methods of achieving wealth and power, and both transmit their naive hopes to the men in their lives. When the men are defeated, women protectively comfort them: that role is played by the mother in the story, and by Clara Butterworth in the novel.

While "The Egg" and *Poor White* reflect Anderson's early view that human effort cannot "subdue the primal, organic forces of nature," as Spencer argues, later writings show that by the thirties he had transferred those mythic assumptions to "a redemptive feminine principle" such as that represented in the girls at work in American factories (13–15). The cleavage may be less definite than Spencer suggests, for *The Triumph of the Egg* is steeped in some such feminine life principle—most plainly in "Motherhood." An adequate study of Anderson's evolving representation of women has not yet appeared.

Critics have remarked that Anderson's portrayal of the father figure here contrasts with the much less sympathetic treatment of similar figures in *Windy McPherson's Son* (1916) and in *Winesburg, Ohio* (David Anderson 64–65; similarly, Howe 170).

The "vein of tragi-comedy" so brilliantly effective in "The Egg" reappears in the sketches Anderson produced for his Virginia newspapers using his persona "Buck Fever" (Weber, "Essence" 136).

Critical Studies

Early reviewers were less enthusiastic about "The Egg" than subsequent critics have been. Many simply did not mention it. O'Brien selected it as one of the author's four best stories in 1920 but thought "The Other Woman" surpassed it. Crawford "was surprised" by the "poignancy of humor" upon an audience listening to the story read aloud (71). Hansen considered the story "less important" than others in the volume (153). Claverton thought it lacked "elegance of form" but recognized the brilliance of its intimate portrait of "the simple-minded rustic impatient and maddened at the prospect of the endless ennui of continuous failure" (104–105).

More recent commentators generally rank the story as one of Anderson's best (for example, Voss 193; Burbank 96; Raymund 140; West 676; D. Anderson 64). Schevill calls it "one of the outstanding tales in American literature" (164). Howe says it "deserves to be placed among the great stories of the world" (168). Even Trilling, one of Anderson's harshest critics, judged it one of the few "first-rate" stories in the canon and noted that it "gets better on each re-reading" (1).

The metaphysical aspect of the tale is indicated by Schevill's statement that it is "a parable for the fate of man" (164). Similarly, Howe observes the stark pessimism implicit in the image of an "arbitrary, unmotivated" universe in which man "is not merely defeated but tricked in his defeat" by his "hunger for life"; the egg, at first a simple commodity, becomes as the story progresses "an increasingly threatening force," grotesque and uncontrollable (171). The egg, Burbank adds, symbolizes the "maddeningly fragile, refractory, and intractable" quality of life (86). And the deformity of the chickens, David Anderson notes, points up the tragic spiritual deformity inherent in human life (64).

The social dimension of the story has been another important interest of critics. Gregory observed that it is "a burlesque of American salesmanship" ("Editor's" 24), and other critics have developed that idea more fully. Joseph analyzes the narrative in terms of its treatment of American aspirations, dramatized in Columbus's egg trick and the father's critique of that trick (134–35). Columbus is the prototype of American success, and there is "imaginative audacity" amounting to genius in his breaking of old conceptions (134). Yet the father's criticism of Columbus's cheating satirizes the "empty cleverness" at the core of the American myth of success. At the same time, the unnaturalness of the father's attempts to emulate Columbus in triumph over an egg reveals something grotesque in American experience and indicates the inevitable triumph of nature over such attempts (135). West comments that the story condemns literature of the Horatio Alger variety, and the American belief in it, as a "perversion" of American ideals that has contributed to making a society "in which the little man has no chance" (690). Stewart, noting similarities between this tale and Chekhov's "In the Ravine" and "The Kiss," emphasizes the "dark comedy of the American peasant trying to handle middle-class values" (37). She makes the important point that the father's dream of a community where "bright happy groups" would come singing with "joy and laughter" to enjoy the "wonders" of life reveals the unconscious thrust of his spirit against "the sterility of [mere] economic success"; beneath his ridiculousness, then, lies a "spiritual grace" missing from the success of Philistine society (37–38; similarly, Joseph 140).

The psychology of the familial relationship has interested other commentators. West details a Freudian element in the narrator's "Oedipal" difficulties, manifested in his "belittlement of his parents," the jingle he sings about going to the barber shop, "the sexual innuendo" in his reference to himself as an infant lying beside his mother, and his pleasure that his father's egg "trick is not 'consummated'" but ends in "quasi-sexual humiliation when 'the contents spurted over his clothes'" (686–88). The final scene, West argues, where the boy "wails with the anguished jealousy of a small boy who . . .

must forever abandon hope of breaking into the closed circle of his parents' love," also marks the moment when he can "begin to love his parents" maturely (688–89). Mesher notices that the narration itself "identifies the son with his father," whereas the barrage of "subjunctives and conditionals" that surround the description of the mother's hopes "distances him" from her; he contends that the final line of the story indicates the narrator's effort to place the blame for his own defeat on his parents' marriage (181). Savin pursues the idea that the narrator feels guilty about "the role his own birth has played" in bringing about his parents' ambition; though he seeks to mask his likeness to his father, the son's "narrative performances" repeat the father's "elaborate posturing and histrionic" performance in the restaurant and reveal a similarly "obsessive desire to amuse and entertain" (455–56). Patrick and Barbara Bassett note differences between the father's "pathological" and the son's "philosophical" interest in eggs (53–54).

There is some truth to Raymund's statement that "Anderson's method is so simple, so devastating, as to defy description" (141). Nevertheless, formalist and stylistic analysis have yielded useful insight into sources of the story's power. Though Wright classifies it as a comic story with a plot of choice, he observes that "strong overtones of pathos" and "levels upon levels of seriousness" enhance the effect (387, 192–93). Howe praises the "bold sort of artlessness" Anderson achieves by using the traditional narrative device of "protestation to perplexity": the narrator's "slightly bewildered" and "mildly wry" tone allays the "grim, despairing" view of life latent in "the bare fable" he tells (150–51, 168). Taylor discusses the point of view and the dramatic irony ensuing from the gap between the child's innocent perspective and the dismal implications of his narrative (50). Mizener comments on the effective interaction between "the casual, commonsense point of view of Joe Kane," which recognizes the ludicrousness of the father's behavior, and the "subjective" emphasis on the father's hopeful longing and crushing disappointment (429).

In a fuller analysis than either of these, Hagopian and Dolch take account of the fact that the narrator is no longer a child but a man viewing events retrospectively: "Anderson makes him something of a home-spun philosopher, a small-town Schopenhauer with the implication that his own life has fully confirmed the meaning of the events he witnessed in his boyhood" (12). Technically, they point out, the story is "old-fashioned" in presenting characters and setting in "an elaborate exposition" as well as in narrating "a dramatic event heavily charged with a moral"; its point of view and its "pessimistic existentialism," however, mark it as modern (12). The narrator's "digression" is actually an integral part of the tale, providing a frame for the "cosmically comic" climactic scene (12–13). They note, as Howe had earlier, that it is a "told" rather than a "written" story and that it is "a parable": they judge the parable to be "one of the lesser forms of literary art" because it "does not *embed* [its] meaning in action" but merely "illustrates" a stated truth (12–13). (It might be argued to the contrary that parables are rich because they invite a variety of interpretations.) Hagopian and Dolch also argue that the story is flawed by the fact that the narrator does not witness the crucial scene (14). Barker had made the same charge twenty years before, complaining that the narrator's "lame" excuse that he inexplicably knows what he has not witnessed betrays the writer's faulty technique (439).

Several interpreters, though, explain the narrator's imaginative reconstruction of his father's experience as no lapse at all but an important aspect of the story's meaning. Savin asserts that the son's knowledge, which comes "from what he knows . . . of himself," is part of an "egg-like" narrative structure that reveals "within the shell of history" the "fertile center" that consists of "the fictions one creates about oneself and one's genesis" (456–57). Stouck, similarly, remarks that the "self-flexive narrative voice" calls attention to the fictionality of the story and links it with postmodern technique (313–14). Lawry finds in the narrator's "participative imagination" a merger of "father and son," "past and present," and "village and town"—and also Anderson's resolution to problems of narration he had been struggling with in his fiction about Winesburg and Bidwell (60–61). Gado notes that as the father's "thinking" was his "undoing," so the son begins to think— and "is undone"; the narrator's pivotal role "illustrates a general principle" of Anderson's art, that form "is a function of the *teller's* reaction to his materials" (Gado 14).

A superb analysis of Anderson's handling of language can be found in West's essay, which looks closely at the ironic mingling of "facile, vaguely evocative phrases of advertising" and other cheap literature of easy optimism with material of an utterly different sort—biblical echoes, reiterated references to sickness, to wonder, and the "resonant repetition" of the image of trembling hands, God's as well as the parents' (680–85). In contrast, Kingsbury's "structural semantic" dissection of one line of the text, which short-circuits possible complexities of meaning, offers more insight into the analyst's presuppositions than into the tale itself.

Several critics discover parallels between "The Egg" and works by other writers—William Faulkner's "Mirror of Chartres Street" (Richardson 306), Franz Kafka's "A Hunger Artist" (Arbuckle and Misenheimer), and Nathanael West's stories (Reid). Schevill finds in it a continuation of the "psychological-introspective tradition" represented by Hawthorne and Melville (159–60). West places it in the American tradition of Twain, Poe, Thoreau, Franklin, Cooper, Crane, Edwards, and even Dickinson (689–90). But, for all that, the story is unique, a complex triumph of art woven from the *lacrimae rerum*.

Works Cited

Anderson, David. 1967. *Sherwood Anderson: An Introduction and Interpretation*. New York: Holt, Rinehart.

Anderson, Sherwood. 1916. *Windy McPherson's Son*. New York: John Lane. Rev. ed., New York: B. W. Huebsch, 1922; Chicago and London: University of Chicago Press, 1965. Introduction by Wright Morris.

——. 1919. *Winesburg, Ohio*. New York: B. W. Huebsch. Rpt. New York: Viking, 1960.

——. 1920. *Poor White*. New York: B. W. Huebsch. Rpt. New York: Viking, 1966. Introduction by Walter B. Rideout.

Arbuckle, Donald E., and James B. Misenheimer, Jr. "Personal Failure in 'The Egg' and 'A Hunger Artist.'" *Winesburg Eagle* 8, no. 2 (1983):1–3.

Barker, Russell H. "The Storyteller Role." *College English* 3 (1942):433–42.

Bassett, Patrick, and Barbara Bassett. "Anderson's 'The Egg.'" *The Explicator* 40 (1981):53–54.

Burbank, Rex. 1964. *Sherwood Anderson*. New York: Twayne. Rpt. in part in *The Achievement of Sherwood Anderson: Essays in Criticism*. Ed. Ray Lewis White. Chapel Hill: University of North Carolina Press, 1966, 32–43. Rpt. in part in *Sherwood Anderson: Collection of Critical Essays*. Ed. Walter B. Rideout. Englewood Cliffs, NJ: Prentice-Hall, 1974, 70–83.

Calverton, V. J. "Sherwood Anderson: A Study in Sociological Criticism." *Modern Quarterly* 2 (1924):82–118. Rpt. in *The Newer Spirit: A Sociological Criticism of Literature*. Introduction by Ernest Boyd. New York: Boni & Liveright, 1925, 52–118.

Crawford, Nelson Antrim. 1981. "Sherwood Anderson, the Wistfully Faithful." In *Critical Essays on Sherwood Anderson*. Ed. David D. Anderson. Boston: G. K. Hall, 65–73. Originally printed in *The Midland* 8 (November 1922):297–308.

Fanning, Michael, ed. 1976. *France and Sherwood Anderson: Paris Notebook, 1921*. Baton Rouge: Louisiana State University Press.

Gado, Frank, ed. 1983. *The Teller's Tales*. Schenectady, NY: Union College Press.

Geismar, Maxwell, ed. 1962. *Sherwood Anderson: Short Stories*. New York: Hill and Wang.

Gregory, Horace. 1949. "Editor's Introduction." *The Portable Sherwood Anderson*. Ed. Horace Gregory. New York: Viking, 1–31. Rev. ed. New York: Viking Penguin, 1972.

———. 1968. "On Sherwood Anderson." In *Talks with Authors*. Ed. Charles F. Madden. Carbondale: Southern Illinois University Press, 12–22.

Gregory, Horace, ed. 1949. *The Portable Sherwood Anderson*. New York: Viking. Rev. ed. New York: Viking Penguin, 1972.

Hagopian, John V., and Martin Dolch. 1962. "The Egg." *Insight I: Analysis of American Literature*. Frankfurt am Main: Hirschgraben-Verlag, 11–14.

Hansen, Harry. 1923. *Midwest Portraits: A Book of Memories and Friendships*. New York: Harcourt, Brace.

Howe, Irving. 1951. *Sherwood Anderson*. New York: William Sloane.

Jones, Howard Mumford, and Walter B. Rideout, eds. 1953. *Letters of Sherwood Anderson*. Boston: Little, Brown.

Joseph, Gerhard. "The American Triumph of The Egg: Anderson's 'The Egg' and Fitzgerald's *The Great Gatsby*." *Criticism* 7 (1965):131–40.

Kingsbury, Stewart A. 1971. "A Structural Semantic Analysis of the Punch Line of Sherwood Anderson's Short Story, 'The Egg.'" *Papers from the Michigan Linguistic Society Meeting October 3, 1970*. Ed. David Lawton. Mount Pleasant: Central Michigan University, 117.

Lawry, Jon S. "The Arts of Winesburg and Bidwell, Ohio." *Twentieth Century Literature* 23 (1977):53–66.

Mesher, David R. "A Triumph of the Ego in Anderson's 'The Egg.'" *Studies in Short Fiction* 17 (1980):180–83.

Miller, William V. 1974. "Earth-Mothers, Succubi, and Other Ectoplasmic Spirits: The Women in Sherwood Anderson's Short Stories." *Midamerica I*. Ed. David D. Anderson. East Lansing, MI: Midwestern Press, 64–81. Rpt. in *Critical Essays on Sherwood Anderson*. Ed. David D. Anderson. Boston: G. K. Hall, 1981, 196–209.

Mizener, Arthur, ed. 1967. *Modern Short Stories: The Uses of Imagination*. Rev. ed. New York: Norton.

Modlin, Charles E., ed. 1992. *Certain Things Last: The Selected Stories of Sherwood Anderson*. New York: Four Walls Eight Windows.

———, ed. 1984. *Sherwood Anderson: Selected Letters*. Knoxville: University of Tennessee Press.

O'Brien, Edward Joseph. 1921. *The Best Short Stories of 1920*. Boston: Small, Maynard.

Raymund, Bernard. "The Grammar of Not-Reason: Sherwood Anderson." *Arizona Quarterly* 12 (1956):48–60, 137–48.

Reid, Randall. 1967. *The Fiction of Nathanael West: No Redeemer, No Promised Land*. Chicago: University of Chicago Press.

Richardson, H. Edward. "Anderson and Faulkner." *American Literature* 36 (1964):298–314.

Rosenfeld, Paul, ed. 1947. *The Sherwood Anderson Reader*. Boston: Houghton Mifflin.

Savin, Mark. "Coming Full Circle: Sherwood Anderson's 'The Egg.'" *Studies in Short Fiction* 18 (1981):454–57.

Schevill, James. 1951. *Sherwood Anderson: His Life and Work*. Denver: University of Denver Press.

Spencer, Benjamin I. "Sherwood Anderson: American Mythopoeist." *American Literature* 41 (1969):1–18.

Stewart, Maaja A. "Skepticism and Belief in Chekhov and Anderson." *Studies in Short Fiction* 9 (1972):29–40.

Stouck, David. "Sherwood Anderson and the Postmodern Novel." *Contemporary Literature* 26 (1985):302–316.

Sutton, William A., ed. 1985. *Letters to Bab: Sherwood Anderson to Marietta D. Finley, 1916–33*. Foreword by Walter B. Rideout. Urbana and Chicago: University of Illinois Press.

Taylor, Welford Dunaway. 1977. *Sherwood Anderson*. New York: Frederick Ungar.

Townsend, Kim. 1987. *Sherwood Anderson*. Boston: Houghton Mifflin.

Trilling, Lionel. "The World of Sherwood Anderson." *New York Times Book Review,* November 9, 1947, pp. 1, 67–69.

Voss, Arthur. 1973. *The American Short Story: A Critical Survey*. Norman: University of Oklahoma Press.

Weber, Brom. "Anderson and the 'The Essence of Things.'" *Sewanee Review* 59 (1951):678–92. Rpt. in *Critical Essays on Sherwood Anderson*. Ed. David D. Anderson. Boston: G. K. Hall, 1981, 125–37.

West, Michael. "Sherwood Anderson's Triumph: 'The Egg.'" *American Quarterly* 20 (1968):675–93.

White, Ray Lewis, ed. 1969. *Sherwood Anderson's Memoirs: A Critical Edition*. Chapel Hill: University of North Carolina Press.

Wright, Austin McGiffert. 1961. *The American Short Story in the Twenties*. Chicago: University of Chicago Press.

Unlighted Lamps

Circumstances of Composition

Anderson reported that, when he moved to Chicago from Elyria, Ohio, in 1913, he brought with him four novels—*Windy McPherson's Son, Marching Men,* "Talbot Whittingham," and "Mary Cochran" (Modlin, *Letters* 43). Of these, the first two were published, in 1916 and 1917 respectively, and the other two were not. In October of 1916 Anderson was working on "Mary Cochran" and writing to his friend Marietta Finley about a revision he was planning (Sutton, *Letters* 7). Finley wrote a review of the manuscript for him. It indicates that Mary Cochran grew up in the routine monotony of a doctor's household in a New England village, then went to a Midwestern university and on to work in Chicago, where she became engaged to Duke Yetter but finally married someone else; Finley's review is included in Sutton's *The Road to Winesburg* (581–83).

In November of 1919 Anderson was again working on this material, referring to it as "the Mary Cochran stories" (Sutton, *Letters* 16); about the same time, he wrote that "the Mary Cochran book" was taking shape as "a group of tales woven about the life of one person [as in *Winesburg*] but each tale will be longer and more closely related to the development of the central character" so that it might be published as a novel (Anderson's letter, printed in Curry, 242). Later, he said that his procedure had not been to excerpt stories from the unpublished novel, but to take the living character in his imagination and put her into a new and different story (Hansen 123; Sutton, *Letters* 45).

In 1928, Anderson was again writing about Mary Cochran (Sutton, *Letters* 308–309).

Sources and Influences

Since this story originated in the author's mind from situations already developed in a manuscript for a novel, it has a density that most of the stories in *The Triumph of the Egg* lack.

Two different biographical sources have been offered for Mary Cochran. Sutton notices that her loneliness, her confusion, and her restless searching "all make her a blood sister of her creator" (*Road* 334). Howe observes that Mary bears a striking resemblance to Tennessee Mitchell, the "New Woman" who became Anderson's wife in 1916 immediately after his divorce from his first wife (82). His suggestion is tantalizing but inconclusive: whereas the character's mother has left her husband and infant daughter and the father dies while Mary is at home, Tennessee's mother died when Tennessee was seventeen and her father died after she left home and went to Chicago (Townsend 124).

Ross remarks several literary influences stamped on the tale: naturalistic domination of the characters by their compulsions, "Chekhovian longing," Gothic echoes, and Freudian motivations (31). Way elaborates slightly on the similarity to Chekhov (114). Hoffman states, however, that in this story the barrier between father and daughter results not from Freudian repression but from simple "timidity" (243).

Publication History

"Unlighted Lamps" first appeared in *Smart Set* in July of 1921 (65:45–55). Mencken had turned down "Queer" in January of 1916 and printed "The Story Writers," which seems slight by comparison, but in 1919 he had praised the *Winesburg* stories (White, "Mencken's") and brought out "I Want to Know Why." Anderson and Mencken were not much alike, and Anderson did not respect Mencken much (Jones-Rideout, *Letters* 37), but Mencken's respect for Anderson seems to have grown with Anderson's reputation.

The story was collected in *The Triumph of the Egg* in 1921 (64–92). Rosenfeld included it in *The Sherwood Anderson Reader* after the author's death (36–52).

Relation to Other Works

In April of 1921, after he had sent off to the publisher the collected stories that would finally be named *The Triumph of the Egg,* Anderson told his correspondents that the book would be called "Unlighted Lamps" (Sutton, *Letters* 152; Campbell and Modlin 5). His intention suggests the central significance of the symbolic title for the whole volume. These stories tell of souls living in spiritual darkness, ailing from emotional cold, and struggling to discover light.

Elements of the original plot of "Mary Cochran" may have evolved into aspects not only of "Unlighted Lamps" and "The Door of the Trap," in both of which Mary Cochran is a character, but also into "The New Englander." An odd symbolic detail links Mary, in "Unlighted Lamps," with Elsie Leander, in "The New Englander": both sit on rocks in an old apple orchard. The two Mary Cochran stories, moreover, along with "Out of Nowhere into Nothing," tell a sort of composite tale of a young woman's growing to maturity in a world where men either ignore or misuse her. The overall pattern in these stories. of movement from childhood in a growing town to adulthood in a modern city, is similar to the progress of many of Anderson's male protagonists. So in some sense these stories in *The Triumph of the Egg* give a female counterpart of George Willard's experience in *Winesburg, Ohio.*

A repeated pattern in Anderson's works is that of motherless girls reared by fathers who express no love for them; examples include Mary Cochran in this story, Clara Butterworth in *Poor White* (1920), Louise Bentley in "Godliness," the child in "Tandy," and Belle Carpenter in "An Awakening" (Chapman 35). The connection between emotional deprivation inflicted by fathers on their daughters and the daughter's subsequent difficulties in forming healthy heterosexual relationships also appears in "The New Englander," *Beyond Desire* (1932), and *Kit Brandon* (1936). The theme receives fullest treatment in the novels, understandably, but it is also important in the stories.

Anderson's wife, Tennessee Mitchell, sculpted the heads pictured in the opening pages of *The Triumph of the Egg,* and it may be that her influence colors a number of the tales and sketches in the volume in other ways as well. Her life story does approximate the various phases of women's lives depicted in several tales in the book.

Howe groups "Unlighted Lamps" with other stories about "the neurotic costs of the unlived life," "The Door of the Trap" and "Out of Nowhere into Nothing" as well as others in *Horses and Men* (173). As in "Mother," "The Teacher," "The Strength of God," and a number of other *Winesburg* tales, characters find it impossible to communicate an emotion that they very much want to express (Wright 58). Miller mentions this as one of three Anderson stories about doctors who are unable to show their feelings ("Portraits" 7).

Critical Studies

Wright classifies "Unlighted Lamps" as a caustic-pathetic story having "a discovery plot with a double protagonist"; the discovery made by both father and daughter is "that they have never properly expressed or understood" their love for each other (230–31n).

There are no articles devoted to this story alone. The two most extended treatments, and the best, are just a few pages long. Burbank mentions a resemblance between Tolstoy's *Death of Ivan Ilych* and this tale, where the doctor and his daughter "examine their lives" in the face of his approaching death (89). He focuses primarily, though, on the technique that makes this tale of buried lives powerful. "Anderson's brilliant blending of counterpoints," as Burbank puts it, consists of the contrast between the stifled lives of the two main characters and the spontaneous life of the townspeople, the author's playing of motifs of light against dark, birth against death, and the shifts of narrative perspective and mood that display the characters' "abrupt" transitions between "timid resolutions" and paralyzing "indecision" (89–91). Burbank's scrutiny of Anderson's "prose pointillism" reveals the careful craft that went into the story.

Way also discusses "the subtle alternations in point of view between [father's and daughter's] parallel trains of thought" and elaborates on the imagery of "flickering light," analyzing particularly the fine passage where a farmer's lighted match triggers the doctor's memory of a great burst of light that flamed forth from a mirror on his knees when his wife told him she was pregnant and he in response was silent (114–15). Way notices the complex texture of the story, which fuses the psychological details of Mary's sexual maturation with the context of her relationship with her father and with that larger context of sociological detail about the infusion of Italian immigrant industrial workers into "the older rural Anglo-Saxon community" (113).

Other commentators have admired the story's "deep and poignant . . . tragedy" (Fagin 131), the dignity Anderson accords his characters in their defeat (Chapman 42) and the symbolism of the lamp (Taylor 57; Miller, "Earth-Mothers" 78). Taylor comments additionally on the author's handling of time, concentrating on a single day but "telescoping details drawn from a broad expanse of time" (56). David Anderson mentions Duke Yetter as one who misunderstands Mary, but does not analyze his role further (65). Understandably, the quiet realistic mode of the story has not attracted intricate readings or passionate response of any kind. The episode it relates leaves questions that a novel could develop in productive ways. Yet the story stands well enough on its own. It would not suffer from somewhat closer scrutiny.

Works Cited

Anderson, David. 1967. *Sherwood Anderson: An Introduction and Interpretation*. New York: Holt, Rinehart.

Anderson, Sherwood. 1921. *The Triumph of the Egg*. New York: B. W. Huebsch. Rpt. New York: Four Walls Eight Windows, 1988. Introduction by Herbert Gold.

Burbank, Rex. 1964. *Sherwood Anderson*. New York: Twayne. Rpt. in part in *The Achievement of Sherwood Anderson: Essays in Criticism*. Ed. Ray Lewis White. Chapel Hill: University of North Carolina Press, 1966,

32–43. Rpt. in part in *Sherwood Anderson: Collection of Critical Essays.* Ed. Walter B. Rideout. Englewood Cliffs, NJ: Prentice-Hall, 1974, 70–83.

Campbell, Hilbert H., and Charles E. Modlin, eds. 1976. *Sherwood Anderson: Centennial Studies.* Troy, NY: Whitston.

Chapman, Arnold. "Sherwood Anderson and Eduardo Mallea." *PMLA* 69 (1954):34–45.

Curry, Martha Mulroy. 1975. *The "Writer's Book" by Sherwood Anderson: A Critical Edition.* Metuchen, NJ: Scarecrow Press.

Fagin, N. Bryllion. 1973. *The Phenomenon of Sherwood Anderson: A Study in American Life and Letters.* New York: Russell & Russell. Originally printed Baltimore: Rossi-Bryn, 1927.

Hansen, Harry. 1923. *Midwest Portraits: A Book of Memories and Friendships.* New York: Harcourt, Brace.

Hoffman, Frederick J. 1957. *Freudianism and the Literary Mind.* Rev. ed. Baton Rouge: Louisiana State University Press. Rpt. in *Sherwood Anderson: Winesburg, Ohio: Text and Criticism.* Ed. John H. Ferres. New York: Viking, 1966, 309–20. Rpt. in *The Achievement of Sherwood Anderson: Essays in Criticism.* Ed. Ray Lewis White. Chapel Hill: University of North Carolina Press, 1966, 174–92.

Howe, Irving. 1951. *Sherwood Anderson.* New York: William Sloane.

Jones, Howard Mumford, and Walter B. Rideout, eds. 1953. *Letters of Sherwood Anderson.* Boston: Little, Brown.

Miller, William V. 1974. "Earth-Mothers, Succubi, and Other Ectoplasmic Spirits: The Women in Sherwood Anderson's Short Stories." In *Midamerica I.* Ed. David D. Anderson. East Lansing, Mich.: Midwestern Press, 64–81. Rpt. in *Critical Essays on Sherwood Anderson.* Ed. David D. Anderson. Boston: G. K. Hall, 1981, 196–209.

———. 1976. "Portraits of the Artist: Anderson's Fictional Storytellers." In *Sherwood Anderson: Dimensions of His Literary Art: A Collection of Critical Essays.* Ed. David D. Anderson. East Lansing: Michigan State University Press, 1–23.

Modlin, Charles E., ed. 1984. *Sherwood Anderson: Selected Letters.* Knoxville: University of Tennessee Press.

Rosenfeld, Paul, ed. 1947. *The Sherwood Anderson Reader.* Boston: Houghton Mifflin.

Ross, Danforth. 1961. *The American Short Story.* University of Minnesota Pamphlets on American Writers, No. 14. Minneapolis: University of Minnesota Press.

Sutton, William A., ed. 1985. *Letters to Bab: Sherwood Anderson to Marietta D. Finley, 1916–33*. Foreword by Walter B. Rideout. Urbana and Chicago: University of Illinois Press.

———. 1972. *The Road to Winesburg: A Mosaic of the Imaginative Life of Sherwood Anderson*. Metuchen, NJ: Scarecrow Press.

Taylor, Welford Dunaway. 1977. *Sherwood Anderson*. New York: Frederick Ungar.

Townsend, Kim. 1987. *Sherwood Anderson*. Boston: Houghton Mifflin.

Way, Brian. 1971. "Sherwood Anderson." In *The American Novel and the Nineteen Twenties*. Malcolm Bradbury and David Palmer (Eds.) Stratford-upon-Avon Studies 13. London: Edward Arnold, 107–126.

White, Ray Lewis. "Mencken's Lost Review of *Winesburg, Ohio*." *Notes on Modern American Literature* 2 (1978): Item 11.

Wright, Austin McGiffert. 1961. *The American Short Story in the Twenties*. Chicago: University of Chicago Press.

Senility

Circumstances of Composition

This story apparently was written in December of 1916. There is a typescript of the story dated December 15, 1916 (Rideout 219). In early January 1917, Anderson sent a draft of the story to Marietta Finley. At that time, it was entitled "Doctor." In the accompanying letter he told her: "You said you sometimes hungered for vulgarity. Here is my 'Doctor.' You will find it vulgar but there is something else in it too. Do you not think so?" (Sutton, *Letters* 39; "Doctor" is printed alongside the letter, 40–42.). Revising this draft for print, Anderson (possibly with the advice of his editors) softened the vulgarity. "The piles protrude from the rectum," for example, became "The sickness that bleeds is a terrible nuisance"; similarly, "called him a son of a bitch" became "called him an ugly name."

During this period, Anderson frequently traveled about the country to meet clients of his employer, the Critchfield Company. On a trip out of Chicago to Kentucky, he may very well have met such a man as the one in the story.

Sources and Influences

The general revolt of the avant-garde against the genteel tradition is plainly evident in this tale. Exact sources, however, have not been mentioned.

Publication History

"Senility" was first published in *Little Review* in September of 1918 (5:37–39). In the same issue appeared an episode of James Joyce's *Ulysses* and several poems by T. S. Eliot. The story was collected in *The Triumph of the Egg* in 1921 (93–96).

Relation to Other Works

In November of 1917, Anderson's "Apology for Crudity" was published, arguing that "crudity is an inevitable quality in the production of a really significant present-day American literature"; since the life of its people is in fact "crude and childlike," writers must have faith in that simple reality and dare to tell that story. The essay expressed one of Anderson's most fundamental beliefs, which is reflected in this experimental tale.

More than any other story in the collection, "Senility" deserves Hart Crane's response that in *The Triumph of the Egg* Anderson "has written of ghastly desolations," that "he has, like a diver, touched bottom" (73). Geismar suggests that the old man's "lugubrious chant" expresses the central idea of a volume more despairing than *Winesburg, Ohio* (1919) and with more "tormented" characters (*Last* 245). Elsewhere Geismar comments that in this story disease is a metaphor for the condition of the ailing America Anderson is representing in *The Triumph of the Egg* ("Introduction" xvi).

Incongruously the old, diseased man is one of three "doctors" in *The Triumph of the Egg*. Doctor Cochran in "Unlighted Lamps" and the psychoanalyst in "Seeds" also devote themselves to trying to cure the ailments of others. All three stories bear the irony that the physician cannot heal himself. As David Anderson notes, the protagonist can cure physical ills "but not the sickness in his own heart" (65). The twisted foot of the old man's pretty young wife links her with the woman from Iowa in "Seeds"; he treats her with tenderness, buying her straight shoes so she will not guess that he has noticed her deformity, but their relationship is hardly a model of the long, patient love recommended as a cure for the neurotic woman in the former story.

The old man is a grotesque of the most obvious sort. His tears link him particularly with the carpenter in "The Book of the Grotesque." His imprisoned, hate-filled brother—his double—is reminiscent of the brothers of that carpenter, of Doctor Parcival in "The Philosopher," and of the murderer in "Brothers."

Critical Studies

This story, hardly more than a sketch, has received little attention. Narrated in the third person, it is a dialogue between an old man in Kentucky and a cordial stranger from the city. The old man, Tom, does most of the talking, rambling in senile fashion. The vivid realism of his portrait is daunting; such a subject is not usually treated in fiction, and there is little apparatus within the story to guide a reader in interpreting the meaning. The old man says he is happy and good, and indeed his words and his actions support his claim that he is good, though his tears and his decrepitude undercut his claim that he is happy. The tone of the episode blends the ludicrous and the pathetic in a way that anticipates the Theatre of the Absurd.

Cargill states: "The impressionistic study called 'Senility,' repulsive though it is, is one of the best things Anderson did" (681). Unfortunately, he does not elaborate.

West charges that "Senility" is poor because it has "neither the incisiveness of allegory nor the completeness of character development or an enclosing action" (46–47). In the context of the whole of *The Triumph of the Egg,* though, the old man's misery stands as the nadir of desolation. It is an important part of the symbolic waste land imagery in that collection and of the Shelleyan call for rebirth.

Works Cited

Anderson, David. 1967. *Sherwood Anderson: An Introduction and Interpretation.* New York: Holt, Rinehart.

Anderson, Sherwood. "An Apology for Crudity." *Dial* 63 (November 8, 1917), 437–38. Rpt. in *Sherwood Anderson's Notebook.* New York: Boni & Liveright, 1926.

———. *The Triumph of the Egg.* 1921. New York: B. W. Huebsch. Rpt. New York: Four Walls Eight Windows, 1988. Introduction by Herbert Gold.

Cargill, Oscar. 1941. *Intellectual America: Ideas on the March.* New York: Macmillan.

Crane, Hart. 1952. *The Letters of Hart Crane 1916–1932.* Ed. Brom Weber. New York: Hermitage House.

Geismar, Maxwell. 1962. "Introduction." *Sherwood Anderson: Short Stories.* New York: Hill and Wang, ix-xxii.

Geismar, Maxwell. 1947. "Sherwood Anderson: Last of the Townsmen." In *The Last of the Provincials: The American Novel, 1915–1925*. Boston: Houghton Mifflin, 223–84. Rpt. in part in *Sherwood Anderson: Winesburg, Ohio: Text and Criticism*. Ed. John H. Ferres. New York: Viking, 1966, 377–82.

Rideout, Walter B. Review of *The "Writer's Book" by Sherwood Anderson: A Critical Edition*. By Martha Mulroy Curry. Metuchen, NJ: Scarecrow Press, 1975. In *Resources for American Literary Study* 10 (1980):217–20.

Sutton, William A., ed. 1985. *Letters to Bab: Sherwood Anderson to Marietta D. Finley, 1916–33*. Foreword by Walter B. Rideout. Urbana and Chicago: University of Illinois Press.

West, Ray B., Jr. 1952. *The Short Story in America: 1900–1950*. Chicago: Regnery. Rpt. New York: Books for Libraries (Division of Arno Press), 1979.

The Man in the Brown Coat

Circumstances of Composition

"The Man in the Brown Coat" was written by the spring of 1920, possibly in 1919. By this time Anderson was no longer living in the Cass Street house where he wrote *Winesburg, Ohio,* which came out in May of 1919. He may have lived on Division Street. He was still in Chicago, working as an advertising copywriter for the Critchfield Company and writing literature on the side, but he had worked out an arrangement with the firm whereby he could keep his own schedule while still sharing his fees with them (Townsend 148). Feeling the taste of literary success, he was increasingly eager to leave his job and devote himself full-time to art. At the end of March 1919, he told Van Wyck Brooks that he was writing, along with tales for a new book (which became *The Triumph of the Egg*), some "insane, experimental" items for *A New Testament:* "It is an attempt to express, largely by indirection, the purely fanciful side of a man's life, the odds and ends of thought . . . and emotions that are so seldom touched. I've a fancy this last experiment would make your hair stand on end" (Jones-Rideout, *Letters* 46). The nature of the story, which is more a prose poem than a story, and especially its last sentence, suggest that it was originally intended for *A New*

Testament (where indeed it appeared) and that only later the author decided that it and other similar pieces would fill out his volume of tales.

A feisty letter from Anderson to Waldo Frank in mid-1919 suggests that the story may have been written about this time: "To the casual eye I am on these days just a fat-cheeked man in a brown coat and a very yellow necktie. In reality I am no such thing. I am a river running down through a valley. I am a princely man with a broken leg. I am one who sits on the roofs of tall buildings in Chicago and sees sheep nibbling grass beside a brook in the state of Missouri" (Jones-Rideout, *Letters* 47).

At the end of 1917, Anderson had been reading history—as "an antidote to the War," he said; he specifically mentions General Grant, who appears in the epigraph of this story (Jones-Rideout, *Letters* 27).

Sources and Influences

This sketch contains manifest biographical elements. Anderson's father, like his character's, was a house painter who "did not rise in the world" as his son did (*TE* 97). Anderson, too, had written hundreds of thousands of words searching for the words to lead into life. But the most important source is Anderson's recollection of the painful distance that existed between him and his first wife, Cornelia, whom he liked and respected. He evidently felt that their situation was broadly typical of many contemporary marriages.

Publication History

"The Man in the Brown Coat" was first printed in the January-March issue of the *Little Review* in 1921 (7:18–21). The story had previously been rejected by the *Freeman* on the grounds, as Anderson put it, first, that the story was not any good ("That reason don't go. It is," Anderson fumed to Van Wyck Brooks), and second, that as a "political magazine" they did not care about literature (Jones-Rideout, *Letters* 59). The failure of the *Seven Arts* in 1917 had been a sharp disappointment to Anderson as well as to many others. By this time, he had scant respect for the *Little Review,* calling it and the *Dial* "immature, undignified, pretentious, asinine things; I don't look at *Little Review* at all. I throw such things as '[The] Man in the Brown Coat' into it" (Jones-Rideout, *Letters* 59). The same issue of *Little Review* that printed the story, though, included Margaret Anderson's report of the trial of the magazine for printing obscene material—James Joyce's *Ulysses.*

In October of 1921 Anderson's story was reprinted in *The Triumph of the Egg* (97–101). That version includes several revisions. The historian's father, "a mender of shoes" in *Little Review,* becomes a house painter in the collected tales. A few other sentences are inserted and a few deleted, but the revisions are not substantial.

In 1927 Anderson included "The Man in the Brown Coat" in *A New Testament* (71–76), again with minor revisions. Geismar reprinted it in his collection of Anderson's stories (30–32).

Relation to Other Works

This is a version of one of Anderson's favorite themes, the life buried behind the walls that separate people from one another, even those they love. Fagin mentions the historian as one of Anderson's many lonely characters (135). The gulf between husband and wife in particular occurs in many of the author's novels and stories, notably *Dark Laughter* (1925), which depicts the domestic life of Fred and Aline Grey in these terms: "In the evening after dinner he looked at her and she looked at him. What was to be said? There was nothing to talk about. Often the minutes passed with infinite slowness" (282). The historian's longing to establish contact with his wife aligns him especially with the protagonist of "The Other Woman," in the same volume. The tone of the two stories, though, is markedly different: this lyrical first-person rumination is only lightly touched by the ironies surrounding the self-shielding explanations and equivocations of the husband in the preceding third-person narration.

Miller notes that the historian in this sketch is one of three college professors in Anderson's tales; like the professor in "The Flood," he shows "the limitations of strictly intellectual communication" (7). (The third professor is in "In A Strange Town.") Ironically, this educated man, author of three books that stand up on library shelves, is shy of his wife and longs to find words with which he might break through to her.

The historian's idea that he knows his wife's thoughts links him with the boy in "I Want to Know Why" (who "knows" the horse's and the trainer's thoughts), with the writer in "Brothers," and with Melville Stoner in "Out of Nowhere into Nothing." Outside this volume, the same idea appears in other stories as well, but never to better ends than in "Death in the Woods."

Most important, "The Man in the Brown Coat" participates in the pattern encompassing *The Triumph of the Egg* of life stirring within the apparently dead husks that populate the world. Dreaming of heroes—Napoleon, Grant, Alexander—the timid historian contemplates taking the heroic action that might lead him into authentic life—speaking to his wife. The incongruity is preposterous, yet Anderson's language leaves no doubt that beneath the dreary brown coat lies an aspiration that, properly understood, is worthy of the comparison.

Critical Studies

Fagin makes the reasonable assumption that the historian is Anderson himself (135); there are obvious differences, of course, but Anderson here deliberately introduces the personal note.

Most recent critics ignore "The Man in the Brown Coat" entirely. Some comment that though the professor has written three history books, he cannot find words to bring him into communication with life (Burbank 95; similarly, Cargill 680; and D. Anderson 65). Burbank adds that the character is "two-dimensional," a problem that he traces to Anderson's inability to handle the "urbane tone of the sophisticated narrator" (95).

Critics writing in the twenties, however, were far more responsive, evidently refreshed by Anderson's lack of urbanity. That civilized New Yorker Paul Rosenfeld applauded the symbolic "overtones" and the "play of word-timbres" and "verbal shapes and colours" of a prose handled so delicately that it was almost poetry; a brown coat, he noted, was "conventionally tinted stuff" that represents an inescapable inner reality inhibiting the mind's "bright colours" (36–37). Gilman, likewise, praised the story for an effect "curiously like that achieved by Stravinsky or Bloch or Schönberg or Ornstein in one of those haunting and intangible projections in tone which hold the quintessence of an experience" (413).

Works Cited

Anderson, David. 1967. *Sherwood Anderson: An Introduction and Interpretation*. New York: Holt, Rinehart.

Anderson, Sherwood. 1921. *The Triumph of the Egg.* New York: B. W. Huebsch. Rpt. Introduction by Herbert Gold. New York: Four Walls Eight Windows, 1988.

——. 1925. *Dark Laughter.* New York: Boni & Liveright; Grosset and Dunlap.

——. 1927. *A New Testament.* New York: Boni & Liveright.

Burbank, Rex. 1964. *Sherwood Anderson.* New York: Twayne. Rpt. in part in *The Achievement of Sherwood Anderson: Essays in Criticism.* Ed. Ray Lewis White. Chapel Hill: University of North Carolina Press, 1966, 32–43. Rpt. in part in *Sherwood Anderson: Collection of Critical Essays.* Ed. Walter B. Rideout. Englewood Cliffs, NJ: Prentice-Hall, 1974, 70–83.

Cargill, Oscar. 1941. *Intellectual America: Ideas on the March.* New York: Macmillan.

Fagin, N. Bryllion. 1973. *The Phenomenon of Sherwood Anderson: A Study in American Life and Letters*. New York: Russell & Russell. Originally printed Baltimore: Rossi-Bryn, 1927.

Geismar, Maxwell, ed. 1962. *Sherwood Anderson: Short Stories*. Ed. Maxwell Geismar. New York: Hill and Wang.

Gilman, Lawrence. "The Book of the Month: An American Masterwork." *North American Review* 215 (1922):412–16. Rpt. in *Critical Essays on Sherwood Anderson*. Ed. David D. Anderson. Boston: G. K. Hall, 1981, 38–41.

Jones, Howard Mumford, and Walter B. Rideout, eds. 1953. *Letters of Sherwood Anderson*. Boston: Little, Brown.

Miller, William V. 1976. "Portraits of the Artist: Anderson's Fictional Storytellers." In *Sherwood Anderson: Dimensions of His Literary Art: A Collection of Critical Essays*. Ed. David D. Anderson. East Lansing: Michigan State University Press, 1–23.

Rosenfeld, Paul. "Sherwood Anderson." *Dial* 72 (1922):29–42. Rpt. in *The Port of New York*. New York: Harcourt, Brace, 1924, 175–98. Rpt. in *Critical Essays on Sherwood Anderson*. Ed. David D. Anderson. Boston: G. K. Hall, 1981, 74–85.

Townsend, Kim. 1987. *Sherwood Anderson*. Boston: Houghton Mifflin.

Brothers

Circumstances of Composition

This story was written in October 1920 when James M. Cox (mentioned in the story) was running for president against Warren G. Harding and Eugene V. Debs. In the late spring of that year, Anderson moved to Palos Park, a town twenty-five miles southwest of Chicago surrounded by rolling hills and fields; the house he rented for $12.50 a month was tiny, but Anderson was glad to be away from the city (Townsend 170). His wife, Tennessee Mitchell, now a sculptor, came from Chicago for part of each week, and Anderson still worked "occasionally" in the advertising office of the Critchfield advertising company in the city (Townsend 171). His second marriage was disintegrating, though, and the story's "indictment of marriage" may be an outgrowth of the author's discouragement (Miller, "Earth-Mothers" 75, "Portraits" 9).

Sources and Influences

Geismar suggests the influence of Whitman on this story, in particular its portrait of the old man who claims brotherhood with a murderer; Whitman "linked himself with all the criminals, the sinners, and the outcasts of the New World" (xvi).

Anderson's reading of Henry Adams must have contributed to the foreman's adoration of the secretary in the bicycle factory as "virginal and pure, . . . far off and unattainable" (*TE* 112). The world of the story is the world of the dynamo, dominated by the fragmenting force of industrialization. Its denizens are left yearning for unity, for beauty, for life-giving meaning.

Publication History

"Brothers" was published in April of 1921 in *Bookman* (53:110–15). The following October it appeared in *The Triumph of the Egg* (102–15), with several additions and deletions of sentences and phrases. Edward O'Brien chose it for *The Best Short Stories of 1921* (3–12). When Anderson became a newspaper editor in Marion, Virginia, he reprinted the story in the *Smyth County News* (September 27, 1928, pp. 1–2). After the author's death, Rosenfeld included it in *The Sherwood Anderson Reader* (218–25). It also is printed in Geismar's edition of Anderson's stories (33–40) and in Modlin's recent collection *Certain Things Last* (39–47).

Relation to Other Works

This story turns on the inner lives of three quite different men. The rich romantic imaginings of the factory foreman in the midst of his humdrum life in the city merge with the sympathetic fantasies of a loony old man from the forest and with the developed, creative imaginings of a cultivated writer who lives, significantly, between forest and city. Through intuitive leaps that take off from dry newspaper reports of the one man's crime, the three of them become "brothers." The imaginative life is an important theme in many of Anderson's tales. The narrator of "The Egg," for example, imaginatively reconstructs his father's experience much as the narrator here creates the inner world of the factory foreman. Particularly close to this story is the portrayal of Doctor Parcival (in "The Philosopher"), who also identifies himself with a murderer, a cruel brother, and Christ crucified. In both instances, intuitive understanding overcomes barriers of time and space and class and morality. Thus this story epitomizes a trait, characteristic of Anderson's art,

that Rosenfeld admires: "Removing the sense of individual guilt and responsibility for insufficiency and failure, that poisoned spring, he transmutes it to
a source of miracle–reconciliation with the fellow citizen, with existence,
with oneself" (xxv).

The Whitman-like unifying sympathy that Rosenfeld so admires has
proved less congenial to others. Townsend discusses the "sense that marriage deadens men's and women's spirits" that runs through several stories
in *The Triumph of the Egg*—"The Door of the Trap," "The Other Woman,"
"Out of Nowhere into Nothing," and "Brothers" (168–69). These stories, says
Townsend, reveal the author's "intimate knowledge of lovers and husbands"; the men are sometimes tender and mystical but also have the capacity to hurt, even kill (169). But though Anderson's success is in making these
characters understandable, forgivable, Townsend argues, his writing would
have been stronger if he had been sterner in his judgments, less forgiving.

The falling leaves are a motif linking the story with recurrent images from
Shelley's "Ode to the West Wind" that shape *The Triumph of the Egg* as a
prophetic call for rebirth (see "Seeds," "Relation to Other Works"). Fog and
factory smoke are twin symbols of layers of confusion surrounding life in
both country and city; minds try to break through this haze. Also symbolic
is the murderer's statement of his motive—the gas was not lighted; the import of the symbol is plainly the same as in "Unlighted Lamps." Hands, too,
function effectively here as symbols, as they do throughout *Winesburg;* in
the mind of the foreman, whose hands are always dirty, the secretary's white
hands are transformed into a mythic vision of unattainable beauty.

Critical Studies

Critics in the twenties praised "Brothers" with little qualification. Lovett said,
"The last paragraph . . . is a lyric cry of the artist's soul" (83). Hansen called
it "a powerful story" of a circumscribed soul longing for beauty and forced
by "circumstances" into murder (154). Beach admired "the structural movement of the narrative" (from the author speaking of present, to his account
of meeting the old man in the fog the day before, to the story of the factory
foreman whose story has been in the newspapers for months, then back to
the old man, and finally back to the authorial voice), calling it a "poetic
arrangement" that conveys life's "counterpoint" (258). Even in 1950, Flanagan remarked that the story paints "a mood . . . with the perfection of the
miniaturist" (175).

More recent critics have been less enthusiastic. Burbank criticizes the narrator for speaking of "trivia" such as "I am sitting in my house and it rains";
this, he thinks, is typical of Anderson's incapacity for handling narrators who
are neither "naive" nor "groping" (95). From the passage he quotes, Burbank

omits the phrase "in the country"; he ignores the important link between dreary city and dreary country, and the importance of mood. David Anderson merely notes the despair that accompanies the idea that anyone who tries to break down barriers and declare kinship with others is labeled "insane" (65). Geismar interprets: behind the ostensible motive for the crime (the janitor did not turn on the light), he observes, are deeper causes that led up to the sudden explosion of a desperate man. The murderer was a simple country man who came to the big city to find a new life and who found instead "only a degraded kind of urban existence, a kind of living death" (xv). This is quite right, of course, but the story is more complex than any of these critics allows. As a story artfully balancing a tightly controlled narrative and symbolic structure against a dreamily intuitive lyricism, "Brothers" deserves attention more along the lines that Beach once sketched out.

Works Cited

Anderson, David. 1967. *Sherwood Anderson: An Introduction and Interpretation.* New York: Holt, Rinehart.

Anderson, Sherwood, 1921. *The Triumph of the Egg.* New York: B. W. Huebsch. Rpt. Introduction by Herbert Gold. New York: Four Walls Eight Windows, 1988.

Beach, Joseph Warren. 1926. *The Outlook for American Prose.* Chicago: University of Chicago Press.

Burbank, Rex. 1964. *Sherwood Anderson.* New York: Twayne. Rpt. in part in *The Achievement of Sherwood Anderson: Essays in Criticism.* Ed. Ray Lewis White. Chapel Hill: University of North Carolina Press, 1966, 32–43. Rpt. in part in *Sherwood Anderson: Collection of Critical Essays.* Ed. Walter B. Rideout. Englewood Cliffs, NJ: Prentice-Hall, 1974, 70–83.

Flanagan, John J. "The Permanence of Sherwood Anderson." *The Southwest Review* 35 (1950):170–77. Rpt. in *Critical Essays on Sherwood Anderson.* Ed. David D. Anderson. Boston: G. K. Hall, 1981, 111–119.

Geismar, Maxwell, ed. 1962. *Sherwood Anderson: Short Stories.* New York: Hill and Wang.

———. 1962. "Introduction." *Sherwood Anderson: Short Stories.* New York: Hill and Wang, ix-xxii.

Hansen, Harry. 1923. *Midwest Portraits: A Book of Memories and Friendships.* New York: Harcourt, Brace.

Lovett, Robert Morss. "The Promise of Sherwood Anderson." *Dial* 72

(1922):79–83. Rpt. in *Literary Opinion in America*. Ed. Morton Dauwen Zabel. New York: Harper, 1934, 327–32. Rpt. in *Sherwood Anderson: A Collection of Critical Essays*. Ed. Walter B. Rideout. Englewood Cliffs, NJ: Prentice-Hall, 1974, 65–69.

Miller, William V. "Earth-Mothers, Succubi, and Other Ectoplasmic Spirits: The Women in Sherwood Anderson's Short Stories." *Midamerica I*. Ed. David D. Anderson. East Lansing, MI: Midwestern Press, 1974, 64–81. Rpt. in *Critical Essays on Sherwood Anderson*. Ed. David D. Anderson. Boston: G. K. Hall, 1981, 196–209.

——. "Portraits of the Artist: Anderson's Fictional Storytellers." In *Sherwood Anderson: Dimensions of His Literary Art: A Collection of Critical Essays*. Ed. David D. Anderson. East Lansing: Michigan State University Press, 1976, 1–23.

Modlin, Charles E., ed. 1992. *Certain Things Last: The Selected Stories of Sherwood Anderson*. New York: Four Walls Eight Windows.

O'Brien, Edward J., ed. *The Best Short Stories of 1921*. Boston: Small, Maynard, 1922.

Rosenfield, Paul, ed. 1947. *The Sherwood Anderson Reader*. Boston: Houghton Mifflin.

Townsend, Kim. 1987. *Sherwood Anderson*. Boston: Houghton Mifflin.

The Door of the Trap

Circumstances of Composition

Anderson had begun a novel he called "Mary Cochran" when he was president of a company in Elyria, Ohio. He brought the manuscript with him in 1913 to Chicago, where he took a job writing advertisements for the Critchfield Company but actually devoted himself primarily to writing fiction, getting it published, and establishing a literary reputation. In 1916 he was at work on the "Mary Cochran" material again, and in the fall of 1919, evidently, he was reshaping it into stories. (For details, see "Unlighted Lamps," "Circumstances of Composition." Both stories were reworked from that unpublished novel.)

Sources and Influences

Howe suggests that Tennessee Mitchell, who became Anderson's wife in 1916, may have been a model for Mary Cochran (82).

A more important influence on this story was Anderson's memory of his first marriage, politely friendly but stifling, with a nice wife, three nice children, and a nice job to fund it all. Long walks were Anderson's way of coping with his desperation, as they are the professor's.

The metaphorical "trap" may mean more than simply marriage, however. Broader implications are suggested in a letter of 1918 in which Anderson says, "what is maturity beyond a realization that life is a trap into which we are thrown and no one knows the way out" (*Letters*, Sutton 102).

Publication History

"The Door of the Trap" was first published in the *Dial* in May of 1920 (68:567–76). Dedicating *The Best Short Stories of 1920* to Sherwood Anderson, Edward O'Brien referred to this story as "among the finest imaginative contributions to the short story" in America that year. The story was collected the following year in *The Triumph of the Egg* (116–33).

The *Dial* had published Anderson's "Apology for Crudity" in 1917, and after moving its editorial offices to New York, it had published the story called "The Triumph of the Egg" in March of 1920. In 1921 its editors awarded Anderson the first *Dial* prize, which was accompanied by a sum of $2,000 and immense prestige.

Relation to Other Works

This story is most obviously related to "Unlighted Lamps," in which Mary Cochran is presented as a younger woman still in her hometown of Huntersburg, Illinois. But subtler ties link it to other tales in *The Triumph of the Egg*. It is plainly connected to other stories concerned with the emotional sterility of conventionally genteel marriage—"The Other Woman," "Out of Nowhere into Nothing," and "Brothers" (Townsend 168–89). "The Man in the Brown Coat," too, is associated with this story since both deal with professors who are separated from their wives by a metaphoric wall, but the history professor in the more poetic sketch intuitively reaches out to know his wife's innermost thoughts, whereas the materialist math professor here tries to "face facts" and to accept his wife as a lifeless lump. The soft songs of the Negro servant, which suggest a simpler, more natural life than that of her employers, develop a motif introduced in "I Want to Know Why" and also important in "Out of Nowhere into Nothing." The symbolism of trees connects this story particularly with "Seeds" and with "Out of Nowhere into Nothing." The primary symbol of "The Egg" reappears in the professor's longing to break out of his "shell" (*TE* 118). Even his quarrel with the "German who had the chair of modern languages" points to a connection between this episode and the story "War." All these interrelationships indicate an overall thematic unity in the volume's concern with life struggling to free itself from its dead husks. Life stirs within the entrapping shell.

The forms of the stories in the volume, however, are extremely varied, far more so than in *Winesburg, Ohio* (1919). Anderson's experiments with technique include shifts in narrative point of view, in arrangement of chronology, in amount of dialogue, and, most pronounced of all, in modes ranging from straightforward prose to lyrical poeticism. Of all the stories in the book, "The Door of the Trap" is the most conventional in approach, using a third-person omniscient narrator to present, in chronological order, thoughts and actions that rise to a distinct turning point and move to a denouement with a bitter twist at the end. Maybe that is why critics have paid so little attention to it.

Critical Studies

Wright classifies "The Door of the Trap" as a caustic-pathetic episode of suffering; the protagonist's "gesture of accommodation" to his trapped circumstances, Wright explains, provides "poignant evidence" of his suffering (389, 232–33). As in some earlier stories by Dreiser, psychic restraints hinder the character's quest for love so that he "makes only a half-hearted effort to find it"; he reveals his emotional need "primarily in his attempt to conceal that need" by kissing Mary and then ordering her to leave his house for good (71). The reader is left to infer what feelings govern the man's bizarre behavior (407).

Howe mentions the story as one of those focused on "the neurotic costs of the unlived life" and especially on timidity about sex (173–74). He considers it an example of the characteristic weaknesses of those of Anderson's stories patterned on "written" rather than oral narration: "devoid . . . of any account of external experience," "hazy in evocation of place and thing," and tender in presentation of a lost soul hardly differentiated from all the other lost souls in the author's fiction, such stories are "neither descriptively faithful nor symbolically coherent" (173, 176).

Other critics are less harsh in their written judgments. Yet in the final analysis, the unconcern they display by either ignoring the story or dispensing with it in a brief, poorly prepared comment is the severest condemnation of all. David Anderson's remarks are irrelevant (95). Leary's are not much better; he declares that the professor "spends his life waiting for the meaning of his life to be revealed, with the result that his life is ultimately meaningless" (141). Burbank's interpretation reflects some attention to the facts of the story but offers a fundamental misreading: the reader is to understand, he states, that the professor saves Mary "from a life of failure" by making her "aware of her sexual desires" (95, 111). Burbank's conclusion is skewed by his reading of *Many Marriages*. Actually the ending of "The Door of the Trap" indicates plainly that the math professor has wounded Mary, taught her to lie, and deadened her spirit: "The voice was dull and heavy. It was not the voice of a young girl. 'She is no longer like a young tree,' he thought" (*TE* 133). The irony of the final lines is acute as the suffering man takes sadistic "grim pleasure" in the fact that Mary "will be imprisoned" and that it will not be his fault. On the contrary, it will. It is.

Works Cited

Anderson, David. 1967. *Sherwood Anderson: An Introduction and Interpretation*. New York: Holt, Rinehart.

Anderson, Sherwood. 1919. *Winesburg, Ohio*. New York: B. W. Huebsch. Rpt. New York: Viking, 1960.

———. *The Triumph of the Egg*. 1921. New York: B. W. Huebsch. Rpt. New York: Four Walls Eight Windows, 1988. Introduction by Herbert Gold.

Burbank, Rex. 1964. *Sherwood Anderson*. New York: Twayne. Rpt. in part in *The Achievement of Sherwood Anderson: Essays in Criticism*. Ed. Ray Lewis White. Chapel Hill: University of North Carolina Press, 1966, 32–43. Rpt. in part in *Sherwood Anderson: Collection of Critical Essays*. Ed. Walter B. Rideout. Englewood Cliffs, NJ: Prentice-Hall, 1974, 70–83.

Howe, Irving. 1951. *Sherwood Anderson*. New York: William Sloan.

Leary, Lewis. 1969. "Sherwood Anderson: *The Man Who Became a Boy Again*." In *Literatur und Sprache der Vereinigten Staaten: Aufsätze zu Ehren von Hans Galinsky*. Hans Helmcke, Klaus Lubbers, Renate Schmidt-von Bardeleben (Eds.) Heidelberg: Carl Winter, 135–43.

O'Brien, Edward Joseph. 1921. *The Best Short Stories of 1920*. Boston: Small, Maynard..

Sutton, William A., ed. 1985. *Letters to Bab: Sherwood Anderson to Marietta D. Finley, 1916–33*. Foreword by Walter B. Rideout. Urbana and Chicago: University of Illinois Press.

Townsend, Kim. 1987. *Sherwood Anderson*. Boston: Houghton Mifflin.

Wright, Austin McGiffert. 1961. *The American Short Story in the Twenties*. Chicago: University of Chicago Press.

The New Englander

Circumstances of Composition

Anderson read "The New Englander" to his friend Paul Rosenfeld during the Christmas of 1919, in its almost final version (Rosenfeld, *Reader* xxvii). But the story was written very early in 1919 while Anderson was still living in Chicago and still writing advertisements for the Critchfield Company. He had lived in New York City for several months in 1918, and he had established a growing reputation with his *Winesburg* stories. He had also entered into a friendly exchange of ideas with Waldo Frank and Van Wyck Brooks. He was deeply impressed by these men and their cultivated minds, and his relationship with them was to have important consequences for his writing career.

He may have written this story "at a railroad station at Detroit," so deeply absorbed in it that he missed his train, as he says in his fictionalized autobiography *A Story Teller's Story* (155). Curry speculates, however, that Anderson mixed up his facts and that he may really have written it at a railroad station in Harrodsburg, Kentucky (xli, 224n, 301–302n), since in his memoirs he tells of writing an unnamed story there (Rosenfeld, *Memoirs* 341–43); West, on the other hand, guesses that the story written in Harrodsburg was "The Egg" (678–79).

Sources and Influences

Anderson had grown up in Clyde, Ohio, a town situated in the agricultural country of northern Ohio; the area, still known as the Western Reserve, had been settled mainly by New Englanders migrating west. His consciousness of himself as a regional writer, nurtured from 1913 on by his association with other members of the Chicago Renaissance, was made more acute after 1916 by his contacts with editors of the New York little magazine *Seven Arts,* Yale-educated Waldo Frank and Harvard-educated Van Wyck Brooks, and also with the *Seven Arts* music critic, Yale-educated Paul Rosenfeld. Anderson himself had barely completed high school. His fears that he was provincial were alleviated in part by a widespread recognition that the economic, political, and cultural eminence of New England was being supplanted by the Midwest's increasing power. The new role of the Midwest in national politics might be measured by the presidential election of 1920, in which the opponents, Warren Harding and James Cox, were two men from Ohio. The literary dominance of New England was also a thing of the past, having yielded to a lively insurgent growth of writing from other regions, especially the Midwest. Then, too, the adulation the cultivated Eastern intellectuals of *Seven Arts* heaped on Anderson sharpened his consciousness of his role in an evolving national culture. He was gratified but also rather unsettled by their perspective: late in 1920 he confided to a friend that it made him "ill" to think that he always had lived and always would live "in the middle west, in a raw new civilization" (Sutton, *Letters* 141). His Eastern friends, for their part, when they met the forty-year-old advertising man and storyteller, could not help seeing him in terms of their own theories of American culture. Waldo Frank, whose *Our America* appeared in 1919, said of Anderson: "he personified for me the fecund sap of what he loved to call Mid-America. . . . To me, the young New Yorker who knew his Europe well and had scarce seen his own land beyond the Eastern seaboard, Sherwood Anderson was America; the discovery of him was an exhilarating part of my discovery of my own country" (40–41). And Van Wyck Brooks let Anderson know that "nations had become great, and life burned high, because men had done what he was labouring to do" (Rosenfeld, "Sherwood" 41).

During these years, conversation with Brooks, who was writing *The Ordeal of Mark Twain* (1920), clarified Anderson's sense of himself as a Mid-westerner, a kinsman of Twain. Twain had "honesty," Anderson said, and a "wholesome disregard of literary precedent"; having begun as a "crude buffoon," still he had developed "tenderness and subtlety" and, at his best in *Huck Finn*, had forgotten those who wanted to tame him (including William Dean Howells and an excessively "good" wife) and had kept the fine innocence of "the half-savage, god-worshiping, believing boy" (Jones-Rideout, *Letters* 31, 32, 33). In some such combination of the crude and the subtle, Anderson believed, must lie the secret of a triumphant new American art. Transparently expressing fears that he himself might be ruined by the highbrows, Anderson told Brooks that Twain had been injured among "that New England crowd, the fellows from barren hills," those "cultural fellows"; tragically, Twain had been caught by concern with his reputation and by "smartness" and "shrillness" (Jones-Rideout, *Letters* 32, 33, 34). In December of 1918, Anderson recommended that Brooks should include in his discussion of Twain "a chapter on the American going East into that tired, thin New England atmosphere and being conquered by its feminine force" (Jones-Rideout, *Letters* 43). Possibly these letters yield evidence that Anderson was growing "too sophisticated in his primitivism," as Howe declares (118). Certainly they show how conscious he was of it and how determined he was to maintain it.

Anderson's reading of *The Education of Henry Adams* in late 1918 contributed further to his understanding of the decline of New England's cultural hegemony; he began to see it as his mission to reverse Adams's pessimism by showing possible sources of reverential love in Midwestern culture (Crowley 186–87).

Moreover, it seems likely that Anderson's awareness of such New England regionalists as Mary E. Wilkins Freeman played a role in shaping this story. Anderson's New England women bear a strong resemblance to Freeman's portraits of women isolated in a rocky land that hardier men have deserted in search of richer soil and better opportunity. Anderson's aim, though, was to probe a deeper reality than that contained in the work of the local colorists, who were, not by coincidence, mostly women.

The evident influence of Freudian ideas on this story has been debated. Michaud, who calls the story "almost technically Freudian," considers its description of "the tortures of inhibition" to be not only dramatic but scientific (188–91). Hoffman objects, however, that, although "Anderson was hailed as the leader in the American fight against conventional repression," his knowledge of Freud was general rather than specific, that he "developed his themes quite independently of Freud," and that he always maintained "a skeptical attitude toward the new psychology" (239–41). Anderson may have known more about Freud than Hoffman's analysis indicates; he was an avid reader, and his conversations with a leading psychoanalyst, Trigant Burrow, must have conveyed more than a general knowledge of repression (see "Seeds," "Sources and Influences"). He certainly accepted Freud's theory that unconscious motivations govern much human behavior. On the other hand, his skepticism that Freud had provided the answer to human problems is plain. Critics commit a fundamental error if they miss the sharply ironic tone of this statement, from *Dark Laughter:* "If there is anything you do not understand in human life consult the works of Dr. Freud" (230; for criticism that accepts this as a literal expression of Anderson's view, see Glicksberg 20). Any notion that the mysteries of love and life could be scientifically explained was anathema to Anderson; as the passage from *Dark Laughter* indicates, he thought only old, dead-hearted men would try.

Publication History

"The New Englander" first appeared in print in February of 1921 in the *Dial* (70:143–58). It was reprinted in *The Triumph of the Egg* that October (134–60). After Anderson's death, Rosenfeld included it in *The Sherwood Anderson Reader* (54–69).

Relation to Other Works

In *A New Testament* (1927), which Anderson began writing in 1919, one section is also entitled "The New Englander" (92–94). Lines from this loose poetic effusion read: "I have made a stone god of myself, at my back a house, at my hand an open door./ My dream is I shall pass through you into the dawning of new days." The imagery of stone and door is similar to that in the story of the same title, as is the pressing desire for a new and fuller life.

This story's emphasis on the fertility of Midwestern cornfields reiterates a major theme of *Mid-American Chants* (1918). Corn there becomes a sacramental symbol, invested with "an elemental vitality to counteract the sterile religious tradition of New England"; avoiding both "the elegiac disenchantment with the region to be found in Masters's *Spoon River Anthology* and the virile bravado of Sandburg's contemporaneous *Cornhuskers*," these poems envision a "vernal rebirth in the West" (Spencer 12–13, 10–11). Caught between two worlds, Elsie Leander stands as a symbol of American malaise. The possibility of redemption of the barren civilization of New England by the vigorous spirit of rich, earthy Midwestern culture is hinted in her ecstasy in the corn. The ending is highly indeterminate, but when Elsie ignores her New England parents' "thin voices" and elects to stay in the wind and the rain as the door of their home shuts "with a bang," she has in some sense turned her back on a dead past and begun to awaken to life (*TE* 159–60).

In his *Memoirs* Anderson tells of writing *Tar* (1926) in a Virginia cornfield; tenderly he recalls his own raptures on the warm ground under the corn and, with some amusement, describes himself as "a kind of corn field mystic" (White, *Memoirs* 486–87).

He treats American society's transition away from a rigidly Puritan New England culture in other works as well. "Godliness" devotes primary attention to the specific problems caused by religious fanaticism and secular materialism, neither of which is important in "The New Englander." Both stories, though, display the pathos of lives starved by hard material conditions and flinty habits of emotional restraint. *Poor White* (1920) describes the mixed results of a well-meaning New Englander's effort to awaken the mind of a dreamy, indolent Ohio boy to consciousness and self-cultivation. Sarah Shepard, "the puritan tradition personified," trains Hugh McVey to be "clean, industrious, restless and ambitious" and to use his mind toward practical ends; in the process, though, he becomes so completely cut off from his natural instincts that "his capacity for love or any kind of sexual relationship is atrophied" (Way 117–18). In a sense, Elsie Leander is unlearning those lessons, awakening to the deep life of the unconscious and of the earth.

Elsie Leander's plight, of course, resembles that of certain grotesques in *Winesburg, Ohio* (1919). Her acute need for love, suppressed by fear, as Wright points out, erupts in an outburst of passion like that in "Adventure" and "The Strength of God" (71, 138, 231). Her sensitivity and the intensity of her quest for self-fulfillment, as Miller notes, link her with the protagonists of "Mother" and "The Teacher" (77).

Within *The Triumph of the Egg*, Elsie Leander's story shares the dominant pattern of frustrated efforts to find understanding (David Anderson 65). Several of the stories are concerned with the predicament of women repressed by the forces of Puritanism and deprived of spiritual nourishment—notably, "Seeds," "Unlighted Lamps" and "Out of Nowhere into Nothing." The story that follows this one, "War," shows a woman acting successfully to overcome oppressive force. In "Motherhood," the episode after "War," a woman conceives a child. Symbolically, these two tales point toward a resolution of the problems that bring Elsie to her storm of grief. Symbols of rock and tree, which recur in other stories, also link Elsie's story to patterns of meaning implicit in the whole volume. The killed rabbit, incidentally, Anderson had used in his first published story, "The Rabbit-pen."

Critical Studies

There are no extended critical analyses of "The New Englander." Taylor, however, offers a useful discussion of its narrative technique, its significantly detailed contrasts between the Vermont and Iowa settings, and its sexual imagery (52–53). He also elucidates the ambiguous tone of the ending, where Elsie Leander unleashes "a storm of grief that was only partially grief": "This indicates, apparently, that in expressing unbridled emotion for the first time in her life—albeit an emotion of frustration and anguish—she has realized that she possesses a greater capacity for emotion than she has ever suspected" (54).

Evaluation of the story has ranged widely. In a 1923 review essay Gregory charged that, though "moving and poetically conceived," the story is "weakened by a groping intellect" and lacks understanding of the repressed "minds of certain women" (245). Howe noted the "extraordinary skein of symbols" but objected that "the story itself lacks the conviction of reality"; instead of "genuinely conceived characters," he argued, what the story offers is a symbolic redecoration of "the legend of Puritan repression" (176–77). West, for similar reasons, thinks that "The New Englander" represents Anderson "at his worst" (46).

Among the story's admirers, Cargill proposes that it is "[t]he best 'Freudian' study in the volume" (680). His judgment is based, unfortunately, on nothing more substantial than a simplistic observation that the story is one of Anderson's "case histories of frustrated love" and an absurd claim that Elsie "satisfied her sexual longings by lying in a cornfield in the rain" (680). Hoffman is also sympathetic to the story, interpreting its conflict as one "between nature itself and the world of power, wealth, and religion," between impulse and inhibition (244–45). Weber, however, has presented the only solid defense against Howe's criticism. Accusing Howe of "utter misreading," Weber asserts that the story is "one of the finest embodiments of the merits potentially contained in Anderson's lyrical symbolic method"

(132–33). Since "the main action is psychological," Weber argues, the rationalist-moralist demand for external realism misses the real point—namely, Elsie's release "from her chrysalis . . . onto the hot sensual prairie" and her "bitter symbolic rejection of the New England past" (133). This insight deserves emphasis. Anderson's experiments in narrative may have frequently been judged by alien standards.

One nice complexity in the story has been overlooked. Though the New Englander, Elsie Leander, looks enviously at the raw energy and strength and wild abandon of her niece Elizabeth, the young Midwestern woman secretly wishes "to be a lady"; "in desperation," afraid her brothers will laugh at her if she tries "to walk demurely," Elizabeth behaves more roughly and boisterously than ever, and then is ashamed when her aunt sees her holding a killed rabbit (*TE* 149–50, 152). This detail is not only psychologically acute. By depicting dessicated Easterners looking with longing at the robust vigor of the Midwest while crude Midwesterners look with longing at the refinement of the East, Anderson here also enriches the historical-cultural dimension of a tale that is his fullest examination of regional attitudes in the early part of the century. The contrast between the two cultures is vividly encapsulated in the image of the bloody rabbit on "the delicate flowers of a white crocheted table cover" (*TE* 152). But the kinship of New England and the Midwest is evident in the kindred names "Elsie" and "Elizabeth." Most important, each woman—and each culture—needs the other's virtues to become balanced and whole.

Works Cited

Anderson, David. 1967. *Sherwood Anderson: An Introduction and Interpretation*. New York: Holt, Rinehart.

Anderson, Sherwood. 1919. *Winesburg, Ohio*. New York: B. W. Huebsch. Rpt. New York: Viking, 1960.

——. 1921. *The Triumph of the Egg*. New York: B. W. Huebsch. Rpt. New York: Four Walls Eight Windows, 1988. Introduction by Herbert Gold.

——. 1924. *A Story Teller's Story*. New York: B. W. Huebsch. Rpt. in *A Story Teller's Story: A Critical Text*. Ed. Ray Lewis White. Cleveland: Press of Case Western Reserve University, 1968. Rpt. New York: Viking, 1969.

——. 1925. *Dark Laughter*. New York: Boni & Liverright; Grosset and Dunlap, 1925.

——. 1927. *A New Testament*. New York: Boni & Liveright.

Cargill, Oscar. 1941. *Intellectual America: Ideas on the March*. New York: Macmillan.

Crowley, John W. 1976. "The Education of Sherwood Anderson." In *Sherwood Anderson: Centennial Studies*. Ed. Hilbert H. Campbell and Charles E. Modlin. Troy, NY: Whitston, 185–201.

Curry, Martha Mulroy. 1975. *The "Writer's Book" by Sherwood Anderson: A Critical Edition*. Metuchen, NJ: Scarecrow Press.

Frank, Waldo. "Sherwood Anderson: A Personal Note." *Newberry Library Bulletin* 2, no. 2 (December 1948):39–43.

Glicksberg, Charles J. 1971. *The Sexual Revolution in Modern American Literature*. The Hague: Martinus Nijhoff.

Gregory, Alyse. "Sherwood Anderson." *Dial* 75 (1923):243–46.

Hoffman, Frederick J. 1957. *Freudianism and the Literary Mind*. Rev. ed. Baton Rouge: Louisiana State University. Rpt. in *Sherwood Anderson: Winesburg, Ohio: Text and Criticism*. Ed. John H. Ferres. New York: Viking, 1966, 309–20. Rpt. in *The Achievement of Sherwood Anderson: Essays in Criticism*. Ed. Ray Lewis White. Chapel Hill: University of North Carolina Press, 1966, 174–92.

Howe, Irving. 1951. *Sherwood Anderson*. New York: William Sloane.

Jones, Howard Mumford, and Walter B. Rideout, eds. 1953. *Letters of Sherwood Anderson*. Urbana and Chicago: University of Illinois Press.

Michaud, Régis. 1928. *The American Novel To-day: A Social and Psychological Study*. Boston: Little, Brown.

Miller, William V. 1974. "Earth-Mothers, Succubi, and Other Ectoplasmic Spirits: The Women in Sherwood Anderson's Short Stories." In *Midamerica I*. Ed. David D. Anderson. East Lansing, MI: Midwestern Press, 64–81. Rpt. in *Critical Essays on Sherwood Anderson*. Ed. David D. Anderson. Boston: G. K. Hall, 1981, 196–209.

Rosenfeld, Paul. "Sherwood Anderson." *Dial* 72 (1922):29–42. Rpt. in *The Port of New York*. New York: Harcourt, Brace, 1924, 175–98. Rpt. in *Critical Essays on Sherwood Anderson*. Ed. David D. Anderson. Boston: G. K. Hall, 1981, 74–85.

——, ed. 1947. *The Sherwood Anderson Reader*. Boston: Houghton Mifflin.

Spencer, Benjamin I. "Sherwood Anderson: American Mythopoeist." *American Literature* 41 (1969):1–18.

Sutton, William A., ed. 1985. *Letters to Bab: Sherwood Anderson to Maretta D. Finley, 1916–33*. Forword by Walter B. Rideout. Urbana and Chicago: University of Illinois Press.

Taylor, Welford Dunaway. 1977. *Sherwood Anderson*. New York: Frederick Ungar.

Way, Brian. 1971. "Sherwood Anderson." In *The American Novel and the Nineteen-Twenties*. Malcolm Bradbury and David Palmer (Eds.). Stratford-upon-Avon Studies 13. London: Edward Arnold, 107–26.

Weber, Brom. "Anderson and the 'The Essence of Things.'" *Sewanee Review* 59 (1951):678–92. Rpt. in *Critical Essays on Sherwood Anderson*. Ed. David D. Anderson. Boston: G. K. Hall, 1981, 125–37.

West, Ray B., Jr. 1952. *The Short Story in America: 1900–1950*. Chicago: Regnery. Rpt. New York: Books for Libraries (Division of Arno Press), 1979.

White, Ray Lewis, ed. 1969. *Sherwood Anderson's Memoirs: A Critical Edition*. Chapel Hill: University of North Carolina Press.

Wright, Austin McGiffert. 1961. *The American Short Story in the Twenties*. Chicago: University of Chicago Press.

War

Circumstances of Composition

The original publication date of this story suggests that it was written in Chicago late in 1915 or, at the latest, early in 1916. The central events in the tale seem to be set during World War I. But the precise circumstances of its composition have not been established. Possibly, Anderson *did,* as the narrator states, hear the story told by a woman he had met on a train, who had actually experienced the events. As he and his friends freely admitted, he gathered his stories from many such sources.

Sources and Influences

When the story mentions "the German philosophy of might" (in which the German in charge of the Polish refugees has "steeped his soul"), it refers not only to German militarism generally but also to the Nietzschean philosophy of will to power. Anderson's interest in Nietzsche during the period when this tale apparently was written is mentioned by his friend Daugherty (37). Schevill states that even earlier, during the year 1899–1900, when Anderson was studying at Wittenberg Academy, discussions about Nietzsche and other topics "resounded through" the boardinghouse where he lived with "a fermenting mixture of teachers, publishers, editors and artists" (29).

In describing the character of the German leader of the refugees as "such a man as might be professor of foreign languages in a college in our country," Anderson may have been thinking of Dr. K. F. R. Hochdoerfer, professor of modern languages and specialist in German literature at Wittenberg College in Springfield, Ohio, whom Anderson knew during the year he studied at Wittenberg Academy.

Publication History

This story was first published with the title "The Struggle" in the May 1916 issue of *Little Review* (3:7–10). By this time Anderson had published several essays, sketches, and stories in this avant-garde "little magazine" edited by Margaret Anderson (no relation). The story was reprinted in *Little Review Anthology* (55–59).

When Anderson compiled *The Triumph of the Egg* (1921), he included this tale and changed its name to "War." A few minor changes of words were also made at that time. Anderson still liked the story well enough in 1927 to reprint it in his Virginia newspaper *The Smyth County News* (November 24, 1927, p. 5). Recently, the *Little Review* version of the tale has been reprinted in White's collection of Anderson's early works (159–63).

Relation to Other Works

The inclusion of this rather early story with later-composed stories in *The Triumph of the Egg* highlights a dimension of the tale that is virtually allegorical. Through the whole volume runs a struggle between death and life, which is announced in the opening prose poem, "The Dumb Man," and which culminates in the final, prophetic prose poem, "The Man with the Trumpet": "I told my people life was sweet, that men might live" (*TE* 269). In some of the stories, the struggle takes shape as a battle of the life-impulse against deathly repression and materialism. The epigraph of "The Man in the Brown Coat" particularly anticipates the circumstances of "War" by placing a long history of military conquest (Napoleon, Alexander, Grant, Hindenburg) in explicit contrast to the rising moon (representing beauty and poetic imagination) and the historian's longing for shared life and love. Then in "War" the same fundamental battle assumes heightened dramatic form as an inhuman military force threatens to extinguish the force of life represented by a weary old mother and her straggling refugees. When at last she summons the sheer force of will to vanquish the oppressor, the direction of the cycle is reversed. So in the whole sequence, this tale is pivotal: the stories preceding it show various deathly forces stifling weak souls longing for love and beauty, and in the two stories following it the creative force of upsurgent life moves toward ascendancy. Especially clear in "War" is Anderson's conviction that ideological battles are waged first and foremost in the psyche.

The triumph of the old Polish mother in "War" is particularly significant in relation to the title of the story immediately after it—"Motherhood." For *The Triumph of the Egg* associates the life force primarily with a female principle that wants "to create in love" (*TE* 2). These stories contain the germ of Anderson's idea, fully developed in *Perhaps Women* (1931), that the machine age has made men impotent and that women have the potential for revitalizing Western culture.

White notes correctly that in this tale Anderson first used "the device of the story presented as told to him by a participant in the action," but his contention that it also contains Anderson's first "use of the sympathetic grotesque as an element in storytelling" is less tenable (159).

Critical Studies

This tale has been mostly ignored by critics. David Anderson's remark that it is a story of "despair" is inadequate and perhaps mistaken (65). Likewise, Burbank's comment that it has an "omniscient author" is not helpful, though his statement that the narrative is "essayistic" in approach rather than a dramatic presentation of lifelike characters is more to the point (95).

The narrator tells a story, which he says was told to him by a Polish woman on a train, of a forced march she had endured with her mother, her lover, and the peasants who had worked on their small estate. One climactic moment of the woman's story absorbs the narrator's attention and provides a sort of epiphany for him; it is a mystical moment of transformation, when the soul of the German soldier leading the refugees and the soul of the Polish mother seem mysteriously to switch places.

The characters are described in abstract terms—"the old tired mother-in-Poland" (*TE* 167), the hard, militaristic German, and the passive young couple who stand by and watch. But Anderson has humanized the German to the extent of explaining his inner struggle. Beneath his cruel surface he is just a man, "such a man as might be professor of foreign languages in a college in our country," a man who has to read regularly in books of "the German philosophy of might" in order to steel himself against his own humane moral impulses (*TE* 162–63). Even then his conscience keeps him "from hitting the old woman with his fist" (*TE* 165). The man's inner struggle is crucial in determining the result of his outward struggle with the old woman, who resists being torn from her homeland. When the German adopts the weak attitude that the old woman has previously held, muttering as she had earlier that all he wants is to be left alone, she adopts his previous toughness, brutally driving her weary people back towards home. The story evokes approbation of an injustice corrected, a measure of pity for a beaten man who is also in some sense a victim of the war machine, and lingering questions about the harsh virtue that wins.

From one standpoint, the story records a psychological battle for dominance between two individuals and a victory achieved by the sheer force of a superior will. The defeat of the German, made possible in part by his fundamental humanity, is a spiritual triumph for the old Polish mother, who musters the strength of will to win the battle. Beyond that, the story is a parable with social implications of obvious relevance to the war in Europe and, more broadly, to oppressed people everywhere. Beyond even that, by exploring an episode in which good and evil are not easily separable, the story provides a glimpse of the moral complexity of war. Finally—and the story only bears this much weight within the larger framework of *The Triumph of the Egg*—it registers faith in the perennial power of life to prevail over whatever forces attempt to snuff it out.

Works Cited

Anderson, David. 1967. *Sherwood Anderson: An Introduction and Interpretation*. New York: Holt, Rinehart.

Anderson, Margaret, ed. 1953. *Little Review Anthology*. New York: Hermitage House.

Anderson, Sherwood. 1921. *The Triumph of the Egg*. New York: B. W. Huebsch. Rpt. Introduction by Herbert Gold. New York: Four Walls Eight Windows, 1988.

——. 1931. *Perhaps Women*. New York: Horace Liveright, Rpt. Mamaroneck, NY: Appel, 1970.

Burbank, Rex. 1964. *Sherwood Anderson*. New York: Twayne. Rpt. in part in *The Achievement of Sherwood Anderson: Essays in Criticism*. Ed. Ray Lewis White. Chapel Hill: University of North Carolina PRess, 1966, 32–43. Rpt. in part in *Sherwood Anderson: A Collection of Critical Essays*. Ed. Walter B. Rideout. Englewood Cliffs, NJ: Prentice-Hall, 1974, 70–83.

Daugherty, George H. "Anderson, Advertising Man." *Newberry Library Bulletin* 2, no. 2 (December 1948):29–38.

Schevill, James. 1951. *Sherwood Anderson: His Life and Work*. Denver: University of Denver Press.

White, Ray Lewis, ed. 1989. *Sherwood Anderson: Early Writings*. Kent, OH, and London: Kent State University Press.

Motherhood

Circumstances of Composition

The date this sketch was written is uncertain. Presumably Anderson wrote it while he was married to Tennessee Mitchell and working as a writer of advertising copy for the Critchfield firm in Chicago, as he was when most of the other tales in *The Triumph of the Egg* were composed. Its symbolic nature and its function as a pivotal point in the volume may indicate that it was written later than most of the other stories, when he was gathering them together and arranging them for press, that is, early in 1921.

Sources and Influences

Anderson often made analogies between physical pregnancy and imaginative pregnancy, commonly envisioning artistic production as being the same kind of fulfillment of man's nature that (he thought) biological production is of woman's nature. "My head is filled with fancies that cannot get expressed. A thousand beautiful children are unborn to me," he wrote to a correspondent in November of 1916 (Sutton, *Letters* 15). Numerous such remarks abound in his writing, suggesting that the pregnant woman in this tale represents both kinds of creation.

Ironically enough, Anderson did not want his wife, Tennessee, to have children and never "gave [her] the chance," he later confessed to his fourth wife, Eleanor (Modlin, *Love Letters* 300).

Publication History

"Motherhood" was first published in 1921 in *The Triumph of the Egg* (168–70). It is the only story in the collection that did not receive prior periodical publication.

Relation to Other Works

The dominant idea of *The Triumph of the Egg* concerns the life impulse, which is symbolized by seeds, eggs, and stones. Beneath deathly appearances, the germ of vital life stirring within is the basis of hope for mankind.

Seed imagery obviously associates this story with "Seeds," which diagnoses a universal disease; the woman's pregnancy here functions metaphorically to imply hope for the barren land depicted throughout the volume. Of the other tales in the volume, "The New Englander" is most nearly related to "Motherhood." Elsie Leander desires life and love as she lies in the cornfield listening to the cries of unborn children calling to her; likewise in this sketch the seeds planted in the womb of the archetypal woman, and struggling toward birth, prophetically represent the fulfillment of the New England spinster's longing as vital new forces promise to emerge in a nation long dominated by an effete New England culture. Furthermore, in "War," the story immediately preceding, the victory of the "old tired mother-in-Poland" leads in to the triumph of elemental life represented in "Motherhood" and widens its symbolic sense to the universal.

The sorrow of the pregnant mother over those still awaiting birth, which mutes the triumphant note in the tale, makes sense in terms of the idea in the whole volume that, as temples are built stone by stone, the process of cultural awakening happens one individual at a time. (This idea is clearest in the prophetic epilogue, "The Man with the Trumpet")." Many stony lives still await rebirth, and the woman's sadness is also the artist's sadness that the words he plants like seeds leave so much yet unborn.

Anderson's mystical sense of the vitality of the land and his tendency to depict women as earth mothers has led some critics to deride him for weak characterization (Gold 555; Miller). The mode of this story is almost purely symbolic, however; characterization is nearly beside the point. Feminists have grounds to object, though, that the child in the mother's womb is (of course!) a son.

Even after Anderson had abandoned the more mythic attitudes expressed in his writing in the twenties, he retained his belief in "a redemptive feminine principle" that might counteract the crippling effects of machine technology; *Perhaps Women* (1931) presents that theory most clearly (Spencer 14–15).

Critical Studies

Few critics mention "Motherhood." Those who do disagree fundamentally about its interpretation. As if sexual liberation were the story's point, Fagin comments that the woman in "Motherhood" is one of Anderson's many lonely souls but that she is "fulfilled by what happened in the grass" (135). Ignoring the positive import of pregnancy, David Anderson, however, remarks that the story reiterates "the despair" of "Brothers" and "The Door of the Trap" (65).

Evaluators disparage the sketch. Burbank suggests that its "essayistic" texture, which makes it fail as a story, is typical of Anderson's attempts to write from the standpoint of a "sophisticated, omniscient author" (95). West objects that it has neither a clear allegory nor a developed character nor a coherent action, merely "an atmosphere of social revolt, a revolt aimed particularly against the conventional taboos concerning sex" (46–47). The silence of other critics suggests their agreement with these negative evaluations. Nevertheless, in the context of the whole volume, the allegory may be clearer than critics have seen, with optimistic implications that the forces of a still buried life might be stirring within the universal culture.

Works Cited

Anderson, David. 1967. *Sherwood Anderson: An Introduction and Interpretation*. New York: Holt, Rinehart.

Anderson, Sherwood. 1921. *The Triumph of the Egg*. New York: B. W. Huebsch. Rpt. New York: Four Walls Eight Windows, 1988. Introduction by Herbert Gold.

Burbank, Rex. 1964. *Sherwood Anderson*. New York: Twayne. Rpt. in part in *The Achievement of Sherwood Anderson: Essays in Criticism*. Ed. Ray Lewis White. Chapel Hill: University of North Carolina PRess, 1966, 32–43. Rpt. in part in *Sherwood Anderson: A Collection of Critical Essays*. Ed. Walter B. Rideout. Englewood Cliffs, NJ: Prentice-Hall, 1974, 70–83.

Fagin, N. Bryllion. 1973. *The Phenomenon of Sherwood Anderson: A Study in American Life and Letters*. New York: Russell & Russell. Originally printed Baltimore: Rossi-Bryn, 1927.

Gold, Herbert. "The Purity and Cunning of Sherwood Anderson." *Hudson Review* 10 (1957–58):548–57. Rpt. in *the Age of Happy Problems*. New York: Dial Press, 1962, 56–67. Rpt. in part in *Sherwood Anderson: Winesburg, Ohio: Text and Criticism*. Ed. John H. Ferres. New York: Viking, 1966, 396–404. Rpt. in *Critical Essays on Sherwood Anderson*. Ed. David D. Anderson. Boston: G. K. Hall, 1981, 138–45.

Miller, William V. 1974. "Earth-Mothers, Succubi, and Other Ectoplasmic Spirits: The Women in Sherwood Anderson's Short Stories." In *Midamerica I*. Ed. David D. Anderson. East Lansing, MI: Midwestern Press, 64–81. Rpt. in *Critical Essays on Sherwood Anderson*. Ed. David D. Anderson. Boston: G. K. Hall, 1981, 196–209.

Modlin, Charles E., ed. 1989. *Sherwood Anderson's Love Letters to Eleanor Copenhaver Anderson*. Athens and London: University of Georgia Press.

Spencer, Benjamin I. "Sherwood Anderson: American Mythopoeist." *American Literature* 41 (1969):1–18.

Sutton, William A., ed. 1985. *Letters to Bab: Sherwood Anderson to Marietta*

D. Finley, 1916–33. Foreword by Walter B. Rideout. Urbana and Chicago: University of Illinois Press.

West, Ray B., Jr. 1952. *The Short Story in America: 1900–1950*. Chicago: H Regnery. Rpt. New York: Books for Libraries (Division of Arno Press), 1979.

Out of Nowhere into Nothing

Circumstances of Composition

Toward the end of November 1920, Anderson wrote to Marietta Finley that he was "deep in" a story he then called "Out of Nothing into Nowhere" (Sutton, *Letters* 138). By December 20, it had become "somewhat longer" than he expected, "very intricate and . . . delicate" (Sutton, *Letters* 140–41). Early in 1921, still at work, he described his story: "By the recital of a few common place thoughts that have long been hidden away in a woman's mind, her mind is startled into unusual thinking. Like a flying machine her mind flits off into space, looses [*sic*] itself in a maze of sharp new reactions to life. . . . It is such a delicately adjusted thing that I am uncertain whether or not I shall be able to pull it off" (Sutton, *Letters* 149). By January 23, 1922, he wrote Paul Rosenfeld that it was finished (Modlin, *Letters* 22).

During this time, Anderson lived in a small house in Palos Park, a town situated amid pretty countryside twenty-five miles outside of Chicago. His wife, Tennessee Mitchell, spent part of each week in Chicago and part with him there, but their marriage was under strain. Still writing some advertising copy for the Critchfield Company and troubled by recurrent respiratory problems, Anderson struggled to find time for his fiction (Schevill 131–32). But public recognition of his work was growing steadily, and he believed he was improving in his art.

In 1923, he told a friend that he considered "Out of Nowhere into Nothing" his "next best" story, after "The Egg" and "The Untold Lie" (Jones-Rideout, *Letters* 110).

Sources and Influences

Bishop detects the possible influence of D. H. Lawrence in the phrasing of this story and notes a deeper resemblance in its concept of the soul struggling "between some dream of impossible loveliness, which the dreamer wishes to attach to the body of the beloved, and the inane fecundity of life" (11). More broadly speaking, the story develops Anderson's idea that life is "a struggle with death" and that one must cultivate "the growing thing" within oneself (Sutton, *Letters* 149).

Anderson's reading of *The Education of Henry Adams* is reflected in Rosalind Westcott's thoughts about sexual force and worship of the Virgin. Adams had written, "An American Virgin would never dare command; an American Venus would never dare exist." Rosalind is a modern American woman trying to figure out how to break through that cultural barrier, to recover a vital power deeper than mere "sex expression" in order to counter the deathly force of a man who has capitulated to materialism and allowed his creative powers to atrophy (*TE* 204). But Anderson's story goes much further than Adams in exploring the crisis of gender roles that American women faced in the early twentieth century as they moved out of the domestic sphere and into the workforce, as they acquired new mobility, and as they struggled to gain personal autonomy and to forge new kinds of relationships with men.

The title may be related to the opening lines of George MacDonald's poem "Baby," from his famous volume *At the Back of the North Wind:* "Where did you come from, baby dear?/Out of the everywhere into the here." The poem's genteel prettification of the facts of life is one manifestation of the cultural context the story depicts and against which it reacts. Anderson's negative version of MacDonald's poetic line serves to unmask the aching void behind the reigning Puritan belief that sex is ugly and sinful. It is perhaps difficult for modern readers to appreciate how widespread and intense was the kind of rejection of sexual relations that Rosalind Wescott's mother expresses. This is no sentimental notion of feminine purity. It is a profound aversion to intimate physical contact with men. Knowing sex only as the "brutal assault" of the predatory male upon the female or as the demand imposed with routine cruelty by husbands upon wives, Ma Wescott has long and lovingly harbored as her best hope for her daughter that Rosalind be triumphantly independent of men. Here, cloaked beneath the surface of American respectability, Anderson reveals a combination of biological ignorance and religious dogma that grew easily and often into physical disgust. Avant-garde artists and intellectuals called it pathological, but to many it was not only normal—it was righteous, practical, and self protective.

Anderson mentioned his first wife's distaste for sex in a letter to his fourth wife (Modlin *Love Letters* 251). His second wife, Tennessee Mitchell, was more adventuresome. She had had, before her marriage, at least one affair with a married man (Edgar Lee Masters), and she and Anderson endeavored to maintain an unencumbering marriage that would allow both partners to develop freely. But like society as a whole, the author was still struggling to understand how sex and love might be made harmonious, how the needs and desires of individual men and women might be made compatible, and how complex personal emotions should be related to the institution of marriage.

Several other aspects of the story are plainly developed from Anderson's own autobiography. He had known first-hand Rosalind's youthful excitement about the cultural life of Chicago, Walter Sayers's weary disinterest in the profits and losses of the business world, and Melville Stoner's detached observation of other people's lives. He may have wondered at times if he were not, like Melville Stoner, something of a vulture feeding on the filth of the world as he tried to pluck beauty from it. Rosalind's vision of dancing trees also evidently originated in the author's adolescent experiences, which he describes in his *Memoirs* (White 109–10) and in his autobiographical novel *Tar* (104–05). Finally, Anderson himself, like Rosalind, had run away from home, suddenly, desperately, blindly seeking.

The name Melville Stoner seems to have derived from that of the prominent Melville Stone, founder of Chicago's *Daily News*. It is not clear, though, what significance that connection has, if any.

Publication History

From July to September of 1921 "Out of Nowhere into Nothing" was serialized in the *Dial* (71:1–18, 153–69, 325–46). For this, one of his longest stories, the magazine paid the author two cents a word (Schevill 151). Later that year "Out of Nowhere into Nothing" appeared as the final story in *The Triumph of the Egg* (171–267). After Anderson's death, Rosenfeld reprinted it in *The Sherwood Anderson Reader*, including it with other selections under the heading "The Wonders of Chaos" (157–210).

Relation to Other Words

Bishop notes that both "Out of Nowhere into Nothing" and "I Want to Know Why" dramatize the "conflict between the desire of the young for a seen or imagined beauty, and the cruel ugliness of life and the meaningless need for perpetuating it" (118). In fact, if the statement is revised to allow for the persistence of "young" desire in older people, that theme is fundamental to the whole volume *The Triumph of the Egg*. The sense of a living seed buried within the husk of existence, or—in an alternative symbol—of a living egg hidden within the shell, pervades the book. The image of the stone (Melville Stoner) works similarly: in "Motherhood" stones are likened to "children" straining to emerge from the earth where they lie half-buried, and in the poetic epilogue, "The Man with the Trumpet," the speaker hurls a stone "that [humankind] might build temples to themselves" (*TE* 170, 269). A stone may be a seed that will flower, as in the ancient riddle. Rosalind's meditation on the cycle of recurring life and death is in a sense the culminating epiphany of the book, an answer to the question posed by the horse-struck boy in "I Want to Know Why" and to the question of the dying Doctor Cochran in "Unlighted Lamps"—"Why are babies always being born?" (*TE* 91). It is the same philosophical riddle on which "The Egg" is based. As an answer, it hardly satisfies the mind. But like many paradoxes, it leaves the heart hope amid its pain. For the wasteland imagery that runs throughout the book converges in Rosalind's climactic vision of dry Willow Creek filled with water. The water, symbolic of the wellsprings of life in a tradition descending from the Neoplatonic philosopher Plotinus, is luminous with the vigor of ineffable Being. Like the similar visionary moment in T. S. Eliot's *Four Quartets,* the mystical spring that Rosalind imagines is a redemptive symbol of everpresent possibility, a glimpse of eternal plenitude within the perpetual flux.

Anderson's understanding of the historical roots of American cultural distress surfaces in an interesting parallel between remarks about Christopher Columbus's "duplicity" in "The Egg" (*TE* 58–59) and Walter Sayers's theory that the white men of America do not really own the land they inhabit: "The red men, although they are practically all gone, still own the American continent" (*TE* 245). These passages pinpoint the national original sin in historical events of imperialism and genocide committed against a primitive, indigenous people by Europeans convinced of their own superiority. The section of the story that treats Mrs. Sayers's black gardener, the ongoing oppression of the African-American in America, and the long history of black slavery traces a parallel instance of oppression. Other stories in the collection extend the geographical reach of the paradigm. "The Man in the Brown Coat," by referring to Alexander, Napoleon, Grant, and Hindenburg, calls up a history of conquest reaching beyond American shores, and "War" shows modern European struggles for power as another phase of the same age-old story. Against this large background of death-dealing mankind takes place the individual quest to awaken to fullness of life. The latent imperative is recovery of some vital integrity the red men represented.

Fagin states that the story "summarizes all phases of Sherwood Anderson's work"—the dreary town, the inarticulate characters, the sense of missing out on life, the rebellion against standard definitions of success, the Strindbergian battle between the sexes; "finally," says Fagin, "we have Anderson himself in the figure of Melville Stoner, who 'would not write as others do' and who has come to a conviction that 'we know little enough here in America, either in the towns or in the cities,'" and who startles people with the honesty of his vision (88–89, quoting *TE* 190, 191–92). The pattern of escape, too, appears throughout Anderson's work ("Departure," "The Man Who Became a Woman," and many others). Though in this story there seems to be no *place* for Rosalind to escape to, the sheer fact of "recoil and recommitment" is, as Régis Michaud commented, a "renewal of existence" akin to the conversion experience (Fanning 77).

Also, there is the attention to sex, a theme Anderson introduced in his earliest stories. The father's repressive response in "Sister" to his daughter's plan of taking a lover particularly resembles the mother's response in this story to a similar situation. But the closest parallels to this story appear in *Many Marriages,* serialized in the *Dial* between October 1922 and March 1923. In the novel as in the story, puritanical attitudes have created "the general atmosphere of fear in which so many modern women live and breathe" (*Marriages* 64). Trying to break out of that inhibiting atmosphere, John Webster, the protagonist of the novel, parades naked in front of the statue of the Virgin; similarly, Rosalind Westcott undresses to admire her lovely body and ponders the sexual element in worship of the Virgin (Hansen 160–61). The Carlylean idea of stripping off garments also emerges as Rosalind flees into the night at the end of the story. The novel stresses sexual freedom so strongly that for the most part it seems to propose sex as a panacea. Rosalind, however, emphatically rejects such simplistic notions: "If the sex impulse within it [my body] had been gratified in what way would my problem be solved? I am lonely now. It is evident that after that had happened I would still be lonely" (*TE* 205). Her conclusion is consistent with explicit statements in "Seeds" (in the same collection) and with ideas implicit in stories such as "Nobody Knows" in *Winesburg, Ohio.* Read closely, the ending of *Many Marriages* suggests a similar irony: as Webster runs off with his secretary, he begins discontentedly to nag her.

An approximation of the title phrase appears both in "the Philosopher"—Doctor Parcival's tales "began nowhere and ended nowhere" (*WO* 51), and in "A Chicago Hamlet"—where ugly streets "go on and on forever, out of nowhere into nothing" (*HM* 139–40).

Critical Studies

This story was "much praised in its time" (Raymund 142). Crawford's 1922 review applauded its "poignancy" and its lack of sentimentality (71). Hansen, in 1923, admired the way it caught "overtones and the subtle influences of the subconscious" (153). Fagin responded to its call "to life and beauty" (89). And Chase, though less enthusiastically, accepted it as a story where a man's human sympathy lends a woman the courage she needs (44).

As changing critical tides began to turn against Anderson, response to "Out of Nowhere into Nothing" became less favorable. For Edmund Wilson, the story was too much like *Many Marriages,* too "subjective" in method and too limp and rambling in structure (91). Howe approved of Rosalind

Westcott and Melville Stoner as two of Anderson's "more individualized and memorable characters" and of its treatment of "male inadequacy, . . . a good man's refusal to enter the dangerous relationships of love and sex" (175). But he criticized the "long murky flashbacks" and the "perverse romanticism" of its view that life is "a mere occasional explosion in the darkness" (175). Schevill's complaints are more extensive: "the narration becomes diffuse, and the symbolism of the title remains murky. The style leaves only a clouded impression of overloaded symbols" (165). In their train, Burbank finds the story "tiresome" and "prolix," weakened by "foggy characters" and lack of "concreteness, rich suggestiveness, and compression of a symbolic structure" (91, 94). For him, Rosalind's groping is virtually synonymous with the author's groping. Subsequent critics have not disputed these claims.

Indeed, nobody has considered the story worthy of extended discussion or detailed analysis. What discussion there has been centers on two topics: the ending and the depiction of the African-American.

Interpretations of the ending diverge sharply. Walcutt declares it an epiphanic discovery by which Rosalind "comes into possession of a delicious confidence in her powers" (226). David Anderson, in contrast, regards Rosalind's flight as a "futile rebellion" reflecting her "hopeless confusion" and the "despair" of the whole volume in which she appears (66). Wright surmises that the ending implies a future in which the heroine will be exploited by a man who will use her love "for his sexual advantage, without giving to her any of the things—child, home, married respectability—that she wants" (78; similarly, Miller 78). Furthermore, Wright argues, readers can see that Rosalind is responsible for "deliberately and wilfully" deciding to begin this unwise affair, though this "caustic" element is relieved by the "courage" of her "determination to have love at any cost" (214). These conflicting assessments do not cancel each other out, for the story is open-ended. Williams offers the most perceptive commentary on this matter. Observing that both village and city deny Rosalind's "chances for love and success," Williams notes that the optimism of the last sentence (where Rosalind is described as a "'creator of light'" driving away the darkness with her spiritual force) is offset by "an actual void" (226–28). Hence, argues Williams, "Out of Nowhere into Nothing" is "one of [Anderson's] outstanding statements on the ambiguity of modern life" (228).

The story's handling of a black character has aroused controversy. Emphasizing the theme of flowing, instinctual life, John Peale Bishop spoke approvingly of the story's expression of "sympathy with the simple unthinking life of the African negro" (12). Since the character is a college graduate and has practiced law, that interpretation is untenable at best. In a letter to Anderson, Jean Toomer accurately called the portrait itself "superficial" and unrealistic. Black people "who are interested in the 'progress' of the Negro would take violent exception to such a statement as, 'By educating himself he had cut himself off from his own people,'" objected Toomer; however, he added, the "emotion" evoked by the portrait and the "sense of beauty" are deeply true, "easily more Negro than almost anything I have seen" (Turner 459). Matthews adds a further rebuke: by suggesting that a black man is "unnatural" to pursue intellectual and professional development and by depicting his "ready acceptance of a slave status" as a white woman's gardener, Anderson reveals a racist belief in "the innate inferiority of black people" (408). Actually, since the story is critical of industrial urban development, often misnamed "progress," and affirmative of spontaneous, vital forces of the earth, it could be argued that Anderson's story primitivistically asserts the innate superiority of black (and red) people. Either of those interpretations is simplistic, though. The dilemma of the Negro lawyer-become-gardener is much like Rosalind's: in seeking to emerge from stifling traditional roles, the woman and the black man both confront stifling new pressures that also deny inward fulfillment.

Several aspects of this long narrative deserve more attention. Particularly fine is its examination of the mental processes of a twentieth-century woman caught between traditional town and modern city, threatened by conflicting cultural definitions of what she ought to be, and trying to create herself anew—out of nothing. The psychologically acute studies of daughter, mother, and father are also worth fuller analysis. Likewise, Anderson's complex interweaving of multiple points of view should be explicated and evaluated. And those supposedly "murky" symbols should be probed. Burbank briefly discusses the bird symbolism used to describe Melville Stoner:

> In a structure built upon contrasts between death and life, night and day, shadows and light, dead trees and vibrant plant and insect life, Stoner himself is characterized by resembling alternately a vulture and a sea gull. He appears to Rosalind as death, but he actually holds out to her the promise of life through his imaginative consciousness. . . . (92)

Another overlooked symbol yields special insight into the meaning of the story and the volume *The Triumph of the Egg*. Three times in Rosalind's meditations she thinks of water as being "the color of chrysoprase" (*TE* 217, 255, 266). The richly significant word "chrysoprase," prominent by its difference from the more commonplace diction surrounding it, is made more prominent by repetition. Sounding faintly like "Christ-praise," it hints of spiritual joy. More important, the word denotes not only a golden-green hue but also a golden-green stone that has since medieval times been said to shine in the dark. The many references to stones and to darkness thus come together as Rosalind runs forward into the night, feeling the darkness spring back before her as within herself she generates radiant light. The human self, then, is instinct with the power of resurrection. Furthermore, that mystically enabling life force is shown to operate partly through the murmur of words in the mind. This is the ground of the artist's hope, expressed in "The Man with the Trumpet," that words may be like seeds or like stones, living instruments for bringing about the dawn of new consciousness.

Works Cited

Anderson, David. *Sherwood Anderson: An Introduction and Interpretation.* New York: Holt, Rinehart, 1967.

Anderson, Sherwood. "Sister." *Little Review* 2 (December 1915):3–4. Rpt. in *Sherwood Anderson: Early Writings.* Ed. Ray Lewis White. Kent, OH, and London: Kent State University Press, 1989, 138–40.

——. 1921. *The Triumph of the Egg.* New York: B. W. Huebsch. Rpt. New York: Four Walls Eight Windows, 1988. Introduction by Herbert Gold.

——. 1923. *Many Marriages.* New York: B. W. Huebsche. Rpt. in critical ed., by Douglas G. Rogers. Metuchen, NJ: Scarecrow, 1978.

——. 1923. *Horses and Men.* New York: B. W. Huebsch.

——. 1926. *Tar: A Midwest Childhood.* New York: Boni & Liveright. Rpt. *Tar: A Midwest Childhood: A Critical Text.* Ed. Ray Lewis White. Cleveland: Press of Case Western Reserve University, 1969.

Bishop, John Peale. "The Distrust of Ideas: D. H. Lawrence and Sherwood Anderson—and Their Qualities in Common." *Vanity Fair* 22 (December 1921):10–12, 118. Rpt. in *The Collected Essays of John Peale Bishop.* Ed. Edmund Wilson. New York: Scribners, 1948, 233–40.

Burbank, Rex. 1964. *Sherwood Anderson.* New York: Twayne. Rpt. in part in *The Achievement of Sherwood Anderson: Essays in Criticism.* Ed. Ray Lewis White. Chapel Hills: University of North Carolina Press, 1966, 32–43. Rpt. in part in *Sherwood Anderson: Collection of Critical Essays.* Ed. Walter B. Rideout. Englewood Cliffs, NJ: Prentice-Hall, 1974, 70–83.

Chase, Cleveland B. 1927. *Sherwood Anderson.* New York: Robert M. McBride. Rpt. Folcroft, PA: Folcroft Press, 1969.

Crawford, Nelson Antrim. 1981. "Sherwood Anderson, the Wistfully Faithful." In *Critical Essays on Sherwood Anderson.* Ed. David D. Anderson. Boston: G. K. Hall, 65–73. Originally printed in *The Midland* 8 (November 1922):297–308.

Fagin, N. Bryllion. 1973. *The Phenomenon of Sherwood Anderson: A Study in American Life and Letters.* New York: Russell & Russell. Originally printed Baltimore: Rossi-Bryn, 1927.

Fanning, Michael, ed. 1976. *France and Sherwood Anderson: Paris Note-book, 1921*. Baton Rouge: Louisiana State University Press.

Hansen, Harry. 1923. *Midwest Portraits: A Book of Memories and Friend-ships*. New York: Harcourt, Brace.

Howe, Irving. 1951. *Sherwood Anderson*. New York: William Sloane.

Jones, Howard Mumford, and Walter B. Rideout, eds. 1953. *Letters of Sher-wood Anderson*. Boston: Little, Brown.

Matthews, George C. "Ohio's *Beulah Land* or Plantation Blacks in the Fic-tion of Sherwood Anderson." *College Language Association Journal* 25 (1982):405–413.

Miller, William V. 1974. "Earth-Mothers, Succubi, and Other Ectoplasmic Spirits: The Women in Sherwood Anderson's Short Stories." In *Mid-america I*. Ed. David D. Anderson. East Lansing, MI: Midwestern Press, 64–81. Rpt. in *Critical Essays on Sherwood Anderson*. Ed. David D. An-derson. Boston: G. K. Hall, 1981, 196–209.

Modlin, Charles E., ed. 1989. *Sherwood Anderson's Love Letters to Eleanor Copenhaver Anderson*. Athens and London: University of Georgia Press.

———, ed. 1984. *Sherwood Anderson: Selected Letters*. Knoxville: University of Tennessee Press.

Raymund, Bernard. "The Grammar of Not-Reason: Sherwood Anderson." *Arizona Quarterly* 12 (1956):48–60, 137–48.

Rosenfeld, Paul, ed. 1947. *The Sherwood Anderson Reader*. Boston: Houghton Mifflin.

Schevill, James. 1951. *Sherwood Anderson: His Life and Work*. Denver: Uni-versity of Denver Press.

Sutton, William A., ed. 1985. *Letters to Bab: Sherwood Anderson to Marietta D. Finley, 1916–33*. Foreword by Walter B. Rideout. Urbana and Chi-cago: University of Illinois Press.

Turner, Darwin T. "An Intersection of Paths: Correspondence Between Jean Toomer and Sherwood Anderson." *College Language Association Jour-nal* 17 (1973–74):455–67.

Walcutt, Charles Child. "Sherwood Anderson: Impressionism and the Buried Life." *Sewanee Review* 60 (1952):28–47. Rpt. in *American Literary Natu-ralism, a Divided Stream*. Minneapolis: University of Minnesota Press, 1956, 222–39. Rpt. in part in *Sherwood Anderson:* Winesburg, Ohio: *Text and Criticism*. Ed. John H. Ferres. New York: Viking, 1966, 432–43.

White, Ray Lewis, ed. 1969. *Sherwood Anderson's Memoirs: A Critical Edi-tion*. Chapel Hill: University of North Carolina Press.

Williams, Kenny J. 1988. *A Storyteller and a City: Sherwood Anderson's Chicago*. De Kalb: Northern Illinois University Press.

Wilson, Edmund. 1952. "Sherwood Anderson's *Many Marriages.*" In *The Shores of Light: A Literary Chronicle of the Twenties and Thirties*. New York: Farrar, Straus, & Young, 91–93. Originally printed as "Many Marriages." *Dial* 74 (1923):399–400.

Wright, Austin McGiffert. 1961. *The American Short Story in the Twenties*. Chicago: University of Chicago Press.

Horses and Men

I'm a Fool

Circumstances of Composition

The precise date of this story's composition has not been determined, but it seems to have been written in the fall of 1920 or shortly thereafter. The Prohibition amendment, referred to in the story, had gone into effect in January of that year. Beginning in January, too, Anderson had spent over four months in Alabama, away from his Chicago advertising job, happily writing fiction and experimenting with painting. He had been deeply impressed with the black folk of Alabama, who seemed to him beautiful, natural, "the sweetest souled people in America" (Sutton, *Letters* 121). In August, vacationing in Wisconsin, he began working on a manuscript about a boy named Tom Edwards, grandson of a Welsh poet, and found it expanding into a novel, which he called "Ohio Pagans" (Jones-Rideout, *Letters* 60–61; Sutton, *Letters* 125–26). After he returned to Chicago and the advertising agency, recollections of his freer, simpler life in Alabama intensified his resentment against the commercial world where he was obliged to earn his living. He felt personally corrupted by his participation in the lies of the advertising business and in the struggle for success. During this period Anderson realized that his new book was disintegrating into a group of separate tales (Jones-Rideout, *Letters,* 65). References by the narrator of "I'm a Fool" to his Welsh grandfather (a figure in "An Ohio Pagan," which was extracted from the manuscript of the novel) suggest that the first-person story came of a burst of inspiration that occurred while the characters of the unfinished third-person novel were vivid in the author's mind. Anderson said that he had written the tale "at the copy desk one morning while I was presumed to be writing copy for a gas engine company" (Campbell and Modlin 10; slightly different accounts appear in White, *Memoirs,* 122–23, 432–33).

Deeper conflicts Anderson was experiencing at this period concerned his sense of himself as an American writer and his desire to be esteemed by literary critics whom he genuinely respected. During the period preceding the writing of "I'm a Fool," Anderson had been engaged in literary discussions with Van Wyck Brooks, whose *The Ordeal of Mark Twain* appeared in 1920. Brooks represented for Anderson a world of wealth, education, and cultivation from which he himself had been excluded. Anderson especially revered Brooks's mind, so Brooks's acceptance of Anderson's work had been profoundly gratifying. Yet as a Midwesterner confronting the world of high New England culture, Anderson identified strongly with Twain. At times he had pleaded with Brooks to be more sympathetic to his subject, not to judge Twain too harshly for succumbing to the "cheapness" that surrounded him (Jones-Rideout, *Letters* 40). Reading Brook's finished book in late August, Anderson admired it tremendously yet was incensed by Brooks's criticism of Twain, which Anderson knew encompassed him too somehow. Stung by a sense of personal slight, he fired off an angry letter to Brooks; almost immediately he felt ashamed of what he had done (Jones-Rideout, *Letters* 59–63). Disappointed hopes for an understanding brotherhood of artists were made only more bitter by disgust with himself. A November letter reflects his mood: "Aren't we all a lot of damn fools? There you are, and someday you'll get the itch to come out [to visit me]. You'll get to imagining yourself listening to beautiful talk, dining with beautiful people, finding love and comradeship among your own kind. Then you'll come back here and find the same moneygrubbing asses, the same sentimental fools you left. . . . The Lord made us fools. How shall we escape, O Lord?" (Jones-Rideout, *Letters* 64–65).

Sources and Influences

When he was a boy in Clyde, Ohio, Anderson took a job as groom in the stables of Thomas C. Whitehead, "owner of a string of race horses and one of the directors of the Clyde Fair" (Schevill 16). Surveying the scene at the Clyde Race Track, Anderson was fascinated by the gamblers and flashy men, and he acquired an abiding love for horses and admiration for the men who drove them. In his *Memoirs* he tells of his youthful ambition to be a racehorse driver, his stirring pride when he was allowed to take "a bay gelding named Doctor Fritz" for a jog around the track, and his mournful intuition that he lacked the cool steadiness essential in a good driver (White 121–22). Anderson uses the name Doctor Fritz for one of the horses in the story.

The name of the stallion "Bucephalus," too, which derives ultimately from Alexander the Great's beloved steed, evidently is remembered from that of a real horse Anderson had known; a horse of that name raced at the Clyde Fair Grounds on August 10, 1893 (Rideout, "Borrowing" 173 n. 14). The narrator exposes his ignorance of books when he refers to another race horse, a gelding, as "'About Ben Ahem' or something like that"; the real name, undoubtedly, came from Leigh Hunt's famous romantic poem "Abou Ben Adhem," which concerns a Mohammedan saint whose humanitarian love earned him a divine blessing. The horses' names, along with the difference in their ability to breed, correspond with the narrator's conflicting romantic ideals—his longing to be a conquering hero on the one hand and his generous love on the other. Placed in the mundane setting of a smalltown racetrack, the ideals seem wryly ridiculous but also poignantly genuine.

Other autobiographical elements appear in the groom's ambivalent attitudes about social class, his defensiveness about not going to college, his desire to "put up a good front," and his hostility to social pretensions in others. Similarly, a prominent side of Anderson's personality appeared throughout his life in his poor man's ambivalence about the things that accompany wealth and his love of flashy clothes. "There is in me something that likes to strut before men," Anderson wrote (*Notebook*, 171). The groom's bitter regret over such shallow impulses, though, corresponds to Anderson's anxiety about his adman's tendency to "slickness."

Anderson himself was the first of many who have pointed out the stylistic indebtedness of "I'm a Fool" to Mark Twain: "After all, isn't it [the story], say, Mark Twain at his best, the Huckleberry Finn Mark Twain?" (Jones-Rideout, *Letters* 102). Anderson's first-person narrator and his idiom, even the friendship of black man and white youth, are frankly borrowed from Twain's masterpiece. Furthermore, as Westbrook argues, Anderson may have got his central idea for "I'm a Fool" from Twain's *Roughing It*, where a youth tells a similarly disastrous "'whopper' of a lie about ownership of a horse to impress a young lady": in both episodes a young man's affectation leads to humiliation, but Anderson transforms Twain's "hilarious comedy" into something "more serious, even pathetic" (236, 237).

Publication History

"I'm a Fool" first appeared in February of 1922 in the *Dial* (72:119–29). Anderson had difficulty marketing this tale, which, ironically, has proved to be one of his most popular. He sent it to *Vanity Fair*, which had accepted the piece he later entitled "Milk Bottles," but on December 2, 1921, they returned it with the explanation that they did not publish fiction (*Vanity Fair* letters). After the story was rejected by several mass market periodicals, the *Dial* agreed to print it "for less than a hundred dollars" (Pecile 149). The *Dial*, which awarded Anderson their prestigious prize in 1921, evidently accepted the folksy oral narrative with a measure of reluctance after the publisher, James Sibley Watson, told the editor, Gilbert Seldes, "This can't do us any harm" (Wasserstrom 81).

The following May, the story was published in the *London Mercury* (6:19–27). In October of 1923, it was collected in *Horses and Men*. Subsequently, it was much reprinted, beginning with O'Brien's *Best Short Stories of 1922,* so that in the spring of 1927 Anderson reported selling the tenth reprint (Modlin, *Letters* 91). It was "Anderson's most popular story by far in the 1930s"; he received payment for reprints "at least eighteen times in addition to royalties received for a few radio broadcasts of the story" (Campbell 168). Orson Welles made a radio play of the story in 1938, and Cecil B. DeMille considered using the story for a movie (Curry 195–96n). It has continued to receive numerous reprints in anthologies, and it is included in Martha Foley's *Fifty Best American Short Stories, 1915–1965* (38–48). A television production—with screenplay by Ron Cowan, directed by Noel Black, and starring Ron Howard and Santiago Gonzales—was presented on PBS in 1978. Recently it was reprinted in Modlin's collection *Certain Things Last* (48–59).

Relation to Other Works

"I'm a Fool" is one of three racetrack stories Anderson produced. "I Want to Know Why" and "The Man Who Became a Woman" similarly exploit the world of the boys and men who work with the horses. "I'm a Fool" is the simplest, most straightforward of the three. The story, in its focus on the bewildered adolescent trying to come to terms with experience, typifies an important segment of Anderson's work. Most closely related to it is "I Want to Know Why," which also features a racetrack swipe as first-person narrator. Even the adults in many of Anderson's tales, novels, and poems, though, tend to be groping and confused as they search through the muddles of modern society and their own tangled impulses for more genuine life.

Bridgman suggests that in *Horses and Men* Anderson was trying "to work out the main problem of the vernacular—how to drop the speaker yet retain the speaking style"; beginning in "I'm a Fool" with the youthful voice that, in Huck Finn, Twain had found to be "vernacular at its purest," Anderson then progressed to the voice of the adult looking back at adolescent experience in "The Man Who Became a Woman" and with less success to the adult voice narrating adult experience in "The Triumph of a Modern" (159–61). As the narrator is effaced and finally disappears in such tales as "A Chicago Hamlet" and "An Ohio Pagan," Bridgman contends, the prose loses its vitality (162). Actually, as David Anderson points out, the narrator of "I'm a Fool" may be an adult; the remark that it all happened "before prohibition and all that foolishness" suggests that considerable time has elapsed, even though the style is "consciously adolescent" (73).

The largely autobiographical *Tar* (1926) also draws upon Anderson's memories of the racetracks. More important in connection with "I'm a Fool," *Tar* includes a similar account of a boy's humiliation when, as a result of his own admitted folly, he loses all hope of establishing a relationship with a pretty and wealthy girl, far above him in social station, to whom he is romantically attracted (239–68).

Anderson's handling of Burt in "I'm a Fool" bears comparison with the portrayal of African-American characters in "I Want to Know Why," "Out of Nowhere into Nothing," "The Man Who Became a Woman," and *Dark Laughter* (1925). This tale in particular—and the television production based on it—has elicited complaint that it presents the black man as a creature of natural instinct, in accord with racial stereotypes (Matthews 407, 410). To some extent, of course, that is true, but it is important to remember, as Horace Gregory has said, that Anderson uses the Negro as "a vitalizing yet ambiguous symbol" ("On Sherwood" 19–20). Burt is a more complex character than has been acknowledged: he is a tough fighter; he has "kind eyes" and sings old spirituals; a victim of white prejudice, he might have "got to the top . . . if he hadn't been black"; and he is as capable of putting on a swaggering air in saloons as are the white characters. Although the white boy associates Burt with a dream of freedom from everything he detests about middle-class existence, two quite different things are also clear. First, the details the white youth offers about Burt's life show that he knows Burt is not really free from society and its wrongs. Second, the boy simultaneously holds contrary ideals: when you find the girl you want to marry, he says, "you want nice things around her like flowers and swell clothes, and want her to have the kids you're going to have, and you want good music played and no rag time" (*Horses and Men* 15). His dilemma, in part, springs from his vague understanding that neither the primitive (black) idyll nor the domestic (white) idyll is exempt from the distresses and hypocrisies of the whole culture.

Critical Studies

Sherwood Anderson's own criticism of this story has more or less set the frame for subsequent critical discussion. In a 1923 letter to Van Wyck Brooks, he wrote: "I think also that 'I'm a Fool' is a piece of work that holds water, but do you not think its wide acceptance is largely due to the fact that it is a story of immaturity and poses no problem"; remarking its link with Twain's style (see "Sources and Influences" above), he proceeded, "I do not want you to like best of my things the things easiest to like" (Jones-Rideout, *Letters* 89–90). Again in 1924, writing to John Gould Fletcher, he called the story "first class but not important" (Modlin, *Letters* 55).

A few months later, however, William Faulkner in the *Dallas Morning News* called "I'm a Fool" "the best short story in America." Other critics have observed in Faulkner's "Cheest" and *The Reivers* the influence of the techniques and subject matter of Anderson's story (Richardson 307; Adams 124).

Evaluations by more recent commentators have been similarly divided. Calverton agrees with Anderson, calling the story "exceptionally appealing" and "deliciously flavored" but "not powerful" (106). Scheville admires "the Twain idiom" and the direct, colloquial style but discovers "little depth" or real substance (187; similarly, Tanner 215). Howe, more harshly, finds the "coy" narration "inconceivable from the lips of" a nineteen-year-old well schooled in drinking and swearing; too self-conscious in approach and too "merely adolescent" in content, the story, he concludes, resembles Tarkington more than Twain (154). Way likewise judges it inept in technique and "stereotyped" in effect (120–21). Others, though, have followed Faulkner in praising the story. Gregory calls it "one of Anderson's masterpieces in the art of making a dramatic monologue turn into a story" and "the best of his very short short stories": he singles out the slangy glibness of the narrator as a superb indicator of a desire "to hide his innocence behind a guise of being tough and worldly" (463). Pecile applauds Anderson's artful "finesse" in using the narrator's colloquial, "artless rambling" to advance the action and reveal the character (148). Miller argues that Howe's failure to consider the story "in the comic tradition" causes him to miss its real "charm and poignance" (12). And Raymund, suggesting that Anderson's effort to emulate the sophistication of urban Eastern culture led him to undervalue the story, praises the author's deft management of irony (142).

Surprisingly, however, this very famous story has received few detailed or extended analyses. Fagin reads the story, too simply but still usefully, in terms of the narrator's discovery of "an ideal": having devoted himself, "boasting, swaggering," to cheap and tawdry values, the youth attains both "a glimpse of" an ideal already latent within him and comes to a painful realization of his folly (91). Walcutt's discussion, also brief, is valuable for its explanation of Anderson's "impressionism," which renders "the *quality* of experience" through the "disorderly," "rambling," associative style of its uneducated narrator; this technique reveals the narrator's "ludicrous confusion of values" but also his "fundamental goodhearted sincerity," it indicates the difficulties posed by by the provincial "absence of 'manners'" along with the universal tendency of men "to brag before girls and be ashamed of themselves afterwards," and finally it questions commonly held assumptions about reality itself (232–33). Wright classifies the story as a romantic comedy with a plot of choice (387). He correctly states that the protagonist, when "exposed to the unpleasant realities of life, fails to achieve a mature understanding of them" but perhaps goes too far when he suggests that the reader possesses the understanding the protagonist lacks (211). The comic effect of the story depends on readers' knowledge exceeding the character's, but its deeper substance derives from issues less easy to resolve.

Burbank seems to have been the first critic to remark the story's theme of initiation and to trace the narrator's confusion to vacillation between the values of genteel respectability embraced by his lower middle-class family and the more primitive values represented by "the freedom of the tracks"

(100–101; similarly Taylor 62, 64). Burbank emphasizes the swipe's knowledge that the races are fixed and laments his "inability to make moral discriminations" (102). Moral discriminations are not so simple as that, though. Pecile, in an otherwise similar analysis, stresses the "false respectability" of the middle-class family and the pompous "airs of the dude." In effect combining those emphases, Ross persuasively argues that the story dramatizes a broad social failure of America itself, for the narrative evinces an endless web of hypocrisies and corruptions committed by respectable and unrespectable alike as the boy "naïvely exposes the lying that goes on in small-town America, little realizing that his own lying, like Huck's, has grown out of the community lying" (30). The story's strength, as Ross puts it, inheres in its "Chekhovian longing for life as it might be" and "acceptance of life as it is" (31).

Works Cited

Adams, Richard P. "The Apprenticeship of William Faulkner." *Tulane Studies in English* 12 (1962):113–56.

Anderson, David. 1967. *Sherwood Anderson: An Introduction and Interpretation*. New York: Holt, Rinehart.

Anderson, Sherwood. 1923. *Horses and Men*. New York: B. W. Huebsch.

——. 1926. *Tar: A Midwest Childhood*. New York: Boni & Liveright. Rpt. in *Tar: A Midwest Childhood: A Critical Text*. Ed. Ray Lewis White. Cleveland: Press of Case Western Reserve University, 1969.

——. 1970. *Sherwood Anderson's Notebook*. Mamaroneck, NY: Appel. Originally printed New York: Boni & Liveright, 1926.

Bridgman, Richard. 1966. *The Colloquial Style in America*. New York: Oxford University Press.

Burbank, Rex. 1964. *Sherwood Anderson*. New York: Twayne. Rpt. in part in *The Achievement of Sherwood Anderson: Essays in Criticism*. Ed. Ray Lewis White. Chapel Hill: University of North Carolina Press, 1966, 32–43. Rpt. in part in *Sherwood Anderson: Collection of Critical Essays*. Ed. Walter B. Rideout. Englewood Cliffs, NJ: Prentice-Hall, 1974, 70–83.

Calberton, V. J. "Sherwood Anderson: A Study in Sociological Criticism." *Modern Quarterly* 2 (1924):82–118. Rpt. in *The Newer Spirit: A Sociological Criticism of Literature*. Introduction by Ernest Boyd. New York: Boni & Liveright, 1925, 52–118.

Campbell, Hilbert H. "Sherwood Anderson and the Viking Press, 1925–1941." *Resources for American Literary Study* 10 (1980):167–72.

Campbell, Hilbert H., and Charles E. Modlin, eds. 1976. *Sherwood Anderson: Centennial Studies*. Troy, NY: Whitston.

Curry, Martha Mulroy. 1975. *The "Writer's Book" by Sherwood Anderson: A Critical Edition*. Metuchen, NJ: Scarecrow Press.

Fagin, N. Bryllion. 1973. *The Phenomenon of Sherwood Anderson: A Study in American Life and Letters*. New York: Russell & Russell. Originally printed Baltimore: Rossi-Bryn, 1972.

Faulkner, William. "Prophets of the New Age II. Sherwood Anderson." *Dallas Morning News* 26 April 1925. Rpt. as "Sherwood Anderson." *Princeton University Library Chronicle* 18 (Spring 1957):89–94.

Foley, Martha, ed. 1965. *Fifty Best American Short Stories, 1915–1965*. Boston: Houghton Mifflin.

Gregory, Horace. "On Sherwood Anderson." In *Talks with Authors*. Ed. Charles F. Madden. Carbondale: Southern Illinois University Press, 1968, 12–22.

———, ed. 1949. *The Portable Sherwood Anderson*. New York: Viking. Rev. ed. New York: Viking Penguin, 1972.

Howe, Irving. 1951. *Sherwood Anderson*. New York: William Sloane.

Jones, Howard Mumford, and Walter B. Rideout, eds. 1953. *Letters of Sherwood Anderson*. Urbana and Chicago: University of Illinois Press.

Matthews, George C. "Ohio's *Beulah Land* or Plantation Blacks in the Fiction of Sherwood Anderson." *College Language Association Journal* 25 (1982):405–13.

Miller, William V. 1976. "Portraits of the Artist: Anderson's Fictional Storytellers." In *Sherwood Anderson: Dimensions of His Literary Art: A Collection of Critical Essays*. Ed. David D. Anderson. East Lansing: Michigan State University Press, 1–23.

Modlin, Charles E., ed. 1992. *Certain Things Last: The Selected Stories of Sherwood Anderson*. New York: Four Walls Eight Windows.

———, ed. 1984. *Sherwood Anderson: Selected Letters*. Knoxville: University of Tennessee Press.

Pecile, Jordan. 1977. "On Sherwood Anderson and 'I'm a Fool.'" In *The American Short Story*. Ed. Calvin Skaggs. New York: Dell, 145–49.

Raymund, Bernard. "The Grammar of Not-Reason: Sherwood Anderson." *Arizona Quarterly* 12 (1956):48–60, 137–48.

Richardson, H. Edward. "Anderson and Faulkner." *American Literature* 36 (1964):298–314.

Rideout, Walter B. 1976. "A Borrowing from Borrow." In *Sherwood Anderson: Centennial Studies*. Hilbert H. Campbell and Charles E. Modlin (Eds.). Troy, NY: Whitston, 162–74.

Ross, Danforth. 1961. *The American Short Story*. University of Minnesota Pamphlets on American Writers, no. 14. Minneapolis: University of Minnesota Press.

Schevill, James. 1951. *Sherwood Anderson: His Life and Work*. Denver: University of Denver Press.

Sutton, William A., ed. 1985. *Letters to Bab: Sherwood Anderson to Marietta D. Finley, 1916–33*. Foreword by Walter B. Rideout. Urbana and Chicago: University of Illinois Press.

Tanner, Tony. 1965. "Sherwood Anderson's Little Things." *The Reign of Wonder: Naïvety and Reality in American Literature*. Cambridge: Cambridge University Press, 205–227.

Taylor, Welford Dunaway. 1977. *Sherwood Anderson*. New York: Frederick Ungar.

Vanity Fair letters to Anderson. Sherwood Anderson Collection. Newberry Library, Chicago.

Walcutt, Charles Child. "Sherwood Anderson: Impressionism and the Buried Life." *Sewanee Review* 60 (1952):28–47. Rpt. in *American Literary Naturalism, a Divided Stream*. Minneapolis: University of Minnesota Press, 1956, 222–39. Rpt. in part in *Sherwood Anderson:* Winesburg, Ohio: *Text and Criticism*. Ed. John H. Ferres. New York: Viking, 1966, 432–43.

Wasserstrom, William. 1963. *The Time of the Dial*. Syracuse, NY: Syracuse University Press.

Way, Brian. 1971. "Sherwood Anderson." In *The American Novel and the Nineteen Twenties*. Malcolm Bradbury and David Palmer (Eds.). Stratford-upon-Avon Studies 13. London: Edward Arnold, 107–126.

Westbrook, Wayne W. "'I'm a Fool': A Source in Roughing It." *Studies in Short Fiction* 22 (1985):234–37.

White, Ray Lewis, ed. 1969. *Sherwood Anderson's Memoirs: A Critical Edition*. Chapel Hill: University of North Carolina Press.

Wright, Austin McGiffert. 1961. *The American Short Story in the Twenties*. Chicago: University of Chicago Press.

The Triumph of a Modern
or, Send for the Lawyer

Circumstances of Composition

Anderson wrote "The Triumph of a Modern" in August 1922. At that time he was staying in the New York City apartment of Ben Huebsch, his friend and publisher. Anderson wrote to his brother Karl late in August that he had been writing "like a crazy man"; he was trying to develop a new "satirical vein," and among five stories he had produced was "a satire on the new movement in the arts" (Jones-Rideout, *Letters* 89). Townsend's conclusion that this story is the satire referred to there is convincing (193). Other satirical pieces Anderson composed around the same time include the story "There She Is—She Is Taking Her Bath" and an article, "Ohio: I'll Say We've Done Well." That summer, Anderson had resigned his position with the Critchfield advertising agency. He had accepted the *Dial* award of $2,000 in January, and his fiction was selling well. In February, Anderson rejoiced that the Modern Library edition of *Winesburg, Ohio* had "sold in a month as much as in its first year" and that *The Triumph of the Egg* was "going into its third printing" (Modlin, *Letters* 29). This success, along with a revulsion toward the world of business, gave him hope that at last he could earn his living by his art alone. But he was uneasy about the failure of his second marriage, and he worried that success might spoil him.

Sources and Influences

Passing time has blunted the satiric thrust of this tale, and its targets have been largely forgotten. When he wrote "The Triumph of a Modern" Anderson had been reading Clive Bell's *Since Cézanne,* a series of essays on various modern artists and artistic movements. He sent a copy of Bell's book to his brother Karl, a modernist painter of some stature, and in their letters they discussed Bell's ideas. Thoughts generated by Bell's book provided an impetus for this story.

But the major influence on the story was Anderson's response to the success of the writers and artists of the Chicago Renaissance. His early hopes had been disillusioned as he discovered that members of "the Dell group of Fifty-seventh Street . . . had been co-opted, as had Anderson, by the glitter and glamour" of the modernist movement and by the tendency to present ideas "for their shock value" (Williams 234). Anderson was disappointed that the enthusiastic reception of *Winesburg, Ohio* and *Many Marriages* depended so much on "narrow interpretations" regarding their "liberated" view of sexuality (D. Anderson 73–74). He also wondered, with a persistent self-lacerating anxiety about his own propensities toward the advertising man's "slickness," just how much he was succumbing to "the temptation, always present, to try to get into the big money by attempting to give [the public] what [he thought] they want[ed]" (White, *Memoirs* 344). "As a modern, Anderson was always uncomfortably and self-consciously a failure" (Hoffman 5). In "The Triumph of a Modern" he distanced himself from the excesses and the shallowness he saw in the contemporary literary scene.

Especially, this satire targets Waldo Frank, whom Anderson considered breast fixated. After Frank's novel *Dark Mother* appeared in 1920, Anderson vented his exasperation with the book's "silly intellectuality": "It is of course all right to write a book about the mother complex and to involve it with other complexes. Life is surely so involved. The point is that Waldo should have told his story simply, straightly. . . . The matter of woman's breasts. There again I think the man was afraid we would not get it he was putting over the mother complex. One knows instinctively there is a deep seated connection in both a physical and a psychic way between the male and the breasts of women. . . . Waldo in his book however suckles too much. One feels him being, or striving to be bold, to startle" (Sutton, *Letters* 134). A more general account of Anderson's feelings about Waldo Frank, disapproving of Frank's excessive desire to be "great," appears in the *Memoirs* (White, 445–51).

Publication History

"The Triumph of a Modern," a somewhat journalistic satire, first appeared on January 31, 1923, in the *New Republic* (33:245–47). The previous year that liberal magazine of opinion had published Anderson's articles on Gertrude Stein, Paul Rosenfeld, Ring Lardner, Sinclair Lewis, and Alfred Stieglitz, later collected in *Sherwood Anderson's Notebook* (47–55, 242–26). In October of 1923 the story was collected in *Horses and Men* (21–27), which reappeared the following year in London in an edition by Jonathan Cape. Maxwell Geismar included the tale in his 1962 edition of Anderson's stories (53–57).

Relation to Other Works

David Anderson observes that the stories in *Horses and Men* are arranged so that they alternate "between a rural, agricultural setting and an urban, commercial setting; and with the exception of the last story, each one is designed to be mutually complementary" (74). "The Triumph of a Modern," then, is paired with "I'm a Fool"; in both, according to David Anderson, the narrator "distorts reality in order to gain in appearance"—social acceptance for the country youth, an inheritance for the city man—and so sacrifices the possibility of genuine fulfillment (74). The contrast between the two narrators is significant, however. Whereas the boy in "I'm a Fool" repents of his lie and yearns for an authentic life of sincere human relationship, the confidence man in this tale delights in his ability to manipulate and deceive. He is a shape-shifter, having gone "right down through the movements," becoming in turn an impressionist, a cubist, a post–impressionist, and a vorticist as art fashions have changed (*HM* 27). He is all pose. He apes the role of the artist, representing the inauthenticity of his society even as he touches the note that strikes those around him as deeply true and authentic. The dark core of the satire at last inheres in the fact that while the comedy of "I'm a Fool" exposes the dream of romantic youth as impossible, the base duplicity of the more thoroughly alienated modern artist here turns out to be, in one sense, the perfect means of social adjustment.

Dark Laughter (1925) develops some of the same concerns as "The Triumph of a Modern." That novel exclaims against the "debauch of lying" that during the war characterized every level of society—governments, priests, writers, and children (178). In large measure, too, both novel and tale depict the artistic life of the 1920s as falsely sophisticated and caught up in shallow new notions of success.

The dedication of *Horses and Men* and its prefatory tribute to Theodore Dreiser mark not only Anderson's gratitude for Dreiser's healthy frankness about the place of sex in people's lives but also reverence for his good old "thoroughbred" simplicity and honesty.

Critical Studies

The theme of "The Triumph of a Modern" is discussed briefly by two critics. David Anderson states that the narrator's pride in having risen above "puritanical standards" and his insincere use of words are Anderson's means of satirizing the modernist confusion whereby "rebellion against the dead ideas of the past" has become corrupted by "crude and selfish purposes" (73). Similarly, Williams comments that the story is "an exposé of the deluding aspects of modern art, an art whose assumed fidelity to truth is itself a distortion of life" (Williams 234).

The prose style of this first-person narrative, so strikingly different from the colloquial Huck Finn style of "I'm a Fool" (immediately preceding it in *Horses and Men*), has been disparaged by critics. Burbank considers this story representative of Anderson's failure whenever he attempted to use "an urbane tone of the sophisticated narrator" (95). Bridgman, more generously, sees the style as an experiment Anderson conducted in an effort to develop the possibilities of the vernacular beyond the level where Twain had left it—the level Anderson had used in some of his racetrack stories. Brigman holds that, as Anderson "raised the [narrator's] level of maturity," an accretion of "synthetic constructions and qualifications" made the style unwieldy (159–61). Nevertheless, in fairness it should be said that while the style that Anderson readers love best is simple, pungent, and poetic, the prissy, inflated style of "The Triumph of a Modern" is perfectly appropriate for its satirical aim. It effectively characterizes the effete, pretentious narrator, whose sentimental effusions successfully extract an inheritance from a love-starved old woman. Readers have failed to recognize how wittily and well the story thus mocks second-rate "modern" writing and its commercial success.

Works Cited

Anderson, David. 1967. *Sherwood Anderson: An Introduction and Interpretation*. New York: Holt, Rinehart.

Anderson, Sherwood. 1970. *Sherwood Anderson's Notebook*. Mamaroneck, NY: Appel. Originally printed New York: Boni & Liveright, 1926.

———. "Ohio: I'll Say We've Done Well." *Nation* 115 (August 9, 1922): 146–48.

———. 1923. *Horses and Men*. New York: B. W. Huebsch.

———. 1925. *Dark Laughter*. New York: Boni & Liveright; Grosset and Dunlap.

Bell, Clive. 1922. *Since Cézanne*. London: Chatto & Windus.

Bridgman, Richard. 1966. *The Colloquial Style in America*. New York: Oxford University Press.

Burbank, Rex. 1964. *Sherwood Anderson*. New York: Twayne. Rpt. in part in *The Achievement of Sherwood Anderson: Essays in Criticism*. Ed. Ray Lewis White. Chapel Hill: University of North Carolina Press, 1966, 32–43. Rpt. in part in *Sherwood Anderson: Collection of Critical Essays*. Ed. Walter B. Rideout. Englewood Cliffs, NJ: Prentice-Hall, 1974, 70–83.

Geismar, Maxwell, ed. 1962. *Sherwood Anderson: Short Stories*. New York: Hill and Wang.

Hoffman, Frederick J. "The Voices of Sherwood Anderson." *Shenandoah* 13 (1962):5–19. Rpt. in *The Achievement of Sherwood Anderson: Essays in Criticism*. Ed. Ray Lewis White. Chapel Hill: University of North Carolina Press, 1966, 232–44.

Jones, Howard Mumford, and Walter B. Rideout, eds. 1953. *Letters of Sherwood Anderson*. Boston: Little, Brown.

Sutton, William A., ed. 1985. *Letters to Bab: Sherwood Anderson to Marietta D. Finley, 1916–33*. Foreword by Walter B. Rideout. Urbana and Chicago: University of Illinois Press.

Townsend, Kim. 1987. *Sherwood Anderson*. Boston: Houghton Mifflin.

White, Ray Lewis, ed. 1969. *Sherwood Anderson's Memoirs: A Critical Edition*. Chapel Hill: University of North Carolina Press.

Williams, Kenny J. 1988. *A Storyteller and a City: Sherwood Anderson's Chicago*. De Kalb: Northern Illinois University Press.

"Unused"

Circumstances of Composition

Sherwood Anderson spent the early months of 1920 in Alabama, enjoying freedom from the daily grind of his advertising job in the city, painting and writing without unwanted interruptions. During the summer months he returned to his advertising business, sometimes in Chicago and sometimes on the road, visiting clients. In July, though, he joined his wife, Tennessee Mitchell, in Ephraim, Wisconsin, for a vacation. He had been at work on *Many Marriages,* but in Wisconsin he took up an old manuscript and began to turn the story into a novel (Jones-Rideout, *Letters* 60–61). The working title was "Ohio Pagans." On August 6, he said he was rather exhausted from intense labor on this "highly personal tale" about May Edgely, "of Bellevue Ohio," and Tom Edwards, grandson of a Welsh poet; by then he had already written about "laborers, farmers and ice cutters and fishermen of Lake Erie," all of which appear in the finished tale (Sutton, *Letters* 125–26). Settled in a little house in Palos Park, Illinois, in November, he saw the book losing its integration: "can't say yet whether it will be a book of short tales or a long novel. . . . The tales will no doubt win" (Jones-Rideout, *Letters* 65). By January of 1922 he had set the novel aside (Modlin, *Letters* 29). He did not seek to publish any "tales" from this manuscript until, some months later, he gathered the materials for *Horses and Men*. In late April or early May, he reworked material from his novel, changing the setting of May Edgley's story from Bellevue to Bidwell, the scene of *Poor White* (1920). On May 7, he sent the typed manuscript to his agent, Otto Liveright.

During the period of this story's composition, Anderson was deeply disturbed by public responses to his published writings, which too often saw him as "filthy minded" and concluded that his primary subject was sex (White, *Memoirs* 446). Even his friend Van Wyck Brooks, he feared, thought *Winesburg, Ohio* was rather "nasty" (Jones-Rideout, *Letters* 59–60). Though Anderson had been glad enough to participate with Brooks and others in a general movement against puritanical repression, he protested against the narrowness of such judgment. Despite *Many Marriages* (1923), which hails a new dawn of sexual liberation, some of his writing during this period seems aimed to counter the view of his critics (see "Relation to Other Works" below).

One Anderson scholar suggests that Jeanette Franks, a "bold imaginative girl" who tells "wild adventure tales" in Anderson's unfinished "Talbot Whittingham," is an early verson of May Edgley (Rideout 43, 50).

Sources and Influences

For the setting of this story, Anderson drew on memories of Clyde, Ohio, where he had grown up. It was a region mainly of farms (berry farms were plentiful), but also characterized by small businesses, railroad trains, and a respectable ethic of "getting ahead." The Dewdrop, on Sandusky Bay, where the dance in the tale is held, was a real place where Anderson had gone in his youth; he recalled taking an Irish servant girl there, watching "occasional fights," and dancing "the figures for the square dances" called out by a veteran named Rat Gould (White, *Memoirs* 104–105). The land Anderson remembered had its beauties, but life was no idyll amid the harrowing social divisions of the rural community. Anderson's portrayal of that remembered world thus participated in the literary movement termed "the revolt from the village," which attacked the American myth that the town was an innocent "rural paradise" (Hilfer 3).

Publication History

"Unused" was first published in *Horses and Men* in October 1923. That short story collection appeared the following year in a British edition by Jonathan Cape. The individual story, however, has never been republished.

Relation to Other Works

In the paired stories of *Horses and Men,* "Unused" is complemented by "A Chicago Hamlet"; the former has a rural setting and the latter an urban one, but in both "honest rebellion result[s] in tragedy" (D. Anderson 74). As Tom in the latter tale is a modern version of Shakespeare's hero, there is an echo of Ophelia's tragedy in this tale of an Ohio girl who finds reality too much to bear and is drowned among the willows; the final image of "A Chicago Hamlet," of a woman in an "Arctic" country walking along "all broken," also may help to connect the separate stories.

More broadly, May Edgley is typical of many lonely characters in the Anderson canon who spend their lives "desperately yearning" for social relationships; in this regard she particularly resembles the main characters in "Hands" and "Queer" (Wright 58). In a way, she might also be a deeper view of a character like Louise Trunnion, who plays a subordinate role in "Nobody Knows." As her name suggests, May Edgley exists like Louise on the margin of village society, and her fresh desire for life and romance leaves her as vulnerable as spring buds to the rough elements.

Though "Unused" involves an illicit sexual relationship, sex seems far less important here (and indeed throughout *Horses and Men*) than in much of Anderson's earlier work. Whereas many characters in his earlier tales are thwarted by lack of an outlet for their sexual desires, this tale emphasizes the fact that it is not sexual gratification May seeks—she could join her sisters "on the turf" if it were—but a fuller, richer life. "Seeds" makes a similar point, but here it is still plainer. After what proves to be a horrific sexual assault, May's flight from sensuality merely intensifies her quest for beauty and life. The real point is what the story title of an early Anderson tale refers to as "vibrant life." Everywhere that is Anderson's fundamental theme. May Edgley perceives that her sister, like their mother, has let the "thing within herself," the germ of life, be killed; and she refuses to let that happen to her (*HM* 79). That image is reiterated from *Winesburg, Ohio,* where it appears in "The Book of the Grotesque" and in "Mother" (22, 43). In "Unused," as in the opening passages of "The Book of the Grotesque" *Mid-American Chants,* and *A New Testament,* the image is elaborated, metaphorically, as a kind of pregnancy. The heroine conceives an idea and a "new life began to unfold itself": "she could create a life," she learns, in art (*HM* 63).

William V. Miller has observed that May is a "potential artist," one of numerous artist-figures in Anderson's corpus ("Earth-Mothers" 69). Like Tom in "A Chicago Hamlet," she is a compulsive storyteller; similar characters appear in "A Dead Dog," "A Jury Case," and "Why they Got Married" (Miller, "Portraits" 13–14).

Anderson here develops a favorite idea concerning the expressive "truth" of fiction. The stories May produces, while they are lies in one sense, do express the inner truth of her experience: deeply, essentially, it *is* true that a man tried to murder her, though not literally so. May's fictions rebuild "the romance of existence" her neighbors have nearly destroyed, and her vitalizing fantasies differ markedly from the pervasive hypocrisy of a society that condemns vice openly but "in secret looked upon [it] as a mark of virility in young manhood" (*HM* 78, 38). In contrast, "her own lie, told to defeat a universal lie, now seemed a small, a white innocent thing" (*HM* 76). The multiple ironies surrounding these different kinds of lying are important in several of the tales in this collection, especially "I'm a Fool," "The Triumph of a Modern," and "Milk Bottles," as well as in the prefatory tribute, "Dreiser."

The idea that artistic truth develops from creative lying, central as well to the fictionalized autobiography *A Story Teller's Story* (1924), informs the introductory section of "Unused," where a first-person narrator tells how the third-person story that follows originated. The narrator states that seeing May Edgley's body was his "first sight of death" and that the doctor's comments about her life were like "seed" planted in "a boy's awakening imagination" (*HM* 35). By implication, then, the narrator creates the young woman's story out of those fragments in much the same way that she builds her tower of romance. Furthermore, the boy's development of imaginative sympathy with a woman paves the way for the story "The Man Who Became a Woman." Here, also, one can see a phase of the evolution of that great story "Death in the Woods."

Critical Studies

In 1927, Bryllion Fagin, though generally enthusiastic in his praise of Anderson's work, declared that, despite the hints in "Unused" of symbolism showing beauty destroyed by a callous society, the story is "far too long and too ordinary" (90). Most other critics have agreed.

The structure of the story—an introductory section followed by five distinct chapters—betrays its origin in an abortive novel. Formally, the story is "marred by a lack of economy, a deficiency in probability and characterization, and a failure to dramatize some of the important elements upon which the effect depends," according to Austin Wright (229). Its vein of romantic pathos and its "full-fledged plot of misfortune" are uncharacteristic of the 1920s; the shape of the tale is "somewhat comparable to [earlier works such as Stephen] Crane's *Maggie*" (Wright 229, 388, 40). Howe sees even the rhythmic texture of Anderson's prose here disintegrating into "an increasingly stiff cadence and an irritatingly false simplicity" (177).

Almost the sole defender of the story is Welford Taylor, who calls May Edgley "one of Anderson's most completely developed characters" and who points out patterns of recurring images—the stream of life and the tower of fantasy—that represent the heroine's attempts first to connect herself with the communal life and then, when that fails dreadfully, to rise above it in a self-created world (57–61).

The psychological interest of May Edgley's story is explored by Hoffman, who discusses the interplay of "external pressures" and individual weakness in producing the tragedy. The community's harsh judgment of the young woman's sexual mistake leads her to behavior that could be classified by such terms as "repression, projection, 'defense mechanism,' [and] 'substitutive gratification'" (243–44). Wright adds, similarly: "emotional vulnerability" causes the ostracized character to react by further "ostracizing herself" (40).

One fine psychological feature of this tale, however, has not been noted. Anderson demonstrates acute sensitivity to the trauma experienced by a victim of what readers in the 1990s refer to as "acquaintance rape." In Chapter 1 May Edgley is seen from the vantage point of the scandalized town as she goes willingly into the woods with Jerome Hadley for a romantic dalliance. Then, in Chapter 3, the reader sees the same events from May's vantage point: "The actual experience with the man in the forest had been quite brutal. . . . She had consented—yes—but not to what happened" (*HM* 67). Defiled in body and spirit, she tries not to think, and desperately, over and over, scrubs the flesh—neck, breasts, legs—her assailant has touched. Thereafter she perceives other men as just like Jerome, terrible figures wanting to pollute and defeat her, and she becomes altogether afraid of actual life. Thereafter, she channels her energy into the life of fiction.

Works Cited

Anderson, David. 1967. *Sherwood Anderson: An Introduction and Interpretation*. New York: Holt, Rinehart.

Anderson, Sherwood. 1919. *Winesburg, Ohio*. New York: B. W. Huebsch. Rpt. New York: Viking, 1960.

———. 1923. *Horses and Men*. New York: B. W. Huebsch.

———. "A Dead Dog." *Yale Review* 20 (Spring 1931):554–67. Rpt. in *The Sherwood Anderson Reader*. Ed. Paul Rosenfeld. Boston: Houghton Mifflin, 1947, 404–15.

Fagin, N. Bryllion. 1973. *The Phenomenon of Sherwood Anderson: A Study in American Life and Letters*. New York: Russell & Russell. Originally printed Baltimore: Rossi-Bryn, 1927.

Hilfer, Anthony Channel. 1969. *The Revolt from the Village, 1915–1930*. Chapel Hill: University of North Carolina Press.

Hoffman, Frederick J. 1957. *Freudianism and the Literary Mind*. Baton Rouge: Louisiana State University Press. Rev. ed. Rpt. in *Sherwood Anderson: Winesburg, Ohio: Text and Criticism*. Ed. John H. Ferres. New York: Viking, 1966, 309–20. Rpt. in *the Achievement of Sherwood Anderson: Essays in Criticism*. Ed. Ray Lewis White. Chapel Hill: University of North Carolina Press, 1966, 174–92.

Howe, Irving. 1951. *Sherwood Anderson*. New York: William Sloane.

Jones, Howard Mumford, and Walter B. Rideout, eds. 1953. *Letters of Sherwood Anderson*. Boston: Little, Brown.

Miller, William V. 1974. "Earth-Mothers, Succubi, and Other Ectoplasmic Spirits: The Women in Sherwood Anderson's Short Stories." In *Midamerica I*. Ed. David D. Anderson. East Lansing, MI: Midwestern Press, 64–81. Rpt. in *Critical Essays on Sherwood Anderson*. Ed. David D. Anderson. Boston: G.K. Hall, 1981, 196–209.

———. 1976. "Portraits of the Artist: Anderson's Fictional Storytellers." In *Sherwood Anderson: Dimensions of His Literary Art" A Collection of Critical Essays*. Ed. David D. Anderson. East Lansing: Michigan State University Press, 1–23.

Modlin, Charles E., ed. 1984. *Sherwood Anderson: Selected Letters*. Knoxville: University of Tennessee Press.

Rideout, Walter B. 1976. "Talbot Whittingham and Anderson: A Passage to *Winesburg, Ohio*." in *Sherwood Anderson: Dimensions of His Literary Art*. Ed. David D. Anderson. Lansing: Michigan State University Press, 41–60.

Sutton, William A., ed. 1985. *Letters to Bab: Sherwood Anderson to Marietta D. Finley, 1916–33*. Foreword by Walter B. Rideout. Urbana and Chicago: University of Illinois Press.

Taylor, Welford Dunaway. 1977. *Sherwood Anderson*. New York: Frederick Ungar.

White, Ray Lewis, ed. 1969. *Sherwood Anderson's Memoirs: A Critical Edition*. Chapel Hill: University of North Carolina Press.

Wright, Austin McGiffert. 1961. *The American Short Story in the Twenties*. Chicago: University of Chicago Press.

A Chicago Hamlet

Circumstances of Composition

"A Chicago Hamlet" consists of two parts. Each part opens with the narrator's description of weary Chicago evenings he has spent drinking and talking with an advertising colleague named Tom; each part then moves into the narrator's retelling of a story Tom has told concerning his young manhood, which constitutes the central episode. Each part of the story was originally conceived as a separate tale, but Anderson began composing them at about the same time, late in 1916, during the period when he was working for the Critchfield advertising agency in Chicago and writing the stories that would make up *Winesburg, Ohio.*

The main character, Tom, is evidently based on Sherwood Anderson's longtime friend George Daugherty, in 1916 a fellow copywriter at the Critchfield company. It is possible that the first part of "A Chicago Hamlet" did indeed originate as an oral narrative conveyed by Daugherty to Anderson. Daugherty was, like Tom, heavyset, awkward, warm and talkative. Anderson gave Daugherty credit for being one of his best "feeders"—his term for those whose conversation provided material for his fiction (White, *Memoirs* 77, 376–81). The earliest draft of what was to become Part 1 is dated November 24, 1916, and appears in a letter to Marietta D. Finley (Sutton, *Letters* 10–11). The letter concerns an Irishman named "Donaghy," son of an impoverished Ohio farmhand, and it contains in brief the key elements of the finished story—the father and son silently digging potatoes in the cold, the son going to bed without supper and lying feverish and bitter as he listens to his father's zealous prayers, the son's desire to kill his father with the whippletree, and the father's bare feet black with dirt.

In 1918 Anderson mentions his story about a "boy who had been digging potatoes" and who "wanted to kill his father, because he wanted the house to be quiet" (Jones-Rideout, *Letters* 35). Since that motive does not appear in the 1916 sketch, another version of the first part must have been written by that time; but, as there is no evidence that Anderson had shown it to anyone or tried to publish it, he probably did not yet consider it finished. The final version of the story, expanded by the narrator's discussion of the weariness of life in Chicago and of desultory conversations with Tom, was not completed until May 9, 1923, while Anderson was in Reno, Nevada, awaiting his divorce from his second wife. The departures from realism at the end of each section and the experimentation with a looser, more random narrative style are characteristic of Anderson's writing of this period.

A letter to Finley dated December 5, 1916, contains the germ of of Part 2 (Sutton, *Letters* 19–23). Part 2, however, seems to have been developed out of a story told to Anderson not by Daugherty but by an Alfred Tiffany. In the December letter Anderson discusses Tiffany, a (possibly fictitious) friend from Indiana, and includes among other things a short account of Tiffany's adventure one night on a North Dakota farm, where he was surprised by a lonely wife who slipped out of her house, came to the barn, and placed her hand into his—that of a passing traveler. The final version of this part of the story, however, was a product of August 1922, and it was published the following spring. Only later still did Anderson combine the two episodes as related fragments in the life of one Hamlet-like character.

Sources and Influences

Even if Anderson did take the two central episodes of "A Chicago Hamlet" almost directly from oral tales told to him by friends (see "Circumstances of Composition" above), autobiographical influences are also plain. The central character's provincial and impoverished childhood, his fierce resentment of his father, his mother's death and father's remarriage, and his sensitive, vague yearning for a better life are all features Anderson repeatedly recalled from his own youth. Anderson's virtually obsessive rituals of cleansing (White, *Memoirs* 249–50) are reflected in Tom's symbolic self-purification after he sees his father's dirty feet. Tom's curious notion that he held his life in his hand, moreover, appears as Anderson's own in his *Memoirs* (110).

Anderson's idea of depicting a contemporary, common American man in terms that equate him morally with a Shakespearean tragic hero was not a new one. Herman Melville's Ahab is a prominent precursor. A nearer antecedent is Mary E. Wilkins Freeman's story "A Village Lear," in which an old man is rejected by his daughters. Probably, though, Anderson had in mind "The Hamlet of the Shtchigri District," in Ivan Turgenev's *Annals of a Sportsman;* yet, while Anderson held Turgenev's masterpiece in highest esteem, his "A Chicago Hamlet" is not at all an imitation of the Russian author's tale. In Anderson's story, echoes of Shakespeare's *Hamlet* appear in the ineffectual, brooding hero's sense that the time is out of joint, in his intense resentment of his parent's careless, hasty remarriage, in his urge to kill a father-figure who is kneeling at prayer, in his recoil from the murder he contemplates, in his temptation toward (and rejection of) suicide, and in an aversion to women. In Part 2, the silent encounter at the barn perhaps recalls the long gaze Hamlet and the Ophelia exchange in her closet; and the final, mysterious image of a woman "all broken" walking in a "country, where there is summer but for a few weeks each year" may also evoke Shakespeare's tragic heroine (*HM* 182). In Northrop Frye's terms, "Anderson's best writings may be classified as . . . low mimetic tragedy, the modern naturalistic tragedy of ordinary people"; revolting against the cherished American belief in both an innocent "rural paradise" and in a splendidly progressive city, Anderson's work is part of a movement that would restore the tragic dimension to American literature (Hilfer 148–49, 3, 26).

Tom's Oedipal rivalry with his father suggests a Freudian influence on the story, but as Wright says, "there is no indication that Anderson needed Freud to supplement the inspiration received from Shakespeare" (369).

Nietzsche's contempt for religious piety and his advocacy of the superman's will to power is an explicit philosophical feature of the 1916 draft of Part One of "A Chicago Hamlet" (see "Circumstances of Composition" above). In the final version, however, Nietzsche is not mentioned, and the hero's impulse "to crush out impotence and sloth" is checked by a sudden recognition that his own feet, like those of the man he intends to kill, are black with dirt; recalling the New Testament story of the woman who washed Jesus's feet and dried them with her hair, he learns something about keeping sacred his own "clean integrity" (*HM* 151, 152).

Publication History

Part 2 first appeared as a separate story, in March 1923, in the literary magazine *Century* (105:643–56), with the title "Broken." It was then combined with Part 1 (previously unpublished) and added to the collection *Horses and Men,* which came out in October of the same year.

Relation to Other Works

A son's patricidal hatred of his father is a recurrent topic in Anderson's fiction. It is an important feature of *Windy McPherson's Son* (1916), where Sam McPherson half strangles his father and throws him into the road, believing he has actually killed him. In *Kit Brandon* (1936), Gordon Halsey does in fact kill his father. The closest parallel to the situation in "A Chicago Hamlet," though, is in "Godliness," where Jesse Bentley's crude, fanatical zeal causes his grandson to strike him down with a stone—symbolically a slaughter by the youth of old philistine gods and old forces of repression. The vivid image of the farmer kneeling to pray in a fence corner appears in both stories and again in *Hello Towns* (*WO* 72; *HM* 166; *Hello* 323; see also Jones-Rideout, *Letters* 404, and *Mid-American Chants* 58–59).

"Out of Nowhere into Nothing," the title of an Anderson story of 1921, is embedded in the text of "A Chicago Hamlet," where it refers to the dismal streets of Chicago (*HM* 140). In both instances, the phrase conveys a mood of disgust for the ugliness and aimlessness of modern life, a recurrent theme in American literature of the twenties, "from Ring Lardner's Long Island society—where on Saturday night everybody gets dressed up 'like something was going to happen. But it don't'—to Hemingway's celebrated Spanish 'Nada'" (Geismar xvi–xvii).

Townsend detects a broad link between this story and other tales in which Anderson "is exploring the question of manhood"; in particular, the episode involving Tom's encounter with the farmer's wife recalls masculine encounters with "the other woman" in "The Rabbit-pen," "The Door of the Trap," and "The Other Woman" (195).

Miller observes that Tom, who is "orally eloquent" but incapable of rendering his stories effectively in written form, resembles the doctor in "A Moonlight Walk" (16). An interesting inversion of this pattern occurs in a story adjacent to "A Chicago Hamlet" in *Horses and Men*, "The Man Who Became a Woman": there Tom Means is a writer with high aspirations and earnest notions about style, but it is his friend Herman, who is devoid of any such qualities, who brilliantly succeeds in writing a perfect story.

Critical Studies

Soon after the publication of "A Chicago Hamlet," Newton Arvin responded to it appreciatively, commenting on its tragedy: while the hero holds "the cup of his 'identity' as a kind of Grail, . . . there are none but the profane to touch it." All the more poignant, then, is Tom's fleeting experience with the farmer's wife, "which momentarily offered a relationship not hostile to [his] modesty" (46).

In Rex Burbank's opinion "A Chicago Hamlet" is "one of Anderson's most successful Adamic stories." Observing the depicted wretchedness of both country and city, Burbank interprets Tom's ritual cleansing as "Christlike"; the Adamic pattern appears in Tom's "pilgrimage . . . in search of a life" of purity and beauty, "glimpses of beauty and innocence" when Tom spiritually "possesses" the farmer's wife, "the 'fall' (in becoming an advertising writer), resulting from a paucity of alternatives and the enticements of a deceptive, commercial salvation," and a final disillusionment relieved by "hope in an emergent courage and strength gained from isolated glimpses of the 'fine sense of life'" (93–94).

Other critics, though, have given the story little attention, probably because it does not achieve a successful form. Although Burbank approves of the technique Anderson employs—"juxtaposing contrasting images which blend into a single impression in the reader's mind" (93), Williams evaluates that approach as "rambling" and holds that some parts of the story are "inconsequential" (232). Bridgman regrets Anderson's decision to eliminate the first-person narrative voice; presenting the material as a written adaptation of a tale previously told to the writer results in a style that has lost its crispness (162). It is hard to avoid the conclusion that readers would have liked the story better if the two parts had been combined and pared down to their more essential elements. The story includes a meditation on the difficulty of conveying by means of print what gestures and modulations of voice enable an oral storyteller to communicate to a listening audience: "All of our modern fussing with style in writing is an attempt to do the same thing" (*HM* 177). This may be "a cogent observation," as Williams says (233), but it also betrays Anderson's uneasy sense of what is wrong with a sprawling story that fusses too much with peripheral details.

Works Cited

Anderson, Sherwood. 1918. *Mid-American Chants*. New York: John Lane. Rpt. New York: B. W. Huebsch, 1923.

———. 1923. *Horses and Men*. New York: B. W. Huebsch.

———. 1929. *Hello Towns!* New York: Horace Liveright.

Arvin, Newton. 1981. "Mr. Anderson's New Stories." In *Critical Essays on Sherwood Anderson*. Ed. David D. Anderson. Boston: G. K. Hall, 45–47. Rpt. of *The Freeman* 8 (December 5, 1923):307–308.

Bridgeman, Richard. 1966. *The Colloquial Style in America*. New York: Oxford University Press.

Burbank, Rex. 1964. *Sherwood Anderson*. New York: Twayne. Rpt. in part in *The Achievement of Sherwood Anderson: Essays in Criticism*. Ed. Ray Lewis White. Chapel Hill: University of North Carolina Press, 1966, 32–43. Rpt. in part in *Sherwood Anderson: Collection of Critical Essays*. Ed. Walter B. Rideout. Englewood Cliffs, NJ: Prentice-Hall, 1974, 70–83.

Geismar, Maxwell, ed. 1962. *Sherwood Anderson: Short Stories*. New York: Hill and Wang.

Hilfer, Anthony Channel. 1969. *The Revolt from the Village, 1915–1930*. Chapel Hill: University of North Carolina Press.

Jones, Howard Mumford, and Walter B. Rideout, eds. 1953. *Letters of Sherwood Anderson*. Boston: Little, Brown.

Miller, William V. 1976. "Portraits of the Artist: Anderson's Fictional Storytellers." In *Sherwood Anderson: Dimensions of His Literary Art: A Collection of Critical Essays*. Ed. David D. Anderson. East Lansing: Michigan State University Press, 1–23.

Sutton, William A. 1985. *Letters to Bab: Sherwood Anderson to Marietta D. Finley, 1916–33.* Foreword by Walter B. Rideout. Urbana and Chicago: University of Illinois Press.

Townsend, Kim. 1987. *Sherwood Anderson.* Boston: Houghton Mifflin.

White, Ray Lewis, ed. 1969. *Sherwood Anderson's Memoirs: A Critical Edition.* Chapel Hill: University of North Carolina Press.

Williams, Kenny J. 1988. *A Storyteller and a City: Sherwood Anderson's Chicago.* De Kalb: Northern Illinois University Press.

Wright, Austin McGiffert. 1961. *The American Short Story in the Twenties.* Chicago: University of Chicago Press.

The Man Who Became a Woman

Circumstances of Composition

Sherwood Anderson wrote "The Man Who Became a Woman" in the fall of 1922, according to Kim Townsend (195). If Townsend is right, at the time Anderson wrote the story he was living in New York City, having left Chicago and his work with the Critchfield advertising agency. In his biography, however, Walter Rideout will argue that the story was composed in April and May of 1923, while Anderson was in Reno, Nevada, awaiting his divorce from Tennessee Mitchell. Anderson's other two famous racetrack stories had been published in November of 1919 ("I Want to Know Why") and in February of 1922 ("I'm a Fool"). He had received critical recognition for his accomplishments as a writer and had accepted the prestigious *Dial* award in a formal ceremony in January 1922. He had traveled to Europe and in the American South. He had much reason for confidence. The failure of his second marriage, though, undermined his morale. With no very specific goal either as a man or as a writer, Anderson felt a looming uncertainty about his future.

Sources and Influences

Autobiographical influences played an important role in shaping the central character of "The Man Who Became a Woman."

> The parallels are multiple: both Anderson and Herman were born in small towns; both had fathers who were independent small time businessmen; both first sought to make it on their own in Chicago. Herman was nineteen at the time that his father died and his mother deserted him; Anderson was nineteen when his mother died and his father deserted him. Both Anderson and Herman suffered hysterical episodes. Both found in writing a release for unbearable psychological tensions. (Malmsheimer 23–24)

The setting, moreover, is drawn from the author's memories of boyhood days when he fed his ardent imagination with the racehorses and drivers at the Clyde Race Track and when he worked as a groom at a livery stable. (The stench of the Chicago stockyards, too, though, must in some way have contributed to the tale's macabre slaughterhouse behind the racetrack.) Young Anderson had endured the humiliation of having the epithet "livery stable chambermaid" hurled at him (White, *Memoirs* 121). It was all part of his education. The older, rougher companions with whom he worked at the stables sometimes played crude jokes on him, and he was upon at least one occasion "sickened" by an episode of drunken lovemaking when one of them brought a prostitute back to the room where Anderson was sleeping; from these experiences he grew convinced that horses "are infinitely finer and better than many men a boy would have to deal with in living his life" (White, *Memoirs* 111–14).

The voice of Mark Twain's Huckleberry Finn is audible in all three of Anderson's first-person narratives set at the racetrack. Colloquial diction verging on slang, the innocent's revulsion at the cruel ways of men, and responsive openness to life's wonder and mystery are the qualities Anderson recognized as central to Twain's genius in prose, and in this story he achieves his own finest application of that style.

The sexual psychology in this story reflects the influence of Freud, and probably of Havelock Ellis as well (Gregory, "On Sherwood" 19). Perceptible also is the influence of George Borrow, one of Anderson's favorite authors, and his tales of gypsy life (Gregory, "Introduction" 25).

The final scenes, where Herman runs naked through the night, owe something to Thomas Carlyle's *Sartor Resartus*. Anderson had read Carlyle's book and taken to heart an idea about the importance of stripping off layers of lying convention and facing the naked fact of oneself (White, *Memoirs* 250).

Publication History

"The Man Who Became a Woman" was first published in the short story collection *Horses and Men* (1923). Modern reprintings are included in volumes of selected Anderson tales edited by Maxwell Geismar (58–85), Frank Gado (148–86), and Charles Modlin (60–92).

Relation to Other Works

"The Man Who Became a Woman" is most obviously linked with Anderson's two other stories with a racetrack setting, "I Want to Know Why" and "I'm a Fool." In addition, all three stories employ a first-person narrative voice and treat experiences of a male adolescent. They share "the quality of an impotent and bitter introspection and of a trapped and inverted virility," but this story, the third, is "the most bitter" of the three (Geismar, *Last* 246–47). It is also the best, partly because of the plainly retrospective viewpoint: "the addition of the older Dudley's adult sentience adds resonance and perceptiveness to the story" (Miller 12). In all three stories, Anderson's speaker uses the vernacular that Twain perfected in *Huckleberry Finn,* but here he manages the difficult feat of bringing an adult perspective to bear on the narrated events while retaining "a childlike clarity" (Bridgman 160–61).

"Horses and horses racing (before the day of the syndicates and the mobs) were still to Anderson the symbol of the pagan and plenary state, the natural life which industrialization, science and finance capitalism had all conspired to deform or destroy" (Geismar, "Introduction" [*SA: Short Stories*] xvii). Even more than the two earlier racetrack stories, "The Man Who Became a Woman" manifests Anderson's distress with the callousness and confusion of American society. As Spencer has argued, it "reflects something of the psychic effect on Anderson of the destruction of his mythopoeic America," the essentially Jeffersonian pastoral agrarian ideal of his early years; reckoning with forces that seemed to be undermining a proud, pure natural nobility in which he still believed, Anderson looked for sources of renewal—in "an elemental spontaneity and a vital sense of life" that he thought he saw in African-Americans, and increasingly in "a redemptive feminine principle which [he], like Henry Adams, found in his later years the surest counteragent to the distintegrating power of the machine" (14–15).

Though he was not blind to the injustice of racial discrimination, Anderson romanticized Negroes as sweeter than white men, as possessing more inherent power of spirit. His admiration was not unsullied by condescension: "Horses and Negroes seem to be the two things in America that give me the most ascetic [*sic*] pleasure. A flat-nosed, tobacco-chewing man is leading a thoroughbred. In the horse what a noble bearing. . . . We pay something . . . for our silly minds, don't we, always wanting to be great, not daring to just run the cards out and let her ride? . . . What the Negro has to give is rather noble, but is physical, like the running horse or dog. I'm pretty sure of that" (Jones-Rideout, *Letters* 101). Horses as well, he confided to fellow horse lover Alfred Stieglitz, "[w]ill not suffice. The horse is the horse and we are men"; he longed for more—for comradeship with men and for "man and woman love that is also comradeship" (Jones-Rideout, *Letters* 106, 108). Works other than the racetrack stories in which Anderson's attitudes toward black Americans are prominent include "Out of Nowhere Into Nothing" and *Dark Laughter* (1925).

A female perspective is important in many of Anderson's works, from *Winesburg, Ohio* (1919) on. In *Perhaps Women* (1931) he would advance the thesis that, while technology drains men of their manhood, women have a power that resists that dehumanizing force and offers hope for both sexes. Peculiar as that thesis appears in the later work, a subtler version of the theme is effective in "The Man Who Became a Woman," where Herman gazes at coke ovens that threaten like "some man-eating giant" and shivers at "the kind of hell-holes men are satisfied to go on living in": "Come right down to it," he thinks, "I suppose women aren't so much to blame as men. They aren't running the show" (*HM* 206). Herman's alienation from the ugliness and brutality of most men around him and the near-rape that leads him to identify with female fear and helplessness initiate him into a manhood more genuine than the facade of tough self-importance or violence that so often passes for manliness.

This story thus is part of an exploration of male–female relations running through the stories of *Horses and Men*. In the opening tale, "I'm a Fool," a very young man projects an idealized woman, just as Herman at first does, and falls into an absurd, swaggering imitation of manliness. In "The Triumph of a Modern," a Prufrockish man who is afraid of "women in the flesh" uses his understanding of female psychology to manipulate an old woman to his financial advantage. In "Unused" the talk of a sage old doctor stirs "a boy's awakening imagination" to a remarkable understanding of how a woman feels (*HM* 35). In "A Chicago Hamlet" a male character is able to "possess" a woman not bodily, but by gentleness and the force of his intuitive understanding. In "The Man Who Became a Woman" Herman grows from youthful idealization of women into experiences that teach him how it feels to be a woman in a man's world—scared, lonely, powerless, endangered. The stories in the collection do not present an entirely coherent sequence, though: "The Man's Story" probes an obverse situation, its central character's brutal blindness to a woman; "An Ohio Pagan" details a boy's half-erotic, half-religious longing for a woman; and "Milk Bottles" is not interested in the subject at all.

The subject of latent homosexual impulses, significant in "The Man Who Became a Woman," receives fuller attention in "Hands" and *A Story Teller's Story* (1924). More important parallels to this story, perhaps, appear in the recoil of female characters from lesbian overtures in *Poor White* (1920) and *Dark Laughter* (1925).

Critical Studies

Critics have nearly always admired "The Man Who Became a Woman" as true and powerful fiction of the deepest kind. Fagin early hailed it as "the most daring study of adolescent manifestation of the sex instinct in the short story form" (91). Schevill deemed it "a triumph of art in its most difficult and most challenging aspects where the more one reads the more significant do the layers of meaning become" (188). Howe praised it as the "great" story of "a writer in complete imaginative control of his materials," containing "the most dramatic incident in all of Anderson's fiction" (160).

Howe's interpretation, psychological in approach, emphasizes the sexually inexperienced narrator's sensitivity to horses and men and his consequent inability to progress "toward full adult sexuality" (161). The scene where Herman falls into the horse's skeleton Howe interprets as "a brilliant bit of gothic symbolism" representing both "the death of his adolescent love" and "a forbidden homosexual fantasy" (163). Howe suggests that the attack made upon Herman by two black men might be not an actual occurrence but a hysterical projection of homosexual terror, and he attributes the adult narrator's confessional urge to enduring anxiety about his sexual identity (163–64; similarly, Wright 138–39, 214, and Gado 17). Nevertheless, Howe wisely grants the story a broader significance: "Herman Dudley may even be, as he insists, a normal man, but to grant this somewhat desperate claim is to record the precariousness and internal ambiguity of adult normality itself" (164).

Schevill, rather differently, argues that the tale concerns not homosexuality "but the feminine side of a man's nature" (188). Schevill's main interest is sociological—the story's critique of American society and its distorted version of masculine power: "Why is man in this country often so blindly aggressive? Is it because he refuses to value or understand the feminine side of his life?" (189; similarly, Geismar, "Introduction" [*SA: Short Stories*] xviii). Schevill points to Herman's dream of an ideal woman as a projection of "his anima, his sense of the feminine part of his own soul"; in opposition to that ideal stands the brutality of the men in the bar, though even there Schevill observes—beneath the violence—wistful tenderness for the child (188–89; similarly, D. Anderson 76–77).

Babb, also taking issue with Howe's study, asserts that the narrator does grow into fully mature manhood and that the story's primary aim is to delineate his "progress from a conventional existence through a series of fantastic episodes in which he reveals an integrity of being—a responsiveness to every kind of experience" (434). Herman's assimilation of these complex experiences enables him to emerge into adulthood, finally secure enough to admit "his sense of community with Negroes" and his feelings of love for

Tom Means. Burbank, similarly, stresses the story's comic, positive movement and agrees that Herman achieves heterosexual maturity. The fall into the horse's skeleton, Burbank states, symbolizes the death of the boy's innocence, and his emergence shows him "born again," leaving behind both his impossible ideals and "a sordid reality" (105). Burbank offers a perceptive analysis of the role of Tom Means in enabling Herman to "hold on to his comfortable pre-adolescent hero worship"; when Tom leaves, Herman can no longer delay the "irresistible assertion of the dark blood" that thrusts him at last into manhood (104–105). In the same vein, but with a slightly different emphasis, Townsend reads the ending as the successful resolution of an issue with which Anderson, like his character, had long wrestled (195). Herman overcomes his previous stereotypical categorization of women as either whores or virgins, transcends the limits set by "a homophobic culture," and earns manhood by learning "to feel how women really feel" (196–97). The tentative, gentle voice" that speaks of crafting his narrative as "tending to his knitting" is for Townsend further evidence of enlarged, mature manhood (196).

Malmsheimer's psychosocial interpretation is far more negative in emphasis. This analysis is excessive in diagnosing Herman's moony adolescent disturbances as "acute mental illness" symptomized by hallucinations, "hypnoid states, hysterical episodes," and "paranoia," manifesting Oedipal complications and "regressive tendencies" (18–19). But it offers convincing "evidence that homosexuality is not central to" Herman's condition: his sexual fantasies are exclusively about women, and he runs away from the threatened homosexual assault (20–21). The source of his difficulty, Malmsheimer argues, is social: the dreary money-saving friends of his father, the reckless adventurers at the racetrack, and the brutal miners provide the boy no acceptable "male role model," and "the authoritarian father principle" of American culture forces him at last into deathlike submission to a "perniciously" stereotypical "maleness as socially defined" (22–24). Malmsheimer overlooks textual implications of rebirth, focusing instead on the "conformity symbolically represented by [Herman's] sleeping . . . with a dozen (other) sheep" (23).

Gado argues that the story manifests "the peculiar Andersonian condition of antiguity" (rather than ambiguity) in which the narration "unresolves" what it "seems to have resolved" (15). Gado draws attention to significant names that highlight the narrator's sexual ambivalence—Pick-it-boy (the gelding), O My Man (the stallion), and "her," "man," and "dud," components of the narrator's name; he also suggests that the climactic scene represents not only a "fearful passage *in* life" but also "fear about the passage *from* life," so that the ultimate "terror generated by the tale" is anxiety about death (15, 17).

The construction of the story has received some critical attention. Babb comments that the technique (like that of Joseph Conrad's *Heart of Darkness*) is perfectly suited to the drama of "a man engaged in recreating and coming to terms with the critical events of his past": proceeding by "sensitive recording rather than rational analysis," the narrative moves in "a rhythmic ebb and flow as [Herman] repeatedly backs away from and is drawn into telling us about the crucial night" (435). Other formalist commentators, for the most part, concur. Only one suggests that the story might be "a little overplayed, or even a little hammy" (Geismar, "Introduction" xviii), and it can be argued that those qualities, because they serve to personalize the narrator, strengthen rather than weaken the effectiveness of the story. The story has few dramatic scenes and little dialogue but instead is "almost entirely narrated," for its real object is to present a character's thoughts (in his own idiom, it might be added) in such a way that they indicate deeper emotions, which readers must infer for themselves (Wright 292–93, 349–50, 407). Wright classifies the tale as belonging to a category he terms "caustic comedy" (388). As the present discussion shows, astute readers have disagreed about which elements—the caustic or the comic—predominate.

Works Cited

Anderson, David. 1967. *Sherwood Anderson: An Introduction and Interpretation*. New York: Holt, Rinehart.

Anderson, Sherwood. 1923. *Horses and Men*. New York: B. W. Huebsch.

Babb, Howard S. "A Reading of Sherwood Anderson's 'The Man Who Became a Woman.'" *PMLA* 80 (1965):432–35.

Bridgman, Richard. 1966. *The Colloquial Style in America*. New York: Oxford University Press.

Burbank, Rex. 1964. *Sherwood Anderson*. New York: Twayne. Rpt. in part in *The Achievement of Sherwood Anderson: Essays in Criticism*. Ed. Ray Lewis White. Chapel Hill: University of North Carolina Press, 1966, 32–43. Rpt. in part in *Sherwood Anderson: Collection of Critical Essays*. Ed. Walter B. Rideout. Englewood Cliffs, NJ: Prentice-Hall, 1974, 70–83.

Fagin, N. Bryllion. 1973. *The Phenomenon of Sherwood Anderson: A Study in American Life and Letters*. New York: Russell & Russell. Originally printed Baltimore: Rossi-Bryn, 1927.

Gado, Frank, ed. 1983. *The Teller's Tales*. Signature Series. Schenectady, NY: Union College Press.

Geismar, Maxwell, ed. 1962. *Sherwood Anderson: Short Stories*. New York: Hill and Wang.

———. 1947. "Sherwood Anderson: Last of the Townsmen." *The Last of the*

Provincials: The American Novel, 1915–1925. Boston: Houghton Mifflin, 223–84. Rpt. in part in *Sherwood Anderson: Winesburg, Ohio: Text and Criticism*. Ed. John H. Ferres. New York: Viking, 1966, 377–82.

Gregory, Horace. 1949. "Introduction." *The Portable Sherwood Anderson*. Ed. Horace Gregory. New York: Viking, 1–31.

———. 1968. "On Sherwood Anderson." In *Talks with Authors*. Ed. Charles F. Madden. Carbondale: Southern Illinois University Press, 12–22.

Howe, Irving. *Sherwood Anderson*. New York: William Sloane, 1951.

Jones, Howard Mumford, and Walter B. Rideout, eds. 1953. *Letters of Sherwood Anderson*. Boston: Little, Brown.

Malmsheimer, Lonna M. "Sexual Metaphor and Social Criticism in Anderson's *The Man Who Became a Woman*." *Studies in America Fiction* 7 (1979):16–26.

Miller, William V. 1976. "Portraits of the Artist: Anderson's Fictional Storytellers." In *Sherwood Anderson: Dimensions of His Literary Art: A Collection of Critical Essays*. Ed. David D. Anderson. East Lansing: Michigan State University Press, 1–23.

Modlin, Charles E., ed. 1992. *Certain Things Last: The Selected Stories of Sherwood Anderson*. New York: Four Walls Eight Windows.

Schevill, James. 1951. *Sherwood Anderson: His Life and Work*. Denver: University of Denver Press.

Spencer, Benjamin I. "Sherwood Anderson: American Mythopoeist." *American Literature* 41 (1969):1–18.

Townsend, Kim. 1987. *Sherwood Anderson*. Boston: Houghton Mifflin.

White, Ray Lewis, ed. 1969. *Sherwood Anderson's Memoirs: A Critical Edition*. Chapel Hill: University of North Carolina Press.

Wright, Austin McGiffert. 1961. *The American Short Story in the Twenties*. Chicago: University of Chicago Press.

Milk Bottles

Circumstances of Composition

"Milk Bottles" can be dated with considerable accuracy. On November 20, 1920, Sherwood Anderson wrote to Marietta Finley, who had just visited him in Chicago to attend with him an exhibit of his paintings: "I came home to my house here and have worked steadily since. Wrote and typed the story of the half-filled milk bottles and the advertising writer who wanted to write glowingly of his city Chicago" (Sutton, *Letters* 137–38). Anderson at that time lived in Palos Park, a town about twenty-five miles outside of Chicago. His house was a small one, at the edge of the forest. His second wife, Tennessee Mitchell, spent part of each week there, but he had time alone to write. He had long been weary of his job in the city, writing advertisements for the Critchfield firm, and he dreamed of being financially able to devote himself entirely to his art. His novel *Poor White* had just been published, and he had read H. L. Mencken's favorable review in the December issue of *Smart Set.* He had also received an "enthusiastic letter" from Sinclair Lewis.

In another letter written about this time, Anderson mentions a southern schoolteacher who had complained about the realism of something Anderson had written. The teacher's attitude seemed to him to typify "the American philosophy, 'When a thing is ugly we must close our eyes to it'"; that kind of deliberate blindness, Anderson concluded, accounted for the failure of the teacher's creative work (Sutton, *Letters* 138). "Milk Bottles" dramatizes the point, arguing for literary honesty.

Sources and Influences

Van Wyck Brooks speculated that the character "Ed" might have been based on "Anderson himself at a time when" he was mulling over an advertisement for condensed milk (406). Like Anderson, Ed is torn between his job, which demands that he write clever, romanticized ads to promote commercial products, and his desire to write an enduring literary masterpiece. Ironically, Ed produces work of genuine value only when his anger forces him to address reality, and even then he cannot recognize the value of what he has written.

Publication History

"Milk Bottles" was originally published under the title "Why There Must Be a Midwestern Literature" in the March 1921 issue of *Vanity Fair* (16:23–24). The sophisticated *Vanity Fair* did not ordinarily accept fiction; the essayistic title and the addition of subheadings helped fit the tale to the magazine's format. With only minor changes, the article became "Milk Bottles" in the short story collection *Horses and Men* (1923). In 1929 Anderson reprinted it in his Virginia newspaper *The Smyth County News* (January 10:2, 7). Subsequently, Rosenfeld included it in *The Sherwood Anderson Reader,* and Geismar, Gado, and Modlin have reissued it in their more recent editions of Anderson's tales.

Relation to Other Works

The narrator of this thesis-ridden story contrasts writing he considers valid and writing he considers false; the story thus reiterates the idea of the dedicatory preface to *Horses and Men,* entitled "Dreiser," in which Anderson praises the great naturalist for "tramping through the wilderness of lies, making a path" for all the "prose writers of America." Throughout the short story collection, a battle is waged between lies and authentic life. Repeatedly, characters are seduced into lying, seduce others by means of lies, and are trapped in nets of social hypocrisy. Dreiser's simple honesty provides the standard by which they are to be judged. Occasionally, a character attains a glimpse of real "beauty breaking through the husks of life" (xi).

Ed, in this story, has had such a glimpse but has failed to recognize it. Ed is one of several figures in Anderson's works who possess artistic talents but "have sullied their talents by selling out to business"; other examples appear in the uncollected tales "Off-Balance" and "I Get So I Can't Go On" (Miller, "Portraits" 19).

David Anderson suggests that the stories of *Horses and Men* are arranged in pairs, alternating between "a rural, agricultural setting and an urban, commercial setting" (74). In that arrangement, "The Man Who Became a Woman" is paired with "Milk Bottles," and the abandoned slaughterhouse of the former stands as a rural analog to the rubbish heaps of the city in the latter (75).

The original version of this story, published in *Vanity Fair,* uses the brand name "Bottsford's" for the condensed milk in Ed's advertisement instead of the later name "Whitney-Wells." "Bottsford" is the surname of a farmer/thresherman with whom Tom Edwards works in "Ohio Pagans." The coincidence suggests either that "Milk Bottles" actually began as part of the projected novel with the working title "Ohio Pagans" from which both stories and "Unused" were finally extracted, or that Anderson, as he envisioned the process by which his character's anxious imagination was drawn toward images of a pure, healthy, pastoral life, could not resist using a name he himself associated with the bucolic scenery in his unpublished manuscript. Anderson evidently changed the brand name later to prevent readers from connecting the two stories. Yet the broad point remains: as the youth in the country longs for the glories of the city, the city man longs for green hills and fresh air.

Critical Studies

Despite its several reprintings, "Milk Bottles" has elicited only brief critical comment. Geismar aptly observes that the story expresses Anderson's "brooding concern" about the "degraded kind of urban existence" that was increasingly common in America ("Introduction" [*Short Stories*] xv). Gado holds that the story is "an artfully complex performance" in which the central symbol—half-filled bottles of milk—acquires multiple meaning and leads to a significant paradox: "the truth about the city dwellers, which is foul, is beautiful; the lie, which is beautiful, is foul" (12–13). Williams points out the "framework device" that Anderson employs in the story and the crucial juxtaposition of the real city with the false, idealized city which Ed cannot distinguish from the real one (229–30). David Anderson discerns the tragedy of "lost humanity" in the "hopelessness" of the lives in the story. But the tale is too sketchy to convey tragedy, and its tone is wrong. The story touches on important topics: urban frustration, social inequity, linguistic perversion, and aesthetic deformity. But Burbank's evaluation is just: the "symbolism overpowers the flimsy factual structure of the story," the narrator too "clearly speaks for Anderson," and "his parody of the language of Babbittry"—"You've knocked out a regular soc-dolager of a masterpiece here"— is tiresomely smug (94, quoting *HM* 235).

Works Cited

Anderson, David. 1967. *Sherwood Anderson: An Introduction and Interpretation*. New York: Holt, Rinehart.

Anderson, Sherwood. 1923. *Horses and Men*. New York: B. W. Huebsch.

Brooks, Van Wyck. 1955. *The Confident Years: 1885–1915*. New York: Dutton.

Burbank, Rex. 1964. *Sherwood Anderson*. New York: Twayne. Rpt. in part in *The Achievement of Sherwood Anderson: Essays in Criticism*. Ed. Ray Lewis White. Chapel Hill: University of North Carolina Press, 1966,

32–43. Rpt. in part in *Sherwood Anderson: Collection of Critical Essays*. Ed. Walter B. Rideout. Englewood Cliffs, NJ: Prentice-Hall, 1974, 70–83.

Gado, Frank, ed. 1983. *The Teller's Tales*. Signature Series. Schenectady, NY: Union College Press.

Geismar, Maxwell, ed. 1962. *Sherwood Anderson: Short Stories*. New York: Hill and Wang.

Miller, William V. "Portraits of the Artist: Anderson's Fictional Storytellers." In *Sherwood Anderson: Dimensions of His Literary Art: A Collection of Critical Essays*. Ed. David D. Anderson. East Lansing: Michigan State University Press, 1976, 1–23.

Modlin, Charles E., ed. 1992. *Certain Things Last: The Selected Short Stories of Sherwood Anderson*. New York: Four Walls Eight Windows.

Rosenfeld, Paul, ed. 1947. *The Sherwood Anderson Reader*. Boston: Houghton Mifflin.

Sutton, William A., ed. 1985. *Letters to Bab: Sherwood Anderson to Marietta D. Finley, 1916–33*. Foreword by Walter B. Rideout. Urbana and Chicago: University of Illinois Press.

Williams, Kenny J. 1988. *A Storyteller and a City: Sherwood Anderson's Chicago*. De Kalb: Northern Illinois University Press.

The Sad Horn Blowers

Circumstances of Composition

During the period following his greatest success at the outset of the 1920s, Anderson's new hopes led him at last to resign from his job in advertising, but the step was accompanied by increasingly serious uncertainties: "even as the curve of his public success rose, another and more intimate curve began to slope toward crisis" (Howe 198). He was old enough to be slightly embarrassed about receiving the *Dial* prize for young writers, and he was troubled by insecurity about what he had achieved and about where he was going as an artist. Anderson describes his feelings during the months of 1922 and 1923 when he lived and wrote in Ben Huebsch's apartment in New York City: "My own hands had not served me very well. Nothing they had done with words had satisfied me. There was not finesse enough in my fingers. . . . How much was I to blame for that? How much could fairly be blamed to the civilization in which I had lived?" (*Story Teller's* 374–75). As if to compensate for his sense of inadequacy, he wrote at a white heat. In that August of 1922, he wrote not only "The Sad Horn Blowers" but also "The Triumph of a Modern" and Part 2 of "A Chicago Hamlet."

Writing about "The Sad Horn Blowers" a year or two after its composition, Anderson agreed that it is rather "fragmentary." He had considered bringing it to a more definite point of completion, he said, but had decided instead "to touch something off and then let it complete itself in the reader" as in the "old Chinese . . . thing called 'the short stop'"; he admitted that this explanation might be just "an excuse" (Curry, 277–78).

Sources and Influences

Autobiographical sources dominate this story about growing up. Will Appleton is based on the young Sherwood Anderson, and Tom Appleton is plainly modeled on his father, Irwin Anderson. Mother, brother, and sister likewise reflect members of the writer's family. In Camden, Ohio, Irwin Anderson "played the alto horn in the village band," and after the family moved to Clyde, Ohio, he became a house painter and "played the cornet in "Miller's City Band" (Schevill 5, 9). In his *Memoirs,* Sherwood Anderson would recall his father as lively and funny, a great talker popular among the people of their town, and he describes him riding at the front of parades; at the same time, however, he remembers himself shedding bitter tears over his father's foolish behavior and desperately wishing for a father who was "proud silent dignified" (White, *Memoirs* 78–79). According to Sutton's biography, so intense was the adult writer's memory of youthful antipathy to his father that in writing "The Sad Horn Blowers" he twisted the facts of a real accident: in actuality Irwin Anderson had severely scalded himself by pure misfortune when he stepped into an open ditch on his way to a surprise party, but in the story Tom Appleton is scalded as "a result of his own officiousness and clumsiness" (515–16).

Like Will Appleton, Anderson had worked as a laborer in several factories when he was a young man, and after the death of his mother he had lived in roominghouses in various towns and cities. (See also Sutton 566.)

Haines remarks another specific biographical episode that may have entered the tale. In a letter to Alfred Stieglitz, Anderson tells of having burst into tears as he rode alone on a train; he had "had to turn [his] face away from the people in the car for shame of my apparent[ly] causeless grief" (Jones-Rideout, *Letters* 99). As Haines comments, this is "remarkably similar in setting and circumstance" to one of the story's scenes; interestingly enough, though, Anderson makes quite different use of the episode in his letter and in the story (17–18).

Miller states that Mark Twain's influence is discernible in the story (11).

Publication History

"The Sad Horn Blowers" was first published in the February 1923 issue of *Harper's Magazine* (146:273–89). It was the first of Anderson's works to appear there since 1914, when that magazine had published his very first story, "The Rabbit-pen." In October of the same year Anderson incorporated "The Sad Horn Blowers" into the collection *Horses and Men* (245–83). After his death, the story was included in Paul Rosenfeld's *The Sherwood Anderson Reader* (102–127) and, still later, in Maxwell Geismar's edition of Anderson's tales (93–118).

Relation to Other Works

Bidwell, Ohio, the setting of this tale, is also the setting of *Poor White* (1920), "The Egg," "Unused," and "An Ohio Pagan." The characters and situation, as in many of Anderson's other works, are drawn from recollections of his youth. In particular, the feeling of dislocation experienced by the adolescent boy links this story to other tales such as "I'm a Fool," "I Want to Know Why," "The Man Who Became a Woman," and "An Ohio Pagan." Also, George Willard of *Winesburg, Ohio* resembles Will Appleton, and the death of the mother is a "watershed event" for both (Miller 11).

More important, this story illumines "Anderson's changing view of the father–son relationship," for it shows a son coming to identify with the father's frustrations (D. Anderson 77–78). In *Windy McPherson's Son* (1916) "the father figure disgraces himself in his inept attempt to blow reveille," whereas the horn-blowing scene at the end of this story evidences a more compassionate view "toward the human paradox of infinite aspiration and limited ability" (Haines 20n). The semiautobiographical *A Story Teller's Story* (1924) offers a still milder, mellower portrait of the writer's father, "a house-and-barn painter" with a "boyish love" for supervising his sons as they worked; wryly, but with discernible approval, Anderson refers to his father as a romantic dreamer "whose blood and temperament I am to carry to the end of my days" (3–5, 25).

The romantic temperament commonly finds its longings best expressed in music. Memories of his father's horn playing are doubtless connected with a passage describing another sad horn blower who dreams of making the cornet "a classical instrument" in Anderson's *Paris Notebook* (Fanning 37–39). The essential goodness of the soul's impulse toward beauty is never in doubt, but the grotesque impossibility of fulfilling such quixotic dreams casts a mocking shadow. The irony of "The Sad Horn Blowers" is especially self-reflexive as it alludes to "The Man with the Trumpet," the messianic prose poem closing *The Triumph of the Egg,* where Anderson speaks plainly in the authorial first person of his hope that his written words would be a trumpet call to arouse people "in streets and cities" to the knowledge that "life was sweet, that men might live" (*TE* 268–69). It was his message to the world, his fondest dream. Absurdly fond and foolish, he knew. Who had listened or understood? Later, with who knows what bemusement, Anderson would write an editorial in his Smyth County newspaper urging support of the Marion Band: "A good band is the best investment a town can make" (*Hello Towns!* 37–39).

In its account of Will Appleton's factory work—drilling holes in "short, meaningless pieces of iron," "The Sad Horn Blowers" develops an idea from *Poor White,* that industrialism brings endless dull routine for the worker (Williams 231–32). The theme is coupled with a notion Anderson would later amplify in *Perhaps Women* (1931) and elsewhere, that a worker deprived of pride of craftsmanship is deprived of his manhood. Will Appleton is an unheroic representative of an unheroic age in which manhood is severely constrained by the forces of mechanization and dislocating urbanization. The search for manhood is a prominent motif in the stories of *Horses and Men,* notably "I'm a Fool," "The Man Who Became a Woman," "The Man's Story," and "An Ohio Pagan." Shamefully cowed by his wife, the old man in "The Sad Horn Blowers" resembles the central character of the late uncollected tale "His Chest of Drawers."

Critical Studies

"The Sad Horn Blowers" traces Will Appleton's experience as he is uprooted from home and family by the death of his mother and the loss of his father's business after a debilitating injury. When Will goes off to take a job as a factory hand in Erie, Pennsylvania, his eagerness to establish his independence is shaken by his father's and older sister's all-too-evident willingness to let him go off on his own. He allows himself to become attached to a pathetic old man whom he meets on the train after the man ironically misunderstands the youth's "tears of self-pity as those of sympathy" (Haines 17). The old man, like Will's father, is childishly lacking in dignity, and he too is a bad cornet player. Throughout the story Will suffers under "the realization that he is no longer a boy but not yet quite a man"; at last his suffering is eased "when he becomes aware that something of the child remains in all men" (Voss 195). Way praises the story for "remarkably sure control" in conveying the son's "elusive" and "contradictory feelings"—"affection" and "comradeship" on the one hand, humiliation and contempt on the other, and finally, sympathetic acceptance (125–26). "The muted atmosphere, the sad irony, the pessimistic self-knowledge, the unheroic hero," Way states, are distinctively, admirably Andersonian.

Most commentary on the story, however, is biographical in nature (see "Sources and Influences" and "Relation to Other Works" above). In the only extended commentary, Lucow argues that the story depicts the dilemma confronting modern man in "a world in which mature identity paradoxically means absorption into a homogeneous mass" (293). Lucow remarks the "tragic-comic" tone and finds the half-sheared dog in the young man's meditation to be a fitting emblem. After examining Anderson's selection of words in a passage that emphasizes the monotonous sameness of young workingmen's lives, Lucow states that Will Appleton "is attracted by the old man's immaturity" because they both are unwilling to accept the social definition of growing up: their hornblowing is thus both an admission of "defeat" and "an act of defiance."

Works Cited

Anderson, David. 1967. *Sherwood Anderson: An Introduction and Interpretation*. New York: Holt, Rinehart.

Anderson, Sherwood. 1923. *Horses and Men*. New York: B. W. Huebsch.

———. 1924. *A Story Teller's Story*. New York: B. W. Huebsch. Rpt. in *A Story Teller's Story: A Critical Text*. Ed. Ray Lewis White. Cleveland: Press of Case Western Reserve University, 1968. Rpt. New York: Viking, 1969.

———. 1929. *Hello Towns!* New York: Liveright.

———. "His Chest of Drawers." *Household Magazine* 39 (August 1939):4–5. Rpt. in *The Sherwood Anderson Reader*. Ed. Paul Rosenfeld. Boston: Houghton Mifflin, 1947, 831–35. Rpt. in *Sherwood Anderson: Short Stories*. Ed. Maxwell Geismar. 1962, 277–81. Rpt. in *Sherwood Anderson's Memoirs: A Critical Edition*. Ed. Ray Lewis White. Chapel Hill: University of North Carolina Press, 1969, 218–22.

Curry, Martha Mulroy. 1975. *The "Writer's Book" by Sherwood Anderson: A Critical Edition*. Metuchen, NJ: Scarecrow Press.

Fanning, Michael, ed. 1976. *France and Sherwood Anderson: Paris Notebook, 1921*. Baton Rouge: Louisiana State University Press.

Geismar, Maxwell. 1962. "Introduction." *Sherwood Anderson: Short Stories*. New York: Hill and Wang, ix–xxii.

———, ed. 1962. *Sherwood Anderson: Short Stories*. New York: Hill and Wang.

Haines, Robert E. Ned. "Turning Point: Sherwood Anderson Encounters Alfred Stieglitz." *Markham Review* 6 (1976):16–20.

Howe, Irving. 1951. *Sherwood Anderson*. New York: William Sloane.

Jones, Howard Mumford, and Walter B. Rideout, eds. 1953. *Letters of Sherwood Anderson*. Boston: Little, Brown.

Lucow, Ben. "Mature Identity in Sherwood Anderson's 'The Sad Horn-Blowers.'" *Studies in Short Fiction* 2 (1965):291–93.

Miller, William V. 1976. "Portraits of the Artist: Anderson's Fictional Storytellers." In *Sherwood Anderson: Dimensions of His Literary Art: A Collection of Critical Essays*. Ed. David D. Anderson. East Lansing: Michigan State University Press, 1–23.

Modlin, Charles E., ed. 1992. *Certain Things Last: The Selected Stories of Sherwood Anderson*. New York: Four Walls Eight Windows.

Rosenfeld, Paul, ed. *The Sherwood Anderson Reader*. Boston: Houghton Mifflin.

Schevill, James. 1951. *Sherwood Anderson: His Life and Work*. Denver: University of Denver Press.

Sutton, William A. 1972. *The Road to Winesburg: A Mosaic of the Imaginative Life of Sherwood Anderson*. Metuchen, NJ: Scarecrow Press.

Voss, Arthur. 1973. *The American Short Story: A Critical Survey*. Norman: University of Oklahoma Press.

Way, Brian. 1971. "Sherwood Anderson." In *The American Novel and the Nineteen Twenties*. Malcolm Bradbury and David Palmer (Eds.). Stratford-upon-Avon Studies 13. London: Edward Arnold, 107–26.

White, Ray Lewis. "'As His Home Town Knew Him': Sherwood Anderson's Last Trip Home." *Midamerica* 14 (1987):74–88.

———, ed. 1969. *Sherwood Anderson's Memoirs: A Critical Edition*. Chapel Hill: University of North Carolina Press.

Williams, Kenny J. 1988. *A Storyteller and a City: Sherwood Anderson's Chicago*. De Kalb: Northern Illinois University Press.

The Man's Story

Circumstances of Composition

Sherwood Anderson wrote "The Man's Story" one day in mid-December of 1922, after he had moved from Chicago to live alone in New York City. A letter to Harry Hansen dated December 26 gives this account: "I went home the other evening here and on the way home just the form of a longish short story I've been waiting to write for years came to me clearly. I sat down when I got home and wrote until three in the morning—went to bed—slept until seven and got up and went to the house of a friend. I was tired and he had some good whiskey. At his house I sat and wrote in a heat until about 3 that afternoon—that is to say almost 7 hours more. It was a curious experience. When I got through most of a quart of whiskey was gone but the story was fixed as I wanted it. . . . I was perfectly sober until I had written the last word and then suddenly I was drunk and went and fell into bed and slept for several hours like a dead man" (Modlin, *Letters* 44).

Normally Anderson was not a heavy drinker. The unusual circumstances surrounding this story's composition were so significant to Anderson that he repeated the anecdote several times. In his *Memoirs* Anderson identifies the friend as Stark Young, who lived on Vesey Street; this later version of the story's composition differs in minor details but is essentially the same (White, *Memoirs* 434–35). Actually Stark Young lived at 51 Charlton Street, in the basement apartment of a brownstone building owned by Elizabeth Prall, who would later become Anderson's third wife. She lived on the top floor, sharing her apartment with Margaret Lane, sister of Anderson's first wife. In a third (and similar) account, printed in Curry's *"Writer's Book,"* Anderson adds a telling comment: "I have not reread the story for years but I have a kind of faith that something of the half mystic wonder of my day in that apartment still lingers in it" (92).

Anderson had begun trying to tell the story that became "The Man's Story" even before he came to Chicago in 1913. The earliest version can be found in the unpublished manuscript of a novel he called "Talbot Whittingham"; in one scene, after Lucile Bearing is shot, she returns, wounded and having "accepted defeat," to the hero's apartment, where she fulfills his dream of beauty, while firelight "dances on the droplets of mist in her hair" and she dies smiling (Rideout 46, 50).

Sources and Influences

The germ of "The Man's Story," according to Anderson, was a memory of his own father bending over a fire to burn some papers: "the way his half-kneeling figure was outlined in the little flare of light, the little flame and the darkness," he said, inspired the tale (White, *Memoirs* 277–78). He also states that he used for the setting the apartment on Chicago's North Side where, when he was nineteen, he had visited the abject, work-worn woman who was his first "mistress" (158–63).

The story is more confessional, though, than Anderson ever admitted. He must have known that the deeper source of the story lay in his difficulties with women—especially his first two wives. They—and the woman who would become his third wife—all weighed upon his mind as he created this, possibly the most personal of all his stories. It is not only coincidental that the earlier version of the story, in "Talbot Whittingham," was written as he was "rejustifying, glorifying his break with" his first wife, Cornelia Lane Anderson (Townsend 102). When he departed from Chicago at the beginning of July 1922, he was breaking off his long-troubled second marriage to Tennessee Mitchell knowing that he was inflicting enormous pain on her. Then, when he began his affair with Elizabeth Prall, he was aware of the injury both to Tennessee and, once again, to Cornelia, whose sister was there to watch. Doubtless he sensed the self-abnegation that he would require from Elizabeth as well. Significantly, Elizabeth Prall Anderson relates in her memoirs the somewhat bizarre episode of the story's composition and follows it by remarking that when she met him that fall "Sherwood was a man who was unlike anyone I had known before . . . exciting and excitable," a man of moods whom she "was beginning to accept" despite her reluctance to fall in love with him and have her life "shattered" (51–52). If this is not mere hindsight but accurate recollection, her intuition was indeed prophetic.

Yet another episode of Anderson's heartless treatment of a devoted woman is related by Ben Hecht. This woman, his mistress for two years, had "nursed him, coddled him, loaned him money"; she became suicidal when he callously abandoned her (228–30).

A strange passage in one of Anderson's letters, dated August 1922, may relate to the fictional character of the hunchback girl who loves the central figure and who witnesses, through a keyhole, events in his apartment. The letter articulates a notion that, in any relationship between two people, "there is always a third person present":

> This thing, one might call "The Third," is a composit [*sic*] person made up of the two presences. Toward it all things are directed. If both can

> give freely into the Third a contact is really made and a relationship
> established.
>   In most cases the Third becomes a half formed thing, a grotesque.
> (Sutton, *Letters* 185)

Anderson suggests that this theory would account for the universal condition of loneliness; probably it also connects with the deformed relationship of the main couple in "The Man's Story." But the autobiographical roots of the image are easily discernible.

Anderson was troubled by his capacity for what he referred to as brutality or cruelty and often speaks of it, sometimes apologetically, sometimes defensively. (For example, see Sutton, *Letters* 202, 224; Jones-Rideout, *Letters* 8; Modlin, *Letters* 105; *A Story Teller's Story* 318.) Often, he justified his cruelty to women as an inevitable by-product of his artist's devotion to "the intangible," to "some abstract pure beauty" (Jones-Rideout, *Letters* 115, 187; Schevill 302; White, *Memoirs* 7, 8). In a fit of abstraction he would sometimes completely lose touch with his surroundings ("Notes" 130; Sutton, *Letters* 221). "[W]hen we artists are at work, women must weep," he declared (White, *Memoirs* 277). To some extent, perhaps, Anderson in "The Man's Story" was assuaging his guilt by putting the truth of his inner life in such harsh light, by exaggerating his egotism and lack of feeling.

Publication History

"The Man's Story" first appeared in September of 1923 in the *Dial* (75:247–64). The following month it was issued in the short story collection *Horses and Men* (287–312). Eager to secure magazine publication of the story before the book came out, Anderson had written to his agent Otto Liveright on April 25 instructing him, "Let the *Dial* have 'The Man's Story'—if they want it—and will give it publication before October" (Curry 153). By mid-July the story had been accepted.

It is erroneously reported that Anderson received $750 for this story (Jones-Rideout, *Letters* 91n; Townsend 214). The letter on which this mistaken conclusion has been based refers to "the story about the jealous husband" and is dated January 1923; but the role of the jealous husband in "The Man's Story" is inconsequential, and Anderson surely would not have written the April letter to Liveright if he had already received payment for the story three months before.

After Anderson's death, his friend Paul Rosenfeld included it in *The Sherwood Anderson Reader* (248–65), placing it with other short pieces in a section he entitled "The Life of Art."

Relation to Other Works

Many of the stories in *Horses and Men* show the author "exploring the question of manhood," as Townsend observes (195). In the story immediately preceding this one, "The Sad Horn Blowers," a youth venturing out into the world asks the question directly—"'Manhood'— ... What did it mean?" (279); he earns the somewhat melancholy knowledge that grown men retain within themselves a childish self. In "The Man Who Became a Woman" a youth becomes "more of a man" for the experience of feeling as a woman does (Townsend 197). In "Unused," an imaginative boy develops the ability to express the secrets of a woman's inner life, her sexual victimization and artistic romanticizing. "The Man's Story" presents a quite different picture of manhood, one much closer to that in *Many Marriages* (1923), where the hero expounds this philosophy: "One was a male and at the proper time went toward the female and took her. There was a kind of cruelty in nature and at the proper time that cruelty became a part of one's manhood" (Townsend 194–95). *Kit Brandon* presents a similar view but refers it specifically to the male as artist: "A man can't really paint unless he can also be an utter skunk" (27). Doubtless one reason Anderson liked "The Man's Story" so much was that it was tough and hardboiled, unlike the wistful stories that had led some critics to call him "an eternal adolescent" (Modlin, *Letters* 55).

Among the stories of *Winesburg, Ohio* (1919), "Tandy" comes closest to this one. The visionary quester in "Tandy" longs for an ideal woman who is strong enough to receive, support, and endure his impossibly transcendentalizing love, and he casually crushes a little girl in the process. But there is also a psychological link between Edgar Wilson, the center of dramatic interest in "A Man's Story," and George Willard, the maturing youth in *Winesburg, Ohio,* who long ignores his mother's illness and then is troubled by confused guilt after her death. Moreover, it is impossible not to notice the connection between George's mother, the nearly masochistic woman in this story, and the old woman who spends her life feeding men in "Death in the Woods."

Critical Studies

Set in Chicago, "The Man's Story" is narrated by a newspaper reporter who has covered a murder trial in which a poet named Edgar Wilson is accused of killing a woman. She had run away from her husband to live with Wilson, supported him by working as "wardrobe woman in a theatre," and submissively tolerated the small cruelties he callously inflicted during his frequent fits of abstraction. Ironically, Wilson's poetry expresses transcendental yearnings for love and fulfillment, and it centers on "some half-mystic conception" concerning the universal need to overcome isolating barriers and to release the sweet fruits that lie hidden within tough human husks. The couple has been watched through a keyhole by a hunchbacked girl in an adjoining room. The girl, the mistress, and the reporter who covers the trial are all captivated by Wilson's power. Wilson is not guilty of the murder: a love-crazed stagehand shot the woman because he could not have her. But when she was murdered, Wilson was walking with her, and off in a world of his own imagining, he did not notice the shooting, or the policeman who ran up to question her, or her quiet expiration. He even, in his daze, stepped over her body. After he realized what had happened, though, Wilson sank into desolation. The reporter longs to understand and so to heal him.

Anderson's fourth wife, Eleanor Copenhaver Anderson, said in a 1969 interview that her husband had "always . . . maintained" that "The Man's Story" was his favorite (Curry 225). This comment is consistent with his lavish praise for the tale printed elsewhere, notably in his memoirs, where he insists "it is a story that will someday be counted one of the very great and beautiful short stories of the world" (White 278).

Critics in the twenties were considerably less enthusiastic about the tale than Anderson himself, but a good deal more positive than later critics have been. Writing in 1924, Calverton found the story "a haunting study in schizophrenia" (107). Though he objected to a physiologically mistaken symbolic detail—the bullet-severed "cord or muscle . . . that controls the action of the heart," Calverton was fascinated by the "abnormality" of the central character, his "almost solipsistic pessimism" and "his unnaturally callous attitude toward everything not intimate with his peculiar mental world." A few years later, Whipple called "The Man's Story" "the most enigmatic" of Anderson's tales, and "also the most avowedly mystical": "I do not understand this story, but so far as I can decipher a meaning it is that through the love and possession of one woman a man may attain to a similar kind of union with the whole world" (136).

Responses of more recent commentators range from tepid to hostile. Bridgman sees the narrator's admission that he is confused as telling evidence that the author himself neither understands the story nor has found the right medium for conveying it (162). Williams accepts the narrator as adequate and commends the fittingly bleak urban setting, but suggests, in a colossal understatement, that "the specific incidents" of the plot "may tax credibility" (230–31). Townsend, appropriately, is troubled by the confessional aspect of this story "about stepping all over a woman"; all too plainly discernible in it is Sherwood Anderson reassuring himself that though he has been brutal to those "nearest and dearest to him," he is still a "tender and sensitive" man (194, quoting *HM* 288). Miller observes that "The Man's Story" epitomizes the problem shared by many of the artistic characters in Anderson's work—they need women to enable the process of poetic creation but cannot seem to avoid mistreating them (20). What is wrong with this story, Miller implies, is that it asks the reader "to believe that the relationship between Wilson and the weakly developed woman was mutually satisfactory."

Other facets of "The Man's Story" might be usefully explored. Wright asserts that it contains one of the few "active artists in the canon of the twenties" (145). This artist might be related to the tradition in American fiction from Hawthorne to James that glorifies the sacrifice of the (male) artist's (female) muse to the demands of art. Moreover, Anderson has not been given proper credit for this narrator, a newspaper reporter who, during a bizarre and lengthy murder trial, has become emotionally absorbed in the real-life drama he is reporting. Although the reporter is no intellectual, he is capable of being touched by the artist-defendant's strange poems, and his language is chatty and earnest. The title's reference is multiple: first the story is that of Edgar Wilson's life; then it is the reporter's assignment, but it also becomes his story in a deeper sense as his compulsion to understand it grows; by implication, one supposes, it is every man's story (the term is gender specific), a truth rarely told; and finally, of course, it is the author's story—a distressingly revealing portrait of the artist.

Works Cited

Anderson, Elizabeth, and Gerald R. Kelley. 1969. *Miss Elizabeth: A Memoir.* Boston: Little, Brown.

Anderson, Sherwood. 1923. *Horses and Men.* New York: B. W. Huebsch.

——. 1924. *A Story Teller's Story.* New York: B. W. Huebsch. Rpt. in *A Story Teller's Story: A Critical Text.* Ed. Ray Lewis White. Cleveland: Press of Case Western Reserve University, 1968. Rpt. Viking, 1969.

——. 1926. "Notes Out of a Man's Life." *Sherwood Anderson's Notebook.* New York: Boni & Liveright, 129–31.

——. 1936. *Kit Brandon: A Portrait.* New York and London: Scribners.

Bridgeman, Richard. 1966. *The Colloquial Style in America.* New York: Oxford University Press.

Calverton, V. J. "Sherwood Anderson: A Study in Sociological Criticism." *Modern Quarterly* 2 (1924):82–118. Rpt. in *The Newer Spirit: A Sociological Criticism of Literature.* Introduction by Ernest Boyd. New York: Boni & Liveright, 1925, 52–118.

Curry, Martha Mulroy. 1975. *The "Writer's Book" by Sherwood Anderson: A Critical Edition*. Metuchen, NJ: Scarecrow Press.

Hecht, Ben. 1954. *A Child of the Century*. New York: Simon & Schuster.

Jones, Howard Mumford, and Walter B. Rideout, eds. 1953. *Letters of Sherwood Anderson*. Boston: Little, Brown.

Miller, William V. 1976. "Portraits of the Artist: Anderson's Fictional Storytellers." In *Sherwood Anderson: Dimensions of His Literary Art: A Collection of Critical Essays*. Ed. David D. Anderson. East Lansing: Michigan State University Press, 1–23.

Modlin, Charles E., ed. 1984. *Sherwood Anderson: Selected Letters*. Knoxville: University of Tennessee Press.

Rideout, Walter B. 1976. "Talbot Whittingham and Anderson: A Passage to *Winesburg, Ohio*." In *Sherwood Anderson: Dimensions of His Literary Art*. Ed. David D. Anderson. Lansing: Michigan State University Press, 41–60.

Rosenfeld, Paul, ed. 1947. *The Sherwood Anderson Reader*. Boston: Houghton Mifflin.

Schevill, James. 1951. *Sherwood Anderson: His Life and Work*. Denver: University of Denver Press.

Sutton, William A., ed. 1985. *Letters to Bab: Sherwood Anderson to Marietta D. Finley, 1916–33*. Foreword by Walter B. Rideout. Urbana and Chicago: University of Illinois Press.

Townsend, Kim. 1987. *Sherwood Anderson*. Boston: Houghton Mifflin.

Whipple, T. K. 1928. "Sherwood Anderson." *Spokesman: Modern Writers and American Life*. New York and London: D. Appleton, 115–38.

White, Ray Lewis, ed. 1969. *Sherwood Anderson's Memoirs: A Critical Edition*. Chapel Hill: University of North Carolina Press.

Williams, Kenny J. 1988. *A Storyteller and a City: Sherwood Anderson's Chicago*. De Kalb: Northern Illinois University Press.

Wright, Austin McGiffert. 1961. *The American Short Story in the Twenties*. Chicago: University of Chicago Press.

An Ohio Pagan

Circumstances of Composition

Both "An Ohio Pagan" and "Unused" were extracted from a projected novel, begun in 1920, that Anderson never finished. (See "Unused," "Circumstances of Composition.") He had actually begun writing about the character Tom Edwards early in 1917 in another abandoned novel, which he called "Immaturity." It was about a boy on a quest, "an artist at heart" who represents "American culture" (Sutton, *Letters* 57). By August of 1920, the new book, with the working title "Ohio Pagans," was "expanding into a novel of country people and their efforts to find God" (Jones-Rideout, *Letters* 61; similarly, Sutton, *Letters* 127). Anderson wanted to bring into his work a world that seemed to have been destroyed by an industrial age, "a cruel-beautiful pagan world" with all its "splendor" (Sutton, *Letters* 135). In the spring of 1923 he reworked material from the unfinished novel into "An Ohio Pagan." It was finished, or nearly finished, by May 7.

Sources and Influences

In part, this story is a romanticized version of the youth of Sherwood Anderson himself, of whom Waldo Frank would later say: "This untaught religious pagan of Mid-America personified so much of the American Promise! and his present bewilderments personified the American danger" (42). Autobiographical sources for the story include jobs Anderson held in his youth, first as a groom "in the employ of a physically huge 'sporting farmer' named [Thomas] Whitehead" (the Harry Whitehead of this tale), and later in a threshing operation that "moved slowly from farm to farm over the country stretching northward from Clyde to Sandusky and the Lake Erie shore" (Rideout 164).

Almost above all, though, this story involves a specific setting, the Ohio the author had known in his boyhood. Lavishly, tenderly, it details topographical features, the rhythm of the seasons, and the mythic-religious aura breathed in by an unsophisticated, hardworking people. The growing boy imbibes through his senses curvilinear hills, summer rain, shifting clouds, streams flowing into the bay. Feeling everywhere the presence of a power outside himself, he needs no other instruction in reverence. His rapturous appreciation of landscape and of the sounds and smells of nature is doubtless based on actual remembered fact, but it also owes a great deal to literary precedents such as Walt Whitman and Mark Twain.

Rideout has traced some of the story's material to George Borrow's *Wild Wales* (1862). Anderson "drew directly on" the fifty-ninth and sixtieth chapters of Borrow's book, where Borrow gives an account of the historical Thomas Edwards (1739–1810), the poet known as "Twm o'r Nant" among the Welsh (163, 165). Borrow "summarizes Twm's life, quoting extensively in his own English translation from the Welsh poet's" version of his own life, and "two-thirds of the second paragraph of 'An Ohio Pagan' is a kind of summary of that summary" (165). Outlining parallels between Borrow's and Anderson's versions of the poet's life (Anderson spells his name "Twn"), Rideout observes that Anderson magnified the Welshman's feats to lend him "a legendary, even a mythic quality" and to prepare the reader for the visionary gift of his own main character, the poet's "rather inarticulate" grandson (165–68). Rideout further notes the mythological references to Pegasus and Castalia and suggests that Anderson might have derived pertinent information from the 1911 *Encyclopaedia Britannica* (168, 173n).

Publication History

"An Ohio Pagan" was first published in October of 1923 in the collection *Horses and Men*.

Relation to Other Works

An editorial piece called "Virginia Falls" printed in *Hello Towns!* (1929) recalls this story in its images of something sacred in nature—a maple tree dancing "like a young girl" and "Christ walking with his disciples" in vivid sunlight; "[s]ome of the pagan people see God in trees, cattle, weeds, fields of grain," Anderson writes, "I am more than a little pagan myself" (331–32).

Anderson frequently wrote in a pastoral mode. In *A Story Teller's Story* (1924), Anderson argues that Henry Adams had got it wrong when he said, in his *The Education of Henry Adams*, "An American Virgin would never dare command; an American Venus would never dare exist." Perhaps that was true for intellectual New Englanders, Anderson concedes, but concerning the Midwestern people he had known "it was absurd to say they had neither love nor reverence" (380). "An Ohio Pagan" is a kind of testimonial to this faith.

The religious impulse expressed in Tom Edwards's early visions links the story particularly with "Godliness" in *Winesburg, Ohio*. A primitive visionary even more like Tom is young Hugh McVey of *Poor White* (1920), whose dreams in the grass of Mudcat Landing closely resemble his. A parallel sense of wonder in the face of nature penetrates *Mid-American Chants* (1918), Anderson's stories dealing with horses, and the awakening Elsie Leander in "The New Englander."

For Tom Edwards, as for Elsie Leander, unfulfilled sexual passion fires a poetic/erotic vision of nature. Similarly, the visionary capacity of the youth in "The Man Who Became a Woman" surges up out of a turmoil of lonely adolescent sexual need. It is clear, though, that no mere woman will ever satisfy such gigantic transcendental yearnings—indeed, that may be the key to the meaning of "The Man's Story," which precedes "An Ohio Pagan" in *Horses and Men*. "The best men spend their lives seeking truth," says Sam McPherson, hero of Anderson's first published novel (227); Anderson never wavered from this philosophy.

The wanderings of the young hero of "An Ohio Pagan" are propelled by a tension, common to many of Anderson's works, between the romantically irresponsible free life and the respectable world represented here by the truant officer, the Baptist Sunday School, women teachers, commerce, and law. Also operative is tension between attachment to the loveliness of the countryside and attraction to the exciting opportunities of the city, as well as between desire to overcome rural provinciality and aversion to ugly factory towns. The ending of this story has a lingering ambiguity like that of "Departure," at the end of the *Winesburg* cycle, but this ending makes the ambiguity more explicit. It thus provides a nicely unresolved close to the pattern of alternating rural and urban settings that helps to organize the stories collected in *Horses and Men*.

John Telfer is a character also to be found in *Windy McPherson's Son* (1916). Harry Whitehead and the stallion Bucephalus, named after Alexander the Great's horse, also appear in "I'm a Fool," and the central character of that tale has a Welsh grandfather, too; unfortunately, the reason for these links between the first and last selections in *Horses and Men* is not sufficiently clear. Likewise, both the Tom in "An Ohio Pagan" and the Tom in "A Chicago Hamlet" are decisively influenced by a praying farmer—in opposite ways; the connection invites interpretation, but to no particular end.

Critical Studies

Anderson admitted that "An Ohio Pagan" might be too fragmentary (Curry 277–78). In that vein, some critics have held that, while the picaresque tale is unified somewhat by symbols that reveal the psychic life of its young hero, it is marred by "extraneous and uninteresting" material that betrays both its origin in a novel that never attained form and Anderson's subsequent failure to reshape it into an effective short story (Raymund 144–45). Indeed, it seems natural to wish that the story were more tightly structured.

But perhaps unfairly, Bridgman states that the prose of "An Ohio Pagan" is "fuzzy and flat" because the narrator and the colloquial tone of Anderson's better stories have been eliminated (162–63). Actually, the prose has an oral cadence, as Howe observes; even though the story is narrated in the third person, "one clearly feels the presence of a narrator's voice" (173).

Otherwise, "An Ohio Pagan" has elicited only a few isolated comments of bland praise. (Most critics have ignored it altogether.) In its behalf, Calverton allows that it captures something of "the moody mysticism of adolescence" and successfully blends "symbolism with reality" (107). Fagin, defending Anderson against charges of immorality and irreverence, holds up the naïve boyhood fancies of Tom's nature visions: "his yokels are soft, lyrical mystics" (120, 144–45). David Anderson considers the story "excellent" but offers no analysis beyond general remarks about the "optimism" of the ending and its suggestion "that man may find satisfaction in the search [for meaning] even though it never ends" (164, 78). Weber remarks, "The pantheistic embrace of nature in 'An Ohio Pagan' . . . has rarely been equaled in American literature" (35). Perhaps none of Anderson's short stories better deserves Hart Crane's admiring conclusion that "Nature is so strong in all the work of Anderson—and he describes it as one so willingly and happily surrendered to it, that it colors his work with the most surprising grasp of what 'innocence' and 'holiness' ought to mean" (47). Finally, what the story contains of worth seems to lie in the distinctive mood it captures and evokes. As Modlin says, it contains "startlingly imaginative material," impressive "lyrical descriptions of nature," and "understated poignancy" as at the end "the young pagan looks expectantly toward the city" (xi).

Works Cited

Anderson, David. 1967. *Sherwood Anderson: An Introduction and Interpretation*. New York: Holt, Rinehart.

Anderson, Sherwood. 1916. *Windy McPherson's Son*. New York: John Lane. Rev. ed. New York: B. W. Huebsch, 1922; Chicago and London: University of Chicago Press, 1965. Introduction by Wright Morris.

———. 1923. *Horses and Men*. New York: B. W. Huebsch.

Bridgman, Richard. 1966. *The Colloquial Style in America*. New York: Oxford University Press.

Calverton, V. J. "Sherwood Anderson: A study in Sociological Criticism." *Modern Quarterly* 2 (1924):82–118. Rpt. in *The Newer Spirit: A Sociological Criticism of Literature*. Introduction by Ernest Boyd. New York: Boni & Liveright, 1925, 52–118.

Crane, Hart. 1952. *The Letters of Hart Crane 1916–1932*. Ed. Brom Weber. New York: Hermitage House.

Curry, Martha Mulroy. 1975. *The "Writer's Book" by Sherwood Anderson: A Critical Edition*. Metuchen, NJ: Scarecrow Press.

Fagin, N. Bryllion. 1973. *The Phenomenon of Sherwood Anderson: A Study in American Life and Letters*. New York: Russell & Russell. Originally printed Baltimore: Rossi-Bryn, 1927.

Frank, Waldo. 1919. *Our America*. New York: Boni & Liveright.

Howe, Irving. 1951. *Sherwood Anderson*. New York: William Sloane.

Jones, Howard Mumford, and Walter B. Rideout, eds. 1953. *Letters of Sherwood Anderson*. Boston: Little, Brown.

Modlin, Charles E., ed. 1992. *Certain Things Last: The Selected Stories of Sherwood Anderson*. New York: Four Walls Eight Windows.

Raymund, Bernard. "The Grammar of Not-Reason: Sherwood Anderson." *Arizona Quarterly* 12 (1956):48–60, 137–48.

Rideout, Walter B. 1976. "A Borrowing from Borrow." In *Sherwood Anderson: Centennial Studies*. Hilbert H. Campbell and Charles E. Modlin (Eds.). Troy, NY: Whitston, 162–74.

Sutton, William A., ed. 1985. *Letters to Bab: Sherwood Anderson to Marietta D. Finley, 1916–33*. Foreword by Walter B. Rideout. Urbana and Chicago: University of Illinois Press.

Weber, Brom. 1964. *Sherwood Anderson*. Minneapolis: University of Minnesota Press. Rpt. in *Seven Novelists in the American Naturalist Tradition: An Introduction*. Ed. Charles Child Walcutt. Minneapolis: University of Minnesota Press, 1974, 168–204.

Death in the Woods

Death in the Woods

Circumstances of Composition

"Some of my best stories have been written ten or twelve times," Sherwood Anderson said, "and there is one story, 'Death in the Woods,' a magnificent tale, one of the most penetrating written in our times, that was ten years getting itself written. I had to approach and approach. I was like a lover patiently wooing a woman. I wrote and threw away, wrote and threw away" (Curry 28). Even after it was published, Anderson continued to tinker with the text until 1933, when it achieved its final form.

Although, as Anderson reported, some early drafts were simply discarded, several of the preliminary attempts have survived. The earliest of these, evidently, is a typewritten fragment on the reverse side of which Anderson wrote part of *Winesburg, Ohio;* Ray Lewis White dates this fragment "around 1916" ("Death" 1). White summarizes the contents of the ten-page fragment, which concerns a newspaperman's journey home to visit his sick mother, and extracts brief textual passages. One passage describes a terrifying scene the man sees on a snowy moonlit night in the Wisconsin woods, a circle of dogs "dragging the pack and the body of [a] dead woman into the clearing." Other excerpts show a second alarming moment when the man's sight of his sleeping mother merges with his mental image of the dead woman and, finally, years later, the man thinking about "the imagination of men working in circles, all physical life caught in a great circle . . . " (1–3). Even in this early version, the dead woman seems to be saying: "I have fed the animal hungers of man and beast always, since I was a child. My life has been spent doing that and now that life is gone and I still feed animal hungers" (2).

A second fragmentary sketch preliminary to the story was saved in the notebook Anderson kept during his 1921 trip to Paris (Fanning 62–65). The central character of the sketch is named "Mother Winters," and her husband—once a swearing, carousing young rowdy but now grown sullen and wrathful—is the owner of a sawmill several miles from town; these details suggest that the characters evolved in the author's mind as connected to the family of Windpeter Winters, earlier depicted in the *Winesburg* story "The Untold Lie." This fragment focuses on the woman's life and does not include her death, though that seems to be foreshadowed by a long dream sequence in which, old at thirty-six, she struggles for the release of death (62–64). After describing the woman's husband, the notebook entry goes on to give an account of her young life as a servant on the farm of a German family named Swartz; her only friends were the animals she had to feed, and one day when she was seventeen and the farmer's wife had driven off to purchase groceries, "some[thing] happened" (64–65). The fragment breaks off at this point.

Another version of a portion of what came to be "Death in the Woods" was found after Anderson's death among papers in his Marion, Virginia, printshop. It is part of a manuscript called "Father Abraham: A Lincoln Fragment," which Rosenfeld edited for his *Sherwood Anderson Reader;* Rosenfeld concluded that it probably dates from the mid-twenties, when Anderson was in Reno, Nevada (530–602, xxvii). In this semibiographical narrative, Anderson portrays Abraham Lincoln as a thoughtful youth with a poet's temperament. One long segment presents the young lawyer's imaginative reconstruction of events leading up to a criminal case involving the attempted rape and crippling of a young bound girl by a brutal German farmer. The story that transpires in Lincoln's mind is colored by his memories of his mother and of the death of his sweetheart, Ann Rutledge, as well as by a keen perception of his own male lusts. Lincoln's feeling is not outrage but patient, sorrowful, empathetic understanding. In once sense, he knows, he is the girl feeding the farm animals and fleeing in terror from her attacker; at the same time and in the same way he is the blindly determined farmer tearing the girl's dress, and also the farmer's scheming wife.

Another surviving manuscript is "Death in the Forest." This holograph, bearing Eleanor Anderson's note, "Early version of short story Death in the Woods," has been edited by William V. Miller and published as an appendix to White's critical edition of *Tar.* The fragment begins, "It was December and snowing when Mrs. Ike Marvin . . . died in the little hollow in the center of Grimes' woods, about two miles south of our Ohio town" (232). Immediately the focus shifts to the first-person narrator's memories of his experiences on the day it happened—memories of activities in the store where he worked, the arrival of the news, the trek of the excited townsfolk out to see the body, the dogs' having ripped the salt pork out of the woman's bag, and the child's delight in holding a luxurious overcoat for a man who helped carry away the body. But Anderson must have realized that his story had become sidetracked, for the fragment ends awkwardly: "As to the actual story of Ma Marvin's death—I found all about it in a rather queer way nearly twenty years later. Now I will tell you of that" (236).

A Story Teller's Story (1924) mentions the many inhabitants of the storyteller's world of fancy. One of those he would like to tell his readers about is "the old woman accompanied by the gigantic dogs who died alone in a wood on a winter day" (121). But Anderson was not yet ready.

At last, in the spring of 1926, Anderson got it told, drawing upon various elements of earlier versions and combining the story of the woman's death with the story of her life and with a condensed account of the townspeople who witness scattered scenes from her brief tragedy. The woman's name now was Grimes. The story was finished by May (Sutton, *Letters* 263). Anderson mailed typed fair copy to his agent, Otto Liveright, during the first week of June. That spring, Anderson left New Orleans for the farm near Troutdale, Virginia, where, with the money he earned from his bestseller *Dark Laughter* 1925, he and his wife Elizabeth began to build the only house he ever owned. He had drawn closer to his brothers during that spring after his brother Earl was felled by a stroke. Thoughts about his childhood, stirred by these renewed contacts, absorbed him further as he finished a draft of *Tar*, sections of which began to appear in *Woman's Home Companion* in June. He threw himself into writing a new novel, tentatively entitled "Another Man's House." In April he wrote to his old friend Marietta Finley: "I write in a new mood for me. Acceptance. Something that has happened to all of us these last few years. It may be because we are older. That has its dramatic value also. . . . Sometimes I think—just to accept a little dog trotting at my heels. Accept women trees skies places. Flesh is flesh, it hungers always. To acceot [*sic*] the hunger also" (Sutton, *Letters* 255–56). That note contains hints that point to "Death in the Woods," which may have been composed either in April in New Orleans or a few weeks later in Virginia, or perhaps both.

Sources and Influences

Anderson always believed that "the imagination must constantly feed upon reality or starve" ("Note" 73). "Death in the Woods" is preeminently a story about the workings of the creative imagination as over and over it circles around a specific event, at length transforming all the confused disorder of experience into art. As the story explicitly indicates, its sources were manifold.

First, there were events in the author's own life, some of them remembered distinctly, some of them so vague as to skirt the borders of dreamlife. Surely contributing to the character Mrs. Grimes was Anderson's own mother, selfless, silent, workworn, gone to an early grave (Howe 166; but see D. Anderson 131 for an opposing view). Anderson often stretched actual facts by saying that Emma Anderson had been a "bound girl" before her marriage (White, *Memoirs* 44–45; *Story Teller's* 7; Howe 11–12; Kramer 37). Anderson's experiences as a laborer on the farm of a German during the summer of 1899 doubtless played a role in the story's portrayal of mind-numbing agricultural toil and the sexual exploitation of female workers. Anderson reported that in creating the story he drew also from a boyhood memory of standing in the cold, peeking into a window at a girl undressing before a stove and from another, later memory of witnessing a young girl's nude body lying on an operating table ("Girl" 21). In his *Memoirs* he wrote that he "got the impulse" for the story that eventually became "Death in the Woods" from a strangely surreal experience he had in Palos Park, Illinois (probably early in 1921); having walked out on a snowy, moonlit night accompanied by a group of neighborhood dogs and lying down to think for a while in the woods, he was suddenly startled by a "German police dog" staring down at him, whereupon he looked up to see all the dogs running in a circle in a clearing (White, *Memoirs* 310–12). The manuscript on the back of the Winesburg stories, if White's 1916 dating is correct ("Death" 1), indicates that this memory may have been somewhat embellished. (See "Circumstances of Composition.")

Numerous literary sources have also been proposed. Howe declares that this is "the only one of Anderson's stories that may accurately be compared . . . to Russian fiction" (164). Like Turgenev and Chekhov, Anderson depends on "effects of mood and devices of pacing rather than conflict between characters to pull his story into climax." Moreover, Anderson achieves here something of the Russians' sense of "the ultimate unity" of all natural things "bunched in the hand of death" (164). Gregory points out Wordsworthian elements: the recollection of childhood, the use of the diction of common people, the emphasis on the dignity of the poor, the "moonlit rural scene," and the transcendental evocations ("Editor's" 27–28). Elsewhere, Gregory observes that the scene "where Death makes a counterfeit of Sleep" recalls Shelley's "Queen Mab" ("On Sherwood" 14–15). Way detects the trace of Whitman in the "complex structure of images" woven like musical motifs into a beautiful poetic fabric (123–25); and there are other conceptual and technical elements that show how much Anderson may have absorbed from Whitman. Rideout suggests that Anderson may have been influenced by George Borrow's *Wild Wales,* in which there is a chapter about a "Death in the Snow" (174 n. 20). Surprisingly, no one has mentioned the influence here of Jack London's wilderness tales. Somewhere in the background lies the immensely popular *The Call of the Wild,* which traces a dog's reversion to wolfish savagery. And more palpable analogues appear in London's "To Build a Fire," a detailed story of death by freezing, and "The Law of Life," where an aged Indian abandoned by his tribe sits in the snow awaiting death—which in the end is accomplished by an encircling ring of hungry wolves. Wagner finds a precursor in Gertrude Stein; the old woman resembles Stein's Lena and Anna, and Anderson uses "Stein-like" techniques of repetition (84, 85). Plainly, some residue of Henry Adams's adoration of the Virgin appears in the tale, as it does more explicitly in *Dark Laughter* (1925).

Even Rembrandt's painting seems to have entered into Anderson's carefully pictorial treatment of the death scene: in the *Paris Notebook* the author enthusiastically admires Rembrandt's art and his "half barbaric, splendid, mystic conception of death" (Fanning 30). Certainly innumerable other sources in some way contributed to the finished tale. But the tale itself is sui generis.

Publication History

When Anderson mailed "Death in the Woods" to his agent, Otto Liveright, Liveright warned him that it would be difficult to sell to "the better-paying magazines" because they would consider some of its content to be "illicit"; but hoping that *Harper's Magazine* might revoke half of Anderson's thousand-dollar debt to them, Liveright submitted it there (Curry 97). As he predicted, *Harper's* rejected it. Schevill conjectures that the rejection had serious consequences for Anderson's art, discouraging him from pursuing the "style and form" the story so brilliantly displays (230).

"Death in the Woods" made its first appearance in September of 1926 in the *American Mercury* (9:7–13). The only work Anderson had published previously in this antiestablishment magazine was the uncollected story "Caught," which came out in February 1924. In December of 1925, Anderson received a letter from H.L. Mencken, the magazine's editor, requesting a submission: "Put your price on it," it said (Mencken 287). The payment was $325; after Liveright took his fee, Anderson received $292.50 for the story.

The following November, Anderson published a revised version of the story as the twelfth chapter of *Tar: A Midwest Childhood* (199–222). To make it consistent with the book's overall scheme, he changed the original first-person narration to a third-person perspective. He also deleted the final two paragraphs of the *Mercury* text and made other small revisions throughout.

As winner of the O. Henry Memorial Award Prize, "Death in the Woods" appeared as one of the *Prize Stories of 1926* (23–35). Anderson grasped the irony of the situation; he wrote to Gilbert Seldes, who had been associate editor of the *Dial* when Anderson received that magazine's far more prestigious prize, "Don't you know that I have been making funny cracks about O. Henry as a short story writer for years?" (Curry 135n–136n). But he accepted the award.

Finally, the story became the first and title story for Anderson's fourth collection of tales, *Death in the Woods* (issued in April 1933). Anderson again made revisions of the text, evidently not from the *Tar* version but from the one that had appeared in the *American Mercury*. This final published version retains the first-person point of view and the last paragraphs of the original; there are about twenty alterations of words and phrases, all minor except for one—the addition of a short paragraph at the end of the first marked section, which comments about the treatment of "bound children." This volume, unfortunately, came out during the depths of the Depression. Anderson's publisher, Horace Liveright, went bankrupt almost immediately thereafter; consequently, the book did not receive the attention it deserved. "With adequate circulation, the book would have done much to halt the decline of [Anderson's] reputation" (Schevill 301; see also D. Anderson 121, 122).

Passing years have increased the popularity of this story, and it has been very widely anthologized, translated into other languages, and reprinted in selections of Anderson's works.

Relation to Other Works

The central figure of "Death in the Woods" somehow embodies all the women Sherwood Anderson ever wrote about. She epitomizes Anderson's recurrent female character type he referred to as the "feeders" (Miller, "Portraits" 10). Into her portrait he poured all the "love" and "guilt" he attached to "the memory of his over-burdened mother" (Miller, "Earth" 76). The story thus recalls particularly the patient suffering of Elizabeth Willard in the *Winesburg* tales "Mother" and "Death." Like Louise Bentley of "Godliness," too, Mrs. Grimes is "rejected, ignored, or grossly misunderstood" by all the men she knows (O'Neill 81). In girlhood and youth, she excites men's emotional and sexual hungers, as do dozens of young women in Anderson's fiction. But men cripple her, in effect. Sexual cruelty teaches her, as it does Ma Wescott in "Out of Nowhere into Nothing," that married life is better when a husband quits making that kind of demand. Noble and pitiable, she feeds others perpetually but receives too little nourishment herself to sustain her soul. Death transforms her into a sculpture-like image of idealized beauty. A similar pattern of transformation, in a visionary moment rather than in death, recurs in "Death," "Respectability," "The Teacher," "Like a Queen," and *Kit Brandon* (1936).

Anderson does not use the word "breasts" in this story, though breasts and all their intricate associations are evoked again and again. The subtlety of technique here thus makes an interesting contrast with that in the satiric tale "The Triumph of a Modern," in which a modern writer cynically flaunts the word "breasts" for sensational effect and easy profit. That readers vividly envision much that Anderson leaves unsaid in "Death in the Woods" is a testimony to his art.

Anderson did not, however, believe in women artists. All his life he made a distinction between what he considered to be the fundamental nature of woman and the fundamental nature of the artist, and he was fond of the tired old analogy between childbearing and artistic production (see Jones-Rideout, *Letters* 242, for one example). This analogy is significant in "Death in the Woods" in the implied hierarchical parallel between the woman's destiny—to feed animal life—and the male narrator's destiny—to create artistic beauty. The same analogy is basic to the rather cockeyed theory of the sexes in an industrial era that Anderson put forth in *Perhaps Women* (1931). But "Death in the Woods" is not reducible to theory, happily. It honors the silent, self-sacrificing toil of countless unknown generations of abused and mortal flesh as much as it celebrates the mind's enduring power to weave the raw pain of human existence into stories that can, like music, uplift and redeem battered spirits.

The story is the author's "most brilliant application" of his idea about how the writer's imagination should deal with external reality, "a method which he endeavored to explain in *A Story Teller's Story* and elsewhere," but with less success (Voss 197). "In the world of fancy, life separates itself with slow movements and with many graduations into the ugly and the beautiful. What is alive is opposed to what is dead. . . . All morality then becomes a purely aesthetic matter. What is beautiful must bring aesthetic joy. . . . In the world of fancy, you must understand, no man is ugly. Man is ugly in fact only. Ah, there is the difficulty!" (*Story Teller's* 78).

Critical Studies

"Death in the Woods" has perhaps become Anderson's most popular short story. It was not always so. By 1933, the author's reputation had long since passed its peak, and only a few early reviewers recognized its worth. One critic, for example, found the story "marred by the usual self-consciousness of Mr. Anderson" and lamented the failure to render sufficiently the "objective circumstances" of Mrs. Grimes's life (Troy 508). But with few exceptions, later critical consensus has inclined toward agreement with Norman Holmes Pearson, who in 1948 announced that the story was Anderson's "masterpiece and the narration of his artistic fulfillment" (55; see also Taylor 17; Voss 195; West 47; Burbank 125; Spencer 3; Ferguson 217). Even Lionel Trilling, who was antagonistic to Anderson, discovered in the tale "the kind of grim quaintness which is, I think, Anderson's most successful mood" (25). This short story has been, on the whole, unusually well served by scholars and interpreters.

Pearson's brief but astute analysis is still exemplary. The "chief character," he observes, "is not the old woman who dies, but the boy who sees her dead" (56). "Bit by bit" the boy grows into understanding of the meaning of the woman's life and death. "Not until all of these bits are fused is the story complete. Then there is achieved form." That is what the narrator means when he says near the story's close, "A thing so complete has its own beauty." Pearson quotes a letter in which Anderson elaborated for him this notion of artistic form:

> I presume that we all, who begin the practice of an art, begin out of a great hunger for order. We want brought into consciousness something that is always there but that gets so terribly lost. . . . I have the belief that, in this matter of form, it is largely a matter of depth of feeling. How deeply do you feel it? Feel it deeply enough and you will be torn inside and driven on until form comes.
>
> I think this whole thing must be in some way tied up with something I can find no other word to describe aside from the word morality. I suppose I think that the author who doesn't struggle all his life to achieve this form, let it be form, betrays this morality. It is terribly important because, to my way of thinking, this morality may be the only true morality there is in the world." (56; also in Jones-Rideout, *Letters* 387–88)

Schevill remarked the "many different points of view" from which the narrative describes Mrs. Grimes; "the narrator, her good-for-nothing husband, the butcher who gives her the meat, and the various townspeople who find her body" all contribute to "the portrait" of "the tragedy of a 'grotesque'" (230).

Howe observed that the story "is gaunt and elemental"; with "brilliant . . . pacing," it builds up to a climax of awe that "makes the death of even this most miserable creature seem significant and tragic" (166–67). Furthermore, says Howe, the "language, neither colloquial nor literary, is the purest Anderson ever summoned, and its gravely undulating rhythms successfully take its prose to that precarious point which is almost poetry" (167; similarly, Burbank 125–28).

Lawry elaborated the idea that "it is the narrator who 'creates' the meaning of the story," which is "a revelation created upon memory by contemplation" (306). Initially Lawry states that the "explicit interior statement" of the story's "meaning" is inadequate; since he selects the statement that "the life of the old woman of the story was given over to 'feeding animal life,'" it is easy for him to prove that a great many story details are extraneous to that theme. But Lawry's discussion is more worthwhile for its explanation of the process by which the narrator goes about "receiving" and "creating" a conscious "wholeness of realization" (307). Through convergences the narrator detects between the old woman's experience and his own, his sympathetic imagination "absorbs" aspects of both the "real" Mrs. Grimes and of her "ideal beauty"; he stands "revealed as an artist" as he forges from diverse fragments of her experience and his own a coherent "form" (307). Readers likewise are "invited to enter as individuals into a process almost identical with that of the narrator and to reach with him for contact with another life" (308).

Although the flow of its telling seems perfectly simple and natural, actually the structure of "Death in the Woods" is extremely intricate—"as complicated as that of any story" of the period, according to Wright (263). Two early critics objected to its most daring departure from conventional technique. First Barker and then Howe judged it a fault that readers of a first-person narrative should become witnesses to a scene that no living person saw: "the most vivid scene in the story is the fully conceived, gruesome death-scene," and the narrator's "belated effort" to contrive an explanation of how he knew the details of that scene is "lame," according to Barker (439–40; similarly, Howe 167). Formalist critics have refuted that charge with considerable success, arguing that the narrator's explanations of how he acquired his knowledge serve to "emphasize the improvisatory character of the art process," in which imaginative invention adds vital elements to "mere fact" (Joselyn 257).

The narrator's supposedly "weak" explanations are not to be understood as the author's explanations; they are a device the author employs to insist that art is not properly journalistic documentation, transcription of outward reality, even mimetic illusion. Art grows from the merger between outward reality and inward experience; it is half perceived and half created. That is a deeply Romantic notion, and it has been a profound if not central element of modernism. The narrator betrays some perplexity when he says, "I wonder how I know all this" (*DW* 6). But the author would have readers see that stories are, always, *made up.* Whereas "most short stories conceal the mechanics of their structure," Robinson describes the way that Anderson's story reverses that norm in order to show how art is created through the complex interaction of memory, "gossip overheard," "personal experience," and "desire to understand life and put its pieces together."

Joselyn's formalist analysis focuses on a pattern of "four transformations" in the story. Mrs. Grimes undergoes a "metamorphosis . . . from girl to woman, feeder, and victim, then to the perpetual, 'frozen' embodiment of the young girl, caught in 'marble'" (255). The narrator moves from boyhood to young manhood (in Illinois, where he sees circling dogs) to older manhood. The dogs are nearly, though not completely, transformed into wolves. Most important, in this "story about the creation of a story," "facts" are transformed "into a work of art" through a process "of choice and selection" (256–57). Though the transformations of the artistic process in one sense are "forever unfinished," Jocelyn declares that the story is "a perfectly integrated work of art" (257, 259).

In another formalist interpretation, Guerin also argues that "Death in the Woods" is an "art object"; specifically, he likens it to "Keats's Grecian urn." All the patterned elements in the narrative move toward a final "epiphany" (4). Guerin locates four points of view; the agitated "rabbit hunter" who found the body tells the story first, then the narrator's brother tells it, the young narrator who knows that those tellings are "wrong" is unable to tell it, and at last "the matured narrator tells us 'the real story.'" Guerin points out "the initiation archetype" in the boy's first view of a woman's body, which coincides with an encounter with "the mystery and awesomeness of death" (4). Even the name Mrs. Grimes, he observes, underscores her role as "Earth

Mother." Particularly acute is Guerin's explanation of Anderson's handling of verb tenses: frequent shifts between past tense and "the historical present" blur the border at which the facts of time enter "timelessness" (4–5; similarly, Ferguson 222–23). Everything attains shape. The narrator repeatedly mentions "how the death scene forms itself into a picture." The woman's nude body is sculptural, frozen into perpetual youth and loveliness, "like marble" (5). "The circle the dogs have described suggests an artistic completeness." The story becomes "an artifact in [the narrator's] mind"—complete, beautiful, "a cold pastoral, a sylvan historian that tells us that beauty is truth, truth beauty" (5).

Although Gregory once cautioned against applying the Freudian label to Anderson's "mysticism" ("Editor's" 10), psychological criticism has not been lacking. One Freudian interpreter understands the tale as "a breast fantasy" and holds that its hidden center is an associated "infantile complex" recalling oral eroticism and oral aggression (Hepburn 11). When the narrator states that he "saw everything," euphemistically referring to his view of the woman's breasts, "it is possible to infer that the entire scene covertly concerns breast-feeding"; both narrator and reader harbor unconscious memories of nursing at their mothers' breasts and have rediscovered "breasts as sexual objects" in their adolescence (10). Freud's theory of the uncanny accounts for the anxiety and the sense of magic experienced when the woman's partially naked body suddenly recalls a host of repressed emotions; the dogs, moreover, trigger "infantile fear" of castration (10–11). This analysis spotlights significant details of the narrative, albeit somewhat reductively.

Another Freud-inspired commentator views the story as a recounting of a failed initiation ritual. Scheick contends that the narrator, disturbed by connections he perceives "between feeding, sex, and death" and neurotically anxious about "the adult male's hunger for the sexual victimization of women," displays symptoms of an "arrested state of psychological development" resulting from his unconscious "identification with the old woman" (142–43). The "trauma" the narrator experiences in the masculine ritual carried out in the forest involves his "realization . . . that he is already guilty of victimizing women in terms of feeding," for he remembers that because he and his brother will return home late, " 'Either mother or our older sister would have to warm our supper' " (144). Consequently, he cannot allow himself to progress to mature masculinity. Instead, as he imaginatively feeds on the woman, his mind "must continually circle around the woman's frozen body in a manifestation of what Freud described as a compulsion toward repetition" (145).

Rohrberger traces the mystical aura of the story to "a prehistoric past" (50). In this mythic reading, the "primitive instinctual behavior of the dogs" is one indicator of the imbedded symbolic pattern. The narrator's struggle to account for "how he has managed to locate the information which he needs in order to tell the story" also suggests that its source reaches into "his subconscious memory" and indeed into a mysterious dim memory of "a past far beyond the dawn of civilization" (49–50). Ultimately, the tale is the narrator's created myth "of rebirth and regeneration" much like the "complex of myths" about Demeter, Proserpine, and Hecate that were connected with ancient Greece's "Eleusinian mysteries" (52–53). Like Demeter, the old woman carries a grain bag and performs her role as one who feeds the creatures of the earth. Like Proserpine, she "is carried away" during the harvest "amid much violence." Like Hecate, she is associated with the moon and "the elemental forces of life and the inevitability of death" symbolized by "phases of the moon." Out of his wonder at life's mysterious cycles, the narrator constructs a new version of the ancient story in which "old mother" and "young maiden" are one eternal "entity" (52–53).

Some poststructuralists have been interested in the story's narrative technique. Gerlach notes that "linear effects are minimized" (98). Gado observes that "the presumption of certainty is steadily erased" until at last "the facticity of Mrs. Grimes's story has evanesced" (18). Kennedy considers "Death in the Woods" as "metafiction"; though he says little that is really new, his discussion is eminently lucid and makes an important contribution by examining the story in the context of more recent experimental fiction.

Feminist critics, understandably, have had reservations about Anderson's story, despite its sympathy for a victimized woman. Ferguson points out that the finished story has altered a detail from the preliminary "Death in the Forest" ; in the earlier manuscript the group of townsfolk who hurry out to the death scene includes women, but the later story makes the group exclusively male (223). This change, she suggests, enhances the sense that a "ritual" is being enacted. While the dead woman "becomes the archetype of female experience," Ferguson notes that the "egocentricity" of the male artist ("absorbing the external world into" his mind) is evident (223, 231).

Far more explicitly, Colquitt directs attention to Anderson's "polarized worldview," in which "woman's destiny is circumscribed by biology, [while] man's destiny transcends the purely physical and finds consummate expression only in the creation of art" (176, 177). Furthermore, she charges not only that Anderson was haunted by "a legacy of unresolved guilt" but also that "the narrator reveals his sympathy with brutal forms of masculine expression" and discovers in art a way to "ignore the political realities" around him (180, 183). More tenuously, she holds that "the threat Mrs. Grimes faces" from the dogs "is the threat of rape" (186). But the final thrust of her argument is directed at "the interpretive web Anderson's narrator seductively dangles before" his readers in an effort to "implicate" them "in that 'vast . . . calamity' of masculinist convention that proceeds to dehistoricize woman by objectifying her into art" (189–90).

Unlike much of Anderson's earlier fiction, "Death in the Woods" shows "true resignation" (Wright 113). It looks at pain and wrong feelingly but with classic quiet. A recent critic attacks the story by raising the old objections about "violation of point of view" and "forced coincidence" and by protesting the inhumanity of "Anderson's callous use of the woman's pitiable life and death as a symbol of 'completeness'" (Coulthard 32, 37). The critic is only one of those to whom, in an era of heavily politicized literary criticism, the absence of rebellion has seemed to be an act of complicity with the oppressive cruelties of the status quo. But the story seems likely to outlast this era, too.

Works Cited

Anderson, David. 1967. *Sherwood Anderson: An Introduction and Interpretation*. New York: Holt, Rinehart.

Anderson, Sherwood. 1924. *A Story Teller's Story*. New York: Huebsch. Rpt. *A Story Teller's Story: A Critical Text*. Ed. Ray Lewis White. Cleveland: Press of Case Western Reserve University, 1968.

——. "A Note on Realism." *Sherwood Anderson's Notebook*. 71–78. Originally published in *The Literary Review*, Section 3, 1–2 (October 25, 1924).

——. 1926. *Tar: A Midwest Childhood*. New York: Boni & Liveright. Rpt. in *Tar: A Midwest Childhood: A Critical Text*. Ed. Ray Lewis White. Cleveland: Press of Case Western Reserve University, 1969.

——. "Girl by the Stove." *Decision* 1 (1941):19–22. Rpt. in *The Sherwood, Anderson Reader*. Ed. Paul Rosenfeld. Boston: Houghton Mifflin, 1947, 704–707.

——. 1969. "Death in the Forest." Ed. William V. Miller. In *Tar: A Midwest Childhood, A Critical Text*. Ed. Ray Lewis White. Cleveland and London: Press of Case Western Reserve University, 231–36. Originally in "The Technique of Sherwood Anderson's Short Stories." Ph.D. diss., University of Illinois, 1969. *DAI,* 30, 03–A, pp. 1175–1176.

Barker, Russell H. "The Storyteller Role." *College English* 3 (1942):433–42.

Burbank, Rex. 1964. *Sherwood Anderson*. New York: Twayne. Rpt. in part in *The Achievement of Sherwood Anderson: Essays in Criticism*. Ed. Ray Lewis White. Chapel Hill: University of North Carolina Press, 1966, 32–43. Rpt. in part in *Sherwood Anderson: Collection of Critical Essays*. Ed. Walter B. Rideout. Englewood Cliffs, NJ: Prentice-Hall, 1974, 70–83.

Colquitt, Claire. "The Reader as Voyeur: Complicitous Transformations in 'Death in the Woods.'" *Modern Fiction Studies* 32, no. 2 (Summer 1986):175–90.

Coulthard, A. R. "The Failure of Sherwood Anderson's 'Death in the Woods.'" *Interpretations* 14 (1983):32–38.

Curry, Martha Mulroy. 1975. *The "Writer's Book" by Sherwood Anderson: A Critical Edition*. Metuchen, NJ: Scarecrow Press.

Fanning, Michael, ed. 1976. *France and Sherwood Anderson: Paris Notebook, 1921*. Baton Rouge: Louisiana State University. Press.

Ferguson, Mary Anne. 1981. "Sherwood Anderson's *Death in the Woods*: Toward a New Realism." In *Critical Essays on Sherwood Anderson*. Ed. David D. Anderson. Boston: G. K. Hall, 217–34. Originally printed in *Midamerica VII*. East Lansing, MI: Midwestern Press, 1980, 73–95.

Gado, Frank. 1983. "Introduction." *The Teller's Tales*. Schenectady, NY: Union College Press.

Gerlach, John. 1985. *Toward the End: Closure and Structure in the American Short Story*. University: University of Alabama Press, 94–100.

Gregory, Horace. 1949. "Editor's Introduction." *The Portable Sherwood Anderson*. Ed. Horace Gregory. New York: Viking, 1–31. Rev. ed. New York: Viking Penguin, 1972.

———. 1968. "On Sherwood Anderson." *Talks with Authors*. Ed. Charles F. Madden. Carbondale: Southern Illinois University Press, 12–22.

Guerin, Wilfred L. " 'Death in the Woods': Sherwood Anderson's 'Cold Pastoral.' " *College English Association Critic* 30 (May 1968):4–5.

Hepburn, James G. "Disarming and Uncanny Visions: Freud's 'The Uncanny' with Regard to Form and Content in Stories by Sherwood Anderson and D. H. Lawrence." *Literature and Psychology* 9 (1959):9–12.

Howe, Irving. 1951. *Sherwood Anderson*. New York: William Sloane.

Joselyn, Sister Mary. "Some Artistic Dimensions of Sherwood Anderson's 'Death in the Woods.' " *Studies in Short Fiction* 4 (1967):252–59.

Kennedy, Thomas E. "Fiction as Its Own Subject: An Essay and Two Examples—Anderson's 'Death in the Woods' and Weaver's 'The Parts of Speech.' " *Kenyon Review* n.s. 9, no. 3 (Summer 1987):59–70.

Kramer, Dale. 1966. *Chicago Renaissance: The Literary Life in the Midwest, 1900–1930*. New York: Appleton-Century.

Lawry, Jon S. " 'Death in the Woods' and the Artist's Self in Sherwood Anderson." *PMLA* 74 (1959): 306–11. Rpt. in *Sherwood Anderson: A Collection of Critical Essays*. Ed. Walter B. Rideout. Englewood Cliffs, NJ: Prentice-Hall, 1974, 120–29.

Martin, Robert A. "Primitivism in Stories by Willa Cather & Sherwood Anderson." *Midamerica* 3 (1976):39–45.

Mencken, H. L. 1981. *The Letters of H. L. Mencken*. Ed. Guy J. Forgue. Boston: Northeastern University Press.

Miller, William V. 1976. "Portraits of the Artist: Anderson's Fictional Storytellers." In *Sherwood Anderson: Dimensions of His Literary Art: A Collection of Critical Essays*. Ed. David D. Anderson. East Lansing: Michigan State University Press, 1–23.

———. 1974. "Earth-Mothers, Succubi, and Other Ectoplasmic Spirits: The Women in Sherwood Anderson's Short Stories." In *Midamerica I*. Ed. David D. Anderson. East Lansing, MI: Midwestern Press, 64–81. Rpt. in *Critical Essays on Sherwood Anderson*. Ed. David D. Anderson. Boston: G. K. Hall, 1981, 196–209.

Modlin, Charles E., ed. 1984. *Sherwood Anderson: Selected Letters*. Knoxville: University of Tennessee Press.

O. Henry Memorial Award: Prize Stories of 1926. 1927. Garden City, NY: Doubleday.

O'Neill, John. "Anderson Writ Large: 'Godliness' in *Winesburg, Ohio*." *Twentieth Century Literature* 23 (1977):67–83.

Pearson, Norman Holmes. "Anderson and the New Puritanism." *Newberry Library Bulletin* Second Series 2, no. 2 (December 1948):52–63. Rpt. in *Critical Essays on Sherwood Anderson*. Ed. David D. Anderson. Boston: G. K. Hall, 1981, 102–110.

Raymund, Bernard. "The Grammar of Not-Reason: Sherwood Anderson." *Arizona Quarterly* 12 (1956):48–60, 137–48.

Rideout, Walter B. 1976. "A Borrowing from Borrow." In Hilbert H. Campbell and Charles E. Modlin (Eds.). *Sherwood Anderson: Centennial Studies*. Troy, NY: Whitston, 162–74.

Robinson, Eleanor M. "A Study of 'Death in the Woods.'" *College English Association Critic* 30, no. 4 (January 1968):6.

Rohrberger, Mary. "The Man, the Boy, and the Myth: Sherwood Anderson's 'Death in the Woods.'" *Midcontinent American Studies Journal* 3 (Fall 1962):48–54.

Rosenfeld, Paul, ed. 1942. *Sherwood Anderson's Memoirs*. New York: Harcourt, Brace.

———, ed. 1942. *The Sherwood Anderson Reader*. New York: Harcourt, Brace.

Scheick, William J. "Compulsion Toward Repetition: Sherwood Anderson's 'Death in the Woods.'" *Studies in Short Fiction* 11 (1974):141–46.

Schevill, James. 1951. *Sherwood Anderson: His Life and Work*. Denver: University of Denver Press.

Spencer, Benjamin T. "Sherwood Anderson: American Mythopoeist." *American Literature* 41 (1969):1–18.

Sutton, William A., ed. 1985. *Letters to Bab: Sherwood Anderson to Marietta D. Finley, 1916–33*. Foreword by Walter B. Rideout. Urbana and Chicago: University of Illinois Press.

Taylor, Welford Dunaway. 1977. *Sherwood Anderson*. New York: Frederick Ungar.

Townsend, Kim. 1987. *Sherwood Anderson*. Boston: Houghton Mifflin.

Trilling, Lionel. 1950. "Sherwood Anderson." *The Liberal Imagination: Essays on Literature and Society*. New York: Viking, 22–33. Originally in *Kenyon Review* 3 (1941):293–302. Rpt. in *Sherwood Anderson: Winesburg, Ohio: Text and Criticism*. Ed. John H. Ferres. New York: Viking, 1966, 455–67. Rpt. in *Achievement of Sherwood Anderson: Essays in Criticism*. Ed. Ray Lewis White. Chapel Hill: University of North Carolina Press, 1966, 212–24. Rpt. in *Sherwood Anderson: A Collection of Critical Essays*. Ed. Walter B. Rideout. Englewood Cliffs, NJ: Prentice-Hall, 1974, 130–38.

Troy, William. "Fragmentary Ends." *Nation* 136 (1933):508.

Voss, Arthur. 1973. *The American Short Story: A Critical Survey*. Norman: University of Oklahoma Press.

Wagner, Linda W. 1976. "Sherwood, Stein, the Sentence, and Grape Sugar and Oranges." In *Sherwood Anderson: Dimensions of His Literary Art: A Collection of Critical Essays*. Ed. David D. Anderson. East Lansing: Michigan State University Press, 75–89.

Way, Brian. 1971. "Sherwood Anderson." In Malcolm Bradbury and David Palmer (Eds.), *The American Novel and the Nineteen Twenties*. Stratford-upon-Avon Studies 13. London: Edward Arnold, 107–126.

Weber, Brom. 1964. *Sherwood Anderson*. Minneapolis: University of Minnesota Press. Rpt. in *Seven Novelists in the American Naturalist Tradition: An Introduction*. Ed. Charles Child Walcutt. Minneapolis: University of Minnesota Press, 1974, 168–204.

West, Ray B., Jr. 1952. *The Short Story in America: 1900–1950*. Chicago: Regnery. Rpt. New York: Books for Libraries (Division of Arno Press), 1979.

White, Ray Lewis. "Death in the Woods: Anderson's Earliest Version." *Winesburg Eagle* 7, no. 2 (April 1982):1–3.

———, ed. 1969. *Sherwood Anderson's Memoirs*. Chapel Hill: University of North Carolina Press.

Wright, Austin McGiffert. 1961. *The American Short Story in the Twenties*. Chicago: University of Chicago Press.

The Return

Circumstances of Composition

By the time he wrote "The Return," during the first week of November 1924, Sherwood Anderson had become a famous author. Much of his fiction had received high acclaim, and he had mingled with intellectuals and artists in Chicago, New York, Paris, and London. In July he and his wife, Elizabeth, had moved to New Orleans, where he enjoyed his celebrity and his association with the literary crowd there. But he had various worries, personal and artistic. He was still looking for security.

Sources and Influences

"The Return" almost certainly springs from the author's own life. The fictional town of Caxton is based primarily on Clyde, where Anderson spent most of his boyhood, where he played baseball for the local team and occasionally rode on a freight train for adventure, and which—like the central character of "The Return"—he left after his mother died. Once of his close boyhood friends, too, was named Herman [Hurd]. Anderson's father had remarried, and the family had scattered; consequently, after a few visits in the early years after his departure, Anderson had stayed away, and the town of his boyhood gradually became less a reality than "a background on which to paint the dreams of his manhood" (*WO* 247).

But in the later years Anderson went to his hometown again from time to time. The germ of "The Return" must have been provided by one of these trips back to Clyde. After one such trip (in the summer of 1922), he wrote quite cheerfully, with little of the irony that so strongly colors the story: "Yesterday I spent with a group of my boyhood friends, now become lawyers, grocers, laborers, doctors, mechanics. We had a big feed out of doors on the shore of Sandusky bay—with wine and song. It was really charming of them. They had a notion I had done something but weren't very sure what it was so they got up this feast to celebrate anyway. One them said, 'We are proud of you. We don't know what for but we are proud of you anyway[']" (Sutton, *Letters* 184). But in another letter he betrays considerable anxiety: "What I think is that I have allowed people to make me a bit too conscious of myself. A certain humbleness toward life . . . was perhaps getting away from me" (Modlin, *Letters* 38–39). These sentiments are remarkably similar to those of the central character in this story as he heads toward home.

Anderson had teenage sons when he composed "The Return." His concerns about them also seem to be reflected in the musings of the father in the story.

Publication History

"The Return" was originally published in May of 1925 in the *Century Illustrated Monthly Magazine* (110:3–14). The *Century* had published the latter part of Anderson's "A Chicago Hamlet" in 1923 and his "When I Left Business for Literature" in 1924. Long one of the leading mass-market periodicals in America, the magazine was declining in quality and influence in the twenties but was still widely read (Tebbel 128). It also paid well. Anderson received $360 for the story, after his agent took a 10 percent commission.

O'Brien included "The Return" in his volume *The Best Short Stories of 1925* (21–38). In 1933 Anderson collected it with other tales in the volume *Death in the Woods* (27–56). It is one of only two stories from *Death in the Woods* that Rosenfeld selected for the posthumous *The Sherwood Anderson Reader,* where, oddly enough, it is placed in a section entitled "The Life of Art" (285–300). Modlin includes "The Return" in his collection *Certain Things Last* (161–78).

Relation to Other Works

Born of a specific event in Anderson's adulthood, the main action of this tale is virtually without parallel in his fiction. Yet there is a discernible link between the protagonist's fast-speed drive out of town and the wild carriage rides taken by Elizabeth Willard and Louise Bentley to let off emotional steam (in "Mother" and "Godliness," respectively). Daring driving is also a hallmark of Kit Brandon, in the novel of that title (1936); Kit drives fast partly because she has been a bootlegger, and partly because she is in symbolic flight from the pressures life has inflicted on her, but also because by that time Anderson had developed an idea about woman's compatibility with the machine that does not appear in his earlier fiction.

Unspoken thoughts lingering between emotionally separate husbands and wives is a motif that connects this story to many other works in the Anderson canon—notably, for example, "The Man in the Brown Coat" and *Poor White* (1920). This is one of five stories collected in *Death in the Woods* that concern "the death of a woman and its effect upon a male character"; here the central character, a widower "whose marriage for the sake of professional advancement has been sterile," searches for a deeper, more fulfilling relationship (Ferguson 218, 228).

Critical Studies

"The Return" is a third-person narrative about forty-year-old John Holden, a successful New York architect, who comes back to his hometown in the Midwest eighteen years after his original departure. A restrained, self-contained widower with nagging feelings of inadequacy, he returns looking for "time to think" and dreaming vaguely about renewing acquaintance with his old sweetheart. He is eager for adventure, for a life of deeper passion and more intense awareness of others. He finds out, however, that his once-youthful friends have lapsed into drearily unromantic middle age. Though John has contemplated being "a bit wilder, more reckless" (*DW* 36), he recoils from the cheap dissipations his friends offer and, to relieve his distress, races out of town in his roadster.

The events in the story are thoroughly mundane; its drama is that of multiple psychological stresses surging within a purely ordinary middle aged man. In consequence, perhaps, critics have had little to say about it. Howe judges the story to be more effective than most of Anderson's writing not in the "oral-storyteller mode" (173). One critic finds the story's central concern to be the protagonist's discovery that his past has been displaced by "the machine age" (D. Anderson 131–32). Another remarks that the theme is "the futility of returning to childhood scenes . . . in order to find a sense of adult identity"; John seeks something more than "casual sex" (Ferguson 224, 228). Yet the main character's multiple inner conflicts give the story a deeper complexity than these critics have acknowledged.

Wright's comments on the formal structure of "The Return" are similarly succinct but somewhat more illuminating. Wright classifies the story as a simple romance with an episode of discovery; it is romantic because the central character "gets a glimpse of what it means to be emotionally unfettered, to throw his habitual caution to the winds," yet, Wright observes, while the character's experiences lead him to understand better his own ambivalent feelings, there is no "permanent change" in his behavior (386, 184, 137). There is a fine touch of wry comedy in the ending, where the timid, guilt-ridden architect allays his welling anxieties by speeding away from his native town, telling himself with bravado, "Lord! It will be fun! I'll let her out." Readers understand why his trip has been upsetting, but they also know that racing down the highway will do little to alleviate his frustrated longing for a more authentic life.

Works Cited

Anderson, David. 1967. *Sherwood Anderson: An Introduction and Interpretation.* New York: Holt, Rinehart.

Anderson, Sherwood. 1920. *Poor White.* New York: B. W. Huebsch. Rpt. New York: Viking, 1966. Introduction by Walter B. Rideout.

———. 1933. *Death in the Woods and Other Stories.* New York: Liveright. Rpt. New York and London, 1961.

———. 1936. *Kit Brandon: A Portrait.* New York and London: Scribner's.

Ferguson, Mary Anne. 1981. "Sherwood Anderson's *Death in the Woods:* Toward a New Realism." In *Critical Essays on Sherwood Anderson.* Ed. David D. Anderson. Boston: G. K. Hall, 217–34. Originally printed in *Midamerica VII.* East Lansing, MI: Midwestern Press, 1980, 73–95.

Howe, Irving. 1951. *Sherwood Anderson.* New York: William Sloane.

Modlin, Charles E., ed. 1992. *Certain Things Last: The Selected Short Stories of Sherwood Anderson.* New York: Four Walls Eight Windows.

———, ed. 1984. *Sherwood Anderson: Selected Letters.* Knoxville: University of Tennessee Press.

O'Brien, Edward J. 1926. *The Best Short Stories of 1925.* Boston: Small, Maynard.

Rosenfeld, Paul, ed. 1947. *The Sherwood Anderson Reader.* Boston: Houghton Mifflin.

Sutton, William A., ed. 1985. *Letters to Bab: Sherwood Anderson to Marietta D. Finley, 1916–33.* Foreword by Walter B. Rideout. Urbana and Chicago: University of Illinois Press.

Tebbel, John. 1969. *The American Magazine: A Compact History.* New York: Hawthorn.

Wright, Austin McGiffert. 1961. *The American Short Story in the Twenties.* Chicago: University of Chicago Press.

There She Is—She Is Taking Her Bath

Circumstances of Composition

Sherwood Anderson wrote "There She Is—She Is Taking Her Bath" in August 1922. Staying in New York City at an apartment provided by his publisher, Ben Huebsch, he was writing with furious energy—"like a madman," he said (Sutton, *Letters* 184). A couple of months before, he had bought a Ford; now having "sold what was left of the Ford" and going only once a week to Huebsch's office to pick up his mail, he lived alone and kept secret his address—12 Saint Luke's Place (Modlin, *Letters* 40; Sutton, *Letters* 186). Except for a visit from his brother Karl, there were few outward distractions. He had left Tennessee Mitchell, his second wife, left Chicago, left his job as an advertising man. His inner turbulence poured into his work. "Have, since you left," he told his brother, "written five short stories and a poem. . . . I am rather set just now on developing in myself a satirical vein that I have never worked. Satire, delicately handled, can be a quite tremendous thing. The thing has to be handled with entire sympathy, and any taint of patronage would ruin it" (Jones-Rideout, *Letters* 89).

Now a widely recognized author, Anderson had acquired a literary agent, Otto Liveright, and had high hopes that he might be relieved from the difficulties of marketing his own work. This new arrangement, he had been led to believe, would enable him to write in his own way, without regard to publishers' demands, and magazines would pay him "a long price" (Sutton, *Letters* 187). This expectation did not quite pan out.

Sources and Influences

No doubt Anderson's own experience in the business world provided some background for this story, which is written from the perspective of a businessman. An equally important influence, and the target of its satire, was the genre of popular fiction about businessmen. Whereas the formula for writing such fiction, as Anderson well knew, included a depiction of the hero as resolute and courageous, this story mocks that heroic image by presenting the interior musings of a businessman who is revealed to be neurotically sensitive and ridiculously shy in his private life (Curry 35, 162). He harbors notions like Robert Browning's Duke of Ferraro ("A [wife's] tender look . . . should be saved and bestowed only upon her husband"), but his wife has nothing to fear from this timid soul, whose thoughts vacillate between self-vaunting pretension and wretched shame.

One critic has speculated that Anderson's reading of Henry James may have influenced this story as well; Somers perceives a similarity between the narrator of "There She Is—She Is Taking Her Bath" and the narrator of James's "The Aspern Papers" (91–92).

Publication History

Although "There She Is—She Is Taking Her Bath" was accepted for publication fairly quickly, a long delay separated its writing and its appearance in print. By January of 1923 Anderson delighted in his good luck in selling it for a fine sum: "A magazine has paid $750 for the story about the jealous husband. It's odd. Since I've been here [in New York], I've got more for two stories than I ever got for all the stories I've written these years" (Jones-Rideout, *Letters* 91, where "the story about the jealous husband" is erroneously identified as "The Man's Story"). The magazine was *The Pictorial Review,* an illustrated monthly and slick competitor to *Woman's Home Companion.* Having made his reputation primarily in the pages of little magazines, Anderson wondered if he had "sold out," yet he was glad enough of this sign that his "bread and butter struggle" was over (Jones-Rideout, *Letters* 91). Then the magazine staff began to hesitate; during the spring and summer, while Anderson pressed his agent to get the story in print "before October" so that he could include it in the collection *Horses and Men,* a dispute between the editor-in-chief and the circulation department made Liveright's entreaties futile (Curry 1, 153–54). Later Anderson, perhaps embellishing, would write a comic version of this episode. As he told it, the delay came after the story had been set in type and illustrated. First the editor asked that the title be changed ("Roll your own," the author said, but the editor thought that title did not fit, either); then, years later, the story was returned, with the explanation that it was incompatible with the "tone" of the *Pictorial Review;* happily, Anderson was never asked to return his $750 payment (Rosenfeld, *Memoirs* 436–37).

The story finally received publication in 1928 in *The Second American Caravan* (Kreymborg 100–111). Subsequently Anderson added it to the collection *Death in the Woods* (1933). Not surprisingly, it is the earliest composed of the tales in that book. The story has been selected for inclusion in recent editions of Anderson's short fiction by Maxwell Geismar, Frank Gado, and Charlie Modlin.

Relation to Other Works

Writing to Van Wyck Brooks in 1923, Anderson contrasted "There She Is— She Is Taking Her Bath" with "I'm a Fool" (Jones-Rideout, *Letters* 102). Responding to Brooks's praise for "I'm a Fool," Anderson agreed that it "holds water" but protested that Brooks should not "like best of my things the things easiest to like," that is, simple works with the immature perspective of a boy similar to Twain's Huck Finn; instead, Anderson solicited Brooks's appreciation of more complex and sophisticated stories—and he mentioned this story, "The Man Who Became a Woman," and "The Man's Story." The indication is that Anderson was striving to overcome his too-narrow classification as a voice of rural, adolescent experience. Interestingly, "There She Is—She Is Taking Her Bath" seems virtually to allude to "I'm a Fool" by the narrator's repeated self-questioning—when he says, for example, "I could not decide whether I was a fool" (*DW* 79). In one respect, then, Anderson has here translated the anxious uncertainties of boyhood into the anxious uncertainties of manhood. The story would fit easily within the framework of *Horses and Men,* which from many angles probes the vexed question of what it means to be a man.

Anderson's effort to develop "a satirical vein" (see "Circumstances of Composition") also was at least partly an attempt to broaden his reach as a writer; such tales as "There She Is—She Is Taking Her Bath" and "The Triumph of a Modern," written about the same time, are fruits of this effort. In both stories, Anderson's stylistic manipulations of language are skillfully aimed toward the overall satiric purpose and distinctly, instructively different from the lyrical style of *Winesburg, Ohio* and from the Twain-inspired style of "I'm a Fool."

As for thematic connection with Anderson's other fiction, Raymund observes that the "theme of impotence" here also is important in "The Flood" and "Why They Got Married," both likewise in *Death in the Woods* (147); numerous earlier works from *Winesburg* onward also deal with the same theme. More broadly, the whole problem of husbands and wives who cannot communicate with each other is prominent throughout Anderson's work, and the issue of marital infidelity is treated, more soberly, in stories such as "Respectability" and "The Other Woman." Perhaps the closest parallel, however, can be found in the posthumously published "The Persistent Liar," in which an adulterous husband whose wife finds an incriminating love note proceeds to deny repeatedly for years that any such note ever has existed (Papinchak 30).

Critical Studies

Set in New York City, "There She Is—She Is Taking Her Bath" is a monologue written by a desperately worried man who has discovered evidence
that his wife may be having an illicit affair. Nerve-wrenching doubt and
confusion disrupt his self-important complacence and professional competence. The name the husband gives is John Smith, but it "sounds like an
alias" (Papinchak 29). He cannot bear not knowing the truth, nor can he
bear to find it out. His wife remains perfectly nonchalant, and the thought
of an unseemly confrontation with her is so discomfiting that he decides to
"use finesse" instead. His "finesse," however, immediately turns into a series
of clumsy maneuverings and preposterous evasions.

Interpretation of the story has been brief but generally appreciative.
Bland found it a "chortlingly funny" tale, a comedy about a husband who
has led a life of "the sanest, plainest sort" and thus is uncomprehending and
"slightly unbalanced" by his wife's infidelity (133–34). Schevill agreed that it
is one of Anderson's "best humorous pieces" (302; similarly, Townsend 283).

With a sharply different sense of the tone of the story, Geismar once
praised it as "a miniature of the human tragedy inherent in our American
success patterns" (*Last* 272). Later, considering the story at a bit more length
in the introductory essay of his Anderson collection, Geismar partially
amends his earlier view: "Here Anderson raised an episode of 'domestic
drama' to a fine level of tragicomedy" (xix). Still unwilling to emphasize the
satiric and comic elements of the tale, Geismar considers it one of
Anderson's "ironic parables of human weakness and conflict," a translation
of the idea of the grotesque central to *Winesburg* into more "ordinary
human relationships." This assessment of the story has value, but it is not
adequate. Certainly, the narrator is weak and suffers from inner conflict, and
his misery is vividly grotesque. Yet his absurd avoidance of the obvious
solution to his problem—simply asking his wife about the note from Bill—
renders his behavior less pitiable than laughable.

Above all, though, what makes the story funny is the manner of its telling.
An astute analyst observes that the story is "deliciously larded with clichés"
(Raymund 147). The narrator thinks of himself and other businessmen as
persons "of some account in the world" in contradistinction to "young
squirts" with canes and mustaches who go about "ogling women." He repeatedly calls himself "a man whose honor has been tampered with." With
overblown dignity he asserts his principles: "We men must protect the integrity of our homes and our firesides." Milquetoast though he is, what he
repeatedly, pompously "maintains" is "I am right." He is "not to have the
wool pulled over [his] eyes." Unfortunately, his way of (as he says) "vindi-
cating his honor" is only imagined—and in terms as hilarious for the reader
as solemn for him: "There, take that and that. . . . I will muss your mus-

tache. Give me that cane. I will break it over your head" (*DW* 62). He becomes faintly aware of his own reliance on clichés (Ferguson 225). Reluctantly surrendering his delusion that he is "man of the world," he is humiliated because the detectives he hires patronize him and because his wife calmly takes a bath as his world caves in; the reader's appropriate response is "amused sympathy" (Somers 88). Though one critic finds that "humor disappears as the impotent protagonist realizes that his fears will continue, that his hands will shake, and that he will spill his dessert" (D. Anderson 132), it is a mistake to disregard the ludicrous disproportion between the poor man's problem—his wife's apparent adultery—and the result he dreads—spilled dessert.

According to Gado, the husband is not motivated by jealousy so much as by regard for rules and "codes of behavior." His "paragon" is a master of "the rules of whist," and "the thought that his wife believes she can *cheat* with impunity" stirs his admiration (9). He stands outside the bathroom door "feckless before the greater mystery of woman" (10).

A further dimension of the tale is that the reader is scarcely more certain than Smith himself about whether or not the wife is really carrying on a love affair. Is her unfaithfulness "real or a product of Smith's overactive imagination"? (Somers 86). It is not true that "the reader easily perceives the innocence of the wife who is merely taking a bath" (Ferguson 228). Despite the author's own statement (years after the composition of the tale) that the wife is "quite innocent" (Rosenfeld, *Memoirs* 437), the story is anything but conclusive about the matter. On the one hand, a perfumed note signed "Bill" invites her to a rendezvous in the park "when the old goat has gone away." That looks pretty incriminating. On the other hand, Smith's conclusion that two young carpet-sweeper salesmen are confederates in "a pretty slick scheme" to disguise the adulterous liaison seems to be a silly exaggeration (Papinchak 30). Just as Smith hires one detective to tell him the truth and another one to ensure that the first one tells him that Mrs. Smith is faithful whether she is or not, readers are deprived of certainty—and not merely about Mrs. Smith. Mr. Smith repeatedly admonishes the reader, "What do you know of the secret life led by your wife?" The irony may be directed chiefly at him, but some of it is deflected outward as well. The mock heroic mode here gives way to the modernist absurd.

Works Cited

Anderson, David. 1967. *Sherwood Anderson: An Introduction and Interpretation*. New York: Holt, Rinehart.

Anderson, Sherwood. "The Persistent Liar." *Tomorrow* (September 6, 1946):10–12.

Bland, Winifred. 1970. "Through a College Window." In *Homage to Sherwood Anderson, 1876–1941*. Ed. Paul P. Appel. Mamaroneck, NY: Appel, 131–37.

Curry, Martha Mulroy. 1975. *The "Writer's Book" by Sherwood Anderson: A Critical Edition*. Metuchen, NJ: Scarecrow Press.

Ferguson, Mary Anne. 1981. "Sherwood Anderson's *Death in the Woods:* Toward a New Realism." In *Critical Essays on Sherwood Anderson*. Ed. David D. Anderson. Boston: G. K. Hall, 217–34. Originally printed in *Midamerica VII*. East Lansing, MI: Midwestern Press, 1980, 73–95.

Gado, Frank, ed. 1983. *The Teller's Tales*. Signature Series. Schenectady, NY: Union College Press.

Geismar, Maxwell, ed. 1962. *Sherwood Anderson: Short Stories*. New York: Hill and Wang.

———. 1947. "Sherwood Anderson: Last of the Townsmen." *The Last of the Provincials: The American Novel, 1915–1925*. Boston: Houghton Mifflin, 223–84. Rpt. in part in *Sherwood Anderson:* Winesburg, Ohio: *Text and Criticism*. Ed. John H. Ferres. New York: Viking, 1966, 377–82.

Jones, Howard Mumford, and Walter B. Rideout, eds. 1953. *Letters of Sherwood Anderson*. Boston: Little, Brown.

Kreymborg, Alfred, Lewis Mumford, and Paul Rosenfeld, eds. 1928. *The Second Amerian Caravan: A Yearbook of American Literature*. New York: Macaulay.

Modlin, Charles E., ed. 1992. *Certain Things Last: The Selected Stories of Sherwood Anderson*. New York: Four Walls Eight Windows.

———, ed. 1984. *Sherwood Anderson: Selected Letters*. Knoxville: University of Tennessee Press.

Papinchak, Robert Allen. 1992. *Sherwood Anderson: A Study of the Short Fiction*. New York: Twayne.

Raymund, Bernard. "The Grammar of Not-Reason: Sherwood Anderson." *Arizona Quarterly* 12 (1956):48–60, 137–48.

Rosenfeld, Paul, ed. 1942. *Sherwood Anderson's Memoirs*. New York: Harcourt, Brace.

Schevill, James. 1951. *Sherwood Anderson: His Life and Work*. Denver: University of Denver Press.

Somers, Paul P[reston], Jr. 1974. "Anderson's Twisted Apples and Hemingway's Crips." In *Midamerica I*. Ed. David D. Anderson. East Lansing, MI: Midwestern Press, 82–97.

Sutton, William A., ed. 1985. *Letters to Bab: Sherwood Anderson to Marietta*

D. *Finley, 1916–33*. Foreword by Walter B. Rideout. Urbana and Chicago: University of Illinois Press.

Townsend, Kim. 1987. *Sherwood Anderson*. Boston: Houghton Mifflin.

Way, Brian. 1971. "Sherwood Anderson." In *The American Novel and the Nineteen Twenties*. Malcolm Bradbury and David Palmer (Eds.). Stratford-upon-Avon Studies 13. London: Edward Arnold, 107–26.

Wright, Austin McGiffert. 1961. *The American Short Story in the Twenties*. Chicago: University of Chicago Press.

The Lost Novel

Circumstances of Composition

In 1928, Sherwood Anderson lived in Marion, Virginia, with his third wife, Elizabeth Prall Anderson. Since November of 1927, he had been editing two local papers, the *Smyth County News* and the *Marion Democrat,* and these provided him with an income and the interest of involvement in a small town's varied activities. His serious artistic writing, though, was being hindered by journalistic activity, and he knew that his marriage was coming apart.

Failure had become familiar. He was famous, but a younger generation already viewed him as past his prime. Over the years he had begun and abandoned numerous lengthy attempts at novels. As for marriage, Anderson had walked out on his first wife and their three children, had left his second wife not too many years later, and would soon—in December of 1928—send his third wife off to her family in California and tell her not to come back.

A probable date of composition for "The Lost Novel" is suggested by a letter Anderson wrote on March 26 to his friend Roger Sergel, who was then in Chicago, living at the edge of Jackson Park. Sergel's address was very near the apartment where Floyd Dell had lived in 1913, when Anderson had begun to congregate there with the writers and artists of the Chicago Renaissance. It was also close to the apartment where Anderson had lived from 1904 to 1906 with Cornelia, his first wife. Reminiscing about nights when he once wandered about the park with his dreams, Anderson asks Sergel: "Did

I ever tell you the story of my lost novel? That happened on what is called the Japanese island in Jackson Park" (Jones-Rideout, *Letters* 182–83).

Sources and Influences

Understandably, a biographical source has been suggested for "The Lost Novel." Sutton points out the parallel between essential story details and Anderson's "relationship with [his first wife] Cornelia in his artistic crisis in Elyria [Ohio] and Chicago" (564). As Anderson had done, the fictional British novelist has neglected his job and family for his writing. And, though he is ashamed about his ruthlessness, his "casual, brutal" treatment of his wife, he has "kept on writing. . . . " In this story, Anderson changes the locale, rearranges the "time sequences," and simplifies the characters' "reactions," but, Sutton believes, "the meaning of the transcendent artistic experience and the devotion of the artist" at the expense of his personal, domestic relations are drawn fairly directly from the author's own life.

Publication History

"The Lost Novel" first appeared in September 1928 in *Scribner's Magazine* (84:255–58). Anderson reprinted it later the same month in the weekly newspaper he owned and edited, the *Smyth County News* (September 20, p. 5). The following year the story was published along with one other, later to be titled "Like a Queen," in the slender volume *Alice and the Lost Novel,* the tenth in a series of The Woburn Books, issued in 530 numbered copies by the London firm Elkin Mathews & Marot. Edward J. O'Brien also chose the story for his *The Best Short Stories of 1929.* Anderson subsequently collected it into his book *Death in the Woods* (1933). More recently, Maxwell Geismar has included it in *Sherwood Anderson: Short Stories* (1962).

Relation to Other Works

Miller states that "The Lost Novel" is one of only three Anderson stories with a European setting (20). Plausibly, Miller speculates that the author employed the setting "to disguise a very personal subject matter." A similar situation, Miller adds, appears in an Anderson tale published posthumously as "The Yellow Gown," where the artist at work on his masterpiece is unconscious of the life of the woman who loves him. A repetitive feature of Anderson's artist characters is that these men "misuse women but find them indispensable." Above all, as Miller implies, it is "The Man's Story" that presents Anderson's conflicted feelings about art and women and his final quilt-ridden acceptance of the sacrifice of individual women "to the life of the imagination—the focal point of his deepest sense of morality" (20–21).

The situation in "The Lost Novel" bears an especially close resemblance to "Loneliness," in which the entrance of a woman into a room spells tragedy. In both instances, the actuality of a woman collides with the artist's ideal abstractions.

The story also contains an interesting parallel to the *Winesburg* tale "Paper Pills." As Doctor Reefy erects towers of thought which he then later knocks down, so the novelist in this later story builds up in his mind "[w]hat is to be the book" and laughs when it "is destroyed" (*DW* 83, 91). Each character realizes that one can never quite capture the elusive essence he pursues, and both of them accept the dreadful cost of the endless pursuit with something like gaiety.

In this story and in "The Return" William Troy laments what he sees as Anderson's "return to the thinness of characterization and detail, the diffuse lyricism" of his early works, in which can be found the same "monotonous insistence" on the theme of "inarticulateness" (508).

See also the discussion of "Like a Queen."

Critical Studies

Set in England on the Thames Embankment, this story is a first-person narrative in which an English novelist tells an American short story writer about the failure of his marriage and about a strange experience he had one night in Hyde Park, when he "wrote a novel at one sitting" but discovered the next day that his novel "was nothing but blank empty sheets of paper" (*DW* 91). He had poured all his love into the novel, feeling at last that he "had done justice to" the woman and children he had driven away. But once again, reality intruded upon his quest for an unattainable ideal.

The writer has been incapable of "reconciling art with family life"; the "intensity of his commitment" to art becomes clear when, after he knocks his wife down for interrupting his writing, "he is ashamed, but not repentant" (Miller 20–21).

Ferguson proposes that the narrator of the story, "shocked by the injustice of [the] novelist's perception of his wife as an object to be abused and used for literary puposes, perceives the novelist's self-deception" (228). But she does not provide evidence to support that claim, and it seems tenuous. While the text acknowledges the novelist's cruelty, it gives primary emphasis to the poignance of his quixotic devotion.

Critic David Anderson is probably correct in asserting that "The Lost Novel" seeks, in the "genially" rambling style of the oral storyteller, to define "the mystic qualities of the creative experience" as the artist himself experiences it (115). But does the story succeed? It is an understatement to say that that critic's opinion that the story is "one of [Sherwood Anderson's] most pleasant works" is not widely shared. Anderson anticipated such a reception, though. Disconcertingly, the story ends with the narrator's expressed doubt that more than "a dozen" people will understand it.

Works Cited

Anderson, David. 1967. *Sherwood Anderson: An Introduction and Interpretation*. New York: Holt, Rinehart.

Anderson, Sherwood. 1929. *Alice and the Lost Novel*. Number Ten of the Woburn Books. London: Elkin Mathews & Marrot.

Jones, Howard Mumford, and Walter B. Rideout, eds. 1953. *Letters of Sherwood Anderson*. Boston: Little, Brown.

Geismar, Maxwell, ed. 1962. *Sherwood Anderson: Short Stories*. New York: Hill and Wang.

Ferguson, Mary Anne. 1981. "Sherwood Anderson's *Death in the Woods:* Toward a New Realism." In *Critical Essays on Sherwood Anderson*. Ed. David D. Anderson. Boston: G. K. Hall, 217–34. Originally printed in *Midamerica VII*. East Lansing, MI: Midwestern Press, 1980, 73–95.

Miller, William V. 1976. "Portraits of the Artist: Anderson's Fictional Storytellers." In *Sherwood Anderson: Dimensions of His Literary Art: A Collection of Critical Essays*. Ed. David D. Anderson. East Lansing: Michigan State University Press, 1–23.

O'Brien, Edward J. 1929. *The Best Short Stories of 1929*. Boston: Small, Maynard.

Sutton, William A. 1972. *The Road to Winesburg: A Mosaic of the Imaginative Life of Sherwood Anderson*. Metuchen, NJ: Scarecrow Press.

The Fight

Circumstances of Composition

"The Fight" was written during July 1927. Anderson was doing a series of pieces for *Vanity Fair*. The previous September, in one of the biggest fights of all time, Gene Tunney had taken Jack Dempsey's heavyweight boxing title. As the nation made preparation for a rematch, Anderson composed this story. From December of 1926 through March of 1927, he and his wife, Elizabeth, had vacationed in Paris, where he had been received with great fanfare. Headlines had trumpeted his arrival, and parties were held in his honor. But the trip had been depressing in a number of ways, and he was deeply glad to return to America and (after a brief lecture tour) to the hills of Troutdale, Virginia, where his own stone house was under construction. "I went to Paris and found myself close to famous," he wrote his friend Paul Rosenfeld, who had gone with him on an earlier, happier trip; "That's just plain sickening" (Jones-Rideout, *Letters* 170). Anderson was in a slump. On the day his ship returned to the States, his brother Earl died. His third wife could not feed his emotional hungers. He was fifty years old. Past achievement seemed to interfere with present relationships. And his writing for the most part seemed to go nowhere. With terrific energy he began—and then abandoned—one project after another. Despite all the public recognition, his recent books had received sadly mixed reviews. A younger generation of more avant-garde writers was casting him aside. He did not believe that he was finished as a writer, but undoubtedly he was losing his confidence.

Sources and Influences

Ernest Hemingway's *The Torrents of Spring* had been published in May of 1926. It was a parody of Anderson's style and themes in general, and of *Dark Laughter* in particular. Anderson had promoted young Hemingway's career from the time of their earliest acquaintance in Chicago; he had helped to get *In Our Time* accepted by Liveright; and he had sent Hemingway a copy of his own new book *Dark Laughter*. He had not expected the public blow Hemingway dealt him in return.

Just before *Torrents* came out, Hemingway wrote to Anderson to explain. His parody was "a joke," he said, and not "meant to be mean," but it was also "absolutely sincere"; Anderson's recent writing was "rotten" (Baker, *Letters* 205). The terms he used to discuss the book he had written were taken from boxing: he did not think that writers should have to "pull [their] punches." He told Anderson he knew it looked as though "because you had always been swell to me . . . I felt an irresistible need to push you in the face," but really that had nothing to do with it. The satire was simply aimed at bad writing and was supposed to be "funny." Wanting to know whether his attack had made Anderson "sore," Hemingway closed with a couple of chatty paragraphs, in which he mentioned his plans for a trip to Arkansas (206).

On June 14 Anderson responded. First he mentioned his new Virginia farm, inviting Hemingway and his wife to stop for a visit on their way to Arkansas. But he expressed resentment of the "patronizing" tone Hemingway had used in his letter and the implication that the parody would be somehow fatal (Modlin, *Letters* 79–80; see also White, *Memoirs* 463). He continued the metaphor of the fight:

> You speak so regretfully, tenderly, of giving me a punch. . . . Come out of it, man. I pack a little wallop myself. I've been middleweight champion. You seem to forget that. . . . I think the Scribner book will help me and hurt you. Spite of all you say, it's got the smarty tinge. You know it. . . . But in your turn now, man, don't get sore at me. If you are going to wallop, you've got to take yours. You started it. I didn't.

With some politely friendly closing lines and a parting joke, he carried it off. He could take a punch.

Hemingway's next letter (July 1) acknowledged that his elder rival did not have "a glass jaw" (Baker, *Letters* 210). But his own jaw was not made of glass, either, he wanted Anderson to know. He would not "headslip" Anderson's charge that the letter about *Torrents* had perhaps been patronizing; he would "take it on the nose." He would, however, "counter [Anderson's] lead" by explaining that he had more integrity than Anderson had given him credit for. And, yes, he might stop by Anderson's farm; it "would be grand" to see him, either there or in Paris. He would try not to "lead with [his] chin and forget to duck" next time.

Jovial and hostile at the same time, the banter continued. Anderson wrote back on July 17, referring to the light heavyweight bout that had been fought the previous night, when " 'pop 'em' Paul Berlenbach got popped . . . by Jack Delaney" (Modlin, *Letters* 81). But Anderson was generous, too. He was glad Hemingway had "the ability to take it" and glad of Hemingway's growing reputation. Again he invited Hemingway for a visit.

Hemingway responded that the Arkansas trip had been canceled, but he thanked Anderson "for the swell letter" (Baker, *Letters* 218). The proof for his novel *The Sun Also Rises* had been mailed, and he hoped Anderson would like it—it was not "smarty." But a lot of things were going badly, he confided, and he had been troubled by insomnia. There was something like an apology for the tone of his May letter, but also an excuse: "the show is really very tough and it is winning all the time and unless you know everything when you're twenty five you don't stand a chance of knowing anything at all when it's had time to shake down and you're thirty five . . ." (219).

Anderson's reply needled Hemingway. "My God man, I have always thought of you as a horse for strength. It shocks me to hear that you don't sleep. Aren't there any real huskies in the world?" (Modlin, *Letters* 86). But on the whole he was polite, genial, and self-abnegating. Calling Hemingway "old dear," he wrote, "Most of the time I don't know a thing. I get older in my body but can't seem to get it up into my head. No one gets very wise I guess. At least I know I don't" (87).

Anderson arrived in Paris in December, accompanied by his wife and two of his children. It is not clear exactly what happened there. Anderson and Hemingway met in January and maybe again in February. In a letter to Maxwell Perkins, Hemingway told of spending a couple of afternoons with Anderson: "He was not at all sore about *Torrents* and we had a fine time" (Baker, *Letters* 241). Anderson was to remember it differently in his *Memoirs;* by this account, Hemingway had waited till the Andersons' "last day in Paris" to visit, and when they went out for a drink Hemingway offered an awkward "here's how," then "turned and walked rapidly away" (White, *Memoirs* 465). Elizabeth Anderson, who never forgave Hemingway for *Torrents* or for his "repellently patronizing" letter, recalled that when Hemingway had dropped by in Paris, he had made fun of their hotel; she had reciprocated with pointed rudeness (170, 130–31). Whatever happened, Anderson seems to have summed up his feelings in a letter to Rosenfeld, written in late April: "It made me pretty sick seeing Hemingway this winter" (Jones-Rideout, *Letters* 173).

Publication History

"The Fight" appeared in the October 1927 issue of *Vanity Fair* (29:72, 106, 108). During the late summer of 1926, Anderson had contracted with *Vanity Fair* to write a series of articles, one a month. He was to be allowed to pick his own subjects (Jones-Rideout, *Letters* 158). The magazine would pay him $300 apiece for twelve articles (Schevill 236). Anderson's association with *Vanity Fair* went back to 1921, when they had brought forth "Why There

Must Be a Midwestern Literature," later reprinted as "Milk Bottles." The magazine, light, lively, and sophisticated, printed little fiction, but by 1926 Anderson had become a regular contributor, and a few of his contributions were short stories. On August 19, 1927, the editor wrote Anderson to say: "Just reread the story about the fight. Believe me, dear boy, it is one of the best things I have ever read" (Sherwood Anderson Papers).

When Anderson gathered his stories for the collection *Death in the Woods,* published in April of 1933, he chose four of well over a dozen pieces from *Vanity Fair* for inclusion. This is the earliest of those he selected.

Relation to Other Works

In classic Andersonian fashion, "The Fight" enables readers to see the turbid emotional currents surging beneath the surface of ordinary men's lives. As it often happens in Anderson's fiction, the currents burst forth in an act that by "normal" standards is absurd and foolish. In "The Strength of God," for example, a minister thrusts his hand through a glass window. Or, in "The Egg," an earnest shopowner hurls an egg at a customer. In "The Fight" a savage need for self-assertion seething within two intelligent, educated, respectable, professional men explodes unexpectedly in a bloody fistfight.

The theme of the buried life intersects in "The Fight" with another theme characteristic of Anderson's work—the idea that childishness is an important component of manhood as we know it. As early as 1917, in "An Apology for Crudity," Anderson had stated his belief that Americans "are a crude and childlike people" and that America's literature necessarily should reflect the simple reality of its people (437). He went on to write vividly of adolescent experience in powerful stories such as "I Want to Know Why." His partly autobiographical *Tar* (1926) looked at the world through a child's eyes. And, more and more, he probed the childish impulses, thoughts, and fancies that linger into adulthood, rendering mature men—and commonly Anderson's fiction is gender-specific in this regard—strangely or absurdly foolish to themselves and others. The immature, irresponsible father figure, modeled after the author's own father, reappears in Anderson's fiction from *Windy McPherson's Son* (1916) onward and is prominent in stories like "The Egg" and "The Sad Horn Blowers." But the theme of childishness expands to much larger range in the stories collected in *Death in the Woods,* for it includes the businessman's ridiculously helpless jealousy in "There She Is— She Is Taking Her Bath," the Southern poet's need for a comforting mother in "A Meeting South," the mountaineer's touching homesickness in "A Sentimental Journey," the middle-aged doctor's boyish nervousness about love in "Another Wife," and the Wilder cousins' puerile vindictiveness in "The Fight."

Critical Studies

"The Fight" is a story of two men, cousins, who suddenly engage in a dead serious, childishly silly fight. It is told in the third person by a narrator whose point of view is mostly that of one of the cousins, John Wilder, at whose home the other, Alfred Wilder, is a guest. Having grown up more or less together "in the same Middle-Western American small town" (*DW* 96), the Wilder cousins have always performed the customary family civilities, exchanging gifts and courtesy notes. But beneath the surface politeness, they have concealed a heartfelt dislike for each other. They have moved to different cities, and—now professional men of nearly fifty—they have not seen each other for years. When Alfred pays a call on his cousin, only some perverse will involving guilt about his long-harbored hatred moves John to invite him to stay for a longer visit. Though they treat each other with elaborate politeness, their irrational hostility simmers and then without warning erupts into a sudden, intense fight. John gets a black eye. He thinks hopefully that Alfred may be awfully sore tomorrow. Alfred leaves. Nothing is resolved.

This story, though powerful in substance and accomplished in style, has been almost completely overlooked. David Anderson comments: "It is an attempt to point out the senselessness and the irrationality at the heart of human rivalry, which no amount of reason can change. Only a change of heart can do this, Anderson points out, an act of love that cannot be intellectualized" (132). Mary Anne Ferguson states, "'The Flight' [*sic*] shows the necessity of putting aside childish views if one is to be taken seriously" (224). Both critics widely miss the mark. The story does indeed depict the irrationality of rivalry, but it contains not a hint of the didactic. In no way does it recommend love or any other solution to the sheer fact of unreasoned, savage antipathies that sometimes underlie civilized behavior. The story is psychologically insightful, unblinkingly honest in its realism, and masterful in its subtle handling of tone. Devoid of tenderness but replete with understanding, its complex tone emerges from the perception that the fight between these normally sensible, self-controlled men on the one hand is ridiculously petty and childish and on the other hand represents an elemental struggle for masculine dominance.

The structure of the story is reminiscent of that Anderson had used frequently in *Winesburg, Ohio*. The narrative opens in the present and briefly introduces the characters, moves into a long section detailing the background of the present situation, and upon returning to the opening scene, relates a dramatic episode that provides the climax. A particularly interesting aspect of the handling of the material here is that the section of narrative background that deals with the Wilders' childhood conveys a mordant recognition of the vicious cruelty of supposed innocents; when John shot the dog he once had loved, "[i]t was an oddly satisfactory feeling to see him die" because this oblique retaliation would make Alfred suffer (*DW* 100). The emotional content of adulthood is revealed then to be similarly perverse. Both men know how absurd their behavior has been, and they both laugh with counterfeit calm and friendliness, but their hatred continues unabated.

Readers of this story apparently have failed to recognize the biographical interest of this story, as it sheds light on Anderson's feelings about his fight with Hemingway. It is of considerable importance. And some day "The Fight" may prove significant as a document about American culture, which is characterized by the persistence of old patterns of physical aggression within a middle-class code of conduct that seeks to deny or transcend aggression. But even on its own terms, it is a story worth resurrecting.

Works Cited

Anderson, David. 1967. *Sherwood Anderson: An Introduction and Interpretation*. New York: Holt, Rinehart.

Anderson, Elizabeth, and Gerald R. Kelley. 1969. *Miss Elizabeth: A Memoir*. Boston: Little, Brown.

Anderson, Sherwood. "An Apology for Crudity." *Dial* 63 (November 8, 1917):437–38.

Baker, Carlos, ed. 1981. *Ernest Hemingway: Selected Letters, 1917–1961*. New York: Scribners.

Ferguson, Mary Anne. 1981. "Sherwood Anderson's *Death in the Woods*: Toward a New Realism." In *Critical Essays on Sherwood Anderson*. Ed. David D. Anderson. Boston: G. K. Hall, 217–34. Originally printed in *Midamerica VII*. East Lansing, MI: Midwestern Press, 1980, 73–95. Rpt. in *Sherwood Anderson: A Study of the Short Fiction*. By Robert Allen Papinchak. New York: Twayne, 1992, 141–62.

Jones, Howard Mumford, and Walter B. Rideout, eds. 1953. *Letters of Sherwood Anderson*. Boston: Little, Brown.

Modlin, Charles E., ed. 1984. *Sherwood Anderson: Selected Letters*. Knoxville: University of Tennessee Press.

Sherwood Anderson Papers. Newberry Library. Chicago, Illinois.

White, Ray Lewis, ed. 1969. *Sherwood Anderson's Memoirs: A Critical Edition*. Chapel Hill: University of North Carolina Press.

Like a Queen

Circumstances of Composition

Sherwood Anderson wrote this story in late June or early July 1928. At the time, he lived in Marion, a small town in the Virginia mountains. In the fall of 1927, with the aid of a loan from Burton Emmett, he had become the owner of two weekly newspapers, and for a while he enjoyed the fun of editing them—meeting local people from all walks of life; covering various issues, celebrations, checker tournaments, and shootings; genially expounding his opinions; and occasionally publishing a piece of fiction. He and his wife, Elizabeth, though they lived together and though she helped handle the business, had long since begun to drift apart. She held herself distant from the local Southerners, whom she considered uncouth, dogmatic, and boring. She tried to refine her husband and stonily tolerated what she saw as his childishness. If once she had given him inspiration, the struggle between them now drained his spirit. They did not talk about the growing rift in their relationship, even when he in a moment of despair tried to kill them both by driving over an embankment (Elizabeth Anderson 176–77).

Sources and Influences

"Like a Queen" carries strong suggestions that there were definite real-life models for the several queenly women who figure in it. The "friend" who "had something like a nervous breakdown" and went "to the Ozark Mountains" covertly refers to Anderson himself in 1912 and 1913, during the dissolution of his first marriage. No one has yet offered a guess about specific models for the women characters. David Anderson does, however, trace the qualities of womanly understanding, "intuitive wisdom and feeling," to the "inner beauty" that the author remembered as the essence of his own mother (Sherwood 115). Generally, it can be said that Anderson nearly always considered himself "a lover of abstract womanhood" (Sutton, *Letters* 326).

Publication History

At its first publication the story was named "Beauty," a title assigned by the editor of *Harper's Bazaar,* where it appeared in January of 1929 (63:78–79). Restoring to it his original title, "Alice," Anderson reprinted it in his little country newspaper, the *Smyth County News* (May 2, 1929, p. 2). During the same year, it was paired with "The Lost Novel" for publication as the tenth of the Woburn Books series, *Alice and the Lost Novel,* issued in a limited edition of 530 numbered copies by the London firm Elkin Mathews & Marrot (3–15). Then Anderson chose it from among his stories for inclusion in his 1933 book *Death in the Woods,* renaming it "Like a Queen" (111–23). In 1962, Geismar published it in his collection of Anderson stories (148–55).

Relation to Other Works

Critics have observed the importance of "Like a Queen" as a statement about Anderson's view of women, for it constitutes part of a long meditation, inextricably entangled with his personal experiences, about the importance of the female to the male. The main character, Alice, has the same "ability to give of herself and to project understanding and trust to the men around her" that the title characters of *Windy McPherson's Son* (1916) and *Tar* (1926) find in their mothers; yet the "dream quality" attached to those earlier portrayals has disappeared, and the "wife-mother" has evolved into "a woman of the world" (D. Anderson, *Sherwood* 115). Alice thus marks a transition toward the image of woman that appears in *Perhaps Women* (1931), *Beyond Desire* (1932), and *Kit Brandon* (1936) (D. Anderson, "Myth" 137–38).

The Appalachian woman Alice strongly resembles Aunt Sally in "A Meeting South," another "aging" woman who has "lived and loved" (Geismar, "Introduction" [*SA: Short Stories*] xix). Both of them epitomize "beauty, grace, and courage" (Miller, "Defense" 56) and have dimensions of character that link them with the heroines of "Mother," "The Teacher," "The New Englander," "Unused," "Unlighted Lamps," and "Out of Nowhere into Nothing" (Miller, "Earth-Mothers" 206). Even more than those heroines, Alice nearly fulfills the ideal set forth in "Tandy," for she is a woman "strong to be loved" (*WO* 145). As Ferguson aptly points out, Alice is "more nearly autonomous"; her power is evidenced partly "when she obtains a gift of a thousand dollars to support [the narrator] in his work" (227). She has achieved the beauty that George Willard rather pompously instructs Helen White to strive for in "Sophistication."

The pairing of this story with "The Lost Novel" in *Alice and the Lost Novel* (see "Publication History") suggests that Anderson saw the two together as a kind of statement of his faith. Both strive to represent something metaphysical, to convey Anderson's sense that the artist (male) must perennially quest for some abstract power of beauty and love, which is (more or less) embodied in the female. Anderson, who had found his inchoate perception of this relationship expressed in Henry Adams's discussion of the power of the medieval Virgin, believed it is always man's need to worship this power, however threatened it may be by forces in the modern world. "The male is a doer," he would write in his *Memoirs,* "whereas that whole natural impulse of the female is to be" (550). Ideal beauty might appear, disappear, and reappear in a woman (*DW* 121), and the demands of a real woman might intrude upon a man's artistic quest. But when the transforming power of mythopoeic beauty is alive in a woman, the sensitive man is possessed by wild adoration.

Significant in "Like a Queen" is a vein of primitivism. All three examples of surpassing female beauty given within the text are women of the lower class, peasants. Like so many writers and artists of the twenties, Anderson can be seen here seeking some pagan, natural virtue that promises to redeem dispirited modern man.

Critical Studies

At least one commentator has found "Like a Queen" to be "among our finest short fiction" (White, "Introduction" 15). Nevertheless, criticism of the story has been scant. The critical discussion that exists has been dominated by interest in its relationship to Anderson's other works.

Virtually plotless, hardly more than a sketch, the story is essayistic in texture, but it does culminate in an epiphanic moment, the woman's transfiguration and the narrator's responding passionate love. Freudian symbolism indicates the abashment of the male in the presence of the ineffable power of the female. David Anderson rightly sees the story as "a brief attempt to define the beauty of a woman" (*Sherwood* 115). Such beauty is a thing of the spirit more than of the body; as such, it paradoxically strikes a man with mystic awe and inspires him with confidence.

Works Cited

Anderson, David. 1967. *Sherwood Anderson: An Introduction and Interpretation.* New York: Holt, Rinehart.

———. 1976. "Anderson and Myth." In *Sherwood Anderson: Dimension of His Literary Art.* East Lansing: Michigan State University Press, 118–41. Rpt. in *Critical Essays on Sherwood Anderson.* Boston: G. K. Hall, 1981, 267–83.

Anderson, Elizabeth, and Gerald R. Kelly. 1969. *Miss Elizabeth: A Memoir.* Boston: Little, Brown.

Anderson, Sherwood. 1929. *Alice and the Lost Novel.* Number Ten of the Woburn Books. London: Elkin Mathews & Marrot.

Ferguson, Mary Anne. 1981. "Sherwood Anderson's *Death in the Woods:* Toward a New Realism." In *Critical Essays on Sherwood Anderson*. Ed. David D. Anderson. Boston: G. K. Hall, 217–34. Originally printed in *Midamerica VII*. East Lansing, MI: Midwestern Press, 1980, 73–95.

Geismar, Maxwell, ed. 1962. *Sherwood Anderson: Short Stories*. New York: Hill and Wang.

Miller, William V. 1974. "Earth-Mothers, Succubi, and Other Ectoplasmic Spirits: The Women in Sherwood Anderson's Short Stories." *Midamerica I*. Ed. David D. Anderson. East Lansing, MI: Midwestern Press, 64–81. Rpt. in *Critical Essays on Sherwood Anderson*. Ed. David D. Anderson. Boston: G. K. Hall, 1981, 196–209.

———. "In Defense of Mountaineers: Sherwood Anderson's Hill Stories." *Ball State University Forum* 15 (1974):51–58.

Sutton, William A., ed. 1985. *Letters to Bab: Sherwood Anderson to Marietta D. Finley, 1916–33*. Foreword by Walter B. Rideout. Urbana and Chicago: University of Illinois Press.

White, Ray Lewis, ed. 1969. *Sherwood Andersons Memoirs: A Critical Edition*. Chapel Hill: University of North Carolina Press.

———. 1966. "Introduction." *The Achievement of Sherwood Anderson: Essays in Criticism*. Ed. Ray Lewis White. Chapel Hill: University of North Carolina Press.

That Sophistication

Circumstances of Composition

The date of this story's composition has not been precisely established, but certainly it was written sometime after Sherwood Anderson left Paris in March 1927 (see "Sources and Influences" below) and before the story appeared in print in September of 1928. During that time Anderson lived in the mountains of southwestern Virginia—on his Ripshin farm until the end of 1927, and then, when he took on the editing of two local papers, in the little town of Marion. This was a period of crisis in the author's life, outwardly manifested in the change of career. Anderson dissolved the contract he had made with Horace Liveright in 1925, according to which he had agreed to produce a book a year in return for an advance payment of a hundred dollars weekly (Howe 201). This arrangement had become onerous, as Anderson rankled under the compulsion to create, and create hurriedly. Becoming a country newspaper editor relieved him of having to earn his living by his art and offered interesting contacts with the life of a town. Local issues, sheep shearings, cattle judgings, and murder trials, he wrote to Gertrude Stein, made for "a busy and amusing life" (White, *Sherwood/Gertrude* 64–65)—at least for a while. But until his interest waned, the plain, simple folk of the mountains helped to restore a soul jaded by too much sophistication. "It helps being down here," he said, "I'm done with cities. No more Paris, Europe for me ever" (Jones-Rideout, *Letters* 171).

Sources and Influences

The impulse for this story, and much of its material, was provided by Anderson's visit to Paris in 1927. The trip made him miserable; he had trouble writing, and it did not help at all to discover himself a celebrity abroad. He found the expatriates who gathered in Paris unbearable. It was unpleasant to see Hemingway again after the insult of *Torrents of Spring,* which had enjoyed brisk sales at Sylvia Beach's bookshop. James Joyce, too, made him "ill" (Jones-Rideout, *Letters* 173). Moreover, though Anderson had become friendly with Eugene Jolas in New Orleans, now Jolas seemed "muddled" and foolish, and evenings with the insurgent group of writers collected around Jolas in Paris upset him (Modlin, *Letters* 97). They were preparing to launch the avant-garde little magazine *transition*—to present a synthesis of German expressionism, dadaism, and surrealism; to revolutionize language" by subverting rational structures (Hoffman, *Little* 173, 287). Anderson was repelled.

Also in Paris, probably in January, Anderson went to the literary salon of rich American patroness of the arts Natalie Barney: this experience entered the story as the afternoon at the studio of Madam T. His wife, Elizabeth, who accompanied him, wrote in her autobiography about a poetry reading they attended at Barney's with Gertrude Stein and Alice B. Toklas:

> Everything was oversized and expensive and very antique. There was a small garden in which there sat, to our astonishment and glee, a small Greek temple of love. Here, people sat in rows of rickety chairs, facing the temple and awaiting the poetry reading. . . . A tall, emaciated English lady with burning eyes stood up and droned out her poetry, which had to do with some mystical, complicated concept of love. (162)

When the woman "began chanting some impossible lyric about the Isle of Lesbos," she and Sherwood could scarcely suppress their laughter at the "absurdity" of it all. The poetry reading, the temple of love, and the aura of homosexuality became targets of satire in Anderson's fictional treatment of the episode.

The character Ralph Cook is a thinly disguised portrait of Ralph Church, a former student of Elizabeth's brother, David Prall, who had gone on to study philosophy at Oxford. When Church left California in 1926, Anderson had sent letters of recommendation for him to Stein and Hemingway; they met again when Anderson was in Paris.

The character Henry Longman seems to be a composite portrait of some of the expatriates who congregated in Paris in 1927 and thereafter. Anderson gave Longman the personal background of Hart Crane: "He came from Cleveland. . . . His father was a candy manufacturer out there" (*DW* 134). But of course Crane never married, and he did not arrive in Paris until January of 1929, after this story was published. Anderson evidently used this background because it served to make a point about many of the young American aesthetes of the twenties. They were children of a generation that had acquired wealth by hard work in the world of business; the money their fathers had earned enabled them to go abroad for travel and study and pursuit of culture.

Mabel Cathers may have had a real-life prototype as well, but her literary lineage plainly descends from the American girls of Henry James. Like so many of James's heroines, Mabel goes abroad—equipped with hope, pluck, naïveté, and basic good sense—to absorb the best Europe has to offer. Anderson handles Mabel's disillusionment, however, without Jamesian solemnity.

Anderson's own quest for sophistication had begun early. Even in his youth, he had longed to see the great world beyond the small Ohio town where he grew up. Keenly aware of his provincialism, he went off to Chicago, off to join the Army, and back to school again. During his first marriage, he and his wife (who had toured Europe before their marriage) joined literary reading groups in Elyria, Ohio: "We were all yearning for culture," she said (Sutton, *Road* 182). Even when he became known as a successful writer of the Chicago Renaissance, he continued to feel unsophisticated in comparison with the well-educated, well-traveled intellectuals of New York. It was with delight, then, that in 1921 he had gone with Paul Rosenfeld, an influential New York critic, to France. France represented for him centuries of devotion to beauty, to art, to a culture such as America only dimly imagined (Fanning 79). But by 1925, Anderson's attitude had undergone a change, partly the result of his own middle age, partly of the increasing hysteria of the expatriate scene. He wrote a friend that though he might have gained over the years "a sort of canniness, . . . I am not sophistocated [*sic*], cannot be" (Sutton, *Letters* 212). The excess and affectation of the bohemian intellectuals in Paris in 1927 made him long for the "earthy, folksy people" of Virginia (Elizabeth Anderson 171). Once returned, he decided, "The so-called bigger world is largely illusion. In my own life now I try and try to cut the bigger world out" (Sutton, *Letters* 293).

Publication History

With the title misspelled "That Sophistocation," this story was first published on May 23, 1929, in the *Smyth County News,* which Sherwood Anderson owned and edited (1, 4). This newspaper, based in the little Appalachian town of Marion, Virginia, seems an incongruous forum for a story about aesthetes in Paris. Most people in Smyth County hardly could have grasped its import. As one local woman told Anderson, they did not "buy any books" (White, *Memoirs* 501). Yet, since the story burlesques the artsy crowd madly seeking "culture" abroad, printing it in the local paper must have been somehow for the author a gesture of love and commitment to down-to-earth American values and to the unsophisticated people of Marion.

Anderson previously had tried and failed to place the story in a magazine with a more cosmopolitan audience. A printer's copy of the story in the Newberry Library shows that someone on the staff of *Vanity Fair* had edited the manuscript and scheduled it for the magazine's September issue (evidently September 1927). The editor has added this subtitle: "A Study of a Little Group of Serious Self-Cultivators Gambolling in the Elysian Fields of Paris." On the manuscript, marked editorial deletions of several references to homosexuality suggest reasons that may have led the editors to decide against publishing the story. Though gossip about the activities of various celebrities was a stock-in-trade of *Vanity Fair,* possibly the story's characters were too easily recognizable as well. If Anderson subsequently attempted to market the story elsewhere, that fact has not come to light.

After making numerous minor revisions, Anderson collected the tale in *Death in the Woods* (1933). But both in the version that he printed in his newspaper and in the version that appears in his book, he left out the passages that the *Vanity Fair* editor had excised from the manuscript.

Relation to Other Works

The nearest parallel to the substance of "That Sophistication" is located in *Dark Laughter* (1925) in the section dealing with Aline Grey's trip to Paris after the war. The ingénue on her way to affront her destiny quickly discovers that people who converse about literature and modern painting can also be shallow, greedy, and perverse. She is open to life, and her education includes a glimpse of the sex orgy that took place at the Quatre Arts Ball, attended by war-weary Americans eager to "go the limit." Aline's world is turned upside down, and the sophistication she acquires is not so much culture as it is cynicism (139–203; compare Schevill 208–209).

The recoil from sophistication in Anderson's work, however, reaches its fullest statement in "That Sophistication," which marks a turning point in his career away from his position as a standard bearer of the avant-garde campaign against Puritan repression. His *Winesburg, Ohio* particularly had been extolled and vilified for breaking down old barriers by treating sexual matters with some degree of openness. Since the war, he felt there no longer seemed to be any such thing as "sex repression" (Jones-Rideout, *Letters* 198). Appalled by some manifestations of the modern culture that he himself had helped to spawn, he wondered whether young people might "vulgarize themselves beyond repair" before a new morality evolved to replace the old one that had broken down (*Hello Towns!* 320). The contrast between *Winesburg*'s "Sophistication" and "That Sophistication" is a telling one. The early story looks kindly on a young provincial couple's progress toward maturity; the later story sneers at a generation parading its shallow worldliness abroad. Once, too, Anderson had carried a sort of banner against homophobia in the story "Hands," but now that battle seemed to him to have been won. He would never again have a character parade naked, as he had in *Many Marriages* (1923). Nor would he try to imitate the rhythms of Joyce, as he had in *Dark Laughter* (1925). He retreated from efforts to forge a new, dashingly experimental, fashionably innovative style. Henceforth, as he headed back to the country, he fought to regain his own homespun integrity. Lincoln and Grant were his heroes. He would try to purify his style, but his art would have to be his own (Sutton, *Letters* 309).

Critical Studies

"That Sophistication" paints an unflattering picture of a group of deracinated intellectuals and pretenders to aestheticism herding together in Paris. Composed mostly of Americans, the group is characterized by self-indulgent hedonism and phony refinement. Parasitical "sophisticates" gather at tables laden with expensive food and wine, all of which has been bought by the labors of a preceding generation of manufacturers. The story in part is a "lively" satire of "Chicago ladies looking for culture in Paris" (Townsend 283). Sexual freedom reigns among this liberated set of social derelicts, which is dominated by "mannish women and womanly men" (*DW* 130). Their bohemian revolt is viewed as "futile" and "meaningless" (David Anderson 132). And the vulgarly naïve heroine "provides an epitaph for the expatriates of the American twenties" (Geismar, *Last* 272): "I might have saved my husband all this money and got all this sophistication I'm getting, or anyway all I needed, right in Chicago" (*DW* 138).

The deliberately meandering first-person narrative presents an acid cultural commentary in the tradition of Mark Twain's *Innocents Abroad*. Rich Americans whose wealth derives from commercial enterprise are ashamed of their background and pretend to be English. Titled Englishmen are ashamed of their titles and consider European civilization effete. The Americans do not grasp the simplest literary allusions but, ashamed of being primitive, consider themselves privileged to be around "swell" intellectual talk as they eagerly lap up the ideas of world-weary Europeans who disparage the childishness of American hope. Affectation is the order of the day. Crudely these children of the middle class ape the dissipations of the old aristocracy. Art, beauty, and urbanity are eclipsed by their frenetic search for pleasure. Thus this parodic portrait of the lost generation shows them in their ignorant search for "culture" to be producing a modern culture in danger of losing everything of real value in the old.

Works Cited

Anderson, David. 1967. *Sherwood Anderson: An Introduction and Interpretation*. New York: Holt, Rinehart.

Anderson, Elizabeth, and Gerald R. Kelley. 1969. *Miss Elizabeth: A Memoir*. Boston: Little, Brown.

Anderson, Sherwood. 1925. *Dark Laughter*. New York: Liveright.

———. 1929. *Hello Towns!* New York: Liveright.

Fanning, Michael, ed. 1976. *France and Sherwood Anderson: Paris Notebook, 1921*. Baton Rouge: Louisiana State University Press.

Geismar, Maxwell. 1947. "Sherwood Anderson: Last of the Townsmen." *The Last of the Provincials: The American Novel, 1915–1925*. Boston: Houghton Mifflin, 223–84. Rpt. in part in *Sherwood Anderson:* Winesburg, Ohio: *Text and Criticism*. Ed. John H. Ferres. New York: Viking, 1966, 377–82.

Hoffmann, Frederick J. "The Voices of Sherwood Anderson." *Shenandoah* 13 (1962):5–19. Rpt. in *The Achievement of Sherwood Anderson: Essays in Criticism*. Ed. Ray Lewis White. Chapel Hill: University of North Carolina Press, 1966, 232–44.

———, Charles Allen, and Carolyn F. Ulrich. 1946. *The Little Magazine: A History and Bibliography*. Princeton: Princeton University Press.

Howe, Irving. 1951. *Sherwood Anderson*. New York: William Sloane.

Jones, Howard Mumford, and Walter B. Rideout, eds. 1953. *Letters of Sherwood Anderson*. Boston: Little, Brown.

Modlin, Charles E., ed. 1984. *Sherwood Anderson: Selected Letters.* Knoxville: University of Tennessee Press.

Schevill, James. 1951. *Sherwood Anderson: His Life and Work.* Denver: University of Denver Press.

Sutton, William A., ed. 1985. *Letters to Bab: Sherwood Anderson to Marietta D. Finley, 1916–133.* Foreword by Walter B. Rideout. Urbana and Chicago: University of Illinois Press.

———. 1972. *The Road to Winesburg: A Mosaic of the Imaginative Life of Sherwood Anderson.* Metuchen, NJ: Scarecrow Press.

Townsend, Kim. 1951. *Sherwood Anderson.* Boston: William Sloane.

White, Ray Lewis, ed. 1972. *Sherwood Anderson/Gertrude Stein: Correspondence and Personal Essays.* Chapel Hill: University of North Carolina Press.

———, ed. 1969. *Sherwood Anderson's Memoirs: A Critical Edition.* Chapel Hill: University of North Carolina Press.

In a Strange Town

Circumstances of Composition

Except for "Brother Death," "In a Strange Town" was the last of the stories in *Death in the Woods* to be composed. It was written in July of 1929, while its author was indeed staying for a while in a strange town. Sherwood Anderson had been deeply depressed. Separated now from his third wife, he had been eager to get away from his home in Marion, Virginia, which was filled with reminders of her. In Marion, he had already begun to woo Eleanor Copenhaver, who would become his fourth wife later on, but she was refusing to embark upon a sexual relationship. Above all, "[h]is failure to complete any long fiction since *Tar* in 1926 continued as the root of his despondency" (Shevill 265). So he had helped to rent a small house in upstate New York where he could get away to write and where his friend Charles Bockler could paint (Townsend 251). As it turned out, Bockler's wife had become pregnant and was beset by attacks of nausea as she tried to cook for the men (Modlin, *Letters* 108). Anderson found that all too distracting and escaped to Danbury, Connecticut, with Mrs. Bockler's sister, Mary Vernon Greer, who had done some secretarial work for him and with whom, intermittently, he was having an affair. It was there that he wrote the story. He was also working on a novel, which went by various working titles (one of them was "No Love"); to get needed money, he continued to write for magazines.

Anderson added final revisions to the manuscript in August.

Sources and Influences

One can only speculate about the psychobiographical import of the women in "In a Strange Town" and their relation to the actual women in Anderson's life. It is not clear what one critic means when he refers to the tale as "wholly autobiographical" (Weber 40). But in his *Memoirs* Anderson makes illuminating comments about what he meant to express in this work, which has to do with his recurrent need to purge himself of "self" (White, *Memoirs* 435–36). He was at various times nearly suicidal, he says, and desperately in need of something akin to religious salvation, but since the only ultimate truth he could believe in was the truth of art, he would at such times find absolving freedom in "a bath of new impressions" as he wandered "in some new and strange town" (436–47). This observation suggests, then, that the substance of the story is grace—that grace by which life (implicitly defined as the meeting between the perceived life of the exterior world and the answering life within the mind) again and again in some mysterious way triumphs over death.

Publication History

By October of 1929, Anderson had sold "In a Strange Town" to *Scribner's Magazine,* and it appeared there the following January (87:20–25). It was one of three *Scribner's* stories that Anderson selected for his 1933 volume *Death in the Woods* (141–57). Posthumously, it has been printed in collections of Anderson's stories edited by Maxwell Geismar, Frank Gado, and Charles Modlin.

Relation to Other Works

The protagonist of "In a Strange Town" is one of several college professors in Anderson's stories, but the only one to have "found a way to social and psychic wholeness" (Miller 7). Introspective, meditative, reticent, and inhibited, this professor of philosophy is awkward in managing his personal relationships, like so many of Anderson's less literate characters. Unlike most of them, however, he has a quiet, calm way of dealing with his moods, and more words to express himself. Interestingly enough, though, the language he uses to describe his innermost experience does not consist of philosophical jargon or even particularly elevated diction but is straightforward, at times primer-like, in its simplicity.

During the period when he wrote the story, Anderson was trying to achieve a kind of prose he had once touched in *Many Marriages* (1923), music-laden, with "laughter like stars laughing, buried down in the prose" (Modlin, *Letters* 18). A few months afterward, he thought in his prose he had "gone as far . . . as a man can go on the road of feeling," and he retreated for a while to a more objective stance, which he tried for particularly in "These Mountaineers" (Jones-Rideout, *Letters* 195–96). But "In a Strange Town" goes down and down into subjective terrain and is awash with the color of feeling.

As Ferguson points out, this is one of the five stories in *Death in the Woods* that "deal with the death of a woman and its effect upon a male character" (218). In fact, the figure of a dead woman shows up repeatedly throughout Anderson's writings, hovering over the stories of *Winesburg* (especially "Paper Pills," "The Philosopher," and "Death") and dominating "Unused" and "The Man's Story." This dialectical pull—between death (usually the death of a woman) and the life of the artist—evidently touches the deepest springs of Anderson's art. Almost always there is the suggestion of some obscure shame in connection with the death, and associated with it yet transcending it, the healing power of the artistic imagination. The sustaining power of imagination is what the narrator of "The Man Who Became a Woman" learns from Tom Means's talks, which "started something inside you that went on and on, and your mind played with it like walking about in a strange town and seeing the sights, and you slipped off to sleep and had splendid dreams and woke up in the morning feeling fine" (*HM* 197). "All the art of life," Anderson would say in *Many Marriages* "perhaps consisted in just letting the fancy wash over and color the facts of life" (203).

"In a Strange Town" is positioned almost in the middle of *Death in the Woods,* and near its midpoint stands this apparently rhetorical question: "Death is an important, a majestic thing, eh?" (145). It is the burden of the story, and of the whole book, to offer up a philosophical response nearly opposite from that which seems, for a moment, to be demanded. Death has only such majesty as we give it. The greater majesty belongs to the unceasing flow of life and its "infinite variety" (*DW* 146). While cynical sophisticates may sneer at the American capacity for belief in the possibility of salvation, as they do in "That Sophistication" (the story immediately preceding this one in *Death in the Woods*), "In a Strange Town" argues for the saving power of immersion in life's perpetual stream.

Critical Studies

Although there are no full-length studies of "In a Strange Town," the story has been fairly well served by the two critics who have offered interpretations. The protagonist, as Ferguson points out, "has fled the familiar in order to renew his creativity" (228). Ferguson analyzes the process by which the professor, through observation of "'little odd fragmentary ends of things,'" moves to apprehend "the mystery of life in general," which provides "a catharsis of despair and self-centeredness" (228; see also D. Anderson 132).

Gado discusses the "idiosyncratic" narrative approach exhibited in the story, which disguises its careful crafting in an apparently "unmoored" floatation of utterances" (5–6). The story first arouses curiosity about why the narrator "repeatedly leaves his home to wander in unfamiliar surroundings," and then offers "a simple answer"—strange places refresh his fancy; yet "this assertion, the reader gradually realizes, masks as well as reveals" (5). Only at length does the real source of his compulsion emerge: a young woman, a student who "had roused thoughts long stilled by his wife and the others who populate his days," has been killed by an automobile. (Gado does not mention that her death looks suspiciously like suicide.) The professor's "wanderlust" is not so much "mourning" for her as "a need to recreate the stirring of vitality he felt . . . when her life touched his" (6).

Gado makes much of the paradox that the professor is preoccupied with death even as he "proclaims his love of life" (7). Certainly that seems to be Anderson's point. Life is always poised over the pit of death, is it not? But rather than dwelling on the character's "crabbed and frightened psyche," his "utter vulnerability and confusion," as Gado does, we might heed the serene optimism of his testimony of spiritual resurrection. For the professor's language is replete with metaphysical promise. "There is no such thing as silence" (*DW* 141). "I am taking this bath in life, as you see, and when I have had enough of it I shall go home feeling refreshed" (*DW* 157).

Works Cited

Anderson, David. 1967. *Sherwood Anderson: An Introduction and Interpretation*. New York: Holt, Rinehart.

Ferguson, Mary Anne. 1981. "Sherwood Anderson's Death in the Woods: Toward a New Realism." In *Critical Essays on Sherwood Anderson*. Ed. David D. Anderson. Boston: G. K. Hall, 217–34. Originally printed in *Midamerica VII*. East Lansing, MI: Midwestern Press, 1980, 73–95. Rpt. in *Sherwood Anderson: A Study of the Short Fiction*. Ed. Robert Allen Papinchak. New York: Twayne, 1992, 141–62.

Gado, Frank, ed. 1983. *The Teller's Tales.* Signature Series. Schenectady, NY: Union College Press.

Geismar, Maxwell, ed. 1962. *Sherwood Anderson: Short Stories.* New York: Hill and Wang.

Miller, William V. 1976. "Portraits of the Artist: Anderson's Fictional Storytellers." In *Sherwood Anderson: Dimensions of His Literary Art: A Collection of Critical Essays.* Ed. David D. Anderson. East Lansing: Michigan State University Press, 1–23.

Modlin, Charles E., ed. 1992. *Certain Things Last: The Selected Short Stories of Sherwood Anderson.* New York: Four Walls Eight Windows.

——, ed. 1984. *Sherwood Anderson: Selected Letters.* Knoxville: University of Tennessee Press.

Shevill, James. 1951. *Sherwood Anderson: His Life and Work.* Denver: University of Denver Press.

Townsend, Kim. 1987. *Sherwood Anderson.* Boston: Houghton Mifflin.

Weber, Brom. "Anderson and the 'Essence of Things.'" *Sewanee Review* 59 (1951):678–92. Rpt. in *Critical Essays on Sherwood Anderson.* Ed. David D. Anderson. Boston: G. K. Hall, 1981, 125–37.

White, Ray Lewis, ed. 1969. *Sherwood Anderson's Memoirs: A Critical Edition.* Chapel Hill: University of North Carolina Press.

These Mountaineers

Circumstances of Composition

Sherwood Anderson composed "These Mountaineers" in mid-October, 1929. In a letter written shortly thereafter, he used the terminology of painting to describe the story as "almost devoid of color, almost pure drawing . . . , just a description of some people, all my own feeling left out" (Jones-Rideout, *Letters* 196). The style of the story, he said, represented a deliberate turning away from an excess of feeling that had characterized his writing: "I have gone as far, I suppose, as a man can go on the road of feeling. . . . I am like the painter who, having gone to color and then to color and then to color, turns suddenly again to line. . . . [I] have to come, for the time at least, out of a world where I depend on feeling (color) and have to begin again to observe with my eyes, hear with my ears, the definite facts. It is the same thing you mean when you go back to drawing" (195–96). He spoke in similar terms to another correspondent, emphasizing his attempt in "These Mountaineers" to achieve a "more objective" tone and calling his artistic treatment of the girl in the story "a portrait" (Modlin, *Love Letters* 24, 27).

These letters indicate that Anderson's desire to curtail the strain of feeling in his prose had something to do with his sense that the battle against Puritan repression had been won, something to do with his anxiety over critics' disparagement of the "sentimentality" of his work, and something to do with his remorse over three failed marriages. He was fairly sick of feeling. At the end of 1928, he had sent his third wife away and told her not to come back. He was left in the mountains of Virginia with the house they had built together and the newspaper business he had been running since the fall of 1927. When he wrote this story, he was courting the woman who would eventually become his fourth wife. She worked in the industrial division of the YWCA, and early that year he had traveled with her to the rayon mills of Elizabethton, Tennessee, and there attended a meeting of workers (Townsend 255). Labor troubles were mounting in the country, and Anderson was increasingly aware of "the plight of the working class" (Williams 57).

Sources and Influences

The narrator of this story is transparently Anderson himself, who had moved to the hill country near Marion, Virginia, in 1926, and had built a house there. The standpoint of the outsider confronting an alien culture with mixed feelings of repulsion, pity, and admiration almost certainly conveys Anderson's own general experience regarding the mountaineers. It is not clear, however, whether the specific events in the story actually occurred.

Geismar notices the influence on "These Mountaineers" of Ivan Turgenev, whose *Sportsman's Sketches* Anderson always admired. The imprint of Turgenev is discernible in Anderson's return in this sketch to "that provincial obscurity, those 'small lives,' whose special chronicler he was" ("Introduction" xix). Whereas most of Anderson's fiction had dwelt upon provincial life in his native Midwest, however, this story tries to convey the peculiar traits of the inhabitants of America's southeastern mountains.

A rough background of Appalachian history gives depth to this portrait of a family of mountaineers. Details concerning the gradual yielding of the old spruce forests, first to lumber camps and then to mill towns, suggest the sociological and economic context of the characters who live far back in the hollows, still largely isolated from technological and commercial development. These highland inhabitants preserve many characteristic traits of the culture they had brought with them from the border country of North Britain: grinding poverty, fierce pride, a warrior ethic combined with a weak work ethic, openness about premarital sexual relations, an earthy dialect, a strong sense of social equality, and belligerence toward outsiders (Fischer 605–782).

Publication History

"These Mountaineers" was first published in January, 1930, in *Vanity Fair* (33:44–45), a fashionable magazine of art and ideas that had carried Anderson's articles and stories regularly since 1926. It was subtitled "an author is drawn into a domestic drama of the blue ridge, and finds his rôle an embarrassing one." In the same month, *Scribner's* carried his "In a Strange Town." *This Quarter,* a literary quarterly published in Paris by Edward W. Titus, reprinted "These Mountaineers" in the spring issue of 1931 (3:602–609). Making minor revisions, Anderson then gathered it into his fourth volume of short stories, *Death in the Woods* (1933). Maxwell Geismar reprinted it in his more recent collection of Anderson's short fiction (164–70).

Relation to Other Works

As Anderson explained, the narrative technique of "These Mountaineers" is different from that of most of his earlier fiction (see "Circumstances of Composition"). *Winesburg, Ohio* (1919) began with a dedication to the memory of Anderson's mother, "whose keen observations on the life about her," he wrote, "awoke in me the hunger to see beneath the surface of lives." The dominant note in his work, henceforth, was subjective and psychological. He sought to unfold the secret recesses of human minds, the hidden impulses scarcely known even to the individuals who harbored them. The disastrous novel *Many Marriages* (1923) took this psychological bent to an extreme and wallowed in forbidden longings brought to light. Usually with more success, Anderson remained committed to probing subtle complexities of feeling in his fiction of the later twenties. His attempt in this story to handle material more objectively marks a new approach. Still, most of the stories of *Death in the Woods*—both those such as "Another Wife" and "A Sentimental Journey," written earlier than "These Mountaineers," and those such as "Brother Death," written later—follow the path that Anderson referred to as subjective.

"These Mountaineers" bears comparison with other stories Anderson wrote about the hill folk in Virginia and Tennessee. It is similar to "A Sentimental Journey," "A Mountain Dance," and "A Mountain Marriage" in the respect it accords the mountaineers "for asserting their humanity in a society circumscribed by poverty and ignorance" (Miller, "Defense" 56; similarly, "Portraits" 8). Nevertheless, "A Sentimental Journey," which records an episode that enables cross-cultural understanding, is markedly different from "These Mountaineers," which centers on a failure of such understanding. Moreover, in the latter story Anderson is less interested than he had been earlier to correct false romantic notions about the mountaineers. As he indicates within the later story, frequent newspaper reports about labor unrest in the region had helped change those notions. Consequently, the story strives less to reveal the inner life of the mountaineers than to show their rough, independent dignity.

The narrator's idea that the young mountain woman is an aristocrat links her with Aunt Sally in "A Meeting South" and with Alice in "Like a Queen." None of these characters even approaches the genteel. Anderson was developing an idea that inner strength and spiritual beauty are the measure of true aristocracy. The title character of *Kit Brandon* (1936), another child of the mountains, shares these qualities.

Critical Studies

Somewhat in the manner of an essay, "These Mountaineers" describes a Northern man's contact with a poor white family of the Southern mountains. Journalistic details introduce a narrative: an initial encounter with "an evil-looking," "tough-bodied old fellow," a visit to the mountain man's dirty, one-room house where the guest is served cold beans and meets an unmarried, pregnant girl—scarcely a woman yet—who lives in the house and whom the old man repeatedly calls "a hell cat," the guest's subsequent return to give the young woman twenty dollars, and her proud refusal—in terms the narrator coyly finds too shocking to repeat. Generally, the narrator's condescension and pity are made to seem understandable at first and ridiculous at last. His respectability thus serves as an ironic foil to enhance the finer virtue of the Appalachian woman.

Hilfer states that the story is "an excellent objective impression of mountain life" focused on a "tough" young woman, "defeated but definite," who refuses charity (241). Miller praises it as one of Anderson's best "hill tales" ("Defense" 51). But it has aroused little commentary, and no interpretive studies.

Works Cited

Ferguson, Mary Anne. 1981. "Sherwood Anderson's *Death in the Woods:* Toward a New Realism." In *Critical Essays on Sherwood Anderson.* Ed. David D. Anderson. Boston: G. K. Hall, 217–34. Originally printed in *Midamerica VII.* East Lansing, MI: Midwestern Press, 1980, 73–95.

Fischer, David Hackett. 1989. *Albion's Seed: Four British Folkways in America.* New York and Oxford: Oxford University Press.

Geismar, Maxwell, ed. 1962. *Sherwood Anderson: Short Stories.* New York: Hill and Wang.

Hilfer, Anthony Channel. 1969. *The Revolt from the Village, 1915–1930.* Chapel Hill: University of North Carolina Press.

Jones, Howard Mumford, and Walter B. Rideout, eds. 1953. *Letters of Sherwood Anderson.* Boston: Little, Brown.

Miller, William V. "In Defense of Mountaineers: Sherwood Anderson's Hill Stories." *Ball State University Forum* 15 (1974):51–58.

———. 1976. "Portraits of the Artist: Anderson's Fictional Storytellers." In *Sherwood Anderson: Dimensions of His Literary Art: A Collection of Critical Essays.* Ed. David D. Anderson. East Lansing: Michigan State University Press, 1–23.

Modlin, Charles E., ed. 1989. *Sherwood Anderson's Love Letters to Eleanor Copenhaver Anderson.* Athens and London: University of Georgia Press.

Morgan, H. Wayne. 1963. "Sherwood Anderson: The Search for Unity." *Writers in Transition: Seven Americans.* New York: Hill and Wang, 82–104.

Townsend, Kim. 1987. *Sherwood Anderson.* Boston: Houghton Mifflin.

Williams, Cratis D. "Kit Brandon, a Reappraisal." *Shenandoah* 13 (1962): 55–61.

Wright, Austin McGiffert. 1961. *The American Short Story in the Twenties.* Chicago: University of Chicago Press.

A Sentimental Journey

Circumstances of Composition

Sherwood Anderson wrote "A Sentimental Journey" in November 1927, after he and his wife, Elizabeth, had settled in the beautiful hill country of southwest Virginia, where, near Troutdale, Anderson had built—at last—a house of his own. Taking some pride in their new status as country gentry, they named their home Ripshin, for the creek that ran through the property. This new residence brought the two cosmopolitan outsiders into the midst of an alien Appalachian culture, where severely impoverished hillbillies and tough moonshiners constituted a real presence along with the more respectable folk of the valley farms and villages. The cross-cultural encounter was unsettling and stimulating to the Andersons, as this story attests.

Sources and Influences

The biographical source for "A Sentimental Journey" is readily apparent. The character David, a scholar who has come with his wife to live amid the hills, is plainly modeled after Sherwood Anderson himself. The emotions David and his wife experience in the presence of the illiterate mountaineer undoubtedly are drawn directly from the Andersons' life as well. As Morgan has observed, the story's broad background was provided by rapid changes that took place in the economy of the South during the twenties, the industrialization that brought with it "a change in social and spiritual values" (93). In his *Memoirs* Anderson discusses his role as part of that change: "It was a new world come into the hills and I was a part of it. To my neighbors I was a rich man." By employing local workers in the construction of his house, he confessed, he had disturbed "a way of life that had its own values," where everyone before his arrival had been "all poor together" (White, *Memoirs* 500–501). The wise humility one discerns in this reflection had been learned gradually, through just such experiences as "A Sentimental Journey" relates.

Publication History

Beginning in 1927, *Vanity Fair* published a series of twelve articles that Anderson submitted for $300 apiece. "A Sentimental Journey" first appeared in January of 1928 in that magazine (29:46, 118). It was accompanied by a subtitle: "Wherein a Stalwart Virginia Mountaineer Ventures Forth into the Great World." Not long thereafter, Anderson reprinted the story in the small-town paper he was editing at the time, the *Smyth County News* (June 21, 1928, p. 5). He reissued it in 1929 in *Hello Towns!* (265–72) and then again in *Death in the Woods* (1933). Plainly, this is a story that the author himself liked very much. After Anderson's death, Paul Rosenfeld included it in his *The Sherwood Anderson Reader.*

After it came out in *Hello Towns!* and before he published the version in *Death in the Woods,* Anderson made some fairly extensive revisions. He added a new first paragraph, introducing a character named David and his wife, Mildred. David then takes the place of the first-person narrator who originally had told about Joe and his story, and a new first-person narrator tells about David telling about Joe. It is slightly awkward, but not terribly so. Mildred's name has been substituted for the "E." who was the original narrator's wife; local people of Smyth County would have understood "E." to mean Elizabeth, from whom Anderson was divorced by the time *Death in the Woods* came out. Anderson also made a number of minor additions and deletions to sharpen the sense of individual passages, and he dropped a final paragraph that too obviously stated the story's point.

Relation to Other Works

"A Sentimental Journey" is one of about thirteen stories that Anderson wrote, between 1926 and 1937, concerning the inhabitants of Appalachia (Miller, "Portraits" 8). The first of these tales, "A Mountain Dance," was subtitled "Showing That the Folk of the Tennessee Hills Are Not as Depicted in Romantic Fiction." "A Sentimental Journey" is similarly motivated by Anderson's "desire to cut through the fog of romance surrounding moun-taineers in order to reveal their essential stubborn courage and pride" (Miller, "Portraits" 8). This is the sweetest of the three stories about moun-taineers that Anderson collected in *Death in the Woods.* The mountaineer who tells of his brave journey through a winter snowstorm with his young son admits that he was propelled by "sentimentality" (*DW* 182). Yet the understated manner of his telling and his self-reflexive humor are not at all sentimental. Likewise, the framing story—of David's meeting with the mountaineer—is completely realistic. Thus, while the character's journey *is* sentimental, "A Sentimental Journey" distinctly is not.

Among Anderson's works, the closest parallel to "A Sentimental Journey" is the novel *Kit Brandon* (1936), which gives an extended sympathetic treat-ment of the lives of mountaineers during the period when Prohibition and the influx of industry radically altered Southern culture.

Miller also discerns a parallel between this story and such earlier works as "Departure," "The Sad Horn Blowers," and "An Ohio Pagan"; the "mythic pattern" of "the young man leaving the small town for the city . . . only to be disillusioned there" is repeated in "the journey of the poor hill man to the industrial towns" both here and in the late novel *Beyond Desire* ("Defense" 53–54). The mountaineer's return to the hills, however, gives this story an unusual happy ending.

Joe's gift for storytelling links this story with "A Meeting South," in which a young Southern poet displays a similar gift. A great oral storyteller himself, Anderson was always alert for the same talent in others. It is noteworthy that he offers the same respect to the illiterate mountaineer who may make some moonshine as he does to the educated gentleman whose father keeps Negroes on his plantation to make his whiskey.

Critical Studies

"A Sentimental Journey" is a first-person narrative in which a second narrator, David, tells of meeting a "fierce-looking" mountaineer named Joe. David, an outsider who has settled in this region of lovely landscape and tough moonshiners, is frightened by Joe's looks and by recollections of stories about civilized folk who get shot in the back when they are mistakenly suspected of being federal agents. Apprehensively, he invites Joe into his house to eat. Joe then abandons his initial reserve and tells a story about having once left his farm to see the outside world and to earn money in the coal mines. As Joe speaks confidingly of his desperate shyness and homesickness in the strange mining town, David and his wife find that their nervous fear evaporates. A friendly bond remains with the stranger they had at first distrusted.

Joe is the center of this drama of cross-cultural contact. Trying to "eke out a precarious living" for his family of fourteen children on poor, hilly land, he is typical of the mountain people (Miller, "Defense" 54). He is unlearned and "unsophisticated," but heroic in his struggle "to maintain his integrity" when the noise and smoke of a mining town and its factories offer a "black assault on his senses" (55–56). His rugged strength and mountain pride are softened by tender feelings and natural human insecurities that make him understandable and lovable.

The critic who says Joe takes "his first pay check" and rides home happy because it will enable him to produce a run of moonshine, is guilty of over-hasty interpretation (Williams 56). The crucial point, and the reason Joe leaves his mining job so precipitously, is that he loves and misses his family and the quiet hills he has always known.

The formal structure of the narrative is unusual. As Raymund observes,

David's story "is told at one remove" (146). David, a literate outsider who is initially afraid of Joe, tells about his own reactions to Joe as he retells the story Joe has told, almost exclusively employing indirect discourse rather than mountain dialect.

Particularly forceful in underlining the central theme of "A Sentimental Journey" is the part of Joe's narrative that describes his forced entry into the house of a couple of "high-toned" outsiders to the mountains who denied his request for shelter from a howling storm as he and his son traveled home from the mining town. At this point, David looks at his wife. The reader infers that David is glad to be different from those people, so nearly like him, who failed to respond to a father's need to warm his freezing child. David's hospitality, one understands, is well rewarded.

Perhaps there is justice in Raymund's remark that this story "of all Anderson's writing most deserves the epithet 'quaint'" (146). But the account it gives of the anxiety that accompanies meetings between individuals from different cultures, and of the overcoming of that anxiety, though charming, is more than quaint. It is substantial.

Works Cited

Anderson, Sherwood. "A Mountain Dance." *Vanity Fair* 29 (1927):59, 110.

———. 1929. *Hello Towns!* New York: Liveright.

———. "Virginia Justice." *Today* 2 (July 21, 1937):6–7, 24. Rpt. as "Justice" in *The Sherwood Anderson Reader*. Ed. Paul Rosenfeld. Boston: Houghton Mifflin, 1947, 398–403.

Ferguson, Mary Anne. 1981. "Sherwood Anderson's *Death in the Woods:* Toward a New Realism." In *Critical Essays on Sherwood Anderson*. Ed. David D. Anderson. Boston: G. K. Hall, 217–34. Originally printed in *Midamerica VII.* East Lansing, MI: Midwestern Press, 1980, 73–95.

Miller, William V. "In Defense of Mountaineers: Sherwood Anderson's Hill Stories." *Ball State University Forum* 15 (1974):51–58.

———. 1976. "Portraits of the Artist: Anderson's Fictional Storytellers." In *Sherwood Anderson: Dimensions of His Literary Art: A Collection of Critical Essays*. Ed. David D. Anderson. East Lansing: Michigan State University Press, 1–23.

Morgan, H. Wayne. 1963. "Sherwood Anderson: The Search for Unity." *Writers in Transition: Seven Americans*. New York: Hill and Wang, 82–104.

Raymund, Bernard. "The Grammar of Not-Reason: Sherwood Anderson." *Arizona Quarterly* 12 (1956):48–60, 137–48.

Rosenfeld, Paul, ed. 1947. *The Sherwood Anderson Reader.* Boston: Houghton Mifflin.

White, Ray Lewis, ed. 1969. *Sherwood Anderson's Memoirs: A Critical Edition.* Chapel Hill: University of North Carolina Press.

Williams, Cratis D. "Kit Brandon, a Reappraisal." *Shenandoah* 13 (1962): 55–61.

A Jury Case

Circumstances of Composition

To escape the heat of New Orleans in the summer of 1925, Sherwood Anderson and his wife, Elizabeth Prall Anderson, visited the mountains of southwestern Virginia. That rural retreat appealed to Anderson, who was almost fifty and had never owned a home of his own, so he decided to put down roots there. In 1926 he and Elizabeth embarked upon the construction of a stone house on farmland near Troutdale, Virginia, and in the summer of 1927 it was completed. During this time, a great many friends and relatives came to Virginia to visit the Andersons. The two of them also spent several months in Europe. He made a brief lecturing tour and received an honorary degree at Wittenberg College. He worked hard on several writing projects: he finished *Tar,* did a series of articles for *Vanity Fair,* sent off *A New Testament,* and spent months on "Another Man's House," a novel that he never finished.

He had made almost enough money on *Dark Laughter* to pay for the house and the trip. But he felt the pressing need for more money, to finish paying for the house and to finance the education of his children. He had worked out an arrangement in April 1925 with Boni & Liveright that obligated him, in return for a hundred dollars a week, to turn out a book a year (Townsend 217). Instead of freeing him as he had hoped, though, the agreement with his publisher increasingly had the opposite effect, making him feel like a hack. To regain his independence, in November of 1927 he bought two local newspapers in Marion, Virginia, and began a career as newspaper editor.

Anderson finished "A Jury Case" in June of 1927. He also thought of writing a book about the Appalachian people, but on that subject he produced only several short stories until, much later, came *Kit Brandon* (1936).

Sources and Influences

Anderson became fascinated with the workmen who were building his house. They were an impressive introduction to Appalachian culture. To a friend in the north, he wrote about these "mountain-men, small farmers, moonshiners" who worked for fifteen or twenty cents an hour and often got drunk and fought among themselves (Sutton, *Letters* 264, 274). They were "simple men" who lived by "the early American code" whereby respect between men was determined on the basis of strength, physical and moral; "Every man must look out for himself. Back of it all real friendliness" (275). Anderson contemplated the mountaineer he had hired to plant grass for his lawn: a few years before, he had murdered someone "in a drunken quarrel," yet Anderson found him "sweet and gentle" (263). The author also observed the subservient position of women in this mountain culture, which he thought resembled the patriarchal world of the Old Testament (275). Sociological interest in the ways of mountain folk joined with Anderson's long-held concern with the issue of male power to influence "A Jury Case."

Possibly, too, the action in this story has a literary antecedent in Mark Twain's writings. Cal Long's power over the weaker will of George Small bears some resemblance to the episode in *Huckleberry Finn* where Colonel Sherburn stands off an enraged mob by sheer personal force. Anderson alludes to that episode in the final chapter of *Beyond Desire* (1932).

Interestingly, Cargill remarked that "A Jury Case," in which a man is "coerced" into committing a murder "by an unconscionable bully," handles material "in the fashion of Hemingway" (330). Indeed the "tough" subject matter here may have borne for its author some connection with the hardboiled Hemingway, for Anderson was still smarting from Hemingway's cruel parody, *The Torrents of Spring*. But Anderson's approach is not terse like Hemingway's, and far more than Hemingway's fiction usually does, this story works to elicit sympathy with the weak rather than with the strong.

The era of Prohibition provides an important general context for the story. When the production and sale of alcoholic beverages were outlawed, illegal businesses sprang up almost immediately to meet the continued public demand for liquor. The business was lucrative, and—as it was unregulated by any legal authority—disputes had to be settled outside the law, by citizens whose instinct for justice often enough got mixed up with greed and a will to power. The small-time moonshiners here are poor cousins of the big-time gangsters that flourished in America's cities during the twenties.

Publication History

"A Jury Case" was first published in December 1927 in *American Mercury* (12:431–34), which had brought out Anderson's "Death in the Woods" the previous year. Both stories were subsequently collected in the 1933 volume *Death in the Woods.*

Relation to Other Works

Anderson wrote a number of stories about the people in the hills of Appalachia. Williams says of these stories that they treat "more barbaric brutality, raw emotions, feral cunning, and primitive living conditions" than Anderson's earlier novels and tales with settings in the Midwest (57). To some extent that is true. Poverty in the Appalachian mountains was more extreme. And the "ferocious violence" of the moonshiners in "A Jury Case" is similar to that of the bootleggers, also mountaineers, in *Kit Brandon* (1936), as Raymund has remarked (147). But Anderson's primary aim in writing about the hillfolk seems to have been to depict their humanity, to emphasize within these apparently exotic creatures emotions that everyone knows and can identify with. He also sought to raise issues important beyond the local region. The power of an individual's will to overmaster other, weaker individuals is a theme prominent in several of Anderson's works, notably the early story "War," which is set primarily in Europe.

Of the three tales in *Death in the Woods* about real mountaineers (as differentiated from the people settled in the valleys amid the mountains), this one presents less appealing characters than those central to "These Mountaineers" and "A Sentimental Journey." If Cal Long is repugnant in his dominant viciousness, George Small is repellent in his neurotic weakness.

Two other stories by Anderson—"A Dead Dog" and "Virginia Justice"— also feature situations involving disputes of justice among the hill people. These were published in magazines but never collected by him in one of his short story volumes.

Critical Studies

"A Jury Case" is a first-person narrative about three moonshiners. One of them steals the still from the other two, and they hunt him down for retribution. Of the two avengers, however, one is a timid, nervous man, torn between his code of morals and loyalty to his family on the one hand and a need to prove his manly toughness on the other. He becomes a pawn in the hands of the stronger, meaner man, who escapes scot-free after getting his weaker cohort to perform the murder. The story ends by offering the question of the murderer's guilt or innocence to the judgment of the jury, and thus to the judgment of readers.

Cargill considered "A Jury Case" one of the two best stories in *Death in the Woods,* the other being the title story (330). But little has been written about it, and no detailed analysis.

Of several brief critical comments, the following deserve mention. Williams discerns in the story "three mountain types: the congenital criminal, the sly troublemaker . . . , and the sensitive but volatile mountaineer who is gentle when sober but a terror of violence and bloodshed when intoxicated" (57). Miller remarks that the author "apparently knew moonshining very well"; though Anderson "does not gloss over the meanness and crudity of such moonshiners as Cal Long," he shows some sympathy with "the small farmer" supporting a family by "this clandestine business" (54). As David Anderson notes, the story calls attention to the "difference between human truth and intellectualized legal truth" (132). Geismar states, accurately, that the story offers a "sense of complexity in human affairs" and, somewhat less accurately, that it poses a central question of whether, under certain circumstances, "a man is justified in committing murder" (272). At issue, really, is not so much whether George Small had a right to kill a business partner who betrayed him as whether he should be exonerated on the grounds that his action was controlled by the superior will of someone else, Cal Long, who may bear equal or greater responsibility for the crime.

The formal structure of the story deserves more attention than it has received. There are two interpolated stories within the story, and additionally an odd narrative maneuver whereby the first-person narrator filters the climactic scene, the murder, through the perspective of yet another character, a village gossip who dramatizes the tragedy using a stick to represent the murder weapon. Not very convincingly, Ferguson explains the technique of this passage as a way of "disarm[ing] disbelief" (225). Miller mentions the comic element provided by "the physical gyrations of Luther Ford in dramatizing the murder scene" (54), and that seems fair enough, so far as it goes. But why should Anderson have chosen to introduce comedy at this point? Such a method of relating the key event, though unquestionably quite deliberate, seems awkward in aesthetic effect. The ending, moreover, is conspicuously weak: "As for myself—being what I am, hearing and seeing all this. . . . How do I know what I think? It's a matter, of course, the jury will have to decide" (*DW* 200).

Works Cited

Anderson, David. 1967. *Sherwood Anderson: An Introduction and Interpretation.* New York: Holt, Rinehart.

Anderson, Sherwood. "A Dead Dog." *Yale Review* 20 (Spring 1931): 554–67. Rpt. *The Sherwood Anderson Reader*. Ed. Paul Rosenfeld. Boston: Houghton Mifflin, 1947, 404–415.

———. "Virginia Justice." *Today* 2 (July 21, 1934):6–7, 24. Rpt. as "Justice" in *The Sherwood Anderson Reader*. Ed. Paul Rosenfeld. Boston: Houghton Mifflin, 1947, 398–403.

Cargill, Oscar. 1941. *Intellectual America: Ideas on the March*. New York: Macmillan.

Ferguson, Mary Anne. 1981. "Sherwood Anderson's *Death in the Woods:* Toward a New Realism." In *Critical Essays on Sherwood Anderson*. Ed. David D. Anderson. Boston: G. K. Hall, 217–34. Originally printed in *Midamerica VII*. East Lansing, MI: Midwestern Press, 1980, 73–95.

Geismar, Maxwell. 1947. "Sherwood Anderson: Last of the Townsmen." *The Last of the Provincials: The American Novel, 1915–1925*. Boston: Houghton Mifflin, 223–84. Rpt. in part in *Sherwood Anderson:* Winesburg, Ohio: *Text and Criticism*. Ed. John H. Ferres. New York: Viking, 1966, 377–82.

Miller, William V. "In Defense of Mountaineers: Sherwood Anderson's Hill Stories." *Ball State University Forum* 15 (1974):51–58.

Raymund, Bernard. "The Grammar of Not-Reason: Sherwood Anderson." Arizona Quarterly 12 (1956):48–60, 137–48.

Sutton, William A., ed. 1985. *Letters to Bab: Sherwood Anderson to Marietta D. Finley, 1916–33*. Foreword by Walter B. Rideout. Urbana and Chicago: University of Illinois Press.

Townsend, Kim. 1987. *Sherwood Anderson*. Boston: Houghton Mifflin.

Williams, Cratis D. "Kit Brandon, a Reappraisal." *Shenandoah* 13 (1962): 55–61.

Another Wife

Circumstances of Composition

"Another Wife" was written during the summer of 1926, and Otto Liveright, Anderson's agent, received it by July 2. Anderson told Alfred Stieglitz on August 5 that it had been bought by *Scribner's Monthly Magazine* (Jones-Rideout, *Letters* 158). Earlier that same summer, Anderson wrote one of his greatest stories, "Death in the Woods." He was also absorbed in the building of his house—the first he had ever owned—in Troutdale, Virginia. And he was working on a novel, "Another Man's House," which he never completed. He did finish a manuscript of his semiautobiographical *Tar: A Midwest Childhood,* which had been appearing in serial form in *Woman's Home Companion,* and he submitted a number of articles and stories to *Vanity Fair.* Though he was famous as a writer and had made enough money on the commercially successful *Dark Laughter* to be able to afford building a fine house, a number of critics and younger writers had attacked his recent work, and he was unsure of his future. He was middle-aged, and in the middle of a major life change.

Sources and Influences

When Sherwood Anderson and his wife, Elizabeth Prall Anderson, came to the hills of western Virginia to get away from the heat of New Orleans in the summer of 1925, they encountered a distinctly different culture. If Anderson had seemed a folksy rural primitive to the Eastern literary-intellectual elite, to the country people around the town of Marion, Virginia, he seemed shockingly sophisticated—perhaps sinfully sophisticated, for he was not only divorced but married to his *third* wife. There was plenty of local gossip about Anderson and the friends who came to visit him. Doubtless there were incidents of mutual suspicion and hostility that influenced the scene in "Another Wife" in which drunken country folk shout insults at a woman the protagonist admires as a modern sophisticate but whom they regard as scandalous and lewd.

The social class difference between Anderson and his third wife also seems to be reflected in the difference between the doctor in this story and the woman who is to become his second wife. Like the doctor, Anderson had grown up in impoverished circumstances and had worked his way up to a measure of wealth, while Elizabeth Prall, like the female character, had always had money, fine clothes, and security. Her charm for Anderson lay partly in the refined, confident self-assurance she had gained from that background. But the difference helped drive them apart later on. Probably, the last line of the story is an intimation of the author's anxiety about his own love for Elizabeth: "Would he get over it after a time?"

Publication History

"Another Wife" first appeared in December of 1926 in *Scribner's Magazine* as part of a series of works by American writers (80:587–94). It was accompanied by illustrations by George Van Werveke. Anderson told Hemingway that the magazine had given him $750 for the story (Baker, *Letters* 241). That was probably the largest payment he had received for a short story, with the exception of an equal amount from the *Pictorial Review* for "There She Is—She Is Taking Her Bath." "Another Wife" was reprinted in O'Brien's *Best Short Stories of 1927* (50–58). Anderson incorporated it into his 1933 collection *Death in the Woods*. But it is significant that he did not publish it in the local Virginia newspapers he bought in 1927, as he did a number of his other stories. Recently the story has appeared in Gado's Anderson selection, *The Teller's Tales* (63–74).

Relation to Other Works

Marriage and its attendant anxieties are important in a large number of works in the Anderson canon. Often, marriage is seen simply as a trap, as for example in "The Door of the Trap" or "The Contract" (an uncollected story). The doctor in "Another Wife," too, fears that his love will lead him to be "caught" in an institutional net of commitments and responsibilities (*DW* 216). In the notorious *Many Marriages* (1923), a husband parades naked to protest the sexual inhibition within his marriage; with far less irony than the subject deserves, the novel applauds his quest to find fulfillment by leaving his wife for his secretary. *Dark Laughter* (1925) treats the issue in broader terms and extends the problems of marriage to both genders. Gado finds a relation between "Another Wife" and the earlier story "The Other Woman," where the narrator is "torn between" love for his respectable bride and attraction to a sexually freer woman (10). In Anderson's fiction, no matter how badly a character has been injured by a marriage, there is a persistent drive to enter another such relationship. (Wash Williams of "Respectability" is a notable exception.) As Ferguson points out, "Another Wife" is one of three stories in *Death in the Woods* about "a widower trying to find a substitute for his dead wife" (218). It is perhaps the most successful of Anderson's many literary attempts to treat the emotional ambivalences of a man contemplating marriage.

The unnamed woman in "Another Wife" belongs to a type of woman in Anderson's fiction that Miller calls "the managers"; Anderson's male characters tend to stand in confused awe "before the wonders of how [such] women manage men" (73). Miller identifies other women of this type in "A Meeting South," "The Egg," and the tales (uncollected by Anderson) "The Rabbit-pen," "Nice Girl," and "Pastoral." In various ways in Anderson's fiction, "women may save men" (Ferguson 219). His fascination with emotionally strong women reached its fullest theoretical expression in *Perhaps Women* (1931).

A coordinate theme in Anderson's work is the persistent boyishness of men. Particularly important in the short stories collected in *Horses and Men* and *Death in the Woods,* this theme is partly a carryover of the Wordsworthian idea that the child is father of the man, but Anderson also sometimes identified immaturity as a peculiarly male trait attributable either to the newness of American culture or to technology's intimidating power. None of these intellectualized explanations seems significant against the sheer intuitive understanding of masculine experience revealed in this narrative. A reader may appreciate, as an irony dimly apparent in the text, that the woman may feel quite as childishly ambivalent and confused as the man. But the Anderson corpus suggests that the author was less aware than he should have been of that simple fact about men and women.

Critical Studies

"Another Wife" is about a middle-aged doctor who comes to the country seeking a summer rest as a cure for a spiritual slump but finds instead the thrill of love and commitment to "another wife." The story lends itself to feminist interpretation. Ferguson provides such a reading, emphasizing the woman's role as active initiator in the relationship with the doctor and describing her as "not above him on a pedestal" but thoroughly "admirable, worthy of his love, and able to renew his self-confidence and vitality" (228).

The form and technique of the story are particularly effective. The third-person narrative concentrates almost entirely on the play of the doctor's consciousness over his past life and present events as, away from his busy medical practice, he is beset by a tumult of thoughts. Only twice is a bit of the woman's conversation interpolated into the stream of his thinking. The story provides a perfect illustration of Geismar's statement that "the apparent 'formlessness'" of Anderson's later stories is actually an artful, meticulously detailed arrangement of "sudden, shifting associations of thought and feeling" ("Introduction" xxi). Geismar in fact has been the most enthusiastic critic to comment on "Another Wife." He remarks its beautiful handling of "desire at fifty" (*Last* 272). He also notes its ironic tone and embrace of the "life, with all its materiality, all its mysteries of the commonplace, all its grace to the very end" ("Introduction" xx).

These remarks, though brief, are more helpful than David Anderson's comment that the story teaches that "true feeling transcends things that can be seen, felt, or measured" (132). The story provides little evidence for his conclusion that the doctor has been able to "penetrate to the essence" of the woman he loves. On the contrary, the doctor's love is giddy, impulsive, delightful, dumbfounding. Just as soon as he thinks, "they were at any rate both mature and grown up enough to know what they were doing," his next thought is "Did they?" (*DW* 215).

Vacillation, in the final analysis, is the key to the story, as Gado's interpretation shows: "The woman is ten years his junior, yet, he imagines, she is far more experienced sexually; consequently, he sees himself in her eyes as at once an unattractive old man and a fumbling boy. He clings to the memory of his undemanding first wife as an amulet; however, he also recalls somewhat ruefully that she had never excited him" ("Introduction" 10). Further steps in this circuitous "mental dance" lead to the "mixed emotion" of the ending, where the doctor thinks, first, how glad and foolish he feels about getting a new wife, and then, on second thought, "Would he get over it after a time?"

Works Cited

Anderson, David. 1967. *Sherwood Anderson: An Introduction and Interpretation*. New York: Holt, Rinehart.

Anderson, Sherwood. "The Contract." *Broom* 1 (December 1921):148–53. Rpt. in *The Sherwood Anderson Reader*. Ed. Paul Rosenfeld. Boston: Houghton Mifflin, 1947, 95–101. Rpt. in *The Portable Sherwood Anderson*. Ed. Horace Gregory. New York: Viking, 1949, 439–48.

——. "Nice Girl." *New Yorker* 12 (July 25, 1936):15–17.

——. "Pastoral." *Redbook* 74 (January 1940):38–39, 59. Rpt. in *Certain Things Last: The Selected Short Stories of Sherwood Anderson*. Ed. Charles E. Modlin. New York: Four Walls Eight Windows, 1962, 288–96.

Baker, Carlos, ed. 1981. *Ernest Hemingway: Selected Letters, 1917–1961*. New York: Scribner's.

Ferguson, Mary Anne. "Sherwood Anderson's *Death in the Woods:* Toward a New Realism." In *Critical Essays on Sherwood Anderson*. Ed. David D.

Anderson. Boston: G. K. Hall, 1981, 217–34. Originally printed in *Mid-america VII*. East Lansing, MI: Midwestern Press, 1980, 73–95.

Gado, Frank, ed. 1983. *The Teller's Tales*. Signature Series. Schenectady, NY: Union College Press.

Geismar, Maxwell. 1947. "Sherwood Anderson: Last of the Townsmen." In *The Last of the Provincials: The American Novel, 1915–1925*. Boston: Houghton Mifflin. 223–84. Rpt. in part in *Sherwood Anderson: Winesburg, Ohio: Text and Criticism*. Ed. John H. Ferres. New York: Viking, 1966, 377–82.

———. 1962. "Introduction." *Sherwood Anderson: Short Stories*. New York: Hill and Wang, ix–xxii.

———, ed. 1962. *Sherwood Anderson: Short Stories*. New York: Hill and Wang.

Jones, Howard Mumford, and Walter B. Rideout, eds. 1953. *Letters of Sherwood Anderson*. Boston: Little, Brown.

Miller, William V. 1974. "Earth-Mothers, Succubi, and Other Ectoplasmic Spirits: The Woman in Sherwood Anderson's Short Stories." In *Midamerica I*. Ed. David D. Anderson. East Lansing, MI: Midwestern Press, 64–81. Rpt. in *Critical Essays on Sherwood Anderson*. Ed. David D. Anderson. Boston: G. K. Hall, 1981, 196–209.

O'Brien, Edward J. 1928. *Best Short Stories of 1927*. New York: Dodd, Mead.

A Meeting South

Circumstances of Composition

Anderson wrote "A Meeting South" in the first week of November 1924. He was living in New Orleans, in the splendidly historic part of the city known as the Vieux Carré. He and his recently wedded third wife, Elizabeth Prall Anderson, with his son Robert, luxuriated in an apartment at 540B St. Peter Street, on the third and fourth floors of the Pontalba Building, overlooking Jackson Square with its equestrian statue of General Andrew Jackson and, beyond that, the broad, deep Mississippi River (Rideout-Meriwether 94). During October, Anderson's autobiographical *A Story Teller's Story* had been published, and he had finished a first draft of a new novel, *Dark Laughter,* which would be in print the following year. Anderson was nourished by the atmosphere of New Orleans and engagement with its literary and artistic activity, and he felt the confidence of a writer whose work is mostly going well.

This story he wrote with considerable speed. On Saturday, November 1, William Faulkner arrived in New Orleans and came to Anderson's apartment hoping to meet him. That visit occasioned "A Meeting South," which Anderson completed within a week after Faulkner's arrival and mailed off to a New York literary agent by November 8 (Rideout-Meriwether 99).

Sources and Influences

William Faulkner is plainly the model for the character that Anderson's narrator chooses to call David. At the time the story was written, Faulkner was twenty-seven years old and had just been removed from his job as postmaster at the University of Mississippi. Virtually unknown as a writer, he had signed a contract for the publication of *The Marble Faun,* a slim book of heavily romanticized pastoral verse that would appear in mid-December. Two years before, Faulkner had worked in the Doubleday Doran Bookstore that Elizabeth Prall (now Anderson's wife) managed in New York City; long afterward, she would remember that he "was frightfully aristocratic and had the kind of gallant Southern manners that intimidated customers" into buying whatever books he selected for them. This charming Southerner, she recalled, even then "drank himself to sleep every night" and fascinated her by telling "amazing, lurid tales about his life"; when she inquired if his stories were "really true," he would defend his veracity, "Would I lie to you, Miss Elizabeth?" Quickly she learned that the novelist-to-be "would lie" indeed, "whenever it struck his fancy" (Elizabeth Anderson 40–41).

Faulkner arrived at the Andersons' New Orleans apartment ostensibly to visit Elizabeth, his former employer, but really to meet her husband, whose short stories he greatly admired, and Sherwood Anderson asked the aspiring young poet to stay to dinner with other, previously invited, guests (Blotner 367; Rideout 97). During this period of his life, Faulkner cultivated a poignant limp, accompanied by a heroic story about his career as a wartime flyer. "Most of the new friends he made in New Orleans remained convinced for years that [an] airplane accident had left him with a silver plate in his head" as well as a serious leg injury; he liked to give the impression that he drank in order to soothe the constant pain of his wounds (Blotner 369). Faulkner's story, of course, was completely false: he had probably never flown a plane and had certainly never been in combat. Other stories he told about his father's plantation emerged similarly from fancy and desire: Faulkner's background was distinctly—for him embarrassingly—middle class. Faulkner "could combine at will his separately developed personalities," as this story demonstrates: the multiple poses he adopted—"aesthete, bohemian, wounded veteran, Englishman, poet, drunkard, even the Southern gentleman"—may have sprung, as some biographers have speculated, from a deep psychic need for maternal affection (Grimwood 20–21, 35–39).

The character Aunt Sally, who provides a semblance of maternal affection for the character David, is based on a woman known to New Orleans as Aunt Rose Arnold, a "big-bosomed" redhead "over six feet tall" who owned a house in what had been until 1917 "the red-light district" of the Vieux Carré (Blotner 370). She lived on Chartres Street, "only steps away from the Anderson apartment" (Rideout-Meriwether 98).

Scholars have always assumed that Anderson was completely taken in by Faulkner's lies (see, for example, Blotner 371; Rideout-Meriwether 98; Townsend 221; Ferguson 225). There is indeed no incontrovertible evidence that Anderson suspected Faulkner of inventing these purportedly autobiographical yarns. But Faulkner's close friends knew that "after a few drinks, he would tell people anything" (Blotner 371), and Elizabeth certainly may have helped her husband to a similar skepticism. Furthermore, Anderson himself was a seasoned, notorious embroiderer of his own autobiography and had just produced a heavily imagined life story that flaunted its fictionality in its title—*A Story Teller's Story*. It is credible that he quickly recognized in Faulkner the same gift of fancy, the same disregard for facts on which he prided himself. It is certain that he and Faulkner were soon engaged jointly (in conversation in New Orleans and in letters) in making up a series of fantastic tales about legendary webfooted descendants of Andrew Jackson, herders of a breed of half-sheep–half-alligators (Faulkner, "Sherwood" 28–29; Jones-Rideout, *Letters* 162–64; Rideout and Meriwether; Richardson 287–89; Phillips 208; Blotner 402–405; White 5–8). One humorous feature of the collaborative tall tale would be that the Jackson descendants always wore "congress shoes" to hide their webbed feet; the emphasis on the deceptive pose was a joke both yarn-spinners enjoyed. Faulkner included a portion of the collaborative Al Jackson saga in his *Mosquitoes* (66–68, 277–81), and Anderson printed some in the Virginia newspapers he later owned and edited (Elizabeth Anderson 96). Surely Anderson was convinced "that one's fanciful life is of as much significance as one's real flesh-and-blood life and that one cannot tell where the one cuts off and the other begins. . . . 'It is only by lying to the limit one can come at truth'" (Jones-Rideout, *Letters* 100).

The story itself, however, presents the best evidence that Anderson appreciated young Faulkner as a storyteller—in both senses of that word. For Anderson's story begins, "He told me the story of his ill fortune." Not the more colloquial "bad luck" or "trouble" or "injury" or even "misfortune"— the heightened diction of the phrase "ill fortune" rings with un-Andersonian eloquent gentility. Then, too, David's plaintive story of "ill fortune" has a suspiciously hyperbolic flavor. He cannot sleep indoors, he says, but finds it is better outdoors: "The mosquitoes bite me some, but I don't mind much. . . . The little pain makes a kind of rhythm for the great pain—like poetry" (*DW* 236). The pose is transparent, however charming. Anderson's story concludes—after establishing several parallels between David and the character named Aunt Sally—with the narrator's smiling remark, "I don't think I had better inquire too closely into her past." One may infer that David's stories about his past, artful and poignant though they are, also might not withstand close inquiry.

Publication History

"A Meeting South" first appeared in April 1925 in the *Dial* (78:269–79), a major forum for the 1920s experimentalists. The *Dial* had published several of Anderson's stories, awarded him its prestigious literary prize in 1921, and serialized his *Many Marriages* in 1922. For this story they paid $90. Anderson collected "A Meeting South" in *Sherwood Anderson's Notebook* in 1926 and in the volume *Death in the Woods* in 1933. Subsequently it has been reprinted in Rosenfeld's *The Sherwood Anderson Reader* (274–84), in Gregory's *The Portable Sherwood Anderson* (517–32), in Geismar's selection of Anderson stories (170–80), and in Modlin's more recent selection (210–21).

Relation to Other Works

One aspect of "A Meeting South" that links it closely to other works in the Anderson canon is that a key role is played by a mother figure. Elizabeth Willard of "Mother" exerts a force over the collection *Winesburg, Ohio* far exceeding her simple presence: her dreams, her sufferings, and her hopes for the son who will feel the pressure of her need for vicarious fulfillment animate the story cycle. Women figure significantly in the collection *Death in the Woods* as well, from Ma Grimes of "Death in the Woods" to Mary Grey of "Brother Death." Aunt Sally in "A Meeting South" is like Ma Grimes in her earthy connection with fundamental life forces, and both of them in their different ways feed men's needs. But Aunt Sally is also like Mary Grey in her acuity, her intuitive understanding. And she is strong and beautiful, as is Alice in "Like a Queen." "Anderson's portraits of women" often radiate a coloring of "chivalry," so mingled with "sexual candor" that he became known as "the 'Ohio Pagan'" (Gregory 21–22). As Ferguson suggests, because Aunt Sally and Alice are more generous and noble than men, they adumbrate the "exaltation of women" that Anderson expressed most lavishly in *Perhaps Women* (1931) (227). Aunt Sally serves as a kind of foster mother for the Southern poet who falls asleep like a child on her patio. Beneath the brave demeanor of the talented young artist, Anderson discerns the longing for a nurturing, nonjudgmental, sensual, but idealized woman—someone to come home to in one's dreams.

Further, this story, which was written on the verge of the Harlem Renaissance, is particularly significant for the light it sheds on Anderson's attitudes toward race and the difficulties of white writers attempting to depict black characters in fiction. African-Americans appear in some of Anderson's prior fiction, notably "I Want to Know Why" and "Out of Nowhere into Nothing." The criticism Anderson directs at Northern "writers of nigger stories" in "A Meeting South" reflects his dissatisfaction not only with popular writers cashing in on the vogue of Negro stories but also with his own failure to penetrate the surface of black lives. In December 1922, upon reading Jean Toomer's works in the New Orleans little magazine *Double Dealer,* Anderson wrote to Toomer praising his work; he confessed that he had wanted "to express something clear and beautiful I felt coming up out of your race" but had found himself unable to write not "of the Negro but out of him" (Modlin, *Letters* 42–43). When Toomer sent Anderson an inscribed copy of the newly published *Cane,* Anderson enthusiastically responded that he could feel in it both the gloriously unsophisticated voice of black workers and also the "nervous distraught" voice of the modern author: "It dances. . . . It is very very fine to me" (Townsend 226; Modlin, *Letters* 52–53). Anderson thus recognized that Toomer was pioneering new dimensions of American experience and bringing depth to literary treatment of blacks. Indeed, Toomer was producing the kind of unconventional fiction encouraged by the editors of the *Double Dealer,* who had called for a new Southern literature to replace traditional "treacly sentimentalities," proclaiming: "New peoples, customs prevail. . . . A storied realm of dreams, lassitude, pleasure, chivalry, and the Nigger no longer exists" (Friend).

The novel *Dark Laughter,* which Anderson was writing during the summer before he met Faulkner, does not achieve the deeper understanding of black life that Anderson admired in Toomer's work. Associating Negroes with natural pagan vitality and earthy, pastoral health, Anderson offers the stereotypical black primitive as a superior alternative to the inhibited, alienated, conformist lives of most whites; the African-American's value remains primarily symbolic. But Anderson's attitude toward the Negro is not so condescending as that of the Northern "writer of nigger stories" mentioned in "A Meeting South," who writes to please an audience that finds them "so amusing" (*DW* 225). Moreover, Anderson's view contrasts sharply with the reactionary view espoused by David, who talks blandly about docile darkies happily working for his father, a white master with unquestioned power to control and even kill them.

David's attitude represents something Anderson almost certainly found offensive in Faulkner. A 1934 book review by Anderson strenuously objects to fiction that casually promotes a perniciously quaint Southernness; the review makes explicit what is implicit in "A Meeting South": "These Alabamans are so persistently and so confoundedly cute, even in their cruelties, the old aristocracy is so aristocratic and the niggers so niggery. Thank you kindly. Hand me the Bill Faulkner" ("Paying" 49). It is worth noting that Faulkner, in his novel *Sartoris*, developed the scene in "A Meeting South" where singing Negroes work with a mule "making the 'lasses" out of sugar cane (*DW* 236–37); in the novel Faulkner asserts that the mule's "mental processes most closely resemble" those of "the nigger who drives him" (279). Despite his admiring appreciation of Faulkner, Anderson saw in him the cruelty that lurks beneath Southern white paternalism. In later years Anderson would say of Faulkner, "he exposed a lot of Southern bunk. After all, there is a lot of insanity in the South. Everywhere there are those decayed families making claim to aristocracy. . . . There is a kind of cruelty thought necessary to keep the Negro, as they say, 'in his place' . . . ; still, at the same time, there is in him also a lot of the same old bunk about the South" (Rosenfeld, *Memoirs* 474). That "old bunk" looms up in David's smugly "aristocratic" attitude toward black Americans.

Critical Studies

Many biographers and critics have commented on "A Meeting South," noting its connection with the historic meeting between two important twentieth-century authors, the older of whom helped the younger toward a career that would overshadow his own. At the time of their meeting, Sherwood Anderson was a literary giant, and one wonders if he divined any prophetic significance in the name "David," which he selected for the small-statured poet with great storytelling talent, whom he modeled after William Faulkner.

The story itself, however, has not received careful analysis. Interpretation has been fairly cursory. Bland in 1933 called the story "bewitchingly beautiful," admiring its atmospheric details and "softened mood" (134). Cargill liked "A Meeting South" because it displays so effectively the "tenderness" that characterized Anderson (330). Schevill merely remarked that the tale is "a fine example of his closely observed, objective style of the *Winesburg* period" (220). Howe thought the story "skirts sentimentality and lacks dramatic incident" but succeeds as a lyrical "character sketch" (159). Voss, similarly, remarks that it is "one of several pieces" in *Death in the Woods* that are "more nearly impressionistic autobiographical sketches than stories, and it is the only successful one" (197). Burbank agrees that the story is "idyllic" and "almost devoid of plot" (124).

Commentators have noted the sensuous New Orleans setting and observed that David, of Southern patrician stock, and Aunt Sally, experienced in an underworld of gamblers and prostitutes, "reveal depths and shades of sensibility" that make them true aristocrats (Burbank 125; similarly, Rideout 99). Miller remarks on David's courageous struggle to write despite his pain, viewing it as an instance of Anderson's stress on the morality of the artist ("Portraits" 19). Everyone seems to agree that, as Burbank says, the story is characterized by its "absence of grotesqueness" (125). This, the prevailing view, ought to be questioned.

No one has discerned any dramatic tension in "A Meeting South," or any shade of irony, or any purpose to the narrator's several digressions. Rideout simply mentions "the controlled casualness of the oral narrative" (99). Nevertheless, if the story is examined more closely, that casually digressive narrative style can be seen as directed toward a subtle drama that contains not only sympathetic tenderness but also an understated but penetrating critique of the two "aristocrats" and, through them, of modern society. The meaning of "A Meeting South" is more pointed than has been supposed. Readers have so long pigeonholed Anderson as a sentimentalist lacking in fine intelligence that they have not been alert to his satiric wit and deadpan comedy. Half-appreciative, half-parodic, "A Meeting South" reveals that Anderson's early view of Faulkner was far more complex than anyone ever guessed.

The distinction between the story David tells and the story the narrator tells is crucial. The pivotal drama inheres not in David's story but in the narrator's attempt to make sense of his experience meeting David and listening to David and Aunt Sally. The narrator's story moves back and forth in time; David's story is included within it at several different points. The narrator's attitude undergoes several transformations: from initial liking for David, to satisfaction at the immediate understanding he sees between David and Aunt Sally, to quiet withdrawal and a growing feeling of isolation as the intimacy between the other two increases, and at last to a "delicious" but unspecified "notion" that brings him cleansing laughter and a delighted sense of understanding. Each phase of the story moves toward this final epiphany.

Early in the story, David and the narrator stand before the statue of General Andrew Jackson and drink to the preservation of the "Union." The word "Union" characterizes the initial phase of this meeting and echoes through a whole series of meetings that follow. Metaphorical overtones resonate first as Midwesterner and Southerner together make the symbolic gesture honoring their nascent friendship. The scene also serves to forecast the meeting between Aunt Sally and David, a motherly old woman and a young poet who seeks motherly sympathy, she a sensible industrious Midwestern plebeian who has risen to prosperity (like a modern-day Moll Flanders) and he an alcoholic scion of a decaying Southern aristocracy. An apparently offhand reference to Darwin near the beginning of the story further indicates

the large cultural movements of North and South that this meeting typifies—
the decline of the South, the rise of the Midwest. By implication, another
ironic meeting appears in the parallel between the Northern author's "nigger
stories," mentioned in an early digression, and the Southerner's stories of the
"niggers" on his daddy's plantation; both are debased, for both exploit the
Negro to give the white audience "what they want" (*DW* 226). Moreover, a
similar parallel links the businesslike, profit-oriented Northern author with
Aunt Sally, who likewise matter-of-factly sells her customers what they
want—in her case, whiskey, gambling, illicit sex.

In another digression, drunken sailors sing a ditty:

> "I've got to get it,
> You've got to get it,
> We've all got to get it
> In our own good time." (*DW* 229)

This peculiar refrain draws attention to the repetition of forms of the word
"get" throughout the narrative, and it raises a question: what is it that "we've
all got to get"? Burbank interprets the song as indicating "frank, free, una-
shamed lustiness" (125), but the "it" in the song could apply equally to
liquor or, more probably, to death. What Aunt Sally "gets"—and Anderson
employs that word—is money and security (*DW* 232, 234). David, in contrast, "got into a crash" (*DW* 227). What the narrator gets is insight; declaring
"I got it," at first he grasps the point David is insinuating about the connection between his injuries and his drinking, and at last he apprehends "something to do with aristocrats" (*DW* 239). He does not define the "something"
that constitutes his final revelation.

Readers, left to grasp the hinted meaning of the climactic epiphany, have
been slow to "get it." The narrative makes the reader responsible for completing the tale in a leap of understanding comparable to the narrator's, but
it also points the way to that goal. The narrator's statement that he has
understood "something" relating to "aristocrats" immediately follows a digression juxtaposing Aunt Sally's heroes (John L. Sullivan, P. T. Barnum, and
a big gambler) and David's hero (Percy Bysshe Shelley). This digression,
tracing the narrator's wandering train of thought, shows that her boasted
monuments are low-brow and David's are high-brow, but the juxtaposition
sets up ironies that operate in both directions. At this point, the narrator,
having been ushered out alone into the dark street as David falls asleep on
Aunt Sally's patio, feels excluded from the union she honors by announcing
that she will send a magnum of champagne to David's father. Her grand
aristocratic gesture leaves the narrator feeling anxious and lonely. But suddenly his thoughts release his tension, and he laughs as he understands the
ironic parallel between his two friends: fine though they are, their aristocratic bearing is ridiculously pretentious. The insight is liberating. Smiling to

himself, he goes on to say that Aunt Sally's past will not bear scrutiny; he implies that David's past is equally suspect. Aunt Sally's wealth and pride, like that of the North she represents, are based on hard-scrabbling, shrewd business dealings, many of them illegal, that exploit lust and greed. David's gentility and pride, like that of the South he represents, are based on a history of slaveholding that still casts its dark shadow over a society where effete whites cling wistfully to nineteenth-century English literary models and continue to lord it over vigorous blacks.

The setting for the meeting, appropriately, is a decayed Southern mansion refurbished by an enterprising Midwesterner to cater to age-old human sins. At one point, the narrator muses, "we do seem attached to sin" (*DW* 231). Indeed, for all the beauty and Latin charm of New Orleans, Anderson describes it as a faintly grotesque world of deracinated souls, where Northerners and Southerners alike are steeped in the sins of the past. Symbolically, even the chinaberry tree has suffered from "a lot of different sicknesses" and has not gotten enough sunlight. David, the gentleman poet, is physically and emotionally crippled. Aunt Sally, fat and ridiculous in her flowery nightclothes, betrays a need to strut. The narrator is fond of these people, and he admits that he hopes Aunt Sally is from his native state. Anderson's narrative tone is tender. But, albeit gently, he exposes the characters' pretensions. Aristocratic graces scarcely disguise the ancient human fellowship. Ironically, despite their heroics and patrician airs, all these folk meet on common ground. Andrew Jackson, backwoods rowdy, war hero, Indian killer, and President, is a fitting symbol of that union.

Faulkner may have grasped the parodic note in "A Meeting South." Not long after it was published, he wrote a short parody of Anderson's style in a foreword to *Sherwood Anderson & Other Famous Creoles* (1926). He begins by imitating almost directly the prose of "A Meeting South": "First, let me tell you something about our Quarter, the Vieux Carré. Do you know our Quarter, with its narrow streets, its old wrought-iron balconies and its southern European atmosphere? An atmosphere of richness and soft laughter, you know" (Spratling and Faulkner). Then Faulkner dwells on brotherhood and fellowship, the themes that seemed to him a mark of Anderson's sentimentality. It is a gently humorous return for Anderson's gently humorous handling of him, tit for tat.

Works Cited

Anderson, Elizabeth, and Gerald R. Kelley. 1969. *Miss Elizabeth: A Memoir*. Boston: Little, Brown.

Anderson, Sherwood. 1970. *Sherwood Anderson's Notebook*. Mamaroneck, NY: Appel. Originally printed New York: Boni & Liveright, 1926.

————. "Paying for Old Sins." *The Nation* 139 (July 11, 1934:49–50. Rev. of Carl Carmer, *Stars Fell on Alabama* and Langston Hughes, *The Ways of White Folks*.

Bland, Winifred. 1970. "Through a College Window." In *Homage to Sherwood Anderson, 1876–1941*. Ed. Paul P. Appel. Mamaroneck, NY: Appel, 131–37.

Blotner, Joseph. 1974. *Faulkner: A Biography*. Vol. 1. New York: Random House.

Burbank, Rex. 1964. *Sherwood Anderson*. New York: Twayne. Rpt. in part in *The Achievement of Sherwood Anderson: Essays in Criticism*. Ed. Ray Lewis White. Chapel Hill: University of North Carolina Press, 1966, 32–43. Rpt. in part in *Sherwood Anderson: Collection of Critical Essays*. Ed. Walter B. Rideout. Englewood Cliffs, NJ: Prentice-Hall, 1974, 70–83.

Cargill, Oscar. 1941. *Intellectual America: Ideas on the March*. New York: Macmillan.

Faulkner, William. 1927. *Mosquitoes: A Novel*. New York: Liveright.

————. 1929. *Sartoris*. New York: Random House.

————. "Sherwood Anderson: An Appreciation." *Atlantic* 191 (June 1953):27–29.

Ferguson, Mary Anne. 1981. "Sherwood Anderson's *Death in the Woods*: Toward a New Realism." In *Critical Essays on Sherwood Anderson*. Ed. David D. Anderson. Boston: G. K. Hall, 217–34. Originally printed in *Midamerica VII*. East Lansing, MI: Midwestern Press, 1980, 73–95.

Friend, Julius Weis. "Southern Letters." *Double Dealer* 1 (June 1921):214.

Geismar, Maxwell, ed. 1962. *Short Stories*. New York: Hill and Wang.

Gregory, Horace. 1949. "Editor's Introduction." *The Portable Sherwood Anderson*. Viking, 1–31. Rev. ed. New York: Viking Penguin, 1972.

Grimwood, Michael. 1987. *Heart in Conflict: Faulkner's Struggles with Vocation*. Athens and London: University of Georgia Press.

Howe, Irving. 1951. *Sherwood Anderson*. New York: William Sloane.

Jones, Howard Mumford, and Walter B. Rideout, eds. 1953. *Letters of Sherwood Anderson*. Boston: Little Brown.

Miller, William V. 1976. "Portraits of the Artist: Anderson's Fictional Storytellers." In *Sherwood Anderson: Dimensions of His Literary Art: A Collection of Critical Essays*. Ed. David D. Anderson. East Lansing: Michigan State University Press, 1–23.

Modlin, Charles E., ed. 1992. *Certain Things Last: The Selected Short Stories of Sherwood Anderson*. New York: Four Walls Eight Windows.

——, ed. 1982. *Sherwood Anderson: Selected Letters*. Knoxville: University of Tennessee Press.

Phillips, William L. "Sherwood Anderson's Two Prize Pupils." *The Achievement of Sherwood Anderson: Essays in Criticism*. Ed. Ray Lewis White. Chapel Hill: University of North Carolina Press, 1966, 202–210. [Originally printed in *University of Chicago Magazine* 47 (1955): 9–12.]

Richardson, H. Edward. "Anderson and Faulkner." *American Literature* 36 (1964):298–314.

Rideout, Walter B., and James B. Meriwether. "On the Collaboration of Faulkner and Anderson." *American Literature* 35 (1963):85–87.

——. "The Most Cultural Town in America': Sherwood Anderson and New Orleans." *The Southern Review* 24 (Winter 1988):79–99.

Rosenfeld, Paul, ed. 1947. *The Sherwood Anderson Reader*. Boston: Houghton Mifflin.

——, ed. 1942. *Sherwood Anderson's Memoirs*. New York: Harcourt, Brace.

Schevill, James. 1951. *Sherwood Anderson: His Life and Work*. Denver: University of Denver Press.

Spratling, William, and William Faulkner. 1966. *Sherwood Anderson & Other Famous Creoles: A Gallery of Contemporary New Orleans*. New Orleans: Pelican Bookshop, 1926. Rpt. Austin and London: University of Texas Press.

Townsend, Kim. 1987. *Sherwood Anderson*. Boston: Houghton Mifflin.

Voss, Arthur. 1973. *The American Short Story: A Critical Survey*. Norman: University of Oklahoma Press.

White, Ray Lewis. "Anderson, Faulkner, and a Unique Al Jackson Tale." *Winesburg Eagle* 16, no. 2 (Summer 1991):5–8.

The Flood

Circumstances of Composition

Sherwood Anderson wrote "The Flood" in the last week of June 1930, and sent it off to be typed (Modlin, *Letters* 124). He was living then near Troutdale, Virginia, at Ripshin Farm. He had been working on the little book that would be *Perhaps Women* and had been involved in various projects concerning the lives of factory workers and the influence of the machine on modern life. A couple of months before, the woman who would later be his fourth wife, Eleanor Copenhaver, had become his lover.

Sources and Influences

A biographical influence on this story was Anderson's personal consideration of the problem of values. When he created the main character, he must have had in mind the brother of his third wife, David Prall, a college professor in California who had written a book titled *Study in the Theory of Value* (1921). But Anderson's letters show that around the time of the story's composition he himself had been discussing questions of value with Burton Emmett, a wealthy patron and collector who was providing him with funds in return for his discarded manuscripts. While he accepted Emmett's money, Anderson protested his notions of value, arguing a bit stridently against "immediate value" in favor of "ultimate value," against "market value" in favor of artistic value, against "money" value in favor of spiritual value or the value of affection (Modlin, *Selected Letters* 114–15, 118–20). He had even proposed to Emmett that they collaborate on a book aimed at "young people who were searching for values in modern-day life" (125 n. 4).

The major influence on the story's tone and substance, though, was the buoyant happiness ushered into Anderson's life by Eleanor Copenhaver's love. The end of 1929 had been a period of severe depression for him; guilt about three failed marriages and dejection about an attempted novel that he finally threw away in despair grew into despondency when Tennessee Mitchell, his second wife, was found dead in her apartment (Modlin, "Introduction" xvii). He brooded, knowing that her suicide was partly (perhaps largely) his fault. But Eleanor made him feel alive again. (From a psychological perspective, it seems significant that the woman who saves the fictional professor is his dead wife's younger sister.) Eleanor seemed a salvation after long, lonely failure. Once again, he felt he could write. His letters to Eleanor became more and more rapturous as his theories gave way to the presence of love. He told her in May that, although sometimes in the fury of composition he almost sensed that he could "conquer the world, . . . find the very central truth and loveliness of all life," actually he knew better: all he or she could do was "to surrender to something outside self" (Modlin, *Love Letters* 113–14).

Publication History

"The Flood" was first published in *Death in the Woods,* the fourth and last collection of short stories that Anderson compiled (1933). It has recently been reprinted in the collection *Certain Things Last* (222–30).

Relation to Other Works

In the series of stories that Anderson wrote over the years about the clash between men's need for work and their need for women, this story indicates a change of mood. In *Winesburg, Ohio* "Loneliness" shows Enoch Robinson crushed by the intrusion of a real woman into the room where he plays with the creatures of his imagination. Similarly, in *Death in the Woods,* "The Lost Novel" shows a marriage destroyed and a creative gift crippled by a wife's entrance into the room where her husband is writing a novel. In "The Flood," however, the latest composed of these stories, a woman's sudden invasion of a man's room and her interruption of his writing are treated with benign humor. The difference in tone, evidently, is attributable to a change in the author's personal experience, primarily to the different personality of the new woman in his life.

One critic finds the protagonist's surrender to the metaphoric floods of life to be a measure of Anderson's retrogression "into his old 'groping'" (Troy 508). But the judgment is perhaps unjust. While it is true that the characters in "The Flood"—the two wives in particular—are not very complex, the style suits the story's comic mood. A more sympathetic interpreter states that "The Flood" conveys a "note of ironical surrender to life [which] pervades *Death in the Woods*" (Geismar, "Introduction" xx; similarly, "Last" 273). Specifically, Geismar perceives a link between this story and "Another Wife," which also probes the "mysteries of the commonplace," the "grace" of life that transcends "the illusions of reason . . . or of human control over human destiny, as established by man's vaunted intellectual power." With a similar emphasis, David Anderson remarks that the theme of "the futility of intellectualized human relations" connects this story with "In a Strange Town" and "A Jury Case" as well (132). Ferguson detects here and in other stories in the collection the recurrent pattern of "men's weakness and consequent need for the saving grace of women" (228–29).

Critical Studies

"The Flood" is the story of a lonely, widowed professor of philosophy who has retreated into thought for a sabbatical year. He plans to culminate his lifetime of study by producing his "magnum opus," in which he will set forth the definition of value (*DW* 250). When at last he feels he has arrived at the verge of ultimate truth, his wife's sister bursts into his room and drags him downstairs to a party, whereupon he proposes to her. He is quite happy about "letting go." The theorizer thus yields to the vital force of life.

"The Flood" has elicited very little critical commentary. Two critics who do discuss it differ widely in interpretation. Geismar suggests that in surrendering "a vision of perfection to the compulsions of experience," the protagonist has "unconsciously solved" the problem of value after all (*Last* 273). Ferguson grudgingly allows that the woman "is a tie to life more important than professional achievement," but since the woman "is not admirable" but "frivolous" Ferguson concludes that, when the professor "succumbs" to marrying her, he is merely repeating an earlier mistake (228). Indeed feminists can hardly approve of this flighty new wife, and any serious reader can predict that a marriage between such an "old stick" (as she calls him) and such a woman will be anything but tension-free. But the story is not meant to be taken in deadly earnest.

Works Cited

Anderson, David. 1967. *Sherwood Anderson: An Introduction and Interpretation*. New York: Holt, Rinehart.

Ferguson, Mary Anne. 1981. "Sherwood Anderson's *Death in the Woods:* Toward a New Realism." In *Critical Essays on Sherwood Anderson*. Ed. David D. Anderson. Boston: G. K. Hall, 217–34. Originally printed in *Midamerica VII*. East Lansing, MI: Midwestern Press, 1980, 73–95.

Geismar, Maxwell. 1947. "Sherwood Anderson: Last of the Townsmen." In *The Last of the Provincials: The American Novel, 1915–1925*. Boston: Houghton Mifflin, 223–84. Rpt. in part in *Sherwood Anderson:* Winesburg, Ohio: *Text and Criticism*. Ed. John H. Ferres. New York: Viking, 1966, 377–82.

———. 1962. "Introduction." *Sherwood Anderson: Short Stories*. New York: Hill and Wang, ix–xxii.

———, ed. 1962. *Sherwood Anderson: Short Stories*. New York: Hill and Wang.

Modlin, Charles E., ed. 1984. *Sherwood Anderson: Selected Letters*. Knoxville: University of Tennessee Press.

———, ed. 1989. *Sherwood Anderson's Love Letters to Eleanor Copenhaver Anderson*. Athens and London: University of Georgia Press.

———. 1992. "Introduction." *Certain Things Last: The Selected Short Stories of Sherwood Anderson*. New York: Four Walls Eight Windows, vii–xxiv.

———, ed. 1992. *Certain Things Last: The Selected Short Stories of Sherwood Anderson*. New York: Four Walls Eight Windows.

Troy, William. "Fragmentary Ends." *Nation* 136 (1933):508.

Why They Got Married

Circumstances of Composition

Sherwood Anderson evidently wrote this story in December 1928. He lived in Marion, Virginia, and worked as editor of two local papers, which he also owned, the *Smyth County News* and the *Marion Democrat*. His serious writing was being crowded out by the obligations of the newspaper business and by personal pressures. His third marriage, to Elizabeth Prall Anderson, had become gradually more distressing to them both. At the close of the year, he sent her off to visit her family in California and told her not to come back.

Sources and Influences

"Why They Got Married" obviously derives partly from Anderson's own deepening concern about the problem of marriage. He surely wondered why he had ever married Elizabeth, who was so unlike him, and the note of hostility expressed in the characters' initial dialogue reflects tensions the author and his wife both knew only too well. But the tone of this story is light, not deeply troubled. A more important influence, undoubtedly, was the countless conversations Anderson had heard in which married couples told acquaintances how they had met and "why they got married."

Publication History

"Why They Got Married" was accepted by *Vanity Fair* on January 9, 1929, and first appeared in that year's March issue (32:74, 116). Anderson's payment was $300, from which his agent deducted 10 percent. Anderson had contributed articles and occasional fiction to *Vanity Fair* regularly since 1926. Anderson felt mildly compromised by selling his work to this trendily stylish New York magazine instead of to more avant-garde literary magazines, but it was a dependable source of income. He had "reason[ed] himself into" commercializing his art "for a house and a woman," he would later confide: "The stink of it isn't out of me yet" (Jones-Rideout, *Letters* 236–37). Almost immediately after the first publication, Anderson placed the story in his own small weekly paper, the *Smyth County News* (March 28, pp. 1, 4, and April 4, p. 2). Then he gathered it among the stories collected in *Death in the Woods* (1933).

Relation to Other Works

Ferguson observes that the "realistic view of women" offered by this story represents a departure from the mystical "exaltation" of women in *Perhaps Women* (1931) and in such stories as "Like a Queen" and "Death in the Woods."

Critical Studies

"Why They Got Married" is a fairly slight performance, entertaining but lacking in substance. Mary Anne Ferguson seems to be the only critic to have discussed it. As she points out, it is "playful" in tone, and it shows the woman as active initiator of a happy marriage in which the wife "is on a par with the man" (228). Ferguson's rather feminist analysis lauds "the woman's skill in winning the man's love" and in manipulating things so that his parents (actually, her parents) will approve. But the story is equally susceptible of a completely different, and negative, reading, for the woman's maneuverings uncomfortably approximate the standard jokes about marriage mentioned in the sardonic opening paragraph.

The most appealing aspect of the story may be the proficient handling of the narration, which replicates feats of "conversational swimming" regularly enacted in matrimonial storytelling, where husband and wife alternately take over the telling of their mutual story, with frequent interruptions and impromptu asides. Playing to their audience of friends and guests one night, the two spouses here give their joint story just the right mixture of sincerity and theatricality. Anderson is famous for his first-person narratives and their fine oral flavor; here he also captures brilliantly this highly specialized genre of oral storytelling, with dual narrators and varied tones of affection, friction, and jest.

Works Cited

Ferguson, Mary Anne. 1981. "Sherwood Anderson's *Death in the Woods:* Toward a New Realism." In *Critical Essays on Sherwood Anderson.* Ed. David D. Anderson. Boston: G. K. Hall, 217–34. Originally printed in *Midamerica VII.* East Lansing, MI: Midwestern Press, 1980, 73–95.

Jones, Howard Mumford, and Walter B. Rideout, eds. 1953. *Letters of Sherwood Anderson.* Boston: Little, Brown.

Brother Death

Circumstances of Composition

Sherwood Anderson finished "Brother Death" during the first week of February, 1933. He was at the Hotel Puritan in Kansas City, Missouri, where he stayed between January and March of 1933 (Curry xliv–xlv, 223). Anderson had already sent the manuscripts for the collection *Death in the Woods* to the printer (Appel 198). But as he told Laura Copenhaver, he "got rather dissatisfied with the short story book, feeling it still needed something to give it more distinction," and therefore "wrote a new short story" (Modlin, *Letters* 165). To write "Brother Death," he explained, he "took the heart out of the novel [he] had started—about the people on the cattle farm—and condensed it into the short story. . . . "

The novel was "Thanksgiving," notes from which have been preserved at the Newberry Library along with six drafts of the short story. Earl Hilton concludes from a study of those manuscripts that the genesis of the story was a phrase Anderson had written as he sketched out a scene for the novel—"legs like trees" (127). According to Hilton, the phrase arrested Anderson's attention, the novel stopped, and the story began, with two children gazing at newly cut tree stumps and wondering whether "they had perhaps bled, like amputated legs." In the first draft, young Ted, who has an incurable heart ailment, is consoled by the stumps, which become for him "Brother Death" (128). The second version adds the idea "that 'something' had died" in Ted's brother, to whom Hilton refers as "Dan" but who is "Don" in the published tale (129). Only in the third version does it become clear that Dan's (Don's) spiritual death results from his drive for property and power; the "original symbol" of the stumps henceforth became subordinate (130).

Subsequently published letters indicate that Anderson was writing about "the Grey farm in Kentucky" and "a question of authority, in the matter of cutting down two young oak trees" as early as November 13, 1932 (White, *Secret* 261). A few days earlier, he had completed a first draft of "Thanksgiving" (White, *Secret* 258). This evidence indicates that some of Hilton's conclusions ought perhaps to be reexamined.

Letters that Anderson wrote to several friends express his conviction that "Brother Death" was a first-rate accomplishment, "one of the finest and most significant [stories] anyone has ever done" (Jones-Rideout, *Letters* 277–78, 292, 295; Sutton, *Letters* 331; Modlin, *Letters* 167, 168).

Sources and Influences

In the letter mentioned above, in which Anderson tells of writing about the "cutting down [of] two young oak trees," he says that his narrative derived from "Mary's reaction to a story heard when she was a child"; White identifies "Mary" as Anderson's friend Mary Emmett (*Secret* 261 and n.).

One critic suggests that Anderson's symbolic use of cut trees may owe something to Anton Chekhov, presumably to his drama *The Cherry Orchard* (Raymund 146). Papinchak extends that insight, noting that in both works the cutting of the trees represents "the end of one era and the beginning of the next" (43).

The idea of the sensitive plant, which shows up in the symbol of the oaks, echoes Shelley's poem of that title. Shelley envisions a garden in which the plants are endowed with human feeling. Though the garden goes through the seasonal drama of decline and death, the poem concludes with optimistic reassurance: "death" is "a mockery" because "love, and beauty, and delight" cannot ever pass away. That is one essential point of Anderson's story.

Anderson attributed the story's strength to Eleanor Copenhaver, whom he was planning to marry at the time he wrote it (Modlin, *Love Letters* 283). The character Mary Grey may be partly a version of her. But Eleanor's father, Bascom E. Copenhaver, probably influenced the story more directly. The idea of writing about the Copenhaver family had long appealed to Anderson, and he was particularly fascinated by the "determined," "inflexible," "sturdy peasant" character of Mr. Copenhaver (White, *Secret* 34). His "Germanic, somewhat rude virtues" seemed at the opposite pole from Anderson's own irresponsibility and subtle sensitivity to beauty (White, *Secret* 78). A powerful rivalry between Eleanor's father and her lover continued throughout the period of their courtship, and that is reflected in the fictional struggle between John Grey and his sons.

Publication History

Redbook magazine rejected "Brother Death," telling Anderson it was "very beautiful but too sad" (Campbell 106). The story's first publication was in Anderson's fourth volume of short stories, *Death in the Woods* (1933). Posthumous collections of Anderson's stories edited by Maxwell Geismar, Frank Gado, and Charles Modlin also include the story.

Relation to Other Works

"Brother Death" was written to round out the volume *Death in the Woods*. As a companion piece to the title story, it helps to frame the whole volume. Together, the first and final stories contemplate the looming threat of death in order to emphasize the abundant wealth of human life (Taylor 67). In "Death in the Woods" the artist's memory acts on actual experience much as Mary Grey's memory does in "Brother Death." In both stories, memory absorbs experience, ruminates over it, sifts it, and—as the years go by—gathers understanding. It is the mind that perpetuates fleeting experience and discovers its significance. In a sense, the perennial triumph of life over death was Anderson's most fundamental belief, the most persistent doctrine that his fiction ever offered. It is the core of that weird early tale "Vibrant Life." It is the Shelleyan undertone that whispers a promise throughout Anderson's most pessimistic volume, *The Triumph of the Egg* (1921). And it is the meaning of the maxim that Anderson composed for his epitaph: "Life not death is the great adventure." Significantly, the sexual content that dominates those earlier works has all but disappeared from "Brother Death." The brooding mind is the source of life.

This story also dwells on the question of success and the terrible cost of placing too much value on money (Modlin, *Letters* 167, 168). As Miller has observed, "The most frequent objects of contempt in Anderson's stories are businessmen" ("Portraits" 6). The shrewd, self-promoting side of himself, however, Anderson knew only too well, and he had spent much of his life as an advertising man. All his life he fought an inner battle between a need to fend off the specter of poverty and a need to think and dream, between the will to wield power and the desire to savor existence, between acquisitiveness and sensitiveness. The primary force of his fiction works against the characters who deplete themselves in pursuit of what he called "bigness"; the deeper commitment always is to feeling, to experience, and beyond that, to art.

Another theme prominent in this story and in a number of Anderson's other works concerns the struggle for power waged by children against their fathers. Anderson inaugurates this theme in *Windy McPherson's Son* (1916), where it assumes a distinctly Oedipal slant. In a closer parallel to "Brother Death," the *Winesburg* story "Godliness" presents a conflict between a child and a strong-willed father who strives determinedly for material success on the land. There, a boy of poetic temperament blindly revolts against his fanatical grandfather, hurling a stone at him like the young biblical David. "Brother Death" orchestrates a variation on the same theme: here, the son of artistic temperament stands somewhat aside from the generational struggle, and the active revolt is carried out by a second son, who is more like his father, and—in a lovely counterpoint—by the daughter against the mother. Both "Godliness" and "Brother Death" convey a sense that some primal drama is being enacted. "The father is all fathers, all authority, all established ownership and command; the older son is all assertive youth, all young and willful ambition; the younger son is all who do not compete and so do not have to surrender" (Havighurst xii–xiii). Both stories are filled with sullen respect for and stronger aversion against the death-in-life associated with hard-driving effort to wrest a living from the soil.

Anderson had used the idea of the sensitive plant previously in *Dark Laughter* (1925). Like Mary Grey in "Brother Death," Aline Grey in the novel thinks of injured trees as "bleed[ing]" or "weep[ing]." When her father talks about extracting sap for the production of turpentine, the child Aline grieves bitterly; later, when the World War ravages the young male population, the dead men seem to the woman Aline like trees, "bleeding, far off, in some strange place" (140–141). The image, by implication, embraces all created things in a mystic unity known to the visionary eye of the innocent but tragically forgotten by practical, materialistic realists.

Howe points out that the "rapport" between the two children, Mary and her brother, Ted, links this story to others with the same theme—"I Want to Know Why," "The Corn Planting," and "A Meeting South" (158–59). One might add "Brothers" to that list. Anderson's fiction again and again features the motif of empathy between fellow human beings, between human beings and animals (horses, of course, mostly) and between human beings and plants (trees here, but more often corn—for example, in "The New Englander"). Anderson's stress on empathy has conduced toward the labeling of him as "sentimental." The label has stuck for a long time. But when the social and psychological substance of his fiction penetrates deep, as it does here, and when the prose flows right, the feeling is powerfully genuine, not maudlin.

Critical Studies

Praise for "Brother Death" has been almost unanimous. Taylor calls it one of Anderson's "two finest" tales (17; similarly, Miller, "Defense" 57). Weber considers it "superior in artistry to almost any one of his earlier short pieces" (136). Townsend finds it "extraordinary," "intricate and wide-ranging, controlled and easeful and moving" (281–82). Even an unfriendly critic applauds it, though he finds the "artistic unity" it exhibits so rare in Anderson's fiction that he thinks such "triumphs are accidental" (Troy 508). Considering the almost undisputed merit of the story, it has received surprisingly little analysis.

Most commentators emphasize the final lines of "Brother Death."

> But while [her younger brother] lived, there was always, Mary afterwards thought, a curious sense of freedom, something that belonged to him that made it good, a great happiness, to be with him. It was, she finally thought, because having to die his kind of death, he never had to make the surrender his brother had made—to be sure of possessions, success, his time to command—would never have to face the more subtle and terrible death that had come to his older brother. (*DW* 298)

As Voss puts it, "there can be more than one kind of death" (197). The elder brother, who yields to his father in order to "secure his material inheritance," suffers a worse death than his younger brother (Bland 135). The ideal the story upholds is the life "free from restrictions imposed by anyone else" (Taylor 72). Even more, the story shows that requisite to the fulfilled life is freedom from greed, power-hunger, and insensitivity (Miller, "Defense" 57, 58). Those are traits that isolate kindred souls and drain one's lifeblood.

A subordinate theme is mentioned by Schevill, who interprets the story as an attack on the American "fear of death," which was manifested in Anderson's day in various taboos forbidding references to the topic (299–300).

Formal features of "Brother Death" have been considered by several critics. Schevill admires the prose technique, which is "free of the curtailed, impressionistic flow of [Anderson's] novels" of the same period and marked by a "rhythmic fusion of style and idea" (300). The technique has been questioned, though, by Howe; he judges that the story is "fine" but marred by "an irrelevant middle" (157–59). Miller demurs briefly ("Defense" 55). Gado allows that the tale is "well-wrought" but regrets its "conventional" structure, symbolism, and "narrative conception" (19). It is "homiletic," "didactic," "a parable": "the etching of a statement supersedes the unfolding of an antiquity"—Gado's coinage, a poststructuralist version of ambiguity (19). Ferguson, in contrast, sees the tale as "going beyond the authoritative voice" and as open to each reader's participation in the creation of the text (230).

Ferguson's feminist interpretation makes much of the fact that the "central consciousness" is that of "a young woman wise beyond her years" (228, 231). This reading finds an exemplary heroine in Mary, who "guards Ted" from their parents' "overprotectiveness," and is assertive, "creative," warm, and "rational" (228–30). Ferguson proceeds to argue that the story succeeds because Anderson had "fully release[ed] the woman within himself" (231). Contrasting it with "Death in the Woods," Anderson's "greatest achievement in mythopoesis," this study plainly prefers "Brother Death" because, instead of being a story "about writing a story," it is a "meticulously reported" story "about living a life" (231).

Townsend agrees with Gado in calling the story "more fable than tale," but he also asserts that it contains the distillation of everything Anderson's "social conscience had told him over the years"; all the battles of "husband against wife, old families against new . . . ," father against son, and even mother against son rise to the surface in the family's quarrel over the oaks (282). These remarks touch upon the rich layer of historical and sociological material within the tale. As Townsend observes, "Brother Death" shows that even in the midst of Depression pressures to align himself with radical political movements, Anderson could not subscribe to a materialist code but remained loyal to art and to feeling. In the rise of John Grey, Anderson represents with keen social and psychological perception the gradual historical transfer of a nation's wealth and power from a class of patricians who cherish beauty and "do not soil [their] hands at the plow" (*DW* 289) to a class of ex-peasants become successful bourgeois landowners who dismiss beauty as "sentimentality" and with solid, shrewd, persistence "get things done" (*DW* 287, 288). The virtues and defects of John Grey typify the moral strengths and weaknesses of America. Grey's sons reflect a conflict Anderson wrestled with all of his life. Mary is simply the one who loves and understands.

Works Cited

Anderson, David. 1967. *Sherwood Anderson: An Introduction and Interpretation*. New York: Holt, Rinehart.

Anderson, Sherwood. "Vibrant Life." *Little Review* 3 (March 1916):10–11. Rpt. in *Sherwood Anderson: Early Writings*. Ed. Ray Lewis White. Kent, OH: Kent State University Press, 1989, 155–57.

Appel, Paul P., ed. 1970. *Homage to Sherwood Anderson, 1876–1941.* Mamaroneck, NY: Appel.

Bland, Winifred. 1970. "Through a College Window." In *Homage to Sherwood Anderson, 1876–1941.* Ed. Paul P. Appel. Mamaroneck, NY: Appel, 131–37.

Campbell, Hilbert H., ed. 1987. *The Sherwood Anderson Diaries, 1936–1941.* Athens and London: University of Georgia Press.

Curry, Martha Mulroy. 1975. *The "Writer's Book" by Sherwood Anderson: A Critical Edition.* Metuchen, NJ: Scarecrow Press.

Ferguson, Mary Anne. 1981. "Sherwood Anderson's *Death in the Woods:* Toward a New Realism." In *Critical Essays on Sherwood Anderson.* Ed. David D. Anderson. Boston: G. K. Hall, 217–34. Originally printed in *Midamerica VII.* East Lansing, MI: Midwestern Press, 1980, 73–95.

Gado, Frank, ed. 1983. *The Teller's Tales.* Signature Series. Schenectady, NY: Union College Press.

Geismar, Maxwell, ed. 1962. *Sherwood Anderson: Short Stories.* New York: Hill and Wang.

Havighust, Walter. 1955. "Introduction." *Masters of the Modern Short Story.* New York: Harcourt, Brace and World, vii–xvii.

Hilton, Earl. "The Evolution of Sherwood Anderson's 'Brother Death.'" *Northwest Ohio Quarterly* 24 (1952):125–30.

Howe, Irving. 1951. *Sherwood Anderson.* New York: William Sloane.

Jones, Howard Mumford, and Walter B. Rideout, eds. 1953. *Letters of Sherwood Anderson.* Boston: Little, Brown.

Miller, William V. "In Defense of Mountaineers: Sherwood Anderson's Hill Stories." *Ball State University Forum* 15 (1974):51–58.

———. 1976. "Portraits of the Artist: Anderson's Fictional Storytellers." In *Sherwood Anderson: Dimensions of His Literary art: A Collection of Critical Essays.* Ed. David D. Anderson. East Lansing: Michigan State University Press, 1–23.

Modlin, Charles E., ed. 1984. *Sherwood Anderson: Selected Letters.* Knoxville: University of Tennessee Press.

———, ed. 1989. *Sherwood Anderson's Love Letters to Eleanor Copenhaver Anderson.* Athens and London: University of Georgia Press.

———, ed. 1992. *Certain Things Last: The Selected Short Stories of Sherwood Anderson.* New York: Four Walls Eight Windows.

Papinchak, Robert Allen. 1992. *Sherwood Anderson: A Study of the Short Fiction*. New York: Twayne.

Raymund, Bernard. "The Grammar of Not-Reason: Sherwood Anderson." *Arizona Quarterly* 12 (1956):48–60, 137–48.

Schevill, James. 1951. *Sherwood Anderson: His Life and Work*. Denver: University of Denver Press.

Taylor, Welford Dunaway. 1977. *Sherwood Anderson*. New York: Frederick Ungar.

Townsend, Kim. 1987. *Sherwood Anderson*. Boston: Houghton Mifflin.

Troy, William. "Fragmentary Ends." *Nation* 136 (1933):508.

Sutton, William A., ed. 1985. *Letters to Bab: Sherwood Anderson to Marietta D. Finley, 1916–33*. Foreword by Walter B. Rideout. Urbana and Chicago: University of Illinois Press.

Voss, Arthur. 1973. *The American Short Story: A Critical Survey*. Norman: University of Oklahoma Press.

Way, Brian. 1971. "Sherwood Anderson." In *The American Novel and the Nineteen Twenties*. Malcolm Bradbury and David Palmer (Eds.). Stratford-upon-Avon Studies 13. London: Edward Arnold, 107–26.

Weber, Brom. "Anderson and the 'The Essence of Things.'" *Sewanee Review* 59 (1951):678–92. Rpt. in *Critical Essays on Sherwood Anderson*. Ed. David D. Anderson. Boston: G. K. Hall, 1981, 125–37.

White, Ray Lewis, ed. 1991. *Sherwood Anderson's Secret Love Letters: For Eleanor, a Letter a Day*. Baton Rouge and London: Louisiana State University Press.

Index of Anderson's Works

437

General Index